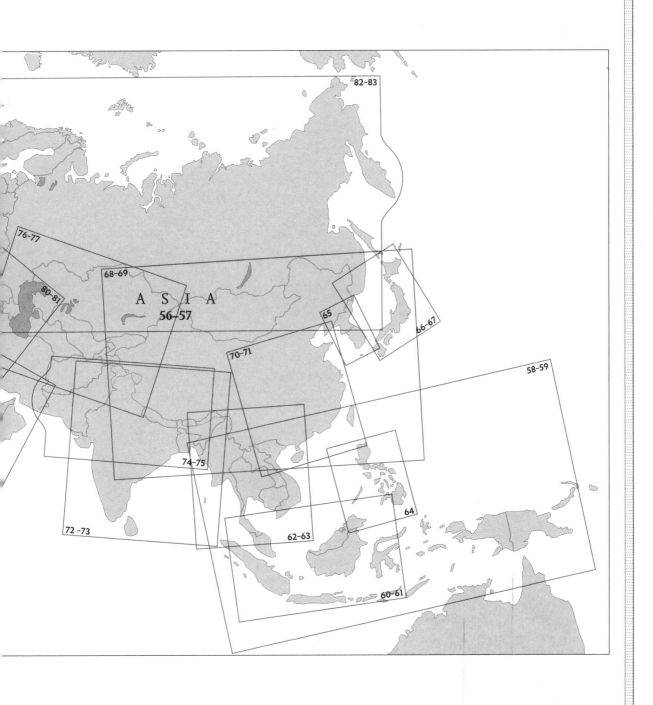

DESKTOP

ATLAS

OF THE

WORLD

THE TIMES DESKTOP ATLAS OF THE WORLD

Times Books, 77-85 Fulham Palace Road, London W6 8JB

First published 2006
Second Edition 2009

Third Edition 2012

Copyright © HarperCollins Publishers 2012

Maps © Collins Bartholomew Ltd 2012

The Times is a registered trademark of Times Newspapers Ltd

Printed in Hong Kong

British Library Cataloguing in Publication Data.
A catalogue record for this book is available from the British Library.

ISBN 978 0 00 745266 8
Imp 001

All mapping in this atlas is generated from Collins Bartholomew digital databases.
Collins Bartholomew, the UK's leading independent geographical information supplier,
can provide a digital, custom, and premium mapping service to a variety of markets.
For further information:
tel: +44 (0) 208 307 4515
e-mail: collinsbartholomew@harpercollins.co.uk
or visit our website at: www.collinsbartholomew.com

If you would like to comment on any aspect of this atlas, please write to
Times Atlases, HarperCollins Publishers, Westerhill Road, Bishopbriggs, Glasgow, G64 2QT
email: timesatlases@harpercollins.co.uk
or visit our website at: www.timesatlases.com
or follow us on Twitter @TimesAtlas

THE TIMES

DESKTOP

ATLAS

OF THE

WORLD

TIMES BOOKS
LONDON

CONTENTS

4

All independent countries and populated dependent and disputed territories are included in this list of the states and territories of the world; the list is arranged in alphabetical order by the conventional name form. For independent states, the full name is given below the conventional name, if this is different; for territories, the status is given. The capital city name is the same form as shown on the reference maps.

The statistics used for the area and population are the latest available and include estimates. The information on languages and religions is based on the latest information on 'de facto' speakers of the language or 'de facto' adherents to the religion. The information available on languages and religions varies greatly from country to country. Some countries include questions in censuses, others do not, in which case best estimates are used. The order of the languages and religions reflect their relative importance within the country; generally, languages or religions are included when more than one per cent of the population are estimated to be speakers or adherents.

Membership of selected international organizations is shown for each independent country. Territories are not shown as having separate memberships of these organizations.

ABBREVIATIONS

CURRENCIES

CFA	Communauté Financière Africaine
CFP	Comptoirs Français du Pacifique

ORGANIZATIONS

APEC	Asia-Pacific Economic Cooperation
ASEAN	Association of Southeast Asian Nations
CARICOM	Caribbean Community
CIS	Commonwealth of Independent States
COMM.	The Commonwealth
EU	European Union
OECD	Organization of Economic Co-operation and Development
OPEC	Organization of Petroleum Exporting Countries
SADC	Southern African Development Community
UN	United Nations

Abkhazia
Disputed Territory (Georgia)

Area Sq Km	8 700
Area Sq Miles	3 360
Population	180 000
Capital	Sokhumi (Aq"a)

AFGHANISTAN
Islamic State of Afghanistan

Area Sq Km	652 225	Religions	Sunni Muslim, Shi'a Muslim
Area Sq Miles	251 825		
Population	32 358 000	Currency	Afghani
Capital	Kābul	Organizations	UN
Languages	Dari, Pushtu, Uzbek, Turkmen	Map page	76–77

ALBANIA
Republic of Albania

Area Sq Km	28 748	Religions	Sunni Muslim, Albanian Orthodox, Roman Catholic
Area Sq Miles	11 100		
Population	3 216 000		
Capital	Tirana (Tiranë)	Currency	Lek
Languages	Albanian, Greek	Organizations	UN
		Map page	109

ALGERIA
People's Democratic Republic of Algeria

Area Sq Km	2 381 741	Religions	Sunni Muslim
Area Sq Miles	919 595	Currency	Algerian dinar
Population	35 980 000	Organizations	OPEC, UN
Capital	Algiers (Alger)	Map page	114–115
Languages	Arabic, French, Berber		

American Samoa
United States Unincorporated Territory

Area Sq Km	197	Religions	Protestant, Roman Catholic
Area Sq Miles	76		
Population	70 000	Currency	United States dollar
Capital	Fagatogo	Map page	49
Languages	Samoan, English		

ANDORRA
Principality of Andorra

Area Sq Km	465	Religions	Roman Catholic
Area Sq Miles	180	Currency	Euro
Population	86 000	Organizations	UN
Capital	Andorra la Vella	Map page	104
Languages	Spanish, Catalan, French		

ANGOLA
Republic of Angola

Area Sq Km	1 246 700	Religions	Roman Catholic, Protestant, traditional beliefs
Area Sq Miles	481 354		
Population	19 618 000		
Capital	Luanda	Currency	Kwanza
Languages	Portuguese, Bantu, local languages	Organizations	OPEC, SADC, UN
		Map page	120

Anguilla
United Kingdom Overseas Territory

Area Sq Km	155	**Religions**	Protestant, Roman
Area Sq Miles	60		Catholic
Population	16 000	**Currency**	East Caribbean dollar
Capital	The Valley	**Map page**	147
Languages	English		

ANTIGUA AND BARBUDA

Area Sq Km	442	**Religions**	Protestant, Roman
Area Sq Miles	171		Catholic
Population	90 000	**Currency**	East Caribbean dollar
Capital	St John's	**Organizations**	CARICOM,
Languages	English, creole		Comm., UN
		Map page	147

ARGENTINA
Argentine Republic

Area Sq Km	2 766 889	**Religions**	Roman Catholic,
Area Sq Miles	1 068 302		Protestant
Population	40 765 000	**Currency**	Argentinian peso
Capital	Buenos Aires	**Organizations**	UN
Languages	Spanish, Italian,	**Map page**	152–153
	Amerindian		
	languages		

ARMENIA
Republic of Armenia

Area Sq Km	29 800	**Religions**	Armenian Orthodox
Area Sq Miles	11 506	**Currency**	Dram
Population	3 100 000	**Organizations**	CIS, UN
Capital	Yerevan (Erevan)	**Map page**	81
Languages	Armenian, Azeri		

Aruba
Self-governing Netherlands Territory

Area Sq Km	193	**Religions**	Roman Catholic,
Area Sq Miles	75		Protestant
Population	108 000	**Currency**	Aruban florin
Capital	Oranjestad	**Map page**	147
Languages	Papiamento, Dutch,		
	English		

Ascension
Part of St Helena, Ascension and Tristan da Cunha

Area Sq Km	88	**Religions**	Protestant, Roman
Area Sq Miles	34		Catholic
Population	884	**Currency**	Pound sterling
Capital	Georgetown	**Map page**	113
Languages	English		

AUSTRALIA
Commonwealth of Australia

Area Sq Km	7 692 024	**Religions**	Protestant, Roman
Area Sq Miles	2 969 907		Catholic, Orthodox
Population	22 606 000	**Currency**	Australian dollar
Capital	Canberra	**Organizations**	APEC, Comm.,
Languages	English, Italian,		OECD, UN
	Greek	**Map page**	50–51

Australian Capital Territory (Federal Territory)

Area Sq Km	2 358	**Population**	359 700
Area Sq Miles	910	**Capital**	Canberra

Jervis Bay Territory (Territory)

Area Sq Km	73	**Population**	611
Area Sq Miles	28		

New South Wales (State)

Area Sq Km	800 642	**Population**	7 253 400
Area Sq Miles	309 130	**Capital**	Sydney

Northern Territory (Territory)

Area Sq Km	1 349 129	**Population**	230 200
Area Sq Miles	520 902	**Capital**	Darwin

Queensland (State)

Area Sq Km	1 730 648	**Population**	4 532 300
Area Sq Miles	668 207	**Capital**	Brisbane

South Australia (State)

Area Sq Km	983 482	**Population**	1 647 800
Area Sq Miles	379 725	**Capital**	Adelaide

Tasmania (State)

Area Sq Km	68 401	**Population**	508 500
Area Sq Miles	26 410	**Capital**	Hobart

Victoria (State)

Area Sq Km	227 416	**Population**	5 567 100
Area Sq Miles	87 806	**Capital**	Melbourne

Western Australia (State)

Area Sq Km	2 529 875	**Population**	2 306 200
Area Sq Miles	976 790	**Capital**	Perth

AUSTRIA
Republic of Austria

Area Sq Km	83 855	**Religions**	Roman Catholic,
Area Sq Miles	32 377		Protestant
Population	8 413 000	**Currency**	Euro
Capital	Vienna (Wien)	**Organizations**	EU, OECD, UN
Languages	German, Croatian,	**Map page**	102–103
	Turkish		

AZERBAIJAN
Republic of Azerbaijan

Area Sq Km	86 600	**Religions**	Shi'a Muslim, Sunni
Area Sq Miles	33 436		Muslim, Russian and
Population	9 306 000		Armenian Orthodox
Capital	Baku	**Currency**	Azerbaijani manat
Languages	Azeri, Armenian,	**Organizations**	CIS, UN
	Russian, Lezgian	**Map page**	81

Azores (Arquipélago dos Açores)
Autonomous Region of Portugal

Area Sq Km	2 300	**Religions**	Roman Catholic,
Area Sq Miles	888		Protestant
Population	245 374	**Currency**	Euro
Capital	Ponta Delgada	**Map page**	112
Languages	Portuguese		

THE BAHAMAS
Commonwealth of The Bahamas

Area Sq Km	13 939	**Religions**	Protestant, Roman
Area Sq Miles	5 382		Catholic
Population	347 000	**Currency**	Bahamian dollar
Capital	Nassau	**Organizations**	CARICOM, Comm.,
Languages	English, creole		UN
		Map page	146–147

BAHRAIN
Kingdom of Bahrain

Area Sq Km	691	**Religions**	Shi'a Muslim, Sunni
Area Sq Miles	267		Muslim, Christian
Population	1 324 000	**Currency**	Bahraini dinar
Capital	Manama	**Organizations**	UN
	(Al Manāmah)	**Map page**	79
Languages	Arabic, English		

BANGLADESH
People's Republic of Bangladesh

Area Sq Km	143 998	**Religions**	Sunni Muslim, Hindu
Area Sq Miles	55 598	**Currency**	Taka
Population	150 494 000	**Organizations**	Comm., UN
Capital	Dhaka (Dacca)	**Map page**	75
Languages	Bengali, English		

BARBADOS

Area Sq Km	430	**Religions**	Protestant, Roman
Area Sq Miles	166		Catholic
Population	274 000	**Currency**	Barbados dollar
Capital	Bridgetown	**Organizations**	CARICOM,
Languages	English, creole		Comm., UN
		Map page	147

BELARUS
Republic of Belarus

Area Sq Km	207 600	**Religions**	Belorussian Orthodox,
Area Sq Miles	80 155		Roman Catholic
Population	9 559 000	**Currency**	Belarus rouble
Capital	Minsk	**Organizations**	CIS, UN
Languages	Belorussian, Russian	**Map page**	88–89

BELGIUM
Kingdom of Belgium

Area Sq Km	30 520	**Religions**	Roman Catholic,
Area Sq Miles	11 784		Protestant
Population	10 754 000	**Currency**	Euro
Capital	Brussels (Bruxelles)	**Organizations**	EU, OECD, UN
Languages	Dutch (Flemish),	**Map page**	100
	French (Walloon),		
	German		

BELIZE

Area Sq Km	22 965	**Religions**	Roman Catholic,
Area Sq Miles	8 867		Protestant
Population	318 000	**Currency**	Belize dollar
Capital	Belmopan	**Organizations**	CARICOM, Comm.,
Languages	English, Spanish,		UN
	Mayan, creole	**Map page**	147

BENIN
Republic of Benin

Area Sq Km	112 620	**Religions**	Traditional beliefs,
Area Sq Miles	43 483		Roman Catholic,
Population	9 100 000		Sunni Muslim
Capital	Porto-Novo	**Currency**	CFA franc
Language	French, Fon,	**Organization**	UN
	Yoruba, Adja,	**Map page**	114
	local languages		

Bermuda
United Kingdom Overseas Territory

Area Sq Km	54	**Religions**	Protestant, Roman
Area Sq Miles	21		Catholic
Population	65 000	**Currency**	Bermuda dollar
Capital	Hamilton	**Map page**	125
Languages	English		

BHUTAN
Kingdom of Bhutan

Area Sq Km	46 620	**Religions**	Buddhist, Hindu
Area Sq Miles	18 000	**Currency**	Ngultrum,
Population	738 000		Indian rupee
Capital	Thimphu	**Organizations**	UN
Languages	Dzongkha,	**Map page**	75
	Nepali, Assamese		

BOLIVIA
Plurinational State of Bolivia

Area Sq Km	1 098 581	**Religions**	Roman Catholic,
Area Sq Miles	424 164		Protestant, Baha'i
Population	10 088 000	**Currency**	Boliviano
Capital	La Paz/Sucre	**Organizations**	UN
Languages	Spanish, Quechua,	**Map page**	152
	Aymara		

Bonaire
Netherlands Special Municipality

Area Sq Km	288	**Religions**	Roman Catholic,
Area Sq Miles	111		Protestant
Population	13 389	**Currency**	United States dollar
Capital	Kralendijk	**Map page**	147
Languages	Dutch, English,		
	Papiamento, Spanish		

Bonin Islands (Ogasawara-shotō)
part of Japan

Area Sq Km	104	**Religions**	Shintoist, Buddhist,
Area Sq Miles	40		Christian
Population	2 772	**Currency**	Yen
Capital	Ōmura	**Map page**	69
Languages	Japanese		

BOSNIA-HERZEGOVINA
Republic of Bosnia and Herzegovina

Area Sq Km	51 130	Religions	Sunni Muslim, Serbian Orthodox, Roman Catholic, Protestant
Area Sq Miles	19 741		
Population	3 752 000		
Capital	Sarajevo	Currency	Marka
Languages	Bosnian, Serbian, Croatian	Organizations	UN
		Map page	109

BOTSWANA
Republic of Botswana

Area Sq Km	581 370	Religions	Traditional beliefs, Protestant, Roman Catholic
Area Sq Miles	224 468		
Population	2 031 000		
Capital	Gaborone	Currency	Pula
Languages	English, Setswana, Shona, local languages	Organizations	Comm., SADC, UN
		Map page	120

BRAZIL
Federative Republic of Brazil

Area Sq Km	8 514 879	Religions	Roman Catholic, Protestant
Area Sq Miles	3 287 613		
Population	196 655 000	Currency	Real
Capital	Brasília	Organizations	UN
Languages	Portuguese	Map page	150–151

BRUNEI
State of Brunei Darussalam

Area Sq Km	5 765	Religions	Sunni Muslim, Buddhist, Christian
Area Sq Miles	2 226		
Population	406 000	Currency	Brunei dollar
Capital	Bandar Seri Begawan	Organizations	APEC, ASEAN, Comm., UN
Languages	Malay, English, Chinese	Map page	61

BULGARIA
Republic of Bulgaria

Area Sq Km	110 994	Religions	Bulgarian Orthodox, Sunni Muslim
Area Sq Miles	42 855		
Population	7 446 000	Currency	Lev
Capital	Sofia (Sofiya)	Organizations	EU, UN
Languages	Bulgarian, Turkish, Romany, Macedonian	Map page	110

BURKINA FASO
Democratic Republic of Burkina Faso

Area Sq Km	274 200	Religions	Sunni Muslim, traditional beliefs, Roman Catholic
Area Sq Miles	105 869		
Population	16 968 000		
Capital	Ouagadougou	Currency	CFA franc
Languages	French, Moore (Mossi), Fulani, local languages	Organizations	UN
		Map page	114

BURUNDI
Republic of Burundi

Area Sq Km	27 835	Religions	Roman Catholic, traditional beliefs, Protestant
Area Sq Miles	10 747		
Population	8 575 000		
Capital	Bujumbura	Currency	Burundian franc
Languages	Kirundi (Hutu, Tutsi), French	Organizations	UN
		Map page	119

CAMBODIA
Kingdom of Cambodia

Area Sq Km	181 000	Religions	Buddhist, Roman Catholic, Sunni Muslim
Area Sq Miles	69 884		
Population	14 305 000		
Capital	Phnom Penh	Currency	Riel
Languages	Khmer, Vietnamese	Organizations	ASEAN, UN
		Map page	63

CAMEROON
Republic of Cameroon

Area Sq Km	475 442	Religions	Roman Catholic, traditional beliefs, Sunni Muslim, Protestant
Area Sq Miles	183 569		
Population	20 030 000		
Capital	Yaoundé		
Languages	French, English, Fang, Bamileke, local languages	Currency	CFA franc
		Organizations	Comm., UN
		Map page	118

CANADA

Area Sq Km	9 984 670	Religions	Roman Catholic, Protestant, Eastern Orthodox, Jewish
Area Sq Miles	3 855 103		
Population	34 350 000		
Capital	Ottawa	Currency	Canadian dollar
Languages	English, French, local languages	Organizations	APEC, Comm., OECD, UN
		Map page	126–127

Alberta (Province)

Area Sq Km	661 848	Population	3 742 753
Area Sq Miles	255 541	Capital	Edmonton

British Columbia (Province)

Area Sq Km	944 735	Population	4 338 106
Area Sq Miles	364 764	Capital	Victoria

Manitoba (Province)

Area Sq Km	647 797	Population	1 243 653
Area Sq Miles	250 116	Capital	Winnipeg

New Brunswick (Province)

Area Sq Km	72 908	Population	753 232
Area Sq Miles	28 150	Capital	Fredericton

Newfoundland and Labrador (Province)

Area Sq Km	405 212	Population	509 148
Area Sq Miles	156 453	Capital	St John's

Northwest Territories (Territory)

Area Sq Km	1 346 106	Population	43 554
Area Sq Miles	519 734	Capital	Yellowknife

Nova Scotia (Province)

Area Sq Km	55 284	Population	943 414
Area Sq Miles	21 345	Capital	Halifax

Nunavut (Territory)

Area Sq Km	2 093 190	Population	33 303
Area Sq Miles	808 185	Capital	Iqaluit (Frobisher Bay)

CANADA

Ontario (Province)

Area Sq Km	1 076 395	Population	13 282 444
Area Sq Miles	415 598	Capital	Toronto

Prince Edward Island (Province)

Area Sq Km	5 660	Population	143 481
Area Sq Miles	2 185	Capital	Charlottetown

Québec (Province)

Area Sq Km	1 542 056	Population	7 942 983
Area Sq Miles	595 391	Capital	Québec

Saskatchewan (Province)

Area Sq Km	651 036	Population	1 052 050
Area Sq Miles	251 366	Capital	Regina

Yukon Territory (Territory)

Area Sq Km	482 443	Population	34 306
Area Sq Miles	186 272	Capital	Whitehorse

Canary Islands (Islas Canarias)
Autonomous Community of Spain

Area Sq Km	7 447	Religions	Roman Catholic
Area Sq Miles	2 875	Currency	Euro
Population	2 103 992	Map page	114
Capital	Santa Cruz de Tenerife/Las Palmas		
Languages	Spanish		

CAPE VERDE
Republic of Cape Verde

Area Sq Km	4 033	Religions	Roman Catholic, Protestant
Area Sq Miles	1 557		
Population	501 000	Currency	Cape Verde escudo
Capital	Praia	Organizations	UN
Languages	Portuguese, creole	Map page	46

Cayman Islands
United Kingdom Overseas Territory

Area Sq Km	259	Religions	Protestant, Roman Catholic
Area Sq Miles	100		
Population	57 000	Currency	Cayman Islands dollar
Capital	George Town	Map page	146
Languages	English		

CENTRAL AFRICAN REPUBLIC

Area Sq Km	622 436	Religions	Protestant, Roman Catholic, traditional beliefs, Sunni Muslim
Area Sq Miles	240 324		
Population	4 487 000		
Capital	Bangui	Currency	CFA franc
Languages	French, Sango, Banda, Baya, local languages	Organizations	UN
		Map page	118

Ceuta
Autonomous Community of Spain

Area Sq Km	19	Religions	Roman Catholic, Muslim
Area Sq Miles	7		
Population	78 674	Currency	Euro
Capital	Ceuta	Map page	106
Languages	Spanish, Arabic		

CHAD
Republic of Chad

Area Sq Km	1 284 000	Religions	Sunni Muslim, Roman Catholic, Protestant, traditional beliefs
Area Sq Miles	495 755		
Population	11 525 000		
Capital	Ndjamena	Currency	CFA franc
Languages	Arabic, French, Sara, local languages	Organizations	UN
		Map page	115

Chatham Islands
part of New Zealand

Area Sq Km	963	Religions	Protestant
Area Sq Miles	372	Currency	New Zealand dollar
Population	640	Map page	49
Capital	Waitangi		
Languages	English		

CHILE
Republic of Chile

Area Sq Km	756 945	Religions	Roman Catholic, Protestant
Area Sq Miles	292 258		
Population	17 270 000	Currency	Chilean peso
Capital	Santiago	Organizations	APEC, OECD, UN
Languages	Spanish, Amerindian languages	Map page	152–153

CHINA
People's Republic of China

Area Sq Km	9 584 492	Religions	Confucian, Taoist, Buddhist, Christian, Sunni Muslim
Area Sq Miles	3 700 593		
Population	1 332 079 000		
Capital	Beijing (Peking)	Currency	Yuan, Hong Kong dollar, Macao pataca
Languages	Mandarin, Wu, Cantonese, Hsiang, regional languages	Organizations	APEC, UN
		Map page	68–69

Anhui (Province)

Area Sq Km	139 000	Population	61 350 000
Area Sq Miles	53 668	Capital	Hefei

Bejing (Municipality)

Area Sq Km	16 800	Population	16 950 000
Area Sq Miles	6 487	Capital	Beijing (Peking)

Chongqing (Municipality)

Area Sq Km	23 000	Population	28 390 000
Area Sq Miles	8 880	Capital	Chongqing

Fujian (Province)

Area Sq Km	121 400	Population	36 040 000
Area Sq Miles	46 873	Capital	Fuzhou

nsu (Province)

Area Sq Km	453 700	Population	26 280 000
rea Sq Miles	175 175	Capital	Lanzhou

angdong (Province)

Area Sq Km	178 000	Population	95 440 000
rea Sq Miles	68 726	Capital	Guangzhou (Canton)

angxi Zhuangzu Zizhiqu (Autonomous Region)

Area Sq Km	236 000	Population	48 160 000
rea Sq Miles	91 120	Capital	Nanning

izhou (Province)

Area Sq Km	176 000	Population	37 930 000
rea Sq Miles	67 954	Capital	Guiyang

inan (Province)

Area Sq Km	34 000	Population	8 540 000
rea Sq Miles	13 127	Capital	Haikou

ebei (Province)

Area Sq Km	187 700	Population	69 890 000
rea Sq Miles	72 471	Capital	Shijiazhuang

eilongjiang (Province)

Area Sq Km	454 600	Population	38 250 000
rea Sq Miles	175 522	Capital	Harbin

enan (Province)

Area Sq Km	167 000	Population	94 290 000
rea Sq Miles	64 479	Capital	Zhengzhou

ong Kong (Special Administrative Region)

Area Sq Km	1 075	Population	6 978 000
rea Sq Miles	415	Capital	Hong Kong

ubei (Province)

Area Sq Km	185 900	Population	57 110 000
rea Sq Miles	71 776	Capital	Wuhan

unan (Province)

Area Sq Km	210 000	Population	63 800 000
rea Sq Miles	81 081	Capital	Changsha

angsu (Province)

Area Sq Km	102 600	Population	76 770 000
rea Sq Miles	39 614	Capital	Nanjing

angxi (Province)

Area Sq Km	166 900	Population	44 000 000
rea Sq Miles	64 440	Capital	Nanchang

in (Province)

Area Sq Km	187 000	Population	27 340 000
rea Sq Miles	72 201	Capital	Changchun

aoning (Province)

Area Sq Km	147 400	Population	43 150 000
rea Sq Miles	56 911	Capital	Shenyang

Macao (Special Administrative Region)

Area Sq Km	17	Population	552 000
Area Sq Mile	7	Capital	Macao

Nei Mongol Zizhiqu (Inner Mongolia) (Autonomous Region)

Area Sq Km	1 183 000	Population	24 140 000
Area Sq Miles	456 759	Capital	Hohhot

Ningxia Huizu Zizhiqu (Autonomous Region)

Area Sq Km	66 400	Population	6 180 000
Area Sq Miles	25 637	Capital	Yinchuan

Qinghai (Province)

Area Sq Km	721 000	Population	5 540 000
Area Sq Miles	278 380	Capital	Xining

Shaanxi (Province)

Area Sq Km	205 600	Population	37 620 000
Area Sq Miles	79 383	Capital	Xi'an

Shandong (Province)

Area Sq Km	153 300	Population	94 170 000
Area Sq Miles	59 189	Capital	Jinan

Shanghai (Municipality)

Area Sq Km	6 300	Population	18 880 000
Area Sq Miles	2 432	Capital	Shanghai

Shanxi (Province)

Area Sq Km	156 300	Population	34 110 000
Area Sq Miles	60 348	Capital	Taiyuan

Sichuan (Province)

Area Sq Km	569 000	Population	81 380 000
Area Sq Miles	219 692	Capital	Chengdu

Tianjin (Municipality)

Area Sq Km	11 300	Population	11 760 000
Area Sq Miles	4 363	Capital	Tianjin

Xinjiang Uygur Zizhiqu (Sinkiang) (Autonomous Region)

Area Sq Km	1 600 000	Population	21 310 000
Area Sq Miles	617 763	Capital	Ürümqi

Xizang Zizhiqu (Tibet) (Autonomous Region)

Area Sq Km	1 228 400	Population	2 870 000
Area Sq Miles	474 288	Capital	Lhasa

Yunnan (Province)

Area Sq Km	394 000	Population	45 430 000
Area Sq Miles	152 124	Capital	Kunming

Zhejiang (Province)

Area Sq Km	101 800	Population	51 200 000
Area Sq Miles	39 305	Capital	Hangzhou

Christmas Island
Australian External Territory

Area Sq Km	135	Religions	Buddhist, Sunni
Area Sq Miles	52		Muslim, Protestant,
Population	1 403		Roman Catholic
Capital	The Settlement	Currency	Australian dollar
Languages	English	Map page	58

Cocos Islands (Keeling Islands)
Australian External Territory

Area Sq Km	14	Religions	Sunni Muslim,
Area Sq Miles	5		Christian
Population	621	Currency	Australian dollar
Capital	West Island	Map page	58
Languages	English		

COLOMBIA
Republic of Colombia

Area Sq Km	1 141 748	Religions	Roman Catholic,
Area Sq Miles	440 831		Protestant
Population	46 927 000	Currency	Colombian peso
Capital	Bogotá	Organizations	UN
Languages	Spanish, Amerindian	Map page	150
	languages		

COMOROS
United Republic of the Comoros

Area Sq Km	1 862	Religions	Sunni Muslim, Roman
Area Sq Miles	719		Catholic
Population	754 000	Currency	Comoros franc
Capital	Moroni	Organizations	UN
Languages	Shikomor (Comorian),	Map page	121
	French, Arabic		

CONGO
Republic of the Congo

Area Sq Km	342 000	Religions	Roman Catholic,
Area Sq Miles	132 047		Protestant, traditional
Population	4 140 000		beliefs, Sunni Muslim
Capital	Brazzaville	Currency	CFA franc
Languages	French, Kongo,	Organizations	UN
	Monokutuba, local	Map page	118
	languages		

CONGO, DEMOCRATIC REPUBLIC OF THE

Area Sq Km	2 345 410	Religions	Christian, Sunni
Area Sq Miles	905 568		Muslim
Population	67 758 000	Currency	Congolese franc
Capital	Kinshasa	Organizations	SADC, UN
Languages	French, Lingala,	Map page	118–119
	Swahili, Kongo,		
	local languages		

Cook Islands
Self-governing New Zealand Overseas Territory

Area Sq Km	293	Religions	Protestant, Roman
Area Sq Miles	113		Catholic
Population	20 000	Currency	New Zealand dollar
Capital	Avarua	Map page	49
Languages	English, Maori		

COSTA RICA
Republic of Costa Rica

Area Sq Km	51 100	Religions	Roman Catholic,
Area Sq Miles	19 730		Protestant
Population	4 727 000	Currency	Costa Rican colón
Capital	San José	Organizations	UN
Languages	Spanish	Map page	146

CÔTE D'IVOIRE (IVORY COAST)
Republic of Côte d'Ivoire

Area Sq Km	322 463	Religions	Sunni Muslim, Roma
Area Sq Miles	124 504		Catholic, traditonal
Population	20 153 000		beliefs, Protestant
Capital	Yamoussoukro	Currency	CFA franc
Languages	French, creole, Akan,	Organizations	UN
	local languages	Map page	114

CROATIA
Republic of Croatia

Area Sq Km	56 538	Religions	Roman Catholic,
Area Sq Miles	21 829		Serbian Orthodox,
Population	4 396 000		Sunni Muslim
Capital	Zagreb	Currency	Kuna
Languages	Croatian, Serbian	Organizations	UN
		Map page	109

CUBA
Republic of Cuba

Area Sq Km	110 860	Religions	Roman Catholic,
Area Sq Miles	42 803		Protestant
Population	11 254 000	Currency	Cuban peso
Capital	Havana (La Habana)	Organizations	UN
Languages	Spanish	Map page	146

Curaçao
Self-governing Netherlands Territory

Area Sq Km	444	Religions	Roman Catholic,
Area Sq Miles	171		Protestant
Population	142 180	Currency	Caribbean guilder
Capital	Willemstad	Map page	147
Languages	Dutch, Papiamento		

CYPRUS
Republic of Cyprus

Area Sq Km	9 251	Religions	Greek Orthodox,
Area Sq Miles	3 572		Sunni Muslim
Population	1 117 000	Currency	Euro
Capital	Nicosia (Lefkosia)	Organizations	Comm., EU, UN
Languages	Greek, Turkish,	Map page	80
	English		

CZECH REPUBLIC

Area Sq Km	78 864	**Religions**	Roman Catholic, Protestant
Area Sq Miles	30 450		
Population	10 534 000	**Currency**	Czech koruna
Capital	Prague (Praha)	**Organizations**	EU, OECD, UN
Languages	Czech, Moravian, Slovakian	**Map page**	102–103

DENMARK
Kingdom of Denmark

Area Sq Km	43 075	**Religions**	Protestant
Area Sq Miles	16 631	**Currency**	Danish krone
Population	5 573 000	**Organizations**	EU, OECD, UN
Capital	Copenhagen (København)	**Map page**	93
Languages	Danish		

DJIBOUTI
Republic of Djibouti

Area Sq Km	23 200	**Religions**	Sunni Muslim, Christian
Area Sq Miles	8 958		
Population	906 000	**Currency**	Djibouti franc
Capital	Djibouti	**Organizations**	UN
Languages	Somali, Afar, French, Arabic	**Map page**	117

DOMINICA
Commonwealth of Dominica

Area Sq Km	750	**Religions**	Roman Catholic, Protestant
Area Sq Miles	290		
Population	68 000	**Currency**	East Caribbean dollar
Capital	Roseau	**Organizations**	CARICOM, Comm., UN
Languages	English, creole		
		Map page	147

DOMINICAN REPUBLIC

Area Sq Km	48 442	**Religions**	Roman Catholic, Protestant
Area Sq Miles	18 704		
Population	10 056 000	**Currency**	Dominican peso
Capital	Santo Domingo	**Organizations**	UN
Languages	Spanish, creole	**Map page**	147

Easter Island (Isla de Pascua)
part of Chile

Area Sq Km	171	**Religions**	Roman Catholic
Area Sq Miles	66	**Currency**	Chilean peso
Population	4 888	**Map page**	157
Capital	Hanga Roa		
Languages	Spanish		

EAST TIMOR
Democratic Republic of Timor-Leste

Area Sq Km	14 874	**Religions**	Roman Catholic
Area Sq Miles	5 743	**Currency**	United States dollar
Population	1 154 000	**Organisations**	UN
Capital	Dili	**Map page**	59
Languages	Portuguese, Tetun, English		

ECUADOR
Republic of Ecuador

Area Sq Km	272 045	**Religions**	Roman Catholic
Area Sq Miles	105 037	**Currency**	United States dollar
Population	14 666 000	**Organizations**	OPEC, UN
Capital	Quito	**Map page**	150
Languages	Spanish, Quechua, Amerindian languages		

EGYPT
Arab Republic of Egypt

Area Sq Km	1 000 250	**Religions**	Sunni Muslim, Coptic Christian
Area Sq Miles	386 199		
Population	82 537 000	**Currency**	Egyptian pound
Capital	Cairo (Al Qāhirah)	**Organizations**	UN
Languages	Arabic	**Map page**	116

EL SALVADOR
Republic of El Salvador

Area Sq Km	21 041	**Religions**	Roman Catholic, Protestant
Area Sq Miles	8 124		
Population	6 227 000	**Currency**	El Salvador colón, United States dollar
Capital	San Salvador		
Languages	Spanish	**Organizations**	UN
		Map page	146

EQUATORIAL GUINEA
Republic of Equatorial Guinea

Area Sq Km	28 051	**Religions**	Roman Catholic, traditional beliefs
Area Sq Miles	10 831		
Population	720 000	**Currency**	CFA franc
Capital	Malabo	**Organizations**	UN
Languages	Spanish, French, Fang	**Map page**	118

ERITREA
State of Eritrea

Area Sq Km	117 400	**Religions**	Sunni Muslim, Coptic Christian
Area Sq Miles	45 328		
Population	5 415 000	**Currency**	Nakfa
Capital	Asmara	**Organizations**	UN
Languages	Tigrinya, Tigre	**Map page**	116

ESTONIA
Republic of Estonia

Area Sq Km	45 200	**Religions**	Protestant, Estonian and Russian Orthodox
Area Sq Miles	17 452		
Population	1 341 000	**Currency**	Euro
Capital	Tallinn	**Organizations**	EU, OECD, UN
Languages	Estonian, Russian	**Map page**	88

ETHIOPIA
Federal Democratic Republic of Ethiopia

Area Sq Km	1 133 880	**Religions**	Ethiopian Orthodox, Sunni Muslim, traditional beliefs
Area Sq Miles	437 794		
Population	84 734 000		
Capital	Addis Ababa (Ādīs Ābeba)	**Currency**	Birr
		Organizations	UN
Languages	Oromo, Amharic, Tigrinya, local languages	**Map page**	117

Falkland Islands
United Kingdom Overseas Territory

Area Sq Km	12 170	**Religions**	Protestant, Roman
Area Sq Miles	4 699		Catholic
Population	2 955	**Currency**	Falkland Islands
Capital	Stanley		pound
Languages	English	**Map page**	153

Faroe Islands
Self-governing Danish Territory

Area Sq Km	1 399	**Religions**	Protestant
Area Sq Miles	540	**Currency**	Danish krone
Population	49 000	**Map page**	94
Capital	Tórshavn		
Languages	Faroese, Danish		

FIJI
Republic of Fiji

Area Sq Km	18 330	**Religions**	Christian, Hindu,
Area Sq Miles	7 077		Sunni Muslim
Population	868 000	**Currency**	Fiji dollar
Capital	Suva	**Organizations**	Comm., UN
Languages	English, Fijian,	**Map page**	49
	Hindi		

FINLAND
Republic of Finland

Area Sq Km	338 145	**Religions**	Protestant, Greek
Area Sq Miles	130 559		Orthodox
Population	5 385 000	**Currency**	Euro
Capital	Helsinki	**Organizations**	EU, OECD, UN
	(Helsingfors)	**Map page**	92–93
Languages	Finnish, Swedish		

FRANCE
French Republic

Area Sq Km	543 965	**Religions**	Roman Catholic,
Area Sq Miles	210 026		Protestant, Sunni
Population	63 126 000		Muslim
Capital	Paris	**Currency**	Euro
Languages	French, Arabic	**Organizations**	EU, OECD, UN
		Map page	104–105

French Guiana
French Overseas Department

Area Sq Km	90 000	**Religions**	Roman Catholic
Area Sq Miles	34 749	**Currency**	Euro
Population	237 000	**Map page**	151
Capital	Cayenne		
Languages	French, creole		

French Polynesia
French Overseas Territory

Area Sq Km	3 265	**Religions**	Protestant, Roman
Area Sq Miles	1 261		Catholic
Population	274 000	**Currency**	CFP franc
Capital	Papeete	**Map page**	49
Languages	French, Tahitian,		
	Polynesian languages		

GABON
Gabonese Republic

Area Sq Km	267 667	**Religions**	Roman Catholic,
Area Sq Miles	103 347		Protestant, traditonal
Population	1 534 000		beliefs
Capital	Libreville	**Currency**	CFA franc
Languages	French, Fang, local	**Organizations**	UN
	languages	**Map page**	118

Galapagos Islands (Islas Galápagos)
part of Ecuador

Area Sq Km	8 010	**Religions**	Roman Catholic
Area Sq Miles	3 093	**Currency**	United States dollar
Population	22 770	**Map page**	125
Capital	Puerto Baquerizo		
	Moreno		
Languages	Spanish		

THE GAMBIA
Republic of The Gambia

Area Sq Km	11 295	**Religions**	Sunni Muslim,
Area Sq Miles	4 361		Protestant
Population	1 776 000	**Currency**	Dalasi
Capital	Banjul	**Organizations**	Comm., UN
Languages	English, Malinke,	**Map page**	114
	Fulani, Wolof		

Gaza
Semi-autonomous region

Area Sq Km	363	**Religions**	Sunni Muslim, Shi'a
Area Sq Miles	140		Muslim
Population	1 535 120	**Currency**	Israeli shekel
Capital	Gaza	**Map page**	80
Languages	Arabic		

GEORGIA
Republic of Georgia

Area Sq Km	69 700	**Religions**	Georgian Orthodox,
Area Sq Miles	26 911		Russian Orthodox,
Population	4 329 000		Sunni Muslim
Capital	Tbilisi	**Currency**	Lari
Languages	Georgian, Russian,	**Organizations**	CIS, UN
	Armenian, Azeri,	**Map page**	81
	Ossetian, Abkhaz		

GERMANY
Federal Republic of Germany

Area Sq Km	357 022	**Religions**	Protestant, Roman
Area Sq Miles	137 847		Catholic
Population	82 163 000	**Currency**	Euro
Capital	Berlin	**Organizations**	EU, OECD, UN
Languages	German, Turkish	**Map page**	102

GHANA
Republic of Ghana

Area Sq Km	238 537	**Religions**	Christian, Sunni
Area Sq Miles	92 100		Muslim, traditional
Population	24 966 000		beliefs
Capital	Accra	**Currency**	Cedi
Languages	English, Hausa,	**Organizations**	Comm., UN
	Akan, local	**Map page**	114
	languages		

Gibraltar
United Kingdom Overseas Territory

Area Sq Km	7	Religions	Roman Catholic, Protestant, Sunni Muslim
Area Sq Miles	3		
Population	29 000		
Capital	Gibraltar	Currency	Gibraltar pound
Languages	English, Spanish	Map page	106

GREECE
Hellenic Republic

Area Sq Km	131 957	Religions	Greek Orthodox, Sunni Muslim
Area Sq Miles	50 949		
Population	11 390 000	Currency	Euro
Capital	Athens (Athina)	Organizations	EU, OECD, UN
Languages	Greek	Map page	111

Greenland
Self-governing Danish Territory

Area Sq Km	2 175 600	Religions	Protestant
Area Sq Miles	840 004	Currency	Danish krone
Population	57 000	Map page	127
Capital	Nuuk (Godthåb)		
Languages	Greenlandic, Danish		

GRENADA

Area Sq Km	378	Religions	Roman Catholic, Protestant
Area Sq Miles	146		
Population	105 000	Currency	East Caribbean dollar
Capital	St George's	Organizations	CARICOM, Comm., UN
Languages	English, creole		
		Map page	147

Guadeloupe
French Overseas Department

Area Sq Km	1 780	Religions	Roman Catholic
Area Sq Miles	687	Currency	Euro
Population	463 000	Map page	147
Capital	Basse-Terre		
Languages	French, creole		

Guam
United States Unincorporated Territory

Area Sq Km	541	Religions	Roman Catholic
Area Sq Miles	209	Currency	United States dollar
Population	182 000	Map page	59
Capital	Hagåtña		
Languages	Chamorro, English, Tagalog		

GUATEMALA
Republic of Guatemala

Area Sq Km	108 890	Religion	Roman Catholic, Protestant
Area Sq Miles	42 043		
Population	14 757 000	Currency	Quetzal, United States dollar
Capital	Guatemala City	Organizations	UN
Languages	Spanish, Mayan languages	Map page	146

Guernsey
United Kingdom Crown Dependency

Area Sq Km	78	Religions	Protestant, Roman Catholic
Area Sq Miles	30		
Population	65 264	Currency	Pound sterling
Capital	St Peter Port	Map page	95
Languages	English, French		

GUINEA
Republic of Guinea

Area Sq Km	245 857	Religions	Sunni Muslim, traditional beliefs, Christian
Area Sq Miles	94 926		
Population	10 222 000		
Capital	Conakry	Currency	Guinea franc
Languages	French, Fulani, Malinke, local languages	Organizations	UN
		Map page	114

GUINEA-BISSAU
Republic of Guinea-Bissau

Area Sq Km	36 125	Religions	Traditional beliefs, Sunni Muslim, Christian
Area Sq Miles	13 948		
Population	1 547 000		
Capital	Bissau	Currency	CFA franc
Languages	Portuguese, crioulo, local languages	Organizations	UN
		Map page	114

GUYANA
Co-operative Republic of Guyana

Area Sq Km	214 969	Religions	Protestant, Hindu, Roman Catholic, Sunni Muslim
Area Sq Miles	83 000		
Population	756 000		
Capital	Georgetown	Currency	Guyana dollar
Languages	English, creole, Amerindian languages	Organizations	CARICOM, Comm., UN
		Map page	150

HAITI
Republic of Haiti

Area Sq Km	27 750	Religions	Roman Catholic, Protestant, Voodoo
Area Sq Miles	10 714		
Population	10 124 000	Currency	Gourde
Capital	Port-au-Prince	Organizations	CARICOM, UN
Languages	French, creole	Map page	147

HONDURAS
Republic of Honduras

Area Sq Km	112 088	Religions	Roman Catholic, Protestant
Area Sq Miles	43 277		
Population	7 755 000	Currency	Lempira
Capital	Tegucigalpa	Organizations	UN
Languages	Spanish, Amerindian languages	Map page	147

HUNGARY
Republic of Hungary

Area Sq Km	93 030	Religions	Roman Catholic, Protestant
Area Sq Miles	35 919		
Population	9 966 000	Currency	Forint
Capital	Budapest	Organizations	EU, OECD, UN
Languages	Hungarian	Map page	103

ICELAND
Republic of Iceland

Area Sq Km	102 820	**Religions**	Protestant
Area Sq Miles	39 699	**Currency**	Icelandic króna
Population	324 000	**Organizations**	OECD, UN
Capital	Reykjavík	**Map page**	92
Languages	Icelandic		

INDIA
Republic of India

Area Sq Km	3 064 898	**Religions**	Hindu, Sunni Muslim,
Area Sq Miles	1 183 364		Shi'a Muslim, Sikh,
Population	1 241 492 000		Christian
Capital	New Delhi	**Currency**	Indian rupee
Languages	Hindi, English, many	**Organizations**	Comm., UN
	regional languages	**Map page**	72–73

INDONESIA
Republic of Indonesia

Area Sq Km	1 919 445	**Religions**	Sunni Muslim,
Area Sq Miles	741 102		Protestant, Roman
Population	242 326 000		Catholic, Hindu,
Capital	Jakarta		Buddhist
Languages	Indonesian, local	**Currency**	Rupiah
	languages	**Organizations**	APEC, ASEAN, UN
		Map page	58–59

IRAN
Islamic Republic of Iran

Area Sq Km	1 648 000	**Religions**	Shi'a Muslim, Sunni
Area Sq Miles	636 296		Muslim
Population	74 799 000	**Currency**	Iranian rial
Capital	Tehrān	**Organizations**	OPEC, UN
Languages	Farsi, Azeri, Kurdish,	**Map page**	81
	regional languages		

IRAQ
Republic of Iraq

Area Sq Km	438 317	**Religions**	Shi'a Muslim, Sunni
Area Sq Miles	169 235		Muslim, Christian
Population	32 665 000	**Currency**	Iraqi dinar
Capital	Baghdād	**Organizations**	OPEC, UN
Languages	Arabic, Kurdish,	**Map page**	81
	Turkmen		

IRELAND
Republic of Ireland

Area Sq Km	70 282	**Religions**	Roman Catholic,
Area Sq Miles	27 136		Protestant
Population	4 526 000	**Currency**	Euro
Capital	Dublin	**Organizations**	EU, OECD, UN
	(Baile Átha Cliath)	**Map page**	97
Languages	English, Irish		

Isle of Man
United Kingdom Crown Dependency

Area Sq Km	572	**Religions**	Protestant, Roman
Area Sq Miles	221		Catholic
Population	83 000	**Currency**	Pound sterling
Capital	Douglas	**Map page**	98
Languages	English		

ISRAEL
State of Israel

Area Sq Km	20 770	**Religions**	Jewish, Sunni Musl
Area Sq Miles	8 019		Christian, Druze
Population	7 562 000	**Currency**	Shekel
Capital	Jerusalem*	**Organizations**	OECD, UN
	(Yerushalayim)	**Map page**	80
	(El Quds)		
Languages	Hebrew, Arabic		

*De facto capital. Disputed.

ITALY
Italian Republic

Area Sq Km	301 245	**Religions**	Roman Catholic
Area Sq Miles	116 311	**Currency**	Euro
Population	60 789 000	**Organizations**	EU, OECD, UN
Capital	Rome (Roma)	**Map page**	108–109
Languages	Italian		

JAMAICA

Area Sq Km	10 991	**Religions**	Protestant, Roman
Area Sq Miles	4 244		Catholic
Population	2 751 000	**Currency**	Jamaican dollar
Capital	Kingston	**Organizations**	CARICOM, Comm.
Languages	English, creole		UN
		Map page	146

JAPAN

Area Sq Km	377 727	**Religions**	Shintoist, Buddhist
Area Sq Miles	145 841		Christian
Population	126 497 000	**Currency**	Yen
Capital	Tōkyō	**Organizations**	APEC, OECD, UN
Languages	Japanese	**Map page**	66–67

Jersey
United Kingdom Crown Dependency

Area Sq Km	116	**Religions**	Protestant, Roman
Area Sq Miles	45		Catholic
Population	92 500	**Currency**	Pound sterling
Capital	St Helier	**Map page**	95
Languages	English, French		

JORDAN
Hashemite Kingdom of Jordan

Area Sq Km	89 206	**Religions**	Sunni Muslim,
Area Sq Miles	34 443		Christian
Population	6 330 000	**Currency**	Jordanian dinar
Capital	'Ammān	**Organizations**	UN
Languages	Arabic	**Map page**	80

Juan Fernández Islands
part of Chile

Area Sq Km	179	**Religions**	Roman Catholic,
Area Sq Miles	69		Protestant
Population	832	**Currency**	Chilean peso
Capital	San Juan Bautista	**Map page**	157
Languages	Spanish, Amerindian		
	languages		

KAZAKHSTAN
Republic of Kazakhstan

Area Sq Km	2 717 300	Religions	Sunni Muslim, Russian Orthodox, Protestant
Area Sq Miles	1 049 155		
Population	16 207 000	Currency	Tenge
Capital	Astana (Akmola)	Organizations	CIS, UN
Languages	Kazakh, Russian, Ukrainian, German, Uzbek, Tatar	Map page	76–77

 KENYA
Republic of Kenya

Area Sq Km	582 646	Religions	Christian, traditional beliefs
Area Sq Miles	224 961		
Population	41 610 000	Currency	Kenyan shilling
Capital	Nairobi	Organizations	Comm., UN
Languages	Swahili, English, local languages	Map page	119

KIRIBATI
Republic of Kiribati

Area Sq Km	717	Religions	Roman Catholic, Protestant
Area Sq Miles	277		
Population	101 000	Currency	Australian dollar
Capital	Bairiki	Organizations	Comm., UN
Languages	Gilbertese, English	Map page	49

KOSOVO
Republic of Kosovo

Area Sq Km	10 908	Religions	Sunni Muslim, Serbian Orthodox
Area Sq Miles	4 212		
Population	2 180 686	Currency	Euro
Capital	Prishtinë (Priština)	Map page	109
Languages	Albanian, Serbian		

 KUWAIT
State of Kuwait

Area Sq Km	17 818	Religions	Sunni Muslim, Shi'a Muslim, Christian, Hindu
Area Sq Miles	6 880		
Population	2 818 000	Currency	Kuwaiti dinar
Capital	Kuwait (Al Kuwayt)	Organizations	OPEC, UN
Languages	Arabic	Map page	78

KYRGYZSTAN
Kyrgyz Republic

Area Sq Km	198 500	Religions	Sunni Muslim, Russian Orthodox
Area Sq Miles	76 641		
Population	5 393 000	Currency	Kyrgyz som
Capital	Bishkek (Frunze)	Organizations	CIS, UN
Languages	Kyrgyz, Russian, Uzbek	Map page	77

 LAOS
Lao People's Democratic Republic

Area Sq Km	236 800	Religions	Buddhist, traditional beliefs
Area Sq Miles	91 429		
Population	6 288 000	Currency	Kip
Capital	Vientiane (Viangchan)	Organizations	ASEAN, UN
Languages	Lao, local languages	Map page	62–63

 LATVIA
Republic of Latvia

Area Sq Km	64 589	Religions	Protestant, Roman Catholic, Russian Orthodox
Area Sq Miles	24 938		
Population	2 243 000		
Capital	Rīga	Currency	Lats
Languages	Latvian, Russian	Organizations	EU, UN
		Map page	88

 LEBANON
Republic of Lebanon

Area Sq Km	10 452	Religions	Shi'a Muslim, Sunni Muslim, Christian
Area Sq Miles	4 036		
Population	4 259 000	Currency	Lebanese pound
Capital	Beirut (Beyrouth)	Organizations	UN
Languages	Arabic, Armenian, French	Map page	80

LESOTHO
Kingdom of Lesotho

Area Sq Km	30 355	Religions	Christian, traditional beliefs
Area Sq Miles	11 720		
Population	2 194 000	Currency	Loti, South African rand
Capital	Maseru		
Languages	Sesotho, English, Zulu	Organizations	Comm., SADC, UN
		Map page	123

 LIBERIA
Republic of Liberia

Area Sq Km	111 369	Religions	Traditional beliefs, Christian, Sunni Muslim
Area Sq Miles	43 000		
Population	4 129 000		
Capital	Monrovia	Currency	Liberian dollar
Languages	English, creole, local languages	Organizations	UN
		Map page	114

LIBYA

Area Sq Km	1 759 540	Religions	Sunni Muslim
Area Sq Miles	679 362	Currency	Libyan dinar
Population	6 423 000	Organizations	OPEC, UN
Capital	Tripoli (Ṭarābulus)	Map page	115
Languages	Arabic, Berber		

LIECHTENSTEIN
Principality of Liechtenstein

Area Sq Km	160	Religions	Roman Catholic, Protestant
Area Sq Miles	62		
Population	36 000	Currency	Swiss franc
Capital	Vaduz	Organizations	UN
Languages	German	Map page	105

LITHUANIA
Republic of Lithuania

Area Sq Km	65 200	Religions	Roman Catholic, Protestant, Russian Orthodox
Area Sq Miles	25 174		
Population	3 307 000		
Capital	Vilnius	Currency	Litas
Languages	Lithuanian, Russian, Polish	Organizations	EU, UN
		Map page	88

Lord Howe Island
part of Australia

Area Sq Km	17	Religions	Protestant,
Area Sq Miles	6		Roman Catholic
Population	364	Currency	Australian dollar
Languages	English	Map page	51

LUXEMBOURG
Grand Duchy of Luxembourg

Area Sq Km	2 586	Religions	Roman Catholic
Area Sq Miles	998	Currency	Euro
Population	516 000	Organizations	EU, OECD, UN
Capital	Luxembourg	Map page	100
Languages	Letzeburgish, German, French		

MACEDONIA (F.Y.R.O.M.)
Republic of Macedonia

Area Sq Km	25 713	Religions	Macedonian Orthodox,
Area Sq Miles	9 928		Sunni Muslim
Population	2 064 000	Currency	Macedonian denar
Capital	Skopje	Organizations	UN
Languages	Macedonian, Albanian, Turkish	Map page	111

MADAGASCAR
Republic of Madagascar

Area Sq Km	587 041	Religions	Traditional beliefs,
Area Sq Miles	226 658		Christian, Sunni
Population	21 315 000		Muslim
Capital	Antananarivo	Currency	Malagasy ariary,
Languages	Malagasy, French		Malagasy franc
		Organizations	SADC, UN
		Map page	121

Madeira
Autonomous Region of Portugal

Area Sq Km	779	Religions	Roman Catholic,
Area Sq Miles	301		Protestant
Population	247 399	Currency	Euro
Capital	Funchal	Map page	114
Languages	Portuguese		

MALAWI
Republic of Malawi

Area Sq Km	118 484	Religions	Christian, traditional
Area Sq Miles	45 747		beliefs, Sunni Muslim
Population	15 381 000	Currency	Malawian kwacha
Capital	Lilongwe	Organizations	Comm., SADC, UN
Languages	Chichewa, English, local languages	Map page	121

MALAYSIA
Federation of Malaysia

Area Sq Km	332 965	Religions	Sunni Muslim,
Area Sq Miles	128 559		Buddhist, Hindu,
Population	28 859 000		Christian,
Capital	Kuala Lumpur/		traditional beliefs
	Putrajaya	Currency	Ringgit
Languages	Malay, English,	Organizations	APEC, ASEAN,
	Chinese, Tamil,		Comm., UN
	local languages	Map page	60–61

MALDIVES
Republic of the Maldives

Area Sq Km	298	Religions	Sunni Muslim
Area Sq Miles	115	Currency	Rufiyaa
Population	320 000	Organizations	Comm., UN
Capital	Male	Map page	56
Languages	Divehi (Maldivian)		

MALI
Republic of Mali

Area Sq Km	1 240 140	Religions	Sunni Muslim,
Area Sq Miles	478 821		traditional beliefs,
Population	15 840 000		Christian
Capital	Bamako	Currency	CFA franc
Languages	French, Bambara,	Organizations	UN
	local languages	Map page	114

MALTA
Republic of Malta

Area Sq Km	316	Religions	Roman Catholic
Area Sq Miles	122	Currency	Euro
Population	418 000	Organizations	Comm., EU, UN
Capital	Valletta	Map page	84
Languages	Maltese, English		

MARSHALL ISLANDS
Republic of the Marshall Islands

Area Sq Km	181	Religions	Protestant, Roman
Area Sq Miles	70		Catholic
Population	55 000	Currency	United States dollar
Capital	Delap-Uliga-Djarrit	Organizations	UN
Languages	English, Marshallese	Map page	48

Martinique
French Overseas Department

Area Sq Km	1 079	Religions	Roman Catholic,
Area Sq Miles	417		traditional beliefs
Population	407 000	Currency	Euro
Capital	Fort-de-France	Map page	147
Languages	French, creole		

MAURITANIA
Islamic Arab and African Republic of Mauritania

Area Sq Km	1 030 700	Religions	Sunni Muslim
Area Sq Miles	397 955	Currency	Ouguiya
Population	3 542 000	Organizations	UN
Capital	Nouakchott	Map page	114
Languages	Arabic, French, local languages		

MAURITIUS
Republic of Mauritius

Area Sq Km	2 040	Religions	Hindu, Roman
Area Sq Miles	788		Catholic, Sunni
Population	1 307 000		Muslim
Capital	Port Louis	Currency	Mauritius rupee
Languages	English, creole,	Organizations	Comm., SADC, UN
	Hindi, Bhojpuri,	Map page	113
	French		

Mayotte
French Overseas Department

Area Sq Km	373	Religions	Sunni Muslim, Christian
Area Sq Miles	144		
Population	211 000	Currency	Euro
Capital	Dzaoudzi	Map page	121
Languages	French, Mahorian		

Melilla
Autonomous Community of Spain

Area Sq Km	13	Religions	Roman Catholic, Muslim
Area Sq Miles	5		
Population	76 034	Currency	Euro
Capital	Melilla	Map page	114
Languages	Spanish, Arabic		

MEXICO
United Mexican States

Area Sq Km	1 972 545	Religions	Roman Catholic, Protestant
Area Sq Miles	761 604		
Population	114 793 000	Currency	Mexican peso
Capital	Mexico City	Organizations	APEC, OECD, UN
Languages	Spanish, Amerindian languages	Map page	144–145

MICRONESIA, FEDERATED STATES OF

Area Sq Km	701	Religions	Roman Catholic, Protestant
Area Sq Miles	271		
Population	112 000	Currency	United States dollar
Capital	Palikir	Organizations	UN
Languages	English, Chuukese, Pohnpeian, local languages	Map page	48

MOLDOVA
Republic of Moldova

Area Sq Km	33 700	Religions	Romanian Orthodox, Russian Orthodox
Area Sq Miles	13 012		
Population	3 545 000	Currency	Moldovan leu
Capital	Chişinău (Kishinev)	Organizations	CIS, UN
Languages	Romanian, Ukrainian, Gagauz, Russian	Map page	90

MONACO
Principality of Monaco

Area Sq Km	2	Religions	Roman Catholic
Area Sq Miles	1	Currency	Euro
Population	35 000	Organizations	UN
Capital	Monaco-Ville	Map page	105
Languages	French, Monégasque, Italian		

MONGOLIA

Area Sq Km	1 565 000	Religions	Buddhist, Sunni Muslim
Area Sq Miles	604 250		
Population	2 800 000	Currency	Tugrik (tögrög)
Capital	Ulan Bator (Ulaanbaatar)	Organizations	UN
Languages	Khalka (Mongolian), Kazakh, local languages	Map page	68–69

MONTENEGRO

Area Sq Km	13 812	Religions	Montenegrin, Orthodox, Sunni Muslim
Area Sq Miles	5 333		
Population	632 000	Currency	Euro
Capital	Podgorica	Organizations	UN
Languages	Serbian, (Montenegrin), Albanian	Map page	109

Montserrat
United Kingdom Overseas Territory

Area Sq Km	100	Religions	Protestant, Roman Catholic
Area Sq Miles	39		
Population	4 655	Currency	East Caribbean dollar
Capital	Brades*	Organizations	CARICOM
Languages	English	Map page	147

*Temporary capital. Official capital Plymouth abandoned in 1997 due to volcanic activity.

MOROCCO
Kingdom of Morocco

Area Sq Km	446 550	Religions	Sunni Muslim
Area Sq Miles	172 414	Currency	Moroccan dirham
Population	32 273 000	Organizations	UN
Capital	Rabat	Map page	114
Languages	Arabic, Berber, French		

MOZAMBIQUE
Republic of Mozambique

Area Sq Km	799 380	Religions	Traditional beliefs, Roman Catholic, Sunni Muslim
Area Sq Miles	308 642		
Population	23 930 000		
Capital	Maputo	Currency	Metical
Languages	Portuguese, Makua, Tsonga, local languages	Organizations	Comm., SADC, UN
		Map page	121

MYANMAR (Burma)
Republic of the Union of Myanmar

Area Sq Km	676 577	Religions	Buddhist, Christian, Sunni Muslim
Area Sq Miles	261 228		
Population	48 337 000	Currency	Kyat
Capital	Nay Pyi Taw/ Rangoon (Yangôn)	Organizations	ASEAN, UN
		Map page	62–63
Languages	Burmese, Shan, Karen, local languages		

Nagorno-Karabakh
Disputed Territory (Azerbaijan)

Area Sq Km	6 000
Area Sq Miles	2 317
Population	140 000
Capital	Şuşa (Shusi)

NAMIBIA
Republic of Namibia

Area Sq Km	824 292	Religions	Protestant, Roman Catholic
Area Sq Miles	318 261		
Population	2 324 000	Currency	Namibian dollar
Capital	Windhoek	Organizations	Comm., SADC, UN
Languages	English, Afrikaans, German, Ovambo, local languages	Map page	121

NAURU
Republic of Nauru

Area Sq Km	21	Religions	Protestant, Roman
Area Sq Miles	8		Catholic
Population	10 000	Currency	Australian dollar
Capital	Yaren	Organizations	Comm., UN
Languages	Nauruan, English	Map page	48

NEPAL
Federal Democratic Republic of Nepal

Area Sq Km	147 181	Religions	Hindu, Buddhist,
Area Sq Miles	56 827		Sunni Muslim
Population	30 486 000	Currency	Nepalese rupee
Capital	Kathmandu	Organizations	UN
Languages	Nepali, Maithili,	Map page	75
	Bhojpuri, English,		
	local languages		

NETHERLANDS
Kingdom of the Netherlands

Area Sq Km	41 526	Religions	Roman Catholic,
Area Sq Miles	16 033		Protestant, Sunni
Population	16 665 000		Muslim
Capital	Amsterdam/	Currency	Euro
	The Hague	Organizations	EU, OECD, UN
	('s-Gravenhage)	Map page	100
Languages	Dutch, Frisian		

New Caledonia
French Overseas Territory

Area Sq Km	19 058	Religions	Roman Catholic,
Area Sq Miles	7 358		Protestant, Sunni
Population	255 000		Muslim
Capital	Nouméa	Currency	CFP franc
Languages	French, local	Map page	48
	languages		

NEW ZEALAND

Area Sq Km	270 534	Religions	Protestant, Roman
Area Sq Miles	104 454		Catholic
Population	4 415 000	Currency	New Zealand dollar
Capital	Wellington	Organizations	APEC, Comm.,
Languages	English, Maori		OECD, UN
		Map page	54

NICARAGUA
Republic of Nicaragua

Area Sq Km	130 000	Religions	Roman Catholic,
Area Sq Miles	50 193		Protestant
Population	5 870 000	Currency	Córdoba
Capital	Managua	Organizations	UN
Languages	Spanish, Amerindian	Map page	146
	languages		

NIGER
Republic of Niger

Area Sq Km	1 267 000	Religions	Sunni Muslim,
Area Sq Miles	489 191		traditional beliefs
Population	16 069 000	Currency	CFA franc
Capital	Niamey	Organizations	UN
Languages	French, Hausa,	Map page	115
	Fulani, local		
	languages		

NIGERIA
Federal Republic of Nigeria

Area Sq Km	923 768	Religions	Sunni Muslim,
Area Sq Miles	356 669		Christian, traditional
Population	162 471 000		beliefs
Capital	Abuja	Currency	Naira
Languages	English, Hausa,	Organizations	Comm., OPEC, UN
	Yoruba, Ibo, Fulani,	Map page	115
	local languages		

Niue
Self-governing New Zealand Overseas Territory

Area Sq Km	258	Religions	Christian
Area Sq Miles	100	Currency	New Zealand dollar
Population	1 496	Map page	48
Capital	Alofi		
Languages	English, Nivean		

Norfolk Island
Australian External Territory

Area Sq Km	35	Religions	Protestant, Roman
Area Sq Miles	14		Catholic
Population	2 523	Currency	Australian dollar
Capital	Kingston	Map page	48
Languages	English		

Northern Mariana Islands
United States Commonwealth

Area Sq Km	477	Religions	Roman Catholic
Area Sq Miles	184	Currency	United States dollar
Population	61 000	Map page	59
Capital	Capitol Hill		
Languages	English, Chamorro,		
	local languages		

NORTH KOREA
Democratic People's Republic of Korea

Area Sq Km	120 538	Religions	Traditional beliefs,
Area Sq Miles	46 540		Chondoist, Buddhist
Population	24 451 000	Currency	North Korean won
Capital	P'yŏngyang	Organizations	UN
Languages	Korean	Map page	65

NORWAY
Kingdom of Norway

Area Sq Km	323 878	Religions	Protestant, Roman
Area Sq Miles	125 050		Catholic
Population	4 925 000	Currency	Norwegian krone
Capital	Oslo	Organizations	OECD, UN
Languages	Norwegian	Map page	92–93

OMAN
Sultanate of Oman

Area Sq Km	309 500	Religions	Ibadhi Muslim, Sunni
Area Sq Miles	119 499		Muslim
Population	2 846 000	Currency	Omani riyal
Capital	Muscat (Masqat)	Organizations	UN
Languages	Arabic, Baluchi,	Map page	79
	Indian languages		

PAKISTAN
Islamic Republic of Pakistan

Area Sq Km	803 940	Religions	Sunni Muslim, Shi'a Muslim, Christian, Hindu
Area Sq Miles	310 403		
Population	176 745 000		
Capital	Islamabad	Currency	Pakistani rupee
Languages	Urdu, Punjabi, Sindhi, Pushtu, English	Organizations	Comm., UN
		Map page	74

PALAU
Republic of Palau

Area Sq Km	497	Religions	Roman Catholic, Protestant, traditional beliefs
Area Sq Miles	192		
Population	21 000		
Capital	Melekeok	Currency	United States dollar
Languages	Palauan, English	Organizations	UN
		Map page	59

PANAMA
Republic of Panama

Area Sq Km	77 082	Religions	Roman Catholic, Protestant, Sunni Muslim
Area Sq Miles	29 762		
Population	3 571 000		
Capital	Panama City	Currency	Balboa
Languages	Spanish, English, Amerindian languages	Organizations	UN
		Map page	146

PAPUA NEW GUINEA
Independent State of Papua New Guinea

Area Sq Km	462 840	Religions	Protestant, Roman Catholic, traditional beliefs
Area Sq Miles	178 704		
Population	7 014 000		
Capital	Port Moresby	Currency	Kina
Languages	English, Tok Pisin (creole), local languages	Organizations	APEC, Comm., UN
		Map page	59

PARAGUAY
Republic of Paraguay

Area Sq Km	406 752	Religions	Roman Catholic, Protestant
Area Sq Miles	157 048		
Population	6 568 000		
Capital	Asunción	Currency	Guaraní
Languages	Spanish, Guaraní	Organizations	UN
		Map page	152

PERU
Republic of Peru

Area Sq Km	1 285 216	Religions	Roman Catholic, Protestant
Area Sq Miles	496 225		
Population	29 400 000		
Capital	Lima	Currency	Nuevo sol
Languages	Spanish, Quechua, Aymara	Organizations	APEC, UN
		Map page	150

PHILIPPINES
Republic of the Philippines

Area Sq Km	300 000	Religions	Roman Catholic, Protestant, Sunni Muslim, Aglipayan
Area Sq Miles	115 831		
Population	94 852 000		
Capital	Manila	Currency	Philippine peso
Languages	English, Filipino, Tagalog, Cebuano, local languages	Organizations	APEC, ASEAN, UN
		Map page	64

Pitcairn Islands
United Kingdom Overseas Territory

Area Sq Km	45	Religions	Protestant
Area Sq Miles	17	Currency	New Zealand dollar
Population	48	Map page	49
Capital	Adamstown		
Languages	English		

POLAND
Polish Republic

Area Sq Km	312 683	Religions	Roman Catholic, Polish Orthodox
Area Sq Miles	120 728		
Population	38 299 000	Currency	Złoty
Capital	Warsaw (Warszawa)	Organizations	EU, OECD, UN
Languages	Polish, German	Map page	103

PORTUGAL
Portuguese Republic

Area Sq Km	88 940	Religions	Roman Catholic, Protestant
Area Sq Miles	34 340		
Population	10 690 000	Currency	Euro
Capital	Lisbon (Lisboa)	Organizations	EU, OECD, UN
Languages	Portuguese	Map page	106

Puerto Rico
United States Commonwealth

Area Sq Km	9 104	Religions	Roman Catholic, Protestant
Area Sq Miles	3 515		
Population	3 746 000	Currency	United States dollar
Capital	San Juan	Map page	147
Languages	Spanish, English		

QATAR
State of Qatar

Area Sq Km	11 437	Religions	Sunni Muslim
Area Sq Miles	4 416	Currency	Qatari riyal
Population	1 870 000	Organizations	OPEC, UN
Capital	Doha (Ad Dawḥah)	Map page	79
Languages	Arabic		

Réunion
French Overseas Department

Area Sq Km	2 551	Religions	Roman Catholic
Area Sq Miles	985	Currency	Euro
Population	856 000	Map page	113
Capital	St-Denis		
Languages	French, creole		

Rodrigues Island
part of Mauritius

Area Sq Km	104	Religions	Christian
Area Sq Miles	40	Currency	Rupee
Population	37 837	Map page	159
Capital	Port Mathurin		
Languages	English, creole		

ROMANIA

Area Sq Km	237 500	**Religions**	Romanian Orthodox, Protestant, Roman Catholic
Area Sq Miles	91 699		
Population	21 436 000		
Capital	Bucharest (Bucureşti)	**Currency**	Romanian leu
Languages	Romanian, Hungarian	**Organizations**	EU, UN
		Map page	110

RUSSIAN FEDERATION

Area Sq Km	17 075 400	**Religions**	Russian Orthodox, Sunni Muslim, Protestant
Area Sq Miles	6 592 849		
Population	142 836 000		
Capital	Moscow (Moskva)	**Currency**	Russian rouble
Languages	Russian, Tatar, Ukrainian, local languages	**Organizations**	APEC, CIS, UN
		Map page	82–83

RWANDA
Republic of Rwanda

Area Sq Km	26 338	**Religions**	Roman Catholic, traditional beliefs, Protestant
Area Sq Miles	10 169		
Population	10 943 000		
Capital	Kigali	**Currency**	Rwandan franc
Languages	Kinyarwanda, French, English	**Organizations**	Comm., UN
		Map page	119

Saba
Netherlands Special Municipality

Area Sq Km	13	**Religions**	Roman Catholic, Protestant
Area Sq Miles	5		
Population	1 737	**Currency**	United States dollar
Capital	Bottom	**Map page**	147
Languages	Dutch, English		

St-Barthélémy
French Overseas Collectivity

Area Sq Km	21	**Religions**	Roman Catholic
Area Sq Miles	8	**Currency**	Euro
Population	8 823	**Map page**	147
Capital	Gustavia		
Languages	French		

St Helena, Ascension and Tristan da Cunha
United Kingdom Overseas Territory

Area Sq Km	121	**Religions**	Protestant, Roman Catholic,
Area Sq Miles	47		
Population	5 404	**Currency**	St Helena pound
Capital	Jamestown	**Map page**	113
Languages	English		

ST KITTS AND NEVIS
Federation of St Kitts and Nevis

Area Sq Km	261	**Religions**	Protestant, Roman Catholic
Area Sq Miles	101		
Population	53 000	**Currency**	East Caribbean dollar
Capital	Basseterre	**Organizations**	CARICOM, Comm., UN
Languages	English, creole		
		Map page	147

ST LUCIA

Area Sq Km	616	**Religions**	Roman Catholic, Protestant
Area Sq Miles	238		
Population	176 000	**Currency**	East Caribbean doll
Capital	Castries	**Organizations**	CARICOM, Comm., UN
Languages	English, creole		
		Map page	147

St-Martin
French Overseas Collectivity

Area Sq Km	54	**Religions**	Roman Catholic
Area Sq Miles	21	**Currency**	Euro
Population	37 163	**Map page**	147
Capital	Marigot		
Languages	French		

St Pierre and Miquelon
French Territorial Collectivity

Area Sq Km	242	**Religions**	Roman Catholic
Area Sq Miles	93	**Currency**	Euro
Population	6 290	**Map page**	131
Capital	St-Pierre		
Languages	French		

ST VINCENT AND THE GRENADINE

Area Sq Km	389	**Religions**	Protestant, Roman Catholic
Area Sq Miles	150		
Population	109 000	**Currency**	East Caribbean doll
Capital	Kingstown	**Organizations**	CARICOM, Comm., UN
Languages	English, creole		
		Map page	147

SAMOA
Independent State of Samoa

Area Sq Km	2 831	**Religions**	Protestant, Roman Catholic
Area Sq Miles	1 093		
Population	184 000	**Currency**	Tala
Capital	Apia	**Organizations**	Comm., UN
Languages	Samoan, English	**Map page**	49

SAN MARINO
Republic of San Marino

Area Sq Km	61	**Religions**	Roman Catholic
Area Sq Miles	24	**Currency**	Euro
Population	32 000	**Organizations**	UN
Capital	San Marino	**Map page**	108
Languages	Italian		

SÃO TOMÉ AND PRÍNCIPE
Democratic Republic of São Tomé and Príncipe

Area Sq Km	964	**Religions**	Roman Catholic, Protestant
Area Sq Miles	372		
Population	169 000	**Currency**	Dobra
Capital	São Tomé	**Organizations**	UN
Languages	Portuguese, creole	**Map page**	113

SAUDI ARABIA
Kingdom of Saudi Arabia

Area Sq Km	2 200 000	Religions	Sunni Muslim, Shi'a Muslim
Area Sq Miles	849 425		
Population	28 083 000	Currency	Saudi Arabian riyal
Capital	Riyadh (Ar Riyāḍ)	Organizations	OPEC, UN
Languages	Arabic	Map page	78–79

SENEGAL
Republic of Senegal

Area Sq Km	196 720	Religions	Sunni Muslim, Roman Catholic, traditional beliefs
Area Sq Miles	75 954		
Population	12 768 000	Currency	CFA franc
Capital	Dakar	Organizations	UN
Languages	French, Wolof, Fulani, local languages	Map page	114

SERBIA
Republic of Serbia

Area Sq Km	88 361	Religions	Roman Catholic, Serbian Orthodox, Sunni Muslim
Area Sq Miles	34 116		
Population	7 306 677	Currency	Serbian dinar
Capital	Belgrade (Beograd)	Organizations	UN
Languages	Serbian, Hungarian	Map page	109

SEYCHELLES
Republic of the Seychelles

Area Sq Km	455	Religions	Roman Catholic, Protestant
Area Sq Miles	176		
Population	87 000	Currency	Seychelles rupee
Capital	Victoria	Organizations	Comm., SADC, UN
Languages	English, French, creole	Map page	113

SIERRA LEONE
Republic of Sierra Leone

Area Sq Km	71 740	Religions	Sunni Muslim, traditional beliefs
Area Sq Miles	27 699		
Population	5 997 000	Currency	Leone
Capital	Freetown	Organizations	Comm., UN
Languages	English, creole, Mende, Temne, local languages	Map page	114

SINGAPORE
Republic of Singapore

Area Sq Km	639	Religions	Buddhist, Taoist, Sunni Muslim, Christian, Hindu
Area Sq Miles	247		
Population	5 188 000	Currency	Singapore dollar
Capital	Singapore	Organizations	APEC, ASEAN, Comm., UN
Languages	Chinese, English, Malay, Tamil	Map page	60

Sint Eustatius
Netherlands Special Municipality

Area Sq Km	21	Religions	Protestant, Roman Catholic
Area Sq Miles	8		
Population	2 886	Currency	United States dollar
Capital	Oranjestad	Map page	147
Languages	Dutch, English, Spanish		

Sint Maarten
Self-governing Netherlands Territory

Area Sq Km	34	Religions	Protestant, Roman Catholic
Area Sq Miles	13		
Population	37 429	Currency	Caribbean guilder
Capital	Philipsburg	Map page	147
Languages	Dutch, English		

SLOVAKIA
Slovak Republic

Area Sq Km	49 035	Religions	Roman Catholic, Protestant, Orthodox
Area Sq Miles	18 933		
Population	5 472 000	Currency	Euro
Capital	Bratislava	Organizations	EU, OECD, UN
Languages	Slovak, Hungarian, Czech	Map page	103

SLOVENIA
Republic of Slovenia

Area Sq Km	20 251	Religions	Roman Catholic, Protestant
Area Sq Miles	7 819		
Population	2 035 000	Currency	Euro
Capital	Ljubljana	Organizations	EU, OECD, UN
Languages	Slovenian, Croatian, Serbian	Map page	108–109

SOLOMON ISLANDS

Area Sq Km	28 370	Religions	Protestant, Roman Catholic
Area Sq Miles	10 954		
Population	552 000	Currency	Solomon Islands dollar
Capital	Honiara	Organizations	Comm., UN
Languages	English, creole, local languages	Map page	48

SOMALIA
Somali Democratic Republic

Area Sq Km	637 657	Religions	Sunni Muslim
Area Sq Miles	246 201	Currency	Somali shilling
Population	9 557 000	Organizations	UN
Capital	Mogadishu (Muqdisho)	Map page	117
Languages	Somali, Arabic		

Somaliland
Disputed Territory (Somalia)

Area Sq Km	140 000	Map page	117
Area Sq Miles	54 054		
Population	3 500 000		
Capital	Hargeysa		

SOUTH AFRICA, REPUBLIC OF

Area Sq Km	1 219 080	Religions	Protestant, Roman Catholic, Sunni Muslim, Hindu
Area Sq Miles	470 689		
Population	50 460 000		
Capital	Pretoria (Tshwane)/ Cape Town	Currency	Rand
		Organizations	Comm., SADC, UN
Languages	Afrikaans, English, nine official local languages	Map page	122–123

SOUTH KOREA
Republic of Korea

Area Sq Km	99 274	**Religions**	Buddhist, Protestant,
Area Sq Miles	38 330		Roman Catholic
Population	48 391 000	**Currency**	South Korean won
Capital	Seoul (Sŏul)	**Organizations**	APEC, OECD, UN
Languages	Korean	**Map page**	65

South Ossetia
Disputed Territory (Georgia)

Area Sq Km	4 000
Area Sq Miles	1 544
Population	70 000
Capital	Tskhinvali

SOUTH SUDAN
Republic of South Sudan

Area Sq Km	644 329	**Religions**	Traditional beliefs,
Area Sq Miles	248 775		Christian
Population	8 260 490	**Currency**	South Sudan pound
Capital	Juba	**Organizations**	UN
Languages	English, Arabic,	**Map page**	117
	Dinka, Nuer, local		
	languages		

SPAIN
Kingdom of Spain

Area Sq Km	504 782	**Religions**	Roman Catholic
Area Sq Miles	194 897	**Currency**	Euro
Population	46 455 000	**Organizations**	EU, OECD, UN
Capital	Madrid	**Map page**	106–107
Languages	Spanish, Castilian,		
	Catalan, Galician,		
	Basque		

SRI LANKA
Democratic Socialist Republic of Sri Lanka

Area Sq Km	65 610	**Religions**	Buddhist, Hindu,
Area Sq Miles	25 332		Sunni Muslim,
Population	21 045 000		Roman Catholic
Capital	Sri Jayewardenepura	**Currency**	Sri Lankan rupee
	Kotte	**Organizations**	Comm., UN
Languages	Sinhalese, Tamil,	**Map page**	73
	English		

SUDAN
Republic of the Sudan

Area Sq Km	1 861 484	**Religions**	Sunni Muslim,
Area Sq Miles	718 725		traditional beliefs,
Population	36 371 510		Christian
Capital	Khartoum	**Currency**	Sudanese pound
Languages	Arabic, Dinka,		(Sudani)
	Nubian, Beja, Nuer,	**Organizations**	UN
	local languages	**Map page**	116–117

SURINAME
Republic of Suriname

Area Sq Km	163 820	**Religions**	Hindu, Roman
Area Sq Miles	63 251		Catholic, Protestant,
Population	529 000		Sunni Muslim
Capital	Paramaribo	**Currency**	Suriname guilder
Languages	Dutch,	**Organizations**	CARICOM, UN
	Surinamese,	**Map page**	151
	English,Hindi		

Svalbard
part of Norway

Area Sq Km	61 229	**Religions**	Protestant
Area Sq Miles	23 641	**Currency**	Norwegian krone
Population	2 400	**Map page**	82
Capital	Longyearbyen		
Languages	Norwegian		

SWAZILAND
Kingdom of Swaziland

Area Sq Km	17 364	**Religions**	Christian,
Area Sq Miles	6 704		traditional beliefs
Population	1 203 000	**Currency**	Emalangeni,
Capital	Mbabane		South African rand
Languages	Swazi, English	**Organizations**	Comm., SADC, UN
		Map page	123

SWEDEN
Kingdom of Sweden

Area Sq Km	449 964	**Religions**	Protestant,
Area Sq Miles	173 732		Roman Catholic
Population	9 441 000	**Currency**	Swedish krona
Capital	Stockholm	**Organizations**	EU, OECD, UN
Languages	Swedish	**Map page**	92–93

SWITZERLAND
Swiss Confederation

Area Sq Km	41 293	**Religions**	Roman Catholic,
Area Sq Miles	15 943		Protestant,
Population	7 702 000	**Currency**	Swiss franc
Capital	Bern	**Organizations**	OECD, UN
Languages	German, French,	**Map page**	105
	Italian, Romansch		

SYRIA
Syrian Arab Republic

Area Sq Km	185 180	**Religions**	Sunni Muslim, Shi'a
Area Sq Miles	71 498		Muslim, Christian
Population	20 766 000	**Currency**	Syrian pound
Capital	Damascus (Dimashq)	**Organizations**	UN
Languages	Arabic, Kurdish,	**Map page**	80
	Armenian		

TAIWAN
Republic of China

Area Sq Km	36 179	**Religions**	Buddhist, Taoist,
Area Sq Miles	13 969		Confucian, Christian
Population	23 164 000	**Currency**	Taiwan dollar
Capital	Taibei	**Organizations**	APEC
Languages	Mandarin, Min,	**Map page**	71
	Hakka, local		
	languages		

The People's Republic of China claims Taiwan as its 23rd province

TAJIKISTAN
Republic of Tajikistan

Area Sq Km	143 100	**Religions**	Sunni Muslim
Area Sq Miles	55 251	**Currency**	Somoni
Population	6 977 000	**Organizations**	CIS, UN
Capital	Dushanbe	**Map page**	77
Languages	Tajik, Uzbek, Russian		

TANZANIA
United Republic of Tanzania

Area Sq Km	945 087	**Religions**	Shi'a Muslim, Sunni Muslim, traditional beliefs, Christian
Area Sq Miles	364 900		
Population	46 218 000		
Capital	Dodoma	**Currency**	Tanzanian shilling
Languages	Swahili, English, Nyamwezi, local languages	**Organizations**	Comm., SADC, UN
		Map page	119

THAILAND
Kingdom of Thailand

Area Sq Km	513 115	**Religions**	Buddhist, Sunni Muslim
Area Sq Miles	198 115		
Population	69 519 000	**Currency**	Baht
Capital	Bangkok (Krung Thep)	**Organizations**	APEC, ASEAN, UN
		Map page	62–63
Languages	Thai, Lao, Chinese, Malay, Mon-Khmer languages		

TOGO
Republic of Togo

Area Sq Km	56 785	**Religions**	Traditional beliefs, Christian, Sunni Muslim
Area Sq Miles	21 925		
Population	6 155 000		
Capital	Lomé	**Currency**	CFA franc
Languages	French, Ewe, Kabre, local languages	**Organizations**	UN
		Map page	114

Tokelau
New Zealand Overseas Territory

Area Sq Km	10	**Religions**	Christian
Area Sq Miles	4	**Currency**	New Zealand dollar
Population	1 466	**Map page**	49
Capital	none		
Languages	English, Tokelauan		

TONGA
Kingdom of Tonga

Area Sq Km	748	**Religions**	Protestant, Roman Catholic
Area Sq Miles	289		
Population	105 000	**Currency**	Pa'anga
Capital	Nuku'alofa	**Organizations**	Comm., UN
Languages	Tongan, English	**Map page**	49

Transnistria
Disputed Territory (Moldova)

Area Sq Km	4 200	**Map page**	90
Area Sq Miles	1 546		
Population	520 000		
Capital	Tiraspol		

TRINIDAD AND TOBAGO
Republic of Trinidad and Tobago

Area Sq Km	5 130	**Religions**	Roman Catholic, Hindu, Protestant, Sunni Muslim
Area Sq Miles	1 981		
Population	1 346 000		
Capital	Port of Spain	**Currency**	Trinidad and Tobago dollar
Languages	English, creole, Hindi		
		Organizations	CARICOM, Comm., UN
		Map page	147

Tristan da Cunha
Part of St Helena, Ascension and Tristan da Cunha

Area Sq Km	98	**Religions**	Protestant, Roman Catholic
Area Sq Miles	38		
Population	263	**Currency**	Pound sterling
Capital	Settlement of Edinburgh	**Map page**	113
Languages	English		

TUNISIA
Republic of Tunisia

Area Sq Km	164 150	**Religions**	Sunni Muslim
Area Sq Miles	63 379	**Currency**	Tunisian dinar
Population	10 594 000	**Organizations**	UN
Capital	Tunis	**Map page**	115
Languages	Arabic, French		

TURKEY
Republic of Turkey

Area Sq Km	779 452	**Religions**	Sunni Muslim, Shi'a Muslim
Area Sq Miles	300 948		
Population	73 640 000	**Currency**	Lira
Capital	Ankara	**Organizations**	OECD, UN
Languages	Turkish, Kurdish	**Map page**	80

TURKMENISTAN
Republic of Turkmenistan

Area Sq Km	488 100	**Religions**	Sunni Muslim, Russian Orthodox
Area Sq Miles	188 456		
Population	5 105 000	**Currency**	Turkmen manat
Capital	Aşgabat (Ashkhabad)	**Organizations**	UN
Languages	Turkmen, Uzbek, Russian	**Map page**	76

Turks and Caicos Islands
United Kingdom Overseas Territory

Area Sq Km	430	**Religions**	Protestant
Area Sq Miles	166	**Currency**	United States dollar
Population	39 000	**Map page**	147
Capital	Grand Turk (Cockburn Town)		
Languages	English		

TUVALU

Area Sq Km	25	**Religions**	Protestant
Area Sq Miles	10	**Currency**	Australian dollar
Population	10 000	**Organizations**	Comm., UN
Capital	Vaiaku	**Map page**	49
Languages	Tuvaluan, English		

UGANDA
Republic of Uganda

Area Sq Km	241 038	Religions	Roman Catholic, Protestant, Sunni Muslim, traditional beliefs
Area Sq Miles	93 065		
Population	34 509 000		
Capital	Kampala		
Languages	English, Swahili, Luganda, local languages	Currency	Ugandan shilling
		Organizations	Comm., UN
		Map page	119

UKRAINE
Republic of Ukraine

Area Sq Km	603 700	Religions	Ukrainian Orthodox, Ukrainian Catholic, Roman Catholic
Area Sq Miles	233 090		
Population	45 190 000		
Capital	Kiev (Kyiv)	Currency	Hryvnia
Languages	Ukrainian, Russian	Organizations	CIS, UN
		Map page	90–91

UNITED ARAB EMIRATES
Federation of Emirates

Area Sq Km	77 700	Religions	Sunni Muslim, Shi'a Muslim
Area Sq Miles	30 000		
Population	7 891 000	Currency	United Arab Emirates dirham
Capital	Abu Dhabi (Abū Ẓabī)		
Languages	Arabic, English	Organizations	OPEC, UN
		Map page	79

Abu Dhabi (Abū Ẓabī) (Emirate)

Area Sq Km	67 340	Population	1 628 000
Area Sq Miles	26 000	Capital	Abu Dhabi (Abū Ẓabī)

Ajman (Emirate)

Area Sq Km	259	Population	250 000
Area Sq Miles	100	Capital	Ajman

Dubai (Emirate)

Area Sq Km	3 885	Population	1 722 000
Area Sq Miles	1 500	Capital	Dubai

Fujairah (Emirate)

Area Sq Km	1 165	Population	152 000
Area Sq Miles	450	Capital	Fujairah

Ra's al Khaymah (Emirate)

Area Sq Km	1 684	Population	241 000
Area Sq Miles	650	Capital	Ra's al Khaymah

Sharjah (Emirate)

Area Sq Km	2 590	Population	1 017 000
Area Sq Miles	1 000	Capital	Sharjah

Umm al Qaywayn (Emirate)

Area Sq Km	777	Population	56 000
Area Sq Miles	300	Capital	Umm al Qaywayn

UNITED KINGDOM
of Great Britain and Northern Ireland

Area Sq Km	243 609	Religions	Protestant, Roman Catholic, Muslim
Area Sq Miles	94 058		
Population	62 417 000	Currency	Pound sterling
Capital	London	Organizations	Comm., EU, OECD, UN
Languages	English, Welsh, Gaelic		
		Map page	94–95

England (Constituent country)

Area Sq Km	130 433	Population	51 809 700
Area Sq Miles	50 360	Capital	London

Northern Ireland (Province)

Area Sq Km	13 576	Population	1 788 900
Area Sq Miles	5 242	Capital	Belfast

Scotland (Constituent country)

Area Sq Km	78 822	Population	5 194 000
Area Sq Miles	30 433	Capital	Edinburgh

Wales (Principality)

Area Sq Km	20 778	Population	2 999 300
Area Sq Miles	8 022	Capital	Cardiff

UNITED STATES OF AMERICA
Federal Republic

Area Sq Km	9 826 635	Religions	Protestant, Roman Catholic, Sunni Muslim, Jewish
Area Sq Miles	3 794 085		
Population	313 085 000		
Capital	Washington D.C.	Currency	United States dollar
Languages	English, Spanish	Organizations	APEC, OECD, UN
		Map page	132–133

Alabama (State)

Area Sq Km	135 765	Population	4 708 708
Area Sq Miles	52 419	Capital	Montgomery

Alaska (State)

Area Sq Km	1 717 854	Population	698 473
Area Sq Miles	663 267	Capital	Juneau

Arizona (State)

Area Sq Km	295 253	Population	6 595 778
Area Sq Miles	113 998	Capital	Phoenix

Arkansas (State)

Area Sq Km	137 733	Population	2 889 450
Area Sq Miles	53 179	Capital	Little Rock

California (State)

Area Sq Km	423 971	Population	36 961 664
Area Sq Miles	163 696	Capital	Sacramento

Colorado (State)

Area Sq Km	269 602	Population	5 024 748
Area Sq Miles	104 094	Capital	Denver

Connecticut (State)

Area Sq Km	14 356	Population	3 518 288
Area Sq Miles	5 543	Capital	Hartford

Delaware (State)

Area Sq Km	6 446	Population	885 122
Area Sq Miles	2 489	Capital	Dover

District of Columbia (District)

Area Sq Km	176	Population	599 657
Area Sq Miles	68	Capital	Washington

Florida (State)

Area Sq Km	170 305	Population	18 537 969
Area Sq Miles	65 755	Capital	Tallahassee

Georgia (State)

Area Sq Km	153 910	Population	9 829 211
Area Sq Miles	59 425	Capital	Atlanta

Hawaii (State)

Area Sq Km	28 311	Population	1 295 178
Area Sq Miles	10 931	Capital	Honolulu

Idaho (State)

Area Sq Km	216 445	Population	1 545 801
Area Sq Miles	83 570	Capital	Boise

Illinois (State)

Area Sq Km	149 997	Population	12 910 409
Area Sq Miles	57 914	Capital	Springfield

Indiana (State)

Area Sq Km	94 322	Population	6 423 113
Area Sq Miles	36 418	Capital	Indianapolis

Iowa (State)

Area Sq Km	145 744	Population	3 007 856
Area Sq Miles	56 272	Capital	Des Moines

Kansas (State)

Area Sq Km	213 096	Population	2 818 747
Area Sq Miles	82 277	Capital	Topeka

Kentucky (State)

Area Sq Km	104 659	Population	4 314 113
Area Sq Miles	40 409	Capital	Frankfort

Louisiana (State)

Area Sq Km	134 265	Population	4 492 076
Area Sq Miles	51 840	Capital	Baton Rouge

Maine (State)

Area Sq Km	91 647	Population	1 318 301
Area Sq Miles	35 385	Capital	Augusta

Maryland (State)

Area Sq Km	32 134	Population	5 699 478
Area Sq Miles	12 407	Capital	Annapolis

Massachusetts (State)

Area Sq Km	27 337	Population	6 593 587
Area Sq Miles	10 555	Capital	Boston

Michigan (State)

Area Sq Km	250 493	Population	9 969 727
Area Sq Miles	96 716	Capital	Lansing

Minnesota (State)

Area Sq Km	225 171	Population	5 266 214
Area Sq Miles	86 939	Capital	St Paul

Mississippi (State)

Area Sq Km	125 433	Population	2 951 996
Area Sq Miles	48 430	Capital	Jackson

Missouri (State)

Area Sq Km	180 533	Population	5 987 580
Area Sq Miles	69 704	Capital	Jefferson City

Montana (State)

Area Sq Km	380 837	Population	974 989
Area Sq Miles	147 042	Capital	Helena

Nebraska (State)

Area Sq Km	200 346	Population	1 796 619
Area Sq Miles	77 354	Capital	Lincoln

Nevada (State)

Area Sq Km	286 352	Population	2 643 085
Area Sq Miles	110 561	Capital	Carson City

New Hampshire (State)

Area Sq Km	24 216	Population	1 324 575
Area Sq Miles	9 350	Capital	Concord

New Jersey (State)

Area Sq Km	22 587	Population	8 707 739
Area Sq Miles	8 721	Capital	Trenton

UNITED STATES OF AMERICA
Federal Republic

New Mexico (State)

Area Sq Km	314 914	Population	2 009 671
Area Sq Miles	121 589	Capital	Santa Fe

New York (State)

Area Sq Km	141 299	Population	19 541 453
Area Sq Miles	54 556	Capital	Albany

North Carolina (State)

Area Sq Km	139 391	Population	9 380 884
Area Sq Miles	53 819	Capital	Raleigh

North Dakota (State)

Area Sq Km	183 112	Population	646 844
Area Sq Miles	70 700	Capital	Bismarck

Ohio (State)

Area Sq Km	116 096	Population	11 542 645
Area Sq Miles	44 825	Capital	Columbus

Oklahoma (State)

Area Sq Km	181 035	Population	3 687 050
Area Sq Miles	69 898	Capital	Oklahoma City

Oregon (State)

Area Sq Km	254 806	Population	3 825 657
Area Sq Miles	98 381	Capital	Salem

Pennsylvania (State)

Area Sq Km	119 282	Population	12 604 767
Area Sq Miles	46 055	Capital	Harrisburg

Rhode Island (State)

Area Sq Km	4 002	Population	1 053 209
Area Sq Miles	1 545	Capital	Providence

South Carolina (State)

Area Sq Km	82 931	Population	4 561 242
Area Sq Miles	32 020	Capital	Columbia

South Dakota (State)

Area Sq Km	199 730	Population	812 383
Area Sq Miles	77 116	Capital	Pierre

Tennessee (State)

Area Sq Km	109 150	Population	6 296 254
Area Sq Miles	42 143	Capital	Nashville

Texas (State)

Area Sq Km	695 622	Population	24 782 302
Area Sq Miles	268 581	Capital	Austin

Utah (State)

Area Sq Km	219 887	Population	2 784 572
Area Sq Miles	84 899	Capital	Salt Lake City

Vermont (State)

Area Sq Km	24 900	Population	621 760
Area Sq Miles	9 614	Capital	Montpelier

Virginia (State)

Area Sq Km	110 784	Population	7 882 590
Area Sq Miles	42 774	Capital	Richmond

Washington (State)

Area Sq Km	184 666	Population	6 664 195
Area Sq Miles	71 300	Capital	Olympia

West Virginia (State)

Area Sq Km	62 755	Population	1 819 777
Area Sq Miles	24 230	Capital	Charleston

Wisconsin (State)

Area Sq Km	169 639	Population	5 654 774
Area Sq Miles	65 498	Capital	Madison

Wyoming (State)

Area Sq Km	253 337	Population	544 270
Area Sq Miles	97 814	Capital	Cheyenne

URUGUAY
Oriental Republic of Uruguay

Area Sq Km	176 215	Religions	Roman Catholic,
Area Sq Miles	68 037		Protestant, Jewish
Population	3 380 000	Currency	Uruguayan peso
Capital	Montevideo	Organizations	UN
Languages	Spanish	Map page	153

UZBEKISTAN
Republic of Uzbekistan

Area Sq Km	447 400	Religions	Sunni Muslim, Russian
Area Sq Miles	172 742		Orthodox
Population	27 760 000	Currency	Uzbek som
Capital	Tashkent	Organizations	CIS, UN
Languages	Uzbek, Russian,	Map page	76–77
	Tajik, Kazakh		

VANUATU
Republic of Vanuatu

Area Sq Km	12 190	Religions	Protestant, Roman Catholic, traditional beliefs
Area Sq Miles	4 707		
Population	246 000		
Capital	Port Vila	Currency	Vatu
Languages	English, Bislama (creole), French	Organizations	Comm., UN
		Map page	48

 VATICAN CITY
Vatican City State or Holy See

Area Sq Km	0.5	Religions	Roman Catholic
Area Sq Miles	0.2	Currency	Euro
Population	800	Map page	108
Capital	Vatican City		
Languages	Italian		

 VENEZUELA
Bolivarian Republic of Venezuela

Area Sq Km	912 050	Religions	Roman Catholic, Protestant
Area Sq Miles	352 144		
Population	29 437 000	Currency	Bolívar fuerte
Capital	Caracas	Organizations	OPEC, UN
Languages	Spanish, Amerindian languages	Map page	150

 VIETNAM
Socialist Republic of Vietnam

Area Sq Km	329 565	Religions	Buddhist, Taoist, Roman Catholic, Cao Dai, Hoa Hoa
Area Sq Miles	127 246		
Population	88 792 000		
Capital	Ha Nôi (Hanoi)	Currency	Dong
Languages	Vietnamese, Thai, Khmer, Chinese, local languages	Organizations	APEC, ASEAN, UN
		Map page	62–63

Virgin Islands (U.K.)
United Kingdom Overseas Territory

Area Sq Km	153	Religions	Protestant, Roman Catholic
Area Sq Miles	59		
Population	23 000	Currency	United States dollar
Capital	Road Town	Map page	147
Languages	English		

Virgin Islands (U.S.)
United States Unincorporated Territory

Area Sq Km	352	Religions	Protestant, Roman Catholic
Area Sq Miles	136		
Population	109 000	Currency	United States dollar
Capital	Charlotte Amalie	Map page	147
Languages	English, Spanish		

Wallis and Futuna Islands
French Overseas Territory

Area Sq Km	274	Religions	Roman Catholic
Area Sq Miles	106	Currency	CFP franc
Population	13 000	Map page	49
Capital	Matā'utu		
Languages	French, Wallisian, Futunian		

West Bank
Disputed Territory

Area Sq Km	5 860	Religions	Sunni Muslim, Jewish, Shi'a Muslim, Christian
Area Sq Miles	2 263		
Population	2 513 283		
Capital	none	Currency	Jordanian dinar, Israeli shekel
Languages	Arabic, Hebrew	Map page	80

 Western Sahara
Disputed Territory (Morocco)

Area Sq Km	266 000	Religions	Sunni Muslim
Area Sq Miles	102 703	Currency	Moroccan dirham
Population	548 000	Map page	114
Capital	Laâyoune		
Languages	Arabic		

 YEMEN
Republic of Yemen

Area Sq Km	527 968	Religions	Sunni Muslim, Shi'a Muslim
Area Sq Miles	203 850		
Population	24 800 000	Currency	Yemeni riyal
Capital	Şan'ā'	Organizations	UN
Languages	Arabic	Map page	78–79

ZAMBIA
Republic of Zambia

Area Sq Km	752 614	Religions	Christian, traditional beliefs
Area Sq Miles	290 586		
Population	13 475 000	Currency	Zambian kwacha
Capital	Lusaka	Organizations	Comm., SADC, UN
Languages	English, Bemba, Nyanja, Tonga, local languages	Map page	120–121

ZIMBABWE
Republic of Zimbabwe

Area Sq Km	390 759	Religions	Christian, traditional beliefs
Area Sq Miles	150 873		
Population	12 754 000	Currency	Zimbabwean dollar (suspended)
Capital	Harare		
Languages	English, Shona, Ndebele	Organizations	SADC, UN
		Map page	121

ANTARCTICA

Total Land Area
12 093 000 sq km
4 669 107 sq miles
(excluding ice shelves)

OCEANIA

Total land area
8 844 516 sq km
3 414 868 sq miles
(includes New Guinea and
Pacific Island nations)

HIGHEST MOUNTAIN
Vinson Massif
4 897 m /16 066 ft

HIGHEST MOUNTAIN
Puncak Jaya

LARGEST ISLAND
New Guinea

LARGEST LAKE AND
LOWEST POINT
Lake Eyre

LONGEST RIVER
AND LARGEST
DRAINAGE BASIN
Murray-Darling

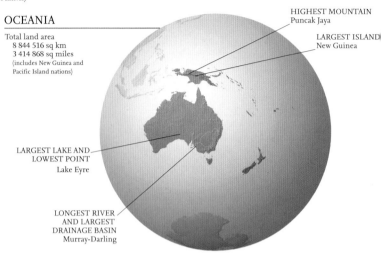

HIGHEST MOUNTAINS	metres	feet
Vinson Massif	4 897	16 066
Mt Tyree	4 852	15 918
Mt Kirkpatrick	4 528	14 855
Mt Markham	4 351	14 275
Mt Jackson	4 190	13 747
Mt Sidley	4 181	13 717

HIGHEST MOUNTAINS	metres	feet	LARGEST ISLANDS	sq km	sq miles	LARGEST LAKES	sq km	sq miles	LONGEST RIVERS	km	mile
Puncak Jaya	5 030	16 502	New Guinea	808 510	312 166	Lake Eyre	0–8 900	0–3 436	Murray-Darling	3 672	2 28.
Puncak Trikora	4 730	15 518	South Island	151 215	58 384	Lake Torrens	0–5 780	0–2 232	Darling	2 844	1 76
Puncak Mandala	4 700	15 420	North Island	115 777	44 701				Murray	2 375	1 47
Puncak Yamin	4 595	15 075	Tasmania	67 800	26 178				Murrumbidgee	1 485	92
Mt Wilhelm	4 509	14 793							Lachlan	1 339	83
Mt Kubor	4 359	14 301							Cooper Creek	1 113	69

ASIA

Total Land Area
45 036 492 sq km
17 388 589 sq miles

LARGEST DRAINAGE BASIN
Ob'-Irtysh

LONGEST RIVER
Yangtze

LARGEST LAKE
Caspian Sea

LOWEST POINT
Dead Sea

HIGHEST MOUNTAIN
Mount Everest

LARGEST ISLAND
Borneo

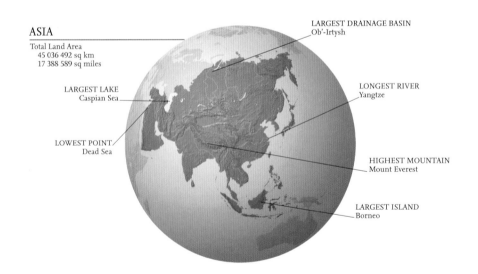

HIGHEST MOUNTAINS	metres	feet	LARGEST ISLANDS	sq km	sq miles	LARGEST LAKES	sq km	sq miles	LONGEST RIVERS	km	miles
Mt Everest	8 848	29 028	Borneo	745 561	287 861	Caspian Sea	371 000	143 243	Yangtze	6 380	3 965
K2	8 611	28 251	Sumatra	473 606	182 859	Lake Baikal	30 500	11 776	Ob'-Irtysh	5 568	3 460
Kangchenjunga	8 586	28 169	Honshū	227 414	87 805	Lake Balkhash	17 400	6 718	Yenisey-Angara-Selenga	5 550	3 449
Lhotse	8 516	27 939	Celebes	189 216	73 056	Aral Sea	17 158	6 625	Yellow	5 464	3 395
Makalu	8 463	27 765	Java	132 188	51 038	Ysyk-Köl	6 200	2 394	Irtysh	4 440	2 759
Cho Oyu	8 201	26 906	Luzon	104 690	40 421						

EUROPE

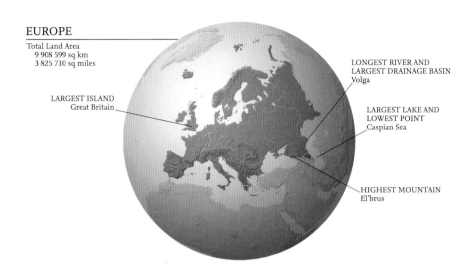

Total Land Area
9 908 599 sq km
3 825 710 sq miles

LARGEST ISLAND
Great Britain

LONGEST RIVER AND
LARGEST DRAINAGE BASIN
Volga

LARGEST LAKE AND
LOWEST POINT
Caspian Sea

HIGHEST MOUNTAIN
El'brus

HIGHEST MOUNTAINS	metres	feet	LARGEST ISLANDS	sq km	sq miles	LARGEST LAKES	sq km	sq miles	LONGEST RIVERS	km	miles
El'brus	5 642	18 510	Great Britain	218 476	84 354	Caspian Sea	371 000	143 243	Volga	3 688	2 292
Gora Dykh-Tau	5 204	17 073	Iceland	102 820	39 699	Lake Ladoga	18 390	7 100	Danube	2 850	1 771
Shkhara	5 201	17 063	Ireland	83 045	32 064	Lake Onega	9 600	3 707	Dnieper	2 285	1 420
Kazbek	5 047	16 558	Ostrov Severnyy (part of Novaya Zemlya)	47 079	18 177	Vänern	5 585	2 156	Kama	2 028	1 260
Mont Blanc	4 810	15 781	Spitsbergen	37 814	14 600	Rybinskoye Vodokhranilishche	5 180	2 000	Don	1 931	1 200
Dufourspitze	4 634	15 203							Pechora	1 802	1 120

AFRICA

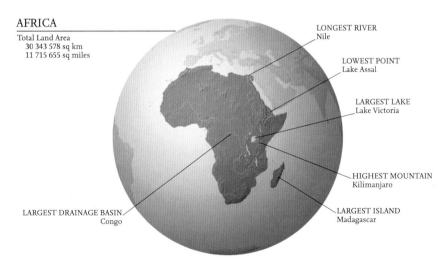

Total Land Area
30 343 578 sq km
11 715 655 sq miles

LONGEST RIVER
Nile

LOWEST POINT
Lake Assal

LARGEST LAKE
Lake Victoria

HIGHEST MOUNTAIN
Kilimanjaro

LARGEST ISLAND
Madagascar

LARGEST DRAINAGE BASIN
Congo

HIGHEST MOUNTAINS	metres	feet	LARGEST ISLANDS	sq km	sq miles	LARGEST LAKES	sq km	sq miles	LONGEST RIVERS	km	miles
Kilimanjaro	5 892	19 330	Madagascar	587 040	226 656	Lake Victoria	68 870	26 591	Nile	6 695	4 160
Mt Kenya	5 199	17 057				Lake Tanganyika	32 600	12 587	Congo	4 667	2 900
Margherita Peak	5 110	16 765				Lake Nyasa	29 500	11 390	Niger	4 184	2 600
Meru	4 565	14 977				Lake Volta	8 482	3 275	Zambezi	2 736	1 700
Ras Dejen	4 533	14 872				Lake Turkana	6 500	2 510	Webi Shabeelle	2 490	1 547
Mt Karisimbi	4 510	14 796				Lake Albert	5 600	2 162	Ubangi	2 250	1 398

NORTH AMERICA

Total Land Area
24 680 331 sq km
9 529 076 sq miles
(includes Hawaiian Islands)

HIGHEST MOUNTAIN
Mt McKinley

LOWEST POINT
Death Valley

LARGEST ISLAND
Greenland

LARGEST LAKE
Lake Superior

LONGEST RIVER AND
LARGEST DRAINAGE BASIN
Mississippi-Missouri

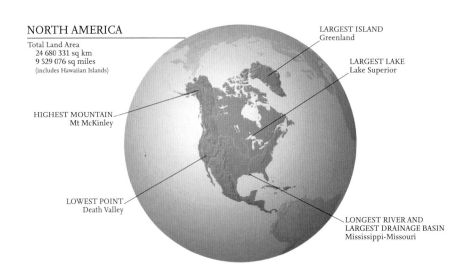

HIGHEST MOUNTAINS	metres	feet	LARGEST ISLANDS	sq km	sq miles	LARGEST LAKES	sq km	sq miles	LONGEST RIVERS	km	mil
Mt McKinley	6 194	20 321	Greenland	2 175 600	839 999	Lake Superior	82 100	31 699	Mississippi-Missouri	5 969	3 7
Mt Logan	5 959	19 550	Baffin Island	507 451	195 927	Lake Huron	59 600	23 012	Mackenzie-Peace-Finlay	4 241	2 6
Pico de Orizaba	5 610	18 405	Victoria Island	217 291	83 896	Lake Michigan	57 800	22 317			
Mt St Elias	5 489	18 008	Ellesmere Island	196 236	75 767	Great Bear Lake	31 328	12 096	Missouri	4 086	2 5
Volcán Popocatépetl	5 452	17 887	Cuba	110 860	42 803	Great Slave Lake	28 568	11 030	Mississippi	3 765	2 3
			Newfoundland	108 860	42 031	Lake Erie	25 700	9 923	Yukon	3 185	1 9

SOUTH AMERICA

Total Land Area
17 815 420 sq km
6 878 534 sq miles

LARGEST LAKE
Lake Titicaca

HIGHEST MOUNTAIN
Cerro Aconcagua

LARGEST ISLAND
Isla Grande de Tierra del Fuego

LONGEST RIVER AND
LARGEST DRAINAGE BASIN
Amazon

LOWEST POINT
Laguna del Carbón

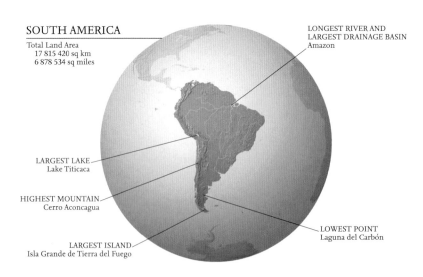

HIGHEST MOUNTAINS	metres	feet	LARGEST ISLANDS	sq km	sq miles	LARGEST LAKES	sq km	sq miles	LONGEST RIVERS	km	mil
Cerro Aconcagua	6 959	22 831	Isla Grande de Tierra del Fuego	47 000	18 147	Lake Titicaca	8 340	3 220	Amazon	6 516	4 0
Nevado Ojos del Salado	6 908	22 664	Isla de Chiloé	8 394	3 241				Río de la Plata-Paraná	4 500	2 7
Cerro Bonete	6 872	22 546	East Falkland	6 760	2 610				Purus	3 218	2 0
Cerro Pissis	6 858	22 500	West Falkland	5 413	2 090				Madeira	3 200	1 9
Cerro Tupungato	6 800	22 309							São Francisco	2 900	1 8

ATLANTIC OCEAN

Total Area
86 557 000 sq km
33 420 000 sq miles

Arctic Ocean

Hudson Bay

Baltic Sea

North Sea

Black Sea

Gulf of
Mexico

Mediterranean Sea

Deepest Point
Milwaukee Deep

Caribbean
Sea

ATLANTIC OCEAN	Area		Deepest Point	
	square km	square miles	metres	feet
Extent	86 557 000	33 420 000	8 605	28 231
Arctic Ocean	9 485 000	3 662 000	5 450	17 880
Caribbean Sea	2 512 000	970 000	7 680	25 197
Mediterranean Sea	2 510 000	969 000	5 121	16 801
Gulf of Mexico	1 544 000	596 000	3 504	11 496
Hudson Bay	1 233 000	476 000	259	850
North Sea	575 000	222 000	661	2 169
Black Sea	508 000	196 000	2 245	7 365
Baltic Sea	382 000	148 000	460	1 509

PACIFIC OCEAN

Total Area
166 241 000 sq km
64 186 000 sq miles

Bering Sea

Sea of Okhotsk

Sea of Japan
(East Sea)

East China Sea
and Yellow Sea

South China Sea

Deepest Point
Challenger Deep

PACIFIC OCEAN	Area		Deepest Point	
	square km	square miles	metres	feet
Extent	166 241 000	64 186 000	10 920	35 826
South China Sea	2 590 000	1 000 000	5 514	18 090
Bering Sea	2 261 000	873 000	4 150	13 615
Sea of Okhotsk	1 392 000	538 000	3 363	11 033
Sea of Japan (East Sea)	1 013 000	391 000	3 743	12 280
East China Sea and Yellow Sea	1 202 000	464 000	2 717	8 914

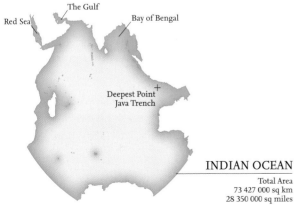

The Gulf

Red Sea

Bay of Bengal

Deepest Point
Java Trench

INDIAN OCEAN

Total Area
73 427 000 sq km
28 350 000 sq miles

INDIAN OCEAN	Area		Deepest Point	
	square km	square miles	metres	feet
Extent	73 427 000	28 350 000	7 125	23 376
Bay of Bengal	2 172 000	839 000	4 500	14 764
Red Sea	453 000	175 000	3 040	9 974
The Gulf	238 000	92 000	73	239

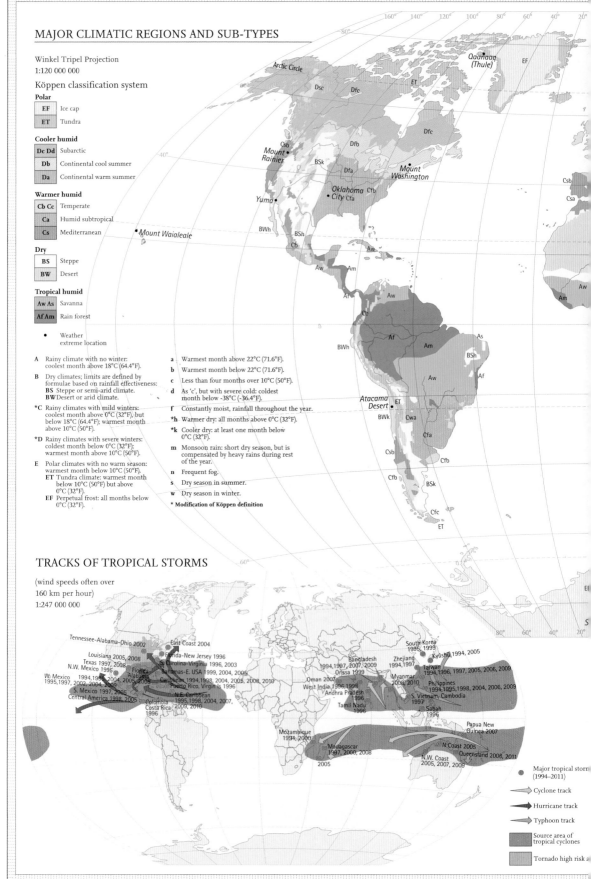

MAJOR CLIMATIC REGIONS AND SUB-TYPES

Winkel Tripel Projection
1:120 000 000

Köppen classification system

Polar

| EF | Ice cap |
| ET | Tundra |

Cooler humid

Dc Dd	Subarctic
Db	Continental cool summer
Da	Continental warm summer

Warmer humid

Cb Cc	Temperate
Ca	Humid subtropical
Cs	Mediterranean

Dry

| BS | Steppe |
| BW | Desert |

Tropical humid

| Aw As | Savanna |
| Af Am | Rain forest |

• Weather extreme location

A Rainy climate with no winter: coolest month above 18°C (64.4°F).

B Dry climates; limits are defined by formulae based on rainfall effectiveness: **BS** Steppe or semi-arid climate. **BW** Desert or arid climate.

*C Rainy climates with mild winters: coolest month above 0°C (32°F), but below 18°C (64.4°F); warmest month above 10°C (50°F).

*D Rainy climates with severe winters: coldest month below 0°C (32°F); warmest month above 10°C (50°F).

E Polar climates with no warm season: warmest month below 10°C (50°F). ET Tundra climate: warmest month below 10°C (50°F) but above 0°C (32°F). EF Perpetual frost: all months below 0°C (32°F).

a Warmest month above 22°C (71.6°F).

b Warmest month below 22°C (71.6°F).

c Less than four months over 10°C (50°F).

d As 'c', but with severe cold: coldest month below -38°C (-36.4°F).

f Constantly moist, rainfall throughout the year.

*h Warmer dry: all months above 0°C (32°F).

*k Cooler dry: at least one month below 0°C (32°F).

m Monsoon rain: short dry season, but is compensated by heavy rains during rest of the year.

n Frequent fog.

s Dry season in summer.

w Dry season in winter.

* Modification of Köppen definition

TRACKS OF TROPICAL STORMS

(wind speeds often over 160 km per hour)
1:247 000 000

● Major tropical storm (1994–2011)

⟹ Cyclone track

➤ Hurricane track

⟹ Typhoon track

Source area of tropical cyclones

Tornado high risk area

WORLD WEATHER EXTREMES

	Location			Location
Highest shade temperature	57.8°C/136°F Al ´Azīzīyah, Libya (13 September 1922)		Highest surface wind speed	
Hottest place — Annual mean	34.4°C/93.9°F Dalol, Ethiopia		High altitude	372 km per hour/231 miles per hour Mount Washington, New Hampshire, USA (12 April 1934)
Driest place — Annual mean	0.1 mm/0.004 inches Atacama Desert, Chile		Low altitude	333 km per hour/207 miles per hour Qaanaaq (Thule), Greenland (8 March 1972)
Most sunshine — Annual mean	90% Yuma, Arizona, USA (over 4 000 hours)		Tornado	512 km per hour/318 miles per hour Oklahoma City, Oklahoma, USA (3 May 1999)
Least sunshine	Nil for 182 days each year, South Pole			
Lowest screen temperature	-89.2°C/-128.6°F Vostok Station, Antarctica (21 July 1983)		Greatest snowfall	31 102 mm/1 224.5 inches Mount Rainier, Washington, USA (19 February 1971 — 18 February 1972)
Coldest place — Annual mean	-56.6°C/-69.9°F Plateau Station, Antarctica		Heaviest hailstones	1 kg/2.21 lb Gopalganj, Bangladesh (14 April 1986)
Wettest place — Annual mean	11 873 mm/467.4 inches Meghalaya, India		Thunder-days average	251 days per year Tororo, Uganda
Most rainy days	Up to 350 per year Mount Waialeale, Hawaii, USA		Highest barometric pressure	1 083.8 mb Agata, Siberia, Rus. Fed. (31 December 1968)
Windiest place	322 km per hour/200 miles per hour in gales, Commonwealth Bay, Antarctica		Lowest barometric pressure	870 mb 483 km/300 miles west of Guam, Pacific Ocean (12 October 1979)

WORLD LAND COVER

© ESA 2010 and UCLouvain
Winkel Tripel Projection
1:120 000 000

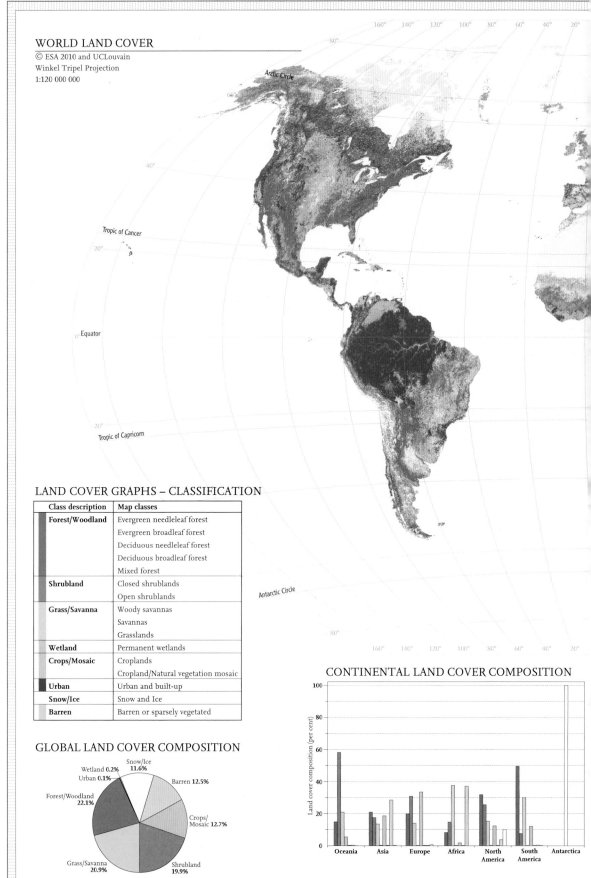

LAND COVER GRAPHS – CLASSIFICATION

Class description	Map classes
Forest/Woodland	Evergreen needleleaf forest
	Evergreen broadleaf forest
	Deciduous needleleaf forest
	Deciduous broadleaf forest
	Mixed forest
Shrubland	Closed shrublands
	Open shrublands
Grass/Savanna	Woody savannas
	Savannas
	Grasslands
Wetland	Permanent wetlands
Crops/Mosaic	Croplands
	Cropland/Natural vegetation mosaic
Urban	Urban and built-up
Snow/Ice	Snow and Ice
Barren	Barren or sparsely vegetated

GLOBAL LAND COVER COMPOSITION

Wetland 0.2%
Urban 0.1%
Snow/Ice 11.6%
Barren 12.5%
Forest/Woodland 22.1%
Crops/Mosaic 12.7%
Grass/Savanna 20.9%
Shrubland 19.9%

CONTINENTAL LAND COVER COMPOSITION

Land cover composition (per cent)

Oceania   Asia   Europe   Africa   North America   South America   Antarctica

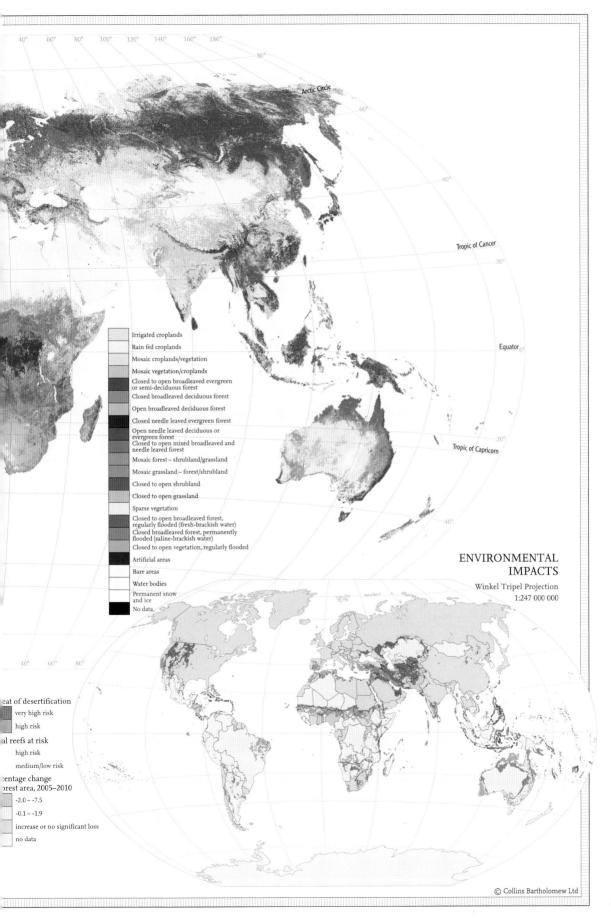

Irrigated croplands
Rain fed croplands
Mosaic croplands/vegetation
Mosaic vegetation/croplands
Closed to open broadleaved evergreen or semi-deciduous forest
Closed broadleaved deciduous forest
Open broadleaved deciduous forest
Closed needle leaved evergreen forest
Open needle leaved deciduous or evergreen forest
Closed to open mixed broadleaved and needle leaved forest
Mosaic forest – shrubland/grassland
Mosaic grassland – forest/shrubland
Closed to open shrubland
Closed to open grassland
Sparse vegetation
Closed to open broadleaved forest, regularly flooded (fresh-brackish water)
Closed broadleaved forest, permanently flooded (saline-brackish water)
Closed to open vegetation, regularly flooded
Artificial areas
Bare areas
Water bodies
Permanent snow and ice
No data

ENVIRONMENTAL IMPACTS

Winkel Tripel Projection
1:247 000 000

[t]eat of desertification
  very high risk
  high risk

[r]al reefs at risk
  high risk
  medium/low risk

[t]centage change
[f]orest area, 2005–2010
  -2.0 – -7.5
  -0.1 – -1.9
  increase or no significant loss
  no data

© Collins Bartholomew Ltd

37

WORLD POPULATION DISTRIBUTION AND THE WORLD'S MAJOR CITIES

Winkel Tripel Projection
1:120 000 000

Major Urban Agglomerations

- over 20 million
- 10 million – 20 million
- 5 million – 10 million

TOP TEN COUNTRIES BY POPULATION AND POPULATION DENSITY 2011

Total population	Country	Rank	Country*	Inhabitants per sq mile	Inhabitants per sq km
1 332 079 000	China	1	Bangladesh	2 707	1 045
1 241 492 000	India	2	Taiwan	1 658	640
313 085 000	USA	3	South Korea	1 262	487
242 326 000	Indonesia	4	Rwanda	1 076	415
196 655 000	Brazil	5	India	1 049	405
176 745 000	Pakistan	6	Netherlands	1 039	401
162 471 000	Nigeria	7	Haiti	945	365
150 494 000	Bangladesh	8	Belgium	913	352
142 836 000	Russian Federation	9	Japan	867	335
126 497 000	Japan	10	Sri Lanka	831	321

* Only countries with a population of over 10 million are considered.

KEY POPULATION STATISTICS FOR MAJOR REGIONS

	Population 2011 (millions)	Growth (per cent)	Infant mortality rate	Total fertility rate	Life expectancy (years)	% aged 60 and over 2010	% aged 60 and over 2050
World	6 974	1.1	42	2.45	69	11	22
More developed regions	1 240	0.3	6	1.7	78	22	32
Less developed regions	5 774	1.3	46	2.6	67	8	20
Africa	1 046	2.3	71	4.4	55	6	10
Asia	4 207	1.0	37	2.2	70	10	24
Europe	739	0.1	6	1.6	77	22	34
Latin America and the Caribbean	597	1.1	19	2.2	75	10	25
North America	348	0.9	6	2.0	79	19	27
Oceania	37	1.5	19	2.5	78	15	24

Except for population and % aged 60 and over figures, the data are annual averages projected for the period 2010–2015.

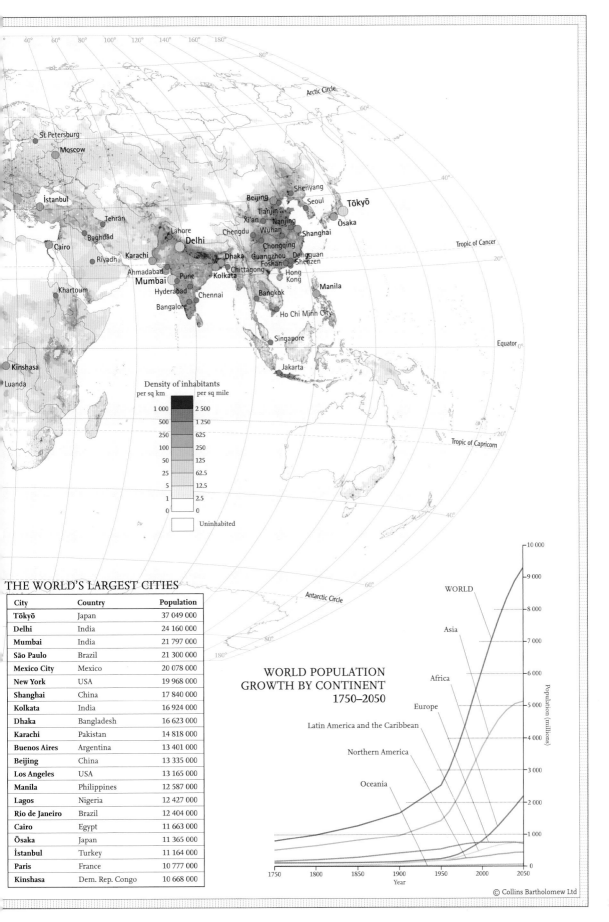

Density of inhabitants

per sq km	per sq mile
1 000	2 500
500	1 250
250	625
100	250
50	125
25	62.5
5	12.5
1	2.5
0	0

Uninhabited

THE WORLD'S LARGEST CITIES

City	Country	Population
Tōkyō	Japan	37 049 000
Delhi	India	24 160 000
Mumbai	India	21 797 000
São Paulo	Brazil	21 300 000
Mexico City	Mexico	20 078 000
New York	USA	19 968 000
Shanghai	China	17 840 000
Kolkata	India	16 924 000
Dhaka	Bangladesh	16 623 000
Karachi	Pakistan	14 818 000
Buenos Aires	Argentina	13 401 000
Beijing	China	13 335 000
Los Angeles	USA	13 165 000
Manila	Philippines	12 587 000
Lagos	Nigeria	12 427 000
Rio de Janeiro	Brazil	12 404 000
Cairo	Egypt	11 663 000
Ōsaka	Japan	11 365 000
İstanbul	Turkey	11 164 000
Paris	France	10 777 000
Kinshasa	Dem. Rep. Congo	10 668 000

WORLD POPULATION GROWTH BY CONTINENT 1750–2050

WORLD

Asia

Africa

Europe

Latin America and the Caribbean

Northern America

Oceania

Population (millions)

Year

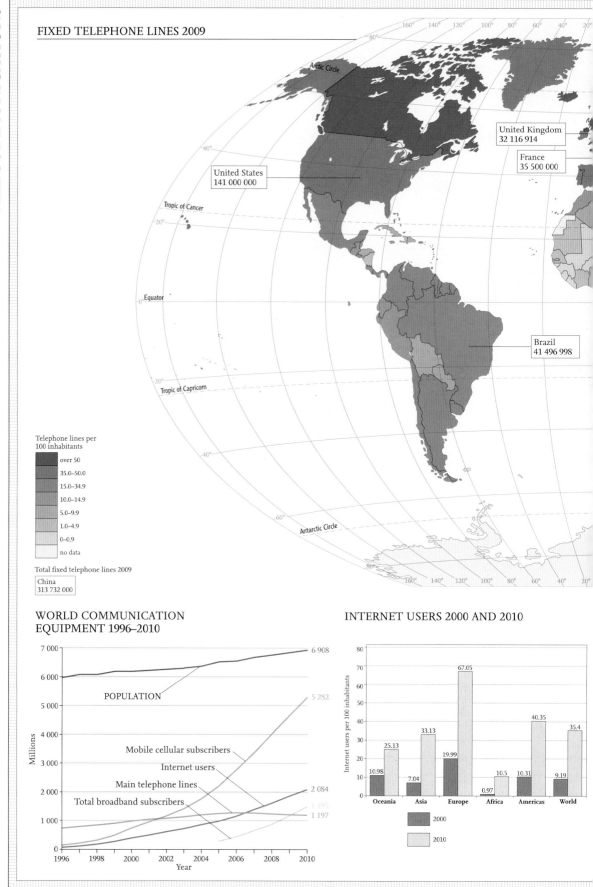

FIXED TELEPHONE LINES 2009

United Kingdom
32 116 914

France
35 500 000

United States
141 000 000

Tropic of Cancer

Arctic Circle

Equator

Brazil
41 496 998

Tropic of Capricorn

Antarctic Circle

Telephone lines per
100 inhabitants

over 50
35.0–50.0
15.0–34.9
10.0–14.9
5.0–9.9
1.0–4.9
0–0.9
no data

Total fixed telephone lines 2009

China
313 732 000

WORLD COMMUNICATION EQUIPMENT 1996–2010

Millions

7 000
6 000
5 000
4 000
3 000
2 000
1 000
0

6 908
5 282
2 084
1 497
1 197

POPULATION

Mobile cellular subscribers

Internet users

Main telephone lines

Total broadband subscribers

1996 1998 2000 2002 2004 2006 2008 2010
Year

INTERNET USERS 2000 AND 2010

Internet users per 100 inhabitants

80
70
60
50
40
30
20
10
0

	Oceania	Asia	Europe	Africa	Americas	World
2000	10.98	7.04	19.99	0.97	10.31	9.19
2010	25.13	33.13	67.05	10.5	40.35	35.4

2000
2010

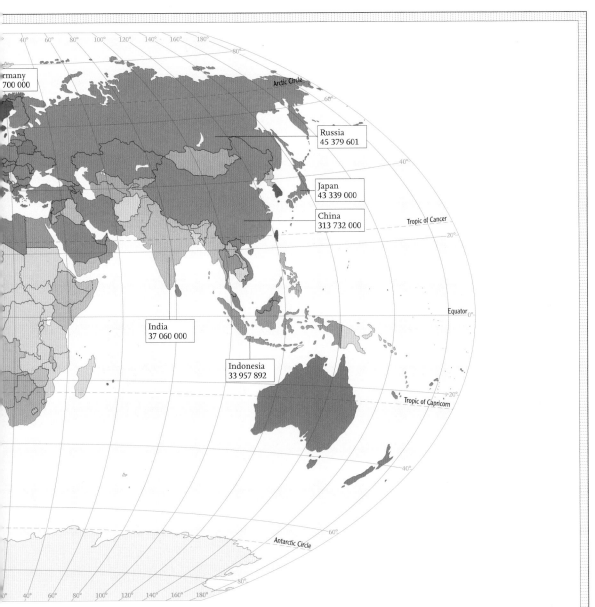

rmany
700 000

Russia
45 379 601

Japan
43 339 000

China
313 732 000

India
37 060 000

Indonesia
33 957 892

Arctic Circle

Tropic of Cancer

Equator

Tropic of Capricorn

Antarctic Circle

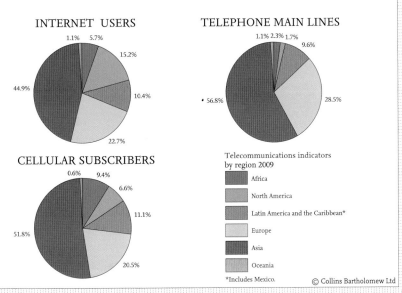

TOP BROADBAND ECONOMIES 2008

Countries with highest broadband penetration rate – subscribers per 100 inhabitants

	Top Economies	Rate
1	Sweden	37.3
2	Denmark	36.8
3	Netherlands	35.0
4	Norway	34.0
5	Switzerland	33.0
6	Iceland	32.9
7	South Korea	32.0
8	Finland	30.6
9	Luxembourg	30.3
10	Canada	29.0
11	France	28.6
12	United Kingdom	28.3
13	Belgium	28.3
14	Germany	27.4
15	Hong Kong, China	26.8

INTERNET USERS

1.1% 5.7% 15.2% 10.4% 22.7% 44.9%

TELEPHONE MAIN LINES

1.1% 2.3% 1.7% 9.6% 28.5% 56.8%

CELLULAR SUBSCRIBERS

0.6% 9.4% 6.6% 11.1% 20.5% 51.8%

Telecommunications indicators by region 2009

- Africa
- North America
- Latin America and the Caribbean*
- Europe
- Asia
- Oceania

*Includes Mexico.

© Collins Bartholomew Ltd

41

MAP POLICIES

PLACE NAMES

The spelling of place names on maps has always been a matter of great complexity, because of the variety of the world's languages and the systems used to write them down. There is no standard way of spelling names or of converting them from one alphabet, or symbol set, to another. Instead, conventional ways of spelling have evolved in each of the world's major languages, and the results often differ significantly from the name as it is spelled in the original language. Familiar examples of English conventional names include Munich (München), Florence (Firenze) and Moscow (from the transliterated form, Moskva).

In this atlas, local name forms are used where these are in the Roman alphabet, though for major cities, and main physical features, conventional English names are given first. The local forms are those which are officially recognized by the government of the country concerned, usually as represented by its official mapping agency. This is a basic principle laid down by the United Kingdom government's Permanent Committee on Geographical Names (PCGN) and the equivalent United States Board on Geographic Names, (BGN). Prominent English-language and historic names are not neglected, however. These, and significant superseded names and alternate spellings, are included in brackets on the maps where space permits, and are cross-referenced in the index.

Country names are shown in conventional English form and include any recent changes promulgated by national governments and adopted by the United Nations. The names of continents, oceans, seas and under-water features in international waters also appear in English throughout the atlas, as do those of other international features where such an English form exists and is in common use. International features are defined as features crossing one or more international boundary.

BOUNDARIES

The status of nations, their names and their boundaries, are shown in this atlas as they are at the time of going to press, as far as can be ascertained. Where an international boundary symbol appears in the sea or ocean it does not necessarily infer a legal maritime boundary, but shows which offshore islands belong to which country. The extent of island nations is shown by a short boundary symbol at the extreme limits of the area of sea or ocean within which all land is part of that nation.

Where international boundaries are the subject of dispute it may be that no portrayal of them will meet with the approval of any of the countries involved, but it is not seen as the function of this atlas to try to adjudicate between the rights and wrongs of political issues. Although reference mapping at atlas scales is not the ideal medium for indicating the claims of many separatist and irredentist movements, every reasonable attempt is made to show where an active territorial dispute exists, and where there is an important difference between 'de facto' (existing in fact, on the ground) and 'de jure' (according to law) boundaries. This is done by the use of a different symbol where international boundaries are disputed, or where the alignment is unconfirmed, to that used for settled international boundaries. Ceasefire lines are also shown by a separate symbol. For clarity, disputed boundaries and areas are annotated where this is considered necessary. The atlas aims to take a strictly neutral viewpoint of all such cases, based on advice from expert consultants.

MAP PROJECTIONS

Map projections have been selected specifically for the area and scale of each map, or suite of maps. As the only way to show the Earth with absolute accuracy is on a globe, all map projections are compromises. Some projections seek to maintain correct area relationships (equal area projections), true distances and bearings from a point (equidistant projections), or correct angles and shapes (conformal projections); others attempt to achieve a balance between these properties. The choice of projections used in this atlas has been made on an individual continental and regional basis. Projections used, and their individual parameters, have been defined to minimize distortion and to reduce scale errors as much as possible. The projection used is indicated at the bottom left of each map page.

SCALE

In order to directly compare like with like throughout the world it would be necessary to maintain a single scale throughout the atlas. However, the desirability of mapping the more densely populated areas of the world at larger scales, and other geographical considerations, such as the need to fit a homogeneous physical region within a uniform rectangular page format, mean that a range of scales have been used. Scales for continental maps range between 1:20 000 000 and 1:44 000 000, depending on the size of the continental land mass being covered. Scales for regional maps are typically in the range 1:12 000 000 to 1:20 000 000. Mapping for most countries is at scales between 1:4 800 000 and 1:12 000 000, although for the more densely populated areas of Europe the scale increases to 1:2 400 000.

ABBREVIATIONS

Arch.	Archipelago		
B.	Bay		
	Bahia, Baía	Portuguese	bay
	Bahía	Spanish	bay
	Baie	French	bay
C.	Cape		
	Cabo	Portuguese, Spanish	cape, headland
	Cap	French	cape, headland
Co	Cerro	Spanish	hill, peak, summit
E.	East, Eastern		
Est.	Estrecho	Spanish	strait
G.	Gebel	Arabic	hill, mountain
Gt	Great		
I.	Island, Isle		
	Ilha	Portuguese	island
	Islas	Spanish	island
Is	Islands, Isles		
	Islas	Spanish	islands
Kep.	Kepulauan	Indonesian	islands
Khr.	Khrebet	Russian	mountain range

L.	Lake		
	Loch	(Scotland)	lake
	Lough	(Ireland)	lake
	Lac	French	lake
	Lago	Portuguese, Spanish	lake
M.	Mys	Russian	cape, point
Mt	Mount		
	Mont	French	hill, mountain
Mt.	Mountain		
Mte	Monte	Portuguese, Spanish	hill, mountain
Mts	Mountains		
	Monts	French	hills, mountains
N.	North, Northern		
O.	Ostrov	Russian	island
Pk	Puncak	Indonesian, Malay	hill, mountain
Pt	Point		
Pta	Punta	Italian, Spanish	cape, point
R.	River		
	Rio	Portuguese	river
	Río	Spanish	river
	Rivière	French	river

Ra.	Range		mountain range
S.	South, Southern		
	Salar, Salina,		
	Salinas	Spanish	salt pan, salt pan
Sa	Serra	Portuguese,	mountain range
	Sierra	Spanish	mountain range
Sd	Sound		
S.E.	Southeast,		
	Southeastern		
St	Saint		
	Sankt	German	Saint
	Sint	Dutch	Saint
Sta	Santa	Italian, Portuguese,	
		Spanish	Saint
Ste	Sainte	French	Saint
Str.	Strait		
Tk	Teluk	Indonesian, Malay	bay, gulf
Tg	Tanjong, Tanjung	Indonesian, Malay	cape, point
Vdkhr.	Vodokhranilishche	Russian	reservoir
W.	West, Western		strait
	Wadi, Wâdi, Wādī	Arabic	watercourse

MAP SYMBOLS

LAND AND WATER FEATURES

- Lake
- Impermanent lake
- Salt lake or lagoon
- Impermanent salt lake
- Dry salt lake or salt pan

- —— River
- - - - Impermanent river
- Ice cap / Glacier
- ⌣123 Pass Height in metres
- ∴ Site of special interest
- ⌄ Oasis
- ⌐⌐⌐⌐ Wall

TRANSPORT

- ═══ Motorway
- —— Main road
- - - - Track
- —— Main railway
- ⊥⊥⊥⊥ Canal
- ✈ Main airport

BOUNDARIES

- ▪▪▪▪ International boundary
- ·▪▪ Disputed international boundary or alignment unconfirmed
- ▪▪ ▪▪ Disputed territory boundary
- Undefined international boundary in the sea. All land within this boundary is part of state or territory named.
- ━━━ Administrative boundary Shown for selected countries only.
- •••• Ceasefire line or other boundary described on the map

RELIEF

Contour intervals used in layer-colouring, for land height and sea depth

METRES FEET	
5000	16404
3000	9843
2000	6562
1000	3281
500	1640
200	656
0	0

Land below sea level

METRES FEET	
200	656
4000	13124
6000	19686

Ocean pages

METRES FEET	
0	0
200	656
2000	6562
3000	9843
4000	13124
5000	16404
6000	19686
7000	22967
9000	29529

123 Ocean deep In metres.

1234 Summit △ Height in metres

1234 Volcano ▲ Height in metres

STYLES OF LETTERING

Cities and towns are explained separately

Country	**FRANCE**
Overseas Territory/Dependency	**Guadeloupe**
Disputed Territory	WESTERN SAHARA
Administrative name Shown for selected countries only.	**SCOTLAND**
Area name	PATAGONIA

Physical features

Island	*Gran Canaria*
Lake	*Lake Erie*
Mountain	*Mt Blanc*
River	*Thames*
Region	*LAPPLAND*

CITIES AND TOWNS

Population	National Capital	Administrative Capital Shown for selected countries only	Other City or Town
over 10 million	DHAKA ▣	Karachi ⊙	New York ⊙
5 million to 10 million	MADRID ▣	Toronto ⊙	Philadelphia ⊙
1 million to 5 million	KĀBUL ▢	Sydney ○	Koahsiung ○
500 000 to 1 million	BANGUI ▢	Winnipeg ○	Jeddah ○
100 000 to 500 000	WELLINGTON ▢	Edinburgh ○	Apucarana ○
50 000 to 100 000	PORT OF SPAIN ▢	Bismarck ○	Invercargill ○
under 50 000	MALABO ▫	Charlottetown ○	Ceres ○

CONTINENTAL MAPS

BOUNDARIES	—— International boundary	------ Disputed international boundary	•••••••• Ceasefire line

CITIES AND TOWNS	National Capital	**Beijing** ▢	Other City or Town	**New York** ○

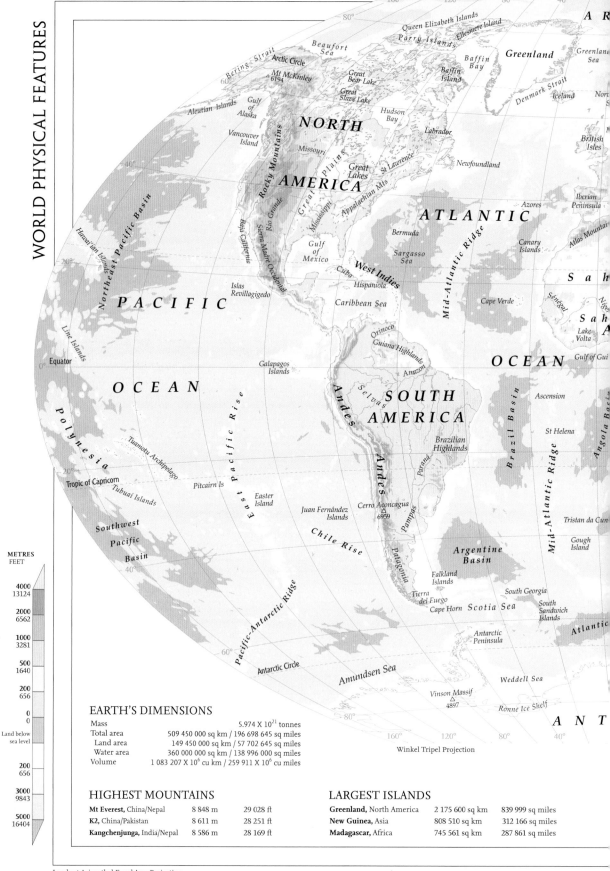

WORLD PHYSICAL FEATURES

METRES
FEET

4000	13124
2000	6562
1000	3281
500	1640
200	656
0	0

Land below
sea level

200	656
3000	9843
5000	16404

EARTH'S DIMENSIONS

Mass	5.974 X 10^{21} tonnes
Total area	509 450 000 sq km / 196 698 645 sq miles
Land area	149 450 000 sq km / 57 702 645 sq miles
Water area	360 000 000 sq km / 138 996 000 sq miles
Volume	1 083 207 X 10^6 cu km / 259 911 X 10^6 cu miles

Winkel Tripel Projection

HIGHEST MOUNTAINS

Mt Everest, China/Nepal	8 848 m	29 028 ft
K2, China/Pakistan	8 611 m	28 251 ft
Kangchenjunga, India/Nepal	8 586 m	28 169 ft

LARGEST ISLANDS

Greenland, North America	2 175 600 sq km	839 999 sq miles
New Guinea, Asia	808 510 sq km	312 166 sq miles
Madagascar, Africa	745 561 sq km	287 861 sq miles

Lambert Azimuthal Equal Area Projection

C **OCEAN**

New Siberia Islands

East Siberian Sea

Novaya Zemlya

Barents Sea

Kara Sea

Arctic Circle

60°

Central Siberian Plateau

West Siberian Plain

Verkhoyanskiy Khrebet

Bering Sea

European Plain

Dnieper

Ural Mountains

Yenisey

Ob

Irtysh

Lena

Kamchatka Pen.

Aleutian Is.

Emperor Seamount Chain

40°

Altai Mountains

Lake Baikal

Amur

Manchurian Plain

Sea of Okhotsk

Hokkaidō

ROPE

Volga

El'brus △ 5642

Black Sea

Aral Sea

Caspian Sea

Turan Lowland

Lake Balkhash

Tien Shan

ASIA

Gobi

Sea of Japan (East Sea)

Honshū

Qilian Shan

Yellow

nean Sea

Euphrates

The Gulf

Zagros Mts

Kunlun Shan

Plateau of Tibet

Himalaya

Mt Everest △ 8848

Yangtze

East China Sea

Ryukyu Is.

Bonin Islands

PACIFIC

Tropic of Cancer

20°

Libyan Desert

Arabian Peninsula

Indus

Ganges

Deccan

Mekong

South China Sea

Philippines

Mid-Pacific Mountains

OCEAN

Nile

Red Sea

Blue Nile

Rub' al Khali

Gulf of Aden

Arabian Sea

Bay of Bengal

Sri Lanka

Peninsular Malaysia

Challenger Deep 10920

Mariana Trench

Marshall Islands

Micronesia

Caroline Islands

Equator 0°

White Nile

Ethiopian Highlands

Lake Victoria

5892 △ Kilimanjaro

Somali Basin

Maldives

Sumatra

Borneo

Celebes

Greater Sunda Islands

Laut Java

Java

Laut Banda

Puncak Jaya △ 5030

New Guinea

Solomon Is.

Tuvalu

Melanesia

Congo Basin

Seychelles

INDIAN

Zambezi

Madagascar

Arafura Sea

Timor Sea

Great Barrier Reef

Coral Sea

Fiji

Tonga Trench

Kalahari Desert

Mauritius

Réunion

OCEAN

AUSTRALIA

Tropic of Capricorn

20°

e of Hope

Crozet Basin

Southeast Indian Ridge

Great Victoria Desert

Darling

Great Dividing Range

Norfolk I.

Lord Howe I.

Great Australian Bight

Murray

Mt Kosciuszko △ 2229

Prince Edward Is

Îles Kerguélen

Tasmania

Tasman Sea

New Zealand

North Island

40°

Mt Cook △ 3754

South Island

Antarctic Basin

Australian-Antarctic Basin

Davis Sea

60°

Antarctic Circle

C **TICA**

Antarctic Mountains

Ross Sea

80°

1: 100 800 000

Equatorial diameter	12 756 km / 7 927 miles
Polar diameter	12 714 km / 7 900 miles
Equatorial circumference	40 075 km / 24 903 miles
Meridional circumference	40 008 km / 24 861 miles

LARGEST LAKES

Caspian Sea, Asia/Europe	371 000 sq km	143 243 sq miles
Lake Superior, North America	82 100 sq km	31 699 sq miles
Lake Victoria, Africa	68 870 sq km	26 591 sq miles

LONGEST RIVERS

Nile, Africa	6 695 km	4 160 miles
Amazon, South America	6 516 km	4 049 miles
Yangtze, Asia	6 380 km	3 965 miles

Arctic Circle

CANADA

Greenland
(Denmark)

Jan Maye
(Norway)

U.S.A.
Anchorage

Nuuk

Reykjavík   ICELAND

Edmonton

Vancouver

UNITED
KINGDOM

REP. OF
IRELAND

London

UNITED STATES

Ottawa   Montreal

Toronto

Paris

FRANC

San Francisco

OF

Chicago

NewYork

AMERICA

Denver

Washington   Philadelphia
D.C.

Azores
(Portugal)

PORTUGAL

SPAIN

Algiers

Los Angeles

Rabat

MOROCCO

TU

Bermuda
(U.K.)

ATLANTIC   Laâyoune

ALGE

Tropic of Cancer

Houston

THE
BAHAMAS

WESTERN
SAHARA

Monterrey

Miami

Nassau

MAURITANIA

Nouakchott

MALI

20°

Hawai'ian
Islands
(U.S.A.)

MEXICO

Havana   CUBA

DOMINICAN
REP.

Mexico City

HAITI

Puerto Rico
(U.S.A.)

CAPE VERDE

SENEGAL

Dakar

THE GAMBIA

GUINEA-BISSAU   GUINEA

BUR.

BELIZE

JAMAICA

GUATEMALA

HONDURAS

Conakry

GH.

EL SALVADOR   NICARAGUA

Caracas

TRINIDAD AND
TOBAGO

SIERRA LEONE

C.D'I.

L

COSTA RICA   San José

Port of Spain

Monrovia

LIBERIA   Accra

PACIFIC

PANAMA

VENEZUELA

Georgetown

Paramaribo

Bogotá

Cayenne

COLOMBIA

FR. G.

Galapagos
Islands
(Ecuador)

Quito

0°   Equator

ECUADOR

BRAZIL

OCEAN

Ascension
(U.K.)

KIRIBATI

OCEAN

Lima   PERU

St Helena
(U.K.)

American
Samoa

French
Polynesia
(France)

BOLIVIA

Brasília

La Paz   Sucre

Cook
Islands
(New Zealand)   Tahiti

St Helena, Ascension
and Tristan da Cunha
(U.K.)

PARAGUAY

Rio de Janeiro

20°

São Paulo

Tropic of Capricorn

Pitcairn Islands
(U.K.)

Easter
Island
(Chile)

Asunción

ARGENTINA

Tristan
da Cunha
(U.K.)

Buenos
Aires   URUGUAY

Santiago

Montevideo

40°

Falkland
Islands
(U.K.)

South Georgia and
the South Sandwich
Islands
(U.K.)

Bouvetøya
(Norway)

60°

Antarctic Circle

80°

ANT

Winkel Tripel Projection

ABBREVIATIONS

A.	ANDORRA	BE.	BENIN	C.A.R.	CENTRAL AFRICAN REPUBLIC
AL.	ALBANIA	BEL.	BELGIUM		
ARM.	ARMENIA	B.H.	BOSNIA-HERZEGOVINA	C.D'I.	CÔTE D'IVOIRE (IVORY COAST)
AUS.	AUSTRIA	BN.	BAHRAIN		
AZ.	AZERBAIJAN	BUR.	BURKINA FASO	CR.	CROATIA
B.	BURUNDI	CAM.	CAMEROON	CYP.	CYPRUS

CZ.R.	CZECH REPUBLIC
DEN.	DENMARK
EQ.G.	EQUATORIAL GUINEA
FR.G.	FRENCH GUIANA
GEOR.	GEORGIA
GER.	GERMANY

C OCEAN

AY
(Svalbard
(Norway))

FINLAND
ESTONIA
LATVIA
LITH.
BELARUS
AND
SEA.
MO.
ROMANIA
K. BULGARIA
istanbul Ankara
GREECE TURKEY
SYRIA
CYP.
LEB.
ISR.
oli Amman
JOR.
Cairo
YA
EGYPT

RUSSIAN FEDERATION

Yekaterinburg
Moscow
Omsk
Astana
KAZAKHSTAN

Novosibirsk
Ulan Bator
MONGOLIA

Magadan

Arctic Circle
60°

Harbin
N.KOREA
P'yŏngyang
Seoul
S.KOREA

40°

Beijing
Tianjin
Xi'an
Wuhan
Shanghai

JAPAN
Tōkyō
Osaka

UZBEK.
Dushanbe
TURKM.
Tbilisi
GEOR.
AZ. ARM.
KYR.
TAJIK.
CHINA

Kâbul
AFGHAN-
Tehrān ISTAN Islamabad
IRAN New
Delhi
Baghdad
IRAQ
PAKISTAN
NEPAL
Kathmandu BHUTAN
BANGLA-
DESH

Lanzhou
Chengdu
Chongqing

PACIFIC

Tropic of Cancer

Taibei
TAIWAN

20°

Riyadh
Q.
SAUDI
ARABIA
BN.
U.A.E. Muscat
OMAN
YEMEN

Karachi
Mumbai

INDIA
Dhaka
MYANMAR
(BURMA)
Nay Pyi Taw
Rangoon

Ha Nôi
Vientiane
THAILAND
Bangkok
CAM-
BODIA

Hong Kong

Manila

PHILIPPINES

OCEAN
Northern
Mariana
Islands
(U.S.A.)

MARSHALL
ISLANDS

Khartoum ERITREA
SUDAN Asmara San'a'
djamena Addis DJIBOUTI
Ababa
C.A.R. SOUTH
SUDAN ETHIOPIA
Bangui
Juba
DEM. UGANDA
REP. KENYA
OF THE Nairobi
CONGO
asa Dodoma
TANZANIA

Chennai

SRI
LANKA

MALDIVES

Kuala Lumpur
Putrajaya
SINGAPORE

BRUNEI

MALAYSIA

FEDERATED STATES
OF MICRONESIA

PALAU

SEYCHELLES
British Indian
Ocean Territory
(U.K.)

INDONESIA

Jakarta

PAPUA
NEW
GUINEA

NAURU

KIRIBATI

TUVALU

COMOROS

INDIAN
Cocos
Islands
(Australia)

Christmas
Island
(Australia)

EAST
TIMOR

Port
Moresby
Coral Sea
Islands
Territory
(Aust.)

SOLOMON
ISLANDS

Equator 0°

Lilongwe
ZAMBIA
MOZAMBIQUE
MADAGASCAR
Antananarivo MAURITIUS
Réunion
(France)
Harare
ZIMBABWE
BOTS-
WANA
lhoek
Maputo
SWAZILAND
Pretoria
Maseru LESOTHO
REP. OF
SOUTH AFRICA

MALAWI

OCEAN

VANUATU

New
Caledonia
(France)

FIJI

SAMOA

TONGA

AUSTRALIA

Perth

Brisbane

Tropic of Capricorn

Norfolk
Island
(Australia)

Sydney
Canberra

French Southern
and Antarctic Lands
Îles Kerguélen
(France)

Wellington
NEW
ZEALAND

40°

C T I C A
80°

40° 80° 120° 160°

Antarctic Circle
60°

1: 100 800 000

GH.	GHANA	KYR.	KYRGYZSTAN	NETH.	NETHERLANDS	SUR.	SURINAME
GUY.	GUYANA	LEB.	LEBANON	NI.	NIGERIA	SW.	SWITZERLAND
HUN.	HUNGARY	LITH.	LITHUANIA	Q.	QATAR	T.	TOGO
ISR.	ISRAEL	LUX.	LUXEMBOURG	R.	RWANDA	TAJIK.	TAJIKISTAN
JOR.	JORDAN	M.	MONTENEGRO	S.	SERBIA	TURKM.	TURKMENISTAN
K.	KOSOVO	MA.	MACEDONIA	SLA.	SLOVAKIA	U.A.E.	UNITED ARAB EMIRATES
KU.	KUWAIT	MO.	MOLDOVA	SL.	SLOVENIA	UZBEK.	UZBEKISTAN

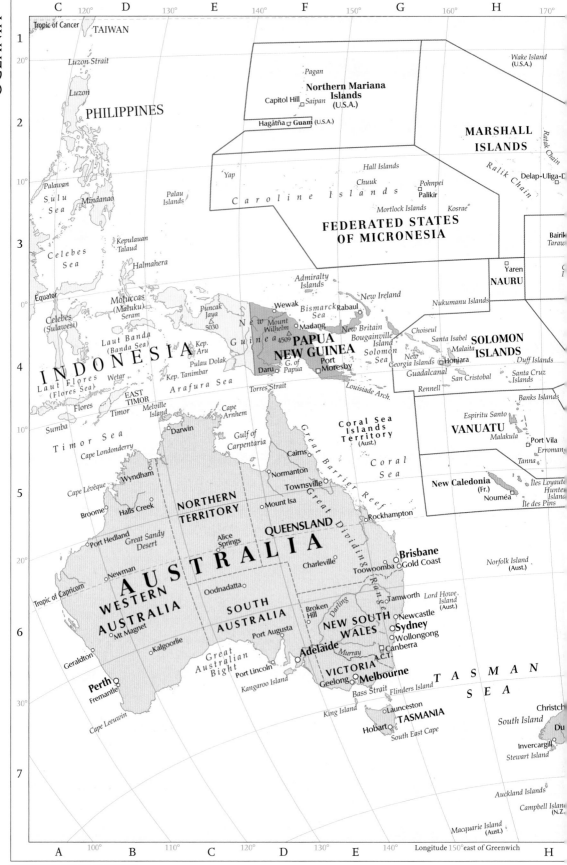

C 120° D 130° E 140° F 150° G 160° H 170°

Tropic of Cancer   TAIWAN

1

Luzon Strait

Luzon

20°

Pagan

Northern Mariana
Islands
(U.S.A.)

PHILIPPINES   Capitol Hill □ Saipan

2   Hagåtña □ Guam (U.S.A.)

MARSHALL
ISLANDS

Ratak Chain

Palawan

Sulu
Sea   Mindanao

Hall Islands

Yap   Chuuk   Pohnpei
Palau   Palikir
Islands

Ralik Chain   Delap-Uliga-D

3

Celebes
Sea

Halmahera

C a r o l i n e   I s l a n d s

FEDERATED STATES
OF MICRONESIA

Mortlock Islands   Kosrae

Bairik
Taraw

Equator   Moluccas
Celebes   (Maluku)
(Sulawesi)   Seram

Puncak
Jaya
△
5030   Mount
Wilhelm
△
4509

Admiralty
Islands

Wewak   Bismarck Rabaul
Sea

New Ireland

Nukumanu Islands

Yaren
NAURU

4

I N D O N E S I A

Kep.
Aru

Laut Banda
(Banda Sea)

Pulau Dolak
Kep. Tanimbar

N e w   G u i n e a

Daru

Madang
PAPUA
NEW GUINEA
G. of   Port
Papua □ Moresby

New Britain
Bougainville
Island
Solomon
Sea

Choiseul
Santa Isabel
New
Georgia Islands Honiara
Guadalcanal   San Cristobal

Malaita

SOLOMON
ISLANDS

Duff Islands

Santa Cruz
Islands

Laut Flores
(Flores Sea)   Wetar

Flores   EAST
TIMOR
Timor   Melville
Island

A r a f u r a   S e a   Torres Strait

Louisiade Arch.

Rennell

Banks Islands

Sumba

Timor

Cape
Arnhem

Cape Londonderry

Coral Sea
Islands
Territory
(Aust.)

Espiritu Santo

Malakula

VANUATU
Port Vila
Erroman

5

T i m o r   S e a

10°

Darwin

Gulf of
Carpentaria

Cairns

Great Barrier Reef

C o r a l
S e a

Tanna

Cape Lévêque

Wyndham

Normanton

Townsville

New Caledonia
(Fr.)
Nouméa

Îles Loyauté
Hunter
Island
Île des Pins

Broome   Halls Creek

NORTHERN
TERRITORY

Mount Isa

Rockhampton

Port Hedland
Great Sandy
Desert

Alice
Springs

QUEENSLAND

Great Dividing Range

Brisbane
Gold Coast

Norfolk Island
(Aust.)

6

Newman   A U S T R A L I A
WESTERN
AUSTRALIA

20°
Mt Magnet

Kalgoorlie

Geraldton

Perth
Fremantle

Oodnadatta

SOUTH
AUSTRALIA

Port Augusta

Great
Australian
Bight

Port Lincoln
Kangaroo Island

Charleville
Toowoomba

Broken
Hill

Darling

NEW SOUTH
WALES

Tamworth Lord Howe
Island
(Aust.)

Newcastle
Sydney
Wollongong
Canberra
A.C.T.

Adelaide

Murray

VICTORIA
Geelong Melbourne

Bass Strait   Flinders Island

T A S M A N

S E A

30°

King Island

Launceston
TASMANIA

Hobart

South East Cape

Christch

South Island

Du

Invercargill

Stewart Island

7

Auckland Islands

Campbell Island
(N.Z.)

Macquarie Island
(Aust.)

A 100° B 110° C 120° D 130° E 140° Longitude 150° east of Greenwich H

Lambert Azimuthal Equal Area Projection

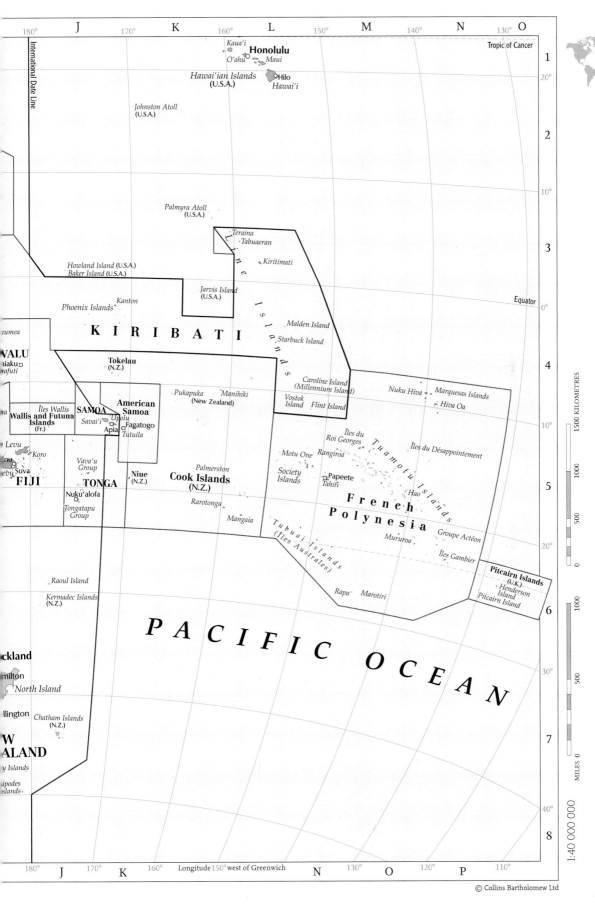

Tropic of Cancer

International Date Line

Kaua'i
Honolulu
O'ahu   Maui
Hawai'ian Islands
(U.S.A.)
Hilo
Hawai'i

1

20°

Johnston Atoll
(U.S.A.)

2

10°

Palmyra Atoll
(U.S.A.)

Teraina
·*Tabuaeran*

3

·*Kiritimati*

Howland Island (U.S.A.)
Baker Island (U.S.A.)

Jarvis Island
(U.S.A.)

Equator   0°

Kanton
Phoenix Islands

K I R I B A T I

Malden Island
Starbuck Island

4

uumea

TUVALU
aiaku□
nafuti

Tokelau
(N.Z.)

Caroline Island
(Millennium Island)

Nuku Hiva   *Marquesas Islands*
·*Hiva Oa*

Pukapuka   *Manihiki*
(New Zealand)

Vostok
Island *Flint Island*

Îles Wallis
Wallis and Futuna
Islands
(Fr.)

SAMOA
Savai'i   *Upolu*
Apia *Tutuila*

American
Samoa
Fagatogo
Tutuila

Îles du
Roi Georges
Motu One   *Rangiroa*
Society
Islands

Îles du Désappointement

· Levu
·nu *Koro*
·eby Suva
FIJI

Vava'u
Group

Niue
(N.Z.)

Palmerston

Papeete
Tahifi

T u a m o t u   I s l a n d s

F r e n c h
P o l y n e s i a

10°

5

TONGA
Nuku'alofa
□
Tongatapu
Group

Cook Islands
(N.Z.)

Rarotonga

Mangaia

Hao

Groupe Actéon

20°

Mururoa
Îles Gambier

Raoul Island

Kermadec Islands
(N.Z.)

T u b u a i   I s l a n d s
(Îles Australes)

Rapa   *Marotiri*

Pitcairn Islands
(U.K.)
Henderson
Island
Pitcairn Island

6

·ckland
·milton
· *North Island*

P A C I F I C   O C E A N

30°

·llington
Chatham Islands
(N.Z.)

7

N E W
ZEALAND

·y Islands
·ipodes
·slands

40°

8

1500 KILOMETRES
1000
500
0

1000
500
0
MILES

1:40 000 000

© Collins Bartholomew Ltd

49

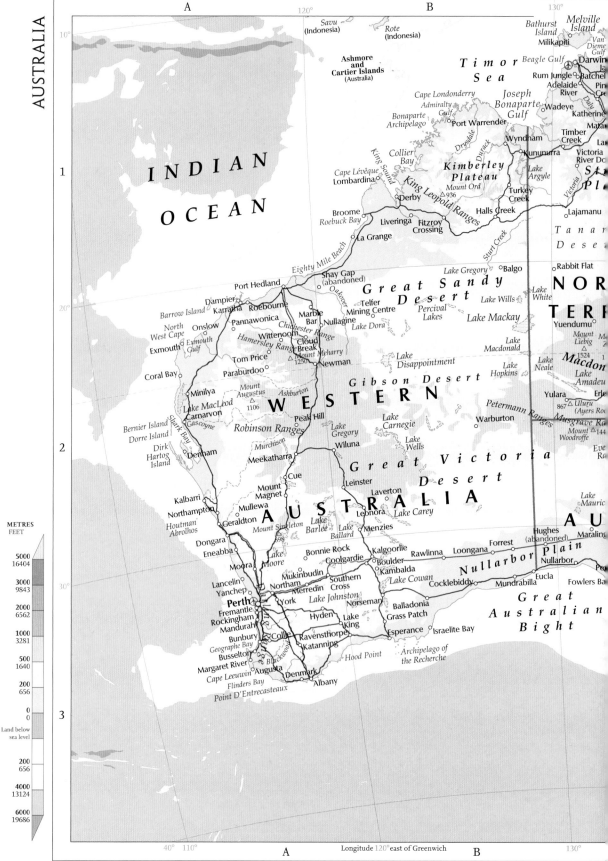

INDIAN

OCEAN

Savu
(Indonesia)
Rote
(Indonesia)

Timor
Sea

Ashmore
and
Cartier Islands
(Australia)

Bathurst
Island
Milikapiti

Melville
Island
Van
Dieme
Gulf
Darwin
Batchel
Pin

Beagle Gulf

Rum Jungle
Adelaide
River

Cape Londonderry
Joseph
Bonaparte
Gulf
Wadeye

Bonaparte
Archipelago
Admiralty
Gulf
Port Warrender

Katherine

Timber
Creek
Mata

Kimberley
Plateau
Mount Ord
△ 936

Wyndham
Kununurra

Victoria
River Do
St
Pl

Collier
Bay
Cape Lévêque
Lombardina

Lake
Argyle

King Leopold Ranges

Turkey
Creek

Derby

Halls Creek

Lajamanu

Victoria

Tanar
Dese

Broome
Roebuck Bay
La Grange
Liveringa
Fitzroy
Crossing

Sturt Creek

Eighty Mile Beach

Shay Gap
(abandoned)

Lake Gregory
Balgo
Rabbit Flat
NO R
TER R H

Great Sandy
Desert

Port Hedland
Dampier
Karratha Roebourne
North
West Cape
Onslow
Pannawonica
Barrow Island

Oakover
Telfer
Mining Centre

Marble
Bar
Nullagine
Chichester Range
Wittenoom
Cloud
Break

Percival
Lakes

Lake Wills
Lake
White

Lake Mackay

Yuendumu

Mount
Liebig
△

Macdon

Exmouth
Exmouth
Gulf
Hamersley Range
Mount Meharry
△ 1250
Newman

Lake Dora

Lake Macdonald
Lake
Neale

Lake
Amadeu

Coral Bay

Tom Price
Paraburdoo

Gibson Desert

Lake
Disappointment

Lake
Hopkins

Yulara
△ Uluru
867 (Ayers Roc

Erle

Mount
Augustus
△
1106
Ashburton

WESTERN

Petermann Ranges

Warburton

Musgrave Ra
Mount △ 144
Woodroffe
Eve
Ra

Minilya
Lake MacLeod
Carnarvon
Gascoyne

Robinson Ranges

Peak Hill

Lake
Carnegie

Lake
Gregory

Bernier Island
Dorre Island
Dirk
Hartog
Island

Shark Bay

Murchison

Wiluna

Great Victoria

Lake
Wells

Lake
Mauric

Denham

Meekatharra
AUSTRALIA
Desert

Cue

AU

Kalbarri
Northampton
Mount
Magnet
Mullewa
Geraldton
Mount Singleton
△98

Leinster

Laverton
Leonora
Lake Carey

Houtman
Abrolhos

Lake
Barlee
Lake
Ballard
Menzies

Dongara
Eneabba

Bonnie Rock
Coolgardie
Kalgoorlie
Boulder

Rawlinna
Loongana
Forrest

Hughes
(abandoned)
Maralin

Moora
Lake
Moore
Mukinbudin
Northam
Southern
Cross
Kambalda
Lake Cowan

Nullarbor
Nullarbor Plain

Eucla
Mundrabilla
Fowlers Ba

Lancelin
Yanchep
Merredin
Perth
Fremantle
Rockingham
Mandurah
York
Lake Johnston
Norseman
Cocklebiddy

Great
Australian
Bight

Hyden
Lake
King
Balladonia
Grass Patch

Bunbury
Collie
Ravensthorpe
Katanning
Esperance
Israelite Bay

Geographe Bay
Busselton
Margaret River
Blackwood
Cape Leeuwin
Augusta
Flinders Bay
Point D'Entrecasteaux

Denmark

Hood Point

Archipelago of
the Recherche

Albany

METRES
FEET

5000	16404
3000	9843
2000	6562
1000	3281
500	1640
200	656
0	0

Land below
sea level

200	656
4000	13124
6000	19686

Lambert Azimuthal Equal Area Projection

PORT MORESBY

Kwikila

Owen Stanley Range

Fergusson Island

D'Entrecasteaux Islands

PAPUA NEW GUINEA

Abau

Conflict Group

Misima Island

Louisiade Archipelago

Rossel Island

Tagula Island

Wessel Islands   Cape Wessel

Buckingham Bay

Nhulunbuy

Cape Arnhem   Arnhem Bay

Prince of Wales Island

Cape York

Bamaga

Cape Grenville

mbi

rnhem Land

Alyangula   Isle Woodah

Cape Cape Arnhem

Cape

York

Peninsula

Weipa

Albatross Bay

Lockhart River

Cape Direction

mbulwar   Groote Eylandt

Archer

Princess Charlotte Bay

Cape Melville

Coen

CORAL

SEA

Borroloola   Sir Edward Pellew Group

Mornington Island

Cape Flattery

Cooktown

astle

Barkly Tableland

Camooweal

Gununa

Burketown

Doomadgee

Wellesley Islands

Kowanyama

Laura

Mossman

Mareeba

Atherton

Cairns

Mount Bartle Frere

Innisfail

10°

GREAT BARRIER REEF

1

rrow Creek

Camooweal

Kajabbi

Cloncurry

Normanton

Forsayth

Tully

Ingham

Hinchinbrook Island

Sylvester

ds

Mount Isa

Richmond

McKinlay

Hughenden

Charters Towers

Townsville

Ayr

Bowen

Proserpine

Whitsunday Island

Tennant Creek

Dajarra

Selwyn Range

Corfield

Lichhardt Range

Mount Dalrymple

1277

Mackay

20°

ings

Georgina

Winton

Belyando

Glenden Sarina

nges

Boulia

Longreach

Barcaldine

Clermont

Dysart

Moranbah

Percy Isles

Arthur Point

QUEENSLAND

Simpson

Desert

Cluny

Lake Philippi

Thomson

Emerald

Blackwater

Yeppoon

Curtis Island

Capricorn Channel

Bilpa Morea Claypan

Betoota

Yaraka

Blackall

Caldervale

Springsure

Moura

Gladstone

Rockhampton

Tropic of Capricorn

Birdsville

Windorah

Buckland Tableland

Monto

Biloela

Bundaberg

Alberga   Macumba

Lake Yamma Yamma

Charleville

Taroom

Maryborough

Hervey Bay

Sandy Cape

Oodnadatta

Quilpie

Mitchell

Roma

Kingaroy

Gympie

Fraser Island

UTH

Lake Eyre (North)

Mungeranie

Copper Creek

Warburton

Wyandra

Bollone

Dalby

Nambour

Tewantin

Maroochydore

2

Cooper Pedy

Lake Eyre (South)

Bulloo Downs

St George

Darling

Toowoomba

Caboolture

RALIA

Marree

Lake Blanche

Hungerford

Cunnamulla

Dirranbandi

Goondiwindi

Warwick

Ipswich

Brisbane

Beenleigh

Gold Coast

oola

Lake Torrens

Leigh Creek

Tibooburra

Downs

Mungindi

Moree

Lismore

Casino

Byron Bay

Ballina

Lake Gairdner

Woomera

Lake Frome

Darling

Brewarrina

Lightning Ridge

Glen Innes

Grafton

Island Lagoon

Barrier Ranges

Wilcannia

Bourke

Narrabri

Walgett

Inverell

Armidale

Coffs Harbour

Macksville

30°

Streaky Bay   Whyalla

Broken Hill

Cobar

Warren

Gunnedah

Tamworth

Port Macquarie

Lord Howe Island

Kyancutta

Port Augusta

Port Pirie

Jamestown

Barnato

Great Range

Dubbo

Muswellbrook

Taree

Eyre Peninsula

Wallaroo

Burra

Ivanhoe

Garnpung Lake

Parkes

Orange

Maitland

Newcastle

Lincoln

Gawler

Murray

Mildura

Wentworth

Hay

Lachlan

Forbes

Lithgow

Penrith

NEW SOUTH WALES

Carnot

Investigator Strait

Adelaide

Murray Bridge

Ouyen

Swan Hill

Wagga Wagga

Griffith

Grenfell

Goulburn

Yass

Sydney

Botany Bay

Wollongong

Nowra

Kingscote

Kangaroo Island

Nhill

Horsham

Mount William

1167

Bendigo

Shepparton

Wangaratta

Albury

Wodonga

CANBERRA

A.C.T.

Cooma

Batemans Bay

Narooma

Cape Jaffa

Stawell

Ballarat

VICTORIA

Melbourne

Mount Kosciuszko

2229

Eden

Bega

3

Mount Gambier

Portland

Geelong

Gippsland

Bairnsdale

Cape Howe

Discovery Bay

Warrnambool

Colac

Frankston

Moe

Sale

TASMAN

SEA

Cape Otway

Bass Strait

Wilson's Promontory

Currie

King Island

Whitemark

Flinders Island

Furneaux Group

Hunter Islands

Cape Barren I.

Banks Strait

Eddystone Point

Burnie

Devonport

Launceston

Mount Ossa

617

Queenstown

Ringal

TASMANIA

Lake Gordon

Sorell

Hobart

Port Arthur

Kingston

C   140°   D   150°   E   160°

© Collins Bartholomew Ltd

600 KILOMETRES

400

200

0

400

300

200

100

MILES 0

1:16 000 000

51

A 140° B

Macumba

Warburton

Cooper Creek

Noccundra Thargominda

Grey Range

Innamincka
Moomba

Bulloo

Mungeranie

Tirari
Desert

Cooper Creek

Sturt Stony
Desert

Bulloo
Downs

QUE

Lake
Eyre
(North)

1

Etadunna

Hungerford

William Creek

Lake
Blanche

Caryapundy
Swamp

Lake Eyre
(South)

Tilcha
(abandoned)

Mount Sturt
427 △

Tibooburra

Milparinka

Wanaaring

Paroo

Marree

Moolawatana

Lake Callabonna

Hawkers Gate

Millers Creek

SOUTH

30°

Lyndhurst

Leigh
Creek

Balcanoona

Lake
Frome

Tongo

Parakylia

Roxby
Downs

Packsaddle

White Cliffs

Momba

Tilpa

Da

Wirraminna

Beltana

Parachilna

Mootwingee

Woomera

Lake
Torrens

AUSTRALIA

Frome Downs

Euriowie

Wilcannia

Island
Lagoon

Pernatty
Lagoon

Mount Robe
486 △

Stephens Creek

Flinders Ranges

Barrier Range

Curnamona

Broken
Hill

Lake
Gairdner

Woocalla

Hawker

Lake
Macfarlane

Cradock

Cockburn
Mingary

Menindee Lake

Menindee

NEW

Nonning

Quorn

Mannahill

Olary

Tandou Lake

Mount Ma

Gawler Ranges

Port Augusta

Stirling North

Yunta

Coombah

Darnick

Ivan

Buckleboo

Iron Knob

Mount
Ramarkabl △ 969

Wilmington

Orroroo

Paratoo

Oakbank

Popiltah

Pooncarie

Mossgiel

Kimba

Whyalla

Wirrabara

Peterborough

Terowie

Canopus

Garnpung
Lake

Hatfield

Boc

Kyancutta

Balumbah

Port Pirie

Jamestown

Lake
Victoria

Burtundy

Darling

Oxley

Lock

Cleve

Crystal
Brook

Gladstone

Burra

Wentworth

Sheringa Eyre
Peninsula

Cowell

Snowtown

Clare

Morgan

Murray

Renmark

Merbein

Mildura

Murrumbidge

Ungarra

Arno
Bay

Wallaroo

Kadina

Blyth

Port Wakefield

Balaklava

Waikerie

Barmera

Berri

Werrimull

Red
Cliffs

Robinvale

Balranald

R

Cockaleechie

Tumby
Bay

Moonta

Maitland

Kapunda
Nuriootpa

Loxton

Hattah

Tooleybuc

Booroorb

Coffin
Bay

Port
Lincoln

Minlaton

Ardrossan

Gawler

Mannum

Alawoona

Mindarie

Moulan

Yorke Peninsula

Gulf St
Vincent

Adelaide

Spencer Gulf

Gambier
Islands

Mount Lofty Range

Ouyen

Swan
Hill

Deni

Cape
Carnot

Yorketown

Mount Barker

Murray Bridge

Pinnaroo

Murrayville

Underbool

Lake
Tyrrell

Sea Lake

Ultima

Murray

Barham

Cohu

Marion
Bay

Willunga

Tailem Bend

Lameroo

Echu

Investigator Strait

Backstairs Passage

Goolwa

Victor
Harbor

Lake
Alexandrina

Coonalpyn

Tintinara

Hopetoun

Birchip

Kerang

Cape Borda

Kingscote

Penneshaw

Meningie

Keith

Lake
Hindmarsh

Warracknabeal
Nhill

Wycheproof

Charlton

Rocheste

Cape
du Couedic

Kangaroo
Island

Youngshusband Peninsula

Bordertown

Kaniva

Dimboola

Donald

St Arnaud

Bendigo

Padthaway

Horsham

Avoca

Castlemaine

VIC

Lacepede Bay
Kingston South East
Cape Jaffa

Naracoorte

Edenhope

Goroke

Stawell
Mount William
△ 1167

Ararat

Kyneton

Daylesford

Sunb

Robe

Lake
George

Penola

Balmoral

Glenelg

The Grampians

Beaufort

Ballarat

Ma

Melton

Beachport

Millicent

Casterton

Coleraine

Skipton

Bacchus Marsh

Wyndham

Werribee

Mount Gambier

Hamilton

Mortlake

Lake
Corangamite

Geelong

Queenscliff

Port MacDonnell

Heywood

Portland

Camperdown
Terang

Colac

Torq

Anglese

Discovery
Bay
Cape Nelson

Port
Fairy

Warrnambool

Lorne

Port Campbell

Apollo Bay
Cape Otway

135°

A

Longitude 140° east of Greenwich

B

METRES
FEET

5000
16404

3000
9843

2000
6562

1000
3281

500
1640

200
656

0
0

Land below
sea level

200
656

4000
13124

6000
19686

Conic Equidistant Projection

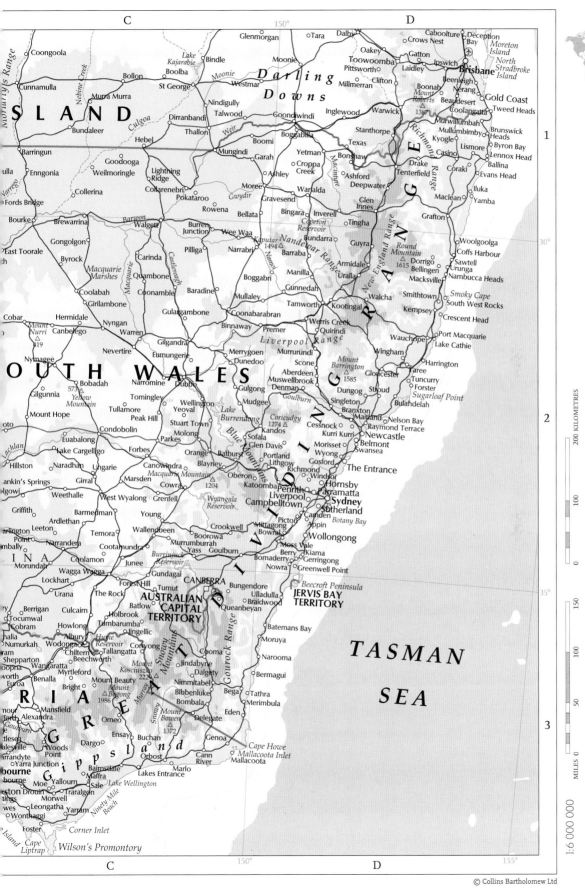

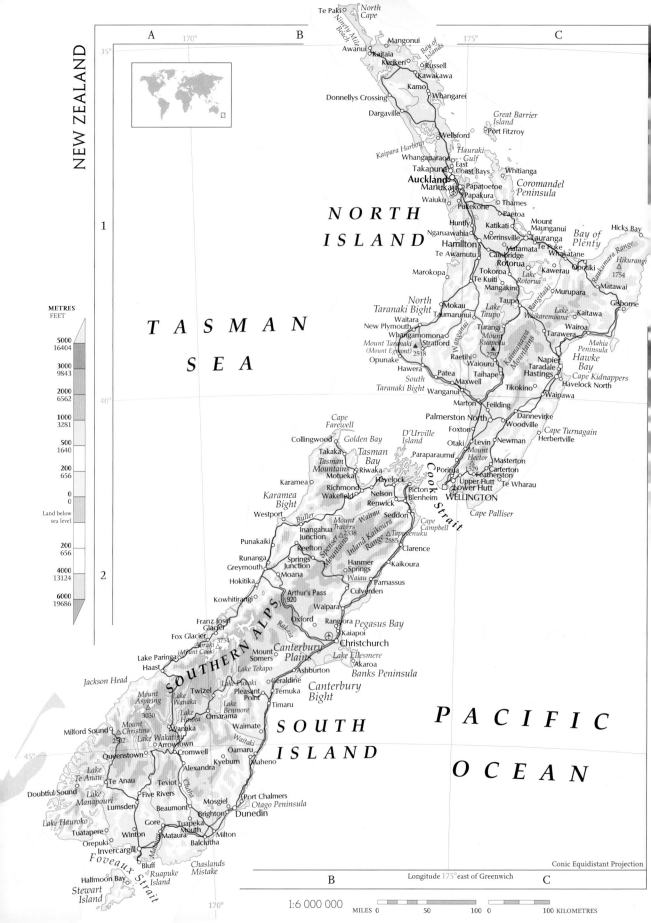

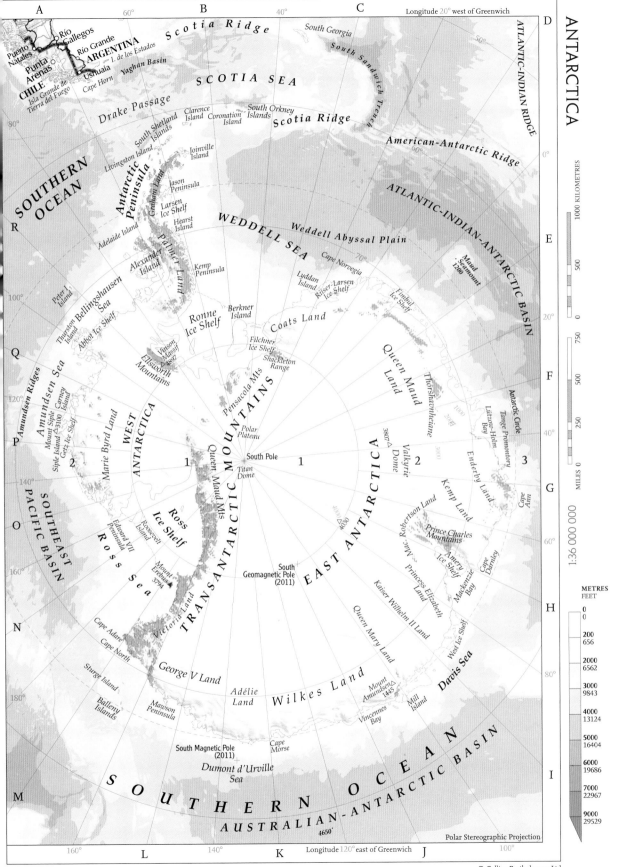

Longitude 20° west of Greenwich

A 60° B 40° C 20°

D

50°

ATLANTIC-INDIAN RIDGE

Scotia Ridge

South Georgia

South Sandwich Trench

South Sandwich Islands

SCOTIA SEA

Puerto
Natales
Río
Gallegos
Río Grande
ARGENTINA
I. de los Estados
Punta
Arenas
Ushuaia
Yaghan Basin
CHILE
Isla Grande de
Tierra del Fuego
Cape Horn

Drake Passage

Clarence
Island
Coronation
Island
South Orkney
Islands

Scotia Ridge

American-Antarctic Ridge

0°

80°

Livingston Island
South Shetland
Islands
Joinville
Island

SOUTHERN
OCEAN

Antarctic
Peninsula
Jason
Peninsula
Graham Land
Larsen
Ice Shelf

ATLANTIC-INDIAN-ANTARCTIC BASIN

60°

R

Adelaide Island

Hearst
Island

WEDDELL SEA

Weddell Abyssal Plain

Cape Norvegia

Maud
Seamount
1200

E

100°

Alexander
Island
Palmer Land

Kemp
Peninsula

70°

Lyddan
Island
Riiser-Larsen
Ice Shelf
Fimbul
Ice Shelf

20°

Peter I
Island
Thurston
Island
Bellingshausen
Sea
Abbot Ice Shelf

Ronne
Ice Shelf
Berkner
Island

Coats Land

Queen Maud
Land

Thorshavnheiane

Antarctic Promontory

Q

Amundsen Ridges
Amundsen Sea
Carney
Island
Getz Ice Shelf
Vinson
Massif
4897
Ellsworth
Mountains

Filchner
Ice Shelf
Shackleton
Range

Lützow-Holm
Bay
Range Promontory

F

120°

Siple Island
Mount Siple
3100
Pensacola Mts

3807

1000

Antarctic Circle

500

P

WEST
ANTARCTICA
Marie Byrd Land

Polar
Plateau
Queen Maud Mts

South Pole

Valkyrie
Dome

2000

Enderby Land

40°

3

2

1

1

2

Cape
Ann

SOUTHEAST
PACIFIC BASIN

140°

Edward VII
Peninsula
Roosevelt
Island
Ross
Ice Shelf

Titan
Dome

EAST ANTARCTICA

3000

Kemp Land

G

160°

Ross
Sea

Mount
Erebus
3794

TRANSANTARCTIC MOUNTAINS

Mac. Robertson Land

Prince Charles
Mountains
Amery
Ice Shelf

60°

Mawson
Escarpment

Cape
Darnley

180°

Cape Adare
Cape North

Victoria Land

South
Geomagnetic Pole
(2011)

Princess Elizabeth
Land
Kaiser Wilhelm II Land

Mackenzie
Bay

H

O

N

George V Land

Queen Mary Land

West Ice Shelf

Davis Sea

80°

Sturge Island

Adélie
Land
Wilkes Land
Mount
Amundsen
1445
Mill
Island

M

Balleny
Islands
Mawson
Peninsula

South Magnetic Pole
(2011)

Cape
Morse

Vincennes
Bay

I

Dumont d'Urville
Sea

SOUTHERN OCEAN

AUSTRALIAN-ANTARCTIC BASIN

4650'

Polar Stereographic Projection

160° L 140° K Longitude 120° east of Greenwich J 100°

© Collins Bartholomew Ltd

55

1000 KILOMETRES
500
0

750
500
250
0

MILES

1:36 000 000

METRES
FEET

0 / 0
200 / 656
2000 / 6562
3000 / 9843
4000 / 13124
5000 / 16404
6000 / 19686
7000 / 22967
9000 / 29529

5 50° **4** 60° **3** 70° **2** 80° **1**

10°

B

C

D

0° E

F

G

H

I J K L

40°

S

R U S S I A N   F E

20° **Yekaterinburg**
Chelyabinsk
Omsk
Novosibirsk
Barnaul Bratsk

Angara

6

SPAIN
FRANCE
IRELAND
UNITED KINGDOM
NETH.
BELGIUM
LUX.
GERMANY
DENMARK
SWITZ.
AUSTRIA
CZECH REP.
POLAND
SWEDEN
NORWAY
FINLAND
North Sea
Baltic Sea
Arctic Circle
North Cape
Svalbard (Nor.)
Barents Sea
Zemlya Frantsa-Iosifa
Severnaya Zemlya
Novaya Zemlya
Kara Sea
Ob
Yenisey
Norilsk
Salekhard
Ural Mountains

30° ITALY
SLOVAKIA
HUNGARY
SLOVENIA
CROATIA
BOSNIA HERZ.
MONT.
SERBIA
K.
ALBANIA
MACE.
GREECE
ROMANIA
BULGARIA
MOLDOVA
UKRAINE
BELARUS
LITHUANIA
LATVIA
ESTONIA
Black Sea
İstanbul
Ankara
T U R K E Y
Volga
Ural (Zhayyq)
Ural'sk
Aktobe
Astana
Pavlodar
Irtysh (Yertis)
Karagandy
K A Z A K H S T A N

CYPRUS
Nicosia
LEBANON
Beirut
SYRIA
Aleppo
GEORGIA
Tbilisi
ARMENIA
Yerevan
AZERBAIJAN
Az.
Baku
Caucasus
Caspian Sea
Aral Sea
Lake Balkhash
Tashkent
Bishkek
Almaty
Ürümqi
MO

EGYPT
ISRAEL
Jerusalem
JORDAN
Amman
Damascus
Mosul
Baghdād
IRAQ
Tigris
Euphrates
Tehrān
I R A N
Mashhad
Aşgabat (Ashkhabad)
TURKMENISTAN
UZBEKISTAN
Dushanbe
TAJIKISTAN
KYRGYZSTAN
SINKIANG
Hotan

7

Mediterranean Sea
Red Sea
SUDAN
Tropic of Cancer
Medina
Kuwait
KUWAIT
Aḥvāz
Eşfahān
Shīrāz
Zāhedān
The Gulf
Ahmadabad (Ahmedabad)

Jeddah
SAUDI
ARABIA
Riyadh
Manama
BAHRAIN
Doha
QATAR
Abu Dhabi
U.A.E.
Muscat
Gulf of Oman
Kābul
AFGHANISTAN
Islamabad
Lahore
Quetta
PAKISTAN
Karachi
Indus
HIMA
TIBET
C H
Mt Everest 8848

8

ERITREA
ETHIOPIA
DJIBOUTI
Aden
Gulf of Aden
Şan'ā
Y E M E N
OMAN
Rub' al Khālī
Socotra (Yemen)
Delhi
New Delhi
Jaipur
Hyderabad
Varanasi
Ganges
Kathmandu
NEPAL
Thimphu
BHUTAN
Brahmaputra
Dhaka
BANGLA-DESH
Mand
MYANM
(BUR

9

SOMALIA
A R A B I A N
S E A
Mumbai (Bombay)
Nagpur
Hyderabad
I N D I A
Nay Pyi Taw
BAY OF
BENGAL
Andaman Islands (India)
Rangoo
(Yangô

0° Equator
Laccadive Islands (India)
Bangalore (Bengaluru)
Chennai (Madras)
Thiruvananthapuram (Trivandrum)
Colombo
SRI LANKA
Sri Jayewardenepura Kotte
Nicobar Islands (India)

10

MALDIVES
Male

SEYCHELLES
Aldabra Islands
Amirante Islands
Mahé
I N D I A N   O C E A N

10°

11

British Indian Ocean Territory
Chagos Archipelago

F 50° **G** 60° **H** 70° **I** Longitude 80° east of Greenwich 90° **K**

Two Point Equidistant Projection

180°
170°

East Siberian Sea
Siberia Islands
Wrangel Island
Arctic Circle

T
S
R
Q
P
O

B E R I N G

S E A

170°

Aleutian Islands (U.S.A.)

Midway Islands (U.S.A.)

N
E
R
I
A

R A T I O N

Lena

Yakutsk

Magadan

Kamchatka Peninsula

Petropavlovsk-Kamchatskiy

Sea of

Okhotsk

Kure Atoll

180°

P A C I F I C

Tropic of Cancer

2500 KILOMETRES

Lake Baikal
sk

Heilong Jiang

Khabarovsk

Sapporo

Hokkaidō

Wake Atoll (U.S.A.)

20°
170°

O C E A N

2000

1500

Qiqihar

Harbin

Vladivostok

Sea of Japan (East Sea)

Sakhalin

Kuril Islands

Amur

1000

Ulan Bator

OLIA
o

NER MONGOLIA

Changchun

Shenyang

NORTH KOREA

P'yŏngyang

Honshū

Tōkyō

J A P A N

8

Bonin Islands (Japan)

500

Baotou

Beijing

Dalian

Seoul

SOUTH KOREA

Ōsaka

0

Tianjin

Yellow

Fukuoka

Kyūshū

Volcano Islands (Japan)

10°
160°

Taiyuan

Huang He

Sea

Lanzhou

Xi'an

Shanghai

East

China

Sea

Ryukyu Islands

N A

Nanjing

engdu

Wuhan

9

Northern Mariana Islands (U.S.A.)

1500

nqing

Yangtze

Changsha

Taibei

Guam (U.S.A.)

Fuzhou

TAIWAN

Kunming

Guangzhou

1000

Nanning

Hong Kong

Caroline Islands

Equator

0°

Ha Nôi

Hainan Dao

Luzon

500

ntiane

VIETNAM

South

Manila

Quezon City

PHILIPPINES

Melekeok

Admiralty Island

New Britain

ILAND

Mekong

C h i n a

PALAU

10

Bangkok

S e a

Mindanao

MILES 0

CAMBODIA

Palawan

Phnom Penh

LAOS

Hô Chi Minh City

Sulu Sea

Davao

Halmahera

Jayapura

New

PAPUA NEW GUINEA

Gulf of Thailand

Celebes Sea

Puncak Jaya △ 5030

Guinea

MALAYSIA

Bandar Seri Begawan

BRUNET

Manado

Moluccas (Maluku)

10°

dan

Kuala Lumpur

Kuching

B o r n e o

Seram

Kepulauan Aru

Pulau Dolak

Putrajaya

SINGAPORE

Balikpapan

Celebes (Sulawesi)

Kepulauan Tanimbar

1:44 000 000

a
t
r
a

Palembang

Banjarmasin

Makassar

Laut Banda

Arafura Sea

Cape Arnhem

11

I N D O N E S I A

Laut Java

Dili

EAST TIMOR

AUSTRALIA

Jakarta

Java

Sumbawa

Laut Sawu

Bandung

Surabaya

Sumba

Timor

O   140°   P   150°

© Collins Bartholomew Ltd

A 105° B 120°

90°

Khulna Lunglei Wuntho Lincang Yuxi Yuxi Kaiyuan Yuxi **CHINA** Hechi **Liuzhou** Longyan **Xiamen** TAIB
Chittagong Namtu Lashio Jinghong Gejiu Wenshan Cao Bang Thai Pingxiang **Nanning** Yulin **Guangzhou** Chaozhou Xin Hual
Cox's Megok Monywa **Mandalay** Lao Son La Nguyen Hai Qinzhou **Shenzhen** (Canton) Hong Kong Gaoxiong
Bazar Myingyan **MYANMAR** Kengtung Phôngsali Cai Duong Beihai Maoming Macao Hong Kong **Gaoxiong**
Sittwe Meiktila Taunggyi **NAY PYI TAW** Chiang Louangphabang **HA NOI** Hai Phong **Zhanjiang**
Kyaukpyu Minbu Pyinmana Rai (Hanoi) Nam Dinh Xuwen Wencheng
Thandwe Pye Taung-ngu Phayao Nan Phôngsavan Vinh Chengmai Qionghai **Hainan** Wanning
Hinthada **(BURMA)** Chiang Lampang Phrae don Thani Ha Tinh Dongfang **Dao**
Bassein Pegu Thaton Uttaradit **VIENTIANE** Savannakhet Hue Laoag
RANGOON Mawlamyaing Tak Phitsanulok Nakhon (Viangchan) Da Nang San Fernando City
(Yangôn) Mouths of Phumi Sakon Salavan Quang Ngai Dagupan Tuguega
the Irrawaddy **THAILAND** Khon Kaen Pakxé Tarlac Vigan Bonto
Ye Lop Buri Surin Ubon Quy Nhon Batanga **MANILA** Quezon C
(Yai) Ayutthaya Ratchasima Ratchathani Play Ku Luc
North Andaman Tavoy Nakhon Phumi Samraong Buon Ma Thuot
Middle Andaman **BANGKOK** Chon Phnum Mindoro
Andaman Islands (Krung Thep) Buri Pattaya Bâtdâmbâng **SOUTH** Calamian
(India) Palaw **CAMBODIA** Nha Trang Group
South Andaman Chanthaburi Pouthisat **PHNOM** Da Lat **CHINA**
Port Blair Tenasserim Kâmpóng **PENH** Phan Rang-Thap Cham
Nachuge Myeik Prachuap Spoe Takêv Biên Phan Thiet **SEA**
Little Andaman Kyúnzu Khiri Khan **Gulf of** Hoa Puerto
(Mergui **Thailand** Sihanoukville Ninh **Ho Chi Minh City** Princesa Roxas
Car Nicobar Archipelago) Chumphon Long Xuyen My Tho Brooke's **Palawan**
Takua Pa Ranong Rach Gia Can Point Sul
Nicobar Islands Phangnga Nakhon Si Tho Balabac Strait Sea
(India) Krabi Thammarat Ca Mau Bac Banggi
Dakoank Phuket Phatthalung Mui Ca Mau Liêu Mouths Kudat Gunung
Great Songkhla of the Mekong Kinabalu Sandakan
Nicobar Hat Yai Yala Kota Kota Kinabalu Semporna
Banda Kangar Bharu **MALAYSIA** **SABAH** Sul
Aceh Alor Star Pasir **BANDAR SERI BEGAWAN** Lahad Datu Archip
Sigli George Taiping Putih **BRUNEI** Lumbis Tawau
Bireun Town Gunung Tahan Kuala Terengganu Miri Tarakan C
Langsa Ipoh 2189 Mukah Tanjungselor
Pangkalansusu Kuala Lipis Kuching Datadian Tanjungredeb
Simeulue Medan **SUMATERA** Kuantan Natuna Igan Bintulu Sambaliung
Sinabang Prapat **PUTRAJAYA** Besar Natuna Sibu **SARAWAK** 2988
Labuhanbilik **KUALA LUMPUR** (Indonesia) Debak Sri Aman Tolito
Gunungsitoli Sibolga Melaka Seremban Kepulauan Sambas Lubok Antu Sangkulirang
Nias Dumai Keluang Anambas Singkawang **BORNEO** Samarinda
Equator Muar **Johor Bahru** Serian Mempawah Muaralembu Donggala Palu
Minas Kepulauan Pontianak Nangahpinoh Balikpapan **CELEBES**
Payakumbuh **SINGAPORE** Tambelan Sukadana (SULAWESI)
Pulau-pulau Pekanbaru Kepulauan Ketapang Sampit Palangkaraya Mamuju
Batu Bukittinggi Riau Kendawangan Banjarmasin Parepare
Padang Sijunjung Belinyu Pangkalanbuun Kotabaru Watampone
Siberut Sipura Bangko Sungailiat Amuntai **Makassar**
Gunung Jambi Bangka Seranyu Tanjung (Ujung Pandang)
Sekayu Pangkalpinang Manggar Sambar Bontosunggu
Pagai Trebingtinggi Belitung Tanjung Pulau Selayar
Utara Palembang Iroboali Selatan **Laut** Tanahjampea
Pagai Lahat Laut Jawa Laut Bali
Selatan Bengkulu Muarabeliti (Java Sea) (Bali Sea) Kepulauan Bonerat
INDONESIA Tanjung Selatan Kepulauan
Gunung Dempo Manggala Kangean
Kotabumi Mataram Dompu Raba
Enggano Bintuhan Krui Madura Denpasar Praya **Sumbawa**
Bandar Lampung **JAKARTA** Lombok
Serang Cirebon Semarang **Surabaya** Waikabubak Waing
Selat Sunda Bandung Surakarta Jember **Sumba**
Sukabumi Cilacap Yogyakarta Malang Bali Selat Lombok
INDIAN Teluk Palabuhanratu **JAVA** Denpasar Lesser Sunda Islan
(JAWA)
OCEAN
Cocos Islands Christmas
(Australia) Island
(Australia)

A Longitude 105° east of Greenwich B 120°

Albers Equal Area Conic Projection

METRES
FEET

5000	16404
3000	9843
2000	6562
1000	3281
500	1640
200	656
0	0
Land below	sea level
200	656
4000	13124
6000	19686

C   135°   D   150°   E

Ryukyu Islands
(Nansei-shotō)
(Japan)

Tropic of Cancer

1

WAN

The People's Republic
f China claims Taiwan
its 23rd Province.

Philippine

Sea

P A C I F I C

Pagan

Northern
Mariana
Islands
(U.S.A.)

O C E A N

zon

CAPITOL HILL ○ Saipan
Tinian

15°

PHILIPPINES

Catanduanes
○ Legazpi
○ Sorsogon
olon ○ Catarman
rosin
Masbate ○ Samar
Roxas ○ Catbalogan
ay ○ Bacolod
○ Tacloban
os ○ Cebu
Bohol
aran *Bohol Sea*
quieta ○ Cagayan de Oro
○ Iligan ○ Butuan
ndian ○ Cotabato
mboanga **Davao**
ela ○ Mati
Moro
Gulf ○ General Santos

Rota
HAGÅTÑA ○ ⊗
Guam
(U.S.A.)

FEDERATED STATES
OF MICRONESIA

Mariana Trench

Ulithi
Fais

2

Yap ⊗
Colonia

Faraulep

Ngulu

Sorol

C a r o l i n e
Eauripik *I s l a n d s*

PALAU
MELEKEOK
Babeldaob

Kepulauan
Talaud
○ Sangir

es

Morotai
Daruba ○
○ Tobelo

East Caroline
Basin

Equator   0°

Kepulauan
Sangir

St Matthias
Group ○ Mussau Island

enanjung ○ **Manado**
inahasa
Gorontalo ○
kwandang
○ Ternate **Halmahera**
○ Sao-Siu

Laut Maluku
(Molucca Sea)

Waigeo

Pelleluhu *Admiralty*
Islands *Islands* ○ Lorengau
Hermit Islands Manus Island
Wuvulu ○ ○ *Ysabel Channel*
Island *Schouten Islands* Umbukul ○

New Hanover
○ Kavieng
New
Ireland

Bismarck Archipelago

Luwuk ○
epulauan
ogian
○ Todeli
ba ○ Peleng
Banggai ○ *Mangole*
ggai ○ *Kepulauan*
ngai *Banggai* *Sula*

○ Labuna
Selat Dampir *Kwoka*
Salawati Sorong ○
Misoöl ○ ○ Fafanlap
Bacan ○ ○ Obi

3000 Jazirah
Doberai
Manokwari ○ *Biak*
○ ○ *Numfoor* ○ *Selat Yapen*
Inanwatan ○ Serui
Ransiki ○ *Yapen* Sarmi ○
Babo ○ Nabire ○

Biak ○
Tanjung d'Urville
Jayapura ○ Vanimo
Aitape ○ Wewak
Sepik ○ Maprik ○ Bogia ○

Manam Island ○
Madang ○

Bismarck Sea
Ulamona ○
Rabaul ○
2438
New Britain

Kimbe ○
Lau

A S I A

Namlea ○
Piru ○ *Gunung Binaiia*
Seram
○ Ambon ○ Bula
Buru *Ambon* Saparua
3019
Kendari ○
Wowoni ○

Manui ○

Laut Seram
(Ceram Sea)
Fakfak ○
Kaimana ○

○ Namua
Moluccas
(Maluku)

Pegunungan Van Rees
Taritatu
PAPUA *Pucak*
(IRIAN JAYA) *Trikora*
Pegunungan Maoke Mandala
Enarotali ○ 5030 4730
Puncak Jaya 4700
Lorentz

NEW
GUINEA

Central Ra.
Mt
Wilhelm 4558 ○
Mendi ○ Goroka ○
○ Mount
Hagen ○

PAPUA

Long
Island
Umboi ○
Huon
Peninsula
Lae ○ Gasmata
New Britain

Morobe ○
Trobriand
Islands
○ Losuia

Buton

Kepulauan
Watubela
Kepulauan
Banda
Kepulauan
Kai
Tual ○ Dobo ○ Wokam
Kai Kecil ○ Benjina
Kepulauan Kobroör ○
Aru ○ Trangan

Amamapare ○
Digul

Kiunga ○
Balimo ○ Kikori ○
Morehead ○

NEW GUINEA
Wau ○
Mount
Victoria 4073 ○
Kerema ○
Gulf Bereina ○
of Papua

Kwikila ○
Alotau ○
Abau ○
PORT
MORESBY
Samarai ○

D'Entrecasteaux Is
Bolubolu ○
Goschen Strait

L a u t   B a n d a
(Banda Sea)

Kepulauan
Tanimbar
Larat ○
Kepulauan Selaru ○
Sermata

Tanjung Deyong

Pulau
Dolok ○
Merauke ○
Daru ○

Manui

res
Sea)

Kepulauan
Barat Daya
Alor Kepulauan Wuliaru ○
Damar Romang Tepa ○ ○ Babar
Kalabahi ○ Huaki ○ *Wetar* Kaiwatu ○
Alor *Kepulauan* Saumlakki ○
DILI ○ Maliana ○ *Kepulauan Leti*
OCUSSI ○ Manatuto ○ **EAST**
Kefamenanu ○ **TIMOR**
2960 **Timor**
Kupang ○

Tanjung Vals

A r a f u r a   S e a

Thursday ○
Island Cape York
Prince of Wales ○ Bamaga
Island

AUSTRALIA

Melville
Island *Croker Island*
Bathurst Island Milikapiti ○
Beagle Gulf *Van Diemen*
Gulf
Batchelor ○ Darwin ○
Adelaide River ○ Pine Creek ○

Nhulunbuy ○
Cape Arnhem
Milingimbi ○
Cape Wessel
Wessel Islands

Arnhem
Land

Jabiru ○
Alyangula ○

Gulf
of
Carpentaria

Weipa ○
○ Lockhart River

Coen ○

Cape York
Peninsula

Cape Grenville

Cape Melville
Cape
Flattery
Laura ○ Cooktown ○

T i m o r   S e a

C   135°   D

500 KILOMETRES
250
0

500
250
0 MILES

1:20 000 000

150°

15°

A B

100°

Phangnga
Ban Khok Kloi
Thalang
Phuket
Krabi
Thung Song
Nakhon Si Thammarat
Mui Ca Mau
Nám Căn
Đao Côn Son

VIETNAM

Trang
Phatthalung
Khao Chum Thong

THAILAND

SOUTH CHI

Hat Yai
Songkhla
Pattani
Thale Luang

Andaman Sea

Satun
Sadao
Narathiwat
Kota Bharu

Pulau We
Sabang
Banda Aceh
Sigli
Bireun
Lhokseumawe

Langkawi
Kangar
Yala
Rangae

Alor Star
Pasir Putih

Sungai Petani
Pinang
Butterworth
Kuala Kerai
Kuala Terengganu

Laut

Natuna Besar

Peureula
George Town
Taiping
Kuala Kangsar
MALAYSIA
Dungun

Takengon
Langsa
Pangkalansusu
Ipoh
Gunung Tahan △2189
PENINSULAR
Cukai

Panarik

Gunung Abongabong △2985
Belawan
Kampar
Tasik Kenyir

Blangkejeren
Gunung Leuser △3145
Binjai
Medan
Bagan Datuk
Kuala Lipis
Teluk Intan
Kuantan

Kepulauan Anambas

Tapaktuan
Tebingtinggi
Pematangsiantar

MALAYSIA
KUALA LUMPUR
Temerluh
Pekan

Jemaja

Kepulauan Natuna (Indonesia)

Subi Besar

Simeulue
Sidikalang
Kisaran
Klang
PUTRAJAYA
Bahau
Padang Endau

Sinabang
Singkil
Prapat
Danau Toba
Balige
Labuhanbilik
Tanjungbalai
Seremban
Melaka
Segamat

Selat Serasan

Liku
Sem

Pulau-pulau Banyak
Rantauprapat
Bagansiapiapi
Dumai
Muar
Batu Pahat
Keluang
Mersing

Sambas
Kueh
Pemangkat
Siluas

Nias
Sirombu
Gunungsitoli
Padangsidimpuan
Sibolga

Duri
Bengkalis

Johor Bahru

Kepulauan Tambelan (Indonesia)

Singkawang
Bengkaya

Ngabang

Telukdalam
Hutanopan
Daludalu
Minas
SINGAPORE

Bintan
Tanjungpinang

Mempawah

Natal
Talu
Bangkinang
Pekanbaru

Kepulauan Riau

Pontianak

Equator
Airbangis
Payakumbuh
Kampar

Lingga
Daik

Pulau-pulau Karimata

Balaiber
Kubu

Tanahmasa
Tanahbala
Pulau-pulau Batu
Padangpanjang
Bukittinggi
Sijunjung
Solok
Rengat
Tembilahan

Singkep
Kepulauan Lingga

Telukbatang

Kagologolo
Padang
Kualatungal

Sukadana

Siberut
Painan
Muarabungo
Gunung Kerinci △3805
Simpang
Batanghari
Jambi
Belinyu

Ketapang

Sipura
Muarasiberut
Sungaipenuh
Bangko
Muaratembesi

Sungailiat
Mentok

Selat Karimata

Suk

Kaliet
Sarolangun
Pangkalpinang
Bangka

Kendawan

Pagai Utara
Mukomuko
Surulangun
Sekayu
Rajik
Koba
Tanjungpandan

Manggar

Tan Sar

Buriai
Pagai Selatan
Lubuklinggau
Musi
Plaju
PALEMBANG
Toboali

Dendang
Belitung

Curup
Tebingtinggi
Kayuagung
Prabumulih

Mega
Bengkulu
Gunung Dempo ▲ 3159
Lahat

Martapura
Menggala

INDI

Gunung Resag △3232
Muaradua

LAUT
(JAV

Bintuhan
Kotabumi
Metro

Enggano
Krui
Kotaagung
Bandar Lampung

Tanjung Cina
Teluk Semangka
Sebesi
JAKARTA
Tanjung Indramayu

Krakatau
Serang
Karawang
Cirebon

Selat Sunda
Rangkasbitung
Bogor
Pekalon

Panaitan
Deli
Sukabumi
Gunung Slamet △3428
Tegal

Teluk Palabuhanratu
Bandung
Garut
Temanggu

Sindangbarang
Ciamis
Gunung △3019

INDIAN

Cilacap
Kebum

JAVA
(JAWA)

OCEAN

Strait of Malacca

SUMATRA

Pesunungan Barisan

Greater Sunda Is

Kepulauan Mentawai

METRES FEET
5000 16404
3000 9843
2000 6562
1000 3281
500 1640
200 656
0 0
Land below sea level
200 656
4000 13124
6000 19686

0°

2

10°

A
Longitude 100° east of Greenwich
B

Albers Equal Area Conic Projection

© Collins Bartholomew Ltd

METRES
FEET

5000	16404
3000	9843
2000	6562
1000	3281
500	1640
200	656
0	0

Land below
sea level

200	656
4000	13124
6000	19686

C 1
B
A

110°
100°
20°
20°

CHINA

HUNAN
Changde
Yuanjiang Anhua
Zhangjiajie Loudi
Lengshuijiang
Xinhua Shaoyang
Yuping Jishou Huaihua
Yongzhou
Lingling
Daoxian
Xing'an
Guilin
Yangshuo Hezhou (Babu)
Lipu
Sanjiang
Rong'an
2081 Shan

GUANGXI
ZHUANGZU ZIZHIQU
Luzhou
Hechi Yizhou
Liuzhou
Bama Heshan
Laibin Guigang
Kongxian
Guiping
Bobai
Maoming
Yulin
Beiliu
Luoding

Qinzhou
Fangcheng
Beihai
Zhanjiang
Hepu
Anpu
Leizhou
Xuwen
Naozhou Dao

Liangjiang Dianbai
Xinying Qiongshan
Haikou
Wencheng
Qionghai
Wanning

HAINAN
Danzhou
Dongfang
Wuzhishan
1867 (Tongshi)
Huangliu Sanya
Lingshui

GUIZHOU
Tongren
Jiangkou
Zhenyuan
Kaili Shiqian Sinan
Zunyi
Xifeng
Guiyang
Qianxi Bijie
Anshun
Liupanshui
Qujing
Kunming
Xingyi
Luodian
Nandan
Dushan
Tianlin
Xilin
Funing

Weining
Weixin
Zhaotong
Xuyong
Xinwen
Tongzi
Weng'an
Duyun
Xingren
Longli
Changshun

SICHUAN
Zigong
Yibin
Luzhou
Mianning
Xichang
Dechang
Huili
Muli
Yongsheng
Panzhihua
Dongchuan

YUNNAN
Dali
Weishan
Chuxiong
Yuxi
Kunming
Mile
Tonghai
Kaiyuan
Mengzi
Gejiu
Yuanjiang
Mojiang
Shiping
Jingdong
Xinping
Simao
Lancang
Lincang
Baoshan
Fengqing
Kangding
Tengchong
Luxi
Longling
Ruili
Shuangjiang

Wuliang Shan
Yuan Jiang

Gulf of Tongking

VIETNAM
HANOI
Hai Phong
Nam Dinh
Ninh Binh
Thai Binh
Thanh Hoa
Vinh
Ha Tinh
Dong Hoi
Diên Châu
Lao Cai
Ha Giang
Yen Bai
Tuyên Quang
Viet Tri
Son La
Diên Biên Phu
Muong
Lang Son
Cao Bang
Mong Cai
Ha Long
Citadel of the
Ho Dynasty

Black River
Red River
3143 Mt

LAOS
VIENTIANE
Louangphabang
Xam Nua
Muang Xai
Pakbeng
Muang Hiam
Phôngsali
Muang Sing

MYANMAR (BURMA)
NAY PYI TAW
Mandalay
Sagaing
Monywa
Meiktila
Magway
Pakokku
Pyay (Prome)
Taungdwingyi
Toungoo
Pyinmana
Lashio
Kengtung
Hsipaw
Mogok
Katha
Bhamo
Myitkyina
Putao
Homalin
Kalewa
Kani
Chauk
Yenangyaung
Thayetmyo
Pyè
Henzada
Thaton
Sittaung
Pegu
Bassein
Pathein

Irrawaddy
Salween
Chindwin

Arakan Yoma
Pegu Yoma
3053
Mount
Victoria

INDIA
ARUNACHAL PRADESH
Pasighat
Tezu
Along
NAGALAND
Kohima
Mokokchung
MANIPUR
Imphal
ASSAM
Guwahati
Dibrugarh
Jorhat
Silchar
Tezpur
Dhubri
Goalpara
Nagaon
MEGHALAYA
Shillong
MIZORAM
Aizawl
Lunglei
Saiha
TRIPURA
Agartala

Brahmaputra

BHUTAN
Tashigang

BANGLADESH
DHAKA (Dacca)
Chittagong
Comilla
Barisal
Khulna
Chandpur
Mymensingh
Rangpur
Sylhet
Cox's Bazar

BAY OF BENGAL
Ramree Island
Man-aung Kyun
Sittwe
Kyaukpyu
Thandwè

Tropic of Cancer

Albers Equal Area Conic Projection

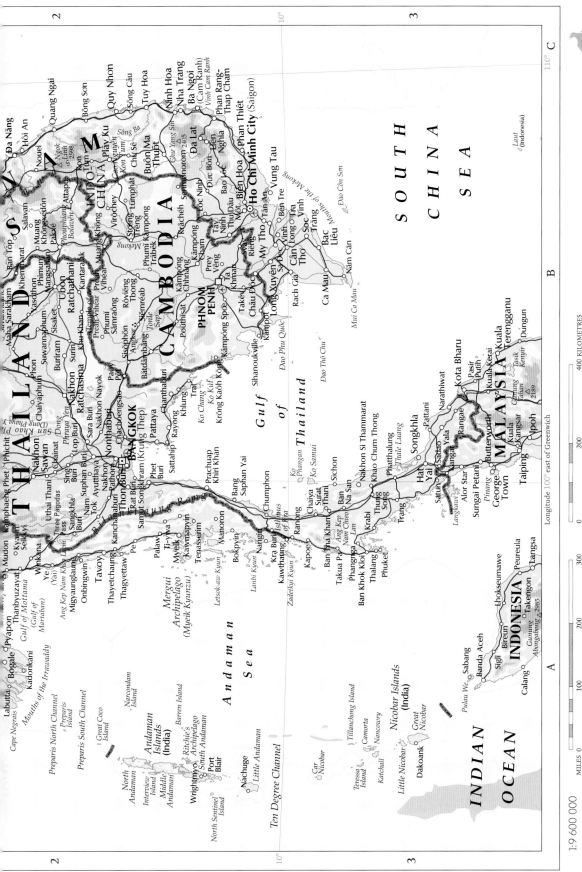

SOUTH CHINA SEA

INDIAN OCEAN

Andaman Sea

Gulf of Thailand

THAILAND

CAMBODIA

MALAYSIA

INDONESIA

BANGKOK

PHNOM PENH

Ho Chi Minh City (Saigon)

Laut (Indonesia)

Da Nẵng
Hội An
Nouei
Quang Ngai
Bồng Sơn
Quy Nhơn
Sông Cầu
Tuy Hòa
Ninh Hòa
Nha Trang
Ba Ngòi (Cam Ranh) *Vịnh Cam Ranh*
Phan Rang-Thap Cham
Phan Thiết

Salavan
Ban Tốp
Khammarat
Muang Khôngxédôn
Pakxé
Muang Mangsahan
Attapu
Phouphiang Bolaven
Ngọc Linh 2598
Kon Tum
Plây Ku
Buôn Ma Thuột
Chu sê
Kon Tum
Pleiku
Chu Yang Sin 2405
Đà Lạt
Đức Bồn Trên
Nghĩa
Biên Hòa
Vũng Tàu

Virôchey
Kémpóng
Tráběk
Phumĭ Sâmraông
Preăh Vihéar
Rôviĕng Tbong
Siĕmréab
Angkor
Batdâmbâng
Sisŏphŏn
Phumĭ Sâmraông
Stœ̆ng Trêng
Kâmpóng Cham
Kâmpóng Chhnăng
Tônle Sab
Poŭthĭsăt
Takêv
Prey Vêng
Kâmpóng Spœ̆
Kâmpót
Sihanoukville
Kaôh Kŏng
Krŏng Kaôh Kŏng

Kâtakral
Kŏng Krailăh
Tây Ninh
Thủ Dầu Một
Bến Cát
Tân An
Bến Tre
Mỹ Tho
Long Xuyên
Châu Đốc
Rạch Giá
Cà Mau
Mũi Cà Mau
Nǎm Cǎn
Bạc Liêu
Sóc Trǎng
Trà Vinh
Cần Thơ
Vĩnh Long

Mouths of the Mekong
Đảo Còn Sơn
Đảo Phu Quốc
Đảo Thổ Chu

THAILAND
Maha Sarakham
Khemmarat
Yasothon
Sewannaphum
Phimun Mangsahan
Ubon Ratchathani
Sisaket
Surin
Buriram
Phon
Chaiyaphum
Nakhon Ratchasima
Nang Rong
Nakhon Nayok
Nakhon Sawan
Phichit
Kamphaeng Phet
Phitsanulok (Dong Phaya Yen)
San Khao Phu
Phraya Yen
Phetchabun
Lop Buri
Saraburi
Ayutthaya
Suphan Buri
Chon Buri
Uthai Thani
Sing Buri
Ang Thong
Chanthaburi
Rat Buri
Nakhon Pathom
Nonthaburi
Samut Songkhram
Samut Sakhon
Samut Prakan
Chachoengsao
Pattaya
Rayong
Trat
Ko Chang
Khlung

Tenasserim
Mergui Archipelago
(Myeik Kyunzu)
Letsok-aw Kyun
Lanbi Kyun
Zadetkyi Kyun

Thanbyuzayat
Kadonkani
Bogale
Labutta
Pyapon
Mouths of the Irrawaddy
Cape Negrais
Gulf of Martaban
(Gulf of Mottama)
Kyaikkami
Mudon
Kyaiktō
Seikkyi
Ye
Whkana
Thagyettaw
Thayetchaung
Migyaunglaung
Onbingwin
Tavoy
Yebyu
Ti-ywa
Pe
Myeik
Kawmapyin
Kawthaung
Three Pagodas Pass
Ang Kep Nam Khla Lem
Nam Tok
Kanchanaburi
Sangkhla Buri
Prachuap Khiri Khan
Bang Saphan Yai
Chumphon
Kra Buri
Ranong
Kapoe
Ban Tha Khun
Phangnga
Takua Pa
Thalang
Ban Khok Kloi
Phuket
Krabi
Sichon
Surat Thani
Chaiya
Ban Na San
Thung Song
Nakhon Si Thammarat
Khao Chum Thong
Phatthalung
Thale Luang
Hat Yai
Songkhla
Pattani
Narathiwat
Yala
Rangae
Bokpyin
Manoron
Lang Suan
Isthmus of Kra

Preparis North Channel
Preparis Island
Preparis South Channel
Great Coco Island
Narcondam Island
Barren Island
North Andaman
Interview Island
Middle Andaman
Andaman Islands (India)
Ritchie's Archipelago
South Andaman
Wrightmyo
North Sentinel Island
Port Blair
Nachuge
Little Andaman
Ten Degree Channel
Tillanchong Island
Teressa Island
Camorta
Katchall
Nancowry
Car Nicobar
Little Nicobar
Nicobar Islands (India)
Dakoank
Great Nicobar

MALAYSIA
Kota Bharu
Pasir Putih
Kuala Kerai
Kuala Terengganu
Dungun
Gunung Tahan 2189
Butterworth
George Town
Pinang
Kuala Kangsar
Ipoh
Taiping
Sungai Petani
Alor Star
Langkawi
Satun
Kangar
Tasik Kenyir

INDONESIA
Lhokseumawe
Peureula
Langsa
Bireun
Sigli
Banda Aceh
Pulau We Sabang
Calang
Gunung Abongabong 2985
Takengon

1:9 600 000

MILES 0   100   200   300

0   200   400 KILOMETRES

Longitude 100° east of Greenwich

110°

100°

10°

A   B   C

2   3

200 KILOMETRES

100

0

MILES 0

100

0

150

0

1:9 600 000

METRES
FEET

5000	16404
3000	9843
2000	6562
1000	3281
500	1640
200	656
0	0

Land below
sea level

200	656
4000	13124
6000	19686

A   120°   B

1

*Dongsha
Quundao*

*Batan
Islands*
Itbayat Basco
Batan

*Luzon
Strait*

Balintang Channel

Babuyan

Calayan *Babuyan
Islands*

Fuga Camiguin

Bangui *Babuyan Channel*

Laoag San Vicente
City Aparri

Bangued Tuguegarao
Vigan *Mount Chico*
Sapocoy
Tagudin Ilagan
Bontoc Palanan

San Fernando *Mount
Pulog* Santiago
La Trinidad △ 2929 Bayombong

Dagupan Baguio **LUZON**
Lingayen San Carlos
Tarlac San Jose
Mount Pinatubo ▲ Cabanatuan
Iba 1660 Gapan
Angeles San Fernando
Olongapo Valenzuela *Polillo Islands*
Balanga **Quezon City**
MANILA □ Pasig
Tagaytay City Santa Cruz Labo
San Pablo Lucena Daet Pandan
*Lubang
Islands* Batangas Lopez Libmanan Naga *Catanduanes*
Calapan Virac
*Mount
Halcon* Boac Oas Tabaco
Mamburao △ 2585 Naujan *Mayon* ▲ 2421
Mindoro Legazpi Sorsogon
Irosin
Roxas *Burias* Catarman
New San Jose Romblon *Sibuyan* Masbate Calbayog
Busuanga *Tablas* *Samar*
*Calamian
Group* *Sibuyan
Sea* *Masbate* Catbalogan
Coron Pandan Roxas
Culion Culasi *Visayan
Sea* Tacloban
Linapacan *Panay* Ormoc Guiuan
El Nido *Cuyo
Islands* Pototan Cadiz *Leyte*
*Dalanganem
Islands* San Jose de Bacolod ▲ 2450 *Cebu*
Taytay Buenavista Iloilo Cebu Maasin
Roxas *Dumaran* *Negros* Talisay *Dinagat*
Bohol *Siargao*
Cauayan Tanjay Tagbilaran Surigao Dapa
Palawan Bayawan Siquijor *Bohol Sea* Mambajao Tandag
Puerto Princesa Dumaguete *Camiguin*
Aprahuan Presidente Cagayan Butuan
*Mount
Mantalingajan* Aborlan Manuel A Roxas Dapitan de Oro Gingoog
△ 2054 Liloy Oroquieta Iligan Malaybalay Bislig
Brooke's Point Ozamis **MINDANAO**
Rio Tuba Siocon Pagadian ▲ *Mount Ragang* Baganga
Bugsuk *Zamboanga* 2815 Tagum
Balabac *Peninsula* *Mount
Balabac* Cotabato Apo* **Davao**
Balabac Strait Zamboanga Datu Piang ▲ Mati
Banggi Isabela 2954 Digos
Kudat *Cagayan de* Lebak *Davao
Tawi-Tawi* Banga Gulf*
Kota Belud Kanibongan *Turtle Islands* *Basilan* General Santos
Kota *(Philippines)* Jolo Kiamba
Kinabalu *Gunung
Kinabalu* Sandakan *Jolo* Batulaki
Ranau △ 4095 Siasi *Sarangani Islands*
MALAYSIA *Gunung
Trus Madi* Lamag Tambisan *Sulu Archipelago*
Tenom △ 2649 Panglima *Sibutu*
Lawas **SABAH** Kuamut Sugala *Tawi-Tawi*
Tomani Pensiangan Lahad *Kepulauan
Datu* *Nanusa*
Semporna *Kepulauan
Talaud*
Lumbis Tawau **C E L E B E S** *Karakelong* Pulutan
INDONESIA **S E A** **INDONESIA**
Mensalong *Sangir* Tahuna
Kubuang Tarakan *Kaburuang*

**PHILIPPINE
SEA**

P H I L I P P I N E S

Cordillera Central

*Scarborough
Shoal*

**S O U T H

C H I N A

S E A**

Mindoro Strait

Mindoro

Palawan Passage

S U L U S E A

Banjaran Crocker

*Moro
Gulf*

A   Longitude 120° east of Greenwich   B

Albers Equal Area Conic Projection

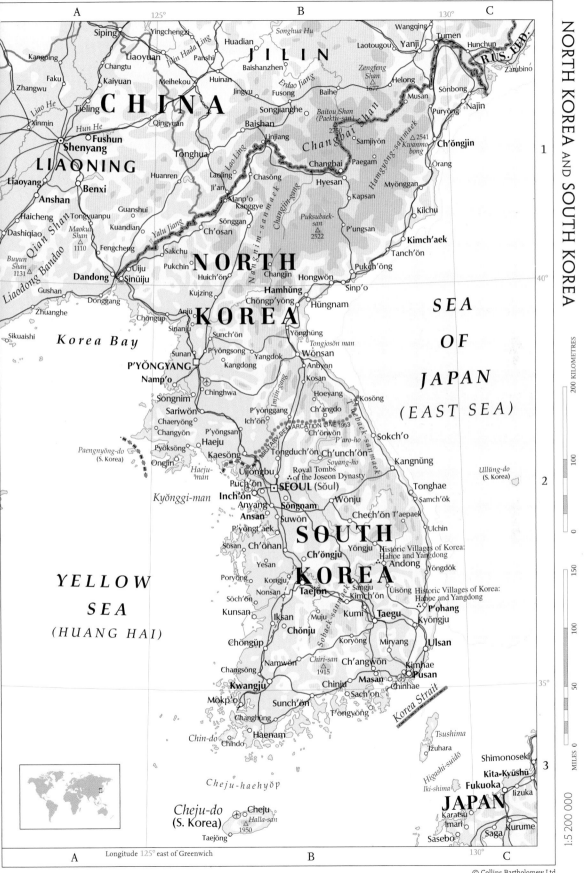

1:5 200 000

© Collins Bartholomew Ltd

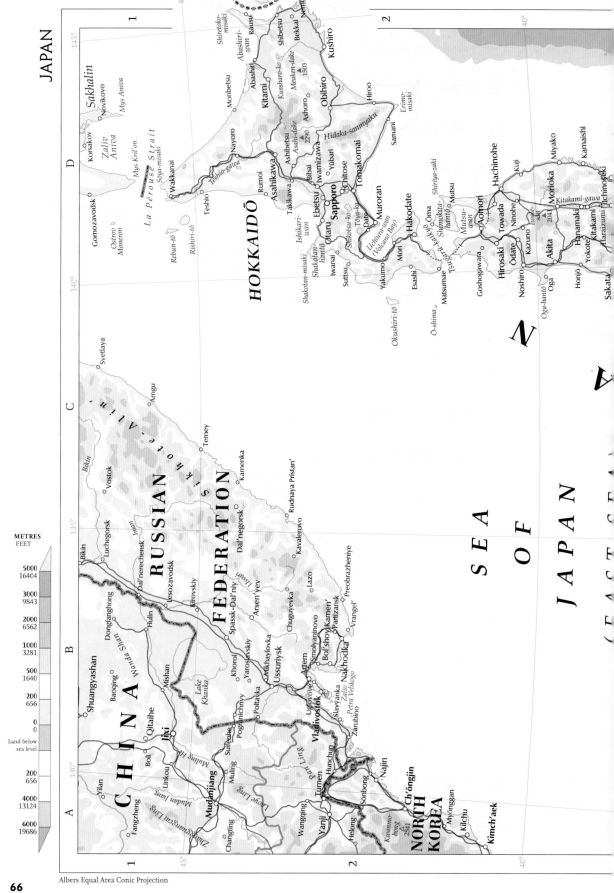

Albers Equal Area Conic Projection

SOUTH
KOREA

Ulchin

Ulling-do
(S. Korea)

Liancourt Rocks
Claimed and administered
by South Korea as *Tok-tŏ*;
claimed by Japan as *Take-shima*

Oki-shotō

Dōgo
Saigō
Dōzen

Ryōtsu

Niigata
Shibata
Niitsu

Sanjō
Nagaoka
Kashiwazaki
Jōetsu
Arai

Natori
Yonezawa
Fukushima

Kōriyama
Iwaki

Aizu-
Wakamatsu

Inawashiro-ko

Sukagawa

Kitaibaraki
Hitachi
Hitachinaka
Mito
Ishioka
Tsuchiura

Kashima-
nada

Chōshi

Sakura
Narita
Katsuura

Nojima-zaki

Tateyama

Katsuyama

Odawara

Numazu
Itō

Shimoda

Iro-zaki

O-shima

Nii-jima

Miyake-jima

Mikura-jima

Izu-shotō

Hachijō-jima

Aoga-shima

Sumisu-jima

Tori-shima

H
O
N
S
H
U

Suzu
Suzu-
misaki
Wajima

Noto-
hantō

Nanao

Himi

Toyama

Takaoka
Kanazawa
Komatsu
Kaga

Ono
Fukui
Sabae

Takefu

Wakasa-
wan

Miyazu

Takayama

Nagano
Ueda

Matsumoto

Ina

Okaya

Gifu
Ogaki
Komaki

Maizuru
Tsuruga

Bituu-ko

Ōtsu
Kyōto

Nagoya

Toyota

Okazaki

Toyohashi

Shirane-san
3192

Fuji-san
3776

Kōfu
Hachiōji
Sagamihara

Kumagaya
Kawagoe

Ōta
Kiryū
Maebashi
Takasaki

Shirane-
san
2578

Mikuni-sammyaku

Utsunomiya
Oyama

Otawara

Sano

TOKYO
Kawasaki
Yokohama

Sagami

O-shima

Chūgoku-sanchi

Tottori

Hyōno-sen
1510

Tsuyama

Kurayoshi

Matsue
Izumo

Gōtsu
Hamada

Masuda

Hagi

Nagato
Yamaguchi

Shimonoseki
Kita-Kyūshū

Ube
Hōfu

Iwakuni

Niimi

Shōbara

Hiroshima

Kure

Suō-nada

Nakatsu

KYŪSHŪ

Fukuoka
Iizuka

Karatsu
Saga
Kurume

Imari

Ōmuta
Arao

Isahaya

Nagasaki
Sasebo
Ōmura

Koshiki-jima-
rettō

Amakusa-
shotō

Akune

Sendai

Makurazaki

Yaku-
shima

Tanega-
shima

Nishino-omote

Ōsumi-kaikyō

Kanoya

Kagoshima
Miyakonojō

Kumamoto

Aso-san
1592

Yatsushiro

Usa
Beppu
Ōita

Saiki

Nobeoka

Hyūga

Miyazaki

Kirishima-
yama
1788

Osumi-
shotō

Tsushima

Izuhara

Iki-shima

Hizen-kaidō

Matsuura
zaki

Ōkawa
Fukagawa
Takachiho

Tsushima-kaikyō

SHIKOKU

Matsuyama

Uwajima

Bungo-suidō

Ōzu
Yawatahama

Niihama
Kōchi

Nankoku

Anan
Tokushima
Naruto
Takamatsu

Kii-suidō

Ishizuchi-san
1981

Tosashimizu

Ashizuri-misaki

Muroto-zaki

Muroto

Kainan
Gobō
Tanabe

Wakayama
Kishiwada
Sakai

Osaka
Kōbe

Kawanishi

Amagasaki

Himeji
Kakogawa

Akō

Okayama
Kurashiki

Fukuyama

Onomichi

Mihara

Tsu

Ise

Owase

Kumano

Shingū

Shiono-misaki

Yaizu

Shizuoka

Hamamatsu

Fujinomiya
Fuji

Matsuzaka

Ise-wan

Nakatsugawa

Tsu

L I A P A N

H O N S H U

K I I

S A N I N

C h ū g o k u - s a n c h i

Wakasa-
wan

P A C I F I C

O C E A N

© Collins Bartholomew Ltd

Longitude 135° east of Greenwich

1:6 000 000

KILOMETRES 0   100   200

MILES 0   50   100   150

130°

140°

3

35°

4

B

C

D

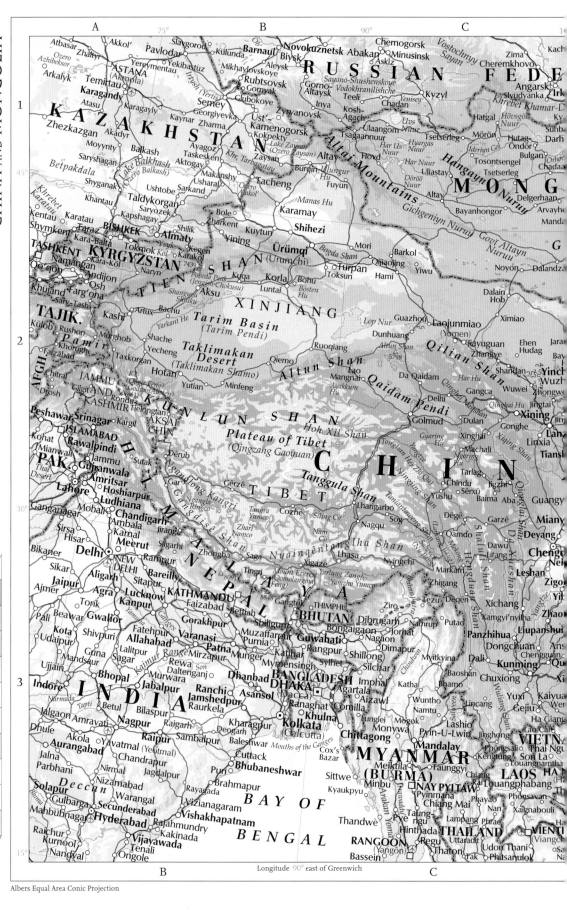

Albers Equal Area Conic Projection

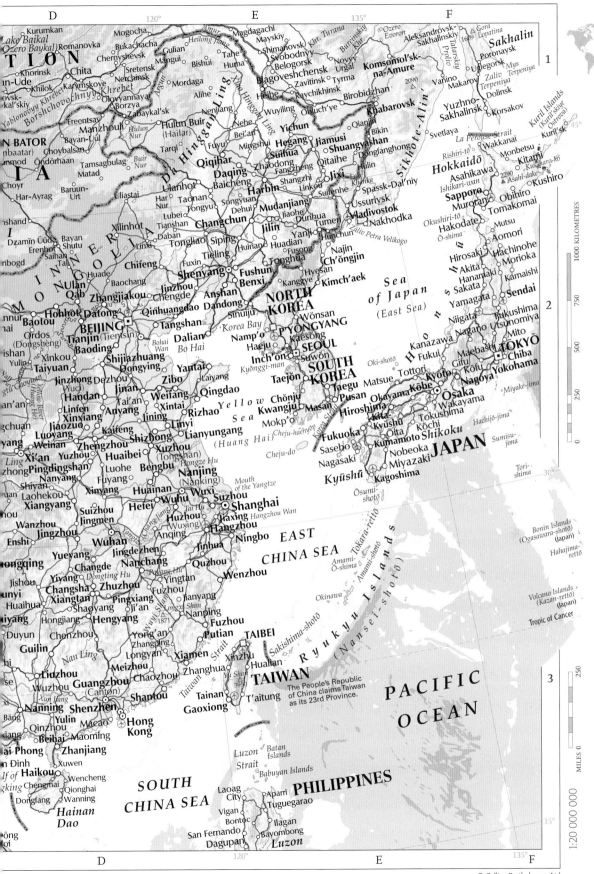

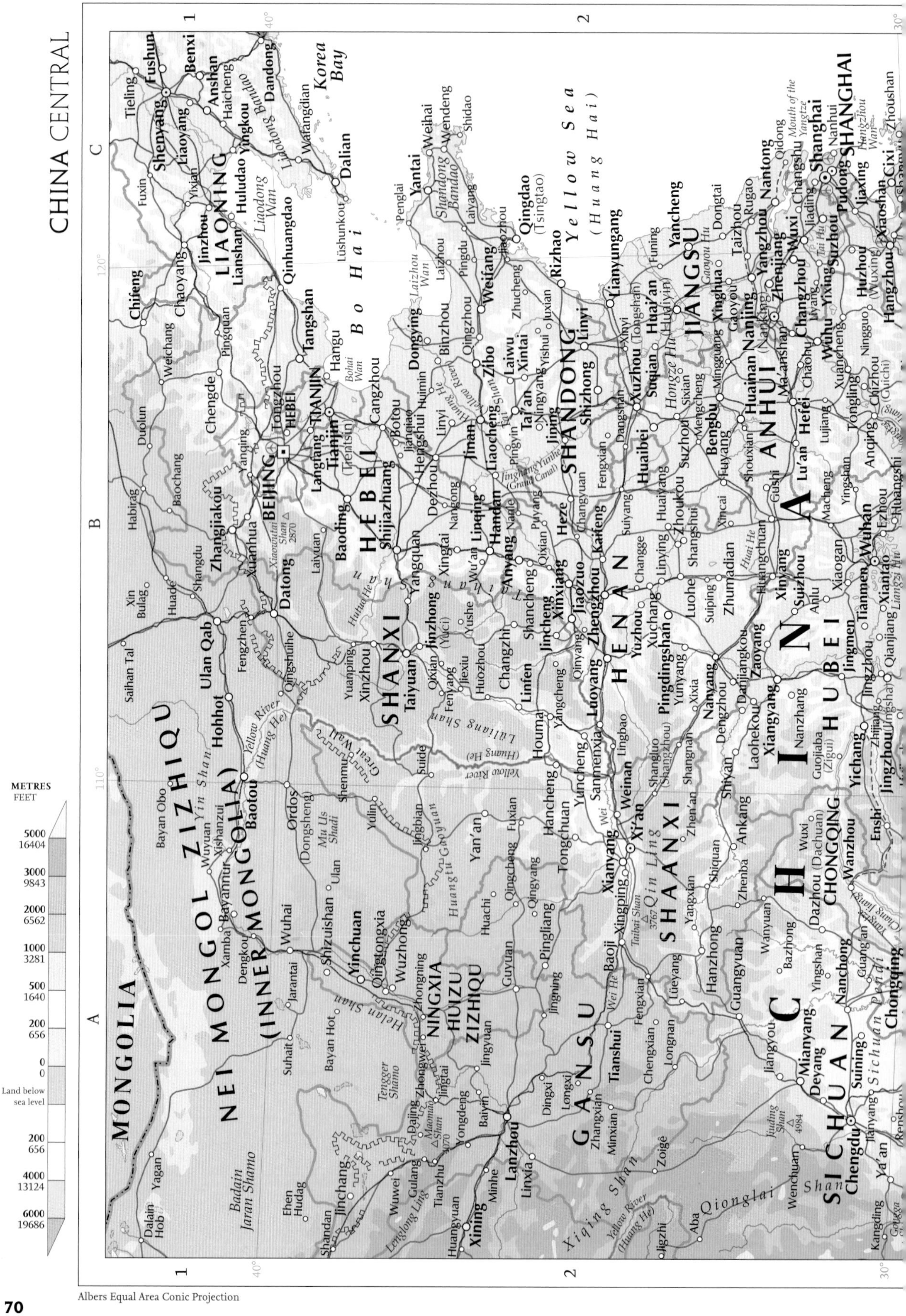

MONGOLIA

NEI MONGOL ZIZHIQU

(INNER MONGOLIA)

LIAONING

HEBEI

SHANXI

SHANDONG

Yellow Sea
(Huang Hai)

Bo Hai

Korea Bay

HENAN

JIANGSU

ANHUI

NINGXIA HUIZU ZIZHIQU

GANSU

SHAANXI

HUBEI

CHONGQING

SICHUAN

SHANGHAI

BEIJING

TIANJIN (Tientsin)

Shenyang, Fushun, Benxi, Anshan, Liaoyang, Haicheng, Yingkou, Dandong, Wafangdian, Dalian, Lüshunkou, Qinhuangdao, Tangshan, Tangshan, Chengde, Zhangjiakou, Datong, Hohhot, Baotou, Ordos, Yinchuan, Wuzhong, Zhongning, Zhongwei, Lanzhou, Linxia, Xining, Wuwei, Jinchang, Jiayuguan, Yining

Qingdao (Tsingtao), Yantai, Weihai, Weifang, Zibo, Jinan, Tai'an, Linyi, Rizhao, Lianyungang, Yancheng, Nantong, Suzhou, Wuxi, Changzhou, Nanjing (Nanking), Zhenjiang, Yangzhou, Hangzhou, Jiaxing, Cixi, Zhoushan, Pudong

Shijiazhuang, Baoding, Cangzhou, Dezhou, Handan, Anyang, Xinxiang, Zhengzhou, Kaifeng, Luoyang, Pingdingshan, Nanyang, Xiangyang, Shiyan, Yichang, Wuhan, Huangshi, Hefei, Bengbu, Huainan, Ma'anshan, Wuhu

Taiyuan, Linfen, Yuncheng, Weinan, Xi'an, Xianyang, Baoji, Hanzhong, Tianshui, Chengdu, Deyang, Mianyang, Chongqing, Suining, Dazhou, Wanzhou, Enshi

Yellow River (Huang He)

Wei He, *Qin Ling*, *Great Wall*

Grand Canal, *Hai He*

METRES / FEET

5000 / 16404
3000 / 9843
2000 / 6562
1000 / 3281
500 / 1640
200 / 656
0 / 0
Land below sea level
200 / 656
4000 / 13124
6000 / 19686

Albers Equal Area Conic Projection

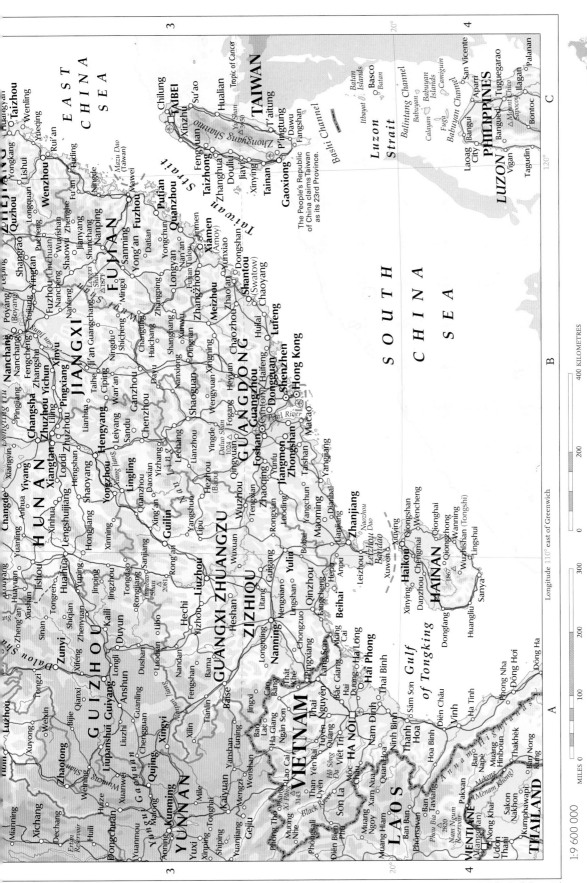

© Collins Bartholomew Ltd

1:9 600 000

MILES 0   100   200   300

0   200   400 KILOMETRES

Longitude 110° east of Greenwich

E A S T   C H I N A   S E A

S O U T H   C H I N A   S E A

Gulf of Tongking

Luzon Strait

Balintang Channel

Babuyan Channel

Bashi Channel

Taiwan Strait

TAIWAN

The People's Republic
of China claims Taiwan
as its 23rd Province.

PHILIPPINES

LUZON

ZHEJIANG

FUJIAN

JIANGXI

HUNAN

GUIZHOU

YUNNAN

GUANGXI ZHUANGZU
ZIZHIQU

GUANGDONG

HAINAN

VIETNAM

LAOS

THAILAND

Tropic of Cancer

20°

120°

110°

AFGHANISTAN

PAKISTAN

C H I N A

QINGHAI

XIZANG ZIZHIQU (TIBET)

PLATEAU OF TIBET (QINGZANG GAOYUAN)

KUNLUN SHAN

Hoh Xil Shan

Tanggula Shan

Ningjing Shan

Taniantaweng Shan

CLAIMED BY CHINA

N E P A L

BHUTAN

THIMPHU

KATHMANDU

I N D I A

BANGLADESH

DHAKA (Dacca)

M Y A N M A R (BURMA)

JAMMU AND KASHMIR

AKSAI CHIN

Line of Control

Karakoram Range

Ladakh Range

Zanskar Mountains

H I M A L A Y A

Himalaya

Ganga (Ganges)

Indus

KABUL

ISLAMABAD

Rawalpindi

Peshawar

Srinagar

Amritsar

Lahore

Faisalabad

Multan

Bahawalpur

Hyderabad

Karachi

Gujranwala

Jhelum

Sargodha

NEW DELHI

Delhi

Jaipur

Jodhpur

Ahmadabad (Ahmedabad)

Vadodara

Rajkot

Bhopal

Indore

Jabalpur

Jaisalmer

Bikaner

Kota

Udaipur

Gwalior

Agra

Mathura

Aligarh

Meerut

Chandigarh

Ludhiana

Jalandhar

Kanpur

Lucknow

Allahabad

Varanasi

Gorakhpur

Patna

Gaya

Ranchi

Jamshedpur

Dhanbad

Asansol

Kolkata (Calcutta)

Khulna

Chittagong

Guwahati

Shillong

Imphal

Aizawl

Agartala

Comilla

Rangpur

Rajshahi

Barisal

Jessore

Darjiling

Gangtok

Patan

Pokhara

Rewa

Satna

Sagar

Bhilwara

Ajmer

Alwar

Tonk

Bundi

Chittaurgarh

Ujjain

Ratlam

Dewas

Bareilly

Moradabad

Shahjahanpur

Sitapur

Faizabad

Rae Bareli

Mirzapur

Bhagalpur

Munger

Darbhanga

Muzaffarpur

Purnia

Ranaghat

Bardhaman

Bankura

Haldwani

Saharanpur

Karnal

Rohtak

Hisar

Sirsa

Ganganagar

Abohar

Bathinda

Ambala

Hoshiarpur

Mandi

Kyelang

Kalpa

Gilgit

Chitral

Kohat

Bannu

Dera Ismail Khan

Quetta

Sukkur

Larkana

Jacobabad

Nawabshah

Mirpur Khas

Gandhidham

Bhuj

Porbandar

Dwarka

Jamnagar

Albers Equal Area Conic Projection

METRES FEET

METRES	FEET
5000	16404
3000	9843
2000	6562
1000	3281
500	1640
200	656
0	0
Land below sea level	
200	656
4000	13124
6000	19686

Tropic of Cancer

Rann of Kachchh

Gulf of Kachchh

Thal Desert

Sulaiman Range

Hindu Kush

Khyber Pass

Mount Everest 8848

K2 (Qogir Feng) 8611

1:12 000 000

© Collins Bartholomew Ltd

A

B

70°

Garabil
Belentligi

TURKMENISTAN

Andkhōy

Shibirghān   Mazar-e
Sharif   Khānābād
Tāshqurghān

Faīzābād   Qullai
iKarl Marks   6726
Ishkoshim   Bāzār
Gonbad

Maīmanah
Sar-e Pul   Aībak   Baghlān
Pul-e Khumrī   Bāzārak
Tirich Mir
7690Δ   Battura
Glacier
Pasu

Mazar

Sālang
Ra(koposhi)   7788   Rondu   K2°(Qogir Feng)
(Godwin Austen)
8611

Bāla
Murghāb
Serhetabat

Darya-ye Morghāb
Dowshī
Gilgit
Nanga Parbat   8126
Chilas
Astor   Skardu   Khaplu   Shyok

Qal'ah-ye Now
Selseleh-ye Sefīd Kūh
(Paropamisus)
Chaghcharān
Bāmyān   Jabal us Sarāj
Chārīkār
Mehtar   Drosh   Dargai
Barī Kōt
Dir
Mongora
Line of
Control
JAMMU
AND
KASHMIR   Srinagar
Leh
Zanskar Ra

Harī Rōd
Koh-e Bābā
5143   Shāh Folad
Mahmud-e Rāqi
Asadābād
Lām
Jalālābād

Abbottābād   Haripur
Sopur   Baramulla
Anantnag   Kargil   Ladakh Ra

Koh-e Chilhī
Abdalān
Nīlī
Δ Qeysar
4182

KABUL
Maīdan Shahr
Sikaram   Khyber Pass
4761   1080
Mardan
Peshāwar
Nowshera
Wah

Daud   Jhelum
Khel   Talagang
Islāmābād
Rawalpindi

Kishtwar
Chamba   Kyelang
Udhampur   HIMACHAL
Nagar   PRADESH
Mandi
Sundarnagar

AFGHANISTAN
HAZĀRAJĀT
Ghaznī

Zarah Sharan
Urgūn-e
Kalān
Khōst

Kohat
Thal

Bannu
Lakki
Marwat
Mianwali
Khushab
Bhera
Jhelum
Gujrat   Jammu
Wazirabad
Sialkot
Kathua
Pathankot
Jammu
Batala
Sujanpur

Dasht-e Mārgo
Helmand
Dīlārām
Tarīn Kōt

Nīlī

Qeysar

Kandahār   Qalāt
Zhob
Takht-i-Sulaimān
3374

Girishk
Arghandāb Rōd   Tarnak Rōd

Tank
Dera
Ismail Khan
Sargodha
Hafizabad
Chiniot
Jhang
Gujranwala
Amritsar
Lahore
Faisalabad
Jalandhar
Firozpur
Ludhiana
Hoshiarpur
Shimla
Mohali
Chandigarh
Ambala
Saharanpur

Lashkar Gah
Kandahār

Toba and Kakar Ranges
Muslimbagh
Pishin
Chaman
Quetta
Loralai
Taunsa
Layyah
Shorkot
Sahiwal
Okara
Fazilka
PUNJAB
Patiala
Bathinda
Roorkee
Nagina

Dasht-e
Arbū-ye Shamāli   30°
Mastung
Mach
Beji   Barkhan
Dera Ghazi
Khan
Khanewal
Multan
Burewala
Abohar
Ganganagar
Tohana
Karnal

Amir
Chah   Chagai
Dalbandin
Hāmūn-i-
Lora
Ras Koh
Δ 3007
Nushki
Kalat   Sibi
Lahri
Dera Bugti
Jampur
Muzaffargarh
Lodhran
Bahawalnagar
Hanumangarh
Sirsa
HARYANA
Hisar
Kairana
Mee

Nok Kundi
Yakmach
Hamun-i-
Mashkel

Central Brahui Range
Sulaiman Range
Rajanpur
Uch
Ahmadpur
East
Fort Abbas
Anupgarh
Suratgarh
Mahajan
Rohtak
Bhiwani
Sonipat

PAKISTAN
Qila Ladgasht
Washuk
Surab
Khuzdar
Nagha Kalat
Karodi
Shikarpur
Shahdad Kot
Jacobabad
Kandh Kot
Ghotki
Kashmore
Rahimyar Khan
Sadiqabad
Barsalpur
Pugal
Bikaner
Sardarshahr
Ratangarh
Rajgarh
Churu
Jhunjhunun
Namaul
Rajgarh
Aligarh
Delhi
Ghaziabad
Morad
NEW DE
Faridaba

Siahan Range
Kamarod
Panjgur
Diz

Pab Range
Girdar Dhor
Kirthar Range
Larkana
Sukkur
Khairpur
Ghotaru
Ramgarh
Jaisalmer
Pokaran
Phalodi
Nokha
Sujangarh
Nagaur
Sikar
Alwar
Mathura
Agra
Firoza

Tump   Turbat
Hoshab
Bhairi
Hol
1454
Bazdar
Wadh
Dadu
Kandiaro
Bela
Diwana
Nawabshah
Shiv
Barmer
Balotra
Jodhpur
Merta
Ajmer
Tonk
Sawai
Madhopur
Jaipur   Bharatpur
RAJASTHAN
Morena
Gwa

Dasht
Central Makran Range
Goshanak
Makran Coast Range
Suntsar
Turbat
Hoshab

Uthal
Sonmiani
Thano
Bula Khan
Sakrand
Khipro
Khokhropar
Pali
Jalore
Deogarh
Bhilwara
Bundi
Kota
Shivpuri
Lalitpur

Gwadar
Pasni
Ormara
Sonmiani
Bay
Hyderabad
Tando Adam
Mirpur Khas
Naukot
Sirohi
Guru
Sikhar
1722
Chittaurgarh
Jhalawar
Baran

METRES
FEET
Karachi
Thatta
Sujawal
Jati
Mithi
Nagar Parkar
Abu Road
Palanpur
Sidhpur
Udaipur
Neemuch
Mandsaur
Garoth
Guna
Bina-Eta

5000
16404

3000
9843
2
Tropic of Cancer
Mouths of the Indus
Rann of Kachchh
Lakhpat
Radhanpur
Dungarpur
Banswara
Jaora
Ratlam
I
N
Agar
Biaora
Bhopal
Vidis

2000
6562
Bhuj
Gandhidham
Mahesana
Gandhinagar
Himatnagar
Godhra
Dahod
Ujjain
Dewas
Indore
MADHYA P
Dhar
Harda
Itarsi
Chhind

1000
3281
Rapur
Kandla
Viramgam
Ahmadabad
(Ahmedabad)
Mahi
Mhow
Khargon
Khandwa
Betu

500
1640
Okha
Dwarka
Surendranagar
GUJARAT
Nadiad
Vadodara
Aliraj pur
Narmada
Satpura Range

200
656
Jamnagar
Rajkot
Kathiawar
Dhasa
Bhavnagar
Bharuch
Nandurbar
Tapti
Jalgaon
Bhusawal
Amravati
Akola
Wardh
Hingang

0
0
Land below
sea level
Porbandar
Gondal
Upleta
Amreli
Khambhat
Gulf of Khambhat
Surat
Vyara
Dhule
Chalisgaon
Khamgaon

200
656   20°
Junagadh
Keshod
Visavadar
Mahuva
Veraval
Diu
Valsad
Daman
Silvassa
Dahanu
Nashik
Manmad
Aurangabad
MAHARASHTRA
Jalna
Nanded N

4000
13124
ARABIAN
SEA
2 Diu
Gulf of Kachchh
Gulf of Khambhat
Daman
Ulhasnagar
Thane
Navi
Mumbai
Kalyan
Narayangaon
Ahmadnagar
(Ahmednagar)
Godavari
Penganga
Pusad
Parbhani
Nanded Ni

6000
19686
3
Administrative areas not named on the map:
INDIA
1. DADRA AND NAGAR HAVELI (B2)
2. DAMAN AND DIU (B2)
Mumbai (Bombay)
Igatpuri
Sangamner
1646
Adla

A   Longitude 70° east of Greenwich   B

74

Albers Equal Area Conic Projection

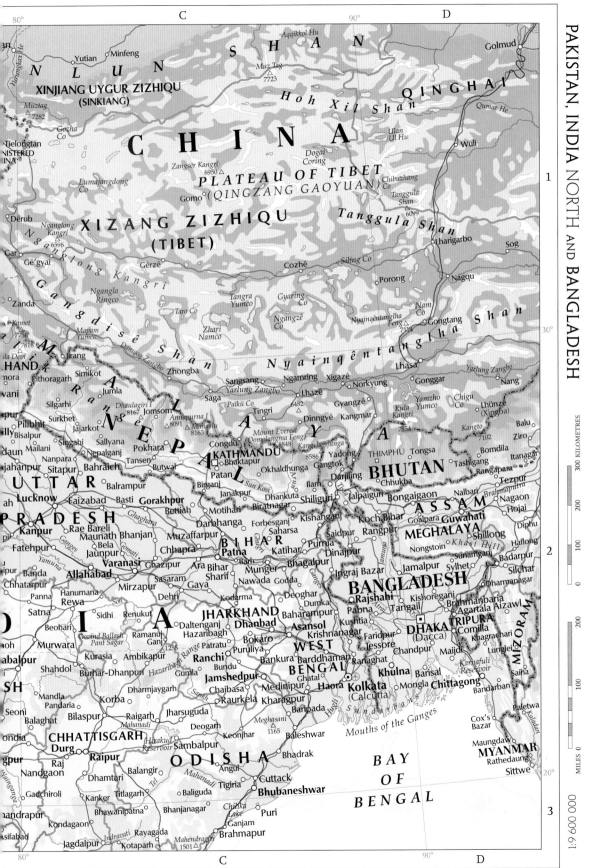

Kirsanov Syzran Tol'yatti Buguruslan Beloretsk Troitsk Borov
Rtishchevo **Penza** Kuznetsk Chapayevsk **Samara** Sterlitamak Karabalyk Kosta
Borisoglebsk Atkarsk Vol'sk Pugachev Buzuluk Grachevka Magnitogorsk Rudnyy
Buturlinovka Balashov **Saratov** Engel's Balakovo Novosergiyevka Kumertau Baymak Kartaly Lisakovsk Tobyl
Mikhaylovka Novoanninskiy Kamyshin Kotovo Ozinki Yershov *Obshchiy Syrt* **Orenburg** Mednogorsk Saraktash Zhitikara Turgayskaya
Serafimovich Frolovo Nikolayevsk *Volga* Taskala Ural'sk Sol'-lletsk Orsk Stolovaya
Ilovlya *Volgogradskoye* Zhanibek Chapayevo Aksay Akbulak Martok Khromtau *Strana*
Kalach-na-Donu *Vodokhranilishche* Zhalpaktal *Ural (Zhayyk)* Aktobe Karabutak

RUSSIAN FEDERATION

Volgograd Akhtubinsk Verkhniy Zhanakala Inderbor (Aktyubinsk) Akshiganak
(Stalingrad) Volzhskiy Baskunchak Miyaly Kandyagash
Kotel'nikovo *Don* Kharabali Aybas *Lowland* Makhambet Makat *Zhem* Emba 635 Yrgyz

K A Z A

Tsimlyanskoye Elista Narimanov *(Prikaspiyskaya* Atyrau Kul'sary Shalkar *Solonchak*
Vodokhranilishche *Nizmennost')* Balykshi *Shalkarteniz*
Proletarskoye -12 Borankul Aral'sk
Vodokhranilishche **Astrakhan'** Kulandy
Stavropol'skaya Ulan-Khol *Mys* Beyneu Ayteke Bi Baykonyr
Vozvyshennost' Lagan' *Tupkaragan* *Vozrozhdenya* (Leninsk)
Divnoye Komsomol'skiy Fort-Shevchenko *Mertvyy Kultuk* *Sor (Peski Karakum)* *Island*
Svetlograd *Mys Sagyndyk* **Aral Sea**
Blagodarnyy Kochubey Shetpe Qoraqalpog'iston

C A S P I A N

Budennovsk *Gora* *Ustyurt* Mo'ynoq *Kyz*
Georgiyevsk Kizlyar *Besshoky* *Plateau* Chimboy *De*
Pyatigorsk Khasavyurt Aktau Mangistau 555 *Borsakelmas* Qo'ng'irot Nukus Uchqu
Nal'chik Groznyy Shetpe -132 *sho'rxogi* Xo'jayli Taxiatosh
Kazbek Makhachkala Zhanaozen (Khodzheyli) Daşoguz
GEORGIA Vladikavkaz Derbent *Kazakhskiy* **UZBEKISTA** (Dashkhovuz)
Tskhinvali *(Bol'shoy Kavkaz)* *Zaliv* *Sarykamyshskoye* Urganch Gazojak
Gori **TBILISI** *Caucasus* Garabogaz Garabogazköl *Ozero* To'rtko'l
GEORGIA *(Tiflis)* 4466 Quba Garabogazköl *Aýlagy* *Amudar'ya* G'ijd
Akhaltsikhe Qazax Şäki *Gora Bazardyuzyu* Garagazli Çagyl Buxo
Gyumri Gäncä Mingäçevir Sumqayit Garsy Bukha
ARMENIA Sevan Şamaxi **BAKU**
Kars *Lake Sevan* **AZERBAIJAN** (Bäkï) T U R A N
Mt. *(Sevana Lich)* Xankändi
Ararat **YEREVAN** **TURKMENISTAN**
Ağrı Dağı Naxçivan Bіläsuvar Türkmenbaşy
5165 **AZER.** *S E A* Balkanabat Kükürtli Türkmenabat
TURKEY Marand Ahar 4810 Ästärä Gumdag Murzechirla (Chardzhev)
Salmas Tabrīz Bereket Serdar **Karakum** Bayramaly Uzb
Lake Urmia Sarab Bandar-e Anzalī Baharly **Desert** Mary
(Daryacheh-ye Orümiyeh) Ardabīl Gonbad-e Bojnürd **AŞGABAT** Garabil
Urmia (Orümiyeh) Rasht *Elburz* Kävüs Shirvän (Ashkhabad) Kaka *Belentli*
Heydarābād Zanjān Behshahr *Küh-e* Mary
Qazvīn *Mountains* Gorgän *Saluk* Tejen
Saqqez Bäbol Sabzevär 2972 Quchän Garabil
As Sulaymānīyah *(Reshteh-ye* Ämol Sārī **Mashhad** Maima
Kirkūk Bījär Karaj *Alborz)* Semnän Torüd Neyshäbür 3416 Torbat-e *Selseleh-ye* Bala
Sanandaj 5671 **TEHRĀN** Torbat-e Jäm *(Paropamis* *Murg*
Hamadān Soltänäbäd Käshmar Heydariyeh Naşräbäd Qal'ah-ye
Kermänshäh Malāyer Qom Khalīläbäd Täybäd Ghürian **HERĀT**
Kerend Nahävand *Daryacheh-ye* *Namak* Täbas *Käshmar* **AFGH**
Borüjerd Aräk *Namak* *Dasht-e Kavīr* Qä'en
Īläm Aligüdarz Käshän Ardestän Dokali Bīrjand
Khorramābād Khvänsär Nä'īn Äqdä Tabas Sarbīsheh Farāh Gir
Dehlorän Najafäbäd **Eşfahān** Qä'en Lashkar Gä
Al Küt Dezfül *(Isfahan)* Ghürian Nehbandän
Shahr-e Äbädeh Yazd Bäfq *Shäh* Zäbol
IRAQ **Kord** Yazd *Küh* Zaranj
Ash Shatrah *Zagros* Näjafäbäd Bāfq 2729 *Dasht-e Märgö*
As Samāwah **Ahvāz** Rämshīr *Mountains* Äbädeh Abarküh Täbäsīn Zarand
Basra Ramshir *Küh-e Dīnär* Anär Zaranj *Helmand* Rüdbär
(Al Başrah) **Ābädān** 4432 Rafsanjän **Kermän** Zäbol *Göd-e Zīrah*
KUWAIT *Marv Dasht* I R A N Behbehän
Al Jahrah

METRES
FEET

5000 16404
3000 9843
2000 6562
1000 3281
500 1640
200 656
0 0
Land below
sea level
200 656
4000 13124
6000 19686

Albers Equal Area Conic Projection

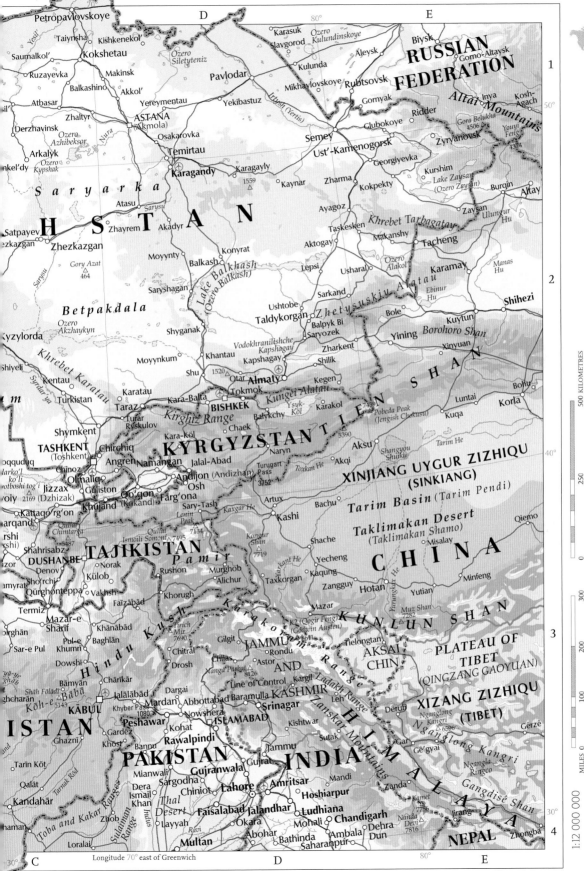

D 80° E

Petropavlovskoye

Taiynsha
Kishkenekol'
Karasuk
Slavgorod
Ozero
Kulundinskoye
Biysk

Saumalkol'
Kokshetau
Makinsk
Kulunda
Aleysk
Gorno-Altaysk

RUSSIAN

1

Ruzayevka
Balkashino
Akkol'
Pavlodar
Mikhaylovskoye
Rubtsovsk

FEDERATION

Atbasar
Yereymentau
Yekibastuz
Irtysh (Yertis)
Gornyak

Altai Mountains

Kosh-Agach

50°

Derzhavinsk
Zhaltyr
ASTANA
(Akmola)
Osakarovka
Semey
Ust'-Kamenogorsk
Ridder
Glubokoye
Zyryanovsk
Gora Belukha
4506
Inya
Youyi
Feng
4374

Arkalyk
Temirtau
Georgiyevka
Kurshim
Lake Zaysan
(Ozero Zaysan)
Burqin

...kel'dy
Ozero
Kypshak
Karagandy
Karagayly
Kaynar
Zharma
Kokpekty
Zaysan
Ulungur
Hu
Altay

Satpayev
Atasu
Sarysu
Zhayrem
1559

Zhezkazgan
Akadyr
Ayagoz
Taskesken
Khrebet Tarbagatay
Makanshy
Tacheng
Manas
Hu

...ezkazgan

Moyynty
Konyrat
Balkash
Lepsi
Usharal
Ozero
Alakol
Karamay

S a r y a r k a
HSTAN

Betpakdala
Gory Azat
464
Saryshagan
Lake Balkhash
(Ozero Balkash)
Sarkand
Bole
Ebinur
Hu
Shihezi

2

...zylorda
Ozero
Akzhaykyn
Shyganak
Ushtobe
Taldykorgan
Balpyk Bi
Saryozek
Yining
Borohoro Shan
xinyuan

...shiyeli
Khrebet Karatau
Moyynkum
Khantau
Vodokhranilishche
Kapshagay
Zharkent
Shilik
Kuytun
Bohu

...m
Kentau
Shu
1520
Kapshagay
Zhalanash
T I E N   S H A N
Luntai
Korla

Turkistan
Karatau
Otar
Almaty
Kegen
Kuqa

Taraz
Kara-Balta
Tokmok
Kungei Alatau
Ysyk-
Köl
Karakol
Pobeda Peak
(Jengish Chokusu)
7439

3

Shymkent
Turar
Ryskulov
BISHKEK
Balykchy
5390
Aksu
Tarim He

TASHKENT
(Toshkent)
Chirchiq
Kara-Köl
Chaek
Naryn
Turugart
Pass
3752
Toxkan He
Akqi
XINJIANG UYGUR ZIZHIQU
(SINKIANG)

...qquduq
...darko'l
...ko'li
...otboshi tog'i
Olmaliq
Angren
Namangan
Jalal-Abad
Artux
Bachu
Tarim Basin (Tarim Pendi)

Jizzax
Guliston
Andijon (Andizhan)
Osh
Kaxgar He
Kashi
Shache
Taklimakan Desert
(Taklimakan Shamo)
Qiemo

...voiy
2169 (Dzhizak)
Go'qon
(Kokand)
Farg'ona
Sary-Tash
Lenin
Peak
7134
Kongur
Shan
7719
CHINA

Kattaqo'rg'on
Khujand
Qullai
Chimtarga
5487
Ismoili Somoni
7495
P a m i r
Shache
Yecheng
Misalay

...qand...
...rshi
Shahrisabz
TAJIKISTAN
Norak
Rushon
Murghob
Taxkorgan
Kaqung
Yarkant He
Zangguy
Hotan
Yutian
Minfeng

...rgan
DUSHANBE
Denov
Kūlob
Alichur
Khorugh
Mazar

Termiz
Mazar-e
Sharif
Khānābād
Faizābād
K2 (Qogir Feng)
(Godwin Austen)
8611
KUNLUN SHAN

...rghān
Pul-e
Khumri
Baghlān
Hindu Kush
Tirich
Mir
7690
Gilgit
Rondu
Tielongtan
Muz Shan
7282

Sar-e Pul
Dowshī
Chitral
Drosh
Karakoram Range
JAMMU
Astor
Kargil
Ladakh Range
Leh
PLATEAU OF
TIBET
(QINGZANG GAOYUAN)

3

...ya-Ye...
...ghāb
Bāmyān
Shāh Foladī
Chārīkār
Nanga Parbat
8126
AND
Line of Control
Baramulla
KASHMIR
Srinagar
Derub

Koh-e Bābā
5143
Jalālābād
Dargai
Chilas
XIZANG ZIZHIQU
(TIBET)

ISTAN
KĀBUL
Khyber Pass
1080
Mardan
Abbottabad
Zanskar Mountains
Kishtwar
Nganglong
Kangri
6596
Gê'gyai

Ghazni
Gardēz
Peshawar
Nowshera
Kohat
ISLAMABAD
Rawalpindi
Jammu
Sutak
Ngangla Ringco

Khōst
Bannu
Gujrat
Ge'gyai
Nganglong Kangri

PAKISTAN
Mianwali
Dera
Ismail
Khan
Sargodha
Gujranwala
INDIA
Amritsar
Hoshiarpur
Mandi
Zanda
Gangdisê Shan

Qalāt
Dera
Ismail
Khan
Thal
Desert
Chiniot
Lahore
Jalandhar
Ludhiana
Chandigarh
Dehra
Dun
Kamet
7756
Jirang

Kandahār
Sulaiman
Range
Faisalabad
Mohali
Ambala
Nanda Devi
7816
NEPAL
Zhongba

...haman
Toba and Kakar Ranges
Zhob
Layyah
Okara
Abohar
Bathinda
Saharanpur

Loralai
Multan
Ravi
Indus
Tarnak Rod

C
Longitude 70° east of Greenwich
D
80°
E

500 KILOMETRES
250
0
300
200
100
MILES 0
1:12 000 000

A
B

Port Said
(Būr Sa‘īd)
GAZA
Al ‘Arīsh
Beersheba
Al Karak
Dead Sea
At Ṭafīlah
Wādī an Sirhān
Al Ismā‘īlīyah
ISRAEL
JORDAN
Ṭurayf
40°
Al Wīdyān
An Najaf
Ad Dīwānīyah
Al Ḥayy
Al
‘Amārah
Ash Shaṭrah
Euphrates
Suez
(As Suways)
30°
Ma‘ān
Petra
As Samāwah
As Sāmāwah
Sūq as
Shuyūʼ
An Nāṣirīyah
IRAQ
Ba
(Al Baṣ
Gulf of Suez
Sinai
Eilat
Al ‘Aqabah
Haql
Wadi Rum
Protected Area
Al ‘Īsāwīyah
‘Ar‘ar
As Samāwah
Ash Shabakah
Hawr al
Ḥammār
Raudha
Zaffaranah
Nuwaybi‘
al Muzayyinah
Jabal Katrina
Mount Catherine
2637
Jabal al Lawz
2579
Al Mudawwarah
Ḥālat ‘Ammār
Al Bi’r
Dawmat
al Jandal
Sakākah
Rafḥā’
Ash
Shu‘bah
Hafar al Bāṭin
Wādī al Bāṭin
Al Jubayl
Ha
K
Raʼs
Ghārib
Jabal Gharib
1751
At Ṭūr
Tabūk
Jabal ad Dubbagh
2350
Raf
979
An Nafūd
Ash Shu‘aybah
Jabal al Kūr
325
Qa
al L
Jamsah
Sharm ash
Shaykh
Al Muwaylih
Dubā
Qaʼat al Mu‘aẓẓam
Taymā’
Mawqaq
Jubbah
Ḥā’il
Ash Shu
AD DAHNA
Ash
Al Ghurdaqah
(Hurghada)
Būr Safājah
Qal‘at al
Azlam
Ad Dār
al Ḥamrā’
Jabal
az Zalma
1258
Ghazzālah
Tābah
Al Kahfah
Al Quwārah
Az Zilfī
Buraydah
Al Arṭāwīyah
Al Majma‘ah
Asharat
Al Quṣayr
Al Wajh
Khaybar
As Sulaymī
Samīrah
Jabal Ṭin
Hulayfah
Uglat
aş Şuqūr
Ar Rass
Nuqrah
‘Unayzah
Az Zilfī
Nafy
SAUDI
2
Marsá al ‘Alam
Ḥanak
Umm
Lajj
Wādī al Ḥamd
Jabal Raḍwá
1814
Sūq
Suwayq
Buwāṭah
Al Ḥanākīyah
Wādī ar Rimah
Jabal Shi‘r
Shubaykīyah
‘Arjah
Ad
Dawādimī
Jabal Tuwayq
Ad Dir‘īyah
RIYADH
(Ar Riyāḍ)
Jabal Hamātah
1977
Baranīs
Tropic of Cancer
Medina
(Al Madīnah)
Al Muşayjīd
Rayyis
Badr Ḥunayn
Umm al
Birak
Mahd adh
Dhahab
‘Afīf
Al Qā‘īyah
Al Quwayyīyah
Ar Ruwaydah
As Salamīyah
Ad Dilam
Al
Hillah
Bi’r Shalatayn
HALAIB
TRIANGLE
ADMINISTERED BY EGYPT,
CLAIMED BY SUDAN
Wadi
al Allaqi
Mastūrah
Rābigh
Jabal Umm
Mukhar
Ad Dafīnah
Halabān
Khashm Māwān
1025
A R A B I A
Jebel Asoteriba
2215
Halaib
Marsa
Delwein
Tuwwal
Khulays
Madrakah
Zalim
Jabal
Hasan
Jabal
Kursh
Layla
ARABI
As Súq
Salāla
Dungunab
Muhammad
Qol
Jeddah
(Jiddah)
Al Ḥawīyah
Al Badi‘
Jabal Tuwayq
Mecca
(Makkah)
At Ṭā’if
Turabah
Wādī Ranyah
Amā’ir
Nubian Desert
Jebel
Oda
2259
Mastābah
Jabal
Abū Şādi
Al ‘Aqīq
Al ‘Aqīq
PENINSULA
20°
SUDAN
Al Līth
Al Junaynah
Al Mindak
Qal‘at
Bishah
Wādī Tathlīth
Khamāsīn
Al Kumdah
As Sulayyil
Port Sudan
Kamob Sanha
Dawqah
Qam
Hadīl
Al ‘Alayyah
Tathlīth
Ḥamḍah
Banī Ma‘āriḍ
‘Urūq al Awārik
R U B
(Em
Al Qunfidhah
An Nimāṣ
Dirs
Sinkat
Suakin
Al Birk
Abhā
Khamīs Mushayṭ
Haraja
Musmar
Erheib
Haiya
Tokar
Ash Shuqayq
Ad Darb
Zahrān
Najrān
Ash
Sharawra
Derudeb
2780
Karora
Algena
ASIR
Ramlat Dahm
3
Athara
Azrout Hills
Wadi Amur
Hagar Nish
Plateau
Suara
2603
Nakfa
Afabet
Jazā’ir
Farasān
Jīzān
Mīdī
Abū ‘Arīsh
Şa‘dah
Khamir
Hajjah
Raydah
Al Hazm al Jawf
Husn Āl
Aroma
Kassala
Akordat
Keren
Dahlak
Archipelago
Aş Şahīl
Al Maḥwīt
Amrān
3760
ŞAN‘Ā’
Ma’rib
New Halfa
Teseney
Barentu
Mendefera
ASMARA
Massawa
Dekemhare
Kamarān
Az Zaydīyah
Bājil
Manākhah
Dhamār
Ma‘bar
Bayhan al Qişab
YEM
Khashm el Girba
Dam
Khashm
el Girba
Showak
Adi
Keyih
Mersa Fatma
Hodeidah
(Al Hudaydah)
Bayt al Faqīh
Zabīd
Radā‘
Yarīm
‘Ataq
Gedaref
Om
Hajēr
Āksum
Inda Silasē
Adwa
Ādī Ārk’ay
Ras Dejen
4533
Sīmēn
Mek’elē
Adigrat
Āşale
3293
Āşale
Ed
Az Zuqur
Al Khawkhah
Hays
Ta‘izz
Ibb
Qa‘ṭabah
Jabal Thamar
2512
Al Baydā’
3267
Lawdar
Hab
ETHIOPIA
Rahad
Gallabat
Athara
Danakil
2131
Assab
Mawza
Mocha
(Al Mukhā)
Dhubāb
Al Nābiyah
Lahij
Musaymir
Shuqrah
Zinjibār
Ash Shaykh ‘Uthman
Aden
(‘Adan)
Bāb al Mandab
At Turbah

Longitude 40° east of Greenwich

Albers Equal Area Conic Projection

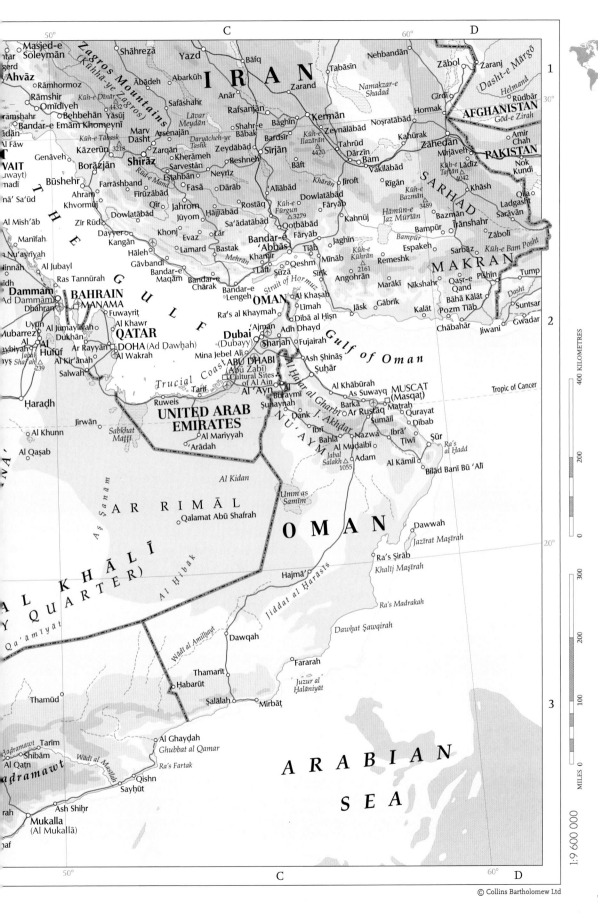

© Collins Bartholomew Ltd

1:9 600 000

C **D**

C **D**

50° 60°

50° 60°

30°

Tropic of Cancer

20°

KILOMETRES
400
200
0

MILES
300
200
100
0

IRAN

Masjed-e
Soleymān
-gerd
Ahvāz
Rāmhormoz
Omīdīyeh
-ramshahr
Bandar-e Emām Khomeynī
-ādān
Al Faw
KUWAIT
(Al Kuwayt)
-madī
Shahrezā
Yazd
Bāfq
Tabāsīn
Nehbandān
Zābol
Zaranj
Dasht-e Mārgō
Ābādeh
Abarkūh
Anār
Helmand
Zarand
Namakzar-e
Shadad
Gīrdī
Hormak
Rūdbār
AFGHANISTAN
Gōd-e Zirah
Amir
Chah
Safāshahr
Rafsanjān
Kermān
Noşratābād
Zāhedān
Mīrjāveh
PAKISTAN
Kāzerūn
3218
Zarqān
SHĪRĀZ
Marv
Dasht
Arsenajān
Kherāmeh
Sarvestān
Bāghīn
Zeynalābād
Tahrūd
Kahūrak
Dārzīn
Bam
Vakīlābād
Zahedan
Kūh-e Lādīz
4042
Taftān
Nok
Kundi
Khāsh
Qila
Ladgasht
Zarqān
Zeydābād
Sīrjān
Bardsīr
Kūh-e
Ilazārān
4420
Borāzjān
Būshehr
Farrāshband
Ahram
Fasā
Dārāb
Estahbān
Neyriz
Aliābād
Jīroft
Kūh-e
Bazmān
3489
Bazmān
Īrānshahr
Zābolī
SARHAD
Dowlatābād
Khvormūj
Zīr Rūd
Qīr
Jahrom
Hājjīābād
Rostāq
Fāryāb
Kahnūj
Hāmūn-e
Jaz Mūriān
Bampūr
Farsh-band
Kūh-e Takask
Kūh-e
Fürgun
3279
Qotbābād
Fāryāb
Jaghīn
Bampūr
MAKRAN
Kūh-e Bam Posht
Dowlatābād
Dayyer
Jūyom
Lār
Bastak
Kūh-e
Kūhrān
2161
Espakeh
Sarbāz
Pīshīn
Tump
Al Mish'āb
Manīfah
Kangān
Lamard
Khonj
Evaz
Bandar-e
'Abbās
Tīāb
Mīnāb
Remeshk
Marākī
Nīkshahr
Qaşr-e
Qand
Bāhā Kalāt
Suntsar
Nu'ayrīyah
Al Jubayl
Gāvbandī
Mehrān
Khamīr
Qeshm
Sīrīk
Angohrān
Jāsk
Gābrīk
Kalāt
Pozm Tīāb
Dasht
-dh
Häleh
Bandar-e
Maqām
Bandar-e
Chārak
Lāft
Sūzā
Strait of Hormuz
Līmah
Chāhbahār
Jiwani
Gwadar
Dhahran
Ras Tannūrah
Bandar-e
Lengeh
OMAN
Dammām
(Ad Dammām)
BAHRAIN
MANAMA
Ra's al Khaymah
Adh Dhayd
Dibā al Hiṣn
Dubai
Ajman
Fuwayrit
Al Khawr
QATAR
DOHA (Ad Dawhah)
(Dubayy)
Sharjah
Fujairah
Gulf of Oman
Mubarrez
Al Jumaylīyah
Dukhān
Ar Rayyān
Mina Jebel Ali
Ash Shināş
Şuḥār
-aybiyah
Al
Hufūf
Al Wakrah
ABU DHABI
Cultural Sites
of Al Ain
Al Khābūrah
As Suwayq
MUSCAT
(Masqat)
-ays
Jabal Sha'ak
239
Al Kir'ānah
(Abū Zabī)
Barkā
Matrah
Salwah
Tarif
Al 'Ayn
Buraymī
Ar Rustāq
Sumāil
Qurayat
Haradh
Ruweis
Trucial Coast
Şunaynah
Dank
J. Akhdar
Ibrī
Nazwa
Ibrā'
Tīwī
Dibab
Şūr
Ra's
al Hadd
Al Khunn
Jirwān
Sabkhat
Matti
Al Mariyyah
Arādah
Bahlā
Al Mudaibī
Adam
Jabal
Salakh
1055
Al Kāmil
Bilad Banī Bū 'Alī
Al Qaşab
As Şanām
AR RIMĀL
Al Kidan
Umm as
Samīm
NU'AYM
AL HAJAR AL GHARBĪ
Qalamat Abū Shafrah
OMAN
Dawwah
Jazīrat Maşīrah
AL KHĀLĪ
(Y QUARTER)
Qa'āmīyāt
Ra's Şīrāb
Al Hibāk
Hajmā'
Jiddat al Harāsīs
Khalīj Maşīrah
Ra's Madrakah
Dawhat Şawqirah
Dawqah
Fararah
Thamarīt
Habarūt
Wādī al Amilhayt
Juzur al
Halāniyāt
Thamūd
Şalālah
Mirbāţ
-adramawt
Tarīm
Shibām
Al Qaţn
Al Ghaydah
Ghubbat al Qamar
Ra's Fartak
Wādī al Maşīlah
ARABIAN
-adramawt
Qishn
Sayhūt
SEA
Ash Shihr
Mukalla
(Al Mukallā)
-naf

METRES
FEET

5000
16404

3000
9843

2000
6562

1000
3281

500
1640

200
656

0
0

Land below
sea level

200
656

4000
13124

6000
19686

Longitude 30° east of Greenwich

Albers Equal Area Conic Projection

cherkassk

Balykshi

Sor
Donyztau

RUSSIAN

Proletarskoye
Vodokhranilishche   Elista

ograd   Utta

Astrakhan

Karakum
Desert
(Peski Karakum)

Borankul

Beyneu

KAZAKHSTAN

Ulan-
Khol

UZBEKISTAN

l'sk

Komsomol'skiy

EDERATION

Lagan'

Mys
Tupkaragan

Fort-Shevchenko

Gora
Bésshoky
△
555

Ustyurt
Plateau

Borsakelmas
sho'rxogi

Uçal Karabaur

1

retsk   Ipatovo   Divnoye
opatkin   Stavropol'skaya   Komsomol'skiy
vir   'Stavropol'   Vozzvyshennost'   Budennovsk
abinsk   Nevinnomyssk
op   Cherkessk
Psebay   Pyatigorsk   Prokhladnyy   Georgiyevsk
Karachayevsk   Kislovodsk   Mozdok

Kochubey

Shetpe

Mangistau
△
132

Aktau

Zhanaozen

Kuryk

Kazakhskiy
Zaliv

Sarykamyshskoye
Ozero

Kizlyar

Khasavyurt

Makhachkala

A'
El'brus
5642
△
U
(BOL'SH

Nal'chik
Alagir
Vladikavkaz

Buynaksk

Izberbash

Sokhumi

OY

KAVKAZ)

Derbent

Garabogaz

Garabogazköl
Aýlagy

Çagyl

T'q'varcheli

Kutaisi

A
S
Khashuri   Gori
Samt'redia   Telavi
Akhaltsikhe

Garabogazköl

TURKMENISTAN

Zugdidi

U

S

Janna

Poti
'umi

GEORGIA

TBILISI
(Tiflis)

Zaqatala
Şәki

Gora
Bazardüzyu
△
1466

Quba

Garşy

Artvin
Akhalkalaki
Ardahan

Lesser C
(Malyy K

Rustavi

Qazax
Gänca   Mingäçevir

Göyçay Şamaxı

Sumqayıt

Abşeron
Yarımadası

Türkmenbaşy

Jebel   Balkanabat

40°

Kaçkar
Dağı
3932   Yusufeli
Oltu

Gyumri   Vanadzor
Sevan

ARMENIA

AZERBAIJAN

Haçıqabul

BAKU
(Bakı)

SEA

Hazar

Bereket

Horasan

Kars
Sarıkamış

□ **YEREVAN**
(Erevan)

Ağdam
(abandoned)

Kür

Şirvan
Salyan

Gumdag

Serdar

rzurum

Ağrı
Iğdır

Mt. Ararat
Ararat

AZER.
Sisian

Xankändi

Bilәsuvar
Cәlilabad

Ogurjaly
Adasy

Magtymguly

Doğubeyazıt

SStephan Dağı
1058

Mәkü

Naxçıvan

Länkäran

Ahar
4810
△

Ardabıl

Tatvan
Ahlat

Van
Salmas

Khvoy

Marand

Aştärä

Muş
Bitlis

Lake Van
(Van Gölü)

Başkale
Semdinli

Urmia
3711
△

Sarab

Tabriz

rbakır
Siirt
tman
Hakkâri

Samai

Lake Urmia
(Daryacheh-ye Orümiyeh)

Mianeh

Bandar-e Anzalı

Rasht

Lahijan

Gomishan

Gonbad-e
Kavus

Gorgan

Mardin
Qamişli
Zakho
Dahuk

Al 'Amadiyah
Oshnoviyeh

Heydarabad
Miandowab

Fowman

Tonkabon

Nowshahr

Amol

Babol

Behshahr

Sari

Mayamey

Emamrud

isakah
Tall
'Afar

Mahabad

Zanjan

Qazvin

Elburz Mountains
(Reshteh-ye Alborz)
△
5671

Damghan

az

Mosul

Arbil

Saqqez

Bijar

Abhar

Karaj   □ **TEHRAN**

Semnan

Torud

2

Mayadin

Ash
Sharqat

As Sulaymaniyah

Kirkük

Sanandaj

Halabja

Qorveh

Soltanabad

Dasht-e Kavir

'Anah

Bayji

Tuz Khurmatu

Ravansar

Hamadan

Qom

Daryacheh-ye
Namak

Jandaq

Al Hadithah
Hit

Tikrit

Qasr-e
Shirin

Kermanshah

Kangavar
Malayer

Arak

Kashan

Samarra'

Kerend

Nahavand

Borujerd

Dorud

Golpayegan

Khvansar

Ardestan

Na'in

Dokali

Al Muqdadiyah
Ba'qubah
Ar Ramadi

Eslamabad-e
Gharb

Ilam

Khorramabad

Aligudarz

Daran

Kuh-e
Karbush
△
4294

Najafabad

Esfahan
(Isfahan)

Aqda

Meybod

□ **BAGHDAD**

Al Kazimiyah

Dehloran

Dezful

Zagros Mountains
(Kühha-ye Zagros)

Shahr-e
Kord

IRAN

Yazd

Bafq

Karbala'

Hillah

Al Küt

Shushtar

Al Hayy

Al 'Amarah

Susangerd

Ramhormoz

Shahreza

Abadeh

Abarküh

Anar

Buhayrat ath
Tharthar

Buhayrat ar
Razazah

An Najaf

Ash Shatrah

Ad Diwaniyah

Ahvaz

Ramshir
Omidiyeh

Masjed-e
Soleyman

Kuh-e
Dinar
△
4432

Yasuj

Safashahr

Shahr-e
Babak

IRAQ

As Samawah

An Nasiriyah

Süq ash
Shuyükh

Khorramshahr

Behbehan

Abadeh Tashk

Marv
Dasht

Arsenajan

Idyan

Hawr al
Hammar

Basra
(Al Başrah)

Abadan

Bandar-e
Emam Khomeyni

Ghenaveh

Kül-e Täbask

Küh-e
Zarqan
△
3215

Daryacheh-ye
Tashk

Kheraneh
Salvestan Neyriz

Beshneh

Ash Shabakah

Raudhatain

Al Faw

KUWAIT

Borazjan

Shiraz

Kazerün
Farrashband

Estahban
Darab

Küd-e Mand

Fasa
Hajjiabad

Rostaq

RABIA

Rafha'

Hawalli
□ **KUWAIT**
(Al Kuwayt)

Al Jahrah

Büshehr

Ahram
Khvormuj

Firüzabad

Qir
Jahrom

Dowlatabad

Jüyom

3

n   Nafūd

Ash
Shu'bah

Aş Şubayhiyah

Wadi al Batin

Al Ahmadi
Mina' Sa'ud

400 KILOMETRES   200   0

300   200   100

MILES   0

1:9 600 000

81

Conic Equidistant Projection

ARCTIC OCEAN

N

M

L

Wrangel Island
(Ostrov Vrangelya)

*Chukchi
Sea*

Bering Strait

U.S.A.

St Lawrence
Island

Arctic Circle
Mys Shmidta

Uelen
Chukotskiy P-ov

Iul'tin

Egvekinot

Providenya
Mys Navarin

Ostrov Komsomolets
Ostrov Oktyabr'skoy
Revolyutsii
Ostrov Bol'shevik

New Siberia Islands
(Novosibirskiye Ostrova)

Ostrova
De-Longa
Ostrov Bennetta
Ostrov Zhokhova

*East Siberian Sea
(Vostochno-Sibirskoye More)*

Proliv Longa

Mys
Shalaurova
Mys Shelagskiy

Pevek

Palyavaam

Belaya

Komsomol'skiy

Anadyr'

Bilibino

Metropil'gyno

Severnaya
Zemlya

Ostrov Kotel'nyy
O. Bol'shoy
Lyakhovskiy

Ostrov
Novaya Sibir'

Ostrov
Malyy
Lyakhovskiy

Ostrov
Medvezh'i

Kolymskaya
Nizmennost'

Chetskiy

Ozero
Krasnoye

Koryakskoye Nagor'ye

Apuka

Ostrov Komsomolets

Mys
Chelyuskin

*Laptev Sea
(More Laptevykh)*

Ostrov
Bel'kovskiy

Yanskiy
Zaliv

Nizhneyansk

Yano-Indigirskaya
Nizmennost'

Indigirka

Srednekolymsk

Kolyma

Yukagirskoye
Ploskogor'ye

Oloy

Seymchan

Evensk

Mys
Olyutorskiy

Ossora

Karaginskiy
Zaliv

Pelag
shnlsk'da

Proliv Vil'kitskogo

Taymyr Peninsula
(Poluostrov Taymyr)

Anabarskiy
Zaliv

Ust'-
Olenek

Tiksi

Deputatskiy

Khonuu

Zyryanka

Omolon

Omsukchan

Penzhinskaya Guba

Zaliv
Korfa

Ozero
Taymyr

Khatanga

Popigay

Olenek

Lena

Kytalyktakh

Batagay

Bytantay

Adycha

Lazo

Khrebet Cherskogo

El'ginskiy

El'gen

Ust'
Nera

Susuman

Yagodnoye

Ust'-
Omchug

Omsukchan

Palatka

Magadan

Zaliv
Shelikhova

Palana

Sredinnyy Khrebet

Esso

Klyuchi
Ust'-Kamchatsk

Komandorskiye
Ostrova

Ostrov
Beringa

Khatanga

Kheta

Saskylakh

Anabar

Olenek

Zhigansk

Verkhoyanskiy Khrebet

Sangar

Tyung

Namtsy

Tomtor

3003

Okhandyga

Allakh-
Yun'

Yun

Ynykchanskiy

Oymyakon

Okhotsk

Mys
Alevina

**Kamchatka
Peninsula**

Milkovo
Nikol'skoye

Petropavlovsk-
Kamchatskiy

Kamchatskiy

Ostrov
Paramushir

FEDERATION

*Central Siberian
Plateau*

Olenek

Udachnyy

Vilyuy

Aykhal

Markha

Mirnyy

Nyuba

Yakutsk

Pokrovsk

Churapcha

Amga

Maya

Aldan

Chyurmikan

Uchur

Ayan

Mys Marii

Okha

Ozero
Orel'

Sakhalin

Noglik

Severo-
Kuril'sk

Oktyabr'skiy

Tembenchi

Tura

Chernyshevskiy

Mokhsogollokh

Lena

Olëkminsk

Chulman

Neryungri

2482

Zeyskoye
Vodokhranilishche

Aleksandrovsk-Sakhalinskiy

Tatarskiy Proliv

Podkamennaya Tunguska

Chunya

Severo-
Yeniseyskiy

Vanavara

Bodaybo

Khani

Stanovoy Khrebet

Tynda

Chul'man

Zeya

Svobodnyy

Khrebet Turana

Amgun'

Poronaysk

Yuzhno-
Sakhalinsk

Boguchany

Angara

Ust'-
Ilimsk

Kirensk

Kirenga

Ust'-Kut

2618

Skovorodino

Mogocha

Amur

Mayskiy

Blagoveshchensk

Birobidzhan

**Komsomol'sk-
na-Amure**

Vanino

sibirsk

Bratsk

Severobaykal'sk

Heilong Jiang

Gulian

Heilong Jiang

Heilong Jiang

Khabarovsk

Sikhote-Alin'

Krasnoyarsk

Kansk

Uyar

Zaozernyy

Nizhneudinsk

Tulun

Kachug

Vitim

Kurumkan

Baykal'skiy Khrebet

Sretensk

Chita

Karymskoye

Borzya

Mangui

Arun

Xiao Hinggan Ling

Nenjiang

Yichun

Hegang

Shuangyashan

Jixi

Spassk-Dal'niy

Bikin

Bikin

**Vostochnyy
Sayan**

Angarsk

Ust'-Ordynskiy

Irkutsk

Lake Baikal
(Ozero Baykal)

Ulan-
Ude

Olovyannaya

Zabaykal'sk

Manzhouli

Hulun Buir
(Hailar)

Hulun
Nur

Da Hinggan Ling

Qiqihar

Daqing

Suihua

Baicheng

Jiamusi

Harbin

Mudanjiang

Vladivostok

Nakhodka

Zaliv Petra
Velikogo

Abakan

Kyzyl

**Hövsgöl
Nuur**

Gusinoozersk

Sühbaatar

Darhan

**ULAN BATOR
(Ulaanbaatar)**

Choybalsan

Baruun-Urt

Ulanhot

Jilin

Changchun

Sipìng

Dunhua

Yanji

Ch'ŏngjin

Kimch'aek

N. KOREA

Angara

Yenisey

Uvs Nuur

gom

Hyargas
Nuur

Tsetserleg

Bulgan

Dzuunmod

Moron

Tosontsengel

Uliastay

Baruun-Urt

Uliastai

Saynshand

GOBI

Xilinhot

Tongliao

Chifeng

Chengde

Shenyang

Fushun

Benxi

Anshan

Jinzhou

Dandong

Sinŭiju

Hyesan

Hamhŭng

Wŏnsan

PYONGYANG

SEOUL

S. KOREA

Hovd

4021

Har Us
Nuur

Altay

Bayanhongor

Arvayheer

Mandalgovi

Erenhot

MONGOLIA

CHINA

Gichgeniyn Nuruu

Uliastay

1:24 000 000

500 KILOMETRES

400

200

0

MILES 0

ATLANTIC OCEAN

Greenland (Denmark)

Arctic Circle

Denmark Strait

Bjørnøya (Nor.)

Jan Mayen (Nor.)

ICELAND
Reykjavík

NORWEGIAN SEA

NORWAY

SWEDEN

Gulf of B

Tron

Faroe Islands (Den.)
Torshavn

Trondheim

Shetland Islands

Orkney Islands

Bergen

Oslo

Stock

NORTH SEA

Vänern

Gothenburg

Gotland

Baltic Sea

SCOTLAND

Glasgow
Edinburgh

N. Belfast
IRELAND

UNITED KINGDOM

DENMARK
Copenhagen

Malmö

RUS.

IRELAND
Dublin

Manchester

ENGLAND

WALES
Cardiff
Birmingham

London

NETHERLANDS

Amsterdam

Hamburg

Berlin

POLAN

English Channel

Channel Is (U.K.)

Brussels
The Hague
Essen

Hannover

Poznań
Warsaw

Łódź

BELGIUM

GERMANY

Frankfurt

Prague

Kato

K.   KOSOVO
LIE.   LIECHTENSTEIN
MACE.   MACEDONIA
MONT.   MONTENEGRO

Paris

Luxembourg
LUXEMBOURG

Rhine

CZECH REPUBLIC

Vienna

SLOVAK

Bratislava

Bay of Biscay

Seine

Loire

Munich

Danube

Buda

Cape Finisterre

FRANCE

Bordeaux

Bilbao

Lyon

Bern   LIE.
SWITZERLAND

Mont Blanc 4808 m

AUSTRIA

SLOVENIA

Ljubljana

Zagreb

HUNGAR

Rhone

Milan

Turin

CROATIA

Belgra

Oporto

SPAIN

Pyrenees

Andorra la Vella   ANDORRA

Marseille

MONACO

SAN MARINO

ITALY

BOSNIA-HERZ.

Adriatic Sea

SE

PORTUGAL

Madrid

Barcelona

Corsica

VATICAN CITY

Rome

Sarajevo

MONT.

Podgorica

Pri

K

Skop

Lisbon

Valencia

Balearic Islands

Sardinia

Naples

Tirana

ALBAN

Cabo de São Vicente

Seville

Gibraltar (U.K.)

Palermo

Sicily

Ionian Sea

MEDITERRANEAN

MALTA
Valletta

SEA

A

MOROCCO

ALGERIA

TUNISIA

Chamberlin Trimetric Projection

2

3

BARENTS
SEA

Novaya
Zemlya

pp

Ostrov
Kolguyev

Vorkuta

Ob'

Murmansk

n d

White Sea

Archangel

Syktyvkar

R U S S I A N   F E D E R A T I O N

Ural Mountains

LAND

Lake
Onega

Perm'

50°

Lake
Ladoga

elsinki

St Petersburg

Nizhniy
Novgorod

Kazan'

Yaroslavl

Volga

ONIA

IA

Orenburg

Moscow

Samara

NIA

Ryazan'

KAZAKHSTAN

4

Minsk

Saratov

BELARUS

Voronezh

Homyel'

Volgograd

Aral Sea

Kiev

Kharkiv

Don

Volga

UZBEKISTAN

U K R A I N E

Donets'k

Astrakhan

Dnipropetrovs'k

Rostov
na-Donu

40°

Chisinău

Dniepr

MOLDOVA

Sea
of Azov

Krasnodar

Odessa

Groznyy

C a u c a s u s

TURKMENISTAN

MANIA

Black Sea

GEORGIA

C a s p i a n   S e a

Bucharest

AZERBAIJAN

ofia

ARMENIA

5

LGARIA

AZER.

İstanbul

ssaloniki

T U R K E Y

I R A N

Aegean
Sea

CE

Athens

30°

Crete

Euphrates

CYPRUS

SYRIA

I R A Q

LEBANON

Tigris

1000 KILOMETRES

750

500

250

0

500

250

MILES 0

1:20 000 000

85

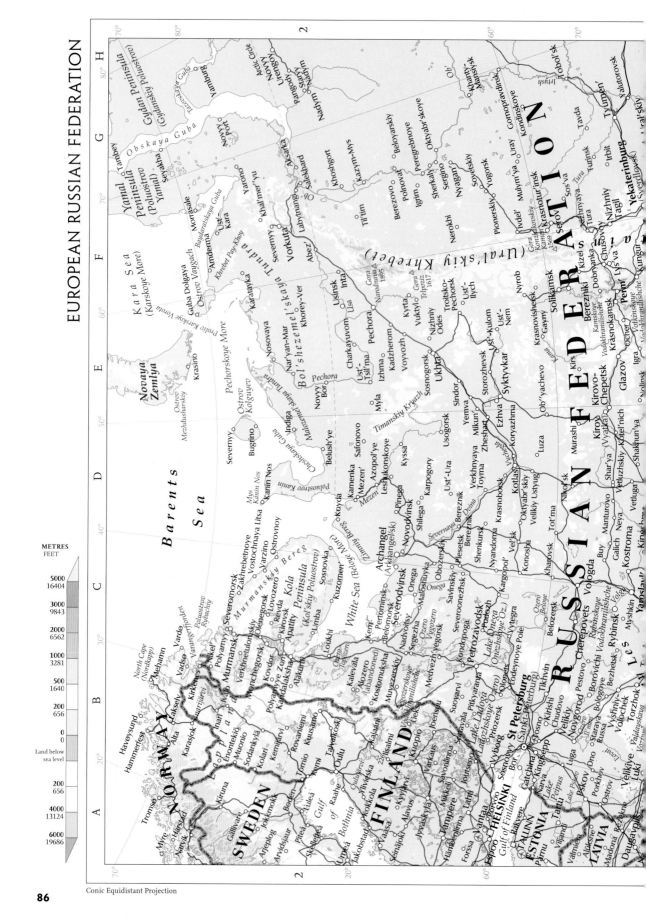

Conic Equidistant Projection

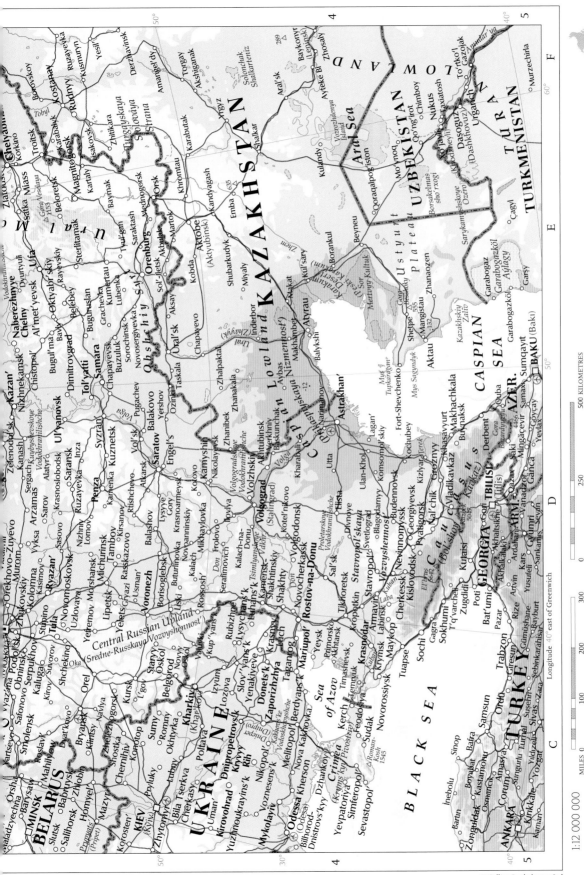

© Collins Bartholomew Ltd

1:12 000 000

MILES 0   100   200   300

0   250   500 KILOMETRES

Longitude 40° east of Greenwich

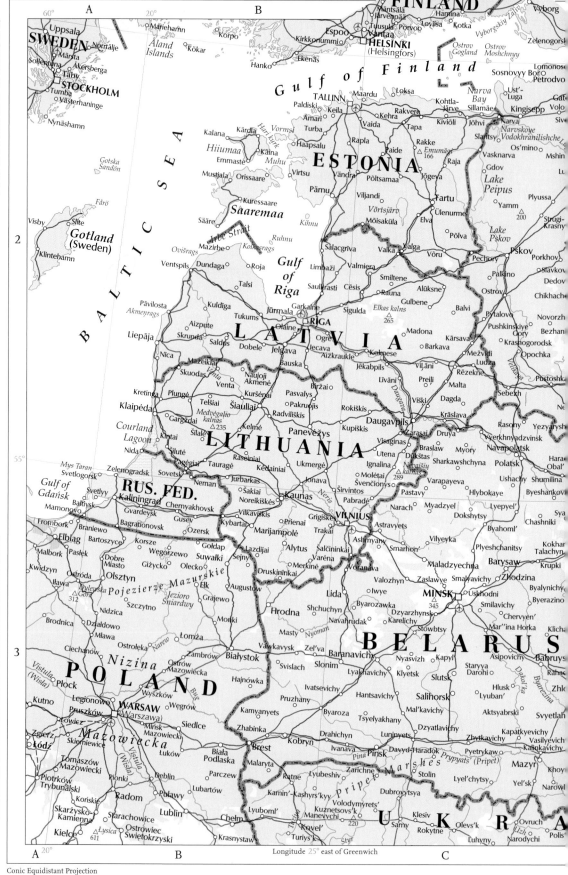

SWEDEN
Uppsala
Norrtälje
Mariehamn
Korpo
Åland
Islands
Kökar
Hanko
Ekenäs

FINLAND
Mäntsälä
Järvenpää
Tuusula
Espoo
Vantaa
Loviisa
Porvoo
Kouvola
Anjalankoski
Hamina
Kotka
Vyborg
Vyborgskiy Zaliv
Zelenogorsk

HELSINKI
(Helsingfors)

Sollentuna
Åkersberga
Märsta
Täby
STOCKHOLM
Tumba
Västerhaninge
Nynäshamn

Kirkkonummio

Ostrov
Gogland
Ostrov
Moshchnyy
Lomonosov
Sosnovyy Bor
Petrodvo

Gulf of Finland

Kalana
Kärdla
Hari kurk
Vormsi
Turba
Haapsalu
Hiiumaa
Emmaste
Kärla
Muhu

Paldiski
Keila
Ämari
TALLINN
Maardu
Loksa

Kehra
Rakvere
Kohtla-
Järve
Sillamäe
Jõhvi
Vaida
Tapa
Rakke
Narva
Kiviõli
Slantsy
Narva
Bay
Kingisepp
Volo

Rapla
Paide

Mustjala
Orissaare
Virtsu
Vändra
Põltsamaa
Jõgeva

Saaremaa
Kuressaare
Pärnu
Viljandi
Võrtsjärv
Tartu

Narvskoye
Vodokhranilishche
Os'mino
Mshin
Gdov
**Lake
Peipus**
Plyussa
Struga-
Krasny

Sääre
Kihnu
Mõisaküla
Ülenurme
Elva
Põlva
Yamm
**Lake
Pskov**

Irbe Strait
Ruhnu
Kolkasrags
Salacgrīva
Valga
Võru
Pechory
Porkhov

Mazirbe
Ovišrags
Limbaži
Valmiera
Valka

Pskov
Palkino
Slavkov
Dedov
Chikhach

Ventspils
Dundaga
Roja
**Gulf
of
Riga**
Saulkrasti
Cēsis
Smiltene
Rauna
Alūksne
Ostrov

Talsi
Līgatne
Gulbene
Balvi
Bytalovo
Novorzh
Bezhani

Pāvilosta
Akmeņrags
Kuldīga
Tukums
Jūrmala
RĪGA
Garkalne
Sigulda
Elkas kalns
△ 265
Madona
Kārsava
Pushkinskiye
Gory
Krasnogorodsk
Opochka

LATVIA
Aizpute
Olaine
Ogre
Barkava
Mežvidi
Ludza

Liepāja
Skrunda
Saldus
Dobele
Jelgava
Iecava
Aizkraukle
Koknese
Viļāni
Preiļi
Malta
Rēzekne
Pustoshka

Nīca
Mažeikiai
Skuodas
Venta
Naujoji
Akmenė
Bauska
Jēkabpils
Līvāni
Viški
Dagda
Sebezh
Ne

Kretinga
Plungė
Telšiai
Šiauliai
Kuršėnai
Pasvalys
Biržai
Rokiškis
Daugavpils
Krāslava
Rasony
Yezyarysh

Klaipėda
Gargždai
Medvėgalio
kalnas
△ 235
Radviliškis
Panevėžys
Kupiškis
Zarasai
Druya
Vyerkhnyadzvinsk

**Courland
Lagoon**
Kintai
Šilalė
Kelmė
Visaginas
Braslaw
Myory
Navapolatsk

Nida
Šilutė
Raseiniai
LITHUANIA
Utena
Dūkštas
Sharkawshchyna
Polatsk

Mys Taran
Pagėgiai
Tauragė
Kėdainiai
Ukmergė
Ignalina
Negešiu
kalnas
△ 289
Varapayeva
Ushachy
Shumilina

Svetlogorsk
Zelenogradsk
Sovetsk
Neman
Jurbarkas
Jonava
Molėtai
Švenčionys
Pastavy
Hlybokaye
Byeshankov

**Gulf of
Gdańsk**
Svetlyy
Baltiysk
RUS. FED.
Kaliningrad
Chernyakhovsk
Šakiai
Kaunas
Širvintos
Narach
Myadzyel
Lyepyel'
Sya

Mamonovo
Gvardeysk
Vilkaviškis
Grigiškes
VILNIUS
Astravyets
Dokshytsy
Chashniki

Frombork
Braniewo
Bagrationovsk
Gusev
Kybartai
Prienai
Trakai
Ashmyany
Smarhon'
Vilyeyka
Plyeshchanitsy
Byaroma'

Elbląg
Bartoszyce
Korsze
Ozersk
Marijampolė
Alytus
Šalčininkai
Varėna
Maladzyechna
Barysaw
Krupki

Malbork
Pasłęk
Dobre
Miasto
Węgorzewo
Giżycko
Gołdap
Suwałki
Lazdijai
Sejny
Merkinė
Voranava
Valozhyn
Zaslawye
Smalyavichy
Zhodzina
Byalynichy

Kwidzyn
Iława
Ostróda
Olsztyn
Olecko
Ełk
Augustów
Druskininkai
Lida
MINSK
Uskhodni
Byerazino

Tylewska
Góra
△ 312
Pojezierze Mazurskie
Jezioro
Śniardwy
Grajewo
Shchuchyn
Byarozawka
△ 345
Smilavichy

Brodnica
Nidzica
Szczytno
Mońki
Hrodna
Navahrudak
Dzyarzhynsk
Chervyen'
Klicha

Działdowo
Mława
Łomża
Zambrów
Vawkavysk
Zel'va
Karelichy
Mar''ina Horka

POLAND
Ciechanów
Ostrołęka
Narew
Ostrów
Mazowiecka
Białystok
Slonim
Baranavichy
BELARUS
Słowbtsy
Asipovichy
Babruys

**Nizina
Mazowiecka**
Płock
Wyszków
Hajnówka
Svislach
Baranavichy
Nyasvizh
Kapyl'
Staryya
Darohi
Rahac
Zhlo

Kutno
Legionowo
WARSAW
(Warszawa)
Wegrów
Siedlce
Ivatsevichy
Pruzhany
Klyetsk
Slutsk
Hlusk
Lyuban'
Svyetlah

Pruszków
Łowicz
Minsk
Mazowiecki
Kamyanyets
Byaroza
Mal'kavichy
Aktsyabrski

Zgierz
Łódź
Skierniewice
Żyrardów
Łuków
Zhabinka
Tsyelyakhany
Salihorsk
Dzyatlavichy
Kapatkyevichy

Tomaszów
Mazowiecki
Rionki
Wisła
Biała
Podlaska
Drahichyn
Ivanava
Davyd-Haradok
Zhytkavichy
Vasilyevich
Kalinkavichy
Mazyr

Piotrków
Trybunalski
Radom
Puławy
Dęblin
Parczew
Lubartów
Kobryn
Pinsk
Luninyets
Pina
Zarichne
Stolin
Lyel'chytsy
Khoy

Mazowiecka
Końskie
Starachowice
Lublin
Chełm
Malaryta
Lyubeshiv
Pripet Marshes
Dubrovytsya
Yel'sk
Narowl

Skarżysko-
Kamienna
Ostrowiec
Świętokrzyski
Lyuboml'
Volodymyrets'
Manevychi
Olevs'k
Ovruch
Polis

Kielce
△ Łysica
611
Krasnystaw
Kovel'
Turiys'k
Klesiv
Sarny
Rokytne
Luhyny
Narodychi

U K R A

Longitude 25° east of Greenwich

Conic Equidistant Projection

METRES
FEET

5000
16404

3000
9843

2000
6562

1000
3281

500
1640

200
656

0
0

Land below
sea level

200
656

4000
13124

6000
19686

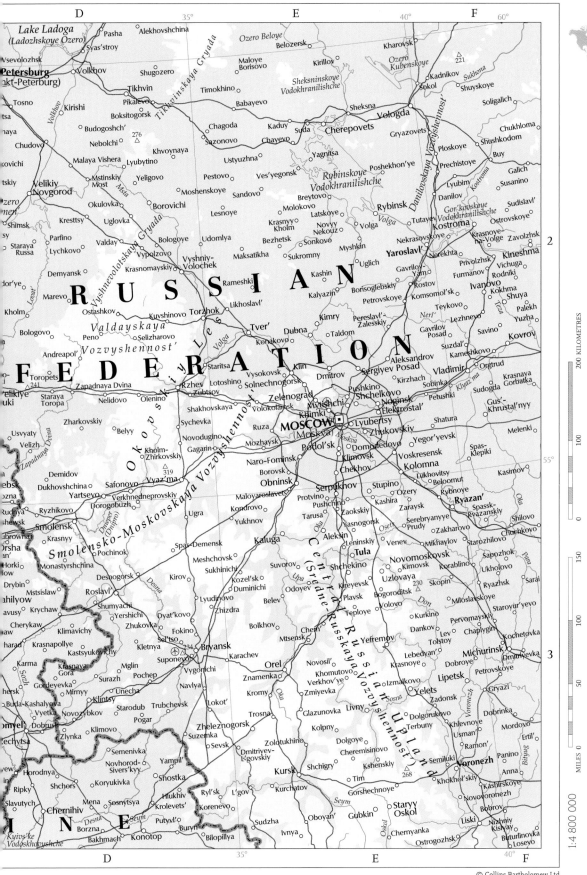

A · B

25° · 30°

Ciechanów Zambrów **Białystok** Hajnówka Vawkavysk Zel'va **Baranavichy** Nyasvizh Asipovichy **Babruysk** Ka

Ostrów Mazowiecka Svislach Slonim Lyakhavichy Klyetsk Kapyl' Staryya Darohi Slutsk Rahachow Zhlobin Chacher Buda-Kasha

Legionowo Wyszków Pruzhany Byaroza Tsyelyakhany Mal'kavichy Hlusk Svyetlahorsk **Homy**

WARSAW (Warszawa) Kamyanyets Zhabinka **Kobryn** Drahichyn Ivanava Luninyets Davyd-Haradok Pyetrykaw Mazyr Khoynyr Narowlya Brahin Rech

Pruszków Mińsk Mazowiecki Siedlce Biała Podlaska **Brest** Pina Pinsk *Prypyats' (Pripet)* Lyel'chytsy Yel'sk Loyew Slav

POLAND Radom Pionki Puławy Lubartów Łuków Parczew Malaryta Lyubeshiv Ratne *Pripet* Zarichne Stolin *Marshes* Kakhovka

Skarżysko-Kamienna Starachowice Lublin Chełm Lyuboml' Kovel' Manevychi 220 Sarny Klesiv Rokytne Olevs'k Ovruch *Uzh* Polis'ke Chornob

Ostrowiec Świętokrzyski Łysica 611 Sandomierz Krasnystaw Zamość Turiys'k Volodymyr-Volyns'k Kivertsi Luts'k Kostopil' Luhyny Korosten' Ivankiv *Kyivs'ke Vodoskhovyshche* Koze

Staszów Tarnobrzeg Mielec Biłgoraj Tomaszów Lubelski Novovolyns'k Mlyniv **Rivne** Zdolbuniv Novohrad-Volyns'kyy Chernyakhiv Yemil'chyne Volodars'k-Volyns'kyy Malyn Borodyanka Makariv Irpin' Br

Dębica Vistula (Wisła) Przeworsk Sokal' Horokhiv Dubno Ostroh Slavuta Baranivka Radomyshl' Vyshho

50° **Tarnów** Rzeszów Jarosław Zhovkva Brody Kremenets' Shepetivka Polonne Chudniv **Zhytomyr** Vasyl'kiv **KIEV** (Kyiv)

Jasło Krosno Przemyśl Yavoriv Kam''yanka-Buz'ka Radyvyliv Pochayiv Izyaslav Starokostyantyniv Berdychiv Andrushivka Fastiv

Gorlice Sanok Ustrzyki Dolne Horodok **L'viv** (L'vov) Zolochiv Peremyshlyany Zbarazh Bilohir''ya Kozyatyn Skvyra **Bila Tserkva** Kaharlyk Myron

Bardejov Svidnik Prešov Humenné Sambir Drohobych Mykolayiv Ternopil' Krasyliv Lityn Pohrebyshche Tetiyiv Zhashkiv Tarashc Ros

SLOVAKIA Košice Michalovce Turka Boryslav Zhydachiv Berezhany Volochys'k △ 362 **Vinnytsya** Illintsi Zvenyhorodka Monastyryshche Tal'ne **UKR**

Trebišov Uzhhorod Svalyava Stryy Kalush Terebovlya **Khmel'nyts'kyy** Bar Zhmerynka Nemyriv Haysyn Teplyk Uman' U'yanov

Hollóháza Mizhhir''ya Dolyna **Ivano-Frankivs'k** Chortkiv Horodok Dunayivtsi Sharhorod Tul'chyn Kryzhopil' Bershad' *Pivdennyy Buh*

Sárospatak Mukacheve Nadvirna Buchach *Dniester (Dnister)* Borshchiv Kam''yanets'-Podil's'kyy Mohyliv-Podil's'kyy Yampil' Kodyma Pervomays'k

Szerencs Kisvárda Berehove Khust Kolomyya Horodenka Zalishchyky Khotyn Sokyryany Ocniţa Soroca Balta Lyubashivka Vradi

Nyíregyháza Vynohradiv Rakhiv Verkhovyna **Chernivtsi** Storozhynets' Briceni Edineţ Floreşti Ananyiv

HUNGARY Hajdúböszörmény Hora Hoverla 2061 Putyla Dorohoi Drochia **Bălţi** Fălești Rîbniţa Kotovs'k Shyryayev Berezi

Debrecen Carei Sighetu Marmaţiei Vişeu de Sus Răduţi Siret Botoşani Hârlău Dealul Mâgura 388 Dubăsari Komintern

2 Hajdúszoboszló **Satu Mare** Acăş Borşa Suceava Fălticeni Paşcani Ungheni **CHIŞINĂU** (Kişinev) **Tiraspol** Rozdil'na **Odes** (Ode

Săcueni Şimleu Silvaniei **Baia Mare** Pietrosa 2305 Vatra Dornei Botoşani Târgu Frumos **Iaşi** Nisporeni Tighina Bilyayivka

Oradea Zalău Dej Bistriţa Pietrosu 2100 Târgu Neamţ **Roman** Vaslui Leova Cimişlia Căuşeni Dnister

Salonta Aleşd Gherla **Cluj-Napoca** Reghin Pasul Bucin 1273 Piatra Neamţ Buhuşi Huşi Comrat Bârlad **Dnistrovs'kyy Lyman** Illichivs'k

Şei Vârful Bihor 1849 Turda Ocna Mureş **Târgu Mureş** Vârful Harghita-Mădaraş 1800 Bacău Moineşti Comăneşti Câdir-Lunga Tarutyne Sarata

Sântana Lipova Aiud Târnăveni Sighişoara Miercurea-Ciuc Oneşti Adjud Mărăşeşti Tecuci Bolhrad Ozero Yalpuh Artsyz Tatarbunary

Hunedoara Alba Iulia Mediaş Agnita Sfântu Gheorghe Focşani Vulcăneşti Cahul Reni Kiliya Vylkove

Deva Sebeş Orăştie Cisnădie **Sibiu** Vârful Moldoveanu 2544 Făgăraş Râşnov Vârful Ciucaş 1954 **Braşov** Mărăşeşti Râmnicu Sărat **Galaţi** Brăila Măcin *Danube Delta*

ROMANIA *Transylvanian Alps* Vârful Moldoveanu Petroşani 1292 Vârful Omu 2505 Râmnic Câmpulung Buzău Ianca **Tulcea** Babadag *Lacul Razim*

Lugoj Caransebeş Bocşa Reşiţa Haţeg Lupeni *Carpaţii Meridionali* Vârful Parângul Mare 2519 Pasul Giuvala Câmpina Buzău Mizil Brăila Măcin Hârşova Baia

45° Vârful Svinecea Mare 1224 Orşova Motru Târgu Jiu Râmnicu Vâlcea Curtea de Argeş Moreni Urlaţi **Ploieşti** Ialomiţa Urziceni Slobozia Ţăndărei Cernavodă **Constanţa**

Vârciorova Strehaia Drăgăşani Costeşti Găeşti Titu Buftea Urziceni Ţăndărei Hârşova Medgidia Basarabi

3 **Drobeta-Turnu Severin** Baia Slatina Bolintin-Vale **Voluntari** Fetești Năvodari

SERBIA Negotin Craiova Balş Drăgăneşti-Olt Videle **BUCHAREST** (Bucureşti) Olteniţa Silistra Călăraşi

Bor Vidin Calafat Băileşti Caracal Roşiori de Vede Vedea Giurgiu Danube (Dunărea) Lom

Zaječar Polana Mare *Danube (Dunărea)* Dăbuleni Alexandria Giurgiu **BULGARIA**

Longitude 25° east of Greenwich

METRES
FEET

METRES	FEET
5000	16404
3000	9843
2000	6562
1000	3281
500	1640
200	656
0	0
Land below sea level	
200	656
4000	13124
6000	19686

234 Suponevo Bryansk Karachev
Mglin Vygonichi Navlya Orel Znamenka Novosil' Khomutovo Verkhov'ye Lebedyan' Dobroye Dmitriyevka Tambov
Surazh Pochep Lokot' Kromy Zmiyevka Izmalkovo Krasnoye Lipetsk Petrovskoye Kotovsk
Unecha Trubchevsk Trosna Glazunovka Livny Dolgorukovo Zadonsk Yelets Gryazi Znamenka Rzhaksa
Klintsy Zheleznogorsk Kolpny Terbuny Khlevnoye Usman' Dobrinka Mordovo Tokarevka
Starodub Pogar Suzemka Dolgoye Semiluki Ramon' Ertil' Zherdevka
Klimovo Semenivka Dmitriyev- Cheremisinovo Shchigry Khokhol'skiy Voronezh Panino Anna Gribanovskiy
Novhorod- L'govskiy Kursk Tim Novovoronezh Buturlinovka
Sivers'kyy Yampil' Shostka Hlukhiv Ryl'sk Korenevo L'gov Kurchatov Gorshechnoye Staryy Oskol Liski Bobrov Talovaya Novokhopersk
Koryukivka Sosnytsya Putyvl' Sudzha Oboyan' Gubkin Chernyanka Nizhniy Kislyay Meshkovskaya
Bakhmach Konotop Buryn' Bilopillya Ivnya Rakitnoye Korocha Ostrogozhsk Losevo Pavlovsk Kalach
Nizhyn Romny Borisovka Belgorod Alekseyevka Novyy Oskol Biryuch Alekseyevka Podgorenskiy Rossosh' Verkhniy Mamon Boguchar
Ichnya Lebedyn Hadyach Shebekino Volokonovka Valuyki Veydelevka Roven'ki Kantemirovka
Pryluky Pyryatyn Lokhvytsya Okhtyrka Zolochiv Vovchans'k Velykyy Burluk Svatove Markivka Milove Chertkovo
Lubny Myrhorod Zin'kiv Bohodukhiv Derhachi Kup"yans'k Novopskov Bilovods'k Degtevo
Khorol Kotel'va Lyubotyn Kharkiv (Khar'kov) Chuhuyiv Kivsharivka Starobil's'k Kreminna Rubizhne Luhans'k Millerovo
Poltava Karliyka Merefa Shevchenkove Izyum Syeyerodonets'k Lysychans'k Kamensk-Shakhtinskiy
Cherkasy Reshetylivka Krasnohrad Pervomays'kyy Barvinkove Slov"yans'k Artemivs'k Stakhanov Krasnodon Gukovo
Smila Chyhyryn Svitlovods'k Komsomol's'k Lozova Kramators'k Druzhkivka Alchevs'k Krasnyy Luch Shakhty
Oleksandriya Dniprodzerzhyns'k Novomoskovs'k Pavlohrad Kostyantynivka Dzerzhyns'k Horlivka Donets'k Novoshakhtinsk
Dnipropetrovs'k Pershotravens'k Dymytrov Makiyivka Krasnyy Luch Kamenolomni
Kryvyy Rih Zhovti Vody P"yatykhatky Vil'nohirs'k Synel'nykove Krasnoarmiys'k Avdiyivka Novocherkassk
Zaporizhzhya Ordzhonikidze Marhanets' Orikhiv Volnovakha Matveyev Kurgan Rostov-na-Donu Aksay Bataysk
Novyy Buh Shyroke Apostolove Enerhodar Vasylivka Polohy Kuybysheve Pokrovskoye Taganrog Azov Kugey
Nikopol' Dniprorudne Tokmak Smyrnove Volodars'ke Novoazovs'k Gulf of Taganrog Yeysk
Mykolayiv Beryslav Nyzhni Sirohozy Melitopol' Prymors'k Berdyans'k Mariupol' Shabel'skoye Zernograd
Kherson Kakhovka Yakymivka Pryazovs'ke Dolgaya Kosa Staroshcherbinovskaya Starominskaya Yegorlykskaya
Nova Kakhovka Syvas'ke Kamyshevatskaya Leningradskaya Kanevskaya Krylovskaya Pavlovskaya

Sea of Azov

BLACK SEA

© Collins Bartholomew Ltd

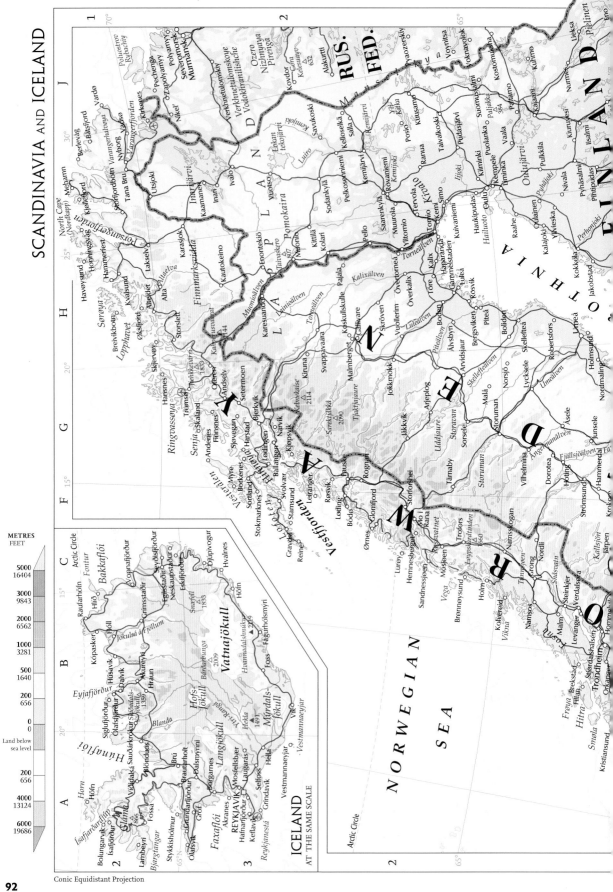

Conic Equidistant Projection

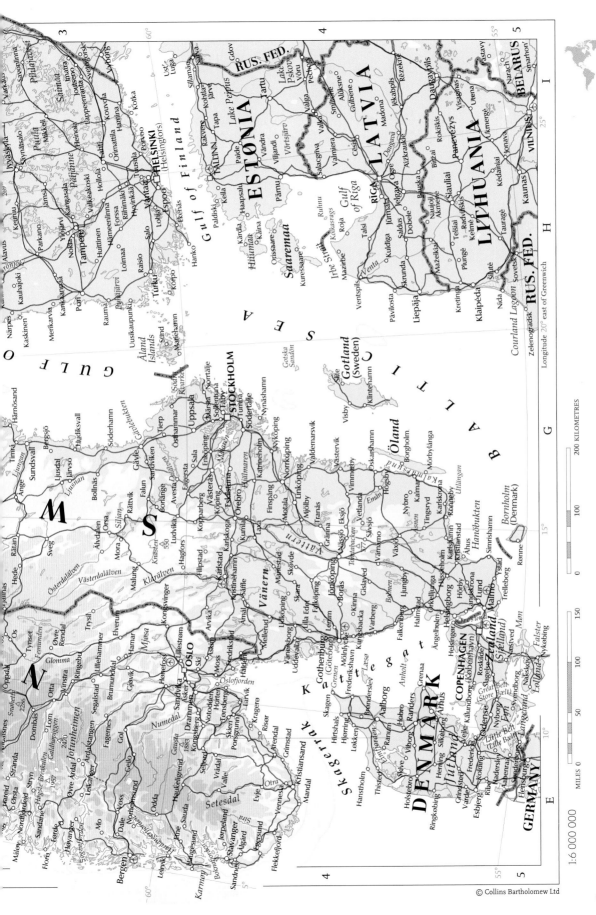

© Collins Bartholomew Ltd

1:6 000 000

MILES 0

KILOMETRES

Longitude 20° east of Greenwich

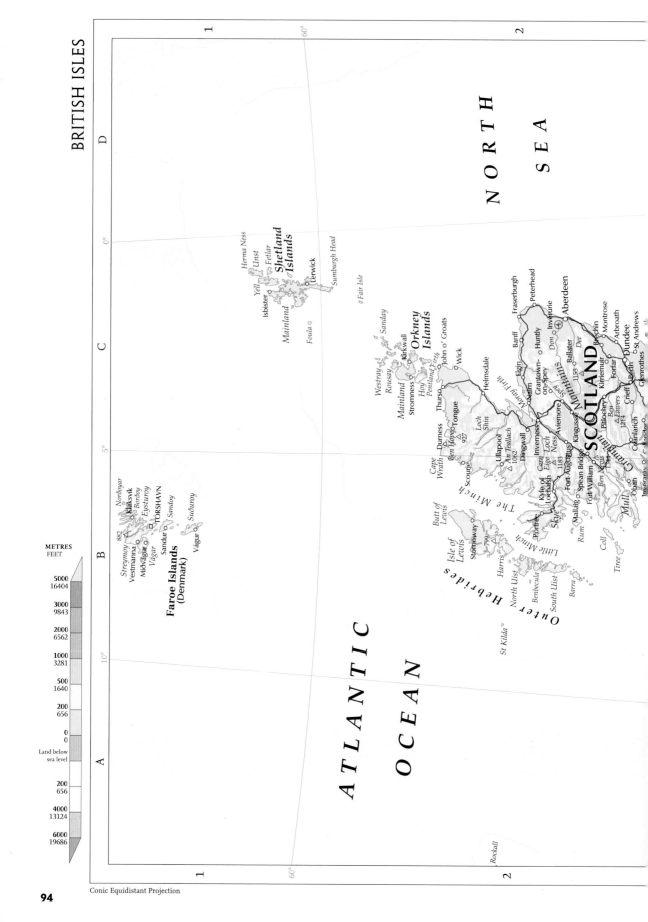

Conic Equidistant Projection

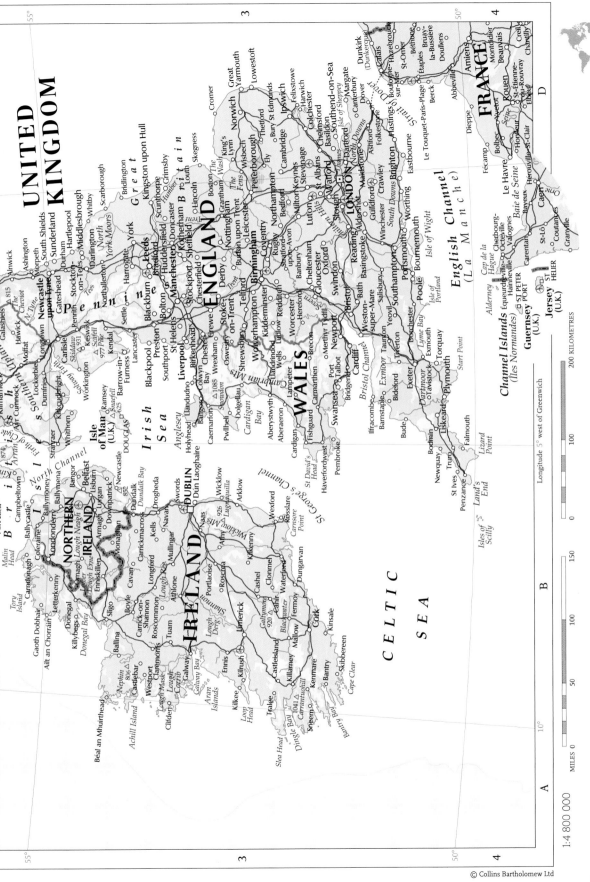

UNITED KINGDOM

FRANCE

IRELAND

NORTHERN IRELAND

ENGLAND

WALES

CELTIC SEA

British Isles

Southern Uplands

P e n n i n e s

G r e a t B r i t a i n

Irish Sea

North Channel

St George's Channel

English Channel (La Manche)

Channel Islands (Îles Normandes)

Guernsey (U.K.)
Jersey (U.K.)
ST PETER PORT
ST HELIER

Coldstream
Galashiels
Hawick
Moffat
Kilmarnock
Ayr
Cumnock
Lockerbie
Dumfries
Longtown
Carlisle
Penrith
Workington
Keswick
Skiddaw 931
Sca Fell 977
Kendal
Barrow-in-Furness
Lancaster
Preston
Blackburn
Blackpool
Southport
Bolton
Settle
Harrogate
Leeds
Bradford
Huddersfield
Manchester
St Helens
Liverpool
Birkenhead
Chester
Crewe
Stoke-on-Trent
Sheffield
Rotherham
Chesterfield
Derby
Nottingham
Newark-on-Trent
Grantham
Leicester
Burton upon Trent
Coventry
Rugby
Birmingham
Kidderminster
Redditch
Stratford-upon-Avon
Banbury
Worcester
Hereford
Gloucester
Cheltenham
Swindon
Oxford
Reading
Bath
Bristol
Weston-super-Mare
Newport
Cardiff
Swansea
Port Talbot
Bridgend
Llanelli
Carmarthen
Haverfordwest
Pembroke
St David's Head
Fishguard
Cardigan
Aberaeron
Aberystwyth
Dolgellau
Barmouth
Pwllheli
Caernarfon
Bangor
Holyhead
Llandudno
Colwyn Bay
Wrexham
Oswestry
Shrewsbury
Telford
Wolverhampton
Dudley

Alnwick
Ashington
Morpeth
Newcastle upon Tyne
Gateshead
South Shields
Sunderland
Hartlepool
Stockton-on-Tees
Middlesbrough
Darlington
Durham
Whitby
Scarborough
Bridlington
York
Northallerton
Thirsk
Kingston upon Hull
Grimsby
Scunthorpe
Doncaster
Lincoln
Louth
Skegness
Boston
Spalding
Peterborough
King's Lynn
Wisbech
Ely
Cambridge
Bedford
Milton Keynes
Luton
Stevenage
St Albans
Watford
Slough
LONDON
Aldershot
Guildford
Crawley
Brighton
Worthing
Eastbourne
Hastings
Maidstone
Chatham
Dartford
Canterbury
Dover
Folkestone
Ashford
Isle of Sheppey
Margate
Southend-on-Sea
Basildon
Chelmsford
Colchester
Harwich
Felixstowe
Ipswich
Bury St Edmunds
Thetford
Norwich
Great Yarmouth
Lowestoft
Cromer

The Wash
North York Moors
The Fens
North Downs
South Downs

Winchester
Basingstoke
Salisbury
Southampton
Portsmouth
Isle of Wight
Bournemouth
Poole
Dorchester
Weymouth
Isle of Portland
Exmouth
Exeter
Torquay
Paignton
Teignmouth
Dartmouth
Start Point
Plymouth
Liskeard
Bodmin
Truro
Newquay
Penzance
St Ives
Land's End
Lizard Point
Falmouth
Isles of Scilly

Lyme Bay
Dartmoor
Exmoor
Bristol Channel

Ilfracombe
Barnstaple
Bideford
Bude
Taunton
Yeovil
Tiverton
Tavistock

Cheviot Hills
Mt Turn
The Cheviot 815

Dunkirk (Dunkerque)
Calais
Boulogne-sur-Mer
Étaples
Le Touquet-Paris-Plage
Berck
Abbeville
Dieppe
Fécamp
Le Havre
Honfleur
Caen
Bayeux
St-Lô
Coutances
Granville
Carentan
Valognes
Cherbourg-Octeville
Octeville
Barfleur
Équeurdreville-Hainneville
Cap de la Hague
Alderney
Bolbec
Rouen
Les Andelys
Heuville-St-Clair
Baie de Seine
Seine
Orne
St-Omer
Hazebrouck
Béthune
Bruay-la-Bussière
Doullens
Amiens
St-Étienne-du-Rouvray
Elbeuf
Montdidier
Beauvais
Creil
Chantilly

Strait of Dover

Stranraer
Port Ellen
Arran 874
Campbeltown
Ballycastle
Ballymoney
Ballymena
Coleraine
Londonderry
Omagh
Strabane
Letterkenny
Enniskillen
Armagh
Lurgan
Craigavon
Lisburn
Belfast
Bangor
Newtownards
Downpatrick
Newcastle
Newry
Dundalk
Drogheda
Swords
DUBLIN
Dún Laoghaire
Wicklow
Arklow
Wexford
Rosslare
Carnsore Point

Lough Neagh
Upper Lough Erne
Lower Lough Erne
Lough Ree
Lough Allen
Lough Derg
Lough Corrib
Lough Mask
Dundalk Bay
Wicklow Mts
Lugnaquilla 926

Malin Head
Carndonagh
Gaoth Dobhair
Ailt an Chorráin
Killybegs
Donegal
Ballybofey
Tory Island
Ballina
Westport
Castlebar
Nephin 806
Achill Island
Béal an Mhuirthead
Claremorris
Castlerea
Roscommon
Carrick-on-Shannon
Longford
Mullingar
Athlone
Tullamore
Kells
Navan
Cavan
Monaghan
Carrickmacross
Boyle
Sligo
Tuam
Galway
Ennis
Kilrush
Kilkee
Loop Head
Tralee
Castleisland
Killarney
Kenmare
Sneem
Bantry
Skibbereen
Cape Clear
Kinsale
Cork
Mallow
Fermoy
Cahir
Clonmel
Cashel
Thurles
Roscrea
Portlaoise
Athy
Kildare
Naas
Kilkenny
Carlow
Waterford
Dungarvan
Youghal
Limerick
Galway Bay
Aran Islands
Clifden
Lough Corrib
Lough Mask
Galway Bay
Dingle Bay
Slea Head
Bantry Bay
Carrauntoohil 1041
Blackwater
Shannon
Suir

Isle of Man (U.K.)
Ramsey
DOUGLAS
Snaefell 625

Firth of Clyde
Solway Firth

1:4 800 000

Longitude 5° west of Greenwich

MILES 0   50   100   150

0   100   200 KILOMETRES

© Collins Bartholomew Ltd

95

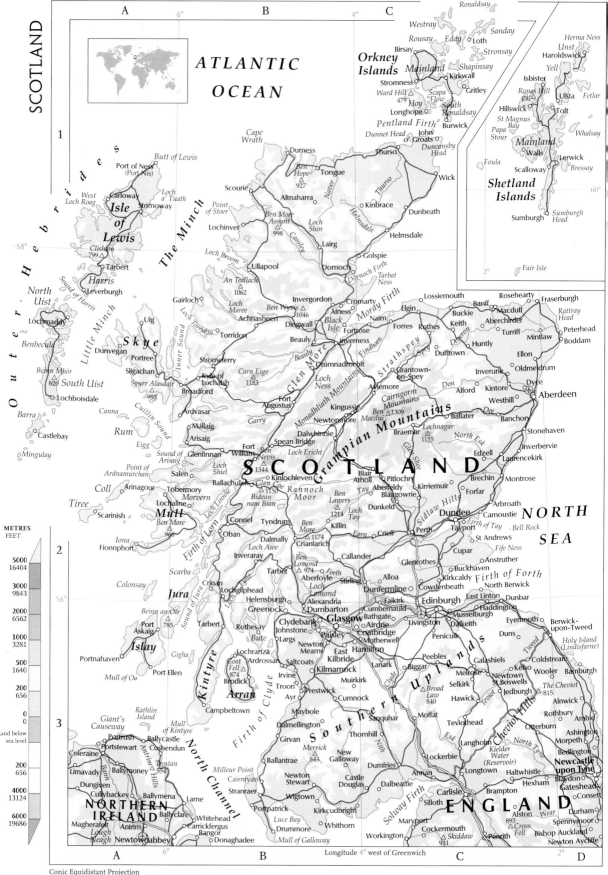

Conic Equidistant Projection

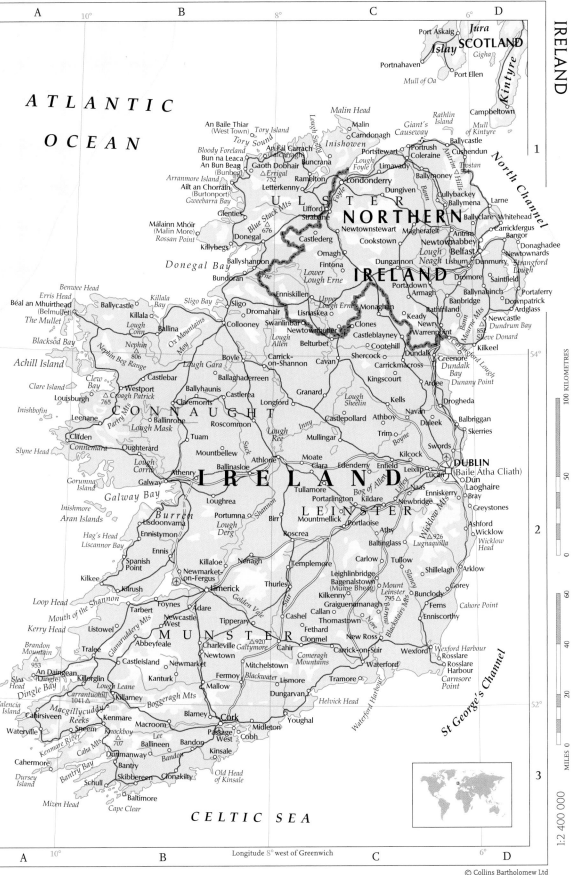

ATLANTIC

OCEAN

SCOTLAND

Port Askaig
Jura
Portnahaven
Islay
Gigha
Mull of Oa
Port Ellen

Kintyre

North Channel

Campbeltown

Malin Head
Malin
Giant's Causeway
Carndonagh
Inishowen
Rathlin Island
Mull of Kintyre
Ballycastle

An Baile Thiar
(West Town) *Tory Island*
Tory Sound
An Fál Carrach
(Falcarragh)
Gaoth Dobhair
Buncrana
Portstewart
Portrush
Coleraine
Cushendun

Bloody Foreland
Bun na Leaca
An Bun Beag
(Bunbeg)
△ Errigal
752
Ramelton
Lough Foyle
Limavady
Ballymoney
Antrim Hills
△ Trostan
554

Arranmore Island
Ailt an Chorráin
(Burtonport)
Gweebarra Bay
Letterkenny
Londonderry
Dungiven
Cullybackey
Ballymena
Larne

Lifford
Strabane
U L S T E R
NORTHERN
Newtownstewart
Magherafelt
Antrim
Ballyclare
Whitehead
Carrickfergus
Bangor

Málainn Mhóir
(Malin More)
Rossan Point
Glenties
Blue Stack Mts
△ 676
Castlederg
Cookstown
Newtownabbey
Donaghadee
Newtownards

Killybegs
Donegal
Omagh
IRELAND
Dungannon
Lough Neagh
Belfast
Lisburn
Dunmurry
Strangford Lough

Donegal Bay
Ballyshannon
Bundoran
Fintona
Portadown
Armagh
Dromore
Saintfield
Portaferry

Erne
Lower Lough Erne
Enniskillen
Upper Lough Erne
Monaghan
Keady
Banbridge
Ballynahinch
Downpatrick
Ardglass

Killala Bay
Sligo Bay
Sligo
Dromahair
Lisnaskea
Swanlinbar
Newtownbutler
Clones
Castleblayney
Newry
Warrenpoint
Newcastle
Dundrum Bay
△ Slieve Donard 852

Benwee Head
Erris Head
Béal an Mhuirthead
(Belmullet)
The Mullet
Ballycastle
Killala
Ballina
Colloney
Lough Allen
Belturbet
Cootehill
Dundalk
Kilkeel
Greenore
Carlingford Lough
Mourne Mts

Blacksod Bay
Lough Conn
Nephin △ 806
Ox Mountains
Moy
Boyle
Carrick-on-Shannon
Cavan
Shercock
Carrickmacross
Dundalk Bay
Dunany Point

Achill Island
Clare Island
Clew Bay
△ Croagh Patrick 765
Westport
Castlebar
Lough Gara
Ballaghaderreen
Lough Sheelin
Kingscourt
Ardee
Drogheda

Inishbofin
Louisburgh
Leenane
Ballinrobe
Claremorris
Castlerea
Longford
Granard
Kells
Navan
Duleek
Balbriggan
Skerries

Slyne Head
Clifden
C O N N A U G H T
Lough Mask
Tuam
Roscommon
Inny
Castlepollard
Athboy
Trim
Boyne
Swords

Connemara
Oughterard
Lough Corrib
Ballinasloe
Lough Ree
Mullingar
Kilcock
Leixlip
Lucan
DUBLIN
(Baile Átha Cliath)

Gorumna Island
Athenry
Ballinasloe
Athlone
Moate
Clara
Edenderry
Enfield
Naas
Newbridge
Enniskerry
Dún Laoghaire
Bray

Galway Bay
Galway
Loughrea
I R E L A N D
Tullamore
Portarlington
Kildare
Bog of Allen
Greystones

Inishmore
Aran Islands
Lisdoonvarna
Burren
Portumna
Lough Derg
Birr
Mountmellick
Portlaoise
L E I N S T E R
Athy
Wicklow Mts
△ 926
Ashford
Wicklow
Wicklow Head

Hag's Head
Liscannor Bay
Ennistymon
Ennis
Shannon
Roscrea
Baltinglass
Lugnaquilla
Carlow
Tullow
Shillelagh
Arklow

Loop Head
Kilkee
Spanish Point
Killaloe
Newmarket-on-Fergus
Nenagh
Templemore
Thurles
Leighlinbridge
Bagenalstown
(Muine Bheag)
Kilkenny
Graiguenamanagh
Mount Leinster 795 △
Blackstairs Mts
Bunclody
Gorey

Kilrush
Mouth of the Shannon
Tarbert
Foynes
Adare
Limerick
Golden Vale
Cashel
Callan
Thomastown
Nore
Ferns
Enniscorthy
Cahore Point

Kerry Head
Listowel
Newcastle West
Tipperary
Suir
Clonmel
Fethard
New Ross
Wexford
Wexford Harbour
Rosslare

Brandon Mountain △ 953
Tralee
Abbeyfeale
M U N S T E R
△ Galtymore 920
Cahir
Comeragh Mountains
Carrick-on-Suir
Waterford
Waterford Harbour
Rosslare Harbour

Slea Head
An Daingean
(Dingle)
Dingle Bay
Killorglin
Castleisland
Newmarket
Charleville
Newtown
Mitchelstown
Blackwater
Lismore
Tramore
Carnsore Point

Valencia Island
Cahirsiveen
Carrantuohill
1041 △
Macgillycuddy's Reeks
Lough Leane
Killarney
Kanturk
Fermoy
Mallow
Dungarvan
Helvick Head

Waterville
Sneem
Kenmare
Kenmare River
Macroom
Boggeragh Mts
Caha Mts
Blarney
Lee
Cork
Midleton
Youghal

Cahermore
△ Knockboy 707
Dunmanway
Bandon
Ballineen
Passage West
Cobh
Kinsale

Dursey Island
Bantry Bay
Bantry
Skibbereen
Clonakilty
Old Head of Kinsale

Schull
Baltimore
Mizen Head
Cape Clear

C E L T I C   S E A

St George's Channel

1:2 400 000

100 KILOMETRES
50
0

MILES
60
40
20
0

54°

52°

Longitude 8° west of Greenwich

© Collins Bartholomew Ltd

97

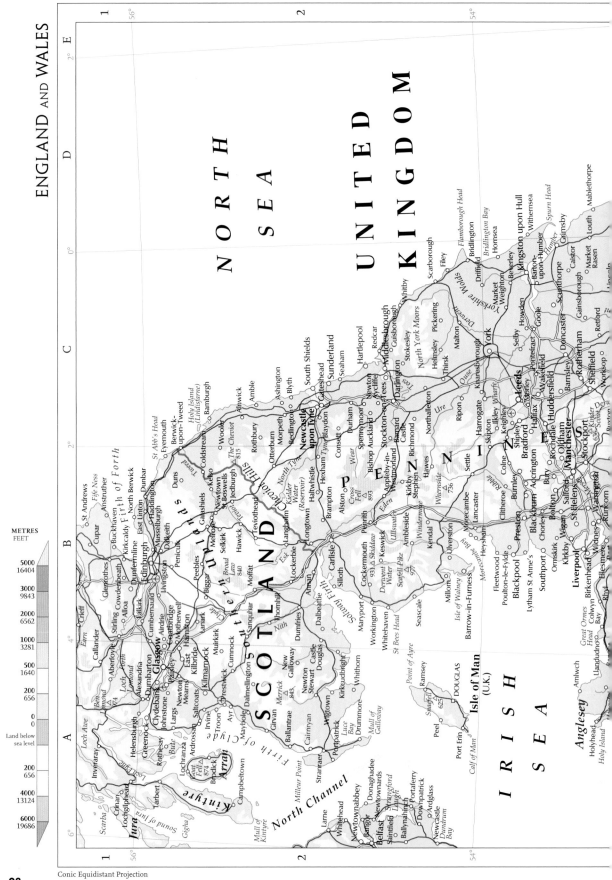

N O R T H   S E A

U N I T E D

K I N G D O M

S C O T L A N D

Southern Uplands

Cheviot Hills

P E N N I N E S

I R I S H

S E A

North Channel

Firth of Forth

Isle of Man
(U.K.)

METRES
FEET

5000	16404
3000	9843
2000	6562
1000	3281
500	1640
200	656
0	0
Land below sea level	
200	656
4000	13124
6000	19686

98

Conic Equidistant Projection

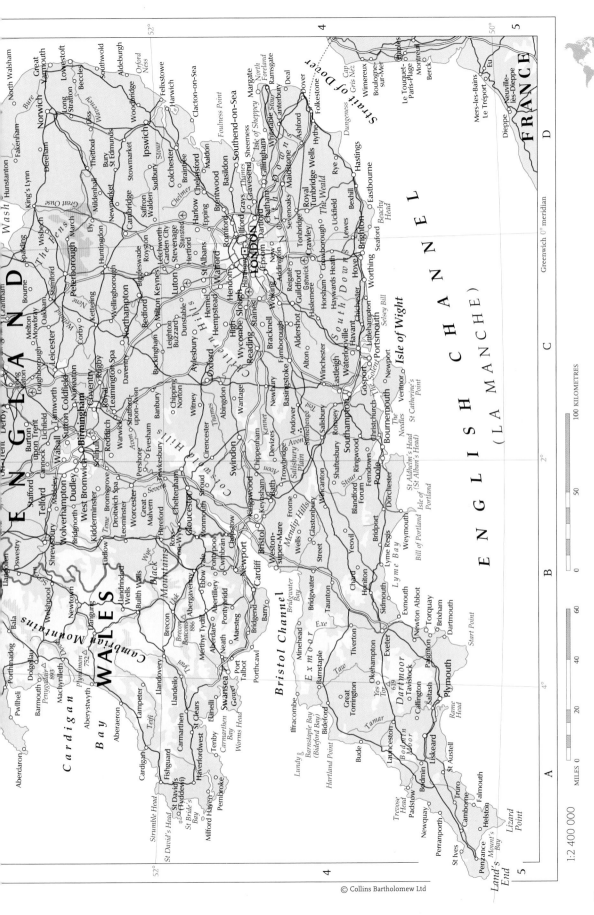

A   4°   B   6°   C

NORTH SEA

East Frisian Islands

Spiekeroog *Langeoog*
Norderney *Lang...*
Juist Norderney
Borkum Norden Westerholt

The Wadden Sea
Uithuizen Hinte Aurich
OSTFRIESL...

West Frisian Islands

West-Terschelling
Oost-Vlieland *Terschelling*
Schiermonnikoog *Ameland*
Hollum
Lauwersmeer Eenrum
Vlieland Burdaard Ferwert Dokkum Bedum Delfzijl Emden Leer West...
Oenkerk Kollum Appingedam Strücklingen (Saterland)
Texel Harlingen Witmarsum Franeker Leeuwarden Hoogezand- Groningen Winschoten Papent...
Den Burg Bolsward Reduzum Sappemeer Veendam Walchum
Marsdiep Sneek Drachten Assen Stadskanaal Sustrum Fries...
Wieringerwerf Sloten Heerenveen Beilen Emmen Haren (Ems) Löning...
Den Helder *IJsselmeer* Wolvega Steenwijk Hoogeveen Coevorden Groß-Hesepe Meppen Lingen (Ems) Fürs...
Schagen Creil Meppel Hardenberg
Nieuwe-Nedorp Enkhuizen Urk Emmeloord Kraggenburg Kloosterhaar
Heerhugowaard Hoorn Kampen Ommen Vriezenveen Almelo Nordhorn
Bergen Berkhout *Markermeer* Lelystad Dronten Zwolle Raalte Gronau (Westfalen) Ibbe...
Alkmaar Purmerend Heerde Nijverdal Borne Rheine
Castricum **NETHERLANDS** Hengelo Oldenzaal Emsdetten
Beverwijk Zaandam Naarden Nijkerk Deventer Enschede Steinfurt Greven...
IJmuiden AMSTERDAM Heerde Apeldoorn Eibergen Ahaus
Zandvoort Amstelveen Driemond Harderwijk *Torenberg* 107△ Zutphen Winterswijk Coesfeld Havixbeck
Haarlem Hilversum Amersfoort Barneveld Doesburg Hoog- Keppel Velen Dülmen
Hillegom Maarssen Utrecht Ede Arnhem Doetinchem Borken
Noordwijk-Binnen Leiden Waddinxveen Veenendaal Zevenaar Bocholt **MÜNSTERLAND**
Katwijk aan Zee Alphen aan den Rijn Nieuwegein Wageningen Andelst (Rhein) Kleve Goch Wesel Dorsten Marl Recklinghausen
THE HAGUE ('s-Gravenhage) (Den Haag) Gouda Nieuwegein Tiel Nijmegen Hoog Mark Gelsenkirchen Herne Lün...
Hook of Holland (Hoek van Holland) Delft Rotterdam Schoonhoven *Waal* 's-Hertogenbosch Wijchen Kevelaer Dinslaken **Duisburg** Bottrop **Essen** Bochum **Dort...**
Vlaardingen Capelle aan de IJssel Culemborg *Maas* Waalwijk Uden Erp St Anthonis Venray Krefeld Moers Mülheim an der Ruhr Hattingen Hagen Ise...
Hellevoetsluis Spijkenisse Gorinchem Tilburg Boxtel Deurne Asten Venlo Ratingen **Düsseldorf** **Wuppertal** Piet...
Scharendijke Dordrecht Oosterhout Best Helmond **Mönchengladbach** Hilden Lüdenscheid
Burgh-Haamstede Zierikzee Zevenbergen Waalwijk Eindhoven Valkenswaard Roermond Wegberg Neuss Remscheid Solingen Att...
Westkapelle Middelburg Roosendaal Breda Etten-Leur Veldhoven Weert Herkenbosch Dormagen Gummers...
Koudekerke Halsteren Best Lommel Maaseik Grevenbroich **Leverkusen**
Vlissingen Hoogerheide Bergen op Zoom Brecht Geel Hechtel Sittard Bergheim (Erft) Bergisch Gladbach
Knokke-Heist Breskens Zandvliet Westmalle Lier Bocholt Weert Genk Hückelhoven Heerlen **Cologne (Köln)**
Blankenberge Sluis Kapellen Lille Lommel Diest Heerlen Eschweiler Kerpen Frechen Troisdorf
Zeebrugge St-Laurins Maldegem St-Niklaas Antwerp (Antwerpen) (Anvers) Willebroek Mechelen Aarschot Hasselt Sittard Maastricht Mechelen Aachen Düren Kerpen Bonn Hennef (Sieg) Sankt Augustin Altm...
Ostend (Oostende) Meetkerke Eeklo Evergem Schaerbeek Leuven Tienen Tongeren Oupeye Liège Raeren Stolberg (Rheinland) Kreuzau Zülpich Königswinter Meckenheim (Weste)
Nieuwpoort Zedelgem Brugge (Bruges) Wingene Deinze Dendermonde Ghent (Gent) Wichelen Aalst **BRUSSELS** (Bruxelles) Borgloon Verviers Mechernich Kallo Bad Neuenahr-Ahrweiler Neuwied
Veurne Torhout Tielt Anderlecht Uccle Halle Waterloo Nivelles Ottignies Eghezée Huy Andenne Spa Malmédy Blankenheim Adenau Mayen Koblenz
Diksmuide Roeselare Zulte Oudenaarde Ronse Ath Soignies Fleurus Namur Assesse Ciney Durbuy Vielsalm St-Vith Dahlem Hillesheim Cochem Emmels...
Ieper Kortrijk Menen Roubaix **BELGIUM** La Louvière Charleroi Montigny-le-Tilleul Marche-en-Famenne Holz Prüm Gerolstein Daun Mosel
Lille Mouscron Tournai Péruwelz Bossu Mons Thuin Châtelet Hastière-Lavaux Dinant Rochefort La Roche-en-Ardenne Houffalize Bastogne Arzfeld Mandersheid Blankenrath Simm... (Hun...
Villeneuve-d'Ascq Lens Soignies Fleurus Assesse Marche-en-Famenne Thommen St-Hubert Clervaux Neuerburg Wittlich Bernkastel-Kues am Hun...
Lens Douai Maubeuge Beaumont Philippeville Couvin Beauraing Libin Libramont **LUXEMBOURG** Wiltz Neuerburg Bitburg Salmtal Bad Kreuzn...
Valenciennes Aulnoye-Aymeries Avesnes-sur-Helpe La Capelle Hirson Rocroi Montherme Bièvre Paliseul Bouillon Neufchâteau Redange Mersch Echternach Kenn Morbach Bad Kreuzn...
Cambrai Caudry Bohain-en-Vermandois La Capelle Couvin Fumay Bogny-sur-Meuse Vresse Libramont Arlon Ettelbruck Bad Bad Kreuz...
Péronne Guise Vervins Marle Rozoy-sur-Serre Charleville-Mézières Sedan Carignan Virton LUXEMBOURG Mersch Konz Trier *Erbeskopf* 818△ Idar-Oberstein Donne...
St-Quentin Chauny Tergnier Montcornet Signy-l'Abbaye △316 Méziers Omont Mouzon Arlon Pétange Redange Reinsfeld Nohfelden
Noyon Laon Rethel Bièvre Stenay Longuyon LUXEMBOURG Esch-sur-Alzette Mettlach Merzig St Wendel Wolfste...
Attichy Soissons **FRANCE** Vouziers Dun-sur-Meuse Spincourt Hayange Orange Thionville Konz Neunkirchen Kaisers...
Courmelles Fismes Guignicourt Bétheny Consenvoye Longuyon Rombas Saarlouis Homburg
Villers-Cotterêts Tinqueux Reims Aisne

Conic Equidistant Projection

A   4°   B   Longitude 6° east of Greenwich   C

METRES / FEET

METRES	FEET
5000	16404
3000	9843
2000	6562
1000	3281
500	1640
200	656
0	0

Land below sea level

200	656
4000	13124
6000	19686

Waddenzee
Westerschelde
Oosterschelde
Albert Kanaal
Leie
Schelde
Dender
Oise
Serre
Meuse
Ourthe
Venn
Eifel
Hohe Venn
Rhine (Rhein)
Sûre
Our
Kyll
Mosel

© Collins Bartholomew Ltd

METRES
FEET

5000
16404

3000
9843

2000
6562

1000
3281

500
1640

200
656

0
0

Land below
sea level

200
656

4000
13124

6000
19686

Conic Equidistant Projection

© Collins Bartholomew Ltd

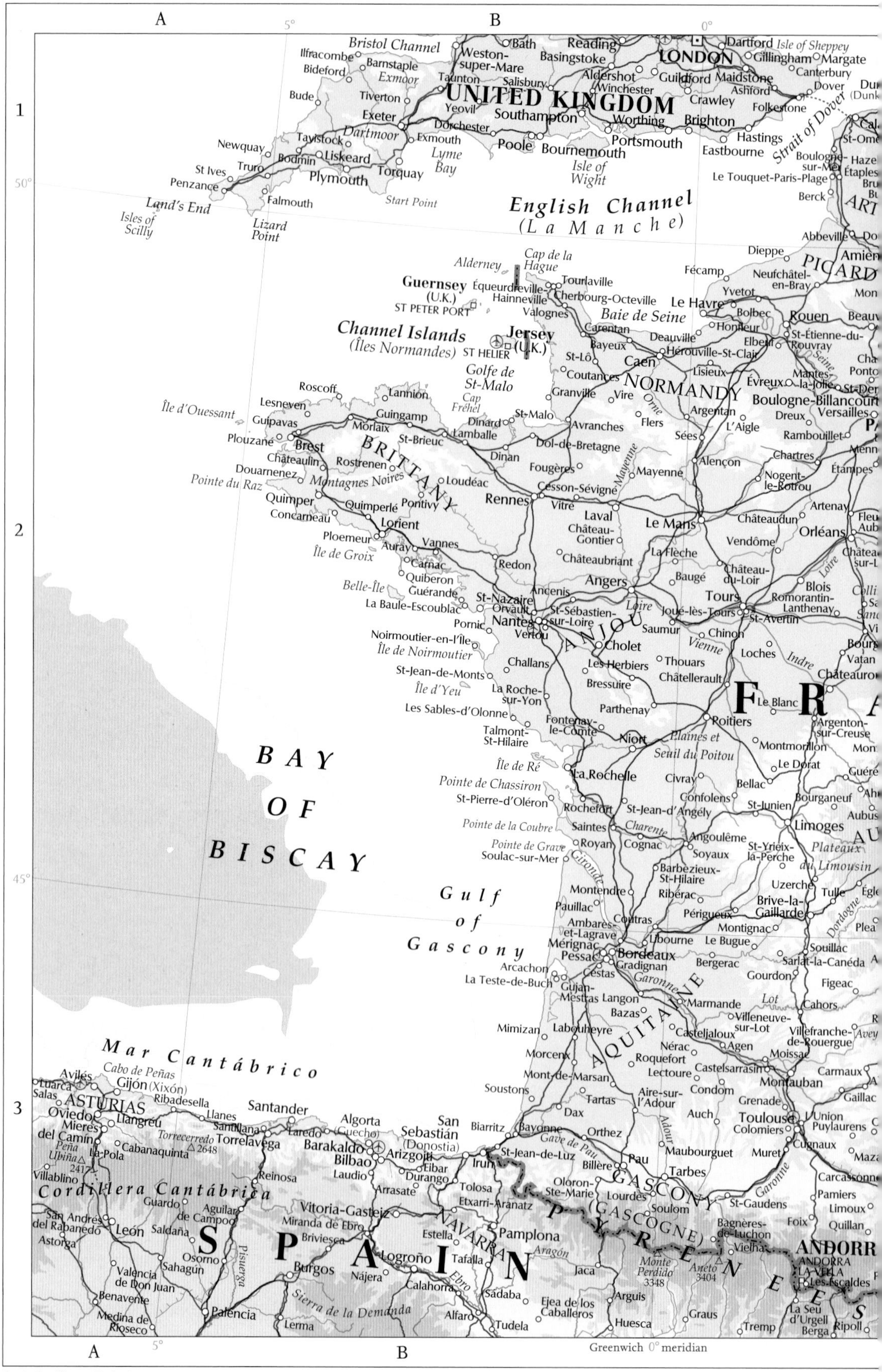

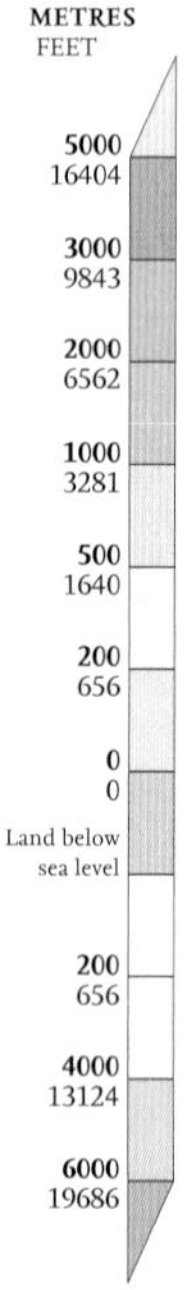

METRES
FEET

5000	16404
3000	9843
2000	6562
1000	3281
500	1640
200	656
0	0

Land below
sea level

200	656
4000	13124
6000	19686

Greenwich 0° meridian

Conic Equidistant Projection

MEDITERRANEAN SEA

1:4 800 000

200 KILOMETRES

100

0

MILES 0

50

100

150

ATLANTIC OCEAN

Mar Cantábrico

GALICIA

ASTURIAS

Cordillera Cantábrica

CASTILLA Y LEÓN

PORTUGAL

SPAIN

CASTILLA-LA MANCHA

EXTREMADURA

Sierra de Gredos

Sierra de Guadarrama

Sierra de Guadalupe

Montes de Toledo

MADRID

ALGARVE

ANDALUCÍA

Sierra Morena

Sierra Nevada

Gibraltar (U.K.)

Golfo de Cádiz

Costa del Sol

Costa de la Luz

Strait of Gibraltar

MOROCCO

Alboran Sea

Cabo Ortegal, Punta de Estaca de Bares, Cervo, Ortigueira, Viveiro, Ribadeo, Luarca, Avilés, Cabo de Peñas, Gijón (Xixón), Ribadesella, Santander, Laredo

A Coruña, Ferrol, Gándara, Salas, Oviedo, Mieres, La Pola Siero, Llanes, Santillana, Torrelavega, Barakaldo, Bilbao

Santiago de Compostela, Betanzos, Ordes, Melide, Lugo, Cangas del Narcea, Villablino, Cabanaquinta, Reinosa, Laudio, Vitoria-Gasteiz

Cape Finisterre (Cabo Fisterra), Vilagarcía de Arousa, Santa Uxía de Ribeira, A Estrada, Lalín, Chantada, Becerreá, Sarria, Ponferrada, León, Astorga, Guardo, Aguilar de Campóo, Osorno, Miranda de Ebro, Briviesca, Burgos

Pontevedra, Marín, Cangas, Redondela, Vigo, Ourense, Monforte de Lemos, Xinzo de Limia, Barco, Truchas, El Teleno, San Andrés del Rabanedo, Valencia de Don Juan, Sahagún, Palencia, Nájera, Logroño

Tui, Fondevila, Verín, Sierra de la Cabrera, Benavente, Medina de Rioseco, Valladolid, Lerma, Aranda de Duero, Ayllón

Viana do Castelo, Braga, Guimarães, Chaves, Bragança, Macedo de Cavaleiros, Zamora, Toro, Tordesillas, Cuéllar, Cerezo de Abajo

Póvoa de Varzim, Maia, Vila Real, Mirandela, Duero, Olmedo, Segovia

Matosinhos, Oporto, Porto, Torre de Moncorvo, Fermoselle, Embalse de Almendra, Ledesma, Medina del Campo, Arévalo, Peñaranda de Bracamonte, Peñalara

Vila Nova de Gaia, Pedroso, Lamego, Meda, Vilar Formoso, Salamanca, Lumbrales, Ciudad Rodrigo, Nuñomoral, Ávila, Alcalá de Henares, Guadalajara, Sigüenza

Ovar, São João da Madeira, Viseu, Mangualde, Aveiro, Ílhavo, Águeda, Guarda, Sabugal, Béjar, Móstoles, Fuenlabrada, Parla, Getafe

Mealhada, Coimbra, Torre, Serra da Estrela, Covilhã, Fundão, Plasencia, Navalmoral de la Mata, Valle del Tiétar, Torrijos, Aranjuez, Ocaña, Tarancón

Figueira da Foz, Lousã, Marinha Grande, Leiria, Pombal, Castelo Branco, Coria, Alcántara, Talavera de la Reina, Toledo

Batalha, Tomar, Cáceres, Trujillo, Embalse de Valdecañas, Sierra de Guadalupe, Madridejos, Alcázar de San Juan

Caldas da Rainha, Peniche, Torres Novas, Abrantes, Ponte de Sor, Portalegre, Herrera del Duque, Herrera del Duque, Ciudad Real, Daimiel, Manzanares, Valdepeñas, Villanueva de los Infantes

Torres Vedras, Santarém, Entroncamento, Campo Maior, Miajadas, Navalvillar de Pela, Almadén, Puertollano

Vila Franca de Xira, Coruche, Elvas, Montijo, Mérida, Don Benito, Villanueva de la Serena, Cabeza del Buey, Hinojosa del Duque, Los Pedroches, Pozoblanco

Amadora, LISBON, Cacém, Estremoz, Redondo, Badajoz, Olivenza, Almendralejo, Peñarroya-Pueblonuevo, Azuaga, Linares, Úbeda

Cascais, Almada, Montijo, Évora, Zafra, Fregenal de la Sierra, Constantina, Andújar, Baeza, Jaén

Cabo Espichel, Setúbal, Alcácer do Sal, Barragem de Alqueva, Torrão, Amareleja, Moura, Rosal de la Frontera, Palma del Río, Córdoba, Martos, Cabra, Alcaudete, Priego de Córdoba, Guadix

Baía de Setúbal, Grândola, Beja, Serpa, Cortegana, Valverde del Camino, Écija, Montilla, Lucena, Puente Genil, Loja

Sines, Cabo de Sines, Aljustrel, Castro Verde, Mértola, Odemira, Almodôvar, Almonte, Coria del Río, Utrera, Carmona, Marchena, Osuna, Antequera, Vélez-Málaga, Motril

Aljezur, ALGARVE, Portimão, Loulé, Huelva, Seville (Sevilla), Morón de la Frontera, Granada, Mulhacén

Cabo de São Vicente, Lagos, Albufeira, Olhão, Tavira, Ayamonte, Almonte, Lebrija, Arcos de la Frontera, Ronda, Málaga, Almuñécar, Adra

Sagres, Cabo de Faro Santa Maria, Playa de Castilla, Sanlúcar de Barrameda, El Puerto de Santa María, Jerez de la Frontera, Marbella, Estepona, Torremolinos

Cádiz, San Fernando, Chiclana de la Frontera, Vejer de la Frontera, Barbate, Algeciras, La Línea de la Concepción, Cabo de Trafalgar, Pta Almina, Ceuta (Spain), Cabo Negro, Cap des Trois Fourches, I. de Alborán

Tangier (Tánger), Asilah, Tétouan

METRES / FEET

METRES	FEET
5000	16404
3000	9843
2000	6562
1000	3281
500	1640
200	656
0	0
Land below sea level	
200	656
4000	13124
6000	19686

A 10°   B   5°

Conic Equidistant Projection

Gulf of Gascony

Arcachon
La Teste-de-Buch
Gujan-Mestras
Mimizan
Morcenx
Soustons
Biarritz
Irun
San
Sebastián
(Donostia)
Etxarri-Aranatz
Pamplona

NAVARRA

Tafalla
Sádaba
Alfaro
Tarazona
Alagón
Calatayud
Daroca
Molina
de Aragón
Perales
del Alfambra

Gradignan
Langon
Bazas
Labouheyre
Roquefort
Mont-de-Marsan
Dax
Orthez
Oloron-
Ste-Marie
Lourdes
Soulom
Jaca
Arguis
Huesca

Figeac
Marvejols
Espalion
Cahors
Villefranche-
de-Rouergue Rodez
Villeneuve-sur-Lot
Agen
Moissac
Montauban
Albi
Carmaux
Gaillac
Toulouse
Castres
Colomiers
Cugnaux
Muret
Pamiers
Carcassonne
Quillan
Foix

FRANCE

AQUITAINE

Marmande
Nérac
Castelsarrasin
Condom
Lectoure
Auch

Bayonne
Aire-sur-
Adour
Tartas
Pau
Billère
Tarbes
Bagnères-
de-Luchon
Vielha
St-Gaudens

GASCONY
(GASCOGNE)

P Y R E N E E S

ANDORRA
ANDORRA
LA VELLA
Les Escaldes
La Seu
d'Urgell
Tremp
Berga
Ripoll
Olot
Torelló
Vic
Salt
Girona

Mende
Les Vans
Pierrelatte
Valréas
Nyons
Bollène
Orange
Sisteron
Digne-
les-Bains
Florac
Bagnols-
sur-Cèze
Carpentras
Uzès
Avignon
Cavaillon
Manosque
Nîmes
Salon-de-
Provence
Pertuis
Draguignan
Arles
Istres
Aix-en-
Provence
Aubagne
Brignoles
Fréjus
Marseille
Toulon
St-Tropez
La Ciotat
Six-Fours-les-Plages
Hyères
Cap
Sicié

LANGUEDOC

The Causses and
the Cévennes
Millau
Ganges
Alès
Lodève
Vauvert
Montpellier
Sète
Béziers
Agde
Narbonne
Durban-Corbières
Limoux
Rivesaltes
Perpignan
Port-Vendres
Étang de Leucate
Céret
Cabo
de Creus
Figueres
Cap
de Begur
Banyoles
Torroella de Montgrí
Palamós

Cabo de Pals

Monte
Perdido
3348
Aneto
3404
Prades
Vielha

CATALUÑA

Manresa
Igualada
Sabadell
Santa Coloma
de Gramenet
Barcelona
El Prat de Llobregat
Vilanova i la Geltrú
Martorell
Mataró
Blanes
Graus
Barbastro
Monzón
Binéfar
Fraga
Lleida
Tàrrega

ARAGÓN

Zaragoza
Cariñena
Quinto
Caspe
Escatrón
Alcañiz
Gandesa
Calamocha
Monreal del Campo
Teruel
Peñarroya
2019
Sarrión
L'Alcora

Valls
Reus
Tarragona
Amposta
Sant Carles
de la Rápita
Vinarós
Torreblanca

Costa Dorada

Golf de Sant Jordi

Costa del Azahar

Cabo de Gata

Serranía
de Cuenca
Sierra de
Javalambre
Santa Cruz
de Moya
Utiel
Minglanilla
La Roda
Albacete
Almansa
Yecla
Hellín
Jumilla
Cieza
Molina de
Segura
Alcantarilla
Murcia
Lorca
Mazarrón
Huércal-
Overa
Vera
Aguilas

Castellón
de la Plana
Burriana
La Vall d'Uixó
Sagunto
Burjassot
Llíria
Manises
Valencia
Catarroja
Torrent
Algemesí
Cullera
Carcaixent
Sueca
Gandia
Oliva
Xàtiva
Ontinyent
Dénia
Alcoy-Alcoi
Villena
Ibi
Benidorm
Elda
Villajoyosa
Novelda
La Vila Joiosa
Alicante
Crevillent
Orihuela
Elche
Elx
Torrevieja

VALENCIA

Golfo de Valencia

Cabo de
la Nao

Costa Blanca

MURCIA

Alhama
de Murcia
Cabo de Palos
Cartagena
Golfo de Mazarrón

Majorca
(Mallorca)
Sóller
Calvià
Sa Dragonera
Palma de
Mallorca
Sa Pobla
Alcúdia
Pollença
La Cabaneta
Manacor
Felanitx
Cap de ses Salines
Cap de
Formentor
Cap des Freu

Minorca
(Menorca)
Punta
Nati
Ciutadella
Es Mercadal
Maó

BALEARIC ISLANDS
(ISLAS BALEARES)
(Spain)

Ibiza
(Eivissa)
Sant Joan de Labritja
Santa Eulalia del Río
Sant Antoni
de Portmany
Ibiza (Eivissa)
Sant Francesc
de Formentera
Formentera

Illa de
Cabrera

M E D I T E R R A N E A N   S E A

ALGIERS
(Alger)
Aïn
Taya
Dellys
Boumerdes
Bejaïa
Jijel
Tipasa
Kolea
Larba
Tizi
Ouzou
Bouira
Bougaa
Sétif
Ténès
Djebel
Bissa
1157
Gouraya
Blida
Médéa
Berrouaghia
Sour el
Ghozlane
Bordj Bou
Arréridj
Sidi
Ali
Aïn Defla
Khemis
Miliana
Miliana
 Ksar el
Boukhari
Aïn
Azel
Aïn Azel
Oued Chelef
Chlef
Sidi
Aïssa
M'Sila
Mostaganem
Arzew
Aïn
Tédélès
Relizane
Bordj Bounaama
Barika
Oran
Oued
Tlélat
Mohammadia
Zemmora
Tissemsilt
Zenzach
Bou Saâda
M'Doukal
Beni Saf
Aïn
Temouchent
Sig
Mascara
Mahdia
Tiaret

ALGERIA

Cap Carbon

200 KILOMETRES
100
0
150
100
50
MILES 0

1:4 800 000

A

ALPS

3738

Merano
Adige Dolomites Cortina
d'Ampezzo
Ortles Bolzano Triglav
3905 Laives 2864 Tolmin
Bonneville Matterhorn Chiavenna Trento Tarvisio SLO
Rumilly Cluses Martigny Mont-Blanc Tirano Belluno Cividale LJUBLJAN
Annecy Mont-Blanc 4478 Verbania Bellinzona Feltre Vittorio del Friuli Logatec
Aix-les- Albertville Chamonix 4810 Lake Lugano Lake Como Sondrio Veneto Udine
Bains Aosta Maggiore Riva del Schio Conegliano Pordenone Gorizia
Voiron Borgosesia Arona Lecco Garda Rovereto Treviso Portogruaro Monfalcone Trieste
Chambery Biella Varese Como Bergamo Lake Vicenza Padua Koper
St-Égrève Ivrea Novara Busto Monza Garda Valdagno Venice (Padova) Poreč Rijek
Grenoble Cuorgne Vercelli Arsizio Rho Brescia Verona Lonigo (Venezia) Istria
45° Barre des Cirie Vigevano Milan Manerbio Laguna Veneta Chioggia Pazin Criky
Ecrins Modane Rivoli Turin (Milano) Lodi Crema Cremona Legnago Adige Porto Tolle Rovinj Labir
Oulx Giaveno (Torino) Po Pavia Adda Mantua Ferrara Codigoro
La Mure 4102 Brianҫon Moncalieri Casale Piacenza (Mantoya) Po Portomaggiore Comacchio Pula Cre
St-Bonnet- Pinerolo Asti Monferrato Tortona Parma Carpi Reno Argenta Veli Los
en-Champsaur Saluzzo Tanaro Alessandria Reggio Modena Bologna Ravenna Loši
Barcelonnette Fossano Alba Acqui Novi Ligure nell'Emilia Monte Imola Forlì Cesenatico
Sisteron Cuneo Terme Genoa Cimone Faenza Cesena Rimini AD
Digne-les- 1871 Mondovi Savona (Genova) 2165 Pesaro R
Manosque Bains Col de Tende Rapallo Sestri Fivizzano Barga Pistoia Prato SAN Fano
Castellane Tende Albenga Levante Carrara MARINO SAN Senigallia
Verdon Maritime San Capo Mele La Spezia Massa Firenze MARINO Ancona
Draguignan MONTE-CARLO Remo Imperia Viareggio Lucca Florence Sansepolcro osimo
Brignoles Grasse Ventimiglia Pisa (Firenze) Cagli Jesi Civitanova
Cannes Nice MONACO Livorno Empoli Scandicci Arezzo Gubbio Fabriano Macerata Marche
Toulon Frejus Antibes Cote d'Azur Ligurian Cecina Siena Cortona Perugia Fermo San Bene
Hyeres St-Raphael Côte d'Azur Sea Isola Potenza del Monte
Cap St-Tropez Cap de St-Tropez di Capraia San Vincenzo Montepulciano Foligno Ascoli
Sicié Îles d'Hyères Cap Corse Piombino Follonica Marsciano Todi Piceno Giulian
Corse Isola Orvieto Corno Teramo
d'Elba Grosseto Viterbo Terni Grande Penne Pes
Monte Lago di 2912
Stello Portoferraio Castiglione Bolsena Narni Tiber L'Aquila Chi
L'Ile-Rousse Bastia della Pescaia Rieti Corno Amaro
St-Florent 1507 Isola Arcipelago Orbetello Tarquinia Guidonia- 2793 Trive
Calvi Pianosa Toscano Civitavecchia Montecelio Avezzano
Corsica Vescovato Isola Tarquinia VATICAN CITY ROME Tivoli Sora
(Corse) Cervione di Montecristo (Roma) Lirí
(France) Corte Pomezia Velletri Frosinone Campob
Capo Rosso 2622 Ghisonaccia Aprilia Sezze Cassino Venaf
Capo di Feno Prunelli-di-Fiumorbo Anzio Latina Fondi Sessa
Ajaccio Zonza Sabaudia Aurunca
Olmeto Punta d'Ovace Golfo Isola Gaeta Naples Case
Sartène 1340 Porto-Vecchio di Gaeta (Napoli)
Capo Pertusato Bonifacio Isole Ponziane Pozzuoli Ves
Strait of Bonifacio Isola di Ischia Sorrento Pompe
Punta Caprara Arzachena La Maddalena Isola di Capri Go
Isola Asinara Capo Ferro Sa
Golfo dell' Punta
Porto Torres Asinara Balestrieri Olbia
Sassari 1359 Budoni
Capo Caccia Oschiri
Alghero Ploaghe Capo Comino
Bonorva Buddusò Siniscola
Sardinia Macomer Nuoro Orosei
(Sardegna) Abbasanta Golfo di Orosei
(Italy) Oristano Punta La Capo di Monte Santu
40° Capo della Frasca Laconi Marmora
1834 Tortoli
Guspini Mandas Tertenia
Monte Linas San Gavino Monreale T Y R R H E N I A N
Iglesias 1236 Terramanna Villaputzu
Portoscuso Assemini S E A
Isola di San Pietro Punta Quartu Sant'Elena
Sant'Antioco Maxia Cagliari Capo Carbonara
Isola di Sant'Antioco 1017 Pula Golfo di
Cagliari

Isol
Isola di Ustica Lipa
Isola Filic
M E D I T E R R A N E A N
Sicily
(Sicilia)
Capo San Vito Partinico Palermo
Monte Sparagio Cefalù
La Galite Trapani 1110 Rocca Termini
Isola Marettimo Alcamo Busambra Imerese Dit
S E A 1613
Marsala Partanna Leonforte
Mazara del Vallo Castelvetrano Caltanissetta Er
Collo Cap Sicilian Channel Capo Granitola Sciacca Canicatti Caltagiro Niscemi
de Fer Chetaibi Menzel Bizerte Agrigento Gela
Skikda Bourguiba Rass Jebel Licata Golfo di Gela
ALGERIA Annaba Cap de Nefza Cap Caltanissetta Vitt
Azzaba El Hadjar Garde El Kala Mateur TUNISIA Bon Golfe de
El Tarf Tabarka Jedeida Tunis

Longitude 10° east of Greenwich

A B

METRES
FEET

5000
16404

3000
9843

2000
6562

1000
3281

500
1640

200
656

0
0

Land below
sea level

200
656

4000
13124

6000
19686

Conic Equidistant Projection

© Collins Bartholomew Ltd

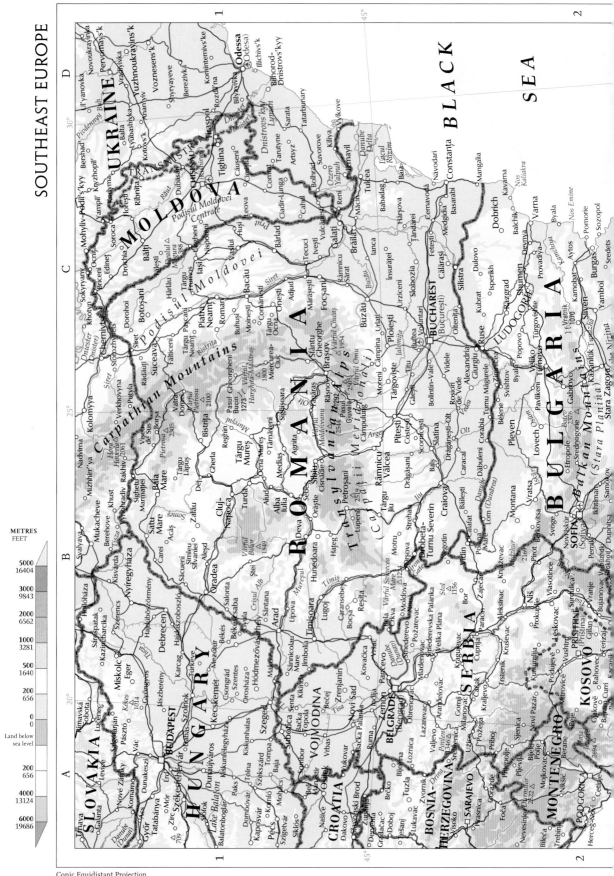

METRES
FEET

5000
16404

3000
9843

2000
6562

1000
3281

500
1640

200
656

0
0

Land below
sea level

200
656

4000
13124

6000
19686

110

Conic Equidistant Projection

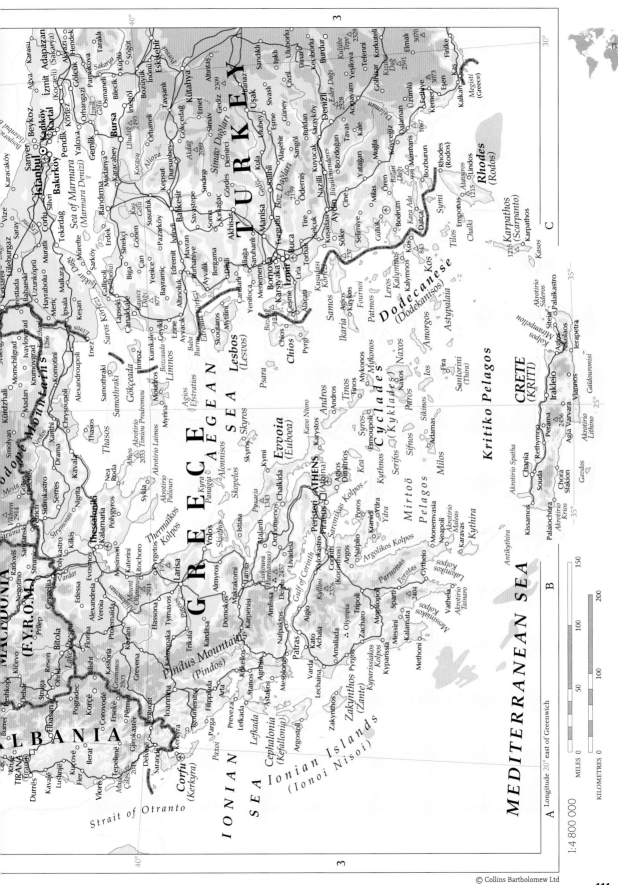

© Collins Bartholomew Ltd

1   2   3   4

A   B   C   D   E   F   G   H   I   J

70°   60°   50°   40°   30°   20°   10°   0°   10°   20°   30°   40°

KAZAKHSTAN

UZBEKISTAN

TURKMENISTAN

Aral Sea

Caspian Sea

RUSSIAN FEDERATION

IRAN

OMAN

Socotra (Yemen)

U.A.E.

QATAR

BAHRAIN

The Gulf

KUWAIT

YEMEN

Gulf of Aden

SOMALILAND

DJIBOUTI

Djibouti

SAUDI ARABIA

Rub' al Khali

IRAQ

SYRIA

JORDAN

ISRAEL

LEBANON

CYPRUS

TURKEY

GEORGIA

ARMENIA

AZERBAIJAN

Caucasus

Volga

UKRAINE

MOLDOVA

ROMANIA

BULGARIA

GREECE

ALBANIA

MACE.

MONT.

SERB.

BOSNIA HERZ.

CROATIA

SLOV.

HUNGARY

SLOVAKIA

CZECH REP.

AUSTRIA

SW.

A L P S

ITALY

BELARUS

POLAND

GERMANY

LITHUANIA

LATVIA

ESTONIA

SWEDEN

NORWAY

DENMARK

North Sea

NETH.

BEL.

LUX.

UNITED KINGDOM

IRELAND

FRANCE

Bay of Biscay

SPAIN

PORTUGAL

Azores (Portugal)

Madeira (Portugal)

Canary Is (Spain)

Black Sea

Mediterranean Sea

MALTA

TUNIS

Tunis

TUNISIA

Tripoli

Benghazi

LIBYA

EGYPT

Alexandria

Cairo

Asyût

Aswân

L. Nasser

Nile

Libyan Desert

S A H A R A

Red Sea

Port Sudan

Asmara

ERITREA

Khartoum

Omdurman

El Obeid

SUDAN

Blue Nile

White Nile

Nile

CHAD

Ndjamena

NIGER

Zinder

Kano

NIGERIA

NIN.

Niamey

BURKINA FASO

Ouagadougou

Niger

MALI

Gao

Bamako

Tamanrasset

ALGERIA

Atlas Mountains

Algiers

Oran

MOROCCO

Tangier

Rabat

Casablanca

Marrakech

WESTERN SAHARA

Laâyoune

MAURITANIA

Nouakchott

SENEGAL

Dakar

THE GAMBIA

Banjul

GUINEA-BISSAU

Bissau

GUINEA

Conakry

SIERRA

Tropic of Cancer

30°   20°   10°   0°   10°   20°   30°   40°

1   2   3   4

Oblated Stereographic Projection

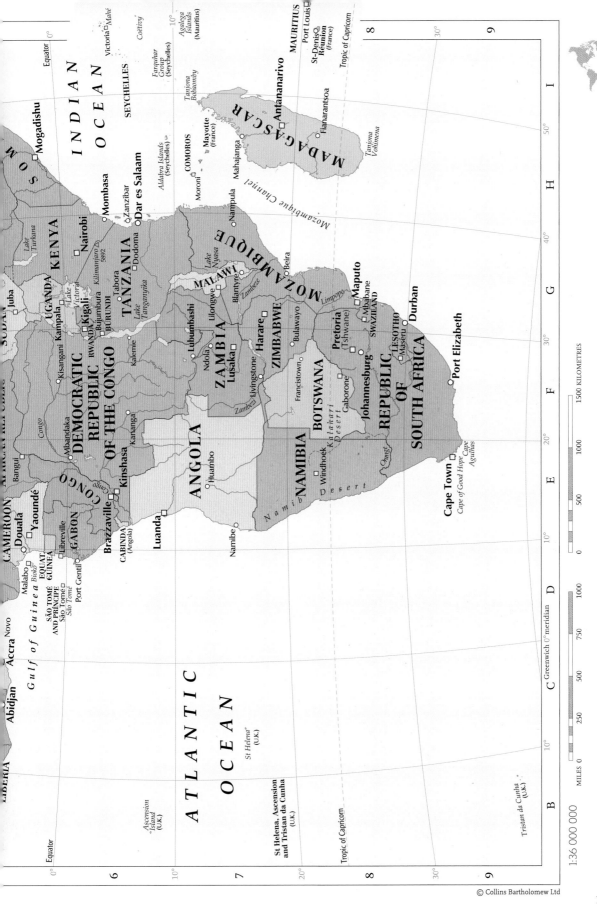

INDIAN OCEAN

SEYCHELLES

Victoria Mahé
Coëtivy

Farquhar Group (Seychelles)

Agalega Islands (Mauritius)

10°

Equator 0°

MAURITIUS
Port Louis
St-Denis Réunion (France)

Tropic of Capricorn

MADAGASCAR

Antananarivo
Fianarantsoa
Tanjona Vohimena
Tanjona Bobaomby

COMOROS
Moroni
Mayotte (France)
Aldabra Islands (Seychelles)

Mozambique Channel

Mogadishu

Mombasa
Zanzibar
Dar es Salaam
Nampula

KENYA
Nairobi
Lake Turkana

UGANDA
Kampala
Kigali
RWANDA
BURUNDI
Bujumbura
Lake Victoria
Kilimanjaro 5892

TANZANIA
Tabora
Dodoma
Lake Tanganyika
Lake Nyasa

MALAWI
Lilongwe
Blantyre

MOZAMBIQUE
Beira
Zambezi

Juba

SUDAN

DEMOCRATIC REPUBLIC OF THE CONGO
Kisangani
Mbandaka
Kananga
Kalemie
Lubumbashi

ZAMBIA
Ndola
Lusaka
Livingstone

ZIMBABWE
Harare
Bulawayo

Maputo
Mbabane
SWAZILAND
Pretoria (Tshwane)
Johannesburg
LESOTHO
Maseru
Durban

Port Elizabeth

REPUBLIC OF SOUTH AFRICA

BOTSWANA
Francistown
Gaborone
Kalahari Desert

NAMIBIA
Windhoek
Namib Desert
Orange
Cape of Good Hope
Cape Agulhas
Cape Town

ANGOLA
Huambo
Luanda
Namibe
CABINDA (Angola)

Bangui

CAMEROON
Douala
Yaoundé

GABON
Libreville
Port Gentil
EQUAT. GUINEA
Malabo Bioko
SÃO TOMÉ AND PRÍNCIPE
São Tomé

CONGO
Brazzaville
Kinshasa
Congo

Gulf of Guinea
Novo
Accra
Abidjan
LIBERIA

ATLANTIC OCEAN

St Helena (U.K.)
Ascension Island (U.K.)
St Helena, Ascension and Tristan da Cunha (U.K.)

Tristan da Cunha (U.K.)

Tropic of Capricorn

Equator

Greenwich 0° meridian

1:36 000 000

MILES 0   250   500   750   1000

0   500   1000   1500 KILOMETRES

A B C D E F G H I

6 7 8 9

0° 10° 20° 30°

© Collins Bartholomew Ltd

113

A   20°   10°

SPAIN
Gibraltar   Cartag
Malaga   Almería
Strait of Gibraltar   Mostaganem
Tangier   Ceuta (Spain)   Oran
(Tanger)   Tétouan   Melilla   Sidi B
Larache   Ksar el Kebir   (Spain)   Abbes
Sidi   Taounate   Oujda   Tlemcen   A
RABAT   Kacem   Fès (Fez)   Taza   Taourirt
Ben Slimane   Meknès   Taza   Figuig   Saha
Casablanca   El Jadida   Oued   Bou   Aïn Sefra
MOROCCO   Settat   Khouribga   Arfa
Safi   Beni Mellal   Zem   Er   Grand Erg
El Kelaâ des Srarhna   Haut Atlas (High Atlas)   Rachida   Occident
Marrakech   Jebel   ATLAS MOUNTAINS   Béchar
Essaouira   Toubkal   4167   Bou   Abadla   Beni Abbès
Taroudannt   Ouarzazate   Zagora
Agadir   Anti-Atlas   Tabelbala   El
Tiznit   Hamada du Drâa   Timim
Sidi Ifni   Ksabi   Adrar   Plate
Guelmim   Erg Iguidi   Sbaa
Tan-Tan   Bordj Flye   ALG
A T L A N T I C   Ste-Marie   Aoulef   In S
Madeira   El Eglab   Reggane
(Portugal)   LAâYOUNE   Chenachane   Sebkha Azzel
FUNCHAL   Al Mahbas   Tindouf   Matti   Sebk
O C E A N   Es Semara   Chegga   Meker
La Palma   Lanzarote   Poste
SANTA   Weygan
Pico del   CRUZ DE   Fuerteventura   'Erg Chech   Bordj
Teide   TENERIFE   Jandía   Tiguesmat   Mokhta
La Gomera   3718   807   Boujdour   Aïn   El Hank   Tanezrouft
El Hierro   Tenerife   Ben Tili   Oued Ilefe
Canary Islands   Gran   LAS PALMAS   Galtat   Bir   Taoudenni
(Islas Canarias)   Canaria   DE GRAN   Zemmour   Mogrein   Aoukâr   'Azaouâd   Adra
(Spain)   CANARIA   **WESTERN**   El Hammâmi   S A   Aguelhc
Skaymat   **SAHARA**   O U R Â N E   Ifôgha
Tropic of Cancer   Ad Dakhla   ADMINISTERED   Zouérat   Araouane   Kidal
BY MOROCCO   Fdérik   Vallée du Tilemsi
Awserd   Maqteïr   M A L I   Anéfis
Tichla   Choûm   'Ayoûn el   Taoudenni
Nouâdhibou   Guelb er Richât   Dhar Oualâta   IRÎGUI
Atâr   485   Timbuktu   Gourma-   Bourem
Akjoujt   (Tombouctou)   Rharous   Ménaka
Nouâmghâr   Akchâr   **MAURITANIA**   Araouane   Gao
NOUAKCHOTT   Sebkhet   Tidjikja   Dhar Tîchît   Lac   Hombori   Ansongo
Te-n-Dghâmcha   Moudjéria   Tîchît   Faguibine
Boutilimit   Magta' Lahjar   HÔD   Néma   Goundam   Doro   Niger
Tiguent   Aleg   Ouâlâta   Lac   Niger
Rosso   Bogué   Kaédi   Kiffa   Bassikounou   Niangay
St-Louis   Dagana   Mbout   Timbedgha   Nara   **S**   Homburi   Fili
Louga   Linguère   Matam   Nioro   Youyarou   Gao   Ménaka   Tillabé
Thiès   Dara   Sélibabi   Ballé   Nampala   Monti   **A**   Gorom-   NIA
DAKAR   Diourbel   Yelimane   Diéma   Kogoni   Douentza   Gorom
Mbour   Fatick   **SENEGAL**   Sandaré   Nioni   Ténenkou   Bandiagara   Dori
Kaolack   Kidira   Kayes   Boron   Macina   Koro   Ouahigouya   Bogandé
Kaffrine   Goudiri   Bafoulabé   Kolokani   Ségou   Djenné   Yako   Gourcy Kaya
BANJUL   Tambacounda   Sandaré   San   Tougan   Nouna   **BURKINA FASO**   Do
Brikama   Gambia   Georgetown   Lac de   Kati   Bla   Koutiala   Koudougou   Zorgho   Gayeri   Diap
THE GAMBIA   Kédougou   Manantali   Satadougou   Kita   Dioila   Sikasso   **OUAGADOUGOU**   Fada-N'Gourma
Sédhiou   Kolda   Mali   Bamako   Kangaba   Mahou   Manga   Tenkodogo   Tô   Pô   Bawku
Ziguinchor   Cacheu   Bafata   Gabú   Koundara   Koubia   Bougouni   Bobo-   Téo   Bolgatanga   Danamo
GUINEA   Buba   Gaoual   Siguiri   Lac de   Dioulasso   Banfora   Lawra   Wa   Bimbila
BISSAU   Bolama   Fouta   Pita   Labé   Selingue   Gaoua   Ferkessédougou   Tchini   Yendi   Kara
BISSAU   Boké   Djallon   Dabola   Kouroussa   Yanfolila   Kolondiéba   Korhogo   Bouna   Salaga   Bassar
Arquipélago   Fria   **GUINEA**   Kankan   Mandiana   Kadiolo   Orodara   Tamale   Bassila
dos Bijagós   Dubréka   Kindia   Mamou   Niger   Minignan   Odienné   Tchini   Damongo   Bimbila   Sokodé
Boké   Faranah   Kankan   Boundiali   Mango   Yendi
CONAKRY   Port   Kissidougou   Touba   Diamra   Korhogo   Bouna   Bolgatanga   Sokodé
Lungi   Loko   Makeni   Kérouané   Beyla   Mankono   White Volta   Tamale   Djoug
FREETOWN   Magburaka   Nzérékoré   Séguéla   Katiola   Sunyani   Salaga   Savalou
SIERRA   Kenema   Bonthe   Bo   Lola   Man   Bouaké   Techiman   Mampong   Krachi   Aného
LEONE   Sefadu   Danané   752   Daoukro   Abengourou   Kintampo   Kete   Abomey   PORTO-N
Bonthe   Zimmi   Tapeta   Daloa   **CÔTE D'IVOIRE**   **GHANA**   Wenchi   Lake Volta   Slave Coast
Robertsport   Kakata   Gbarnga   (IVORY COAST)   Bekwai   Koforidua   LOMÉ
Harbel   Bong   **YAMOUSSOUKRO**   Bongouanou   Obuasi   Tema   ACCRA
MONROVIA   Buchanan   Gagnoa   Divo   **Kumasi**   Winneba
Harper   River Cess   Tiassalé   Aboisso   Takwa   Cape Coast
LIBERIA   Greenville   Sassandra   Abidjan   Bingerville   Axim
Barclayville   Grand-   Sekondi   Gold Coast
Harper   Lahou   Cape   Big
Cape Palmas   San-Pédro   Three Points   of Be
Tabou   **G U L F   O F   G U I N E A**

METRES   FEET
5000   16404
3000   9843
2000   6562
1000   3281
500   1640
200   656
0   0
Land below sea level
200   656
4000   13124
6000   19686

114

Lambert Azimuthal Equal Area Projection

A

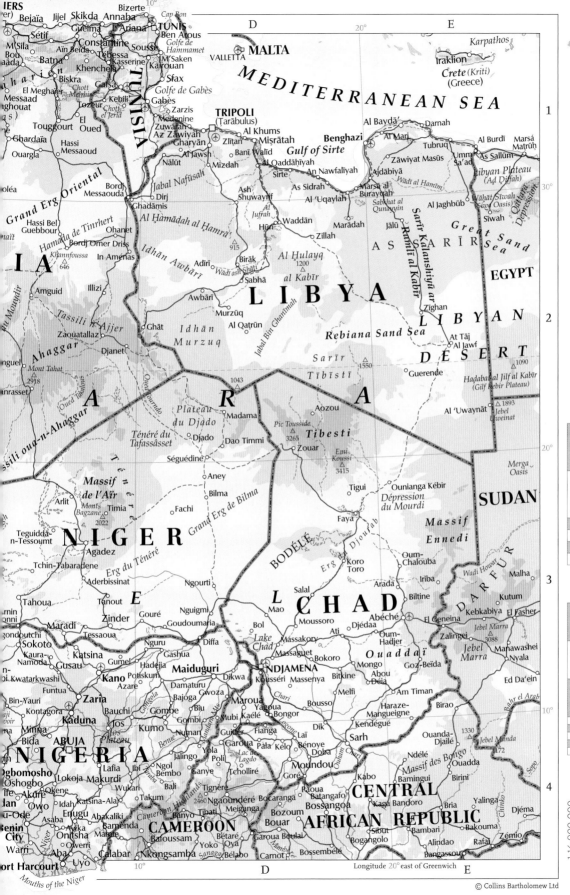

© Collins Bartholomew Ltd

1:16 000 000

METRES FEET

METRES	FEET
5000	16404
3000	9843
2000	6562
1000	3281
500	1640
200	656
0	0
Land below sea level	
200	656
4000	13124
6000	19686

Grid references: A 1, B 1, C 1, D 1, A 2, B 2, C 2, D 2, A 3, B 3, C 3, D 3

IRAN
Yazd, Nā'īn, Eşfahān (Isfahān), Abādeh, Shahr-e Kord, Khvānsār, Khorramābād, Dezfūl, Shīrāz, Neyrīz, Dārāb, Jahrom, Abarkūh, Anār, Fīrūzābād, Borāzjān, Kāzerūn, Būshehr, Ahvāz, Abādān, Khorramshahr, Īlām, An Nāşirīyah, An Nu'mānīyah

IRAQ
BAGHDAD, Ba'qūbah, Ar Ramādī, Al Kūt, Ad Dīwānīyah, An Najaf, As Samāwah, Al Başrah (Al Basrah), Al Hillah, Karbalā', Ar Rutbah, Euphrates, Tigris

THE GULF
U.A.E., ABU DHABI (Abū Zabī), QATAR, DOHA (Ad Dawḥah), BAHRAIN, MANAMA, Dhahrān, Dammām (Ad Dammām), Al Mubarraz, Al Hufūf, Haradh, Tropic of Cancer

KUWAIT (Al Kuwayt), Al Jahrah, Al Aḥmadī, Rafḥā', Sakākah, Dawmat al Jandal, Al Widyān, Ar Ruq'ī

SAUDI ARABIA
RIYADH (Ar Riyāḍ), Ad Dir'īyah, Al Kharj, Al Hillah, Jabal Ţuwayq, Ad Dahnā', Buraydah, 'Unayzah, Shaqrā', Az Zilfī, Majma'ah, Artāwīyah, 'Afīf, As Sulayyil, Najrān, Ash Sharawrah, Sharūrah, As Sūq, NAJD, Ḥā'il, Taymā', Dūbā, Al Wajh, Medina (Al Madīnah), Yanbu' al Baḥr, Rābigh, Mecca (Makkah), Jeddah (Jiddah), At Ţā'if, Al Līth, Al Quniḍhah, Abhā, Turabah, Jīzān, Şabyā, HIJAZ, 'ASĪR, RUB' AL KHALI (EMPTY QUARTER), AR RIMĀL, Wādī Tathlīth, Wādī Ḥanīfah

ARABIAN PENINSULA, An Nafūd

OMAN

YEMEN
ŞAN'Ā', Dhamār, Ibb, Ta'izz, Zabīd, Hodeidah, Al Bayḍā', Shuqrah, Ḥabbān, Shibām, Tarīm, Say'ūn, Al Mukallā (Al Mukalla), Ash Shiḥr, Al Ghaydah, Al Qaṭn, Wādī Ḥaḍramawt, Gulf of Aden, Bāb al Mandab

ERITREA
AŞMARA, Mitsiwa (Massawa), Dekemhare, Keren, Teseney, Barentu, Mendefera, Adigrat, Adwa, Āksum, Mek'elē, Inda Silasē, Dahlak Archipelago, Jazā'ir Farasān

SUDAN
KHARTOUM (El Khartûm), Omdurman (Umm Durmān), Khartoum North, Wad Medanī, Kassalā, Gedaref (Al Qaḍārif), Sennar, Kosti, El Obeid (Al Ubayyiḍ), Ed Dueim, En Nahud, Rabak, Atbara ('Atbarah), Ed Damer, Berber, Shereik, Abū Ḥamad, Karima, Merowe, Dongola, Kerma, Abri, Wadi Halfa (Wādī Ḥalfā'), Selima Oasis, Port Sudan, Sawākin (Suakin), Tokar, Sinkat, Halaib, Haiya, Karora, Aroma, Kassala, Baraka, Gash, El Geteina, El Fasher, Kutum, El Geneina, Nyala, Blue Nile (Bahr), Nile, Atbara

UNDER EGYPTIAN ADMINISTRATION

BIR TAWIL (UNDER SUDAN ADMINISTRATION)

EGYPT
CAIRO (Al Qāhirah), Giza (Al Jīzah), Alexandria (Al Iskandarīyah), Damanhūr, Ţanţā, Shubrā al Khaymah, Būr Sa'īd (Port Said), Būr Sa'īd, Dumyāţ, As Suways (Suez), Ismā'īlīyah, Al Fayyūm, Banī Suwayf, Al Minyā, Mallawī, Asyūţ, Sūhāj, Jirjā, Qinā, Luxor (Al Uqşur), Isnā, Idfū, Aswān, Lake Nasser, Wādī Ḥalfā', Ra's Ghārib, Al Ghurdaqah (Hurghada), Al Quşayr, Marsā al 'Alam, Barānīs, Kawm Umbū, Al Kharjah, Al Qaşr, Mūt, Al Farāfirah, Al Baḥrīyah, Al Bawīţī, Siwah, Sīwah Oasis, Wāḥāt al Baḥrīyah, Wāḥāt al Farāfirah (Farafra Oasis), Wāḥāt ad Dākhilah (Dakhla Oasis), Wāḥāt al Khārijah (The Great Oasis), Al Ballāş, Qaşr al Farāfirah, Qaṭṭārah Depression (Munkhafaḍ al Qaṭṭārah), Western Desert, Eastern Desert, Sinai, Matrūḥ, Marsā Maţrūḥ, Sīdī Barrānī, As Sallūm

JORDAN
AMMAN, Az Zarqā', Irbid, Al Karak, Ma'ān, Al 'Aqabah, Gulf of Aqaba

ISRAEL
JERUSALEM (El Quds), Tel Aviv-Yafo, GAZA, Beersheba (Be'ér Sheva'), Eilat

LEBANON, BEIRUT, Tyre (Şūr)

SYRIA
DAMASCUS (Dimashq), Az Zabadānī, Zaḥlé, Dar'ā, Lake Galilee, Sea of Galilee

Jabal al Lawz 2579, **Jabal ad Dubbayk**, 1258, 1814

MEDITERRANEAN SEA

LIBYA
Benghazi, Al Bayḍā', Darnah, Ţubruq, Al Marj, Ajdābiyā, Marādah, Jālū, Zighān, At Tāj, Al Jaghbūb, Marsā al Burayqah, Zāwiyat Masūs, Umm ar Rizām, Wādī al Ḥamīm, LIBYAN DESERT, Great Sand Sea, Sarīr Kalanshiyū, ar Ramlī al Kabīr, Rebiâna Sand Sea, AS SARĪR, Siwah Oasis, Al Jawf, Guerende

CHAD
Oum-Chalouba, Arada, Iriba, Biltine, Abéché, Ounianga Kébir, Dépression du Mourdi, Massif Ennedi, Wadi Howar, Fada, Faya

FUR, Jebel Marra, Jebel Abyad Plateau, Jebel 'Uwaynāt 1893, Haḍabat al Jilf al Kabīr (Gilf Kebir Plateau), 1090, Al 'Uwaynāt, 465, 1550, Merga Oasis, Wādī al Milk, Baiyuda Desert, Nubian Desert, Jebel Oda 2215, Jebel 'Elba, Jebel Asoteriba 2217, 1977, 2259, 2512, 2580

Lambert Azimuthal Equal Area Projection

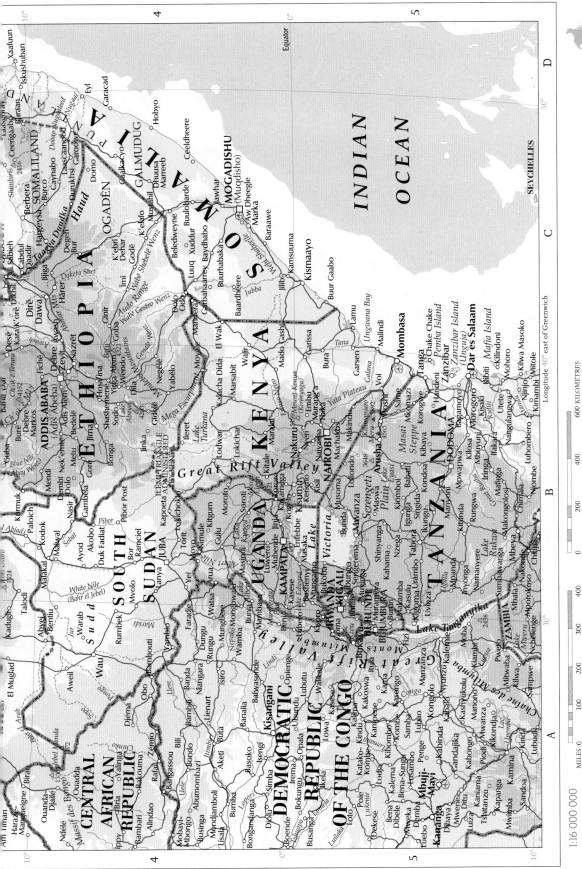

© Collins Bartholomew Ltd

1:16 000 000

Longitude 40° east of Greenwich

MILES 0   100   200   300   400

0   200   400   600 KILOMETRES

INDIAN

OCEAN

SEYCHELLES

A 10° B 20°

CHAD

NIGERIA

CAMEROON

CENTRAL AFRICAN REPUBLI

EQUATORIAL GUINEA

GABON

CONGO

DEMOC REPU OF T CON

ATLANTIC OCEAN

ANGOLA

Tudun Wada · Kari · Bajoga · Damboa · Mora · Massenya · Abou Déia · Bourtoutou
Bauchi · Biu · Gwoza · Maroua · Bousso · Melfi · Am Timan · Plaine de Garar
Gombe · Combi · Mokolo · Yagoua · Bongor · Dik · Kendégué · Haraze-Mangueigne · Birao
Jos · Dindima · Kumo · Kaltungo · Mubi · Kaélé · Chari · Délembé
Pankshin · Benue · Numan · Guider · Fianga · Laï · Koumra · Sarh · Kyabé · Tiroungoulou · Ouanda-Djailé · 1330
Shendam · Jalingo · Garoua · Pala · Kélo · Bénoye · Doba · Maro · Ndélé · Massif des Bongo · Ouadda · Birini
Lafia · Ibi · Ganye · Lac de Lagdo · Béinamar · Moundou · Gore · Kabo · Bamingui · Boulouba · Bani
Wukari · Ngol Bembo · Poli · Tchollire · Koum · Touboro · Baibokoum · Markounda · Batangafo · Kaga Bandoro · Dékoa · Ippy · Bria · Yalinga
Makurdi · Donga · Gashaka · Tignère · Ngaoundéré · Bélèl · Paoua · Bossangoa · Grimari · Bambari · Bakouma · Rafai
Katsina-Ala · Gboko · Takum · Banyo · 2460 · Meiganga · Bocaranga · Bozoum · Damara · Sibut · Alindao · Bangassou
Nkambe · Tibati · Ngaoundal · Garoua Boulai · Bouar · Baoro · Bogangolo · Grimari · Kembé · Uele · Bondo
Ikom · Wum · Bamenda · Foumban · Yoko · Bétaré Oya · Carnot · Bossembélé · Gadzi · Zongo · Bosobolo · Mobayi-Mbongo · Abumombazi
Mamfe · Mbouda · Bafoussam · Lac de Mbakaou · Bouar · Berbérati · BANGUI · Bimbo · Mbaiki · Libenge · Businga · Ebola
Calabar · Kongsamba · Nanga · Bélabo · Kétté · Boda · Mbaiki · Zongo · Gemena · Lisala · Bumba · Lolo
Kumba · Loum · Baffa · Eboko · Bertoua · Nola · Bambio · Salo · Dongou · Kungu · Mondjamboli
Mbanga · Monatélé · Mbandjok · Batouri · Abong Mbang · Yokadouma · Boumba · Impfondo · Makanza · Bongandanga · Lopori
Mont Cameroun 4100 · Buea · Obala · YAOUNDÉ · Akonolinga · Moloundou · Makoua · Mbandaka · Embondo · Bokatala · Basankusu · Djolu · Simba
Limbe · Douala · Edéa · Mbalmayo · Sangmélima · Souanké · Sembé · Ouesso · Epéna · Losombo · Bolomba · Bokele
MALABO · Kribi · Ebolowa · Djoum · Mékambo · Mbomo · Owando · Bikoro · Boende · Watsi · Kengo · Busanga · Bokungu · Ikela
Bioko · Bata · Niefang · Ebebiyin · Oyem · Makokou · Bolobo · Bolia · Ifumo · Eyangu
Cogo · Evinayong · Mitzic · Makokou · Owando · Loukoléla · Lac Tumba · Boleko · Bokele
Ntoum · Monts de Cristal · Alembé · Booué · Makoua · Ntandembele · Inongo · Loto
LIBREVILLE · Bifoun · Lastoursville · Okondja · Obouya · Gamboma · Mushie · Lac Mai Ndombe · Poie
Cap Lopez · Port-Gentil · Lambaréné · Koulamoutou · Akièni · Okoyo · Ngo · Kutu · Dekese · Lodja
Iguéla · Fougamou · Mimongo · Moanda · Franceville · Boumango · Bolobo · Buna · Oshwe · Lukenie · Domiongo · Bena-Sun
Lagune Nkomi · Mouila · Mayoko · Lékana · Djambala · Ngabé · Bandundu · Bagata · Ilebo · Bena Dibele · Kalem
Mossendjo · Komono · BRAZZAVILLE · Bulungu · Mangai · Mweka · Demba · Lusar
Tchibanga · Nyanga · Ndendé · Makabana · Sibiti · Madingou · Mindouli · KINSHASA · Masi-Manimba · Idiofa · Luebo · Kananga · Mbuji-M
Mayumba · Nzambi · Loubomo · Belize · Kasangulu · Kenge · Kikwit · Kingandu · Dibaya · Nal
Pointe-Noire · Luozi · Kisantu · Popokabaka · Gungu · Kilembe · Kamonia · Mwene-Ditu · Gandajika
CABINDA (Angola) · Tshela · Kimpese · Mbanza-Ngungu · Mawanga · Feshi · Tshikapa · Kazumba · Luiza · Kim
Cabinda · Boma · Matadi · Maquela do Zombo · Kasongo-Lunda · Bumba · Kahemba · Chitato · Plateau du Kasaï
Muanda · Kitona · M'banza Congo · Damba · Quimbele · Tembo Aluma · Bindu · Cambulo · Lucapa · Kapanga · Tshi
Tomboco · Lucunga · Songo · Uige · Negage · Massango · Caungula · Cuilo · Lucapa · Sombo · Mwimba
N'zeto · Ambriz · Muxaluando · Camabatela · Capenda-Camulemba · Mona Quimbundo · Saurimo · Sandoa · Kafakum
LUANDA · Catete · Calandula · Chiluage · Muriege · Muconda · Malonga · Kasaj
N'dalatando · Dondo · Lucala · Malanje · Xá-Muteba · Cacolo · Quibundo · Quitapa · Dala · Luau · Dilolo
Calulu · Cuanza 1613 · Quimbundo · Cacolo · Luacano · Caianda
Gabela · Quibala · ANGOLA · Quirima · Camanóngue · Mwhilu
Waku-Kungo · Andulo · N'harea · Luena · Cazombo · Calunda
Sumbe · Planalto do Bié · Camacupa · Sachanga

METRES / FEET

METRES	FEET
5000	16404
3000	9843
2000	6562
1000	3281
500	1640
200	656
0	0
Land below sea level	
200	656
4000	13124
6000	19686

Longitude 20° east of Greenwich

Lambert Azimuthal Equal Area Projection

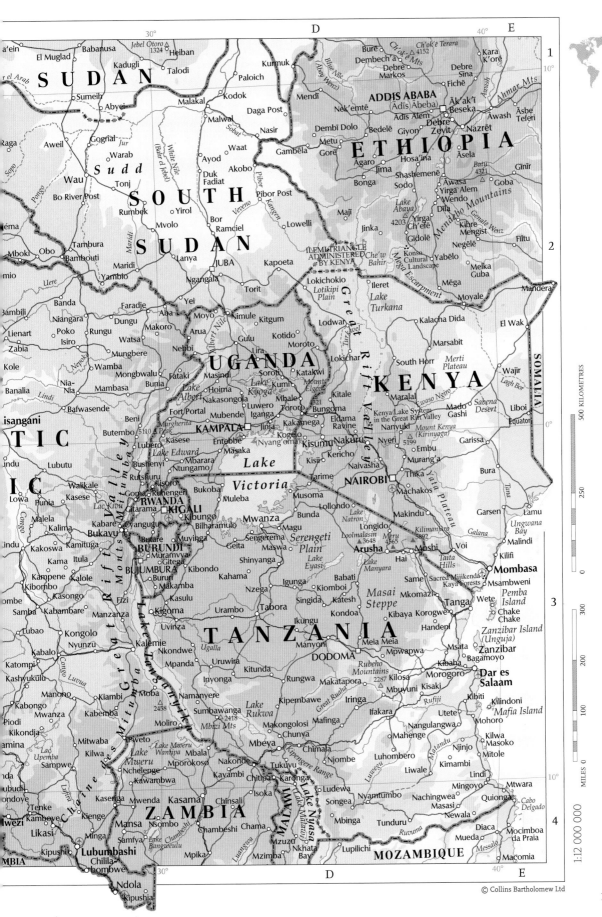

1:12 000 000

500 KILOMETRES

250

0

MILES 0

100

200

300

A · 20° · **B**

DEMOCRATIC REPUBLIC OF THE CONGO

Pointe-Noire
CABINDA (Angola)
Cabinda
Boma
Muanda
Kitona
Matadi
M'banza Congo
Tomboco
N'zeto
Lucunga
Ambriz
Muxaluando
Caxito

Luozi
Tshela
Kisantu
Kimpese
Mbanza-Ngungu
Maquela do Zombo
Damba
Quimbele
Songo
Uíge
Negage
Massango
Camabatela
Calandula

Kenge
Kingandu
Popokabaka
Mawanga
Feshi
Kasongo-Lunda

Masi-Manimba
Idiofa
Kikwit
Gungu
Kilembe
Tshikapa

Mweka
Luebo
Demba

Bena-Sungu
Lusambo
Kananga
Mbuji-Mayi
Penge
Kabinda

Lubao
Kongolo
Ka

Kamonia
Kazumba
Dibaya
Mwene-Ditu
Luiza
Cambulo
Lucapa
Sombo
Chiluage
Sandoa

Gandajika
Kabongo
Kaniama
Tshitanzu
Kapanga
Kamina
Kinda
Kafakumba

Kashyukulu
Piodi
Mwanza
Kikc

Plateau du Kasaï

Kamba
Tenke
Lubudi

Ki
Kambove
Li

LUANDA
N'dalatando
Dondo
Calulu
Gabela
Quibala
Waku-Kungo
Sumbe
Balombo
Lobito
Benguela

Catete
Lucala
Malanje
Xá-Muteba
Andulo
N'harea
Camacupa
Cuemba
Koito

Cuilo
Quitapa
Cacolo
Quirima
Camanongue
Sachanga
Luena

Saurimo
Mona Quimbundo
Muconda
Dala

Muriege
Malonga
Luau
Dilolo

Nasondoye
Kasaji

Kolwezi
Lubumba

Cazombo
Calunda
Lumbala Kaquengue
Lucusse
Mwinilunga
Solwezi

Kipu
Chin

Cuanza
△1613

Planalto do Bié
Chinguar
△2620

ANGOLA

Luvuei
Cangamba
Lumbala N'guimbo
Luacano

Mufumbwe
Ingwe
Zambezi
Kasempa
Kabompo
Mumbeji

Chin
Kasempa

ZAM

Cubal
Huambo
Caconda
Chipindo
Umpulo
Tempué
Menongue
Cuito
Cangombe
Chiume
Mavinga

Caluquembe
Quilengues
Lucira
Bibala
Matala
Kuvango

Cassinga
Cuanavale
Baixo-Longa

Neriquinha
Senanga
Kalabo
Lukulu
Kaoma
Mongu

Namwala
Mumbwa
Ka

Barragem do Gove
△1506

Planalto da Huíla

Cuito
Cuanavale

Kalabo

Namibe
Lubango
Chiange
Cahama
Mucope
Oncócua

Tombua
Virei

Baía dos Tigres
Foz do Cunene
Chitado
Xangongo
Utapi
Ondjiva
Oshikango
Oshakati

Cuvelai
Nankova
Cuito
Uamando
Acampamento de Caça do Mucusso
Katima Mulilo
Luiana
Dirico
Rundu
Bagani
Calai
Cuangar

Rivungo

Mulobezi
Choma
Kalomo

Victoria Falls
Bukalo
Kasane
CAPRIVI STRIP
Victoria Falls

Livingstone
Livingstone
Hwar
Shumba

Kunene
Cunene
Kaokoveld
Hoarusib
Hoanib
Opuwo
Sesfontein
Kamanjab

Etosha Pan
Tsumeb
Otavi
Kombat
Grootfontein
Tsumkwe

Okavango
Okavango Delta
Gumare
Maun

Phuduhudu
Nata
Tutume
Maiten

Namib Desert
Khorixas
Otjiwarongo
Okakarara
Okahandja

Eiseb
Sehithwa
Xhumo
Orapa
Letlhakane

Batti
Makgadikgadi

Serule
Francistown
Pala

NAMIBIA
Uis Mine
Omaruru
Steinhausen

Onjati Mountain
△2050
Omitara
Buitepos
Tshootsha

Ghanzi
Kang
Takatshwaane

BOTSWANA

Hentiesbaai
Swakopmund
Walvis Bay

WINDHOEK
Okahandja
Witvlei
Dordabis
Gobabis
Ncojane

Tsetseng

Serowe
Mahalapye

Tropic of Capricorn

Rehoboth
Solitaire
Nauchas
Tsumis Park
Leonardville
Hoachanas

Kalahari

Hukuntsi
Tshane
Mabutsane
Khakhea

Jwaneng
Molepolole
Mochudi

Lepha
Thabazi

ATLANTIC

Narib
Stampriet
Aranos

Desert

Werda
Kanye
Mabule
GABORONE

Lobatse
Soshang

Maltahöhe
Mariental
Gochas

Tshabong
Terra Firma
Mahikeng

Mmabatho
Johannesb
Sowe

OCEAN

Desert

Helmeringhausen
Tses
Koës
Mologo

NAMAQUALAND
Keetmanshoop

Severn
Vryburg
Delareyville

Sasolb

Lüderitz
Aus
Seeheim
Aroab
Bokspits
Van Zylsrus
Kuruman

Valspan
Phahameng

REPUBLIC OF SOUTH AFRIC

Ai-Ais
△2202
Grünau

Tswelelang
Kgotsong
Magk
Thabon

Oranjemund
Alexander Bay
Karasburg
Ariamsvlei
Upington
Olifantshoek
Postmasburg
Lime Acres
Galeshewe
Kimberley
Masilo

Orange
Keimoes
Bloemhof Dam

Longitude 20° east of Greenwich

A · **B**

Lambert Azimuthal Equal Area Projection

120

METRES / FEET

METRES	FEET
5000	16404
3000	9843
2000	6562
1000	3281
500	1640
200	656
0	0

Land below sea level

200	656
4000	13124
6000	19686

© Collins Bartholomew Ltd

A 20° B

METRES
FEET

5000
16404

3000
9843

2000
6562

1000
3281

500
1640

200
656

0
0

Land below
sea level

200
656

4000
13124

6000
19686

Lambert Azimuthal Equal Area Projection

Khomas Highland
Brakwater
Witvlei
Gobabis
Takatshwaane
WINDHOEK 2489
Doreenville
Kule
Palamakoloi
Tsetseng
Bergland
Dordabis
Ncojane
B O T S W
Wortel
Louwater-Suid
Gross Ums
One
Lehututu
Kang
Salaj
Rehoboth
Leonardville
K A L A H A R I
Khudum
Tropic of Capricorn
Aminuis
Hukuntsi
Motokwe
Takatokwane
Nauchas
Heide
Lokgwabe
Tshane
Tsumis
Park
Hoachanas
D E S E R T
Kokong
Mabutsane
Solitaire
Narib
Aranos
Khakhea
Jwanen
Bullsport
Kuis
Olifants
Salzbrunn
Stampriet
Auob
Maltahöhe
Marental
Werda
Moselebe
Gochas
Makopong
Molopo
Bossiesvlei
Nananib
Plateau
Gibeon
Witbooisvlei
25°
Terra
Firma
Senlac
Tosca
N A M I B I A
Twee
Rivier
Auob
Omaweneno
Schoarzrand
Fish
Berseba
Tses
Koës
Nosop
Tshabong
Morokweng
N O R T
Tiraz
Mountains
2040
Helmeringhausen
Wasser
G R E A T
N A M A Q U A L A N D
Kolonkwaneng
Molopo
Tsaukaib
Bethanie
Keetmanshoop
Aroab
Rietfontein
Severn
Laxey
Vryb
Garub
Aus
Sandverhaar
Hakseen
Pan
Bokspits
Van
Zylsrus
Lolwane
Huf
Seeheim
Kuruman
Hotazel
Tau
Gawachab
Little Karas
Berg
2202
Molopo
Dibeng
Kuruman
Reivile
Holoog
Groot Karas Berg
Gaiab
Sishen
Gakarosa
1855
Vals
Klein Karas
Olifantshoek
Ghaap Plateau
Rosh Pinah
2
Postmasburg
Lime-Acres
Warre
Ai-Ais
Grünau
Ariamsvlei
Lutzputs
Upington
R E P U B L I
Karasburg
Kokerboom
Keimoes
Grootdrink
Griquatown
Campbell
Barkly West
Galeshewe
Kimber
Warmbad
Onseepkans
Kakamas
Kleinbegin
Groblershoop
G R I Q U A L A N D
Ritchie
Oranjemund
Alexander
Bay
Pofadder
Kleinbegin
Putsonderwater
W E S T
Douglas
Bongani
Koffief
Wreck
Point
Eksteenfontein
Pella
Hartbees
Kenhardt
Marydale
E'Thembini
Prieska
Hopetown
Modder
Lekkersing
Aggeneys
Verneuk
Pan
Strydenburg
Port
Nolloth
Steinkopf
Concordia
N O R T H E R N C A P E
Copperton
Houwater
Petrusville
Vander
Nababeep
Carolusberg
Springbok
De Naawte
Van Wyksvlei
Vosburg
Philipstown
De Aar
Kleinsee
Komaggas
Grootvloer
Onderstedorings
Britstown
Nonzwa
Komieskroon
Kamiesberge
Brandvlei
Hanover
Kamiesberg
Swartkolkvloer
Sakrivier
Kareeberge
Carnarvon
Victoria
West
Hanover
Richmond
Hondeklipbaai
30°
Masinyusane
Sabelo
KwaNa
Wallekraal
Garies
Loeriesfontein
S O U T H A
Murraysburg
Sneeuw
Bitterfontein
Kootjieskolk
Sterling
Ongers
Nuwerus
Williston
Graaff-Reinet
Nieuwoudtville
Fish
Hardeveld
Great Karoo
Fraserburg
Aberdeen
Lutzville
Vanrhynsdorp
Calvinia
Beaufort
West
Sidesaviwa
Vredendal
Klawer
Doring
Sutherland
KwaZamukucinga
Jansenvil
Lambert's Bay
Graafwater
Clanwilliam
Salt
Steyterv
ATLANTIC
Sandveld
Wuppertal
Komsberg
Merweville
Leeu-
Gamka
Baboon Point
St Helena
Bay
Citrusdal
Prince Albert Road
Willowmore
OCEAN
Olifants
Laingsburg
Prince
Albert
Cock
Cape St Martin
Velddrif
Piketberg
Prince
Alfred
Hamlet
Groot Swartberg
De Rust
Kougaberge
St Helena Bay
Porterville
2325
Calitzdorp
Dysselsdorp
Joubertina
Vredenburg
Moorreesburg
Ceres
2250
Zoar
Oudtshoorn
Uniondale
Harlem
Kruisfe
Saldanha
W E S T E R N
Ladismith
George
Plettenberg Bay
Malmesbury
Wellington
Montagu
Humans
Atlantis
Paarl
Worcester
C A P E
Little Karoo
Mossel
Bay
Durbanville
Stellenbosch
Robertson
Barrydale
Riversdale
Knysna
Cape
Bellville
Swellendam
Heidelberg
Brakrivier
Seal
CAPE
TOWN
Khayelitsha
Somerset West
Port
Beaufort
Mossel Bay
Kanonpunt
False
Bay
Strand
Caledon
Stilbaai
Cape of
Good Hope
Hawston
Hermanus
20°
Bredasdorp
St
Sebastian
Bay
Gansbaai
Struis Bay
Arniston
Cape Agulhas

ICELAND

Arctic Circle

3

Jan Mayen (Nor)

R

Q (Nor)

70°

Denmark Strait

Ammassalik

P

Kong Christian IX Land

60°

Kong Christian X Land

Kong Frederik VI Kyst

O

80°

10°

Greenland (Denmark)

Kong Frederik VIII Land

N

Sisimiut

40°

50°

M

Ittoqqortoormiit

Labrador Sea

4

Nuuk

NEWFOUNDLAND AND LABRADOR

Newfoundland

St John's

C. Race

Cabot Strait

St Pierre and Miquelon (Fr.)

PRINCE EDWARD ISLAND

NEW BRUNSWICK

NOVA SCOTIA

50°

Gulf of St Lawrence

Île d'Anticosti

St Lawrence

Smallwood Res.

QUÉBEC

Labrador

Montréal

Québec

5

Peary Land

Ellesmere Island

Queen Elizabeth Islands

L

Baffin Bay

Davis Strait

Kuujjuaq

Baffin Island

Iqaluit

Hudson Strait

Inukjuak

Chisasibi

Belcher Is.

Foxe Basin

Southampton I.

Coats I.

Mansel I.

Hudson Bay

ONTARIO

Thunder Bay

Lake Superior

1

Dundas

Qaanaaq (Thule)

Devon Island

J

Somerset Island

Prince of Wales Island

Bathurst Inlet

Repulse Bay

Boothia Pen.

K

H

NUNAVUT

Churchill

Lake Winnipeg

Winnipeg

MANITOBA

MINNESOTA

St Paul

St Paul's

MICH

120°

110°

Melville Island

Parry Islands

I

G

Victoria Island

Amundsen Gulf

Banks Island

130°

140°

F

Sachs Harbour

Great Bear Lake

Great Slave Lake

Yellowknife

Lake Athabasca

SASKATCHEWAN

Saskatoon

Regina

NORTH DAKOTA

Bismarck

SOUTH DAKOTA

Rapid City

80°

150°

160°

E

Inuvik

Mackenzie

NORTHWEST TERRITORIES

CANADA

Peace

ALBERTA

Edmonton

Calgary

MONTANA

Billings

WYOMING

2

ARCTIC OCEAN

Beaufort Sea

D

Barrow

C

YUKON TERRITORY

Whitehorse

ROCKY

BRITISH COLUMBIA

Prince George

MOUNTAIN

Helena

IDAHO

Boise

170°

70°

B

A

U.S.A.

ALASKA

Fairbanks

△ Mt McKinley 6194

Kamloops

Vancouver

Victoria

Vancouver Island

Seattle

WASHINGTON

Olympia

Salt Lake City

Reno

Carson City

3

Arctic Circle

RUS. FED.

Bering Str.

Nome

Anchorage

Juneau

Alexander Archipelago

Haida Gwaii (Queen Charlotte Islands)

Portland

Salem

OREGON

Columbia

Gulf of Alaska

60°

St Lawrence I.

St Matthew Island

Kodiak I.

Sacramento

San Francisco

CALI

Nunivak I.

Alaska Pen.

4

Bering Sea

Pribilof Islands

Aleutian Islands

50°

40°

5

6

Bi-Polar Oblique Projection

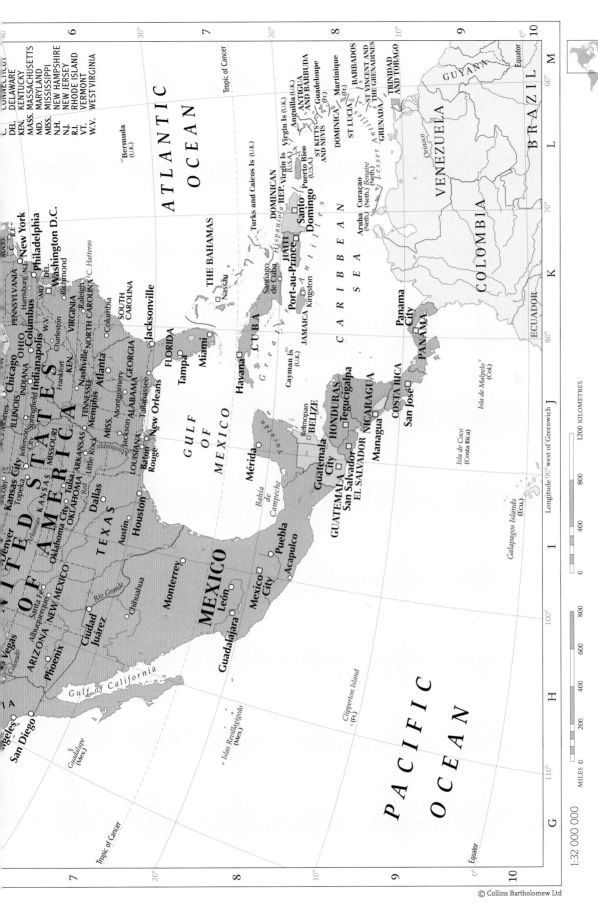

1:32 000 000

Lambert Azimuthal Equal Area Projection

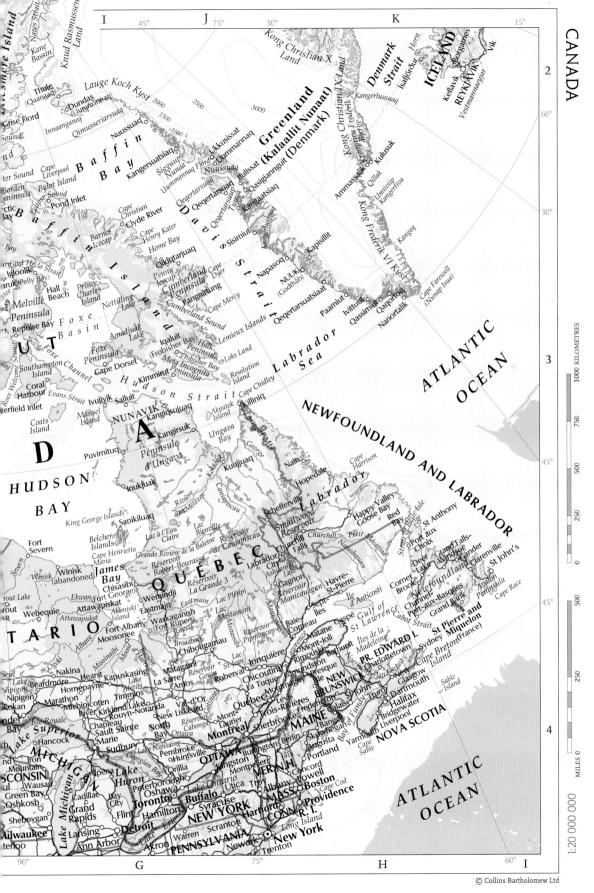

1:20 000 000

A

B

C

1

2

3

140°

130°

120°

YUKON

Beaver Creek
Snag (abandoned)
Koidern
White
Carmacks
Elsa
Mayo
Mount Patterson 2088
Grey Hunter Peak 2214
Stewart
Pelly
Hess
Keele
1600
Mayo

Stewart

Mackenzie Mountains

Selwyn Mountains

Keele Peak 2972

Norman Wells
Tulita (Fort Norman)
Déline

Great Bear Lake

Keith Arm

McTavish Arm

Hottah Lake

Point Lake

Kluane Lake
Faro
Fort Mountain 2404
Ross River
Pelly
Fort Mountain

Wrigley
△ 1574

Blackwater Lake

Keller Lake

Lac Grandin

Gamèti

Wekweètì (Snare Lakes)

Hardisty Lake

Destruction Bay
Haines Junction
Mount Skukum 2382
Whitehorse
Lake Laberge
Johnson's Crossing
Carcross
Teslin
Tuchitua

Mount Sir James MacBrien 2762

North Nahanni

1991

NORTHWEST TER

Whatì

Mackenzie

Belchoko

Yellowkni

Detah

St. Elias Mountains
Mount Logan 5959

Mount Fairweather 4670

Mount St Elias

Gustavus
Hoonah

ALASKA

Yakutat Bay
Yakutat

Kluckwan
Skagway
Haines
Bennett
Carcross
Atlin Lake
Atlin
Teslin Lake

Tungsten (abandoned)

Nahanni Butte
Fort Liard

Jean Marie River
Fort Providence

Great Slave Lake

Fort Resolution
Hay River
Kakisa

Pine Point (abandoned)

Enterprise

Fort Smi

Fitz

△ 899

Tathlina Lake

Devils 2618
Taku

Upper Liard
Watson Lake
Lower Post

Coal River

Liard

Fort Nelson

Liard

Mills Lake

R O C K

Chichagof Island
Juneau
Douglas
Angoon
Admiralty Island

Telegraph Creek
Stikine Plateau

Cassiar

Toad River

Steen River

Bistcho Lake

Zama City

Meander River
△ 1036

Caribou Mountains

Sitka
Kruzof Island
Baranof Island
Kupreanof Island
Petersburg
Wrangell

Dease Lake
Hyland Post

Mount Roosevelt 2896

Rainbow Lake

Chateh
Hay

John D'Or Prairie

Fox Lake

Lake Claire

Alexander Archipelago

Port Alexander

Kate's Needle
Mount Patullo 2739
Stewart
Iskut

Mount Lloyd George 2972

Ware
Muskwa

Prophet River

High Level
La Crete
Fort Vermilion

Peace

Klawock
Prince of Wales Island
Ketchikan

Skeena Mountains

BRITISH

Wonowon

Keg River

Manning

Birch Mountains

Fort Mac

U.S.A.

Dall Island

Dixon Entrance

Masset
Graham Island
Queen Charlotte

Mount Moresby 1138

Hazelton
New Hazelton
Kitwanga
Smithers
Telkwa

COLUMBIA

Takla Landing
Takla Lake

Hudson's Hope

Fort St John
Taylor

Peace

Peace River

Peerless Lake

ALBERT

Grimshaw
Dawson Creek
Fairview
Falher

McLennan

Cadotte Lake

Trout Lake

McM

Wabasca
Desmara

Utikuma Lake

Masset
Masset
Sewell Inlet
Gwaii Haanas

Haida Gwaii (Queen Charlotte Islands)

Prince Rupert
Port Edward
Kitimat
Terrace
Houston
Granisle
Pendleton Bay
Burns Lake

McLeod Lake

Mackenzie

Sentinel Peak 2515

Chetwynd

Beaverlodge
Grande Prairie

Spirit River
Sexsmith

High Prairie

Lesser Slave Lake
Slave Lake

Fox Creek
Swan Hills

Hecate Strait

Banks Island

Princess Royal Island

Ocean Falls

Kitkatla
Bella Coola

Tweedsmuir Island
Hartley Bay

Ootsa Lake
Morice Lake
Kemano (abandoned)
Ootsa Lake
Eutsuk Lake
François Lake

Fort St James
Stuart Lake
Vanderhoof

Summit Lake
Dome Creek

Prince George

Fraser

Grande Cache

McBride

Assiniboine
Barrhead
Whitecourt
Mayerthorpe

Fort

Westlock

La Bic

Red Veg

Fort

Bella Bella

Kalone Peak 2557

Cape St James

Queen Charlotte Sound

Kleena Kleene
Tatla Lake

Chilanko

Fraser Plateau

Williams Lake

Quesnel

Likely

Wells

Cariboo Mts

Valemount

Mount Robson 3954

Jasper

Brûlé
Hinton
Edson

Columbia

Drayton Valley
Devon

Saskatchewan

Edmonton

Leduc

Camrose

Wetaskiwin

Dawsons Landing
Namu
Holberg
Port Hardy
Port McNeill
Alert Bay
Sointula

Mount Waddington 4042
Chilko Lake

Dog Creek

100 Mile House

Clearwater

Blue River

Mica Creek

Mica 3747

Kimbasket Lake

Nordegg

Rimbey
Lacombe
Ponoka

Rocky Mountain House
Red Deer

Columbia

Stettler

Port Alice
Kyuquot
Tahsis
Gold River

Vancouver Island

Golden Hinde 2201

Thompson Sound

Sayward
Campbell River
Powell River

Alexis Creek

Gott Peak

Cache Creek
Clinton
Lillooet

Chilko

Barrière

Shuswap Lake

Salmon Arm
Sicamous

Kamloops

Revelstoke
Galena Bay

Rogers Pass
Golden

Mount Assiniboine 3618

Banff
Canmore

Louise
Sundre
Cochrane

Three Hills
Drumheller
Olds
Airdrie

Calgary

Strathmore
Bassano

Ucluelet
Tofino
Port Alberni
Lake Cowichan
Courtenay
Comox

Squamish
Whistler

Merritt

Vernon

Arrow

New Denver

Kootenay Lake

Invermere

Mount Forham 3457

Kimberley
Fernie

High River
Okotoks

Elkford
Z
Claresh

Nanaimo
Ladysmith
Duncan

Vancouver

Sechelt

North Vancouver

Hope
Chilliwack
Princeton

Kelowna
Penticton

Keremeos

Okanagan Falls

Castlegar
Nelson
Salmo
Trail

Upper Arrow L.
Lower Arrow Lake
Arrow Lake

Cranbrook
Creston

Crowsnest Pass

Lethbridge
Coaldal

Juan de Fuca Strait
Cape Flattery

Port Renfrew
Mission

Cowichan

Mount Baker
Osoyoos
Grand Forks
Rossland

Yahk
Eureka
△ 3184

Cardston

PACIFIC OCEAN

Port Angeles
Port Townsend

Victoria

Lynnwood
Everett

Mount Vernon
Bellingham

Bonners Ferry
Libby
△ 2663

Browning

Whitefish

Mount Olympus 2428
Forks

Seattle
Bremerton

Bellevue
Tacoma

WASHINGTON

Colville
Pend Oreille

Hayden
Kalispell

Flathead Lake
Thompson Falls
Polson

M
Chc

Aberdeen
Shelton

Olympia

Mount Bonaparte 2212

Omak

Grand Coulee

Moses Lake
Ephrata
Wenatchee

Columbia

Spokane
Coeur d'Alene
Kellogg

McDonald 2993

METRES FEET

5000	16404
3000	9843
2000	6562
1000	3281
500	1640
200	656
0	0

Land below sea level

200	656
4000	13124
6000	19686

Lambert Azimuthal Equal Area Projection

130°

B

Longitude 120° west of Greenwich

C

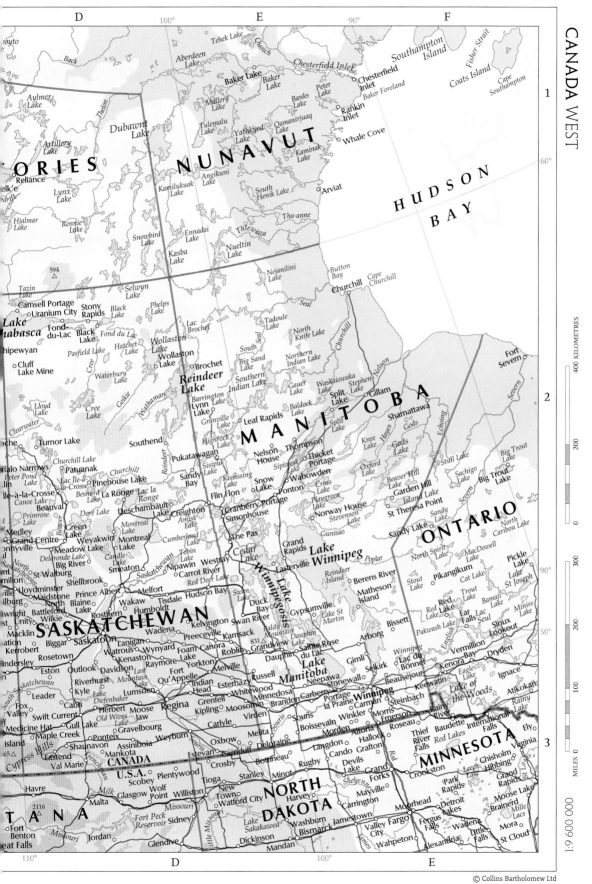

D 100° E 90° F

1

2

3

Tehek Lake
Chorch
Aberdeen Lake
Southampton Island
Fisher Strait
Back
Chesterfield Inlet
Coats Island
Cape Southampton
Baker Lake
Baker Lake
Banks Lake
Peter Lake
Chesterfield Inlet
Baker Foreland
Aylmer Lake
Mallery Lake
Rankin Inlet
Dubawnt Lake
Tulemalu Lake
Yathkyed Lake
Qamanirjuaq Lake
Whale Cove
ORIES
NUNAVUT
Reliance
Kamilukuak Lake
Angikuni Lake
Kaminak Lake
Arviat

elk'e
Lynx Lake
Rennie Lake
South Henik Lake
60°
HUDSON
Hjalmar Lake
Tha-anne
BAY

594

Tazin Lake
Snowbird Lake
Ennadai Lake
Nueltin Lake
Thlewiaza
Nejanilini Lake
Button Bay
Cape Churchill
Selwyn Lake
Kasba Lake
Churchill
Camsell Portage
Stony Rapids
Black Lake
Phelps Lake
Seal
Uranium City
Fond-du-Lac
Lac Brochet
Tadoule Lake
North Knife Lake
Lake Athabasca
Black Lake
Fond du Lac
Wollaston Lake
South Seal
Churchill
hipewyan
Pasfield Lake
Hatchet Lake
Wollaston Lake
Big Sand Lake
Northern Indian Lake
Cluff Lake Mine
Cree Lake
Waterbury Lake
Brochet
Gauer Lake
Waskaiowaka Lake
Stephens Lake
Fort Severn
Reindeer Lake
Southern Indian Lake
Split Lake
Nelson
Gillam
Lloyd Lake
Barrington Lake
Lynn Lake
Granville Lake
Leaf Rapids
Baldock Lake
MANITOBA
Shamattawa
Clearwater
Highrock Lake
Nelson House
Thompson
Knee Lake
Gods Lake
Echoing
oche
Turnor Lake
Southend
Pukatawagan
Sipiwesk Lake
Thicket Portage
Oxford Lake
Beaver Hill Lake
Big Trout Lake
Churchill Lake
Sandy Bay
Sisipuk Lake
Snow Lake
Wabowden
Garden Hill
Big Trout Lake
Peter Pond Lake
Patuanak
Pinehouse Lake
Kississing Lake
Ponton
Cross Lake
Island Lake
Sachigo Lake
lin
Île-à-la-Crosse
Lac Île-à-la-Crosse
La Ronge
Flin Flon
Playgreen Lake
Canoe Lake
Beauval
Lac la Ronge
Creighton
Cranberry Portage
Norway House
St Theresa Point
ONTARIO
Primrose Lake
Dore Lake
Deschambault Lake
Amisk Lake
Simonhouse
Stevenson Lake
Sandy Lake
Medley
Green Lake
Montreal Lake
Cumberland Lake
The Pas
Gunisao Lake
North Caribou Lake
Grand Centre
Weyakwin
Montreal Lake
Tobin Lake
Cedar Lake
Grand Rapids
Lake Winnipeg
Poplar
North Spirit Lake
MacDowell Lake
Pickle Lake
onnyville
Meadow Lake
Candle Lake
Smeaton
Nipawin
Westray
Easterville
Reindeer Island
Berens River
Stout Lake
Pikangikum
Cat Lake
Lake St Joseph
Delaronde Lake
Big River
Red Deer Lake
Swan Lake
Matheson Island
Trout Lake
Ear Falls
St Walburg
Shellbrook
Melfort
Hudson Bay
Duck Bay
Lake Winnipegosis
Bissett
Red Lake
Lac Seul
Sioux Lookout
Miniss Lake
Lloydminster
Maidstone
Prince Albert
North Blaine
Tisdale
Humboldt
Gypsumville
Pakwash Lake
English River
Vermilion Bay
Dryden
Ignace
Battleford
Wilkie
Rosthern
Wadena
Kelvington
Swan River
Lake St Martin
Dauphin Lake
Arborg
Keewatin
Lake of the Woods
Atikokan
Unity
SASKATCHEWAN
Biggar
Saskatoon
Tanigan
Wynyard
Foam Lake
Canora
Roblin
Grandview
831
Sainte Rose du Lac
Gimli
Lac du Bonnet
Kenora
Eagle Lake
Rosetown
Watrous
Kenaston
Raymore
Yorkton
Melville
Dauphin
Lake Manitoba
Neepawa
Stonewall
Selkirk
Beauséjour
Rainy Lake
Eston
Outlook
Davidson
Last Mountain Lake
Fort Qu'Appelle
Indian Head
Russell
Esterhazy
Brandon
Portage la Prairie
Winnipeg
Steinbach
Lake of the Woods
Riverhurst
Lake Diefenbaker
Lumsden
Whitewood
Minnedosa
Carberry
Carman
Kyle
Cabri
Herbert
Moose Jaw
Regina
Grenfell
Kipling
Moosomin
Virden
Souris
Winkler
Morris
Emerson
Roseau
Baudette
International Falls
Ely
Leader
Swift Current
Old Wives Lake
Carlyle
Boissevain
Morden
Altona
Thief River Falls
Red Lakes
Virginia
Fox Valley
Gull Lake
Gravelbourg
Weyburn
Oxbow
Melita
Deloraine
Langdon
Hallock
Grafton
MINNESOTA
Chisholm
Hibbing
Medicine Hat
Maple Creek
Ponteix
Shaunavon
Mankota
Estevan
Carnduff
Bottineau
Rugby
Devils Lake
Crookston
Leech Lake
Grand Rapids
Island
Cypress Hills
Eastend
Val Marie
CANADA
Crosby
Stanley
Minot
Park Rapids
Virginia
65
USA
Scobey
Plentywood
Tioga
New Town
Harvey
Mayville
Moorhead
Detroit Lakes
Moose Lake
Mora
St Cloud
Havre
Glasgow
Wolf Point
Williston
Watford City
NORTH DAKOTA
Carrington
Fergus Falls
Wadena
Brainerd
Mille Lacs
TANA
2116
Malta
Milk
Fort Peck Reservoir
Sidney
Lake Sakakawea
Washburn
Jamestown
Valley City
Fargo
Wahpeton
Alexandria
Little Falls
Fort Benton
eat Falls
Jordan
Glendive
Dickinson
Bismarck
Mandan

Missouri
Little Missouri
Missouri
Sheyenne
Red
James
Crow
St Louis

D 110° D 100° E

© Collins Bartholomew Ltd

1:9 000 000

400 KILOMETRES
200
0

MILES
300
200
100
0

A 90° 60° B 80° C

2

**HUDSON
BAY**

Puvirnituq

Gilmour
Island

Ottawa
Islands

Lac
Payne

Tasia

Lac
Tasiat

Arnaua

Far

Inukjuak

Lac
Le Roy

Hopewell Islands

Lac
Chavigny

Lac
Bacqueville

Lac aux

Rivière aux

NUNAVUT

Sleeper
Islands

Nastapoka Islands

Nastapoca

Lac
Minto

North Belcher
Islands

King-George
Islands

Saniklluaq

Lacs des
Loups Marins

*Belcher
Islands*

Lac
à l'Eau
Claire

Flaherty Island

Kuujjuarapik
(Poste-de-la-Baleine)

Lac
Guillaume-Delisle

Cape Henrietta
Maria

Long Island

Grande Rivière de la Baleine

Lac
Bienville

Churchill

North
Knife Lake

Cape
Churchill

Churchill

Churchill

Stephens
Lake

Nelson

Gillam

MANITOBA

Shamattawa

Knee
Lake

Hayes

Gods

Gods
Lake

Echoing

Fort
Severn

Winisk
(abandoned)

Severn

Winisk

*James
Bay*

Lac Burton

Réservoir
Robert-Bourassa

Réservoir
La Grande 4

Chisasibi
(Fort George)

North
Twin Island

Radisson

Réservoir
La Grande 3

QUÉ

Stull Lake

Severn

Big Trout Lake

Big Trout
Lake

Kasabonika
Lake

Ekwan

Attawapiskat

Akimiski
Island

South
Twin
Island

Wemindji

Sachigo
Lake

North Spirit
Lake

Webequie

Wunnummin
Lake

Winisk
Lake

Attawapiskat

Fort Albany

Eastmain

Réservoir
Opinaca

Eastmain

Sandy
Lake

Sandy Lake

North
Caribou Lake

Missisa
Lake

Kapiskau

Charlton
Island

Rupert Bay

Waskaganish
(Fort Rupert)

Rupert

Lac
Mistassini

Stout
Lake

Pikangikum

MacDowell

Attawapiskat
Lake

Moosonee

Lac Evans

Broadback

North
Red
Lake

Red
Lake

Cat Lake

Trout
Lake

Lake
St Joseph

Pickle Lake

Ogoki
Reservoir

Albany

Moose
Factory

Rivière de l'Harricana

Nottaway

Lac
Comencho

Mistassi

Pakwash Lake

Bamaji
Lake

Whitewater
Lake

Pledger
Lake

Kesagami
Lake

Lac au Godbout

Lac
Opataca

ONTARIO

English

Lac
Seul

Miniss
Lake

Savant
Lake

Ogoki

Otter Rapids

Fraserdale

Lac
Matagami

Chibougam

Vermillion
Bay

Dryden

Sturgeon
Lake

Caribou Lake

Nakina

Missinaibi

Moose

Matagami

Lac Wasswanipi

Kenora

Eagle
Lake

Sioux
Lookout

Armstrong

Lake
Nipigon

Longlac

Hearst

Smooth Rock
Falls

Lebel-sur-
Quévillon

Réservoir
Gouin

Dolbe

Mista

Lake of
the Woods

Ignace

Beardmore

Kapuskasing

Cochrane

Amos

Lac
Parent

St-Félicie

Bota-Métabetch

Fort
Frances

Atikokan

Nipigon

Long
Lake

Hornepayne

Iroquois
Falls

La Sarre

Rouyn-
Noranda

Senneterre

St-M

Rainy Lake

Thunder
Bay

Terrace
Bay

Manitouwadge

Timmins

Malartic

Lac
Simard

La Tuque

**CANADA
U.S.A.**

Thunder
Bay

St Ignace
Island

Kahinakagami
Lake

Marathon

Missinaibi
Lake

Nightawk
Lake

Kirkland
Lake

Englehart

Val-d'Or

Réservoir
Cabonga

Lac
Kempt

Grand
Marais

Pigeon
River

Isle
Royale

Michipicoten
Island

Wawa

Foleyet

New Liskeard

Temagami
Lake

Amos

Mont-
Laurier

St-Michel-
des-Saints

Ma

Lake Superior

Copper
Harbor

Keweenaw
Peninsula

Michipicoten
River

Chapleau

Ramsey
Lake

Lac
Kipawa

Réservoir
Dozois

Mont Tremblant

Trois-
Rivières

Ashland

Gogebic Range

Hancock

Houghton

Batchawana
Mountain

Wanapitei
Lake

Lac
Simard

Maniwaki

Sté-
Adéle

Jolliette

So Ash

Bruce
Crossing

Crystal
Falls

Ishpeming

Marquette

Sault Sainte
Marie

Sault Sainte
Marie

Thessalon

Blind
River

Sudbury

Sturgeon
Falls

North
Bay

Deep River

Petawawa

Pembroke

Shawinigan

Montréal

Park
Falls

Iron Mountain

Newberry

St Joseph Island

North Channel

Espanola

Mattawa

Ottawa

Arnprior

Salaberry-de-
Valleyfield

Sherb

Merrill

Escanaba

St-

Rhinelander

Menominee

MICHIGAN

Manitoulin
Island

Wikwemikong

Lake
Nipissing

South River

Huntsville

Barrys
Bay

Carleton Place

Smiths
Falls

Cornwall

Lac
Champlain

St-Joh

Riche

Wausau

Marinette

Green Bay

Manitoulin
Islands

Cheboygan

Baymouth

Georgian Bay

Parry
Sound

Bracebridge

Bancroft

Gravenhurst

OTTAWA

Ogdensburg

Massena

Plattsburgh

Burlington

Montp

Shawano

WISCONSIN

Green
Bay

Petoskey

Alpena

Tobermory

Owen
Sound

Midland

Rideau
Lake

Brockville

Kingston

Watertown

VERM

Wisconsin
Rapids

Appleton

Oshkosh

Gaylord

Bruce
Peninsula

Port
Elgin

Kawartha
Lakes

Peterborough

Belleville

Lowville

Rutland

Leba

Portage

Fond
du Lac

Sheboygan

Traverse
City

Manistee

Grayling

Tawas
City

Kincardine

Hanover

Barrie

Lindsay

Cobourg

1629

Mount
Marcy

Madison

West Bend

Ludington

Cadillac

Saginaw Bay

Harbor
Beach

Goderich

Orillia

Oshawa

Lake Ontario

Oneida

Oswego

Rome

Utica

Adirondack Mts

Milwaukee

Waukesha

Mount
Pleasant

Big
Rapids

Midland

Bay
City

Port
Huron

Stratford

Guelph

Toronto

Scarborough

Rochester

Syracuse

Auburn

NEW

Troy

Racine

Kenosha

Muskegon

Saginaw

Flint

Kitchener

Hamilton

St Catharines

Geneva

Finger Lakes

Cortland

Schenectady

Albany

Pittsfield

Rockford

Grand
Rapids

Owosso

Pontiac

Brantford

London

St
Thames

Buffalo

Batavia

Ithaca

Elmira

Oneonta

M

Elgin

Battle Creek

Lansing

Livonia

Dunkirk

Hornell

Norwich

Wor

Aurora

Chicago

Kalamazoo

Pontiac

Detroit

Windsor

St Thomas

Erie

Jamestown

Olean

Binghamton

YORK

Springfield

Gary

South Bend

Jackson

Ann
Arbor

Lake Erie

Ashtabula

Bradford

Sayre

Ottawa

Joliet

Michigan
City

Elkhart

Adrian

Sylvania

Pelee
Island

Warren

INDIANA

Plymouth

Fort
Wayne

Toledo

Lorain

Cleveland

Pontiac

Watseka

OHIO

Maumee

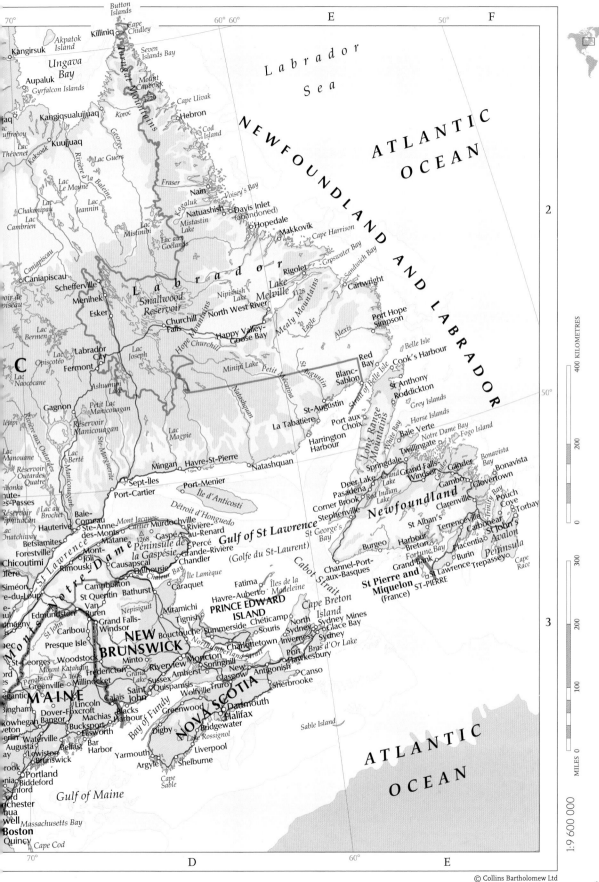

70° 60° 60° E 50° F

Button Islands

Killiniq
Cape Chidley

Akpatok Island

Kangirsuk

Ungava Bay

Aupaluk
Gyrfalcon Islands

Torngat Mountains

Mount Caubvick

Seven Islands Bay

Cape Uivak

Labrador Sea

jaq
uffreboy
Lac Thévenet
Kangiqsualujjuaq
Koroc
Hebron
Cod Island

Kuujjuaq
Koksoak
Rivière à la Baleine

Lac Guers

ATLANTIC

Lac Le Moyne
George
Fraser

Lac Jeannin

Nain

Lac Chakonipau
Lac Cambrien

Lac Mistinibi
Lac aux Goélands

Logaluk

Natuashish

Davis Inlet (abandoned)

Voisey's Bay

Hopedale

OCEAN

Caniapiscau

Scheffierville

Menihek

Esker

Labrador

Smallwood Reservoir

Nipishish Lake

North West River

Churchill Falls

Hope Mountains

Happy Valley-Goose Bay

Lake Melville

Mealy Mountains

Makkovik

Cape Harrison

Rigolet

Groswater Bay

Sandwich Bay

Cartwright

N E W F O U N D L A N D   A N D   L A B R A D O R

1128

Eagle

Alexis

Port Hope Simpson

Belle Isle

Cook's Harbour

Voir du iseau

C

Lac Naococane

Lac Opiscotéo

Labrador City
Fermont

Lac Joseph

Ashuanipi Lake

Minipi Lake

Petit Mécatina

St Augustin

Blanc-Sablon

Red Bay

St Anthony
Roddickton

Grey Islands

50°

Lac Bermen

Gagnon

Petit Lac Manicouagan

Lac Magpie

St-Augustin

La Tabatière

Port aux Choix

Horse Islands

Baie Verte

Notre Dame Bay

Fogo Island

léjipi

Réservoir Manicouagan

Lac Berté

Harrington Harbour

Long Range Mountains

White Bay

Twillingate

Bonavista Bay

anoe

Réservoir Outardes Quatre

Ste-Marguerite

Mingan

Havre-St-Pierre

Natashquan

Springdale

Grand Falls-Windsor

Gander

Clovertown

Bonavista

utes-Passes

Lac au Brochet

Manicouagan

Sept-Îles

Port-Cartier

Port-Menier

Île d'Anticosti

Deer Lake
Pasadena

Grand Lake

Gambo

Réservoir pimuacan

Baie-Comeau

Détroit d'Honguedo

Corner Brook

Red Indian Lake

Clarenville

Trinity Bay

Pouch Cove

ac natchiway

Hauterive

Ste-Anne-des-Monts

Mont Jacques-Cartier

Murdochville

Rivière-au-Renard

Gulf of St Lawrence

St George's Bay

Stephenville

Newfoundland

St Alban's

Terrenceville

Carbonear

St John's

Betsiamites

1268

Gaspé

Torbay

Forestville

Matane

Péninsule de la Gaspésie

Percé

(Golfe du St-Laurent)

Burgeo

Harbour Breton

Placentia

Avalon Peninsula

Chicoutimi

Mont-Joli

Grande-Rivière

Chandler

Fortune Bay

Burin

iere

Rimouski

Causapscal

Dalhousie

Île Lamèque

Cabot Strait

Channel-Port-aux-Basques

Grand Bank

St Lawrence

Trepassey

Cape Race

Siméon
e-du-Loup

Campbellton

Chaleur Bay

Caraquet

Fatima

Îles de la Madeleine

St Pierre and Miquelon
(France) ST-PIERRE

aul

St Quentin
Van Buren

Bathurst

Nepisiguit

Havre-Aubert

Cape Breton

mgny

Edmundston

Grand Falls-Windsor

Miramichi

Tignish

PRINCE EDWARD ISLAND

Chéticamp

Island

Caribou

St John

Presque Isle

Bouctouche

Summerside

Souris

North Sydney

Inverness

Sydney Mines
Glace Bay

pec

St-Georges

Woodstock

NEW BRUNSWICK

Minto

Charlottetown

Northumberland Strait

Sydney

Bras d'Or Lake

Port Hawkesbury

ord

St-Georges

Mount Katahdin

Fredericton

Riverview

Moncton

Springhill

New Glasgow

Antigonish

Canso

egantic

△ 1606

Grand Lake

Sussex

Amherst

Truro

MAINE

Greenville

Millinocket

Lincoln

Saint John

Quispamsis

Wolfville

NOVA SCOTIA

Sherbrooke

ingham

Penobscot

Calais

Bay of Fundy

Greenwood

Dartmouth

Sable Island

kowhegan

Dover-Foxcroft
Bangor

Machias

Blacks Harbour

Digby

Bridgewater

Halifax

veton
erlin

Bucksport

Ellsworth

Bar Harbor

Lake Rossignol

Liverpool

Waterville

Belfast

Yarmouth

Shelburne

ATLANTIC

Augusta
Lewiston
Brunswick

Argyle

Cape Sable

OCEAN

rook

Portland
Biddeford

nia
Sanford
ord
nchester
hua

Quincy

Gulf of Maine

well Massachusetts Bay

Boston

Cape Cod

70° D 60° E

400 KILOMETRES — 200 — 0

300 — 200 — 100 — 0 MILES

1:9 600 000

50° 130° A 120° B 110° C 100°

Port Hardy
Gold River
Campbell River
Powell River
100 Mile House
Mount Waddington 4042
Mount Columbia 3747
Jasper
Leduc Edmonton
Vegreville
Lloydminster
Meadow Lake
The P
Cedar
Lake
Winnipegosis
Swan

Vancouver Island
Nanaimo
Victoria
Kamloops
BRITISH COLUMBIA
Kelowna
Vernon
Nelson
ROCKY
Banff
Red Deer
Airdrie
Okotoks Calgary
ALBERTA
Hanna
Brooks
Medicine Hat
Wetaskiwin
Wainwright
Red Deer
Prince Albert
Saskatoon
SASKATCHEWAN
Unity Biggar
Kindersley
Davidson
Rosthern
Humboldt
Saskatchewan
Nipawin
CANADA
Wynyard
Yorkton
Canora
MA
N

Cape Flattery
Mount Olympus 2428
Bellingham
Everett
Vancouver
Penticton
Cranbrook
Lethbridge
Swift Current
Moose Jaw
Regina
Weyburn
Melville
Moosomin
Virden
Bra
la

Tacoma
Olympia
Mount Rainier 4399
Mount St Helens 2550
Seattle
Spokane
Coeur d'Alene
Kalispell
Shelby
Havre
Glasgow
Estevan
Bottineau
Williston
Minot

Astoria
Portland
Salem
Eugene
Albany
Oregon City
Pendleton
La Grande
Richland
Yakima
WASHINGTON
Moscow
Lewiston
Missoula
Helena
MONTANA
Great Falls
Fort Peck Reservoir
Glendive
Miles City
Dickinson
Bismarck
Bowman
N. DAKO
James

Coos Bay
Grants Pass
Klamath Falls
Upper Klamath Lake
Bend
Burns
Caldwell
Blue Mountains
Salmon
Butte
Bozeman
Dillon
Billings
Yellowstone
Cody
Bighorn
Sheridan
Gillette
Buffalo
Rapid City
Mobridge
Lake Oahe
S. DAKO
Pierre
Aber

Crescent City
Eureka
Redding
Red Bluff
Mount Shasta 4317
Alturas
Lakeview
OREGON
Klamath
Winnemucca
Lovelock
Snake
Idaho Falls
Pocatello
Twin Falls
Jerome
Boise
Nampa
IDAHO
Grand Teton 4190
Garnett Peak 4202
Lander
WYOMING
Green River
Casper
Sweetwater
Laramie
Scottsbluff
Chadron
Niobrara
NEBRAS
North Platte
Ogallala

Point Arena
Ukiah
Santa Rosa
Sacramento
Stockton
San Francisco
Oakland
San Jose
Modesto
Reno
Sparks
Carson City
NEVADA
Great Basin
Humboldt
Pyramid Lake
Elko
Wendover
Great Salt Lake
Brigham City
Logan
Ogden
Salt Lake City
Provo
Evanston
Uinta Mts 4123
Kings Peak
Craig
Cheyenne
Greeley
Boulder
Denver
Aurora
Sidney
North Platte
South Platte
McCook
Burlington
KA
Republican
Kansas
Great Be

Monterey Bay
Salinas
San Jose
Fresno
Visalia
Bakersfield
CALIFORNIA
Sierra Nevada
Mount Whitney 4418
Tonopah
Ely
Wheeler Peak 3982
Sevier Lake
Caliente
St George
Cedar City
Richfield
UTAH
Moab
Grand Junction
UNITED
Mount Elbert 4398
COLORADO
Colorado Springs
Pueblo
STAT
Trinidad
Alamosa
Durango
Liberal
Dodge City
Ulysses
O

Point Conception
Santa Maria
Santa Barbara
Oxnard
Los Angeles
Pasadena
Long Beach
Santa Ana
Riverside
San Diego
Tijuana
Channel Islands
Mount Charleston 3632
Death Valley
Beatty
Las Vegas
Henderson
Barstow
Kingman
Lake Havasu City
Colorado
Grand Canyon
Plateau
Tuba City
Kayenta
Page
Lake Powell
Kanab
Flagstaff
Winslow
Prescott
ARIZONA
Glendale
Phoenix
Mesa
Casa Grande
Tucson
Gallup
Los Alamos
Santa Fe
Albuquerque
St Johns
Baldy Peak 3476
Socorro
NEW MEXICO
Silver City
Deming
Las Cruces
Taos
Las Vegas
Clayton
Tucumcari
Clovis
Portales
Llano Estacado
Amarillo
Dumas
Stratford
Dalhart
Vernon
Wichita
Lubbock
Post
Snyder
San Angelo
Midland
Odessa
TEX

Oceanside
San Diego
Tijuana
Ensenada
Mexicali
Yuma
San Luis Río Colorado
Salton Sea
Rio Colorado
Nogales
Douglas
Agua Prieta
Nuevo Casas Grandes
Alamogordo
Roswell
Lovington
Hobbs
Artesia
Pecos
Fort Stockton
Edwards Plateau

Picacho del Diablo 3096
Cabo San Quintín
San Felipe
Puerto Peñasco
Caborca
Magdalena
Benjamin Hill
Nogales
El Paso
Ciudad Juárez
El Barreal
Moctezuma
Van Horn
Alpine
Ojinaga
Emory Peak
Ciudad Acuña
Del Rio
Ant

Guadalupe (Mexico)
Isla Ángel de la Guarda
Isla Tiburón
Hermosillo
Madera
Chihuahua
Ciudad Delicias
Camargo
Sabinas
Piedras Negras

Bahía Sebastián Vizcaíno
Isla Cedros
Punta Eugenia
Rosarito
Bahía Tortugas
Santa Rosalia
Guaymas
Ciudad Obregón
Yécora
Cuauhtémoc
MEXICO
Conchos
Jiménez
Bolsón de Mapimí
Monclova
Sabinas Hidalgo
Nuevo Laredo
Salado
Lar

Villa Insurgentes
Isla Carmen
Navojoa
Los Mochis
Guasave
Guamúchil
Hidalgo del Parral
Gómez Palacio
Torreón
Matamoros
Monterrey
Rey

Santa Margarita
Isla San José
Isla Cerralvo
Costa Rica
Culiacán
Nazas
Saltillo
Monterelos
Monte

La Paz
Durango
Río Grande
Cerro Peña Nev
Mazatlán
Matehuala 3644
Vic

San José del Cabo

PACIFIC OCEAN

Gulf of California

Baja California

Sierra Madre Occidental

Sonora

MEXICO

Tropic of Cancer

20°

A 120° B Longitude 110° west of Greenwich C 100°

Lambert Azimuthal Equal Area Projection

METRES FEET

5000 / 16404
3000 / 9843
2000 / 6562
1000 / 3281
500 / 1640
200 / 656
0 / 0
Land below sea level
200 / 656
4000 / 13124
6000 / 19686

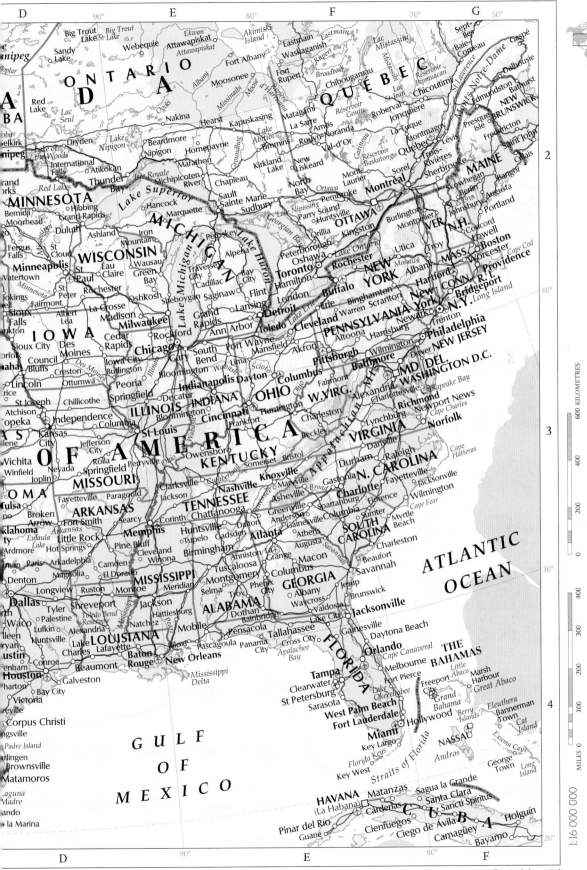

USA WEST

METRES / FEET

METRES	FEET
5000	16404
3000	9843
2000	6562
1000	3281
500	1640
200	656
0	0
Land below sea level	
200	656
4000	13124
6000	19686

Canada

CANADA · U.S.A. · SASKATCHEWAN · ALBERTA · BRITISH COLUMBIA

Val Marie · Frenchman · Milk River · Nelson Reservoir · Cardston · Milk River · Castlegar · Nelson · Trail · Creston · Grand Forks · Rossland · Keremeos · Okanagan Falls · Osoyoos · Oliver

Vancouver Island / British Columbia

Vancouver · Nanaimo · Richmond · Ladysmith · Mission · Chilliwack · Duncan · Sidney · Victoria · Saanich · Port Renfrew · North Vancouver

Washington

Seattle · Bellingham · Anacortes · Mount Vernon · Everett · Lynnwood · Bellevue · Bremerton · Tacoma · Parkland · Lacey · Olympia · Shelton · Aberdeen · Hoquiam · Raymond · Centralia · Chehalis · Kelso · Longview · Oak Harbor · Port Townsend · Port Angeles · Forks

Mount Olympus 2428 · Cape Flattery · Strait of Juan de Fuca · Glacier Peak 3213 · Mount Baker 3285 · Mount Rainier 4392 · Mount St Helens 2550 · Mount Adams · Snohomish · Wenatchee · Chelan · Lake Chelan · Brewster · Okanogan · Omak · Grand Coulee · Ephrata · Moses Lake · Othello · Ellensburg · Roslyn · Yakima · Selah · Toppenish · Sunnyside · Grandview · Prosser · Kennewick · Pasco · Richland · Walla Walla · Dayton · Colfax · Pullman · Ritzville · Cheney · Spokane · Opportunity · Colville · Newport · Kettle Falls

Mount Bonaparte 2212 · Kettle River Range · Franklin D. Roosevelt Lake · Pend Oreille Lake · Sandpoint · Bonners Ferry

Montana

ROCKY MOUNTAINS · MONTANA

Chinook · Havre · Malta · Jordan · Fort Peck Reservoir · Roundup · Bighorn · Hardin · Crow Agency · Lewistown · Harlowton · Big Timber · Livingston · Billings · Laurel · Columbus · Red Lodge

Shelby · Cut Bank · Browning · Gildford · Lothair · Fort Benton · Great Falls · Choteau · Conrad · Augusta · White Sulphur Springs · Big Belt Mountains · Lewis Range · Mount Cleveland 3184 · Flathead Lake · Kalispell · Columbia Falls · Whitefish · Libby · Eureka · Polson · Ronan · Missoula · Deer Lodge · Anaconda · Butte · Boulder · Helena · Townsend · Three Forks · Bozeman · Belgrade · Canyon Ferry Lake · Clarks Fork · Stevensville · Hamilton · Mount Haggin 3230 · Big Hole · Dillon · Salmon

Snowshoe Peak 2663 · McDonald Peak 2993 · Bear Paw Mountain 2116

Wyoming

WYOMING · ROCKY MOUNTAINS · Absaroka Range · Wind River Range · Yellowstone Lake · West Thumb · West Yellowstone · Electric Peak 3343 · Granite Peak 3901 · Cody · Powell · Lovell · Greybull · Worland · Thermopolis · Riverton · Lander · Moran · Grand Teton 4197 · Jackson · Gros Ventre Range · Gannett Peak 4202 · Pinedale · Afton · Montpelier · Kemmerer · Rock Springs · Green River · Flaming Gorge Reservoir · Lyman · Evanston · Sweetwater

Idaho

IDAHO · Snake River Plain · Salmon River Mountains · Sawtooth Range · Bitterroot Range · Clearwater Mountains · Bitterroot · Selway · Mount McGuire 3073 · Challis · Salmon · Cascade · McCall · Payette · Weiser · Council · New Meadows · Grangeville · Kooskia · Kamiah · Orofino · Lewiston · Moscow · Kellogg · Wallace · St Joe · St Maries · Dworshak Reservoir · Coeur d'Alene · Hayden · Selkirk Mountains · Ketchum · Bellevue · Mountain Home · Sun Valley · Arco · Shoshone · Gooding · Jerome · Twin Falls · Burley · Rupert · Glenns Ferry · Contact · Wells · Boise · Meridian · Nampa · Caldwell · Ontario · Parma · Idaho Falls · Rexburg · Rigby · Blackfoot · Pocatello · American Falls · American Falls Reservoir · Malad City · Preston · Soda Springs · Bear · St Anthony · Spencer

Oregon

OREGON · Columbia Plateau · Blue Mountains · Strawberry Mountain 2755 · High Desert · Harney Basin · Steens Mountain · Warner Mountains · Owyhee · Malheur Lake · Harney Lake · Warner Lakes · Lake Abert · Goose Lake · Alkali Lake · Upper Klamath Lake · Crater Lake · Klamath Mountains · Snake · Owyhee · Deschutes · Willamette

Portland · Gresham · Oregon City · Lake Oswego · Woodburn · Keizer · Salem · Albany · Corvallis · Lebanon · Springfield · Eugene · Harrisburg · Cottage Grove · Sutherlin · Roseburg · Myrtle Point · Coos Bay · Port Orford · Brookings · Crescent City · McKinleyville · Grants Pass · Ashland · Medford · Central Point · Klamath Falls · Yreka · Mount Shasta 4317 · Dunsmuir · Canyonville · The Dalles · Hood River · Hermiston · Pendleton · La Grande · Union · Baker · Enterprise · John Day · Burns · Hines · Riley · Brothers · Prineville · Bend · Redmond · Madras · Shaniko · Condon · Goldendale · Oakridge · Chemult · Valley Falls · Lakeview · Lincoln City · Newport · Florence · Reedsport · Tillamook · Astoria · Warrenton · McMinnville · Eagle Cap 2925 · Wallowa Mountains · Santa Rosa Range · Granite Peak 2996 · McDermitt · Denio · Jordan Valley · Juntura · Vale

Mount Hood 3427 · Cape Blanco · Cape Disappointment · Willapa Bay

Lambert Azimuthal Equal Area Projection

40°

COLORADO

NEW MEXICO

35°

Root Plateau

Gunnison

Grand Junction

Crescent Junction

Mount Peale 3877

Moab

Montcello

Cortez

Salida

St Johns

Springerville

Alpine

Glenwood

Clifton

Safford

Chiricahua Peak 2985

Douglas

Duchesne

Price

Wellington

Blanding

Bluff

Shiprock

Gallup

110°

Willcox

Tombstone

Bisbee

UTAH

Green River

Hanksville

Chinle

Kayenta

Many Farms

Ganado

Chambers

Window

Holbrook

Show Low

Mount Baldy Peak 3476

Sierra Vista

Benson

Nogales 2881

2965

Provo

Springville

Spanish Fork

Mount Nebo 3623

Nephi

Delta

Fillmore

Richfield

Escalante

Lake Powell

Page

Tuba City

Polacca

Winslow

Sedona

Camp Verde

Humphreys Peak 3851

Flagstaff

Mogollon Plateau

Williams

Prescott

Prescott Valley

Yarnell

Sedona

Snowflake

Superior

Globe

San Pedro

Kearny

Marana

San Pedro

Green Valley

Mount Wrightson 2881

Colorado

C

Confusion Range

Mount Ellen 3512

Indian Peak 2982

Wheeler Peak 3982

St George

Hurricane

Washington

Cedar City

Parowan

Beaver

Milford

Delano Peak 3710

Sevier Desert

Escalante Desert

Kanab

Grand Canyon

Grand Canyon

BH Williams Mountain 2824

Chino Valley

Bagdad

Wickenburg

Quartzsite

ARIZONA

Phoenix

Glendale

Peoria

Avondale

Buckeye

Gila Bend

Ajo

Lukeville

Casa Grande

Chandler

Tempe

Mesa

Eloy

Florence

Tucson

Sells

Currie

McGill

Schell Creek Range

Pioche

Caliente

Alamo

Lake Mead

Overton

Henderson

Las Vegas

Boulder City

Black Mountains

Bullhead City

Kingman

Mohave Mountains

Lake Havasu City

Parker

Colorado

Blythe

Quartzsite

Wellton

Yuma

San Luis

Rio Colorado

Mexicali

San Luis

D

115°

MEXICO

Egan Range

Ruby Mou

Eureka

Currant

Troy Peak 3443

Warm Springs

Goldfield

Beatty

Shoshone

Baker

Nipton

Needles

Ludlow

Amboy

Twentynine Palms

Indio

Quinta

Colorado

Desert

Brawley

Niland

El Centro

Salton Sea

Calexico

Laguna Salada

Yuma Desert

NEVADA

Great Basin

Mount Callaghan 3105

Austin

Eastgate

Mount Jefferson 3642

Tonopah

Coaldale

Toiyabe Range

Monitor Range

Shoshone Mountains

Death Valley

Panamint Range 3366

Ridgecrest

Mojave Desert

Barstow

Yermo

San Bernardino Mts

Victorville

Hesperia

Palm Springs

La Quinta

Ramona

Escondido

Temecula

Oceanside

Carlsbad

Del Mar

San Clemente

Santee

El Cajon

Chula Vista

Tijuana

Tecate

Rosarito

C

Lovelock

Fallon

Fernley

Reno

Sparks

Virginia City

Carson City

Gardnerville

Dayton

Walker Lake

Hawthorne

Mono Lake

White Mountain Peak 4342

Bishop

Mount Whitney 4418

Lone Pine

Owens Lake

Mount San Antonio 3055

San Bernardino

Riverside

Santa Ana

Palmdale

Lancaster

Mojave

Tehachapi

Mettler

Kern

Bakersfield

Pasadena

Los Angeles

Santa Monica

Torrance

Long Beach

Huntington Beach

San Clemente

Santa Catalina Island

Palo Verde

Blythe

Pyramid Lake

Janesville

Lake Almanor

Quincy

Honey Lake

Susanville

Lake Tahoe

South Lake Tahoe

Sonora

Mammoth Lakes

Fresno

Clovis

Selma

Dinuba

Hanford

Visalia

Tulare

Corcoran

Delano

Wasco

Shafter

Santa Clarita

Simi Valley

Ventura

Oxnard

Santa Barbara

Goleta

Santa Cruz Island

Santa Rosa Island

San Miguel Island

San Nicolas Island

San Clemente Island

Channel Islands

CALIFORNIA

SIERRA NEVADA

Red Bluff

Corning

Chico

Willows

Oroville

Yuba City

Paradise

Auburn

Placerville

Citrus Heights

Arden Town

Sacramento

Davis

Vacaville

Fairfield

Napa

Vallejo

Concord

Berkeley

Oakland

San Francisco

Pacifica

San Mateo

Palo Alto

Sunnyvale

Santa Clara

San Jose

Fremont

Hayward

Stockton

Lodi

Modesto

Turlock

Atwater

Merced

Madera

Los Banos

Gilroy

Hollister

Salinas

Watsonville

Marina

Monterey

Monterey Bay

Santa Cruz

Soledad

King City

Paso Robles

Atascadero

San Luis Obispo

Grover Beach

Arroyo Grande

Santa Maria

Lompoc

Buellton

Point Conception

Healdsburg

Santa Rosa

Point Reyes

Clear Lake

Garberville

Cummings

Fort Bragg

Point Arena

Ukiah

Willits

Eel

Red Bluff

Sacramento Valley

San Joaquin

Kings

California Aqueduct

Lemoore

PACIFIC

OCEAN

B

A

40°

35°

3

4

Longitude 120° west of Greenwich

1:6 400 000

MILES 0

0 50 100 150

0 100 200 KILOMETRES

A 110° B 105° C

SASKATCHEWAN

Val Marie · Estevan · Carnduff · Delor

Browning · Cut Bank · Gildford · Havre · Chinook · Scobey · Plentywood · Crosby · Kenmare · Bottir
Shelby · Lothair · Nelson Reservoir · Glasgow · Wolf Point · Williston · Tioga · Stanley · Minot
Conrad · Choteau · Fort Benton · Bear Paw Mountain 2116 · Malta · Milk · Fort Peck · Missouri · Watford City · New Town · Coteau du Missou

M O N T A N A

Great Falls · Armington · Fort Peck Reservoir · Jordan · Circle · Sidney

R
O
C
K
Y

1

Helena · Lewistown · Rock Springs · Glendive · Beach · Lake Sakakawea · Underwood · Washb
Canyon Ferry Lake · White Sulphur Springs · Harlowton · Belfield · Dickinson · Mandan · Bismarck
Townsend · Boulder · Roundup · Forsyth · Yellowstone · Miles City · Baker · Bowman · Hettinger · Ste
Three Forks · Big Timber · Billings · Bighorn · Hardin · Colstrip · Broadus · Alzada · Lemmon · Grand · Mobridge
Belgrade · Livingston · Columbus · Laurel · Crow Agency · Buffalo · Lake Oahe

N O R T H

Bozeman · Granite Peak 3901 · Red Lodge · Broadus

45° Electric Peak 3490 · West Yellowstone · Lovell · Powell · Sheridan · Belle Fourche · Faith · Dupree · Getty

S O U T H

West Thumb · Yellowstone Lake · Cody · Greybull · Cloud Peak 4016 · Buffalo · Gillette · Sundance · Spearfish · Sturgis · Rapid City · Philip · Pierre
St Anthony · Rexburg · Rigby · Grand Teton 4190 · Moran · Worland · Wright · Newcastle · Black Hills · Lead · Cheyenne · Murdo
Jackson · Gros Ventre Range · Thermopolis · Boysen Reservoir · Custer · Hot Springs · Martin · Win
Gannett Peak 4202 · Wind River Range · Riverton · Cheyenne · Oelrichs · Pine Ridge · Badlands

I
D
A
H
O

2 Afton · Fort Washakie · Mills · Casper · Chadron · Gordon · Merriman · Valentine · Ains
Soda Springs · Pinedale · Lander · Glenrock · Douglas · Lusk · Crawford · Rushville
Montpelier · Sweetwater · Muddy Gap · Pathfinder Reservoir · Torrington · Alliance · Mullen · Hyannis · Middle F · Thedford

W Y O M I N G

Kemmerer · Seminoe Reservoir · Wheatland · Scottsbluff · 1281 Wild Horse Hill · N E B
Green · Green River · Rock Springs · Rawlins · Hanna · Medicine Bow Peak 3661 · Mitchell · Bayard · Bridgeport · North Platte · Sidney · Lake McConaughy · North Platte
Evanston · Lyman · Flaming Gorge Reservoir · Saratoga · Laramie · Cheyenne · Kimball · Ogallala · Sutherland
Kings Peak 4123 · Vernal · Craig · Steamboat Springs · Fort Collins · Wellington · Pine Bluffs · Julesburg · Gothenbur · Lex
Uinta Mountains · Roosevelt · Meeker · Kremmling · Loveland · Greeley · Sterling · Holyoke · Imperial

40° Duchesne · Sheep Mountain 3732 · Estes Park · Longmont · Brush · Akron · Yuma · Wray · Benkelman · McC
Price · Wellington · Glenwood Springs · Rifle · Boulder · Thornton · Fort Morgan
Roan Plateau · Vail · Frisco · Arvada · Aurora · St Francis · Obe

U T A H Green River · Grand Junction · Gypsum · Denver · Lakewood · Colby · Oakley · WaKe
Crescent Junction · Whitewater · Delta · Carbondale · Aspen · Leadville · Woodland Park · Castle Rock · Limon · Burlington · Goodland · Kansas
Moab · Mount Elbert 4399 · Manitou Springs · Colorado Springs · Cheyenne Wells
Hanksville · Mount Peale 3877 · Olathe · Montrose · Gunnison · Garfield · Salida · Canon City · Pikes Peak 4300 · Scott City · Garden City

3 Uncompahgre Peak 4363 · Pueblo · Rocky Ford · Las Animas · Lamar · Arkansas · Ulysses · Satanta · Meade
Lake Powell · Abajo Peak 3462 · Monticello · Silverton · Rio Grande · Monte Vista · Fowler · La Junta · Syracuse · Garden City
Blanding · Del Norte · Walsenburg · Liberal · As
San Juan · Bluff · Cortez · San Juan Mountains · Alamosa · Springfield · Meade

A R I Z O N A Kayenta · Shiprock · Durango · Bayfield · Pagosa Springs · Dulce · Chama · Trinidad · Raton · Cimarron
Farmington · Bloomfield · **N E W M E X I C O** · Sangre de Cristo Range

A 110° B Longitude 105° west of Greenwich C

METRES / FEET scale:

METRES	FEET
5000	16404
3000	9843
2000	6562
1000	3281
500	1640
200	656
0	0
Land below sea level	
200	656
4000	13124
6000	19686

136

Lambert Azimuthal Equal Area Projection

1:6 400 000

200 KILOMETRES

MILES 0

CANADA

ONTARIO

MANITOBA

Morris
Morden Winkler
Emerson

Langdon
Cando
Devils
Lake
Grand
Forks
East
Grand
Forks
Grafton
Hallock
Roseau
Baudette
Rainy
River
Fort
Frances
Rainy Lake
Atikokan
Lake of
the Woods
Iles des
Mille Lacs
Terrace
Bay
Thunder Bay
Thunder
Bay

International
Falls
Thief
River Falls
Upper
Red Lake
Ely
Grand
Marais
Pigeon
River
Copper
Harbor
Keweenaw
Peninsula
Isle Royale

KOTA

Mayville
Crookston
Fosston
Bemidji
Leech Lake
Lake
Winnibigoshish
Grand
Rapids
Red Lakes
Lower
Red Lake
Park Rapids
Nashwauk
Chisholm
Hibbing
Mesabi Range
Virginia
Silver
Bay
Two
Harbors
Apostle
Islands
Lake Superior
Hancock
Houghton
Keweenaw Bay
L'Anse
Marquette
Ishpeming

Valley
City
Moorhead
Fargo
Detroit
Lakes
Wadena
Staples
Brainerd
MINNESOTA
Aitkin
Cloquet
Duluth
Superior
Ashland
Ironwood
Bruce
Crossing
Stambaugh
Gogebic Range
MICHIGAN
Crystal
Falls
Iron Mountain
Escanaba

Wahpeton
Fergus Falls
Alexandria
Little
Falls
Mille
Lacs
Moose
Lake
Mora
St Croix
Park
Falls
Rhinelander
Menominee
Marinette

Ellendale
Aberdeen
Webster
Summit Ortonville
Milbank
Montevideo
Granite
Falls
Redwood
Falls
Sauk
Center
St Cloud
Morris
Cambridge
Elk
River
Litchfield
Coon Rapids
Stillwater
Rush City
Rice
Lake
Spooner
Tomahawk
Merrill
Wausau
Shawano
WISCONSIN
De Pere
Green
Bay
Green Bay
Manitowoc

Redfield
Watertown
Huron
Madison
Brookings
Marshall
Pipestone
New
Ulm
Minneapolis
St Paul
Burnsville
Lakeville
Northfield
Red Wing
Minnesota
Hastings
Faribault
Eau
Claire
Chippewa
Falls
Marshfield
Wisconsin
Rapids
Black
River Falls
Winona
Onalaska
Sparta
Tomah
Petenwell
Lake
Oshkosh
Stevens Point
New
London
Appleton
Lake
Winnebago
Sheboygan
West Bend

Chamberlain
Mitchell
Salem
Hartford
Worthington
Luverne
Windom
Mankato
St Peter
Owatonna
Rochester
Albert Lea
Austin
Decorah
La Crosse
Richland
Center
Wisconsin
Portage
Beaver Dam
Watertown
Madison
Verona
Waukesha
Milwaukee
Fond du Lac

Plankinton
Lake
Francis Case
Wagner
Beresford
Yankton
Sioux
Falls
Sioux
Center
Estherville
Spencer
Algona
Clear
Lake
Mason
City
Charles
City
Waverly
Prairie
du Chien
Platteville
Monroe
Janesville
Machesney
Park
Freeport
Beloit
Waukegan
Arlington
Heights
Racine

O'Neill
Wagner
Vermillion
Sioux City
Cherokee
Le Mars
Storm
Lake
Webster
City
Fort
Dodge
Cedar Falls
Waterloo
Independence
Dubuque
Maquoketa
Rockford
De Kalb
Elgin

Wayne
Norfolk
Sac City
Carroll
Denison
Jefferson
Boone
Ames
Perry
Ankeny
Marshalltown
Grinnell
Newton
IOWA
Anamosa
Cedar
Rapids
Iowa
City
Clinton
Sterling
Dixon
Mendota
Naperville
Aurora
Joliet

West
Point
Fremont
Blair
Council
Bluffs
Atlantic
Indianola
West Des
Moines
Des Moines
Pella
Oskaloosa
Coralville
Davenport
Muscatine
Rock
Island
Geneseo
Kewanee
Galesburg
Chillicothe
Pontiac
Streator
Washington
Bloomington

Columbus
Omaha
Papillion
Wahoo
Red Oak
Villisca
Shenandoah
Creston
Ottumwa
Mount
Pleasant
Burlington
Fort Madison
Macomb
Peoria
Morton
Washington

Central
City
Grand Island
York
Lincoln
Nebraska
City
Clarinda
Lamoni
Princeton
Keokuk
Canton
Quincy
ILLINOIS
Lincoln
Springfield
Decatur
Champaign
Mattoon

Kearney
Aurora
Hastings
Minden
Superior
Beatrice
Fairbury
Auburn
Falls City
Maryville
Kirksville
Trenton
Hannibal
Jacksonville
NSKA

Belleville
Marysville
Hiawatha
St Joseph
Chillicothe
Macon
Marceline
Moberly
Mexico
Bowling
Green
Taylorville
Carlinville
Litchfield
Vandalia
Effingham

psburg
Smith Center
Concordia
Atchison
Cameron
Marshall
Columbia
St Charles
O'Fallon
Chesterfield
Wood River
Salem

noky Hills
Leavenworth
Liberty
Kansas City
Independence
Boonville
Fulton
Jefferson
City
Washington
St Louis
East St Louis
Belleville
Centralia

Hays
Russell
Manhattan
Topeka
Lawrence
Olathe
Overland
Park
Warrensburg
Sedalia
Eldon
Mehlville
Festus
Mount
Vernon

Abilene
Junction
City
Salina
Osage
City
Ottawa
Harrisonville
Clinton
MISSOURI
Sullivan
Du Quoin
West
Frankfort
Carbondale

ANSAS
McPherson
Emporia
Fort
Scott
Lake of
the Ozarks
Camdenton
Rolla
Waynesville
Salem
Perryville
Chester

eat Bend
Hutchinson
St John
Newton
El Dorado
Iola
Nevada
Bolivar
Lebanon
Black
Cape
Girardeau
Mound
City

Pratt
Wichita
Augusta
Chanute
Pittsburg
Springfield
Mountain Grove
Charleston
Sikeston

d Hills
unt
Medicine
Lodge
Derby
Winfield
Wellington
Arkansas City
Parsons
Joplin
Carthage
Monett
Aurora
Neosho
Miami
Coffeyville
Independence
Ozark
Ozark Plateau
West Plains
Poplar Bluff
Alton
Dexter
Kennett
Union
City

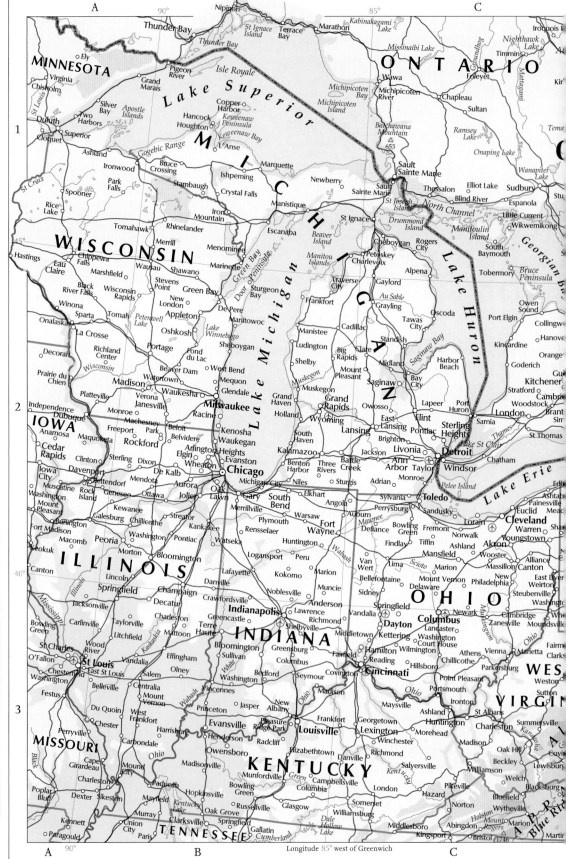

A   90°   B   85°   C

MINNESOTA

Nipigon

Thunder Bay

St Ignace Island   Terrace Bay   Marathon   Kabinakagami Lake   Iroquois

Thunder Bay

Ely   Virginia   Pigeon River   Isle Royale   **O N T A R I O**   Nighthawk Lake   Kir

Chisholm   Grand Marais   Lake Superior   Michipicoten Bay   Wawa   Foleyet   Timmins   Mattagami

Silver Bay   Apostle Islands   Copper Harbor   Michipicoten Island   Michipicoten River   Chapleau   Sultan   Ramsey Lake   Tema   O

Duluth   Two Harbors   Hancock   Keweenaw Peninsula   Batchawana Mountain   Onaping Lake   Wanapitei Lake

1   Superior   Houghton   Keweenaw Bay   △653   Thessalon   Elliot Lake   Sudbury   Stu

Cloquet   Ashland   L'Anse   Sault Sainte Marie   Blind River   Espanola

Ironwood   Gogebic Range   Marquette   Newberry   Sault Sainte Marie   Little Current   Wikwemikong   O

Bruce Crossing   Ishpeming   St Joseph Island   North Channel   Manitoulin Island   South Baymouth

Park Falls   Stambaugh   Crystal Falls   St Ignace   Drummond Island   Rogers City   Tobermory   Georgian Bay   Bruce Peninsula   Collingw

Rice Lake   Spooner   Iron Mountain   Manistique   Beaver Island   Cheboygan   Petoskey   Charlevoix   Alpena   Owen Sound   Hanove

W I S C O N S I N   Rhinelander   Escanaba   Manitou Islands   Gaylord   Lake Huron   Port Elgin   Orange

Hastings   Tomahawk   Menominee   Traverse City   Au Sable   Oscoda   Kincardine   Goderich   Gu

Chippewa Falls   Merrill   Green Bay   Frankfort   Grayling   Tawas City   Collingw

Eau Claire   Wausau   Shawano   Door Peninsula   Sturgeon Bay   Cadillac   Standish   Harbor Beach   Kitchener   Cambr

Marshfield   Stevens Point   Manistee   Big Rapids   Clare   Midland   Saginaw Bay   Bay City   Stratford   Sim

Black River Falls   Wisconsin Rapids   New London   Appleton   Lake Winnebago   Ludington   Shelby   Mount Pleasant   Saginaw   Lapeer   Port Huron   Woodstock

Winona   Sparta   Tomah   Petenwell Lake   De Pere   Manitowoc   Muskegon   Grand Rapids   Owosso   East Lansing   Flint   Sarnia   London   Brant

Onalaska   La Crosse   Oshkosh   Sheboygan   Grand Haven   Wyoming   Lansing   Pontiac   Sterling   Lake St Clair   St Thomas

Decorah   Portage   Fond du Lac   West Bend   Holland   South Haven   Jackson   Brighton   Heights   Detroit   Chatham

Richland Center   Beaver Dam   Mequon   Glendale   Kalamazoo   Battle Creek   Ann Arbor   Livonia   Windsor   Lake Erie

Prairie du Chien   **I O W A**   Madison   Watertown   **Milwaukee**   Benton Harbor   Three Rivers   Taylor   Monroe   Pelee Island

2   Independence   Dubuque   Platteville   Verona   Janesville   Racine   Holland   Sturgis   Adrian   Toledo   Sylvania   Ashtab

Anamosa   Monroe   Beloit   Kenosha   Niles   Perrysburg   Lorain   Painesvi

Maquoketa   Freeport   Belvidere   Waukegan   Michigan City   Elkhart   Angola   Sandusky   Norwalk   Cleveland   Mead

Cedar Rapids   Rockford   Machesney Park   Arlington Heights   South Bend   Auburn   Maumee   Bowling Green   Fremont   Warren   Shar

Clinton   Sterling   Dixon   Elgin   Evanston   Gary   Warsaw   Fort Wayne   Defiance   Findlay   Tiffin   Ashland   Akron   Youngstown

Iowa City   Davenport   De Kalb   Wheaton   **Chicago**   Plymouth   Huntington   Lima   Mansfield   Wooster   Alliance   East Liver

Muscatine   Bettendorf   Mendota   Aurora   Oak Lawn   Merrillville   Rensselaer   Van Wert   Bellefontaine   Mount Vernon   Massillon   Canton   Weirton

Washington   Rock Island   Geneseo   Ottawa   Joliet   Peru   Logansport   Marion   Sidney   Delaware   Philadelphia   New   Steubenville

Mount Pleasant   Kewanee   Streator   Kankakee   Watseka   Kokomo   Muncie   Springfield   Newark   Cambridge   Washingt

Burlington   Galesburg   Chillicothe   Pontiac   Lafayette   Noblesville   Anderson   Vandalia   **Columbus**   Zanesville   Moundsville

Fort Madison   Macomb   Peoria   Morton   Bloomington   Danville   Crawfordsville   Lawrence   Richmond   **Dayton**   Lancaster   Washington Court House   Marietta   Clark

Keokuk   Canton   **I L L I N O I S**   Lincoln   Champaign   Indianapolis   Greencastle   Shelbyville   Middletown   Kettering   Hamilton   Wilmington   Athens   Vienna   Marietta

3   Springfield   Decatur   Charleston   Terre Haute   Greensburg   **O H I O**   Chillicothe   Parkersburg   **WES**

Jacksonville   Taylorville   **INDIANA**   Bloomington   Columbus   Fairfield   Reading   Hillsboro   Point Pleasant   Weston

Bowling Green   Carlinville   Litchfield   Effingham   Sullivan   Bedford   Seymour   Covington   **Cincinnati**   Portsmouth   **VIRGIN**

St Charles   Wood River   Vandalia   Olney   Washington   Madison   Maysville   Ironton   Ashland   St Albans   Summersville

O'Fallon   **St Louis**   East St Louis   Salem   Vincennes   New Albany   Frankfort   Georgetown   Huntington   Charleston

Chesterfield   Belleville   Centralia   Mount Vernon   Jasper   Princeton   Pleasure Ridge Park   **Louisville**   Lexington   Morehead   Oak Hill   Madison   Co

Washington   Festus   Du Quoin   West Frankfort   Evansville   Elizabethtown   Winchester   Richmond   Beckley   Lewisbu

Perryville   Chester   Harrisburg   Henderson   Owensboro   Danville   Salyersville   Williamson   Blacksbu

MISSOURI   Carbondale   Madisonville   Ohio   Munfordville   Campbellsville   **KENTUCKY**   London   Pikeville   Norton   Welch   Bluefield   Blue Rid

Cape Girardeau   Mount City   Paducah   Hopkinsville   Columbia   Bowling Green   Somerset   Hazard   Wytheville   Martin

Poplar Bluff   Charleston   Dexter   Sikeston   Mayfield   Oak Grove   Russellville   Glasgow   Williamsburg   Middlesboro   Abingdon   Mount Rogers △1746   Marion   Bristol   Martir

Kennett   Murray   Union City   Springfield   Gallatin   Dale Hollow Lake   Kingsport   Bristol

Paragould   Clarksville   Paris   **T E N N E S S E E**   Cumberland

A   90°   B   Longitude 85° west of Greenwich   C

Lambert Azimuthal Equal Area Projection

METRES   FEET

5000   16404
3000   9843
2000   6562
1000   3281
500   1640
200   656
0   0
Land below sea level
200   656
4000   13124
6000   19686

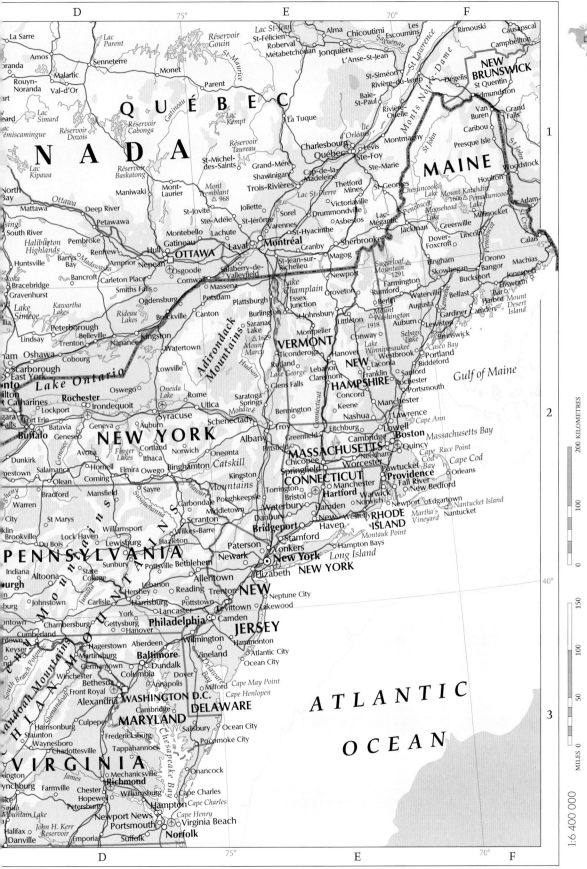

A   95°   B   90°   C

OKLAHOMA
MISSOURI
ARKANSAS
TENNESSEE
KENTU
TEXAS
LOUISIANA
MISSISSIPPI
ALABAM

Tulsa   Owasso   Vinita
Sapulpa   Pryor   Bentonville   Siloam   Rogers   Harrison   West Plains   Poplar Bluff   Charleston   Sikeston   Paducah   Hopkinsville   Glasg
Muskogee   Broken Arrow   Springs   Springdale   Mountain   Alton   Dexter   Mayfield   Murray   Oak   Russellville   Clarksville   Gallat
Okmulgee   Fayetteville   Home   Pocahontas   Kennett   Union City   Paris   Kentucky   Grove   Springfield
Henryetta   Tahlequah   Marshall   Hoxie   Paragould   Dyersburg   McKenzie   Dickson   Nashville   Leb
Chicotah   Sallisaw   Van   Clarksville   Heber Springs   Batesville   Jonesboro   Blytheville   Humboldt   Franklin   Murfreesbo
Eufaula   Buren   Searcy   Newport   Trumann   Jackson   Columbia   McMin
Lake   Fort   Magazine   Russellville   Conway   Wynne   West   Brownsville   Savannah   Linden   Shelbyville   Man
McAlester   Smith   Mountain   Morrilton   Jacksonville   Forrest   Memphis   Bartlett   Bolivar   Lewisburg   Tullaho
Mansfield △ 839   Mountains   City   Millington   Corinth   Lawrenceburg   Fayettevill
Poteau   762   Southaven   Florence   Athens   Huntsville
Atoka   Mena   Little Rock   Marianna   Holly Springs   Booneville   Wheeler   Decatur   Scot
Hugo   Hot   Stuttgart   Helena   Oxford   Russellville   Lake
Idabel   Springs   Amory   Cullman   Gadsden
Paris   Arkadelphia   Pine Bluff   Clarksdale   Batesville   Tupelo   Hamilton   Jasper   Center
Ashdown   De Queen   Malvern   Dumas   Cleveland   Grenada   Point   Birmingham   Chea
Commerce   New Boston   Hope   Fordyce   Monticello   Greenwood   Columbus   Vestavia Hills   Mounta
Texarkana   Camden   Warren   MISSISSIPPI   Winona   Starkville   Bessemer   Sylaca
Sulphur   Mount   El Dorado   Greenville   Indianola   Louisville   Tuscaloosa   Alabaster   Alexande
Springs   Pleasant   Magnolia   Hamburg   Leland   Macon   Eutaw   Clanton
Gladewater   Homer   Crossett   Yazoo   Canton   Demopolis   Prattville   Tusk
Longview   Shreveport   Minden   Bastrop   Lake Providence   City   Pearl   York   Selma   Montgome
Tyler   Athens   Ruston   Monroe   Vicksburg   Meridian
Kilgore   Gibsland   Driskill   Tallulah   Ridgeland   Forest
Henderson   Bossier   Mountain   Jonesboro   163   Jackson   Brandon   Thomasville   Greenville   Troy
Jacksonville   Carthage   City   Winfield   Winnsboro   Crystal Springs   Monroeville   s
Palestine   Mansfield   Natchitoches   Olla   Brookhaven   Jackson   Evergreen   t
Nacogdoches   Toledo   Many   LOUISIANA   Natchez   Laurel   a
Crockett   Lufkin   Bend   Alexandria   Pineville   Hattiesburg   Petal   Andalusia   Enterpr
Reservoir   Leesville   Marksville   McComb   Century   De Fur
Huntsville   Sam Rayburn   Jasper   De Ridder   Lecompte   Kentwood   Lumberton   Crestview   Sprin
Livingston   Reservoir   Corrigan   Oakdale   Ville   Bogalusa   Mobile   Atmore   Fort Walton
Lake   Opelousas   Platte   Picayune   Prichard   Pensacola
Livingston   Conroe   Sulphur   Jennings   Port Allen   Baker   Hammond   Gulfport   Biloxi   Pascagoula   Santa Rosa   Panam
The   Beaumont   Orange   Lake   Crowley   New Roads   Baton   Lake   Gulfport   Mobile   Island
Woodlands   Nederland   Charles   Lafayette   Rouge   Pontchartrain   Mobile   Point
Humble   Vidor   Abbeville   New Iberia   Kenner   Metairie   Mississippi Sound   Bay
Houston   Groves   Plaquemine   New Orleans   Gretna   Chandeleur Islands
Baytown   Port   Thibodaux   Houma   Raceland   Port   Breton
Pasadena   Arthur   White Lake   Morgan   Cut   Sulphur   Sound
Sugar   City   Off   Grand   Mississippi
Land   Marsh   Isle   Delta
Texas City   Island
Lake   Galveston Bay   Atchafalaya Bay   Terrebonne Bay
Jackson   Galveston   Galveston Island
Freeport

Boston Mountains   White   Arkansas   Ouachita Mountains   Lake Ouachita   Ouachita   Red   Sabine   Sam Rayburn Reservoir   Neches   Trinity   Sabine   Red   Yazoo   Mississippi   Pearl   Tombigbee

GULF   OF   MEXICO

1
2
3
4

35°
30°
25°

METRES
FEET

5000
16404

3000
9843

2000
6562

1000
3281

500
1640

200
656

0
0

Land below
sea level

200
656

4000
13124

6000
19686

B   Longitude 90° west of Greenwich   C

Lambert Azimuthal Equal Area Projection

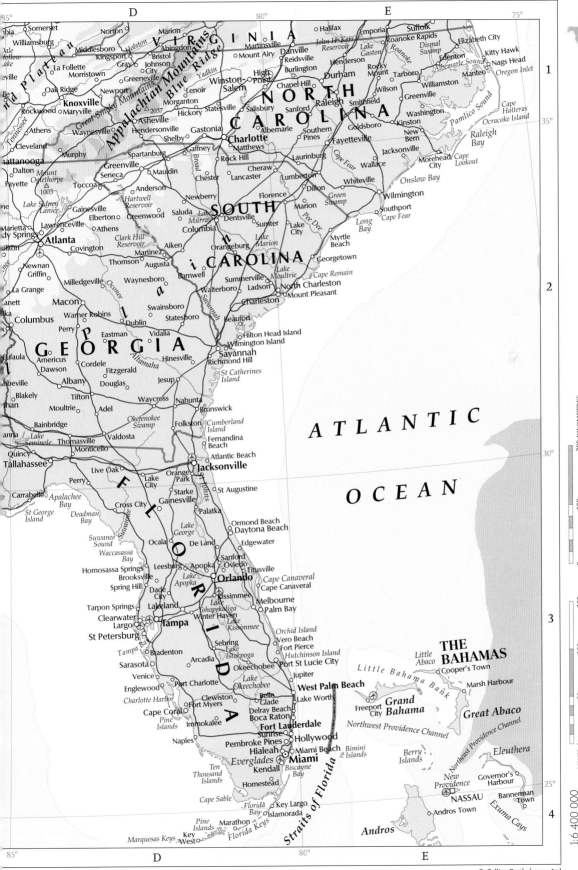

A 115° 110° B 105°

NEVADA

UTAH

Caliente Parowan Escalante
Alamo Escalante Desert Cedar City Lake Powell Colorado Abajo Peak 3462 Monticello Uncompahgre Peak 4363 COLORADO
St George Hurricane Blanding Silverton Del Norte Monte Vista Pueblo
Washington Kanab Page Bluff Cortez Durango Bayfield Alamosa Walse
Virgin San Juan Pagosa Springs San Juan Mountains Sangre de Cristo Range Tri

1

Boulder City Lake Mead Colorado Kayenta Shiprock Farmington Dulce Chama Wheeler Peak 4011 Rato Lar
Dolan Springs Grand Canyon Tuba City Many Farms Bloomfield Los Alamos Taos Espanola
Kingman Grand Canyon Plateau Polacca Chinle Chuska Mountains Chaco Mesa Santa Fe Co
Bullhead City Seligman Williams Bill Williams Mountain 2824 Humphreys Peak 3851 Flagstaff Ganado Gallup Hosta Butte 2693 Santo Domingo Pueblo Rio Rancho Pecos Las Vegas
35° Needles Mohave Mountains Chino Valley Sedona Winslow Holbrook Chambers Thoreau Grants Albuquerque Clines Corners Pecos
Lake Havasu City Bagdad Prescott Camp Verde Snowflake Little Colorado Zuni Mountains Belen Santa Rosa
Parker Prescott Valley Yarnell Show Low St Johns Quemado Bosque Vaughn Su
Quartzite Wickenburg Baldy Peak 3476 Springerville Alpine NEW MEXICO

ARIZONA

Blythe Peoria Glendale Salt Magdalena South Baldy 3287 Socorro Carrizozo Hondo Roswell
Avondale Phoenix Mesa Globe Glenwood Whitewater Baldy 3320 Truth or Consequences Ruidoso Mescalero Artes
Buckeye Tempe Chandler Superior Black Range Silver City Bayard Hatch Tularosa Alamogordo
Yuma Wellton Gila Bend Casa Grande Florence Kearny Clifton Mount Graham 3265 Safford Gila Las Cruces Sacramento Mountains Carls
San Luis Río Colorado Gila Eloy Lordsburg Deming Mesilla Anthony Guadalup Peak 2667

2

Desierto de Altar Ajo Marana Tucson Willcox Columbus El Paso Socorro Diablo Plateau
Sonoita Lukeville Green Valley Benson Chiricahua Peak 2985 Ciudad Juárez Fabens Sierra Blanca Van Hor
Sells Mount Wrightson 2881 Sierra Vista Tombstone Douglas Samalayuca
Puerto Peñasco San Luisito Nogales Sierra Cibuta 2034 Bisbee Agua Prieta Guzmán El Porvenir Villa Ahumada Rio Grande Live
El Socorro Caborca Cananea Fronteras Casa de Janos Rio Bravo del Norte
Desemboque Pitiquito Tubutama Magdalena Nacozari de García Casas Grandes Nuevo Casas Grandes El Sueco Moctezuma
Santa Ana Arizpe Cumpas Bacispe Pacheco Buenaventura San Lorenzo Presic
30° Benjamín Hill Opodepe Moctezuma Tepache Las Varas San Juanito El Sauz Djinar

Gulf of California

Puerto Libertad Carbó Ures SONORA Madera San José de Bavicora CHIHUAHUA Potrei del Llar
Isla Ángel de la Guarda Hermosillo San Pedro el Saucito Alamos Santa María Ciudad Guerrero La Junta Cuauhtémoc Aldama Chihuahua
BAJA CALIFORNIA Isla Tiburón Sonora Mazatán Presa Plutarco Elías Calles Tacupeto Pedernales Doctor Belisario Dominguez Meoqui Ciudad Delicia
Rosarito Bahía Kino Sierra Libre 180 Tecoripa Moreno Yécora Sierra Madre Occidental Carichic San Juanito Saucillo
Santo Domingo Pico Echeverría 1908 Yaqui Creel Conchos MEX
Guerrero Negro Desierto de Vizcaíno Volcán Las Tres Vírgenes 1996 Guaymas Empalme Presa Obregón Rosario Uruáchic Nonoava Presa de la Boquilla Ciudad Camarg Bolsó
3 San Ignacio Santa Rosalía Esperanza Chinipas Conchos Santa Bárbara Jiménez Map
Ciudad Obregón Navojoa Presa Macuzari San Pablo Balleza Hidalgo del Parral
Mulegé Bacobampo Alamos Batopilas Villa Ocampo Escal
BAJA CALIFORNIA SUR Rosarito Choix Presa Miguel Hidalgo Guadalupe y Calvo Nonoava Las Nieves DURANG
Punta Abreojos Huatabampo Don 3150 Camino Real de Tierra A
San José de Comondú Loreto Isla Carmen Punta Rosa El Fuerte Verde Sextín Guanaceví Inde
SINALOA San Blas
Ahome Los Mochis

A Longitude 110° west of Greenwich B 105°

Lambert Azimuthal Equal Area Projection

METRES FEET

METRES	FEET
5000	16404
3000	9843
2000	6562
1000	3281
500	1640
200	656
0	0
Land below sea level	
200	656
4000	13124
6000	19686

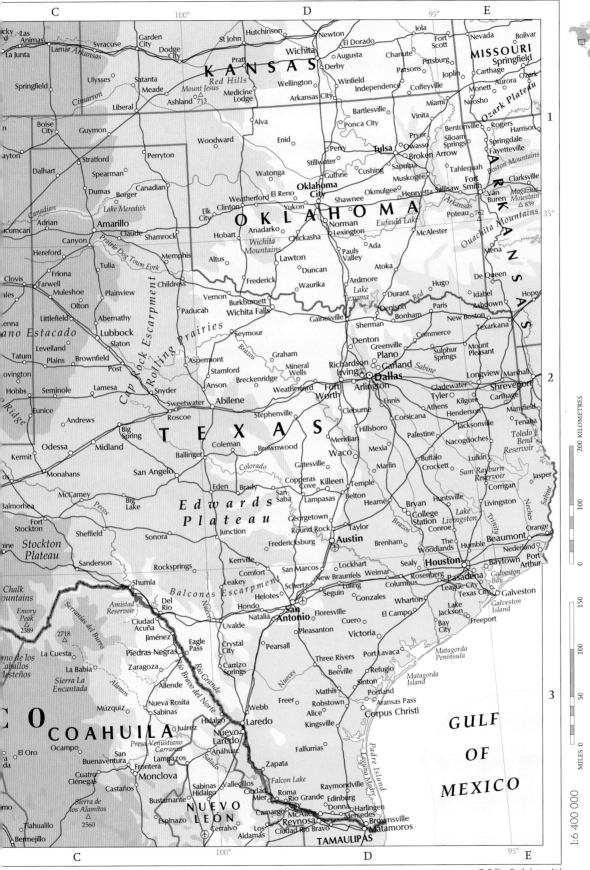

A 110° B

United States / Mexico border region

El Centro · Brawley · Florence · Superior · Kearny · Clifton · Truth or Consequences · Ruidoso · Roswell · Levelland · Brownfield · Lam
Tecate · Yuma · Casa · Grande · Safford · Silver City · Tularosa · Alamogordo · Lovington · Artesia
Tijuana · Mexicali · San Luis · Río Colorado · ARIZONA · Lordsburg · NEW MEXICO · Hobbs · Seminole · Sp
Rosarito · Ajo · Tucson · Green · Valley · Willcox · Benson · Deming · Las Cruces · Carlsbad · Eunice · Andrews · Midland
Ensenada · Desierto de Altar · Puerto · Peñasco · Sierra · Vista · Bisbee · Douglas · Columbus · El Paso · Fabens · UNITE
San · Vicente · Picacho · del Diablo · 3096 · San · Felipe · El Socorro · Nogales · Agua Prieta · Ciudad Juárez · Pecos · Fort · Stockton · Big
Vicente · Guerrero · San · Lázaro · Cárdenas · Tubutama · Santa · Ana · Cananea · Fronteras · Guzmán · Samalayuca · Van · Horn
Cabo San · Quintín · Rosario · Caborca · Magdalena · Arizpe · Nacozari · de García · Casa de Janos · El Porvenir · Villa · Ahumada · Mount Livermore · 2554 · Stockton · Plateau · Sanderson
−30° · Benjamín Hill · Opodepe · Cumpas · Casas · Grandes · Nuevo Casas · Grandes · Moctezuma · Marfa
San Fernando · Puerto · Libertad · Carbó · Moctezuma · Ures · Tepache · Las · Varas · Buenaventura · Presidio · Emory · Peak · 2389 · 2718 · Ojinaga
Isla Ángel · de la Guarda · Bahía · Kino · Álamos · Mazatán · Madera · San José · de Bavicora · Conchos · La Babia
Bahía Rosarito · Pico · Echeverría · 1908 · Hermosillo · Chihuahua · La Junta · Cuauhtémoc · Ciudad · Delicias · Llano de los · Caballos Mesteños · La Cu
Isla · Cedros · Isla · Sebastián · Vizcaíno · Santo · Domingo · Sonora · Tecoripa · Yécora · San · Juanito · Meoqui · Doctor B. · Saucillo · Sierra · Mojada · Ocampo · Buenavent · Múzq
Punta · Eugenia · Guerrero · Negro · Volcán Las · Tres Vírgenes · 1996 · Empalme · Rosario · Uruáchic · Carichic · Creel · Nonoava · Presa de · la Boquilla · Camargo · Jiménez · El Oro · Cuatro Ciénegas · Monch
Bahía · Tortugas · Sierra · Vizcaíno · Ignacio · Guaymas · Esperanza · Ciudad · Obregón · Navojoa · Chinipas · Batopilas · San Pablo · Balleza · Hidalgo · del Parral · Escalón · Ceballos · East
Punta San Hipólito · Santa · Rosalía · Mulegé · Álamos · Huatabampo · Choix · Guadalupe · y Calvo · Bárbara · Las Nieves · Tlahualilo · San Pedro · de las Color
El Fuerte · Presa M. · Hidalgo · Indé · Bermejillo · Camino Real de · Tierra Adentro · 3150 · Ahome · Los Mochis · Guanacevi · Mapimí
Villa Insurgentes · San José · de Comondú · Loreto · Isla · Carmen · Topolobampo · Guasave · Mocorito · Tepehuanes · Gómez Palacio · Matamoros · Torreón · Parras
2 · Ciudad Constitución · Dolores · Isla San José · Guamúchil · Pericos · Tamazula · Topia · Nuevo · Ideal · Canatlán · Guadalupe · Victoria · Viesca · Ge · Ce
Bahía · Magdalena · Puerto · Cortés · Isla Espíritu Santo · La Paz · Pichilingue · Culiacán · Navolato · Costa · Rica · Santiago · Papasquiaro · Cerro · Huehueto · 3150 · Durango · Miguel · Auza · Concep
Isla Santa · Margarita · San Pedro · Isla Cerralvo · El Dorado · Cosalá · Villa · Sombrerete · 3559 · Río Grande · Cañitas · Cama
Tropic of Cancer · Picacho de la Laguna · La Cruz · El Salto · Villa · Unión · Fresnillo · Alto · San · Felipe Pesc
Todos Santos · 2163 · Santiago · La Cruz · 3150 · Mazatlán · Rosario · Jerez · MEX · Zacatecas · Salir
Cabo San Lucas · San José del Cabo · Escuinapa · Teacapán · Villa · Unión · Villanueva · Rincón · Rom
Cabo · Falso · Acaponeta · Nayar · Mezquitic · Colotlán · Aguascalie
20° · Tecuala · Tuxpan · Ruiz · Calvillo · 2981
Laguna Agua Brava · San Martín · de Bolaños · Teul de · Jalpa
Santiago Ixcuintla · González · Ortega · Tepic · Compostela · Las Varas · Islas · Marías · Ixtlán · Yahualica · Tepatitlán · Leor · Irap
Puerto Vallarta · Guadalajara · Ameca · Cocula · La Piedad · Zamora · Hida
Bahía de Banderas · Zacoalco · Laguna de Chapala · Sahuayo · Zacapu · Pátzcua
Cabo Corrientes · Tomatlán · Sayula · Ciudad · Guzmán · Urua
Autlán · Nevado de Colima · 4339 · Colima · 3859 · Tepalcatepec · Apatzin
PACIFIC · Cihuatlán · Manzanillo · Tecomán · Coalcomán · Aguililla · Infie
Armería · Arteaga · Pr
Islas Revillagigedo · (Mexico) · Isla · San Benedicto · Lázaro Cárdenas
Isla · Socorro · Zihuatan
Isla Clarión · Pet

3 · PACIFIC

OCEAN

A · Longitude 110° west of Greenwich · B

Lambert Azimuthal Equal Area Projection

Elevation scale:

METRES
FEET

5000 / 16404
3000 / 9843
2000 / 6562
1000 / 3281
500 / 1640
200 / 656
0 / 0
Land below
sea level
200 / 656
4000 / 13124
6000 / 19686

STATES OF AMERICA

Denton Greenville Commerce Mount Magnolia El Dorado Bastrop Crossett Yazoo City Canton Demopolis Tuskegee
Mineral Wells Richardson Garland Sulphur Pleasant Lake Providence Forest Selma
Graham Springs Shreveport Minden Ruston Jackson Meridian Montgomery
Breckenridge Fort Worth Longview Marshall Monroe Vicksburg **ALABAMA**
Abilene Weatherford Dallas Cleburne Tyler Henderson Jonesboro Winnsboro Laurel Greenville Troy
water Cleburne Ennis Athens Mansfield Alexandria Meridian Andalusia Ozark
Stephenville Waco Palestine Lufkin Toledo Many McComb Hattiesburg Atmore **FLORIDA** Enterprise

T E X A S

Brownwood Gatesville Marlin Crockett Jasper De Ridder Ville Oakdale Bogalusa Mobile Crestview Pensacola
Brady Lampasas Killeen Temple Huntsville Jasper Lake Charles Platte Roads Picayune Biloxi Pascagoula
Georgetown Round Rock Taylor College Conroe **LOUISIANA** Kenner Gulfport Mobile Fort
Austin Station Beaumont Jennings Lafayette Baton Rouge **New Orleans** Bay Walton Beach
San Marcos Brenham Houston The Woodlands Orange Abbeville Houma Port Sulphur Chandeleur
Fredericksburg Kerrville New Braunfels Schertz Lockhart Sealy Pasadena Port Arthur Iberia Morgan Raceland Breton Islands
San Antonio Seguin Gonzales Texas City Galveston Bay City Grand Sound Mississippi

GULF

OF

MEXICO

Tropic of Cancer

G U A T E M A L A

HONDURAS

A   90°   B   80°

UNITED STATES OF AMERICA

Lake Charles Jennings Baton Mobile Pascagoula Pensacola Bainbridge Waycross Brunswick
Orange Lafayette Rouge Biloxi Panama Tallahassee Valdosta
Beaumont LOUISIANA City Lake Jacksonville
Morgan City New Orleans City Gainesville
Houma Cape Apalachee Cross Ocala Daytona Beach
San Blas Bay City Orlando Titusville
Mississippi Waccasassa Tampa Lakeland Cape Canaveral
Delta Bay Clearwater Melbourne
St Petersburg Fort Pierce
Sarasota Lake Grand Little
Port Charlotte Okeechobee Bahama Abaco
Fort Myers West Mar
Palm Beach Freeport City Gre
Everglades Fort Lauderdale Abd
Hollywood Berry NASSAU Eleut
Miami Islands Bannerm
Tov

GULF

OF

MEXICO

FLORIDA

Tropic of Cancer

HAVANA Archipiélago de Sabana
(La Habana) Matanzas
Arrecife Pinar del Río Cárdenas Archipiélago de Camagüey
Alacrán Guane Sagua la Grande George
Progreso Cabo Catoche Golfo de Cienfuegos Santa Clara Placetas
Mérida Tizimín Cancún Batabanó Sancti Spíritus Esmeralda
Muna Valladolid Isla de la Ciego de Ávila Camagüey
Campeche Tekax Juventud CUBA Las Tunas Ho
Bahía de YUCATÁN Cozumel Golfo de
Campeche Isla de Cozumel Guacanayabo Bay San
Champotón Grand Little Manzanillo de
Ciudad MEXICO Cayman Cayman Cabo Cruz
del Carmen Chetumal Cayman Montego Bay Jan
Frontera Escárcega Banco Islands Spanish
Laguna de Chinchorro (U.K.) JAMAICA Town
Términos Ambergris Caye KINGSTON
Villahermosa Belize
Palenque BELMOPAN Turneffe Islands
Teapa Dangriga C
Tenosique Flores BELIZE
San Cristóbal La Libertad Gulf of A
de las Casas Honduras Islas de la Bahía Roatán
Punta Puerto La Ceiba Trujillo R
Gorda Barrios
GUATEMALA Cobán Laguna I
Tapachula Huehuetenango Lago de San Pedro Sula de Caratasca
Quetzaltenango Izabal El Progreso B
Santa Rosa de Copán Patuca Puerto Lempira
Mazatenango GUATEMALA HONDURAS Coco
Santa Ana CITY TEGUCIGALPA Cayos B
Puerto San José Danlí Miskitos
Sonsonate San Cordillera Puerto Cabezas
SAN SALVADOR Vicente Somoto Isabelia Isla de Providencia
EL SALVADOR San Miguel Jinotega (Colombia)
Usulután Matagalpa Río Grande Isla de
Golfo de Fonseca NICARAGUA San Andrés
León Boaco Islas (Colombia)
MANAGUA Juigalpa del Maíz
Jinotepe Granada Bluefields (Nicaragua)
Rivas Lake Nicaragua
Liberia San Juan
PACIFIC COSTA RICA Puerto Limón
Puntarenas SAN JOSÉ
Cartago Canal de Panamá Colón Punta San Blas
OCEAN Chirripó Changuinola Golfo
3819 Bocas Golfo de los PANAMA CITY del Darién
del Toro Mosquitos Mont
La Concepción Aguadulce La Turbo
Puerto Armuelles David Chorrera La Palma
Santiago Chitré Gulf of
Golfo Península Panama
de Chiriquí de Azuero
Península Isla de Coiba Punta
de Osa Mala

METRES
FEET

5000   16404
3000   9843
2000   6562
1000   3281
500   1640
200   656
0   0
Land below
sea level
200   656
4000   13124
6000   19686

Yucatan Channel

Straits of Florida

Great Bahama Bank

Andros

Grand
Bahama

PANAMA

146

Lambert Azimuthal Equal Area Projection

A   90°   B   80°

30°

2

20°

3

10°

4

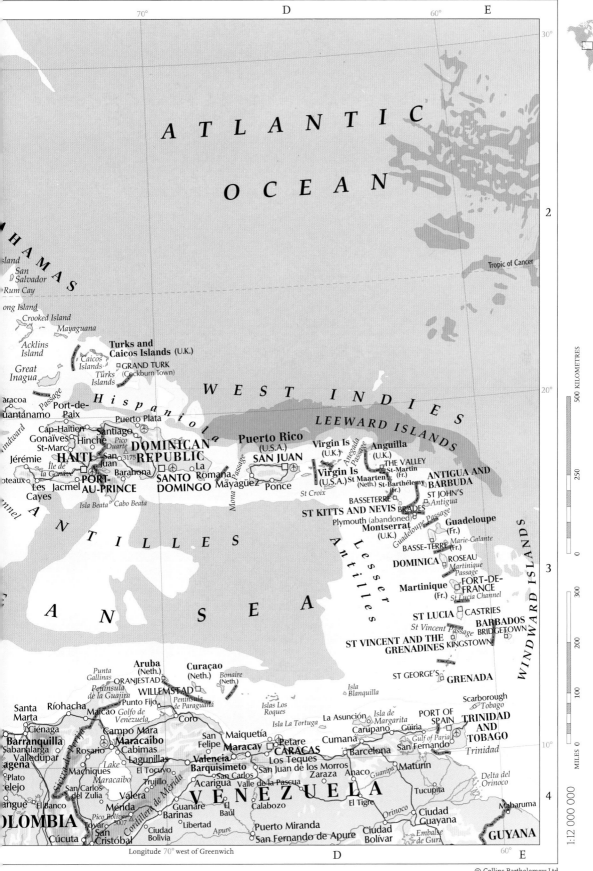

ATLANTIC

OCEAN

Tropic of Cancer

BAHAMAS
Island
San
Salvador
Rum Cay

ong Island
Crooked Island
Mayaguana
Acklins
Island
Great
Inagua

aracoa
Port-de-
Paix
uantánamo

Windward

Hinche
Cap-Haïtien
Santiago
Gonaïves
St-Marc
Jérémie
Île de
la Gonâve
Jacmel
teaux
Les
Cayes
Isla Beata Cabo Beata

hnnel

A   N   T   I   L   L   E   S

A   N

S   E   A

Turks and
Caicos Islands (U.K.)
Caicos
Islands
□ GRAND TURK
(Cockburn Town)
Türks
Islands

W   E   S   T   I   N   D   I   E   S

Hispaniola

Puerto Plata

DOMINICAN
REPUBLIC
Pico
Duarte
3175
San
Juan
Barahona
SANTO
DOMINGO
La
Romana

Mona Passage

Puerto Rico
(U.S.A.)
SAN JUAN
Mayagüez
Ponce

LEEWARD ISLANDS

Virgin Is
(U.K.)
Virgin Is
(U.S.A.)
St Croix

Anguilla
(U.K.)
THE VALLEY
St-Martin
(Fr.)
St Maarten St-Barthélemy
(Neth.) (Fr.)
BASSETERRE
ST KITTS AND NEVIS BRADES
Plymouth (abandoned)□
Montserrat
(U.K.)

Anegada Passage

ANTIGUA AND
BARBUDA
ST JOHN'S
Antigua

Guadeloupe
Passage

Guadeloupe
(Fr.)
BASSE-TERRE (Fr.)
Marie-Galante

DOMINICA
ROSEAU
Martinique
Passage

Martinique
(Fr.)
FORT-DE-
FRANCE
St Lucia Channel
ST LUCIA CASTRIES

L   e   s   s   e   r

A   n   t   i   l   l   e   s

St Vincent Passage
ST VINCENT AND THE
GRENADINES KINGSTOWN

ST GEORGE'S ■ GRENADA

BARBADOS
BRIDGETOWN

WINDWARD ISLANDS

Aruba
(Neth.)
ORANJESTAD
Punta
Gallinas
Peninsula
de la Guajira

Curaçao
(Neth.)
Bonaire
(Neth.)
WILLEMSTAD □
Punto Fijo
Golfo de
Venezuela
Coro
Peninsula
de Paraguaná

Isla
Blanquilla

Isla La Tortuga

Scarborough
Tobago

PORT OF
SPAIN
TRINIDAD
AND
TOBAGO

Santa
Marta
Ríohacha
Maicao
San
Felipe
Maiquetía
Cumaná
Carúpano
Güiria
San Fernando
Trinidad

Ciénaga
Campo Mara
Cabimas
Maracay
CARACAS
Barcelona

Barranquilla
Sabanalarga
Rosario
MARACAIBO
Lagunillas
Valencia
Los Teques
San Juan de los Morros
Maturín

Valledupar
agena
Maracaibo
El Tocuyo
Barquisimeto
San Carlos
Zaraza
Anaco
Guanipa

Plato
elejo
Machiques
Trujillo
Acarigua
Valle de la Pascua
El Tigre
Tucupita
Delta del
Orinoco

Maracaibo

Lake

Isla de
Margarita
La Asunción

Islas Los
Roques

Petare
Los Teques

Guárico

VENEZUELA
El
Baúl
Calabozo
Orinoco
Ciudad
Guayana
Mabaruma

ngüe
El Banco
San Carlos
del Zulia
Mérida
Barinas
Libertad
Puerto Miranda
Ciudad
Bolívar
Embalse
de Guri
GUYANA

OLOMBIA
Pico Bolívar
5007
Toyar
San
Cristóbal
Ciudad
Bolivia
San Fernando de Apure
Apure

Cúcuta

Cordillera de Mérida

500 KILOMETRES
250
0
300
200
100
MILES 0
1:12 000 000

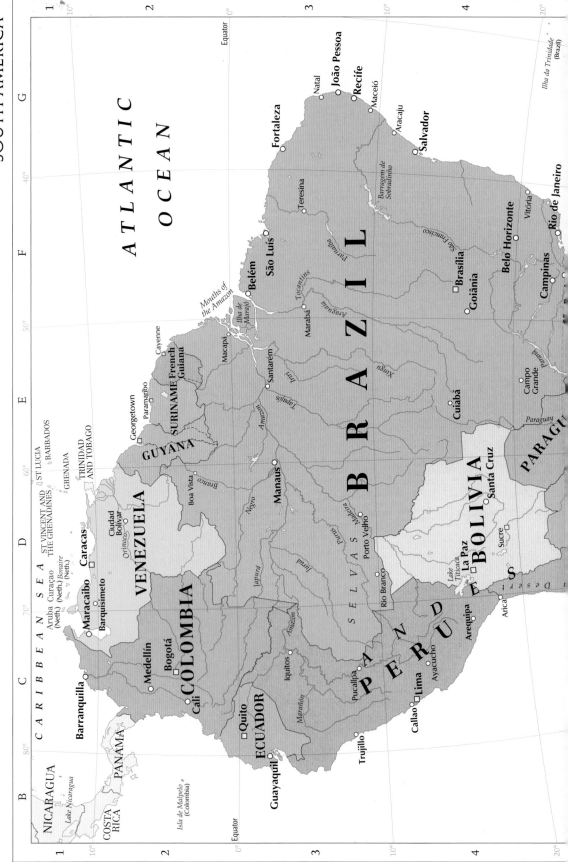

Bi-Polar Oblique Projection

ATLANTIC

OCEAN

PACIFIC

OCEAN

Florianópolis

Porto Alegre

Lagoa
dos Patos

Rio Grande

URUGUAY

Montevideo

Río de la Plata

Mar del Plata

Buenos Aires

La Plata

Corrientes

Paraná

Salado

Rosario

Córdoba

San Miguel
de Tucumán

Mendoza

Cerro
Aconcagua
6959

Valparaíso

Santiago

Concepción

ARGENTINA

Bahía Blanca

Colorado

Negro

Neuquén

ANDES

CHILE

PATAGONIA

Puerto Montt

Isla de Chiloé

Archipiélago
de los Chonos

Golfo de San Jorge

Comodoro
Rivadavia

Río Gallegos

Tierra
del
Fuego

Punta
Arenas

Isla de
los Estados

Cape Horn

Drake Passage

Stanley

Falkland Islands
(U.K.)

South Shetland Islands
(U.K.)

Antarctic
Peninsula

Scotia Sea

South Georgia

South Georgia and the
South Sandwich
Islands
(U.K.)

South Sandwich
Islands

South Orkney
Islands
(U.K.)

Islas
Desventuradas
(Chile)

Archipiélago
Juan Fernández (Chile)

Longitude 20° west of Greenwich

1:28 000 000

0   200   400   600
MILES

0   500   1000 KILOMETRES

© Collins Bartholomew Ltd

A 80°   B   70°   C   60°

CARIBBEAN SEA

Punta Gallinas
Aruba (Neth.)
Curaçao (Neth.)
Bonaire (Neth.)
GRENADA
ST GEORGE'S
TRINIDAD AND TOB

1

Santa Marta   Ríohacha   Golfo de Venezuela   Punto Fijo   Coro   WILLEMSTAD   Isla de Margarita   La Asunción   Tobago   Scarb
Barranquilla   Campo Mara   San   El Faro   Carúpano   PORT OF
Sabanalarga   Sierra de Perijá   **Maracaibo**   Felipe   **CARACAS**   Maiquetía   Cumaná   Güiria   San Fernan
Cartagena   Valledupar   Machiques   Cabimas   Valera   **Barquisimeto**   **Valencia Maracay**   Los Teques   Barcelona   Trinidad
    Sincelejo   Magangué   Lake   Acarigua   Anaco   Maturín
Colón   Golfo del Darién   Maracaibo   Valera   Guanare   Zaraza   Valle de la Pascua   El Tigre   Tucupita   Delta do Orinoco
PANAMA CITY   El Banco   **Mérida** 5007   Barinas   Calabozo   Ciudad Bolívar   Ciudad Guayana   Mab
PANAMA   Montería   Cúcuta   Tovar   Pico Bolívar   San Fernando de Apure   Embalse de Guri   El Callao   Baraman
Aguadulce   La Palma   Turbo   Pamplona   San Cristóbal   Arauca   s   LAIM VENE
Chitré   Gulf of Panama   **Bucaramanga**   5493   Puerto Nuevo   Orinoco   La Paragua   Tumereng   o
Punta Mala   **Medellín**   Socorro   Sierra Nevada del Cocuy   Meta   Puerto Páez   **VENEZUELA**   Angel Falls (Kerepakupai Merú)   Mount Roraima   Ma

2

Coffee Cultural Landscape of Colombia   Tunja   Yopal   Puerto Ayacucho   Guiana Highlands   Pakaraima Mountains   2810   Normandia
Quibdó   Manizales   Zipaquirá   Bisinaca   Cerro Marahuaca 2579   Serra Parima   Boa Vista   Leth
Pereira   **BOGOTÁ**   Arrecifal   Orinoco   Serra Grande   1150
Armenia   Villavicencio   Cerro El Nevado   Guaviare   Pico da Neblina 3014   Caracaraí   Novo Paraíso
Buenaventura   Palmira   Ibagué 4560   **COLOMBIA**   Mitú   Uaupés   Tapurucuara   Branco
Cali   Neiva   San José del Guaviare   Mesa de Yambí   Negro
Popayán   6750   Florencia   Japurá   Barcelos   Repr de Ba
Tumaco   Pasto   Mocoa   Caquetá   Puerto Leguízamo   Lérida   La Pedrera   Maraã   Unini   Iaú   **Manaus**   Itac
Esmeraldas   Ipiales   Apaporis   Negro   Fonte Boa   Manacapuru   Aut
Equator   Ibarra   Lago Agrio   Napo   Cabo Pantoja   El Encanto   Pamar   Santa Clara   Uarini   Codajás   Beruri
QUITO   Volcán Cotopaxi 5896   Putumayo   Tonantins   Amazon (Amazonas)   Coari   Be
Chone   **ECUADOR**   Río Tigre   Amazon   Santo Antônio do Içá   Coari
Manta   Ambato   Riobamba   Amazonas   Letícia   Carauari
Portoviejo   Chimborazo 6310   Alausí   Nauta   Tabatinga   Purus   Novo Aripuanã
Pajàn   Azogues   Río Tigre   Iquitos   Benjamim Constant   Jutaí   Tapauá   Manicoré
Guayaquil   Cuenca   Gualaceo   Marañón   Madeira   Juruá
Isla Puná   **Machala**   Pastaza   Requena   Itui   Jutaí   São M
Golfo de Guayaquil   Tumbes   Barranca   Yavarí   Lábrea   Humaitá   Aripuanã
Macará   Loja   Lagunas   Eirunepé   **SELVAS**   Madeira
Talara   Sullana   Cordillera Oriental   Yurimaguas   Envira   Pauini   Porto Velho   Theodore Roosevelt   Aripuanã
Piura   Catacaos   Jaén   Chachapoyas   Rioja   Tarapoto   Ucayali   Taraucá   Boca do Acre   Abunã   Ariquemes   Jaru
Sechura   Olmos   Contamana   Ipixuna   Feijó   Sena Madureira   Porto Acre   Guayaramerín   Pimenta Bueno   Ju
Punta Negra   Chiclayo   Cajamarca   Cruzeiro do Sul   Taraucá   Rio Branco   Abunã   Vilher
Pacasmayo   Otuzco   Pucallpa   Puerto Portillo   Xapuri   Cobija   Riberalta   Costa Marques   Serra dos Par

3

METRES FEET

METRES	FEET
5000	16404
3000	9843
2000	6562
1000	3281
500	1640
200	656
0	0
Land below sea level	
200	656
4000	13124
6000	19686

Trujillo   Huánuco   Atalaya   Alerta   Puerto   Mategua   Mato Gros
Chimbote   Huaráz   Cerro de Pasco   Uayali   **PERU**   Madre de Dios   Maldonado   Santa Ana de Yacuma   Puerto Alegre   Esperi
Huarmey   Yerupaja 6634   Huancayo   Urubamba   Machu Picchu   Cusco (CUZCO)   Exaltación   Trinidad   Loreto   Pontes e Lacerda   San
Barranca   Sacred City of Caral-Supe   La Merced   Cordillera Vilcanota   Sicuani   Inambari   Beni   San Borja   Ignacio
Huacho   Huaral   Huancavelica   Ayacucho   Abancay   Ayaviri   Sandia   Santa Ana   Puerto Frey   Mamoré   Mato Gros
Callao   **LIMA**   San Vicente de Cañete   Cordillera Occidental   Coracora   Yanaoca   **BOLIVIA**   San Pedro   Bañados del Izozog   Tuc
Chincha Alta   Antabamba   Nudo Coropuna 6425   Juliaca   Lake Titicaca   San Pedro
Pisco   Ica   Nazca   Marcona   **Arequipa**   Chuquibamba   **LA PAZ**   Montero   Pampa Grande   El Cerro   **Santa Cruz**
Chala   Camaná   Moquegua   Colquiri   Cordillera Oriental   Warnes   Cochabamba
PACIFIC OCEAN   Mollendo   Nevado Sajama   Oruro   Huanui   Pampa
Ilo   Tacna   Arica   6542   Corque   Grande   Cabezas

4

A 80°   B   Longitude 70° west of Greenwich   C   60°

Lambert Azimuthal Equal Area Projection

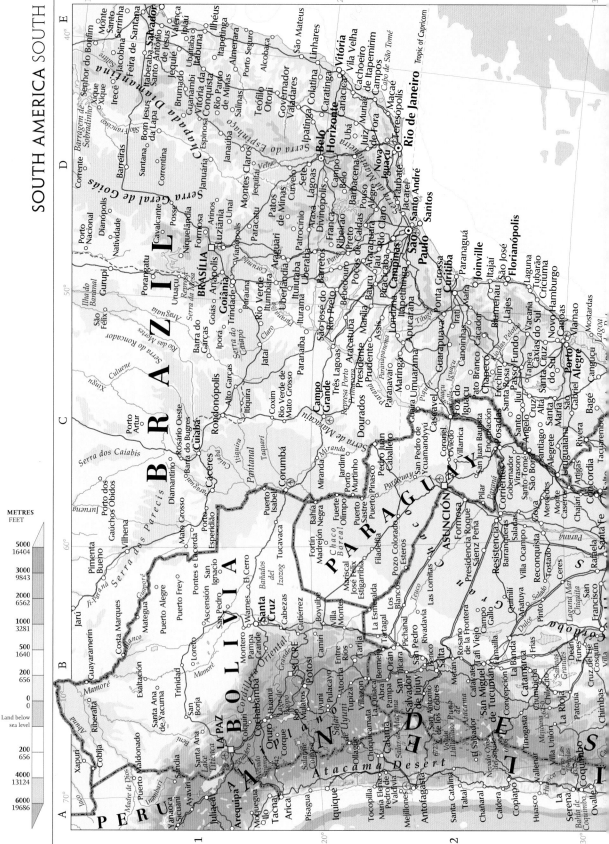

METRES
FEET

5000
16404

3000
9843

2000
6562

1000
3281

500
1640

200
656

0
0

Land below
sea level

200
656

4000
13124

6000
19686

Lambert Azimuthal Equal Area Projection

B C

55° 50°

Rio das Mortes
Serra do Taquaral
Coronel
Ponce
Presidente
Murtinho
Araguaiana
Itapuranga
Ceres
Rialma
Rianópolis
Goianésia
Brasilândia
DISTRITO

Cabeceira
Rio Manso
Poxoréu
Batovi
Barra do Garças
Aragarças
Jussara
Goiás
Jaguá
Pirenópolis
BRASÍLIA
Corumbá
de Goiás
Planaltina
FEDERAL
Form
Cabec

Iaciara
Tesouro
Torixoréu
Bom Jardim
de Goiás
Iporá
Serra
Dourada
Itaberaí
Nerópolis
Anápolis
Gama
Luziânia

M A T O
Rondonópolis
Anhumas
Guiratinga
Diamantino
Piranhas
Aurilândia
Anicuns
Trindade
Silvânia
Vianópolis
Cristalina

São
Lourenço
Ponte de Pedra
Alto Garças
Caiapônia
Paraúna
Goiânia
Hidrolândia
Orizona

G R O S S O
Itiquira
Itiquira
Alto
Araguaia
Santa Rita do Araguaia
Serra do Caiapó
1010
Verde
Edéia
Piracanjuba
G O I A S
Pontalina
Morrinhos
Goiatuba
Caldas
Novas
Buriti Alegre
Goiandira
Catalão

Corrientes
Pedro
Gomes
Mineiros
Jataí
Rio
Verde
Santa Helena
de Goiás
Montividiu
Bois
Ipameri
Guarda
Mor
Vaza

Coxim
Jauru
Alto Taquari
Serranópolis
Serra do Verdinho
Claro
Quirinópolis
Cachoeira
Alta
Santa
Vitória
Monte Alegre
de Minas
Itumbiara
Tupaciguara
Araguari
Coromandel
Represa de
Emborcação
Monte
Carme
Patrocín

Rio Verde de
Mato Grosso
Baús
Costa Rica
Aporé
Itarumã
São Simão
Gurinhatã
Barragem de
São Simão
Ituiutaba
Prata
Uberlândia
Nova
Ponte
Arax

B R A Z
Paraíso
Cassilândia
Aporé
Iturama
Campina
Verde
Campo
Florido
Uberaba
Sacrame

Camapuã
Alto
Sucuriú
Ponte do
Rio Verde
Paranaíba
Inocência
Aparecida
do Tabuado
Santa Fé
do Sul
Santa
Vitória
Itapajipe
Planura
Frutal
Igarapava
Pe

Rochedo
Corguinho
Jaraguari
Garcias
Jales
Cardoso
Grande
Colômbia
Pedregulho
Repres
Peixot

M A T O G R O S S O
Terenos
Ribas do
Rio Pardo
Agua
Clara
Ferreiros
Represa Ilha
Solteíra
Fernandópolis
Votuporanga
Nova
Granada
Barretos
Orlândia
São Joaquim
da Barra
Franca
Jango
Campo
Grande
D O S U L
Sidrolândia
Três
Lagoas
Pereira
Barreto
Represa
Três Irmãos
General
Salgado
Olímpia
Morro
Agudo
São Sebas
do Sul
Bebedouro
Batatais

Aroeira
Rio
Brilhante
Porto
Alegre
Bataguassu
Mirandópolis
Andradina
São José do
Rio Preto
Catanduva
Jaboticabal
Sertãozinho
Cravinhos
Ribeirão
Preto
Moco

Maracaju
Panorama
Valparaíso
Birigüi
Araçatuba
Penápolis
Promissão
Represa
Promissão
Novo
Horizonte
Taquaritinga
Casa Bra

Dourados
Ivinheima
Presidente
Epitácio
Dracena
Lucélia
Lins
Tabatinga
Araraquara
São Carlos
Piraçunung

Ponta
Porã
Bocajá
Caarapó
Teodoro
Sampaio
Santo
Anastácio
Tupã
Cafelândia
Lem
Represa
Porto Primavera
Pirajuí
Garça
Vera
Cruz
S A O
P A U L O
Rio Claro

Aroeira
Juti
Porto São José
Nova
Londrina
Iepê
Rancharia
Marília
Bauru
Jaú
Limeira
Mir
Americ

Amambaí
Loanda
Paranavaí
Porecatu
Assis
Palmital
Serra do Mirante
Agudos
São Manuel
Piracicaba
Campinas

Capitán Bado
Iguatemi
Porto
Camargo
Nova Esperança
Rolândia
Ourinhos
Cornélio
Procópio
Piraju
Botucatu
Avaré
Conchas
Represa de
Jurumirim
Boituva
Salto
Itu

Coronel Sapucaia
Rondon
Maringá
Arapongas
Londrina
Santo Antônio
da Platina
Itaí
Itapetininga
Sorocaba
Pa

Ypé-
Jhú
Umuarama
Cianorte
Apucarana
Tomazina
Vençeslau
Braz
Itapeva
Buri
Piedade
Itanh
Peruíb

Ygatimí
Goio-
Erê
Campo
Mourão
Ibaiti
Itaporanga
Capão
Bonito
Juquiá
1350

Salto del
Guairá
Guaíra
Campos Eré
Telêmaco Borba
Jaguariaíva
Itararé
Dedo
de Deus
Registro
Iguape

Porto Mendes
Toledo
Cândido
de Abreu
Tibagi
Pirái
do Sul
Castro
Apiaí
Eldorado
Jacupiranga

Montes de
Araçangüy
Cascavel
Pitanga
Ipiranga
Reserva
P A R A N Á
Cerro Azul
Ribeira
Cananéia

Represa
de Itaipu
Catanduvas
Serra das
Araras
Serra do Cavern
Prudentópolis
Campo
Largo
Rio Branco do Sul
Antonina
Guaraqueçaba

Represa
de Acaray
Hernandarias
Laranjeiras do Sul
Guarapuava
Ponta
Grossa
Palmeira
Curitiba
Ilha das Peças

Ciudad del Este
Foz do Iguaçu
Chopimzinho
Irati
Lapa
São José
dos Pinhais
Paranaguá

Iguaçu Falls
Represa de
Salto Santiago
Manguerinha
Rio Azul
São Mateus
do Sul
Porto
União
Guaratuba

Wanda
Dionísio
Cerqueira
Rato
Branco
Clevelândia
Palmas
União da
Vitória
Canoinhas
Mafra
Rio Negro
Joinville
Ilha de São Francisco

Eldorado
Montecarlo
Xanxerê
Campos
de Palmas
Caçador
Itaiópolis
São Francisco do Sul
Araquari
Jaraguá do Sul

Puerto
Rico
A R G E N T I N A
S A N T A C A T A R I N A
Serra do Espigão
Blumenau
Itajaí

Lambert Azimuthal Equal Area Projection

Longitude 50° west of Greenwich

METRES
FEET
5000 / 16404
3000 / 9843
2000 / 6562
1000 / 3281
500 / 1640
200 / 656
0 / 0
Land below
sea level
200 / 656
4000 / 13124
6000 / 19686

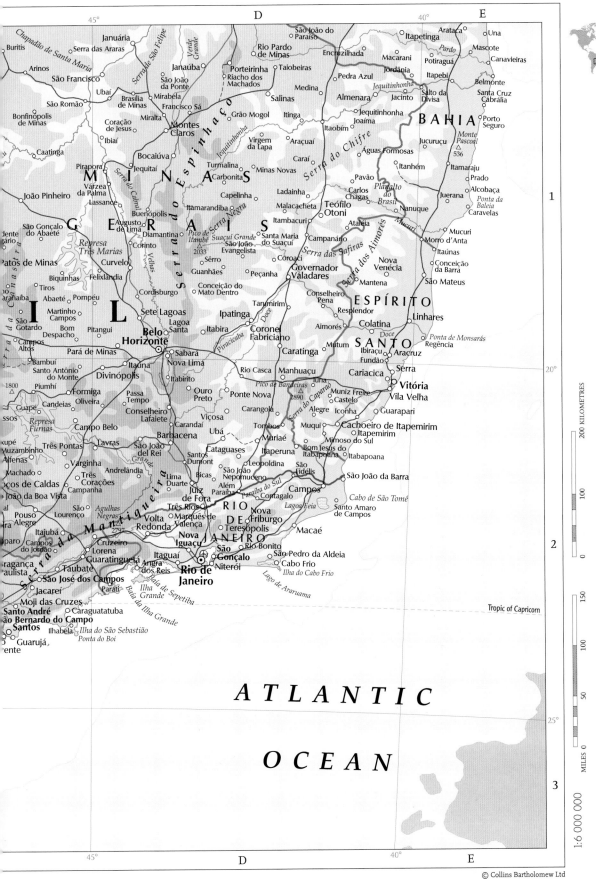

Chapadão de Santa Maria
Buritis
Arinos
São Francisco
São Romão
Bonfinópolis de Minas
Caatinga

Januária
Serra das Araras
Janaúba
São João da Ponte
Ubaí
Brasília de Minas
Mirabéla
Coração de Jesus
Miralta
Ibiaí
Montes Claros
Bocaiúva

Verde Grande
São João do Paraíso
Rio Pardo de Minas
Porteirinha
Riacho dos Machados
Taiobeiras
Salinas
Francisco Sá
Grão Mogol
Itinga
Virgem da Lapa
Araçuaí
Caraí

São João do Paraíso
Encruzilhada
Macarani
Jordânia
Pedra Azul
Medina
Almenara
Jequitinhonha
Joaíma
Itaobím
Águas Formosas
Pavão

Itapetinga
Arataca
Una
Mascote
Canavieiras
Potiraguá
Itapebi
Belmonte
Santa Cruz Cabrália
Jacinto
Salto da Divisa
Porto Seguro
Jequitinhonha
Jucuruçu
Itanhém
Itamaraju
Prado
Alcobaça
Juerana
Caravelas
Mucuri

BAHIA
Monte Pascoal △ 536
Planalto do Brasil
Ponta da Baleia

1

João Pinheiro
Várzea da Palma
Lassance
Buenópolis
Augusto de Lima
Diamantina
Pico de Serra Negra
Itamarandiba
Malacacheta
Teófilo Otoni
Itambacuri
Carlos Chagas
Nanuque
Mucuri
Morro d'Anta
Itaúnas
Conceição da Barra

São Gonçalo do Abaeté
Pirapora
Jequitaí
Carbonita
Capelinha
Ladainha
Santa Maria do Suaçuí
Ataléia
Campanário
Mantena
São Mateus

M I N A S
G E R A I S
Serra do Cabral
Serra do Espinhaço
Serra Negra
Pico de Itambé 2033
Suaçuí Grande
São João Evangelista
Serra das Safiras
Serra dos Aimorés
Mucuri
ESPÍRITO

Represa Três Marias
Corinto
Curvelo
Biquinhas
Felixlândia
Patos de Minas
Tiros
Abaeté
Pompéu
Pitangui
Sêrro
Guanhães
Peçanha
Coroaci
Governador Valadares
Nova Venécia

I L
Martinho Campos
Bom Despacho
Campos Altos
Bambuí
Santo Antônio do Monte
Divinópolis
Itaúna
Itabirito
Pará de Minas
Sete Lagoas
Lagoa Santa
Sabará
Nova Lima
Belo Horizonte
Itabira
Cordisburgo
Conceição do Mato Dentro
Tarumirim
Conselheiro Pena
Resplendor
Aimorés
Colatina
Linhares

1800
Piumhí
Guapé
Formiga
Oliveira
Candeias
Campo Belo
Passa Tempo
Conselheiro Lafaiete
Ouro Preto
Ponte Nova
Rio Casca
Manhuaçu
Caratinga
Iúna
Mutum
Ibiraçu
Fundão
Aracruz
Serra
Cariacica
SANTO
Ponta de Monsarás
Regência

Represa Furnas
Três Pontas
Alfenas
Machado
Poços de Caldas
Varginha
Três Corações
Lavras
Carandaí
Viçosa
Ubá
Carangola
Serra do Caparaó
Pico de Bandeiras 2890
Muniz Freire
Castelo
Alegre
Iconha
Muqui
Cachoeiro de Itapemirim
Guarapari
Vitória
Vila Velha

São Lourenço
Campanha
Andrelândia
Santos Dumont
Cataguases
Muriaé
Itaperuna
Tombos
Leopoldina
Mimoso do Sul
Bom Jesus do Itabapoana
Itabapoana
Itapemirim

Pouso Alegre
São João da Boa Vista
Três Rios
Lima Duarte
Bicas
São João Nepomuceno
Além Paraíba
São Fidélis
São João da Barra

Itajubá
Serra da Mantiqueira
Agulhas Negras 2797
Juiz de Fora
RIO
Paraíba do Sul
Paraíba do Sul
Contagalo
Campos
Cabo de São Tomé
Santo Amaro de Campos

Bragança Paulista
Campos do Jordão
Cruzeiro
Lorena
Guaratinguetá
Taubaté
Volta Redonda
Marquês de Valença
Três Rios
DE
Nova Friburgo
Teresópolis
Lagoa Feia
Macaé

São José dos Campos
Jacareí
Moji das Cruzes
Caraguatatuba
Itaguaí
Angra dos Reis
Parati
Nova Iguaçu
JANEIRO
São Gonçalo
Niterói
Rio de Janeiro
Rio Bonito
São Pedro da Aldeia
Cabo Frio
Ilha do Cabo Frio

Santo André
ão Bernardo do Campo
Santos
Ilhabela
Ilha do São Sebastião
Ponta do Boi
Ilha Grande
Baía de Sepetiba
Baía da Ilha Grande
Lago de Araruama

2

Tropic of Capricorn

Guarujá

A T L A N T I C

O C E A N

25°

3

200 KILOMETRES
100
0
MILES 0
50
100
150

1:6 000 000

© Collins Bartholomew Ltd

A 90° B 120° C 150° D 180°

3 45° 2 60° Arctic Circle

Chukc Sea

Ber

Heilong Jiang

Sea
of Okhotsk

B E R I N G
Sea

Nur
Isla

A S I A

Sakhalin

Ostrov
Beringa

Aleutian Basin

Aleutian Islan

Vladivostok

Kuril
Basin

Kuril Islands
(Kuril'skiye Ostrova)

.7822

Aleutian Tren

4 Tropic of Cancer

Ganges

Hokkaidō

.3510

9550·

Kuril Trench

6671·

Emperor Seamount Chain

1240·

Emperor Trough

Yellow River

Sea
of Japan

.7900

Kolkata

Yangtze

Yellow
Sea

Honshū

8412

Tōkyō

Northwest
Pacific
Basin

Shanghai

East
China
Sea

Shikoku
Kyūshū

Iżu-Ogasawara
Trench

.9780

.6345

18.

Kure Atoll

Midway
Islands

Hawai

Bay
of
Bengal

Rangoon

*Hainan
Dao*

Taiwan

Ryukyu Islands
(Nansei-shotō)

.7181

.7460

Ryukyu
Trench

South Honshu Ridge

Volcano Islands
(Kazan-retto)

Mariana Ridge

Mapmaker
Seamounts

Necke
Island

Hawai

Luzon Strait

15°

Andaman
Islands

South
China
Sea

5560·

Philippine
Basin

Kyushu - Palau Ridge

West
Mariana
Basin

Mid - Pacific Mountains

6530·

Andaman
Basin

Luzon

Saipan

Mariana Trench

Sri Lanka

Philippines

10057

Challenger Deep
10920

Guam·

.1564

MICRONESIA

Central
Pacific
Basin

5 Nicobar
Islands

Palawan

Sulu
Sea

Palau
Islands

8967

Mindanao

.8054

West
Caroline
Basin

East
Caroline
Basin

Caroline Islands

Chuuk

Kwajalein

Marshall Islands

Gilbert Ridge

Gilbert
Islands

Celebes
Sea

·5484

Kosrae

Singapore

Kepulauan
Mentawai

Borneo

Halmahera

7208

Melanesian
Basin

Phoenix Islan

Equator

2302·

Sumatra

Bangka

Celebes

Seram

Admiralty Islands

0°

Cocos
Basin

Laut Jawa

Laut
Banda

·7288

New
Guinea

New
Britain

8940

Solomon
Islands

Solomon
Sea

Funafuti

Fakaofo

.13

Samoa
Basin

Jakarta

Java

Laut Flores

Arafura
Sea

Timor

Torres Strait
Cape York

8322

Savai'i

Investigator Ridge

Java Trench
(Sunda Trench)

7125

Sumba

Timor Sea

Coral Sea
Basin

Espíritu
Santo

Vanua Levu

Niue

6 INDIAN

·6360

North
Australian
Basin

Great Barrier Reef

Coral
Sea

Viti Levu

New
Caledonia

7633

New Hebrides
Trench

Tonga Trench

Horizon Deep
10800

OCEAN

West Australian
Basin

Exmouth
Plateau

North
West Cape

New
Caledonia

Lord Howe Rise

South Fiji
Basin

15°

1924·

AUSTRALIA

Sydney

Norfolk Island

Kermadec Islands

10047·

Kermadec Trench

Sou

Pacif

METRES
FEET

Perth
Basin

Perth

Great
Australian
Bight

Melbourne

Auckland

North Island

Tasman
Sea New
Zealand

Wellington

Chatham
Rise

Chatham
Islands

0
0

Tropic of Capricorn

549·

Cape
Leeuwin

South Australian
Basin

·5670

5176.

200
656

2000
6562

7 Broken Plateau

7102·

Diamantina Deep
6602

·South Tasman Rise

Tasmania

Tasman
Basin

South Island

60·

Campbell
Plateau

Antipodes Islands

3000
9843

Auckland
Islands

4000
13124

5000
16404

Ile Amsterdam
Ile St-Paul

Southeast Indian Ridge

Indian - Antarctic Ridge

SOUTH

6000
19686

1586·

Macquarie
Ridge

1646·

.956

Balleny
Islands

7000
22967

Australian - Antarctic
Basin

·4650

Cape
Adare

R

Ro

9000
29529

8

9

4181·

Antarctic Circle

A N T A

90° 60° 120° 150° 18

Lambert Azimuthal Equal Area Projection

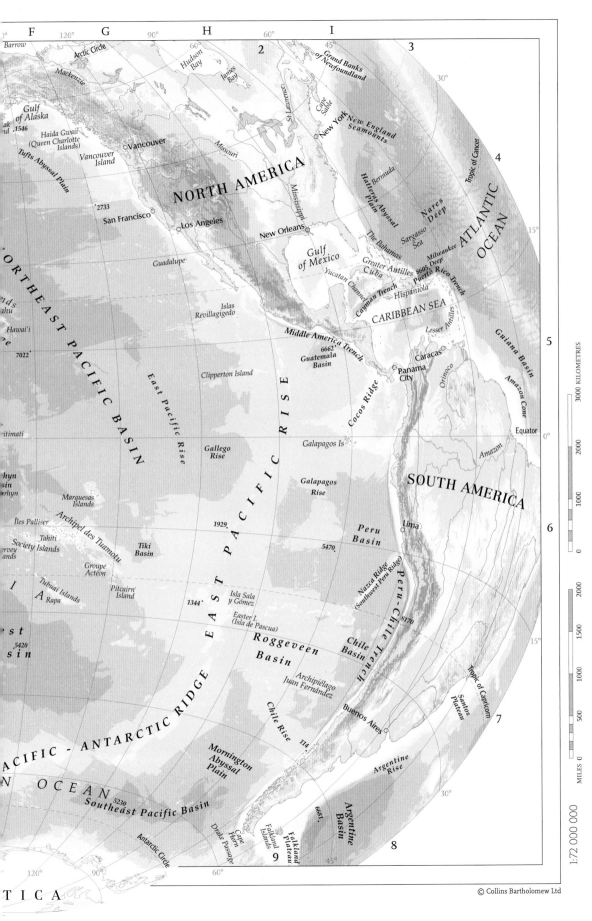

F   120°   G   90°   H   60°   I

2

3

Barrow

Arctic Circle

Mackenzie

Hudson Bay

James Bay

Grand Banks of Newfoundland

Gulf of Alaska

Cape Sable

Haida Gwaii (Queen Charlotte Islands)

ak

.1546

New York

New England Seamounts

30°

Vancouver

Vancouver Island

Missouri

NORTH AMERICA

Bermuda

Tropic of Cancer

4

.2733

Hatteras Abyssal Plain

San Francisco

Los Angeles

Mississippi

Nares Deep

ATLANTIC OCEAN

15°

Guadalupe

New Orleans

Sargasso Sea

Milwaukee 8605 Deep

NORTHEAST PACIFIC BASIN

Gulf of Mexico

The Bahamas

Greater Antilles

Cuba

Yucatan Channel

Puerto Rico Trench

ahu

Islas Revillagigedo

Cayman Trench

Hispaniola

Lesser Antilles

Guiana Basin

5

Hawai'i

Middle America Trench

CARIBBEAN SEA

7022

6662 Guatemala Basin

Caracas

Panama City

Orinoco

Amazon Cone

Equator 0°

itimati

Clipperton Island

Cocos Ridge

Amazon

East Pacific Rise

EAST PACIFIC RISE

Gallego Rise

Galapagos Is

SOUTH AMERICA

6

hyn

sin arhyn

Marquesas Islands

Galapagos Rise

Lima

Peru Basin

Îles Palliser

Archipel des Tuamotu

1929.

Society Islands

Tahiti

5470.

ervey nds

Groupe Actéon

Tiki Basin

Nazca Ridge (Southwest Peru Ridge)

I

A Rapa

Tubuai Islands

Pitcairn Island

1344.

Isla Sala y Gómez

8170

Peru-Chile Trench

15°

.5420

Easter I. (Isla de Pascua)

Chile Basin

t in is

Roggeveen Basin

Archipiélago Juan Fernández

Santos Plateau

Tropic of Capricorn

7

PACIFIC - ANTARCTIC RIDGE

EAST PACIFIC RISE

Chile Rise

114.

Buenos Aires

Argentine Rise

Mornington Abyssal Plain

Argentine Basin

30°

N

OCEAN

5230

5891.

Southeast Pacific Basin

Cape Horn

Falkland Islands

Falkland Plateau

8

Antarctic Circle

Drake Passage

9

45°

120°   90°   60°

TICA

1:72 000 000

3000 KILOMETRES

2000

1000

0

2000

1500

1000

500

0

MILES

© Collins Bartholomew Ltd

157

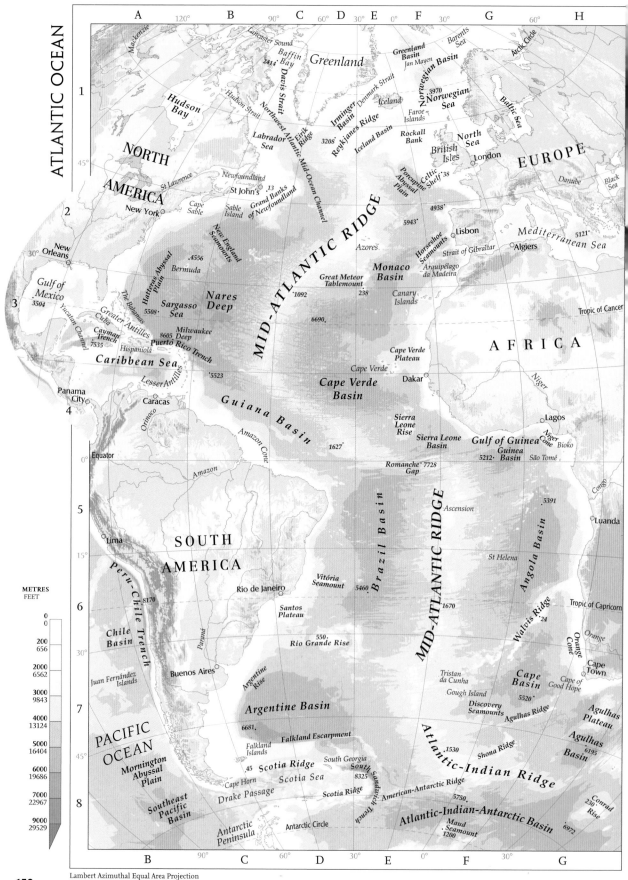

ATLANTIC OCEAN

A 120° B 90° C 60° D 30° E 0° F 30° G 60° H

Mackenzie
Lancaster Sound
Baffin Bay
2414
Greenland
Greenland Basin
Jan Mayen
Barents Sea
Arctic Circle
Hudson Bay
Hudson Strait
Davis Strait
Northwest Atlantic Mid-Ocean Channel
Eirik Ridge
Irminger Basin
Denmark Strait
Iceland
Faroe Islands
Norwegian Basin
3970
Norwegian Sea
Baltic Sea

1

NORTH
Labrador Sea
3208
Reykjanes Ridge
Iceland Basin
Rockall Bank
North Sea
British Isles
London
EUROPE
45°

AMERICA
St Lawrence
Newfoundland
St John's
13
Grand Banks of Newfoundland
Porcupine Abyssal Plain
Celtic Shelf
38
Danube
Black Sea

2

New York
Cape Sable
Sable Island
MID-ATLANTIC RIDGE
4938
Lisbon
Mediterranean Sea
5121
New Orleans
5943
Horseshoe Seamounts
Strait of Gibraltar
Algiers
30°

Gulf of Mexico
3504
New England Seamounts
4556
Bermuda
Azores
Monaco Basin
Arquipélago da Madeira

3

Yucatán Channel
The Bahamas
Hatteras Abyssal Plain
Nares Deep
Sargasso Sea
5508
1092
Great Meteor Tablemount
238
Canary Islands
Cape Verde Plateau
AFRICA
Tropic of Cancer

Cuba
Greater Antilles
Cayman Trench
7535
8605
Milwaukee Deep
Puerto Rico Trench
6690
Niger

Panama City
Hispaniola
Caribbean Sea
Lesser Antilles
5523
Cape Verde
Cape Verde Basin
Dakar

4

Caracas
Orinoco
Guiana Basin
Sierra Leone Rise
Sierra Leone Basin
Gulf of Guinea
Guinea Basin
Lagos
Niger Cone
Bioko

Equator
Amazon Cone
1627
5212
São Tomé
0°

Amazon
Romanche Gap
7728
Congo

SOUTH
Ascension
5391
Luanda

5

Lima
AMERICA
Vitória Seamount
5460
Brazil Basin
St Helena
Angola Basin
15°

Peru-Chile Trench
8170
Rio de Janeiro
1670
MID-ATLANTIC RIDGE
Walvis Ridge
24
Tropic of Capricorn

6

Chile Basin
Santos Plateau
550
Rio Grande Rise
Tristan da Cunha
Cape Basin
5520
Orange Cone
Cape Town
Cape of Good Hope

Buenos Aires
Argentine Rise
Gough Island
Discovery Seamounts
Agulhas Ridge
Orange
30°

7

Juan Fernández Islands
Argentine Basin
6681
Falkland Escarpment
1530
Shona Ridge
Agulhas Plateau
Agulhas Basin
6195

PACIFIC
Falkland Islands
45
Scotia Ridge
South Georgia
South Sandwich Trench
Atlantic-Indian Ridge
45°

OCEAN
Mornington Abyssal Plain
Cape Horn
Scotia Sea
8325
Scotia Ridge
American-Antarctic Ridge
5750
Conrad Rise
230
6972

8

Southeast Pacific Basin
Drake Passage
Atlantic-Indian-Antarctic Basin
Maud Seamount
1200

Antarctic Peninsula
Antarctic Circle

METRES
FEET

0	0
200	656
2000	6562
3000	9843
4000	13124
5000	16404
6000	19686
7000	22967
9000	29529

B 90° C 60° D 30° E 0° F 30° G

158

Lambert Azimuthal Equal Area Projection

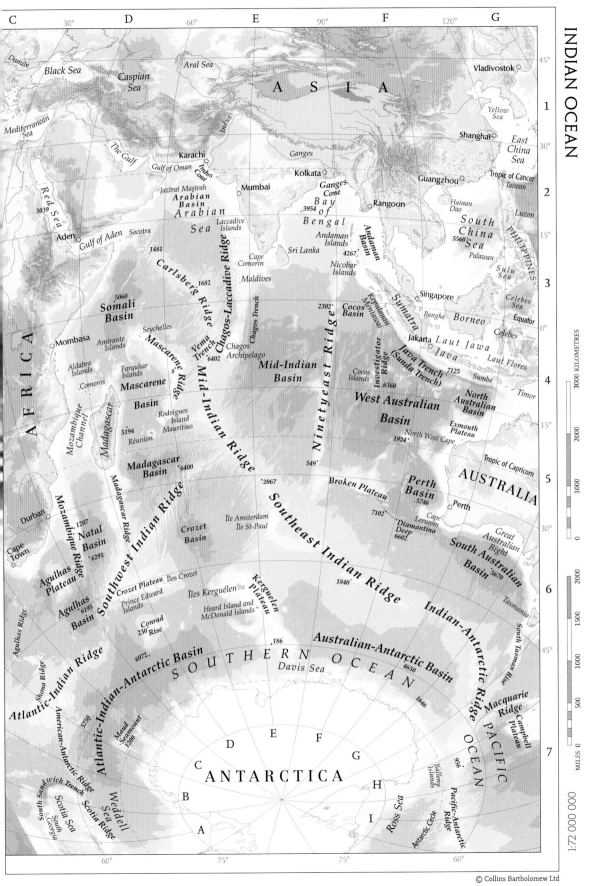

1:72 000 000

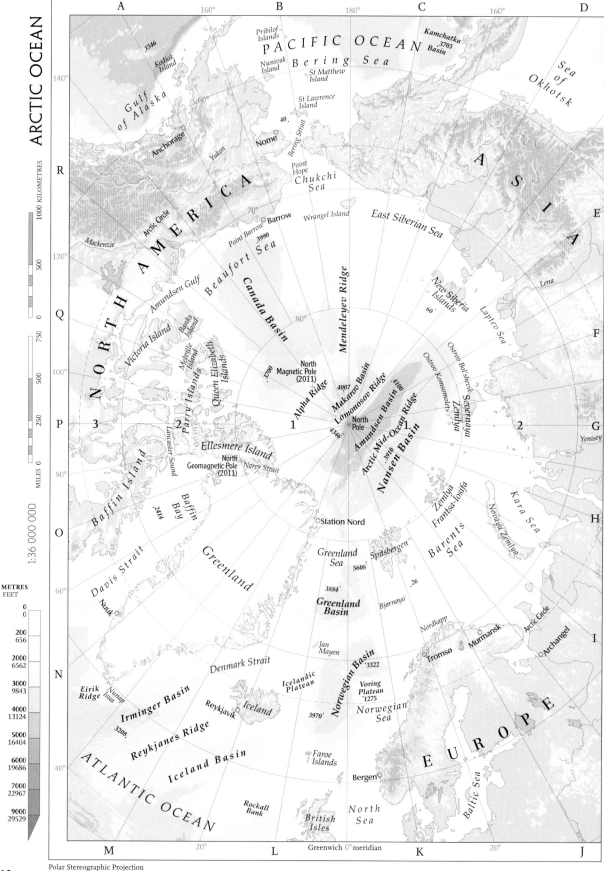

1:36 000 000

1000 KILOMETRES

500

0

750

500

250

MILES 0

METRES
FEET

0
0

200
656

2000
6562

3000
9843

4000
13124

5000
16404

6000
19686

7000
22967

9000
29529

A   160°   B   180°   C   160°   D

PACIFIC OCEAN

Bering   Sea

Pribilof
Islands

Nunivak
Island

St Matthew
Island

St Lawrence
Island

Kamchatka
.3703
Basin

Sea
of
Okhotsk

140°

60°

.1546

Kodiak
Island

Gulf
of
Alaska

Anchorage

Nome

40.

Bering Strait

Point
Hope

Chukchi
Sea

ASIA

NORTH   AMERICA

Mackenzie

Arctic Circle

Yukon

Point Barrow

Barrow

Wrangel Island

East Siberian Sea

Lena

R

E

120°

70°

.3990

Beaufort Sea

Mendeleyev Ridge

New Siberia
Islands

Laptev
Sea

Ostrov Bol'shevik

Ostrov Komsomolets

Severnaya

Zemlya

60

Q

80°

Amundsen Gulf

Victoria Island

Canada Basin

F

.3700

North
Magnetic Pole
(2011)

4007

Makarov Basin

Lomonosov Ridge

4100

Ostrov
Kotel'nyy

Banks
Island

Melville
Island

Parry Islands

Queen Elizabeth
Islands

100°

Alpha Ridge

North
Pole

Amundsen Basin

Arctic Mid-Ocean Ridge

.2910

Nansen Basin

Zemlya
Frantsa-Iosifa

Kara
Sea

Novaya Zemlya

P

3   2   1   4346   1   2   G

Yenisey

80°

Lancaster Sound

Ellesmere Island

North
Geomagnetic Pole
(2011)

Nares Strait

H

O

Baffin Island

Baffin
Bay

.2414

Station Nord

Spitsbergen

Barents
Sea

Davis Strait

Greenland

Greenland
Sea

5608.

60°

Nuuk

.3884

Greenland
Basin

Bjørnøya

.26

Nordkapp

Arctic Circle

Archangel

I

N

Jan
Mayen

Norwegian Basin

.3322

Tromsø

Murmansk

Denmark Strait

Icelandic
Plateau

Voring
Plateau
.1275

Norwegian
Sea

Eirik
Ridge

Nunap
Isua

Irminger Basin

Reykjavik

Iceland

.3970

Bergen

EUROPE

.3208

Reykjanes Ridge

40°

Iceland Basin

Faroe
Islands

North
Sea

Baltic Sea

ATLANTIC OCEAN

Rockall
Bank

British
Isles

M   20°   L   Greenwich 0° meridian   K   20°   J

Polar Stereographic Projection

WORLD FACTS AND FIGURES

	Total Population	2050 Projected Population	Gross National Income (GNI) Per Capita (US$)	Literacy Rate (%)	International Dialling Code	Time Zone	Official Website *Tourism Website*
WORLD	6 937 903 163	9 257 054 000	8732	83.7	...	...	
AFGHANISTAN	32 358 000	76 250 000	310	...	93	+4.5	www.president.gov.af *...*
ALBANIA	3 216 000	2 990 000	4 000	95.9	355	+1	www.km.gov.al *www.albaniantourism.com*
ALGERIA	35 980 000	46 522 000	4 420	72.6	213	+1	www.el-mouradia.dz *www.matet.dz*
ANDORRA	86 000	137 000	41 130	...	376	+1	www.govern.ad *www.andorra.ad*
ANGOLA	19 618 000	42 334 000	3 750	70.0	244	+1	www.governo.gov.ao *www.angola.org/tourism.html*
ANTIGUA AND BARBUDA	90 000	112 000	12 130	99.0	1 268	-4	www.ab.gov.ag *www.antigua-barbuda.org*
ARGENTINA	40 765 000	50 560 000	7 550	97.7	54	-3	www.argentina.gov.ar *www.turismo.gov.ar*
ARMENIA	3 100 000	2 931 000	3 100	99.5	374	+4	www.gov.am *www.armeniainfo.am*
AUSTRALIA	22 606 000	31 385 000	43 770	...	61	+8 to +10.5	www.australia.gov.au *www.australia.com*
AUSTRIA	8 413 000	8 427 000	46 450	...	43	+1	www.bundeskanzleramt.at *www.austria.info*
AZERBAIJAN	9 306 000	11 578 000	4 840	99.5	994	+4	www.president.az *http://azerbaijan.tourism.az*
THE BAHAMAS	347 000	445 000	21 390	...	1 242	-5	www.bahamas.gov.bs *www.bahamas.com*
BAHRAIN	1 324 000	1 801 000	25 420	91.4	973	+3	www.bahrain.bh *www.bahraintourism.com*
BANGLADESH	150 494 000	194 353 000	580	55.9	880	+6	www.bangladesh.gov.bd *www.bangladeshtourism.gov.bd*
BARBADOS	274 000	264 000	...	...	1 246	-4	www.barbados.gov.bb *www.visitbarbados.org*
BELARUS	9 559 000	8 001 000	5 560	99.7	375	+2	www.belarus.by *eng.belarustourism.by*
BELGIUM	10 754 000	11 587 000	45 270	...	32	+1	www.belgium.be *www.visitflanders.com Wallonia: www.opt*
BELIZE	318 000	529 000	3 740	...	501	-6	www.belize.gov.bz *www.travelbelize.org*
BENIN	9 100 000	21 734 000	750	41.7	229	+1	www.gouv.bj *...*
BHUTAN	738 000	962 000	2 020	52.8	975	+6	www.bhutan.gov.bt *www.tourism.gov.bt*
BOLIVIA	10 088 000	16 769 000	1 630	90.7	591	-4	www.bolivia.gov.bo *www.turismobolivia.bo*
BOSNIA-HERZEGOVINA	3 752 000	2 952 000	4 700	97.8	387	+1	www.fbihvlada.gov.ba *www.bhtourism.ba*
BOTSWANA	2 031 000	2 503 000	6 260	84.1	267	+2	www.gov.bw *www.botswanatourism.co.bw*
BRAZIL	196 655 000	222 843 000	8 070	90.0	55	-2 to -4	www.brazil.gov.br *sensational.braziltour.com*
BRUNEI	406 000	602 000	27 050	95.3	673	+8	www.jpm.gov.bn *www.tourismbrunei.com*
BULGARIA	7 446 000	5 459 000	6 060	98.3	359	+2	www.government.bg *www.bulgariatravel.org*
BURKINA FASO	16 968 000	46 721 000	510	28.7	226	GMT	www.primature.gov.bf *www.culture.gov.bf*
BURUNDI	8 575 000	13 703 000	150	66.6	257	+2	... *www.burundiembassy-usa.org/tourism.htm*
CAMBODIA	14 305 000	18 965 000	650	77.6	855	+7	www.cambodia.gov.kh *www.tourismcambodia.com*
CAMEROON	20 030 000	38 472 000	1 190	70.7	237	+1	www.spm.gov.cm *www.cameroon-tourism.org*
CANADA	34 350 000	43 642 000	41 980	...	1	-3.5 to -8	www.canada.gc.ca *www.canada.travel*
CAPE VERDE	501 000	632 000	3 010	84.8	238	-1	www.governo.cv *www.caboverde.com/ilhas/maio/guide-e.htm*
CENTRAL AFRICAN REPUBLIC	4 487 000	8 392 000	450	55.2	236	+1	www.centrafricaine.info *www.centrafricaine.info*
CHAD	11 525 000	27 252 000	600	33.6	235	+1	www.primature-tchad.org *...*
CHILE	17 270 000	20 059 000	9 470	98.6	56	-4	www.gobiernodechile.cl *www.visit-chile.org*

	Total Population	2050 Projected Population	Gross National Income (GNI) Per Capita (US$)	Literacy Rate (%)	International Dialling Code	Time Zone	Official Website *Tourism Website*
HINA	1 332 079 000	1 295 604 000	3 650	94.0	86	+8	www.gov.cn *www.cnto.org*
OLOMBIA	46 927 000	61 764 000	4 990	93.2	57	-5	www.gobiernoenlinea.gov.co *www.colombiaespasion.com*
OMOROS	754 000	1 700 000	810	74.2	269	+3	www.beit-salam.km *www.beit-salam.km/article.php3?id_article=39*
ONGO	4 140 000	8 801 000	2 080	...	242	+1	www.congo-site.com *www.congo-site.com/Tourisme,-Culture,-Art_r4.html*
ONGO DEMOCRATIC PUBLIC OF THE	67 758 000	148 523 000	160	67.0	243	+1 to +2	www.un.int/drcongo *...*
OSTA RICA	4 727 000	6 001 000	6 260	96.1	506	-6	www.casapres.go.cr *www.visitcostarica.com*
ÔTE D'IVOIRE (VORY COAST)	20 153 000	40 674 000	1 070	55.3	225	GMT	www.cotedivoirepr.ci *www.tourismeci.org*
ROATIA	4 396 000	3 859 000	13 770	98.8	385	+1	www.vlada.hr *www.croatia.hr*
UBA	11 254 000	9 898 000	5 550	99.8	53	-5	www.cubagob.gov.cu *www.cubatravel.cu*
YPRUS	1 117 000	1 347 000	30 480	97.9	357	+2	www.cyprus.gov.cy *www.visitcyprus.com*
ZECH REPUBLIC	10 534 000	10 638 000	17 310	...	420	+1	www.czech.cz *www.czechtourism.com*
ENMARK	5 573 000	5 920 000	59 060	...	45	+1	www.denmark.dk *www.visitdenmark.com*
IBOUTI	906 000	1 620 000	1 280	...	253	+3	www.presidence.dj *www.office-tourisme.dj*
OMINICA	68 000	65 000	4 900	...	1 767	-4	www.dominica.gov.dm *www.dominica.dm*
OMINICAN EPUBLIC	10 056 000	12 942 000	4 550	88.2	1 809	-4	www.cig.gob.do *www.godominicanrepublic.com*
AST TIMOR	1 154 000	3 006 000	2 460	50.6	670	+9	www.timor-leste.gov.tl *www.turismotimorleste.com*
CUADOR	14 666 000	19 549 000	3 970	84.2	593	-5	www.presidencia.gov.ec *www.ecuador.travel*
GYPT	82 537 000	123 452 000	2 070	66.4	20	+2	www.egypt.gov.eg *www.egypt.travel*
L SALVADOR	6 227 000	7 607 000	3 370	84.1	503	-6	www.presidencia.gob.sv *www.elsalvador.travel*
QUATORIAL UINEA	720 000	1 493 000	12 420	93.3	240	+1	www.ceiba-equatorial-guinea.org *...*
RITREA	5 415 000	11 568 000	320	66.6	291	+3	www.shabait.com *...*
STONIA	1 341 000	1 233 000	14 060	99.8	372	+2	www.valitsus.ee *www.visitestonia.com*
THIOPIA	84 734 000	145 187 000	330	29.8	251	+3	www.ethiopar.net *www.tourismethiopia.org*
IJI	868 000	1 017 000	3 840	...	679	+12	www.fiji.gov.fj *www.fijime.com*
INLAND	5 385 000	5 611 000	45 940	...	358	+2	www.valtioneuvosto.fi *www.visitfinland.com*
RANCE	63 126 000	72 442 000	42 620	...	33	+1	www.premier-ministre.gouv.fr *www.franceguide.com*
ABON	1 534 000	2 784 000	7 370	87.7	241	+1	www.legabon.org *www.legabon.org*
HE GAMBIA	1 776 000	4 036 000	440	46.5	220	GMT	www.statehouse.gm *www.visitthegambia.gm*
EORGIA	4 329 000	3 186 000	2 530	99.7	995	+4	www.parliament.ge *www.exploregeorgia.org*
ERMANY	82 163 000	74 781 000	42 450	...	49	+1	www.deutschland.de *www.germany-tourism.de*
HANA	24 966 000	49 107 000	1 190	66.6	233	GMT	www.ghana.gov.gh *www.touringghana.com*
REECE	11 390 000	11 647 000	29 040	97.2	30	+2	www.primeminister.gr *www.visitgreece.gr*
RENADA	105 000	95 000	5 580	96.0	1 473	-4	www.gov.gd *www.grenadagrenadines.com*
UATEMALA	14 757 000	31 595 000	2 650	74.5	502	-6	www.congreso.gob.gt *www.visitguatemala.com*
UINEA	10 222 000	23 006 000	370	39.5	224	GMT	www.guinee.gov.gn *...*
UINEA-BISSAU	1 547 000	3 185 000	510	52.2	245	GMT	www.gov.gw *www.minfurgb-gov.com*

	Total Population	2050 Projected Population	Gross National Income (GNI) Per Capita (US$)	Literacy Rate (%)	International Dialling Code	Time Zone	Official Website Tourism Website
GUYANA	756 000	766 000	2 660	...	592	-4	www.gina.gov.gy www.guyana-tourism.com
HAITI	10 124 000	14 178 000	...	48.7	509	-5	www.haiti.org www.haititourisme.org
HONDURAS	7 755 000	12 939 000	1 800	83.6	504	-6	www.congreso.gob.hn www.letsgohonduras.com
HUNGARY	9 966 000	9 243 000	12 980	99.4	36	+1	www.magyarorszag.hu www.hungarytourism.hu
ICELAND	324 000	431 000	43 430	...	354	GMT	www.iceland.is www.visiticeland.com
INDIA	1 241 492 000	1 692 008 000	1 220	62.8	91	+5.5	www.india.gov.in www.incredibleindia.org
INDONESIA	242 326 000	293 456 000	2 050	92.2	62	+7 to +9	www.indonesia.go.id www.my-indonesia.info
IRAN	74 799 000	85 344 000	4 530	85.0	98	3.5	www.president.ir www.tourismiran.ir
IRAQ	32 665 000	83 357 000	2 210	78.1	964	+3	www.cabinet.iq ...
IRELAND	4 526 000	6 038 000	44 280	...	353	GMT	www.gov.ie www.discoverireland.ie
ISRAEL	7 562 000	12 029 000	25 790	...	972	+2	www.gov.il www.goisrael.com
ITALY	60 789 000	59 158 000	35 110	98.9	39	+1	www.governo.it www.enit.it
JAMAICA	2 751 000	2 569 000	4 590	86.4	1 876	-5	www.jis.gov.jm www.visitjamaica.com
JAPAN	126 497 000	108 549 000	38 080	...	81	+9	www.kantei.go.jp www.jnto.go.jp
JORDAN	6 330 000	9 882 000	3 980	92.2	962	+2	www.jordan.gov.jo www.visitjordan.com
KAZAKHSTAN	16 207 000	21 210 000	6 920	99.7	7	+5 to +6	www.government.kz www.kazakhstan-tourist.com
KENYA	41 610 000	96 887 000	760	87.0	254	+3	www.kenya.go.ke www.magicalkenya.com
KIRIBATI	101 000	156 000	1 830	...	686	+12 to +14	www.parliament.gov.ki www.visit-kiribati.com
KOSOVO	2 180 686	...	3 240	...	381	+1	www.rks-gov.net/en-US www.visitkosova.org
KUWAIT	2 818 000	5 164 000	43 930	93.9	965	+3	www.e.gov.kw ...
KYRGYZSTAN	5 393 000	7 768 000	870	99.2	996	+6	www.gov.kg www.president.kg/en/president/about_republic/touris
LAOS	6 288 000	8 384 000	880	72.7	856	+7	www.na.gov.la www.tourismlaos.org
LATVIA	2 243 000	1 902 000	12 390	99.8	371	+2	www.saeima.lv www.latviatourism.lv
LEBANON	4 259 000	4 678 000	8 060	89.6	961	+2	www.presidency.gov.lb www.destinationlebanon.com
LESOTHO	2 194 000	2 788 000	980	89.7	266	+2	www.lesotho.gov.ls www.lesotho.gov.ls/about/tourism.php
LIBERIA	4 129 000	9 660 000	160	59.1	231	GMT	www.emansion.gov.lr ...
LIBYA	6 423 000	8 773 000	12 020	88.9	218	+2	www.libyanmission-un.org http://www.libyan-tourism.org/
LIECHTENSTEIN	36 000	45 000	136 630	...	423	+1	www.liechtenstein.li www.tourismus.li
LITHUANIA	3 307 000	2 813 000	11 410	99.7	370	+2	www.lrv.lt www.travel.lt
LUXEMBOURG	516 000	708 000	76 710	...	352	+1	www.gouvernement.lu www.visitluxembourg.lu
MACEDONIA (F.Y.R.O.M.)	2 064 000	1 881 000	4 400	97.1	389	+1	www.vlada.mk www.exploringmacedonia.com
MADAGASCAR	21 315 000	53 561 000	430	64.5	261	+3	www.madagascar.gov.mg www.madagascar-tourisme.com
MALAWI	15 381 000	49 719 000	290	73.7	265	+2	www.malawi.gov.mw www.guide2malawi.com
MALAYSIA	28 859 000	43 455 000	7 350	92.5	60	+8	www.malaysia.gov.my www.tourism.gov.my
MALDIVES	320 000	405 000	3 970	98.4	960	+5	www.presidencymaldives.gov.mv www.visitmaldives.com
MALI	15 840 000	42 130 000	680	26.2	223	GMT	www.primature.gov.ml www.tourisme.gov.ml

	Total Population	2050 Projected Population	Gross National Income (GNI) Per Capita (US$)	Literacy Rate (%)	International Dialling Code	Time Zone	Official Website / *Tourism Website*
ALTA	418 000	415 000	18 360	92.4	356	+1	www.gov.mt / *www.visitmalta.com*
ARSHALL ISLANDS	55 000	75 000	3 060	...	692	+12	www.rmigovernment.org / *www.visitmarshallislands.com*
AURITANIA	3 542 000	7 085 000	990	57.5	222	GMT	www.mauritania.mr / *...*
AURITIUS	1 307 000	1 367 000	7 250	87.9	230	+4	www.gov.mu / *www.mauritius.net*
EXICO	114 793 000	143 925 000	8 960	93.4	52	-6 to -8	www.gob.mx / *www.visitmexico.com*
ICRONESIA EDERATED STATES OF	112 000	726 000	2 500	...	691	+10 to +11	www.fsmgov.org / *www.visit-fsm.org*
OLDOVA	3 545 000	2 661 000	1 560	98.5	373	+2	www.moldova.md / *www.turism.gov.md*
ONACO	35 000	36 000	197 590	...	377	+1	www.monaco.gouv.mc / *www.visitmonaco.com*
ONGOLIA	2 800 000	4 093 000	1 630	97.5	976	+8	www.pmis.gov.mn / *www.mongoliatourism.gov.mn*
ONTENEGRO	632 000	604 000	6 650	...	382	+1	www.gov.me / *www.visit-montenegro.com*
OROCCO	32 273 000	39 200 000	2 770	56.1	212	GMT	www.maroc.ma / *www.visitmorocco.com*
OZAMBIQUE	23 930 000	50 192 000	440	55.1	258	+2	www.mozambique.mz / *...*
YANMAR	48 337 000	55 296 000	...	92.0	95	+6½	www.mofa.gov.mm / *www.myanmar-tourism.com*
AMIBIA	2 324 000	3 599 000	4 270	88.5	264	+1	www.grnnet.gov.na / *www.namibiatourism.com.na*
AURU	10 000	11 000	...	...	674	+12	www.naurugov.nr / *www.discovernauru.com*
EPAL	30 486 000	46 495 000	440	59.1	977	5.75	www.nepalgov.gov.np / *http://welcomenepal.com*
ETHERLANDS	16 665 000	17 151 000	48 460	...	31	+1	www.overheid.nl / *www.justbeinholland.com*
EW ZEALAND	4 415 000	5 678 000	28 810	...	64	+12 to +12.75	http://newzealand.govt.nz / *www.newzealand.com*
ICARAGUA	5 870 000	7 846 000	1 000	78.0	505	-6	www.asamblea.gob.ni / *www.visit-nicaragua.com*
IGER	16 069 000	55 435 000	340	28.7	227	+1	www.presidence.ne / *www.niger-tourisme.com*
IGERIA	162 471 000	389 615 000	1 190	60.8	234	+1	www.nigeria.gov.ng / *www.tourism.gov.ng*
ORTH KOREA	24 451 000	26 382 000	...	100.0	850	+9	www.korea-dpr.com / *www.korea-dpr.com/travel.htm*
ORWAY	4 925 000	6 063 000	84 640	...	47	+1	www.norway.no / *www.visitnorway.com*
MAN	2 846 000	3 740 000	17 890	86.6	968	+4	www.omanet.om / *www.omantourism.gov.om*
AKISTAN	176 745 000	274 875 000	1 000	55.5	92	+5	www.pakistan.gov.pk / *www.tourism.gov.pk*
ALAU	21 000	28 000	6 220	...	680	+9	www.palaugov.net / *www.visit-palau.com*
ANAMA	3 571 000	5 128 000	6 570	93.6	507	-5	www.pa / *www.visitpanama.com*
APUA EW GUINEA	7 014 000	13 549 000	1 180	60.1	675	+10	www.pm.gov.pg / *www.pngtourism.org.pg/*
ARAGUAY	6 568 000	10 323 000	2 250	94.6	595	-4	www.presidencia.gov.py / *www.senatur.gov.py*
ERU	29 400 000	38 832 000	4 200	89.6	51	-5	www.peru.gob.pe / *www.peru.info*
HILIPPINES	94 852 000	154 939 000	2 050	95.4	63	+8	www.gov.ph / *www.wowphilippines.com.ph*
OLAND	38 299 000	34 906 000	12 260	99.5	48	+1	www.poland.gov.pl / *www.poland.travel*
ORTUGAL	10 690 000	9 379 000	21 910	94.9	351	GMT	www.portugal.gov.pt / *www.visitportugal.com*
QATAR	1 870 000	2 612 000	...	94.7	974	+3	www.mofa.gov.qa / *www.qatartourism.gov.qa*
OMANIA	21 436 000	18 535 000	8 330	97.7	40	+2	www.guv.ro / *www.romaniatourism.com*
RUSSIAN EDERATION	142 836 000	126 188 000	9 340	99.6	7	+2 to +11	www.gov.ru / *www.russiatourism.ru*

	Total Population	2050 Projected Population	Gross National Income (GNI) Per Capita (US$)	Literacy Rate (%)	International Dialling Code	Time Zone	Official Website *Tourism Website*
RWANDA	10 943 000	26 003 000	460	70.7	250	+2	www.gov.rw *www.rwandatourism.com*
ST KITTS AND NEVIS	53 000	68 000	10 150	...	1 869	-4	www.gov.kn *www.stkittstourism.kn*
ST LUCIA	176 000	205 000	5 190	...	1 758	-4	www.stlucia.gov.lc *www.stlucia.org*
ST VINCENT AND THE GRENADINES	109 000	113 000	5 130	...	1 784	-4	www.gov.vc *http://discoversvg.com*
SAMOA	184 000	219 000	2 840	98.8	685	+13	www.govt.ws *samoa.travel*
SAN MARINO	32 000	34 000	50 670	...	378	+1	www.consigliograndeegenerale.sm *www.visitsanmarino.com*
SÃO TOMÉ AND PRÍNCIPE	169 000	299 000	1 130	88.8	239	GMT	www.gov.st *www.stptourism.st*
SAUDI ARABIA	28 083 000	44 938 000	17 210	86.1	966	+3	www.saudiportal.net *www.sauditourism.com.sa*
SENEGAL	12 768 000	28 607 000	1 040	49.7	221	GMT	www.gouv.sn *www.senegal-tourism.com*
SERBIA	7 306 677	8 797 000	6 000	...	381	+1	www.srbija.gov.rs *www.serbia-tourism.org*
SEYCHELLES	87 000	91 000	8 480	91.8	248	+4	www.virtualseychelles.sc *www.seychelles.travel*
SIERRA LEONE	5 997 000	11 088 000	340	40.9	232	GMT	www.statehouse.gov.sl *www.welcometosierraleone.org*
SINGAPORE	5 188 000	6 106 000	37 220	94.7	65	+8	www.gov.sg *www.yoursingapore.com*
SLOVAKIA	5 472 000	5 241 000	16 130	...	421	+1	www.government.gov.sk *www.slovakia.travel*
SLOVENIA	2 035 000	1 994 000	23 520	99.7	386	+1	www.gov.si *www.slovenia.info*
SOLOMON ISLANDS	552 000	1 163 000	910	...	677	+11	www.pmc.gov.sb *www.visitsolomons.com.sb*
SOMALIA	9 557 000	28 217 000	...	...	252	+3	www.tfgsomalia.net *...*
SOUTH AFRICA REPUBLIC OF	50 460 000	56 757 000	5 760	88.7	27	+2	www.gov.za *www.southafrica.net*
SOUTH KOREA	48 391 000	47 050 000	19 830	...	82	+9	www.korea.net *english.visitkorea.or.kr*
SOUTH SUDAN	8 260 490	...	...	...	...	+3	www.goss.org *...*
SPAIN	46 455 000	51 354 000	32 120	97.7	34	+1	www.la-moncloa.es *www.spain.info*
SRI LANKA	21 045 000	23 193 000	1 990	90.6	94	+5.5	www.priu.gov.lk *www.srilankatourism.org*
SUDAN	36 371 510	90 962 000	1 220	70.2	249	+3	www.sudan.gov.sd *...*
SURINAME	529 000	614 000	4 760	94.6	597	-3	www.kabinet.sr.org *www.suriname-tourism.org*
SWAZILAND	1 203 000	1 679 000	2 470	86.9	268	+2	www.gov.sz *www.welcometoswaziland.com*
SWEDEN	9 441 000	10 916 000	48 840	...	46	+1	www.sweden.se *www.visitsweden.com*
SWITZERLAND	7 702 000	7 870 000	65 430	...	41	+1	www.swissworld.org *www.myswitzerland.com*
SYRIA	20 766 000	33 051 000	2 410	84.2	963	+2	www.parliament.gov.sy *www.syriatourism.org*
TAIWAN	23 164 000	...	...	...	886	+8	www.gov.tw *www.go2taiwan.net*
TAJIKISTAN	6 977 000	10 745 000	700	99.7	992	+5	www.prezident.tj *http://tourism.tj*
TANZANIA	46 218 000	138 312 000	500	72.9	255	+3	www.tanzania.go.tz *www.tanzaniatouristboard.com*
THAILAND	69 519 000	71 037 000	3 760	93.5	66	+7	www.mfa.go.th *www.tourismthailand.org*
TOGO	6 155 000	11 130 000	440	56.9	228	GMT	www.republicoftogo.com *...*
TONGA	105 000	138 000	3 260	99.0	676	+13	www.pmo.gov.to *www.tongaholiday.com*
TRINIDAD AND TOBAGO	1 346 000	1 288 000	16 700	98.7	1 868	-4	www.gov.tt *www.gotrinidadandtobago.com*
TUNISIA	10 594 000	12 649 000	3 720	77.6	216	+1	www.ministeres.tn *www.tourismtunisia.com*

	Total Population	2050 Projected Population	Gross National Income (GNI) Per Capita (US$)	Literacy Rate (%)	International Dialling Code	Time Zone	Official Website / *Tourism Website*
TURKEY	73 640 000	91 617 000	8 720	90.8	90	+2	www.tccb.gov.tr / *www.goturkey.com*
TURKMENISTAN	5 105 000	6 639 000	3 420	99.6	993	+5	www.turkmenistan.gov.tm / *www.turkmenistanembassy.org*
TUVALU	10 000	13 000	...	...	688	+12	... / *www.timelesstuvalu.com*
UGANDA	34 509 000	94 259 000	460	...	256	+3	www.statehouse.go.ug / *www.visituganda.com*
UKRAINE	45 190 000	36 074 000	2 800	99.7	380	+2	www.kmu.gov.ua / *www.traveltoukraine.org*
UNITED ARAB EMIRATES	7 891 000	12 152 000	...	90.0	971	+4	www.uae.gov.ae / *www.dubaitourism.ae*
UNITED KINGDOM	62 417 000	72 817 000	41 370	...	44	GMT	www.direct.gov.uk / *www.visitbritain.com*
UNITED STATES OF AMERICA	313 085 000	403 101 000	46 360	...	1	-5 to -10	www.firstgov.gov / *www.discoveramerica.com/ca*
URUGUAY	3 380 000	3 663 000	9 010	98.3	598	-3	www.presidencia.gub.uy / *www.turismo.gub.uy*
UZBEKISTAN	27 760 000	35 438 000	1 100	99.3	998	+5	www.gov.uz / *...*
VANUATU	246 000	513 000	2 620	82.0	678	+11	www.governmentofvanuatu.gov.vu / *http://vanuatu.travel*
VATICAN CITY	800	...	...	...	39	+1	www.vaticanstate.va / *www.vaticanstate.va*
VENEZUELA	29 437 000	41 821 000	10 090	95.2	58	-4.5	www.gobiernoenlinea.ve / *www.venezuelavisitorsbureau.com*
VIETNAM	88 792 000	103 962 000	1 000	92.8	84	+7	www.na.gov.vn / *www.vietnamtourism.com*
YEMEN	24 800 000	61 577 000	1 060	62.4	967	+3	www.yemen-nic.info / *www.yementourism.com*
ZAMBIA	13 475 000	45 037 000	960	70.9	260	+2	www.statehouse.gov.zm / *www.zambiatourism.com*
ZIMBABWE	12 754 000	20 614 000	360	91.9	263	+2	www.parlzim.gov.zw / *www.zimbabwetourism.co.zw*

INDICATOR	DEFINITION
Total population	Interpolated mid-year population, 2011.
2050 projected population	Projected total population for the year 2050.
GNI per capita	Gross National Income per person in U.S. dollars using the World Bank Atlas method, from latest available data.
Literacy rate	Percentage of population aged 15–24 with at least a basic ability to read and write, 2009.
International dialling code	The country code prefix to be used when dialling from another country.
Time zone	Time difference in hours between local standard time and Greenwich Mean Time (GMT).
Official website	The official country website where available.
Tourism website	The country website for tourists where available.

MAIN STATISTICAL SOURCES

United Nations Department of Economic and Social Affairs (UDESA) World Population Prospects: The 2010 Revision

World Bank World Development Indicators online

UNESCO Education Data Centre

International Telecommunications Union (ITU)

WEB LINKS

http://esa.un.org/unpd/wpp/index.htm

http://data.worldbank.org/

http://stats.uis.unesco.org

http://www.itu.int/en/Pages/default.aspx

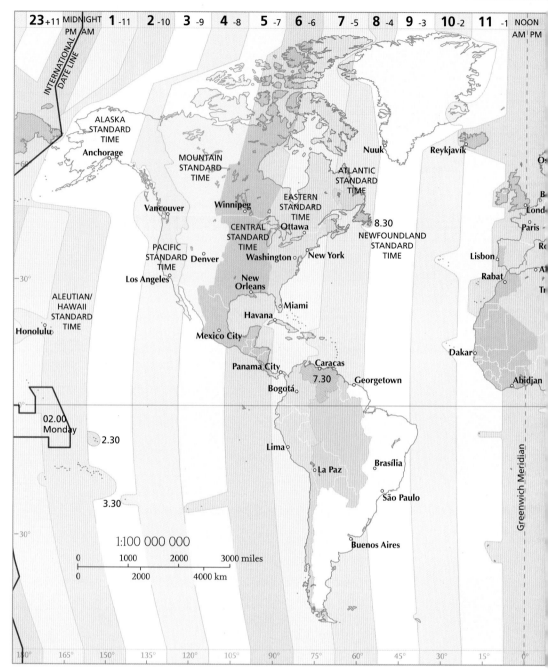

The system of timekeeping throughout the world is based on twenty-four time zones, each stretching over fifteen degrees of longitude – the distance equivalent to a time difference of one hour. The Prime, or Greenwich Meridian (0 degrees west), is the basis for Greenwich Mean Time (GMT) or Universal Coordinated Time (UTC), by which other times are measured. This universal reference point was agreed at an international conference in 1884.

Times are the local Standard Times observed compared with 12:00 (noon) Greenwich Mean Time (GMT). Daylight Saving Time, normally one hour ahead of local Standard Time, which is observed by certain countries for part of the year, is not shown on the map.

	Web Address	Theme
Greenwich Royal Observatory	www.nmm.ac.uk/places/royal-observatory/	The home of time
Greenwich Mean Time	wwp.greenwichmeantime.com	World time since 1884
World time zones	www.worldtimezones.com	Detailed time zones information
The Official US time	www.time.gov/	The home of US time
International Date Line	aa.usno.navy.mil/faq/docs/international_date.php	Understanding the international date line

PM AM

19.00

15.00

21.00

23.00

Anchorage

Moscow

Yekaterinburg

Yakutsk

Magadan

22.00

60°

Novosibirsk

Astana 17.00

18.00

Ulan Bator

Monday Sunday

INTERNATIONAL DATE LINE

30°

harest

16.00

Ankara

Dushanbe

Beijing

Tōkyō

Cairo

Tehrān 15.30 16.30

-20.00

Shanghai

Riyadh

Delhi 17.00

17.45

Chengdu

Hong Kong

17.30

18.30

Mumbai

18.00

Bangkok

Manila

mena

Addis Ababa

-17.30

Singapore

Equator

0°

Nairobi

hasa

Dar es Salaam

Jakarta

Port Moresby

18.30

Hárare

Antananarivo

CENTRAL STANDARD TIME 21.30

23.30

01.00 Monday

etoria

WESTERN STANDARD TIME

EASTERN STANDARD TIME

e Town

Perth

Sydney

22.30

Auckland

30°

-0.45

17.00

30°	45°	60°	75°	90°	105°	120°	135°	150°	165°	180°	165°	150°

ime zone boundaries can be altered to suit international or internal boundaries. China uses only
he time zone although it should theoretically have five, while the Russian Federation stretches
er eleven zones. The four mainland USA time zones do not always follow state boundaries.

he International Date Line is an imaginary line at approximately 180° west (or east) of
reenwich, across which the date changes by one day. The line has no international legal status
d countries near to the line can choose which date they will observe. The line was amended
cently so that it moved to the east of Samoa, to enable the island nation to conduct more
usiness with Australia, New Zealand and Asia, who used to be an entire day ahead of Samoa.

aylight Saving Time allows nations to adjust their clocks to extend daylight during the working
ay. It was first introduced to the UK during the First World War to reduce the demand for
rtificial heating and lighting.

TIME DIFFERENCES FOR
MAJOR CITIES FROM GMT

	hours
Los Angeles	-8
New York	-5
Buenos Aires	-3
Berlin	+1
Cape Town	+2
Mumbai	+5.5
Singapore	+8
Beijing	+8
Tōkyō	+9
Sydney	+10

GEOGRAPHICAL TABLES

HIGHEST MOUNTAINS	Height metres	feet	Location
Mt Everest	8 848	29 028	China/Nepal
K2	8 611	28 251	China/Pakistan
Kangchenjunga	8 586	28 169	India/Nepal
Lhotse	8 516	27 939	China/Nepal
Makalu	8 463	27 765	China/Nepal
Cho Oyu	8 201	26 906	China/Nepal
Dhaulagiri I	8 167	26 794	Nepal
Manaslu	8 163	26 781	Nepal
Nanga Parbat	8 126	26 660	Pakistan
Annapurna I	8 091	26 545	Nepal
Gasherbrum I	8 068	26 469	China/Pakistan
Broad Peak	8 047	26 401	China/Pakistan
Gasherbrum II	8 035	26 361	China/Pakistan
Xixabangma Feng	8 027	26 335	China
Annapurna II	7 937	26 040	Nepal

LONGEST RIVERS	Length km	miles	Continent
Nile	6 695	4 160	Africa
Amazon	6 516	4 049	South America
Yangtze	6 380	3 965	Asia
Mississippi-Missouri	5 969	3 709	North America
Ob'-Irtysh	5 568	3 460	Asia
Yenisey-Angara-Selenga	5 550	3 449	Asia
Yellow River	5 464	3 395	Asia
Congo	4 667	2 900	Africa
Río de la Plata-Paraná	4 500	2 796	South America
Irtysh	4 440	2 759	Asia
Mekong	4 425	2 750	Asia
Heilong Jiang-Argun'	4 416	2 744	Asia
Lena-Kirenga	4 400	2 734	Asia
MacKenzie-Peace-Finlay	4 241	2 635	North America
Niger	4 184	2 600	Africa

LARGEST LAKES	Area sq km	sq miles	Continent
Caspian Sea	371 000	143 243	Asia/Europe
Lake Superior	82 100	31 699	North America
Lake Victoria	68 870	26 591	Africa
Lake Huron	59 600	23 012	North America
Lake Michigan	57 800	22 317	North America
Lake Tanganyika	32 600	12 587	Africa
Great Bear Lake	31 328	12 096	North America
Lake Baikal	30 500	11 776	Asia
Lake Nyasa	29 500	11 390	Africa
Great Slave Lake	28 568	11 030	North America
Lake Erie	25 700	9 923	North America
Lake Winnipeg	24 387	9 416	North America
Lake Ontario	18 960	7 320	North America
Lake Ladoga	18 390	7 100	Europe
Lake Balkhash	17 400	6 718	Asia

LARGEST DRAINAGE BASINS	Area sq km	sq miles	Continent
Amazon	7 050 000	2 722 000	South America
Congo	3 700 000	1 429 000	Africa
Nile	3 349 000	1 293 000	Africa
Mississippi-Missouri	3 250 000	1 255 000	North America
Río de la Plata-Paraná	3 100 000	1 197 000	South America
Ob'-Irtysh	2 990 000	1 154 000	Asia
Yenisey-Angara-Selenga	2 580 000	996 000	Asia
Lena-Kirenga	2 490 000	961 000	Asia
Yangtze	1 959 000	756 000	Asia
Niger	1 890 000	730 000	Africa
Heilong Jiang-Argun'	1 855 000	716 000	Asia
Mackenzie-Peace-Finlay	1 805 000	697 000	North America
Ganges-Brahmaputra	1 621 000	626 000	Asia
St Lawrence-St Louis	1 463 000	565 000	North America
Volga	1 380 000	533 000	Europe

ATLANTIC OCEAN	Area sq km	sq miles	Deepest Point metres	feet
Total extent	86 557 000	33 420 000	8 605	Milwaukee Deep 28 231
Arctic Ocean	9 485 000	3 662 000	5 450	17 880
Caribbean Sea	2 512 000	970 000	7 680	25 197
Mediterranean Sea	2 510 000	969 000	5 121	16 801
Gulf of Mexico	1 544 000	596 000	3 504	11 496
Hudson Bay	1 233 000	476 000	259	850
North Sea	575 000	222 000	661	2 169
Black Sea	508 000	196 000	2 245	7 365
Baltic Sea	382 000	148 000	460	1 509

INDIAN OCEAN	Area sq km	sq miles	Deepest Point metres	feet
Total extent	73 427 000	28 350 000	7 125	Java Trench 23 376
Bay of Bengal	2 172 000	839 000	4 500	14 764
Red Sea	453 000	175 000	3 040	9 974
The Gulf	238 000	92 000	73	239

PACIFIC OCEAN	Area sq km	sq miles	Deepest Point metres	feet
Total extent	166 241 000	64 186 000	10 920	Challenger Deep 35 826
South China Sea	2 590 000	1 000 000	5 514	18 090
Bering Sea	2 261 000	873 000	4 150	13 615
Sea of Okhotsk	1 392 000	538 000	3 363	11 033
Sea of Japan (East Sea)	1 013 000	391 000	3 743	12 280
East China Sea and Yellow Sea	1 202 000	464 000	2 717	8 914

LARGEST ISLANDS	Area sq km	sq miles	Continent
Greenland	2 175 600	839 999	North America
New Guinea	808 510	312 166	Oceania
Borneo	745 561	287 861	Asia
Madagascar	587 040	266 656	Africa
Baffin Island	507 451	195 927	North America
Sumatra	473 606	182 859	Asia
Honshū	227 414	87 805	Asia
Great Britain	218 476	84 354	Europe
Victoria Island	217 291	83 896	North America
Ellesmere Island	196 236	75 767	North America
Celebes	189 216	73 056	Asia
South Island, New Zealand	151 215	58 384	Oceania
Java	132 188	51 038	Asia
North Island, New Zealand	115 777	44 701	Oceania
Cuba	110 860	42 803	North America

DEEPEST LAKES	Depth metres	feet	Continent
Lake Baikal	1 741	5 712	Asia
Lake Tanganyika	1 471	4 826	Africa
Caspian Sea	1 025	3 363	Europe/Asia
Lake Nyasa	706	2 316	Africa
Ysyk-Köl	702	2 303	Asia

LOWEST POINTS ON LAND	Depth below sea level metres	feet	Location
Dead Sea	-423	-1 388	Asia
Lake Assal	-156	-512	Djibouti
Turpan Pendi	-154	-505	China
Qattara Depression	-133	-436	Egypt
Poluostrov Mangyshlak	-132	-433	Kazakhstan

HIGHEST WATERFALLS	Height metres	feet	Location
Angel Falls (Kerepakupai Merú)	979	3 212	Venezuela
Tugela	948	3 110	South Africa
Utigård	800	2 625	Norway
Mongfossen	774	2 539	Norway
Mtarazi	762	2 500	Zimbabwe

EARTH'S DIMENSIONS	
Mass	5.974×10^{21} tonnes
Total area	509 450 000 sq km /196 698 645 sq miles
Land area	149 450 000 sq km / 57 702 645 sq miles
Water area	360 000 000 sq km /138 996 000 sq miles
Volume	$1 083 207 \times 10^{6}$ cubic km /
	$259 911 \times 10^{6}$ cubic miles
Equatorial diameter	12 756 km / 7 927 miles
Polar diameter	12 714 km / 7 900 miles
Equatorial circumference	40 075 km / 24 903 miles
Meridional circumference	40 008 km / 24 861 miles

LARGEST COUNTRIES BY POPULATION	Population
China	1 332 079 000
India	1 241 492 000
United States of America	313 085 000
Indonesia	242 326 000
Brazil	196 655 000
Pakistan	176 745 000
Nigeria	162 471 000
Bangladesh	150 494 000
Russian Federation	142 836 000
Japan	126 497 000

LARGEST COUNTRIES BY AREA	Area sq km	sq miles
Russian Federation	17 075 400	6 592 849
Canada	9 984 670	3 855 103
United States of America	9 826 635	3 794 085
China	9 584 492	3 700 593
Brazil	8 514 879	3 287 613
Australia	7 692 024	2 969 907
India	3 064 898	1 183 364
Argentina	2 766 889	1 068 302
Kazakhstan	2 717 300	1 049 155
Algeria	2 381 741	919 595

LARGEST CITIES	Population	Location
Tōkyō	37 049 000	Japan
Delhi	24 160 000	India
Mumbai	21 797 000	India
São Paulo	21 300 000	Brazil
Mexico City	20 078 000	Mexico
New York	19 968 000	United States of America
Shanghai	17 840 000	China
Kolkata	16 924 000	India
Dhaka	16 623 000	Bangladesh
Karachi	14 818 000	Pakistan
Buenos Aires	13 401 000	Argentina
Beijing	13 335 000	China
Los Angeles	13 165 000	United States of America
Manila	12 587 000	Philippines
Lagos	12 427 000	Nigeria

BUSIEST AIRPORTS (2010)	Location	Passengers
Atlanta (ATL)	USA	89 331 622
Beijing (PEK)	China	73 948 113
Chicago (ORD)	USA	66 774 738
London (LHR)	UK	65 884 143
Tōkyō (HND)	Japan	64 211 074
Los Angeles (LAX)	USA	59 070 127
Paris (CDG)	France	58 167 062
Dallas/Fort Worth Airport (DFW)	USA	56 906 610
Frankfurt (FRA)	Germany	53 009 221
Denver (DEN)	USA	52 209 377
Hong Kong (HKG)	China	50 348 960
Madrid (MAD)	Spain	49 844 596
Dubai (DXB)	UAE	47 180 628
New York (JFK)	USA	46 514 154
Amsterdam (AMS)	Netherlands	45 211 749

Climate is defined by the long-term weather conditions prevalent in any part of the world. The classification of climate types is based on the relationship between temperature and humidity and also on how these are affected by latitude, altitude, ocean currents and wind. Weather is how climatic conditions affect local areas. Weather stations collect data on temperature and rainfall, which can be plotted on graphs as shown here. These are based on average monthly figures over a minimum period of thirty years and can help to monitor climate change.

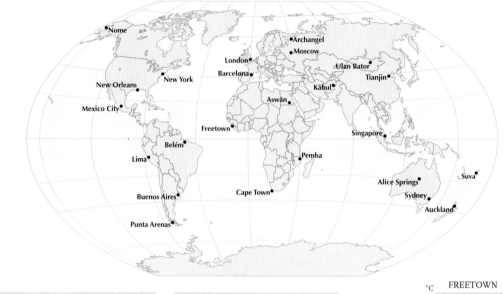

Temperature conversion							
°C	-20	-10	0	10	20	30	40
°F	-4	14	32	50	68	86	104

Rainfall conversion							
mm	25.4	127	254	381	508	635	762
ins	1	5	10	15	20	25	30

AFRICA

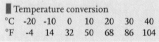

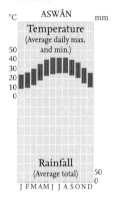

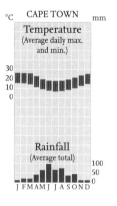

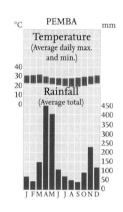

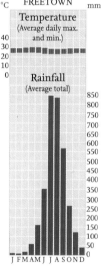

FREETOWN

ASIA

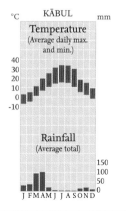

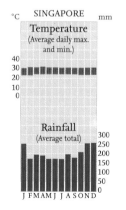

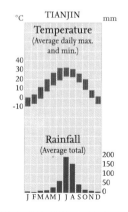

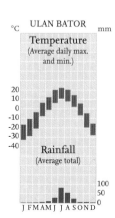

EUROPE

ARCHANGEL
°C / mm
Temperature (Average daily max. and min.)
30 20 10 0 -10 -20 -30
Rainfall (Average total)
100 50
J F M A M J J A S O N D

BARCELONA
°C / mm
Temperature (Average daily max. and min.)
30 20 10 0
Rainfall (Average total)
150 100 50
J F M A M J J A S O N D

LONDON
°C / mm
Temperature (Average daily max. and min.)
30 20 10 0 -10
Rainfall (Average total)
150 100 50
J F M A M J J A S O N D

MOSCOW
°C / mm
Temperature (Average daily max. and min.)
30 20 10 0 -10 -20
Rainfall (Average total)
150 100 50
J F M A M J J A S O N D

NORTH AMERICA

MEXICO CITY
°C / mm
Temperature (Average daily max. and min.)
30 20 10 0
Rainfall (Average total)
200 150 100 50 0
J F M A M J J A S O N D

NEW ORLEANS
°C / mm
Temperature (Average daily max. and min.)
40 30 20 10 0
Rainfall (Average total)
200 150 100 50 0
J F M A M J J A S O N D

NEW YORK
°C / mm
Temperature (Average daily max. and min.)
30 20 10 0 -10
Rainfall (Average total)
150 100 50
J F M A M J J A S O N D

NOME
°C / mm
Temperature (Average daily max. and min.)
20 10 0 -10 -20
Rainfall (Average total)
150 100 50
J F M A M J J A S O N D

SOUTH AMERICA

BELÉM
°C / mm
Temperature (Average daily max. and min.)
40 30 20 10 0
Rainfall (Average total)
350 300 250 200 150 100 50
J F M A M J J A S O N D

BUENOS AIRES
°C / mm
Temperature (Average daily max. and min.)
40 30 20 10 0
Rainfall (Average total)
150 100 50 0
J F M A M J J A S O N D

LIMA
°C / mm
Temperature (Average daily max. and min.)
30 20 10 0
Rainfall (Average total)
50
J F M A M J J A S O N D

PUNTA ARENAS
°C / mm
Temperature (Average daily max. and min.)
30 20 10 0 -10
Rainfall (Average total)
100 50 0
J F M A M J J A S O N D

OCEANIA

ALICE SPRINGS
°C / mm
Temperature (Average daily max. and min.)
40 30 20 10 0
Rainfall (Average total)
100 50 0
J F M A M J J A S O N D

AUCKLAND
°C / mm
Temperature (Average daily max. and min.)
40 30 20 10 0 -10
Rainfall (Average total)
150 100 50
J F M A M J J A S O N D

SUVA
°C / mm
Temperature (Average daily max. and min.)
40 30 20 10 0
Rainfall (Average total)
400 350 300 250 200 150 100 50
J F M A M J J A S O N D

SYDNEY
°C / mm
Temperature (Average daily max. and min.)
30 20 10 0
Rainfall (Average total)
150 100 50
J F M A M J J A S O N D

ENVIRONMENT

The earth has a rich environment with a wide range of habitats. Forest and woodland form the predominant natural land cover and tropical rain forests are believed to be home to the majority of the world's bird, animal and plant species. These forests are part of a delicate land-atmosphere relationship disturbed by changes in land use. Grassland, shrubland and deserts cover most of the unwooded areas of the earth with low-growing tundra in the far northern latitudes. Grassland and shrubland regions in particular have been altered greatly by man through agriculture, livestock grazing and settlements.

Organization	Web address	Theme
Earth Observatory	earthobservatory.nasa.gov	Observing the earth
USGS National Earthquake Information Center	earthquakes.usgs.gov/regional/neic	Monitoring earthquakes
Scripps Institution of Oceanography	sio.ucsd.edu	Exploration of the oceans
NASA Visible Earth	visibleearth.nasa.gov	Satellite images of the earth
USGS Volcano Hazards Program	volcanoes.usgs.gov	Volcanic activity
UNESCO World Heritage Convention	whc.unesco.org	World Heritage Sites
British Geological Survey	www.bgs.ac.uk	Geology
International Union for Conservation of Nature	www.iucn.org	World and ocean conservation
Rainforest Action Network	ran.org	Rainforest information and resources
United Nations Environment Programme	www.unep.org	Environmental protection by the UN
World Conservation Monitoring Centre	www.unep-wcmc.org	Conservation and the environment
World Resources Institute	www.wri.org	Monitoring the environment and resources
IUCN Red List	www.iucnredlist.org	Threatened species

OCEANS

Between them, the world's oceans cover approximately 70 per cent of the earth's surface. They contain 96 per cent of the earth's water and a vast range of flora and fauna. They are a major influence on the world's climate, particularly through ocean currents – the circulation of water within and between the oceans. Our understanding of the oceans has increased enormously over the last twenty years through the development of new technologies, including that of satellite images, which can generate vast amounts of data relating to the sea floor, ocean currents and sea surface temperatures.

Organization	Web address	Theme
International Maritime Organization	www.imo.org/Pages/home.aspx	Shipping and the environment
General Bathymetric Chart of the Oceans	www.gebco.net	Mapping the oceans
National Oceanography Centre, Southampton	www.noc.soton.ac.uk	Researching the oceans
Scott Polar Research Institute	www.spri.cam.ac.uk	Polar research

CLIMATE

The Earth's climate system is highly complex. It is recognized and accepted that man's activities are affecting this system, and monitoring climate change, including human influences upon it, is now a major issue. Future climate change depends critically on how quickly and to what extent the concentration of greenhouse gases in the atmosphere increase. Change will not be uniform across the globe and the information from sophisticated mathematical climate models is invaluable in helping governments and industry to assess the impacts climate change will have.

Organization	Web address	Theme
BBC Weather	news.bbc.co.uk/weather	Worldwide weather forecasts
Climatic Research Unit	www.cru.uea.ac.uk	Climatic research
Met Office	www.metoffice.gov.uk	Weather information and climatic research
National Climatic Data Center	www.ncdc.noaa.gov/oa/ncdc.html	Global climate data
National Hurricane Center	www.nhc.noaa.gov	Tracking hurricanes
National Oceanic and Atmospheric Administration	www.noaa.gov	Monitoring climate and the oceans
World Meteorological Organization	www.wmo.int/pages/index_en.html	The world's climate
NOAA El Niño	www.elnino.noaa.gov	El Niño research and observations

POPULATION

The world's population reached 6 billion in 1999. Rates of population growth vary between continents, but overall, the rate of growth has been increasing and it is predicted that by 2050 another 3 billion people will inhabit the planet. The process of urbanization, in particular migration from countryside to city, has led to the rapid growth of many cities. In mid 2009, for the first time, urban dwellers outnumbered those living in traditionally rural areas. It is estimated that by 2015 there will be 489 cities with over 1 million inhabitants and twenty-two with over 10 million.

Organization	Web address	Theme
Office for National Statistics	www.ons.gov.uk/census/index.html	UK census information
City Population	www.citypopulation.de	Statistics and maps about population
US Census Bureau	www.census.gov	US and world population
UN World Urbanization Prospects	www.esa.un.org/unpd/wup/index.htm	Population estimates and projections
UN Population Information Network	www.un.org/popin	World population statistics
UN Population Division	www.un.org/esa/population/unpop.htm	Monitoring world population

COUNTRIES

The present picture of the political world is the result of a long history of exploration, colonialism, conflict and negotiation. In 1950 there were eighty-two independent countries. Since then there has been a significant trend away from colonial influences and although many dependent territories still exist, there are now 196 independent countries. The newest country is South Sudan which declared independence from Sudan in July 2011. The shapes of countries reflect a combination of natural features, such as mountain ranges, and political agreements. There are still areas of the world where boundaries are disputed or only temporarily settled as ceasefire lines.

Organization	Web address	Theme
European Union	europa.eu	Gateway to the European Union
Permanent Committee on Geographical Names	www.pcgn.org.uk	Place names research in the UK
The World Factbook	www.cia.gov/library/publications/the-world-factbook	Country profiles
US Board on Geographic Names	geonames.usgs.gov	Place names research in the USA
United Nations	www.un.org	The United Nations
International Boundaries Research Unit	www.dur.ac.uk/ibru	International boundaries resources and research
Organisation for Economic Cooperation and Development	www.oecd.org	Economic statistics
The World Bank	data.worldbank.org	World development data and statistics

TRAVEL

Travelling as a tourist or on business to some countries, or travelling within certain areas can be dangerous because of wars and political unrest. The UK Foreign Office provides the latest travel advice and security warnings. Some areas of the world, particularly tropical regions in the developing world, also carry many risks of disease. Advice should be sought on precautions to take and medications required.

Organization	Web address	Theme
UK Foreign and Commonwealth Office	www.fco.gov.uk	Travel, trade and country information
US Department of State	www.state.gov	Travel, trade and country information
World Health Organization	www.who.int/en	Health advice and world health issues
Centers for Disease Control and Prevention	wwwnc.cdc.gov/travel	Advice for travellers
Airports Council International	www.airports.org	The voice of the world's airports
Travel Daily News	www.traveldailynews.com	Travel and tourism newsletter

ORGANIZATIONS

Throughout the world there are many international, national and local organizations representing the interests of individual countries, groups of countries, regions and specialist groups. These can provide enormous amounts of information on economic, social, cultural, environmental and general geographical issues facing the world. The following is a selection of such sites.

Organization	Web address	Theme
United Nations	www.un.org	The United Nations
United Nations Educational, Scientific and Cultural Organization	www.unesco.org/new/en/unesco	International collaboration
United Nations Children's Fund	www.unicef.org	Children's health, education, equality and protection
United Nations High Commissioner for Refugees	www.unhcr.org/uk	The UN refugee agency
Food and Agriculture Organization of the United Nations	www.fao.org	Agriculture and defeating hunger
United Nations Development Programme	www.beta.undp.org/undp/en/home.html	The UN global development network
North Atlantic Treaty Organization	www.nato.int/cps/en/natolive/index.htm	North Atlantic freedom and security
European Environment Agency	www.eea.europa.eu/	Europe's environment
European Centre for Nature Conservation	www.ecncl.org	Nature conservation in Europe
Europa – Gateway to the European Union	europa.eu/index_en.htm	European Union facts and statistics
World Health Organization	www.who.int/en	Health issues and advice
Association of Southeast Asian Nations	www.aseansec.org	Economic, social and cultural development
Joint United Nations Programme on HIV/AIDS	www.unaids.org/en	The AIDS crisis
African Union	www.au.int/	African international relations
World Lakes Network	www.worldlakes.org/	Lakes around the world
Secretariat of the Pacific Commmunity	www.spc.int	The Pacific community
The Maori world	www.maori.org.nz	Maori culture
US National Park Service	www.nps.gov/index.htm	National Parks of the USA
Parks Canada	www.pc.gc.ca	Natural heritage of Canada
Panama Canal Authority	www.pancanal.com	Explore the Panama Canal
Caribbean Community Secretariat	www.caricom.org	Caribbean Community
Organization of American States	www.oas.org/en/default.asp	Inter-American cooperation
The Latin American Network Information Center	lanic.utexas.edu	Latin America
World Wildlife Fund	www.worldwildlife.org/home-full.html	Global environmental conservation
The Amazon Conservation Team	www.amazonteam.org	Conservation in tropical America

DISTANCES

This table shows air distances in both kilometres and *miles* for twenty-seven cities around the world. These are the shortest distances between cities and are known as Great Circle routes.

km / *miles*																										City
8075	9793	5905	6918	4303	11764	5247	11040	3422	3735	10647	14374	11689	5632	13481	5478	2043	2987	2317	7498	2367	13534	4637	5972	4795	14244	Abu Dhabi
5018	*6085*	*3669*	*4299*	*2674*	*7310*	*3260*	*6860*	*2126*	*2321*	*6616*	*8932*	*7263*	*3500*	*8377*	*3404*	*1270*	*1856*	*1440*	*4659*	*1471*	*8410*	*2881*	*3711*	*3091*	*8851*	
8811	2161	8411	9596	18400	12288	18540	14187	13966	16194	14379	10947	2629	19592	10479	18330	16287	17042	12482	11796	16573	10372	17743	10388	9566		Auckland
5475	*1343*	*5227*	*5963*	*11433*	*7636*	*11521*	*8816*	*8678*	*10063*	*8935*	*6802*	*1634*	*12174*	*6512*	*11390*	*10121*	*10590*	*7756*	*7330*	*10298*	*6445*	*11025*	*6455*	*5944*		
4610	7523	1427	3720	8842	16081	9457	13949	7218	7070	13417	15760	7359	10196	13319	9544	6895	7477	2917	10144	7279	16885	8613	3291			Bangkok
2865	*4675*	*887*	*2312*	*5494*	*9993*	*5877*	*8668*	*4485*	*4393*	*8337*	*9739*	*4573*	*6336*	*8276*	*5931*	*4285*	*4646*	*1813*	*6303*	*4523*	*10492*	*5352*	*2045*			
2104	8923	4465	958	8144	17325	8236	11012	9216	5809	10490	12478	9093	9243	10082	8160	7135	7072	3788	12947	7557	19265	7375				Beijing
1307	*5545*	*2775*	*595*	*5061*	*10766*	*5118*	*6843*	*5727*	*3610*	*6518*	*7754*	*5650*	*5744*	*6265*	*5071*	*4434*	*4394*	*2354*	*8045*	*4696*	*11971*	*4583*				
8942	16090	9927	8150	1182	9989	880	6403	6353	1612	6018	9746	15970	1871	9332	934	2903	1739	5791	9588	2891	11890					Berlin
5556	*9998*	*6169*	*5064*	*735*	*6207*	*547*	*3979*	*3948*	*1002*	*3740*	*6056*	*9924*	*1163*	*5799*	*580*	*1804*	*1081*	*3599*	*5958*	*1796*	*7388*					
18365	11821	15889	19429	11135	1968	11029	8490	10416	13461	9001	7366	11629	10024	9828	11105	12236	12235	15800	6891	11811						Buenos Aires
11412	*7345*	*9873*	*12073*	*6919*	*1223*	*6853*	*5276*	*6472*	*8365*	*5593*	*4577*	*7226*	*6229*	*6107*	*6901*	*7603*	*7603*	*9818*	*4282*	*7339*						
9587	14415	8270	8504	2135	9882	3215	9042	3518	2899	8733	12392	13966	3355	12223	3513	426	1234	4436	7208							Cairo
5957	*8957*	*5139*	*5284*	*1327*	*6141*	*1998*	*5618*	*2186*	*1801*	*5427*	*7700*	*8678*	*2085*	*7595*	*2183*	*265*	*767*	*2757*	*4479*							
14737	11034	9671	13710	8417	6075	9307	12551	4090	10101	12744	13703	10338	8536	16054	9635	7481	8367	9284								Cape Town
9157	*6856*	*6009*	*8519*	*5230*	*3775*	*5783*	*7799*	*2542*	*6277*	*7919*	*8515*	*6424*	*5304*	*9976*	*5987*	*4649*	*5199*	*5769*								
5857	10415	4142	4699	5929	14080	6601	11779	5428	4393	11286	14679	10192	7288	12882	6724	4032	4560									Delhi
3640	*6472*	*2574*	*2920*	*3684*	*8749*	*4102*	*7319*	*3373*	*2702*	*7013*	*9121*	*6333*	*4529*	*8005*	*4178*	*2505*	*2834*									
8970	14944	8652	7975	1379	10268	2261	8089	4751	1755	7730	11448	14628	2744	11043	2504	1170										İstanbul
5574	*9286*	*5376*	*4956*	*857*	*6380*	*1405*	*5026*	*2952*	*1091*	*4803*	*7114*	*9090*	*1705*	*6862*	*1556*	*727*										
9171	14126	7924	8083	2310	10308	3339	9190	3662	2671	8854	12552	13713	3602	12210	3615											Jerusalem
5699	*8778*	*4924*	*5023*	*1435*	*6405*	*2075*	*5711*	*2276*	*1660*	*5502*	*7800*	*8521*	*2238*	*7587*	*2246*											
9585	16990	10860	8882	1434	9254	341	5586	6805	5206	5240	8947	16902	1264	8778												London
5956	*10557*	*6748*	*5519*	*891*	*5750*	*212*	*3471*	*4229*	*1557*	*3256*	*5560*	*10503*	*785*	*5455*												
8828	12065	14136	9605	10212	10129	9106	3945	15553	9793	3973	2492	12762	9387													Los Angeles
5486	*7497*	*8784*	*5968*	*6346*	*6294*	*5658*	*2451*	*9664*	*6085*	*2469*	*1549*	*7930*	*5833*													
10789	17687	10021	11396	1365	8118	1054	5785	6177	3446	5551	9083	17315														Madrid
6704	*10990*	*7081*	*6227*	*848*	*5044*	*655*	*3595*	*3838*	*2141*	*3449*	*5644*	*10759*														
8159	711	6050	8551	15987	13227	16793	16671	11513	14418	16730	13557															Melbourne
5070	*442*	*3759*	*5314*	*9934*	*8219*	*10435*	*10359*	*7154*	*8959*	*10396*	*8424*															
11319	12972	16623	12071	10260	7669	9213	3362	14834	10740	3728																Mexico City
7034	*8061*	*10329*	*7501*	*6375*	*4765*	*5725*	*2089*	*9218*	*6674*	*2317*																
10409	16026	14816	10577	6601	8175	5522	533	11692	7077																	Montréal
6468	*9958*	*9207*	*6572*	*4102*	*5080*	*3431*	*331*	*7265*	*4398*																	
7502	14487	8426	6626	2378	11529	2492	7530	6323																		Moscow
4662	*9002*	*5236*	*4117*	*1478*	*7164*	*1549*	*4679*	*3929*																		
11266	12162	7467	10115	5374	8941	6471	11849																			Nairobi
7001	*7557*	*4640*	*6285*	*3339*	*5556*	*4021*	*7363*																			
10870	15990	15349	11078	6907	7729	5851																				New York
6755	*9936*	*9538*	*6884*	*4292*	*4803*	*3636*																				
9738	16959	10743	8990	1108	9146																					Paris
6051	*10538*	*6676*	*5586*	*689*	*5683*																					
18557	13539	15740	18135	9181																						Rio de Janeiro
10288	*8413*	*9781*	*11269*	*5705*																						
9881	16322	10030	8991																							Rome
6140	*10142*	*6232*	*5587*																							
1160	8298	4666																								Seoul
721	*5156*	*2899*																								
5317	6293																									Singapore
3304	*3910*																									
7794																										Sydney
4843																										

Tōkyō

CONVERSION CHARTS

To convert	into	multiply by
LENGTH AND AREA		
millimetres	inches	0.0394
centimetres	inches	0.3937
metres	feet	3.2808
metres	yards	1.0936
kilometres	miles	0.6214
inches	millimetres	25.4
inches	centimetres	2.54
feet	metres	0.3048
yards	metres	0.9144
miles	kilometres	1.6093
acres	hectares	0.4047
hectares	acres	2.4711
square miles	square kilometres	2.5900
square kilometres	square miles	0.3861
TEMPERATURE		
°C	°F	multiply by 1.8 and add 32
°F	°C	subtract 32 and divide by 1.8

To convert	into	multiply by
WEIGHT		
grams	ounces	0.0353
kilograms	pounds	2.2046
metric tonnes (1000 kg)	tons (2 240lbs)	0.9842
ounces	grams	28.3495
pounds	kilograms	0.4536
tons (2 240lbs)	metric tonnes (1000 kg)	1.0161
VOLUME		
pints (20fl oz)	litres	0.5683
imperial gallons	litres	4.5461
litres	pints (20fl oz)	1.7598
litres	imperial gallons	0.2200
SPEED		
km/h	mph	0.6214
mph	km/h	1.6093

INTRODUCTION TO THE INDEX

The index includes all names shown on the maps in the Atlas of the World. Names are referenced by page number and by a grid reference. The grid reference correlates to the alphanumeric values which appear within each map frame. Each entry also includes the country or geographical area in which the feature is located. Entries relating to names appearing on insets are indicated by a small box symbol: □, followed by a grid reference if the inset has its own alphanumeric values.

Name forms are as they appear on the maps, with additional alternative names or name forms included as cross-references which refer the user to the entry for the map form of the name. Names beginning with Mc or Mac are alphabetized exactly as they appear. The terms Saint, Sainte, Sankt, etc., are abbreviated to St, Ste, St, etc., but alphabetized as if in the full form.

Names of physical features beginning with generic geographical terms are permuted – the descriptive term is placed after the main part of the name. For example, Lake Superior is indexed as Superior, Lake; Mount Everest as Everest, Mount. This policy is applied to all languages.

Entries, other than those for towns and cities, include a descriptor indicating the type of geographical feature. Descriptors are not included where the type of feature is implicit in the name itself.

Administrative divisions are included to differentiate entries of the same name and feature type within the one country. In such cases, duplicate names are alphabetized in order of administrative division. Additional qualifiers are also included for names within selected geographical areas.

INDEX ABBREVIATIONS

admin. div.	administrative division	Guat.	Guatemala	r. mouth	river mouth
Afgh.	Afghanistan	hd	headland	reg.	region
Alg.	Algeria	Hond.	Honduras	resr	reservoir
Arg.	Argentina	i.	island	rf	reef
Austr.	Australia	imp. l.	impermanent lake	Rus. Fed.	Russian Federation
aut. comm.	autonomous community	Indon.	Indonesia	S.	South
aut. reg.	autonomous region	is.	islands	salt l.	salt lake
aut. rep.	autonomous republic	isth.	isthmus	sea chan.	sea channel
Azer.	Azerbaijan	Kazakh.	Kazakhstan	special admin. reg.	special administrative
b.	bay	Kyrg.	Kyrgyzstan		region
B.I.O.T.	British Indian Ocean	l.	lake	S. Sudan	South Sudan
	Territory	lag.	lagoon	str.	strait
Bangl.	Bangladesh	Lith.	Lithuania	Switz.	Switzerland
Bol.	Bolivia	Lux.	Luxembourg	Tajik.	Tajikistan
Bos.-Herz.	Bosnia Herzegovina	Madag.	Madagascar	Tanz.	Tanzania
Bulg.	Bulgaria	Maur.	Mauritania	terr.	territory
c.	cape	Mex.	Mexico	Thai.	Thailand
Can.	Canada	Moz.	Mozambique	Trin. and Tob.	Trinidad and Tobago
C.A.R.	Central African Republic	mt.	mountain	Turkm.	Turkmenistan
Col.	Colombia	mts	mountains	U.A.E.	United Arab Emirates
Czech Rep.	Czech Republic	mun.	municipality	U.K.	United Kingdom
Dem. Rep.	Democratic	N.	North	Ukr.	Ukraine
Congo	Republic of the Congo	Neth.	Netherlands	union terr.	union territory
depr.	depression	Nic.	Nicaragua	Uru.	Uruguay
des.	desert	N.Z.	New Zealand	U.S.A.	United States of America
Dom. Rep.	Dominican Republic	Pak.	Pakistan	Uzbek.	Uzbekistan
Equat. Guinea	Equatorial Guinea	Para.	Paraguay	val.	valley
esc.	escarpment	pen.	peninsula	Venez.	Venezuela
est.	estuary	Phil.	Philippines	vol.	volcano
Eth.	Ethiopia	plat.	plateau	vol. crater	volcanic crater
Fin.	Finland	P.N.G.	Papua New Guinea		
for.	forest	Pol.	Poland		
Fr. Guiana	French Guiana	Port.	Portugal		
Fr. Polynesia	French Polynesia	prov.	province		
g.	gulf	pt	point		
Ger.	Germany	r.	river		

100 Mile House

1

128 B2 100 Mile House Can.

A

93 E4 Aabenraa Denmark
100 C2 Aachen Ger.
93 E4 Aalborg Denmark
102 C2 Aalen Ger.
100 B2 Aalst Belgium
93 I3 Äänekoski Fin.
105 D2 Aarau Switz.
100 B2 Aarschot Belgium
70 A2 Aba China
119 D2 Aba Dem. Rep. Congo
115 C4 Aba Nigeria
81 C2 Ābādān Iran
81 D2 Ābādeh Iran
81 D3 Ābādeh Ṭashk Iran
114 B1 Abadla Alg.
155 C1 Abaeté Brazil
Abagnar Qi China see Xilinhot
135 E3 Abajo Peak U.S.A.
115 C4 Abakaliki Nigeria
83 H3 Abakan Rus. Fed.
150 B4 Abancay Peru
81 D2 Abarkūh Iran
66 D2 Abashiri Japan
66 D2 Abashiri-wan b. Japan
59 D3 Abau P.N.G.
Abaya, Lake l. Eth. see Lake Abaya
Ābay Wenz r. Eth. see Blue Nile
83 H3 Abaza Rus. Fed.
108 A2 Abbasanta Italy
104 C1 Abbeville France
141 C2 Abbeville AL U.S.A.
140 B3 Abbeville LA U.S.A.
97 B2 Abbeyfeale Ireland
55 R2 Abbot Ice Shelf Antarctica
74 B1 Abbottabad Pak.
115 E3 Abéché Chad
114 B4 Abengourou Côte d'Ivoire
114 C4 Abeokuta Nigeria
99 A3 Aberaeron U.K.
96 C2 Aberchirder U.K.
Abercorn Zambia see Mbala
99 B4 Aberdare U.K.
99 A3 Aberdaron U.K.
53 D2 Aberdeen Austr.
122 B3 Aberdeen S. Africa
96 C2 Aberdeen U.K.
139 D3 Aberdeen MD U.S.A.
137 D1 Aberdeen SD U.S.A.
134 B1 Aberdeen WA U.S.A.
129 E1 Aberdeen Lake Can.
96 C2 Aberfeldy U.K.
96 B2 Aberfoyle U.K.
99 B4 Abergavenny U.K.
Abergwaun U.K. see Fishguard
Aberhonddu U.K. see Brecon
143 C2 Abernathy U.S.A.
134 B2 Abert, Lake U.S.A.
Abertawe U.K. see Swansea
Aberteifi U.K. see Cardigan
99 B4 Abertillery U.K.
99 A3 Aberystwyth U.K.
86 F2 Abez' Rus. Fed.
78 B3 Abhā Saudi Arabia
81 C2 Abhar Iran
Abiad, Bahr el r. Africa see White Nile
114 B4 Abidjan Côte d'Ivoire
137 D3 Abilene KS U.S.A.
143 D2 Abilene TX U.S.A.
99 C4 Abingdon U.K.
138 C3 Abingdon U.S.A.
91 D3 Abinsk Rus. Fed.
130 B3 Abitibi, Lake Can.
Åbo Fin. see Turku
74 B1 Abohar India
114 B4 Aboisso Côte d'Ivoire
114 C4 Abomey Benin
60 A1 Abongabong, Gunung mt. Indon.
118 B2 Abong Mbang Cameroon
64 A3 Aborlan Phil.
115 D3 Abou Déia Chad
106 B2 Abrantes Port.
152 B2 Abra Pampa Arg.
142 A3 Abreojos, Punta pt Mex.
116 B2 'Abri Sudan
136 A2 Absaroka Range mts U.S.A.
81 C1 Abşeron Yarımadası pen. Azer.
78 B3 Abū 'Arīsh Saudi Arabia
116 A2 Abū Ballāş h. Egypt
79 C2 Abu Dhabi U.A.E.
116 B3 Abu Hamed Sudan
116 B3 Abu Haraz Sudan
115 C4 Abuja Nigeria
81 C2 Abū Kamāl Syria
118 C2 Abumombazi Dem. Rep. Congo
152 B1 Abunã r. Bol./Brazil
150 C3 Abunã Brazil
74 B2 Abu Road India
78 B2 Abū Şādi, Jabal h. Saudi Arabia
116 B2 Abū Sunbul Egypt
116 A3 Abu Zabad Sudan
Abū Ẓabī U.A.E. see Abu Dhabi
117 A4 Abyei Sudan
145 B2 Acambaro Mex.
120 B2 Acampamento de Caça do Mucusso Angola
106 B1 A Cañiza Spain
144 B2 Acaponeta Mex.
145 C3 Acapulco Mex.
151 E3 Acará Brazil
154 A3 Acaray, Represa de resr Para.
150 C2 Acarigua Venez.
110 B1 Acâş Romania
145 C3 Acatlán Mex.
145 C3 Acayucán Mex.
114 B4 Accra Ghana
98 B3 Accrington U.K.
74 B2 Achalpur India
97 A2 Achill Island Ireland
101 D1 Achim Ger.
96 B2 Achnasheen U.K.
91 D2 Achuyevo Rus. Fed.
111 C3 Acıpayam Turkey
109 C3 Acireale Italy
147 C2 Acklins Island Bahamas
153 A3 Aconcagua, Cerro mt. Arg.
106 B1 A Coruña Spain
108 A2 Acqui Terme Italy
103 D2 Ács Hungary
49 N6 Actéon, Groupe is Fr. Polynesia
145 C2 Actopán Mex.
143 D2 Ada U.S.A.
Adabazar Turkey see Adapazarı
79 C2 Adam Oman
111 B3 Adamas Greece
135 B3 Adams Peak U.S.A.
'Adan Yemen see Aden
80 B2 Adana Turkey
111 D2 Adapazarı Turkey
97 B2 Adare Ireland
55 M2 Adare, Cape Antarctica
108 A1 Adda r. Italy
78 B2 Ad Dafīnah Saudi Arabia
78 B2 Ad Dahnā' des. Saudi Arabia
114 A2 Ad Dakhla Western Sahara
Ad Dammām Saudi Arabia see Dammam
78 A2 Ad Dār al Ḥamrā' Saudi Arabia
78 B3 Ad Darb Saudi Arabia
78 B2 Ad Dawādimī Saudi Arabia
Ad Dawḥah Qatar see Doha
Aḍ Ḍiffah plat. Egypt/Libya see Libyan Plateau
78 B2 Ad Dilam Saudi Arabia
78 B2 Ad Dir'īyah Saudi Arabia
117 B4 Addis Ababa Eth.
81 C2 Ad Dīwānīyah Iraq
141 D2 Adel U.S.A.
52 A2 Adelaide Austr.
55 A3 Adelaide Island Antarctica
50 C1 Adelaide River Austr.
101 D2 Adelebsen Ger.
55 K2 Adélie Land reg. Antarctica
78 B3 Aden Yemen
116 C3 Aden, Gulf of Somalia/Yemen
100 C2 Adenau Ger.
115 C3 Aderbissinat Niger
79 C2 Adh Dhayd U.A.E.
59 C3 Adi i. Indon.
116 B3 Ādī Ārk'ay Eth.
108 B1 Adige r. Italy
116 B3 Ādīgrat Eth.
78 A3 Adi Keyih Eritrea
74 B3 Adilabad India
115 D2 Adīrī Libya
139 E2 Adirondack Mountains U.S.A.
Ādīs Ābeba Eth. see Addis Ababa
117 B4 Ādīs Alem Eth.
80 B2 Adıyaman Turkey
110 C1 Adjud Romania
50 B1 Admiralty Gulf Austr.
128 A2 Admiralty Island U.S.A.
59 D3 Admiralty Islands P.N.G.
73 B3 Adoni India
104 B3 Adour r. France
106 C2 Adra Spain
114 B2 Adrar Alg.
138 C2 Adrian MI U.S.A.
143 C1 Adrian TX U.S.A.
108 B2 Adriatic Sea Europe
Adua Eth. see Ādwa
116 B3 Ādwa Eth.
83 K2 Adycha r. Rus. Fed.
91 D3 Adygeysk Rus. Fed.
114 B4 Adzopé Côte d'Ivoire
111 B3 Aegean Sea Greece/Turkey
101 D1 Aerzen Ger.
106 B1 A Estrada Spain
116 B3 Afabet Eritrea
Affreville Alg. see Khemis Miliana
76 C3 Afghanistan country Asia
78 B2 'Afif Saudi Arabia
136 A2 Afton U.S.A.
80 B2 Afyon Turkey
115 C3 Agadez Niger
114 B1 Agadir Morocco
113 I7 Agalega Islands Mauritius
Agana Guam see Hagåtña
74 B2 Agar India
119 D2 Āgaro Eth.
75 D2 Agartala India
81 C2 Ağdam (abandoned) Azer.
105 C3 Agde France
Agedabia Libya see Ajdābiyā
104 C3 Agen France
122 A2 Aggeneys S. Africa
111 C3 Agia Varvara Greece
111 B3 Agios Dimitrios Greece
111 C3 Agios Efstratios i. Greece
111 C3 Agios Kirykos Greece
111 C3 Agios Nikolaos Greece
78 A3 Agirwat Hills Sudan
123 C2 Agisanang S. Africa
110 B1 Agnita Romania
74 B2 Agra India
81 C2 Ağrı Turkey
Ağrı Dağı mt. Turkey see Ararat, Mount
108 B3 Agrigento Italy
111 B3 Agrinio Greece
109 B2 Agropoli Italy
87 E3 Agryz Rus. Fed.
144 B2 Agua Brava, Laguna lag. Mex.
154 B2 Água Clara Brazil
145 C3 Aguada Mex.
146 B4 Aguadulce Panama
144 B2 Aguanaval r. Mex.
144 B1 Agua Prieta Mex.
144 B2 Aguascalientes Mex.
155 D1 Águas Formosas Brazil
154 C2 Agudos Brazil
106 B1 Águeda Port.
114 C3 Aguelhok Mali
106 C1 Aguilar de Campoo Spain
107 C2 Águilas Spain
144 B3 Aguililla Mex.
122 B3 Agulhas, Cape S. Africa
158 F7 Agulhas Basin Southern Ocean
155 D2 Agulhas Negras mt. Brazil
158 F7 Agulhas Plateau Southern Ocean
158 F7 Agulhas Ridge S. Atlantic Ocean
111 C2 Ağva Turkey
115 C2 Ahaggar plat. Alg.
115 C2 Ahaggar, Tassili oua-n- plat. Alg.
81 C2 Ahar Iran
100 C1 Ahaus Ger.
111 C3 Ahlat Turkey
100 C2 Ahlen Ger.
74 B2 Ahmadabad India
74 B3 Ahmadnagar India
74 B2 Ahmadpur East Pak.
74 B1 Ahmadpur Sial Pak.
117 C4 Ahmar Eth.
Ahmedabad India see Ahmadabad
Ahmednagar India see Ahmadnagar
144 B2 Ahome Mex.
81 D3 Ahram Iran
101 E1 Ahrensburg Ger.
104 C2 Ahun France
93 F4 Åhus Sweden
81 C2 Ahvāz Iran
Ahvenanmaa is Fin. see Åland Islands
122 A2 Ai-Ais Namibia
74 A1 Aībak Afgh.
80 B2 Aigialousa Cyprus
111 B3 Aigio Greece
Aihui China see Heihe
Aijal India see Aizawl
141 D2 Aiken U.S.A.
97 B1 Ailt an Chorráin Ireland
155 D1 Aimorés Brazil
155 D1 Aimorés, Serra dos hills Brazil
105 D2 Ain r. France
107 E2 Aïn Azel Alg.
115 C1 Aïn Beïda Alg.
114 B2 'Aïn Ben Tili Maur.
107 D2 Aïn Defla Alg.
114 B1 Aïn Sefra Alg.
136 D2 Ainsworth U.S.A.
Aintab Turkey see Gaziantep
107 D2 Aïn Taya Alg.
107 D2 Aïn Tédélès Alg.
107 C2 Aïn Temouchent Alg.
115 C3 Aïr, Massif de l' mts Niger
60 A1 Airbangis Indon.
128 C2 Airdrie Can.
96 C3 Airdrie U.K.
104 B3 Aire-sur-l'Adour France
101 E3 Aisch r. Ger.
128 A1 Aishihik Lake Can.
100 A3 Aisne r. France
59 D3 Aitape P.N.G.
137 E1 Aitkin U.S.A.
110 B1 Aiud Romania
105 D3 Aix-en-Provence France
Aix-la-Chapelle Ger. see Aachen
105 D2 Aix-les-Bains France
75 D2 Aizawl India
88 C2 Aizkraukle Latvia
88 B2 Aizpute Latvia
67 C3 Aizu-Wakamatsu Japan
105 D3 Ajaccio France
Ajayameru India see Ajmer
115 E1 Ajdābiyā Libya
79 C2 'Ajman U.A.E.
74 B2 Ajmer India
Ajmer-Merwara India see Ajmer
142 A2 Ajo U.S.A.
77 D2 Akadyr Kazakh.
119 D2 Āk'ak'ī Beseka Eth.
Akamagaseki Japan see Shimonoseki
54 B2 Akaroa N.Z.
87 E3 Akbulak Rus. Fed.
80 B2 Akçakale Turkey
114 A3 Akchâr reg. Maur.
111 C3 Akdağ mt. Turkey
80 B2 Akdağmadeni Turkey
88 A2 Åkersberga Sweden
118 C2 Aketi Dem. Rep. Congo
81 C1 Akhalkalaki Georgia
81 C1 Akhaltsikhe Georgia
79 C2 Akhḍar, Jabal mts Oman
111 C3 Akhisar Turkey
87 D4 Akhtubinsk Rus. Fed.
118 B3 Akiéni Gabon
130 B2 Akimiski Island Can.
66 D3 Akita Japan
114 A3 Akjoujt Maur.
Akkerman Ukr. see Bilhorod-Dnistrovs'kyy
77 D1 Akkol' Kazakh.
Ak-Mechet Kazakh. see Kyzylorda
88 B2 Akmenrags pt Latvia
Akmola Kazakh. see Astana
Akmolinsk Kazakh. see Astana
67 B4 Akō Japan
117 B4 Akobo S. Sudan
74 B2 Akola India
118 B2 Akonolinga Cameroon
78 A3 Akordat Eritrea
131 D1 Akpatok Island Can.
77 D2 Akqi China
92 □A3 Akranes Iceland
136 C2 Akron CO U.S.A.
138 C2 Akron OH U.S.A.
75 B1 Aksai Chin terr. Asia
80 B2 Aksaray Turkey
86 F2 Aksarka Rus. Fed.
76 B1 Aksay Kazakh.
91 D2 Aksay Rus. Fed.
80 B2 Akşehir Turkey
76 C2 Akshiganak Kazakh.
77 E2 Aksu China
116 B3 Āksum Eth.
76 B2 Aktau Kazakh.
76 B1 Aktobe Kazakh.
77 D2 Aktogay Kazakh.
88 C3 Aktsyabrski Belarus
Aktyubinsk Kazakh. see Aktobe
67 B4 Akune Japan
115 C4 Akure Nigeria
92 □B2 Akureyri Iceland
Akyab Myanmar see Sittwe
111 D2 Akyazı Turkey
77 C2 Akzhaykyn, Ozero salt l. Kazakh.
140 C2 Alabama r. U.S.A.
140 C2 Alabama state U.S.A.
140 C2 Alabaster U.S.A.
111 C3 Alaçatı Turkey
145 D2 Alacrán, Arrecife rf Mex.
81 C1 Alagir Rus. Fed.
151 F4 Alagoinhas Brazil
107 C1 Alagón Spain
78 B2 Al Aḥmadī Kuwait
77 E2 Alakol', Ozero salt l. Kazakh.
92 J2 Alakurtti Rus. Fed.
78 B3 Al 'Alayyah Saudi Arabia
81 C2 Al 'Amādīyah Iraq
81 C2 Al 'Amārah Iraq
80 A2 Al 'Āmirīyah Egypt
143 C3 Alamítos, Sierra de los mt. Mex.
135 C3 Alamo U.S.A.
142 B2 Alamogordo U.S.A.
144 A2 Alamos Sonora Mex.
144 B2 Alamos Sonora Mex.
144 B2 Alamos r. Mex.
136 B3 Alamosa U.S.A.
Åland is Fin. see Åland Islands
93 G3 Åland Islands is Fin.
80 B2 Alanya Turkey
73 B4 Alappuzha India
80 B3 Al 'Aqabah Jordan
78 B2 Al 'Aqīq Saudi Arabia
107 C2 Alarcón, Embalse de resr Spain
80 B2 Al 'Arīsh Egypt
78 B2 Al Arṭāwīyah Saudi Arabia
61 C2 Alas Indon.
111 C3 Alaşehir Turkey
128 A2 Alaska state U.S.A.
124 D4 Alaska, Gulf of U.S.A.
126 B3 Alaska Peninsula U.S.A.
126 C2 Alaska Range mts U.S.A.
81 C2 Ālāt Azer.
87 D3 Alatyr' Rus. Fed.
150 B3 Alausí Ecuador
93 H3 Alavus Fin.
52 B2 Alawoona Austr.
79 C2 Al 'Ayn U.A.E.
108 A2 Alba Italy
107 C2 Albacete Spain
78 A2 Al Badā'i' Saudi Arabia
78 B2 Al Badī' Saudi Arabia
110 B1 Alba Iulia Romania
109 C2 Albania country Europe
50 A3 Albany Austr.
130 B2 Albany r. Can.
141 D2 Albany GA U.S.A.
139 E2 Albany NY U.S.A.
134 B2 Albany OR U.S.A.
Al Başrah Iraq see Basra
51 D1 Albatross Bay Austr.
116 A2 Al Bawītī Egypt
115 E1 Al Bayḍā' Libya
78 B3 Al Bayḍā' Yemen
141 D1 Albemarle U.S.A.
141 E1 Albemarle Sound sea chan. U.S.A.
108 A2 Albenga Italy
51 C2 Alberga watercourse Austr.
119 D2 Albert, Lake Dem. Rep. Congo/Uganda
128 C2 Alberta prov. Can.
100 B2 Albert Kanaal canal Belgium
137 E2 Albert Lea U.S.A.
117 B4 Albert Nile r. Sudan/Uganda

83 I2 Anabarskiy Zaliv b. Rus. Fed.
150 C2 Anaco Venez.
134 D1 Anaconda U.S.A.
134 B1 Anacortes U.S.A.
143 D1 Anadarko U.S.A.
80 B1 Anadolu Dağları mts Turkey
83 M2 Anadyr' Rus. Fed.
83 M2 Anadyr' r. Rus. Fed.
81 C2 'Ānah Iraq
145 B2 Anáhuac Mex.
73 B3 Anai Mudi India
121 □D2 Analalava Madag.
121 □D3 Analavelona mts Madag.
60 B1 Anambas, Kepulauan is Indon.
137 E2 Anamosa U.S.A.
80 B2 Anamur Turkey
67 B4 Anan Japan
73 B3 Anantapur India
74 B1 Anantnag India
90 B2 Anan'yiv Ukr.
91 D3 Anapa Rus. Fed.
154 C1 Anápolis Brazil
81 D2 Anār Iran
152 B2 Añatuya Arg.
97 B1 An Baile Thiar Ireland
97 B1 An Bun Beag Ireland
65 B2 Anbyon N. Korea
104 B2 Ancenis France
126 C2 Anchorage U.S.A.
108 B2 Ancona Italy
153 A4 Ancud Chile
Anda China see Daqing
97 A2 An Daingean Ireland
93 E3 Åndalsnes Norway
106 C2 Andalucía aut. comm. Spain
Andalusia aut. comm. Spain see Andalucía
140 C2 Andalusia U.S.A.
159 F3 Andaman Basin Indian Ocean
73 D3 Andaman Islands India
63 A2 Andaman Sea Indian Ocean
121 □D2 Andapa Madag.
100 B2 Andelst Neth.
92 G2 Andenes Norway
100 B2 Andenne Belgium
100 B2 Anderlecht Belgium
105 D2 Andermatt Switz.
126 D2 Anderson r. Can.
126 C2 Anderson AK U.S.A.
138 B2 Anderson IN U.S.A.
141 D2 Anderson SC U.S.A.
148 C3 Andes mts S. America
77 D2 Andijon Uzbek.
121 □D2 Andilamena Madag.
121 □D2 Andilanatoby Madag.
Andizhan Uzbek. see Andijon
74 A1 Andkhōy Afgh.
121 □D2 Andoany Madag.
Andong China see Dandong
65 B2 Andong S. Korea
104 C3 Andorra country Europe
104 C3 Andorra la Vella Andorra
99 C4 Andover U.K.
154 B2 Andradina Brazil
89 D2 Andreapol' Rus. Fed.
155 D2 Andrelândia Brazil
143 C2 Andrews U.S.A.
109 C2 Andria Italy
121 □D3 Androka Madag.
Andropov Rus. Fed. see Rybinsk
146 C2 Andros i. Bahamas
111 B3 Andros Greece
111 B3 Andros i. Greece
141 E4 Andros Town Bahamas
73 B3 Andrott i. India
90 B1 Andrushivka Ukr.
92 G2 Andselv Norway
106 C2 Andújar Spain
120 A2 Andulo Angola
114 C3 Anéfis Mali
147 D3 Anegada Passage Virgin Is (U.K.)
114 C4 Aného Togo
107 D1 Aneto mt. Spain
115 D3 Aney Niger
97 B1 An Fál Carrach Ireland
83 H3 Angara r. Rus. Fed.
68 C1 Angarsk Rus. Fed.
93 G3 Ånge Sweden
Angel, Salto del waterfall Venez. see Angel Falls
144 A2 Ángel de la Guarda, Isla i. Mex.
64 B2 Angeles Phil.
150 C2 Angel Falls Venez.
93 F4 Ängelholm Sweden
92 G3 Ångermanälven r. Sweden
104 B2 Angers France
129 E1 Angikuni Lake Can.
52 B3 Anglesea Austr.
98 A3 Anglesey i. U.K.
121 C2 Angoche Moz.
79 C2 Angohrān Iran
120 A2 Angola country Africa
138 C2 Angola U.S.A.
158 F6 Angola Basin S. Atlantic Ocean
128 A2 Angoon U.S.A.
104 C2 Angoulême France
155 D2 Angra dos Reis Brazil
77 D2 Angren Uzbek.
147 D3 Anguilla terr. West Indies
75 C2 Angul India
93 F4 Anholt i. Denmark
71 B3 Anhua China
70 B2 Anhui prov. China
154 B1 Anhumas Brazil

154 C1 Anicuns Brazil
66 D1 Aniva, Mys c. Rus. Fed.
66 D1 Aniva, Zaliv b. Rus. Fed.
88 C1 Anjalankoski Fin.
104 B2 Anjou reg. France
65 B2 Anjū N. Korea
70 A2 Ankang China
80 B2 Ankara Turkey
121 □D3 Ankazoabo Madag.
121 □D2 Ankazobe Madag.
137 E2 Ankeny U.S.A.
102 C1 Anklam Ger.
121 □D2 Ankofa mt. Madag.
70 B2 Anlu China
91 E1 Anna Rus. Fed.
115 C1 Annaba Alg.
101 F2 Annaberg-Buchholtz Ger.
80 B2 An Nabk Syria
78 B2 An Nafūd des. Saudi Arabia
150 D2 Annai Guyana
81 C2 An Najaf Iraq
63 B2 Annam Highlands mts Laos/Vietnam
96 C3 Annan U.K.
139 D3 Annapolis U.S.A.
75 C2 Annapurna I mt. Nepal
138 C2 Ann Arbor U.S.A.
150 D2 Anna Regina Guyana
81 C2 An Nāşirīyah Iraq
115 D1 An Nawfalīyah Libya
105 D2 Annecy France
78 B3 An Nimāş Saudi Arabia
71 A3 Anning China
140 C2 Anniston U.S.A.
105 C2 Annonay France
79 B2 An Nu'ayrīyah Saudi Arabia
121 □D2 Anorontany, Tanjona hd Madag.
71 B3 Anpu China
70 B2 Anqing China
65 B2 Ansan S. Korea
101 E3 Ansbach Ger.
70 C1 Anshan China
71 A3 Anshun China
143 D2 Anson U.S.A.
114 C3 Ansongo Mali
96 C2 Anstruther U.K.
150 B4 Antabamba Peru
80 B2 Antakya Turkey
121 □E2 Antalaha Madag.
80 B2 Antalya Turkey
80 B2 Antalya Körfezi g. Turkey
121 □D2 Antananarivo Madag.
55 A2 Antarctic Peninsula Antarctica
96 B2 An Teallach mt. U.K.
106 C2 Antequera Spain
142 B2 Anthony U.S.A.
114 B2 Anti-Atlas mts Morocco
105 D3 Antibes France
131 D3 Anticosti, Île d' i. Can.
131 D3 Antigonish Can.
147 D3 Antigua i. Antigua
147 D3 Antigua and Barbuda country West Indies
145 C2 Antiguo-Morelos Mex.
111 B3 Antikythira i. Greece
Antioch Turkey see Antakya
49 I8 Antipodes Islands N.Z.
An t-Ob U.K. see Leverburgh
152 A2 Antofagasta Chile
154 C3 Antonina Brazil
António Enes Moz. see Angoche
97 C1 Antrim U.K.
97 C1 Antrim Hills U.K.
121 □D2 Antsalova Madag.
Antseranana Madag. see Antsirañana
121 □D2 Antsirabe Madag.
121 □D2 Antsirañana Madag.
121 □D2 Antsohihy Madag.
100 B2 Antwerp Belgium
Antwerpen Belgium see Antwerp
An Uaimh Ireland see Navan
74 B2 Anupgarh India
73 C4 Anuradhapura Sri Lanka
Anvers Belgium see Antwerp
51 C3 Anxious Bay Austr.
70 B2 Anyang China
65 B2 Anyang S. Korea
108 B2 Anzio Italy
67 C4 Aoga-shima i. Japan
66 D2 Aomori Japan
54 B2 Aoraki N.Z.
108 A1 Aosta Italy
114 B2 Aoukâr reg. Mali/Maur.
114 C2 Aoulef Alg.
115 D2 Aozou Chad
141 D3 Apalachee Bay U.S.A.
150 C3 Apaporis r. Col.
154 B2 Aparecida do Tabuado Brazil
64 B2 Aparri Phil.
86 C2 Apatity Rus. Fed.
144 B3 Apatzingán Mex.
100 B1 Apeldoorn Neth.
100 C1 Apen Ger.
108 A2 Apennines mts Italy
49 J5 Apia Samoa
154 C2 Apiaí Brazil
64 B3 Apo, Mount vol. Phil.
101 E2 Apolda Ger.
52 B3 Apollo Bay Austr.
141 D3 Apopka U.S.A.

141 D3 Apopka, Lake U.S.A.
154 B1 Aporé Brazil
154 B1 Aporé r. Brazil
138 A1 Apostle Islands U.S.A.
80 B2 Apostolos Andreas, Cape Cyprus
91 C2 Apostolove Ukr.
133 F3 Appalachian Mountains U.S.A.
Appennino mts Italy see Apennines
53 D2 Appin Austr.
100 C1 Appingedam Neth.
98 B2 Appleby-in-Westmorland U.K.
138 B2 Appleton U.S.A.
108 B2 Aprilia Italy
62 A1 Aprunyi India
91 D3 Apsheronsk Rus. Fed.
Apsheronskaya Rus. Fed. see Apsheronsk
154 B2 Apucarana Brazil
154 B2 Apucarana, Serra da hills Brazil
83 M2 Apuka Rus. Fed.
64 A3 Apurahuan Phil.
147 D4 Apure r. Venez.
78 A2 Aqaba, Gulf of Asia
81 D2 'Aqdā Iran
75 C1 Aqqikkol Hu salt l. China
154 A1 Aquidauana r. Brazil
104 B3 Aquitaine reg. France
75 C2 Ara India
117 A4 Arab, Bahr el watercourse Sudan
Arabian Gulf g. Asia see The Gulf
78 B2 Arabian Peninsula Asia
56 B4 Arabian Sea Indian Ocean
151 F4 Aracaju Brazil
154 A2 Aracanguy, Montes de hills Para.
151 F3 Aracati Brazil
154 B2 Araçatuba Brazil
155 D1 Aracruz Brazil
110 B1 Arad Romania
115 E3 Arada Chad
79 C2 'Arādah U.A.E.
156 C6 Arafura Sea Austr./Indon.
154 B1 Aragarças Brazil
107 C1 Aragón aut. comm. Spain
107 C1 Aragón r. Spain
151 E3 Araguaia r. Brazil
154 B1 Araguaiana Brazil
151 E3 Araguaína Brazil
154 C1 Araguari Brazil
67 C3 Arai Japan
115 C2 Arak Alg.
81 C2 Arāk Iran
62 A1 Arakan Yoma mts Myanmar
81 C1 Arak's r. Armenia
76 C2 Aral Sea salt l. Kazakh./Uzbek.
76 C2 Aral'sk Kazakh.
Aral'skoye More salt l. Kazakh./Uzbek. see Aral Sea
106 C1 Aranda de Duero Spain
109 D2 Aranđelovac Serbia
97 B2 Aran Islands Ireland
106 C1 Aranjuez Spain
122 A1 Aranos Namibia
143 D3 Aransas Pass U.S.A.
67 B4 Arao Japan
114 B3 Araouane Mali
151 F3 Arapiraca Brazil
154 B2 Arapongas Brazil
154 C3 Araquari Brazil
78 B1 'Ar'ar Saudi Arabia
154 C2 Araraquara Brazil
151 D3 Araras Brazil
154 B3 Araras Brazil
154 B1 Araras, Serra das hills Brazil
154 B3 Araras, Serra das mts Brazil
81 C2 Ararat Armenia
52 B3 Ararat Austr.
81 C2 Ararat, Mount Turkey
155 D2 Araruama, Lago de lag. Brazil
155 E1 Arataca Brazil
Aratürük China see Yiwu
150 B2 Arauca r. Col.
154 C1 Araxá Brazil
81 C2 Arbīl Iraq
129 E2 Arborg Can.
96 C2 Arbroath U.K.
74 A2 Arbū-ye Shamālī, Dasht-e des. Afgh.
104 B3 Arcachon France
141 D3 Arcadia U.S.A.
134 B2 Arcata U.S.A.
145 B3 Arcelia Mex.
86 D2 Archangel Rus. Fed.
51 D1 Archer r. Austr.
49 M5 Archipel des Tuamotu is Fr. Polynesia
149 B6 Archipiélago Juan Fernández S. Pacific Ocean
134 B2 Arco U.S.A.
106 B2 Arcos de la Frontera Spain
127 G2 Arctic Bay Can.
Arctic Institute Islands is Rus. Fed. see Arkticheskogo Instituta, Ostrova
160 J1 Arctic Mid-Ocean Ridge Arctic Ocean
160 Arctic Ocean
126 D2 Arctic Red r. Can.
81 C2 Ardabīl Iran
81 C1 Ardahan Turkey
93 E3 Årdalstangen Norway
97 C2 Ardee Ireland
100 B3 Ardennes plat. Belgium
135 B3 Arden U.S.A.
81 D2 Ardestān Iran
97 D1 Ardglass U.K.

53 C2 Ardlethan Austr.
143 D2 Ardmore U.S.A.
96 A2 Ardnamurchan, Point of U.K.
52 A2 Ardrossan Austr.
96 B3 Ardrossan U.K.
96 B2 Ardvasar U.K.
135 B3 Arena, Point U.S.A.
93 E4 Arendal Norway
100 B2 Arendonk Belgium
101 E1 Arendsee (Altmark) Ger.
150 B4 Arequipa Peru
151 D3 Arere Brazil
106 C1 Arévalo Spain
108 B2 Arezzo Italy
108 B2 Argenta Italy
104 B2 Argentan France
153 C2 Argentina country S. America
158 C7 Argentine Basin S. Atlantic Ocean
157 I8 Argentine Rise S. Atlantic Ocean
153 A5 Argentino, Lago l. Arg.
104 C2 Argenton-sur-Creuse France
110 C2 Argeş r. Romania
74 A1 Arghandāb Rōd r. Afgh.
111 B3 Argolikos Kolpos b. Greece
111 B3 Argos Greece
111 B3 Argostoli Greece
107 C1 Arguis Spain
69 E1 Argun' r. China/Rus. Fed.
131 D3 Argyle Can.
50 B1 Argyle, Lake Austr.
Argyrokastron Albania see Gjirokastër
93 F4 Århus Denmark
122 A2 Ariamsvlei Namibia
152 A1 Arica Chile
96 A2 Arinagour U.K.
155 C1 Arinos Brazil
150 D4 Aripuanã Brazil
150 C3 Aripuanã r. Brazil
150 C3 Ariquemes Brazil
154 B1 Ariranhá r. Brazil
96 B2 Arisaig U.K.
96 B2 Arisaig, Sound of sea chan. U.K.
104 B3 Arizgoiti Spain
142 A2 Arizona state U.S.A.
144 A1 Arizpe Mex.
78 B2 'Arjah Saudi Arabia
61 C2 Arjasa Indon.
92 G2 Arjeplog Sweden
140 B2 Arkadelphia U.S.A.
77 C1 Arkalyk Kazakh.
140 B2 Arkansas r. U.S.A.
140 B1 Arkansas state U.S.A.
137 D3 Arkansas City U.S.A.
Arkhangel'sk Rus. Fed. see Archangel
97 C2 Arklow Ireland
102 C1 Arkona, Kap c. Ger.
82 G1 Arkticheskogo Instituta, Ostrova Rus. Fed.
105 C3 Arles France
143 D2 Arlington U.S.A.
138 B2 Arlington Heights U.S.A.
115 C3 Arlit Niger
100 B3 Arlon Belgium
97 C1 Armagh U.K.
116 B2 Armant Egypt
87 D4 Armavir Rus. Fed.
81 C1 Armenia country Asia
150 B2 Armenia Col.
Armenopolis Romania see Gherla
144 B3 Armeria Mex.
53 D2 Armidale Austr.
134 D1 Armington U.S.A.
130 B2 Armstrong Can.
91 C2 Armyans'k Ukr.
Armyanskaya S.S.R. country Asia see Armenia
Arnaoutis, Cape c. Cyprus see Arnauti, Cape
130 D2 Arnaud r. Can.
80 B2 Arnauti, Cape Cyprus
100 B2 Arnhem Neth.
51 C1 Arnhem, Cape Austr.
51 C1 Arnhem Bay Austr.
51 C1 Arnhem Land reg. Austr.
122 B3 Arniston S. Africa
108 B2 Arno r. Italy
52 A2 Arno Bay Austr.
130 C3 Arnprior Can.
101 D2 Arnsberg Ger.
101 E2 Arnstadt Ger.
122 A2 Aroab Namibia
154 B2 Aroeira Brazil
101 D2 Arolsen Ger.
78 A3 Aroma Sudan
108 A1 Arona Italy
144 B2 Aros r. Mex.
Arquipélago dos Açores aut. reg. Port. see Azores
Arrah India see Ara
81 C2 Ar Ramādī Iraq
96 B3 Arran i. U.K.
97 B1 Arranmore Island Ireland
80 B2 Ar Raqqah Syria
104 C1 Arras France
106 C1 Arrasate Spain
78 B2 Ar Rass Saudi Arabia
79 C2 Ar Rayyān Qatar
150 C2 Arrecifal Col.
145 C3 Arriagá Mex.
79 C2 Ar Rimāl reg. Saudi Arabia
Ar Riyāḍ Saudi Arabia see Riyadh
54 A2 Arrowtown N.Z.

Badlands

136 C1 **Badlands** *reg. ND* U.S.A.
136 C2 **Badlands** *reg. SD* U.S.A.
101 E2 **Bad Lauterberg im Harz** Ger.
101 D2 **Bad Lippspringe** Ger.
101 D3 **Bad Mergentheim** Ger.
101 D2 **Bad Nauheim** Ger.
100 C2 **Bad Neuenahr-Ahrweiler** Ger.
101 E2 **Bad Neustadt an der Saale** Ger.
101 E1 **Bad Oldesloe** Ger.
101 D2 **Bad Pyrmont** Ger.
78 A2 **Badr Ḩunayn** Saudi Arabia
101 D1 **Bad Salzuflen** Ger.
101 E2 **Bad Salzungen** Ger.
102 C1 **Bad Schwartau** Ger.
101 E1 **Bad Segeberg** Ger.
100 C3 **Bad Sobernheim** Ger.
73 C4 **Badulla** Sri Lanka
101 D1 **Bad Zwischenahn** Ger.
106 C2 **Baeza** Spain
114 A3 **Bafatá** Guinea-Bissau
127 H2 **Baffin Bay** *sea* Can./Greenland
127 H2 **Baffin Island** Can.
118 B2 **Bafia** Cameroon
114 A3 **Bafing** *r.* Africa
114 A3 **Bafoulabé** Mali
118 B2 **Bafoussam** Cameroon
81 D2 **Bāfq** Iran
80 B1 **Bafra** Turkey
79 C2 **Bāft** Iran
119 C2 **Bafwasende** Dem. Rep. Congo
119 D3 **Bagamoyo** Tanz.
Bagan Datoh Malaysia *see* **Bagan Datuk**
60 B1 **Bagan Datuk** Malaysia
64 B3 **Baganga** Phil.
120 B2 **Bagani** Namibia
60 B1 **Bagansiapiapi** Indon.
118 B3 **Bagata** Dem. Rep. Congo
91 E2 **Bagayevskiy** Rus. Fed.
142 A2 **Bagdad** U.S.A.
152 C3 **Bagé** Brazil
97 C2 **Bagenalstown** Ireland
81 C2 **Baghdād** Iraq
79 C1 **Bāghīn** Iran
77 C3 **Baghlān** Afgh.
104 C3 **Bagnères-de-Luchon** France
105 C3 **Bagnols-sur-Cèze** France
Bago Myanmar *see* **Pegu**
88 B3 **Bagrationovsk** Rus. Fed.
Bagrax China *see* **Bohu**
64 B2 **Baguio** Phil.
115 C3 **Bagzane, Monts** *mts* Niger
79 D2 **Bāhā Kālāt** Iran
146 C2 **Bahamas, The** *country* West Indies
75 C2 **Baharampur** India
Bahariya Oasis *oasis* Egypt *see* **Wāḩāt al Bahrīyah**
76 B3 **Baharly** Turkm.
60 B1 **Bahau** Malaysia
74 B2 **Bahawalnagar** Pak.
74 B2 **Bahawalpur** Pak.
Bahia Brazil *see* **Salvador**
155 E1 **Bahia** *state* Brazil
146 B3 **Bahía, Islas de la** *is* Hond.
153 B3 **Bahía Blanca** Arg.
144 A2 **Bahía Kino** Mex.
152 C2 **Bahía Negra** Para.
144 A2 **Bahía Tortugas** Mex.
117 B3 **Bahir Dar** Eth.
79 C2 **Bahlā** Oman
75 C2 **Bahraich** India
79 C2 **Bahrain** *country* Asia
89 D3 **Bahushewsk** Belarus
110 C2 **Baia** Romania
120 A2 **Baía dos Tigres** Angola
110 B1 **Baia Mare** Romania
118 B2 **Baïbokoum** Chad
69 E1 **Baicheng** China
Baidoa Somalia *see* **Baydhabo**
Baie-aux-Feuilles Can. *see* **Tasiujaq**
131 D3 **Baie-Comeau** Can.
Baie-du-Poste Can. *see* **Mistissini**
131 C3 **Baie-St-Paul** Can.
131 E3 **Baie Verte** Can.
65 B1 **Baihe** China
69 D1 **Baikal, Lake** Rus. Fed.
Baile Átha Cliath Ireland *see* **Dublin**
110 B2 **Băileşti** Romania
68 C2 **Baima** China
141 D2 **Bainbridge** U.S.A.
Baingoin China *see* **Porong**
48 I3 **Bairiki** Kiribati
Bairin Youqi China *see* **Daban**
53 C3 **Bairnsdale** Austr.
71 A3 **Baise** China
65 B1 **Baishan** *Jilin* China
65 B1 **Baitou Shan** *mt.* China/N. Korea
120 A2 **Baixo-Longa** Angola
70 A2 **Baiyin** China
116 B3 **Baiyuda Desert** Sudan
103 D2 **Baja** Hungary
144 A1 **Baja California** *pen.* Mex.
61 D2 **Bajawa** Indon.
78 B3 **Bājil** Yemen
115 D3 **Bajoga** Nigeria
109 D2 **Bajram Curri** Albania
114 A3 **Bakel** Senegal
135 C3 **Baker** *CA* U.S.A.
140 B2 **Baker** *LA* U.S.A.
136 C1 **Baker** *MT* U.S.A.
134 C2 **Baker** *OR* U.S.A.
134 B1 **Baker, Mount** *vol.* U.S.A.
129 E1 **Baker Foreland** *hd* Can.
49 J3 **Baker Island** *terr.* N. Pacific Ocean
129 E1 **Baker Lake** Can.
129 E1 **Baker Lake** *l.* Can.
135 C3 **Bakersfield** U.S.A.
Bakharden Turkm. *see* **Baharly**
91 C3 **Bakhchysaray** Ukr.
91 C1 **Bakhmach** Ukr.
Bakhmut Ukr. *see* **Artemivs'k**
Bākhtarān Iran *see* **Kermānshāh**
Bakı Azer. *see* **Baku**
111 C2 **Bakırköy** Turkey
92 □C2 **Bakkaflói** *b.* Iceland
118 C2 **Bakouma** C.A.R.
81 C1 **Baku** Azer.
99 B3 **Bala** U.K.
64 A3 **Balabac** Phil.
64 A3 **Balabac** *i.* Phil.
61 C1 **Balabac Strait** Malaysia/Phil.
75 C2 **Balaghat** India
60 C2 **Balaiberkuak** Indon.
52 A2 **Balaklava** Austr.
91 C3 **Balaklava** Ukr.
91 D2 **Balakliya** Ukr.
87 D3 **Balakovo** Rus. Fed.
76 C3 **Bālā Murghāb** Afgh.
145 C3 **Balancán** Mex.
111 C3 **Balan Dağı** *h.* Turkey
64 B2 **Balanga** Phil.
75 C2 **Balangir** India
87 D3 **Balashov** Rus. Fed.
Balaton, Lake *l.* Hungary *see* **Lake Balaton**
103 D2 **Balatonboglár** Hungary
150 D3 **Balbina, Represa de** *resr* Brazil
97 C2 **Balbriggan** Ireland
52 A2 **Balcanoona** Austr.
110 C2 **Balchik** Bulg.
54 A3 **Balclutha** N.Z.
143 C3 **Balcones Escarpment** U.S.A.
129 E2 **Baldock Lake** Can.
138 D2 **Baldwin** U.S.A.
129 D2 **Baldy Mountain** *h.* Can.
142 B2 **Baldy Peak** U.S.A.
Baleares, Islas *is* Spain *see* **Balearic Islands**
107 D2 **Balearic Islands** *is* Spain
155 E1 **Baleia, Ponta da** *pt* Brazil
130 C2 **Baleine, Grande Rivière de la** *r.* Can.
131 D2 **Baleine, Rivière à la** *r.* Can.
75 C2 **Baleshwar** India
108 A2 **Balestrieri, Punta** *mt.* Italy
50 B2 **Balgo** Austr.
79 B3 **Bālḩaf** Yemen
61 C2 **Bali** *i.* Indon.
115 D4 **Bali** Nigeria
60 A1 **Balige** Indon.
75 C2 **Baliguda** India
111 C3 **Balıkesir** Turkey
61 C2 **Balikpapan** Indon.
59 D3 **Balimo** P.N.G.
102 B2 **Balingen** Ger.
64 B2 **Balintang Channel** Phil.
Bali Sea *sea* Indon. *see* **Laut Bali**
78 B3 **Baljurshī** Saudi Arabia
76 B3 **Balkanabat** Turkm.
110 B2 **Balkan Mountains** Bulg./Serbia
77 D2 **Balkash** Kazakh.
Balkash, Ozero *l.* Kazakh. *see* **Balkhash, Lake**
77 C1 **Balkashino** Kazakh.
77 D2 **Balkhash, Lake** Kazakh.
Balla Balla Zimbabwe *see* **Mbalabala**
96 B2 **Ballachulish** U.K.
50 B3 **Balladonia** Austr.
97 B2 **Ballaghaderreen** Ireland
92 G2 **Ballangen** Norway
96 B3 **Ballantrae** U.K.
52 B3 **Ballarat** Austr.
50 B2 **Ballard, Lake** *imp. l.* Austr.
96 C2 **Ballater** U.K.
114 B3 **Ballé** Mali
55 M3 **Balleny Islands** Antarctica
53 D1 **Ballina** Austr.
97 B1 **Ballina** Ireland
97 B2 **Ballinasloe** Ireland
97 B3 **Ballineen** Ireland
143 D2 **Ballinger** U.S.A.
97 B2 **Ballinrobe** Ireland
97 B1 **Ballycastle** Ireland
97 C1 **Ballycastle** U.K.
97 D1 **Ballyclare** U.K.
97 B2 **Ballyhaunis** Ireland
97 C1 **Ballymena** U.K.
97 C1 **Ballymoney** U.K.
97 D1 **Ballynahinch** U.K.
97 B1 **Ballyshannon** Ireland
95 B2 **Ballyvoy** U.K.
52 B3 **Balmoral** Austr.
143 C2 **Balmorhea** U.S.A.
120 A2 **Balombo** Angola
51 D2 **Balonne** *r.* Austr.
74 B2 **Balotra** India
77 D2 **Balpyk Bi** Kazakh.
75 C2 **Balrampur** India
52 B2 **Balranald** Austr.
110 B2 **Balş** Romania
151 E3 **Balsas** Brazil
145 C3 **Balsas** Mex.
145 B3 **Balsas** *r.* Mex.
90 B2 **Balta** Ukr.
90 B2 **Bălţi** Moldova
93 G4 **Baltic Sea** *g.* Europe
80 B2 **Balṭīm** Egypt
97 B3 **Baltimore** Ireland
123 C1 **Baltimore** S. Africa
139 D3 **Baltimore** U.S.A.
97 C2 **Baltinglass** Ireland
88 A3 **Baltiysk** Rus. Fed.
75 D2 **Balu** India
52 A2 **Balumbah** Austr.
88 C2 **Balvi** Latvia
77 D2 **Balykchy** Kyrg.
87 E4 **Balykshi** Kazakh.
79 C2 **Bam** Iran
71 A3 **Bama** China
51 D1 **Bamaga** Austr.
130 A2 **Bamaji Lake** Can.
114 B3 **Bamako** Mali
118 C2 **Bambari** C.A.R.
101 E3 **Bamberg** Ger.
119 C2 **Bambili** Dem. Rep. Congo
118 B2 **Bambio** C.A.R.
119 C2 **Bambouti** C.A.R.
155 C2 **Bambuí** Brazil
98 C2 **Bamburgh** U.K.
118 B2 **Bamenda** Cameroon
118 C2 **Bamingui** C.A.R.
79 D2 **Bampūr** Iran
79 C2 **Bampūr** *watercourse* Iran
77 C3 **Bāmyān** Afgh.
119 C2 **Banalia** Dem. Rep. Congo
71 A3 **Banan** China
151 D4 **Bananal, Ilha do** *i.* Brazil
74 B2 **Banas** *r.* India
111 C3 **Banaz** Turkey
62 B2 **Ban Ban** Laos
97 C1 **Banbridge** U.K.
99 C3 **Banbury** U.K.
96 C2 **Banchory** U.K.
130 C3 **Bancroft** Can.
Bancroft Zambia *see* **Chililabombwe**
119 C2 **Banda** Dem. Rep. Congo
75 C2 **Banda** India
59 C3 **Banda, Kepulauan** *is* Indon.
59 C3 **Banda, Laut** Indon.
60 A1 **Banda Aceh** Indon.
Bandar India *see* **Machilipatnam**
Bandar Abbas Iran *see* **Bandar-e 'Abbās**
75 D2 **Bandarban** Bangl.
79 C2 **Bandar-e 'Abbās** Iran
81 C2 **Bandar-e Anzalī** Iran
79 C2 **Bandar-e Chārak** Iran
81 C2 **Bandar-e Emām Khomeynī** Iran
79 C2 **Bandar-e Lengeh** Iran
79 C2 **Bandar-e Maqām** Iran
Bandar-e Pahlavī Iran *see* **Bandar-e Anzalī**
Bandar-e Shāhpūr Iran *see* **Bandar-e Emām Khomeynī**
60 B2 **Bandar Lampung** Indon.
61 C1 **Bandar Seri Begawan** Brunei
Banda Sea *sea* Indon. *see* **Banda, Laut**
155 D2 **Bandeiras, Pico de** *mt.* Brazil
123 C1 **Bandelierkop** S. Africa
144 B2 **Banderas, Bahía de** *b.* Mex.
114 B3 **Bandiagara** Mali
111 C2 **Bandırma** Turkey
Bandjarmasin Indon. *see* **Banjarmasin**
97 B3 **Bandon** Ireland
97 B3 **Bandon** *r.* Ireland
118 B3 **Bandundu** Dem. Rep. Congo
60 B2 **Bandung** Indon.
128 C2 **Banff** Can.
96 C2 **Banff** U.K.
114 B3 **Banfora** Burkina Faso
64 B3 **Banga** Phil.
73 B3 **Bangalore** India
118 C2 **Bangassou** C.A.R.
61 D2 **Banggai** Indon.
61 D2 **Banggai, Kepulauan** *is* Indon.
61 C1 **Banggi** *i.* Malaysia
Banghāzī Libya *see* **Benghazi**
60 B2 **Bangka** *i.* Indon.
60 B2 **Bangka, Selat** *sea chan.* Indon.
61 C2 **Bangkalan** Indon.
60 B1 **Bangkinang** Indon.
60 B2 **Bangko** Indon.
63 B2 **Bangkok** Thai.
75 C2 **Bangladesh** *country* Asia
63 B2 **Ba Ngoi** Vietnam
97 D1 **Bangor** *Northern Ireland* U.K.
98 A3 **Bangor** *Wales* U.K.
139 F2 **Bangor** U.S.A.
63 A2 **Bang Saphan Yai** Thai.
64 B2 **Bangued** Phil.
118 B2 **Bangui** C.A.R.
64 B2 **Bangui** Phil.
121 B2 **Bangweulu, Lake** Zambia
80 B2 **Banhā** Egypt
62 B2 **Ban Huai Khon** Thai.
118 C2 **Bani** C.A.R.
80 B3 **Banī Mazār** Egypt
116 B2 **Banī Suwayf** Egypt
115 D1 **Banī Walīd** Libya
80 B2 **Bāniyās** Syria
109 C2 **Banja Luka** Bos.-Herz.
61 C2 **Banjarmasin** Indon.
114 A3 **Banjul** Gambia
63 A3 **Ban Khok Kloi** Thai.
128 A2 **Banks Island** B.C. Can.
126 D2 **Banks Island** N.W.T. Can.
48 H5 **Banks Islands** Vanuatu
129 E1 **Banks Lake** Can.
54 B2 **Banks Peninsula** N.Z.
51 D4 **Banks Strait** Austr.
75 C2 **Bankura** India
62 A1 **Banmauk** Myanmar
62 B2 **Ban Mouang** Laos
97 C1 **Bann** *r.* U.K.
62 B2 **Ban Napè** Laos
63 A3 **Ban Na San** Thai.
146 C2 **Bannerman Town** Bahamas
Banningville Dem. Rep. Congo *see* **Bandundu**
71 A4 **Ban Nong Kung** Thai.
74 B1 **Bannu** Pak.
62 B2 **Ban Phôn-Hông** Laos
103 D2 **Banská Bystrica** Slovakia
111 B2 **Bansko** Bulg.
74 B2 **Banswara** India
62 B2 **Ban Taviang** Laos
63 A3 **Ban Tha Kham** Thai.
62 A2 **Ban Tha Song Yang** Thai.
63 B2 **Ban Tôp** Laos
97 B3 **Bantry** Ireland
97 B3 **Bantry Bay** Ireland
60 A1 **Banyak, Pulau-pulau** *is* Indon.
118 B2 **Banyo** Cameroon
107 D1 **Banyoles** Spain
61 C2 **Banyuwangi** Indon.
Banzyville Dem. Rep. Congo *see* **Mobayi-Mbongo**
Bao'an China *see* **Shenzhen**
70 B1 **Baochang** China
70 B2 **Baoding** China
70 A2 **Baoji** China
62 B1 **Bao Lac** Vietnam
63 B2 **Bao Lôc** Vietnam
66 B1 **Baoqing** China
118 B2 **Baoro** C.A.R.
62 A1 **Baoshan** China
70 B1 **Baotou** China
74 B2 **Bap** India
81 C2 **Ba'qūbah** Iraq
109 C2 **Bar** Montenegro
90 B2 **Bar** Ukr.
116 B3 **Bara** Sudan
117 C4 **Baraawe** Somalia
147 C2 **Baracoa** Cuba
53 C2 **Baradine** Austr.
147 C3 **Barahona** Dom. Rep.
116 B3 **Baraka** *watercourse* Eritrea/Sudan
106 C1 **Barakaldo** Spain
61 C1 **Baram** *r.* Malaysia
150 D2 **Baramanni** Guyana
74 B1 **Baramulla** India
89 D3 **Baran'** Belarus
74 B2 **Baran** India
88 C3 **Baranavichy** Belarus
116 B2 **Baranīs** Egypt
90 B1 **Baranivka** Ukr.
128 A2 **Baranof Island** U.S.A.
Baranowicze Belarus *see* **Baranavichy**
59 C3 **Barat Daya, Kepulauan** *is* Indon.
155 D2 **Barbacena** Brazil
147 E3 **Barbados** *country* West Indies
107 D1 **Barbastro** Spain
106 B2 **Barbate** Spain
123 D2 **Barberton** S. Africa
104 B2 **Barbezieux-St-Hilaire** France
51 D2 **Barcaldine** Austr.
107 D1 **Barcelona** Spain
150 C1 **Barcelona** Venez.
105 D3 **Barcelonnette** France
150 C3 **Barcelos** Brazil
114 B4 **Barclayville** Liberia
51 D2 **Barcoo** *watercourse* Austr.
Barcoo Creek *watercourse* Austr. *see* **Cooper Creek**
103 D2 **Barcs** Hungary
92 □B3 **Bárðarbunga** *mt.* Iceland
75 C2 **Barddhaman** India
103 E2 **Bardejov** Slovakia
Bardera Somalia *see* **Baardheere**
79 C2 **Bardsīr** Iran
75 B2 **Bareilly** India
82 D1 **Barents Sea** Arctic Ocean
78 A3 **Barentu** Eritrea
72 C1 **Barga** China
108 B2 **Barga** Italy
75 C2 **Barh** India
52 B3 **Barham** Austr.
139 F2 **Bar Harbor** U.S.A.
109 C2 **Bari** Italy
107 E2 **Barika** Alg.
74 B1 **Barī Kōṯ** Afgh.
150 B2 **Barinas** Venez.
75 C2 **Baripada** India
75 D2 **Barisal** Bangl.
60 B2 **Barisan, Pegunungan** *mts* Indon.
61 C2 **Barito** *r.* Indon.
79 C2 **Barkā** Oman
88 C2 **Barkava** Latvia
74 A2 **Barkhan** Pak.
51 C1 **Barkly Tableland** *reg.* Austr.
122 B2 **Barkly West** S. Africa
68 C2 **Barkol** China
110 C1 **Bârlad** Romania
105 D2 **Bar-le-Duc** France
50 A2 **Barlee, Lake** *imp. l.* Austr.
109 C2 **Barletta** Italy
53 C2 **Barmedman** Austr.
Barmen-Elberfeld Ger. *see* **Wuppertal**
74 B2 **Barmer** India
52 B2 **Barmera** Austr.
99 A3 **Barmouth** U.K.

Bennetta, Ostrov

101 D1 **Barmstedt** Ger.
98 C2 **Barnard Castle** U.K.
53 B2 **Barnato** Austr.
82 G3 **Barnaul** Rus. Fed.
127 H2 **Barnes Icecap** Can.
100 B1 **Barneveld** Neth.
98 C3 **Barnsley** U.K.
99 A4 **Barnstaple** U.K.
99 A4 **Barnstaple Bay** U.K.
141 D2 **Barnwell** U.S.A.
Baroda India *see* **Vadodara**
150 C1 **Barquisimeto** Venez.
96 A2 **Barra** *i.* U.K.
53 D2 **Barraba** Austr.
151 D4 **Barra do Bugres** Brazil
151 E3 **Barra do Corda** Brazil
154 B1 **Barra do Garças** Brazil
150 D3 **Barra do São Manuel** Brazil
Barraigh *i.* U.K. *see* **Barra**
150 B4 **Barranca** Peru
150 B3 **Barranca** Peru
152 C2 **Barranqueras** Arg.
150 B1 **Barranquilla** Col.
105 D3 **Barre des Écrins** *mt.* France
151 E4 **Barreiras** Brazil
63 A2 **Barren Island** India
154 C2 **Barretos** Brazil
128 C2 **Barrhead** Can.
130 C3 **Barrie** Can.
128 B2 **Barrière** Can.
52 B2 **Barrier Range** *hills* Austr.
53 D2 **Barrington, Mount** Austr.
129 D2 **Barrington Lake** Can.
53 C1 **Barringun** Austr.
97 C2 **Barrow** *r.* Ireland
126 B2 **Barrow** U.S.A.
126 B2 **Barrow, Point** U.S.A.
51 C2 **Barrow Creek** Austr.
98 B2 **Barrow-in-Furness** U.K.
50 A2 **Barrow Island** Austr.
126 F2 **Barrow Strait** Can.
99 B4 **Barry** U.K.
122 B3 **Barrydale** S. Africa
130 C3 **Barrys Bay** Can.
74 B2 **Barsalpur** India
101 D1 **Barsinghausen** Ger.
135 C4 **Barstow** U.S.A.
105 C2 **Bar-sur-Aube** France
102 C1 **Barth** Ger.
80 B1 **Bartın** Turkey
51 D1 **Bartle Frere, Mount** Austr.
143 D1 **Bartlesville** U.S.A.
137 D2 **Bartlett** *NE* U.S.A.
140 C1 **Bartlett** *TN* U.S.A.
98 C3 **Barton-upon-Humber** U.K.
103 E1 **Bartoszyce** Pol.
61 C2 **Barung** *i.* Indon.
69 D1 **Baruun-Urt** Mongolia
91 D2 **Barvinkove** Ukr.
53 C2 **Barwon** *r.* Austr.
88 C3 **Barysaw** Belarus
118 B2 **Basankusu** Dem. Rep. Congo
110 C2 **Basarabi** Romania
64 B1 **Basco** Phil.
105 D2 **Basel** Switz.
71 C3 **Bashi Channel** Phil./Taiwan
91 C2 **Bashtanka** Ukr.
64 B3 **Basilan** *i.* Phil.
99 D4 **Basildon** U.K.
99 C4 **Basingstoke** U.K.
81 C2 **Başkale** Turkey
130 C3 **Baskatong, Réservoir** *resr* Can.
Basle Switz. *see* **Basel**
118 C2 **Basoko** Dem. Rep. Congo
81 C2 **Basra** Iraq
128 C2 **Bassano** Can.
114 C4 **Bassar** Togo
63 A2 **Bassein** Myanmar
147 D3 **Basse-Terre** Guadeloupe
147 D3 **Basseterre** St Kitts and Nevis
114 B3 **Bassikounou** Maur.
114 C4 **Bassila** Benin
51 D3 **Bass Strait** Austr.
79 C2 **Bastak** Iran
101 E2 **Bastheim** Ger.
75 C2 **Basti** India
105 D3 **Bastia** France
100 B2 **Bastogne** Belgium
140 B2 **Bastrop** U.S.A.
Basuo China *see* **Dongfang**
Basutoland *country* Africa *see* **Lesotho**
118 A2 **Bata** Equat. Guinea
146 B2 **Batabanó, Golfo de** *b.* Cuba
83 J2 **Batagay** Rus. Fed.
154 B2 **Bataguassu** Brazil
74 B1 **Batala** India
106 B2 **Batalha** Port.
64 B1 **Batan** *i.* Phil.
118 B2 **Batangafo** C.A.R.
64 B2 **Batangas** Phil.
60 B2 **Batanghari** *r.* Indon.
64 B1 **Batan Islands** Phil.
154 C2 **Batatais** Brazil
139 D2 **Batavia** U.S.A.
91 D2 **Bataysk** Rus. Fed.
130 B3 **Batchawana Mountain** *h.* Can.
50 C1 **Batchelor** Austr.
63 B2 **Bătdâmbâng** Cambodia
118 B3 **Batéké, Plateaux** Congo
53 D3 **Batemans Bay** Austr.
140 B1 **Batesville** *AR* U.S.A.
140 C2 **Batesville** *MS* U.S.A.
89 D2 **Batetskiy** Rus. Fed.
99 B4 **Bath** U.K.
96 C3 **Bathgate** U.K.
74 B1 **Bathinda** India
53 C2 **Bathurst** Austr.
131 D3 **Bathurst** Can.
Bathurst Gambia *see* **Banjul**
126 E2 **Bathurst Inlet** *inlet* Can.
126 E2 **Bathurst Inlet (abandoned)** Can.
50 C1 **Bathurst Island** Austr.
126 F1 **Bathurst Island** Can.
78 B1 **Bāţin, Wādī al** *watercourse* Asia
53 C3 **Batlow** Austr.
81 C2 **Batman** Turkey
115 C1 **Batna** Alg.
140 B2 **Baton Rouge** U.S.A.
144 B2 **Batopilas** Mex.
118 B2 **Batouri** Cameroon
154 B1 **Batovi** Brazil
Batrā' *tourist site* Jordan *see* **Petra**
92 I1 **Båtsfjord** Norway
73 C4 **Batticaloa** Sri Lanka
109 B2 **Battipaglia** Italy
128 D2 **Battle** *r.* Can.
138 B2 **Battle Creek** U.S.A.
135 C2 **Battle Mountain** U.S.A.
74 B1 **Battura Glacier** Pak.
117 B4 **Batu** *mt.* Eth.
60 A2 **Batu, Pulau-pulau** *is* Indon.
61 D2 **Batuata** *i.* Indon.
61 D2 **Batudaka** *i.* Indon.
64 B3 **Batulaki** Phil.
Batum Georgia *see* **Bat'umi**
81 C1 **Bat'umi** Georgia
60 B1 **Batu Pahat** Malaysia
61 D2 **Baubau** Indon.
115 C3 **Bauchi** Nigeria
137 E1 **Baudette** U.S.A.
Baudouinville Dem. Rep. Congo *see* **Moba**
104 B2 **Baugé** France
105 D2 **Baume-les-Dames** France
154 C2 **Bauru** Brazil
154 B1 **Baús** Brazil
88 B2 **Bauska** Latvia
102 C1 **Bautzen** Ger.
144 B2 **Bavispe** *r.* Mex.
87 E3 **Bavly** Rus. Fed.
62 A1 **Bawdwin** Myanmar
61 C2 **Bawean** *i.* Indon.
114 B3 **Bawku** Ghana
Baxian China *see* **Banan**
146 C2 **Bayamo** Cuba
Bayan Gol China *see* **Dengkou**
68 C1 **Bayanhongor** Mongolia
70 A2 **Bayan Hot** China
70 A1 **Bayannur** China
70 A1 **Bayan Obo** China
69 D2 **Bayan Shutu** China
69 D1 **Bayan-Uul** Mongolia
136 C2 **Bayard** *NE* U.S.A.
142 B2 **Bayard** *NM* U.S.A.
64 B3 **Bayawan** Phil.
81 C1 **Bayburt** Turkey
138 C2 **Bay City** *MI* U.S.A.
143 D3 **Bay City** *TX* U.S.A.
86 F2 **Baydaratskaya Guba** Rus. Fed.
117 C4 **Baydhabo** Somalia
102 C2 **Bayern** *reg.* Ger.
104 B2 **Bayeux** France
136 B3 **Bayfield** U.S.A.
78 B3 **Bayḩan al Qişab** Yemen
Bay Islands *is* Hond. *see* **Bahía, Islas de la**
81 C2 **Bayjī** Iraq
Baykal, Ozero *l.* Rus. Fed. *see* **Baikal, Lake**
Baykal Range *mts* Rus. Fed. *see* **Baykal'skiy Khrebet**
83 I3 **Baykal'skiy Khrebet** *mts* Rus. Fed.
76 C2 **Baykonyr** Kazakh.
87 E3 **Baymak** Rus. Fed.
64 B2 **Bayombong** Phil.
104 B3 **Bayonne** France
76 C3 **Baýramaly** Turkm.
111 C3 **Bayramiç** Turkey
101 E3 **Bayreuth** Ger.
78 B3 **Bayt al Faqīh** Yemen
143 D3 **Baytown** U.S.A.
106 C2 **Baza** Spain
106 C2 **Baza, Sierra de** *mts* Spain
74 B1 **Bāzā'ī Gonbad** Afgh.
74 A1 **Bāzārak** Afgh.
76 A2 **Bazardyuzyu, Gora** *mt.* Azer./Rus. Fed.
104 B3 **Bazas** France
74 A2 **Bazdar** Pak.
70 A2 **Bazhong** China
79 D2 **Bazmān** Iran
79 D2 **Bazmān, Kūh-e** *mt.* Iran
Bé, Nossi *i.* Madag. *see* **Bé, Nosy**
121 □D2 **Bé, Nosy** *i.* Madag.
136 C1 **Beach** U.S.A.
52 B3 **Beachport** Austr.
99 D4 **Beachy Head** *hd* U.K.
123 C3 **Beacon Bay** S. Africa
50 B1 **Beagle Gulf** Austr.
121 □D2 **Bealanana** Madag.
97 B1 **Béal an Mhuirthead** Ireland
121 □D3 **Beampingaratra** *mts* Madag.
134 D2 **Bear** *r.* U.S.A.
130 B3 **Beardmore** Can.
Bear Island *i.* Arctic Ocean *see* **Bjørnøya**
134 E1 **Bear Paw Mountain** U.S.A.
147 C3 **Beata, Cabo** *c.* Dom. Rep.
147 C3 **Beata, Isla** *i.* Dom. Rep.
137 D2 **Beatrice** U.S.A.
135 C3 **Beatty** U.S.A.
53 D1 **Beaudesert** Austr.
52 B3 **Beaufort** Austr.
61 C1 **Beaufort** Malaysia
141 D2 **Beaufort** U.S.A.
126 D2 **Beaufort Sea** Can./U.S.A.
122 B3 **Beaufort West** S. Africa
96 B2 **Beauly** U.K.
96 B2 **Beauly** *r.* U.K.
100 B2 **Beaumont** Belgium
54 A3 **Beaumont** N.Z.
143 E2 **Beaumont** U.S.A.
105 C2 **Beaune** France
100 B2 **Beauraing** Belgium
129 E2 **Beauséjour** Can.
104 C2 **Beauvais** France
129 D2 **Beauval** Can.
129 D2 **Beaver** *r.* Can.
135 D3 **Beaver** U.S.A.
128 A1 **Beaver Creek** Can.
138 B2 **Beaver Dam** U.S.A.
129 E2 **Beaver Hill Lake** Can.
138 B1 **Beaver Island** U.S.A.
128 C2 **Beaverlodge** Can.
74 B2 **Beawar** India
154 C2 **Bebedouro** Brazil
101 D2 **Bebra** Ger.
99 D3 **Beccles** U.K.
109 D1 **Bečej** Serbia
106 B1 **Becerreá** Spain
114 B1 **Béchar** Alg.
Bechuanaland *country* Africa *see* **Botswana**
138 C3 **Beckley** U.S.A.
117 B4 **Bedelē** Eth.
99 C3 **Bedford** U.K.
138 B3 **Bedford** U.S.A.
98 C2 **Bedlington** U.K.
100 C1 **Bedum** Neth.
53 C3 **Beechworth** Austr.
53 D2 **Beecroft Peninsula** Austr.
101 F1 **Beelitz** Ger.
53 D1 **Beenleigh** Austr.
80 B2 **Beersheba** Israel
Be'ér Sheva' Israel *see* **Beersheba**
143 D3 **Beeville** U.S.A.
121 □D2 **Befandriana Avaratra** Madag.
53 C3 **Bega** Austr.
107 D1 **Begur, Cap de** *c.* Spain
81 D2 **Behbehān** Iran
128 C1 **Behchokǫ̀** Can.
81 D2 **Behshahr** Iran
69 E1 **Bei'an** China
71 A3 **Beihai** China
70 B2 **Beijing** China
100 C1 **Beilen** Neth.
118 B2 **Béinamar** Chad
96 B3 **Beinn an Oir** *h.* U.K.
96 A2 **Beinn Mhòr** *h.* U.K.
Beinn na Faoghlia *i.* U.K. *see* **Benbecula**
121 C2 **Beira** Moz.
80 B2 **Beirut** Lebanon
123 C1 **Beitbridge** Zimbabwe
106 B2 **Beja** Port.
115 C1 **Bejaïa** Alg.
106 B1 **Béjar** Spain
74 A2 **Beji** *r.* Pak.
103 E2 **Békés** Hungary
103 E2 **Békéscsaba** Hungary
121 □D3 **Bekily** Madag.
66 D2 **Bekkai** Japan
114 B4 **Bekwai** Ghana
75 C2 **Bela** India
74 A2 **Bela** Pak.
123 C1 **Bela-Bela** S. Africa
118 B2 **Bélabo** Cameroon
109 D2 **Bela Crkva** Serbia
61 C1 **Belaga** Malaysia
88 C3 **Belarus** *country* Europe
121 C3 **Bela Vista** Moz.
60 A1 **Belawan** Indon.
83 M2 **Belaya** *r.* Rus. Fed.
103 D1 **Bełchatów** Pol.
Belchatow Pol. *see* **Bełchatów**
130 C2 **Belcher Islands** Can.
87 E3 **Belebey** Rus. Fed.
117 C4 **Beledweyne** Somalia
118 B2 **Bélèl** Cameroon
151 E3 **Belém** Brazil
142 B2 **Belen** U.S.A.
110 C2 **Belene** Bulg.
89 E3 **Belev** Rus. Fed.
97 D1 **Belfast** U.K.
139 F2 **Belfast** U.S.A.
136 C1 **Belfield** U.S.A.
105 D2 **Belfort** France
73 B3 **Belgaum** India
Belgian Congo *country* Africa *see* **Congo, Democratic Republic of the**
100 B2 **Belgium** *country* Europe
91 D1 **Belgorod** Rus. Fed.
109 D2 **Belgrade** Serbia
134 D1 **Belgrade** U.S.A.
109 C1 **Beli Manastir** Croatia
60 B2 **Belinyu** Indon.
60 B2 **Belitung** *i.* Indon.
118 B3 **Belize** Angola
146 B3 **Belize** Belize
146 B3 **Belize** *country* Central America
83 K1 **Bel'kovskiy, Ostrov** *i.* Rus. Fed.
128 B2 **Bella Bella** Can.
104 C2 **Bellac** France
128 B2 **Bella Coola** Can.
73 B3 **Bellary** India
53 C1 **Bellata** Austr.
138 C2 **Bellefontaine** U.S.A.
136 C2 **Belle Fourche** U.S.A.
136 C2 **Belle Fourche** *r.* U.S.A.
141 D3 **Belle Glade** U.S.A.
104 B2 **Belle-Île** *i.* France
131 E2 **Belle Isle** *i.* Can.
131 E2 **Belle Isle, Strait of** Can.
130 C3 **Belleville** Can.
138 B3 **Belleville** *IL* U.S.A.
137 D3 **Belleville** *KS* U.S.A.
134 D2 **Bellevue** *ID* U.S.A.
134 B1 **Bellevue** *WA* U.S.A.
Bellin Can. *see* **Kangirsuk**
53 D2 **Bellingen** Austr.
134 B1 **Bellingham** U.S.A.
55 R2 **Bellingshausen Sea** Antarctica
105 D2 **Bellinzona** Switz.
96 C2 **Bell Rock** *i.* U.K.
108 B1 **Belluno** Italy
122 A3 **Bellville** S. Africa
53 D2 **Belmont** Austr.
155 E1 **Belmonte** Brazil
146 B3 **Belmopan** Belize
Belmullet Ireland *see* **Béal an Mhuirthead**
69 E1 **Belogorsk** Rus. Fed.
121 □D3 **Beloha** Madag.
155 D1 **Belo Horizonte** Brazil
138 B2 **Beloit** U.S.A.
86 C2 **Belomorsk** Rus. Fed.
89 E3 **Beloomut** Rus. Fed.
91 D3 **Belorechensk** Rus. Fed.
Belorechenskaya Rus. Fed. *see* **Belorechensk**
87 E3 **Beloretsk** Rus. Fed.
Belorussia *country* Europe *see* **Belarus**
Belorusskaya S.S.R. *country* Europe *see* **Belarus**
Belostok Pol. *see* **Białystok**
121 □D2 **Belo Tsiribihina** Madag.
86 F2 **Beloyarskiy** Rus. Fed.
89 E1 **Beloye, Ozero** *l.* Rus. Fed.
Beloye More *sea* Rus. Fed. *see* **White Sea**
89 E1 **Belozersk** Rus. Fed.
52 A2 **Beltana** Austr.
143 D2 **Belton** U.S.A.
Bel'ts' Moldova *see* **Bălţi**
Bel'tsy Moldova *see* **Bălţi**
97 C1 **Belturbet** Ireland
77 E2 **Belukha, Gora** *mt.* Kazakh./Rus. Fed.
86 D2 **Belush'ye** Rus. Fed.
138 B2 **Belvidere** U.S.A.
51 D2 **Belyando** *r.* Austr.
89 D2 **Belyy** Rus. Fed.
82 F2 **Belyy, Ostrov** *i.* Rus. Fed.
101 F1 **Belzig** Ger.
137 E1 **Bemidji** U.S.A.
118 C3 **Bena Dibele** Dem. Rep. Congo
53 C3 **Benalla** Austr.
Benares India *see* **Varanasi**
115 D1 **Ben Arous** Tunisia
118 C3 **Bena-Sungu** Dem. Rep. Congo
106 B1 **Benavente** Spain
96 A2 **Benbecula** *i.* U.K.
134 B2 **Bend** U.S.A.
123 C3 **Bendearg** *mt.* S. Africa
Bender Moldova *see* **Tighina**
Bendery Moldova *see* **Tighina**
52 B3 **Bendigo** Austr.
121 C2 **Bene** Moz.
102 C2 **Benešov** Czech Rep.
109 B2 **Benevento** Italy
73 C3 **Bengal, Bay of** *sea* Indian Ocean
Bengaluru India *see* **Bangalore**
70 B2 **Bengbu** China
115 E1 **Benghazi** Libya
60 B1 **Bengkalis** Indon.
60 B1 **Bengkayang** Indon.
60 B2 **Bengkulu** Indon.
120 A2 **Benguela** Angola
Benha Egypt *see* **Banhā**
96 B1 **Ben Hope** *h.* U.K.
152 B1 **Beni** *r.* Bol.
119 C2 **Beni** Dem. Rep. Congo
114 B1 **Beni Abbès** Alg.
107 C2 **Benidorm** Spain
114 B1 **Beni Mellal** Morocco
114 C3 **Benin** *country* Africa
114 C4 **Benin, Bight of** *g.* Africa
115 C4 **Benin City** Nigeria
107 C2 **Beni Saf** Alg.
Beni Suef Egypt *see* **Banī Suwayf**
153 C3 **Benito Juárez** Arg.
150 C3 **Benjamim Constant** Brazil
144 A1 **Benjamín Hill** Mex.
59 C3 **Benjina** Indon.
136 C2 **Benkelman** U.S.A.
96 B2 **Ben Lawers** *mt.* U.K.
96 B2 **Ben Lomond** *h.* U.K.
96 C2 **Ben Macdui** *mt.* U.K.
96 A2 **Ben More** *h.* U.K.
96 B2 **Ben More** *mt.* U.K.
54 B2 **Benmore, Lake** N.Z.
96 B1 **Ben More Assynt** *h.* U.K.
128 A2 **Bennett** Can.
83 K1 **Bennetta, Ostrov** *i.* Rus. Fed.

Bennett Island i. Rus. Fed. see Bennetta, Ostrov
96 B2 Ben Nevis mt. U.K.
139 E2 Bennington U.S.A.
123 C2 Benoni S. Africa
115 D4 Bénoyé Chad
101 D3 Bensheim Ger.
114 B1 Ben Slimane Morocco
142 A2 Benson U.S.A.
61 D2 Benteng Indon.
117 A4 Bentiu S. Sudan
138 B2 Benton Harbor U.S.A.
140 B1 Bentonville U.S.A.
63 B2 Bến Tre Vietnam
115 C4 Benue r. Nigeria
97 B1 Benwee Head hd Ireland
96 B2 Ben Wyvis mt. U.K.
70 C1 Benxi China
Beograd Serbia see Belgrade
75 C2 Beohari India
114 B4 Béoumi Côte d'Ivoire
67 B4 Beppu Japan
109 C2 Berane Montenegro
109 C2 Berat Albania
59 C3 Berau, Teluk b. Indon.
116 B3 Berber Sudan
117 C3 Berbera Somalia
118 B2 Berbérati C.A.R.
104 C1 Berck France
91 D2 Berdyans'k Ukr.
90 B2 Berdychiv Ukr.
90 A2 Berehove Ukr.
59 D3 Bereina P.N.G.
76 B3 Bereket Turkm.
129 E2 Berens River Can.
137 D2 Beresford U.S.A.
91 D2 Berezanskaya Rus. Fed.
90 A2 Berezhany Ukr.
90 C2 Berezivka Ukr.
90 B1 Berezne Ukr.
86 D2 Bereznik Rus. Fed.
86 E3 Berezniki Rus. Fed.
Berezov Rus. Fed. see Berezovo
86 F2 Berezovo Rus. Fed.
107 D1 Berga Spain
111 C3 Bergama Turkey
108 A1 Bergamo Italy
102 C1 Bergen Ger.
101 D1 Bergen Ger.
100 B1 Bergen Neth.
93 E3 Bergen Norway
100 B2 Bergen op Zoom Neth.
104 C3 Bergerac France
100 C2 Bergheim (Erft) Ger.
100 C2 Bergisch Gladbach Ger.
122 A1 Bergland Namibia
93 G3 Bergsjö Sweden
92 H2 Bergsviken Sweden
Berhampur India see Baharampur
83 M3 Beringa, Ostrov i. Rus. Fed.
100 B2 Beringen Belgium
124 A4 Bering Sea N. Pacific Ocean
124 B3 Bering Strait Rus. Fed./U.S.A.
100 C1 Berkel r. Neth.
135 B3 Berkeley U.S.A.
100 B1 Berkhout Neth.
55 B2 Berkner Island Antarctica
110 B2 Berkovitsa Bulg.
92 I1 Berlevåg Norway
101 F1 Berlin Ger.
139 E2 Berlin U.S.A.
101 E2 Berlingerode Ger.
53 D3 Bermagui Austr.
144 B2 Bermejíllo Mex.
152 B2 Bermejo Bol.
131 D2 Bermen, Lac l. Can.
125 L6 Bermuda terr. N. Atlantic Ocean
105 D2 Bern Switz.
101 E2 Bernburg (Saale) Ger.
127 G2 Bernier Bay Can.
50 A2 Bernier Island Austr.
100 C3 Bernkastel-Kues Ger.
121 □D3 Beroroha Madag.
52 B2 Berri Austr.
115 C1 Berriane Alg.
53 C3 Berrigan Austr.
107 D2 Berrouaghia Alg.
53 D2 Berry Austr.
146 C2 Berry Islands Bahamas
122 A2 Berseba Namibia
101 C1 Bersenbrück Ger.
90 B2 Bershad' Ukr.
131 D2 Berté, Lac l. Can.
118 B2 Bertoua Cameroon
150 C3 Beruri Brazil
98 B2 Berwick-upon-Tweed U.K.
91 C2 Beryslav Ukr.
121 □D2 Besalampy Madag.
105 D2 Besançon France
81 D3 Beshneh Iran
129 D2 Besnard Lake Can.
140 C2 Bessemer U.S.A.
76 B2 Besshoky, Gora h. Kazakh.
100 B2 Best Neth.
121 □D2 Betafo Madag.
106 B1 Betanzos Spain
118 B2 Bétaré Oya Cameroon
122 A2 Bethanie Namibia
100 B3 Bétheny France
139 D3 Bethesda U.S.A.
123 C3 Bethlehem S. Africa
139 D2 Bethlehem U.S.A.
123 C3 Bethulie S. Africa
105 C1 Béthune France

121 □D3 Betioky Madag.
51 D2 Betoota Austr.
77 D2 Betpakdala plain Kazakh.
121 □D3 Betroka Madag.
131 D3 Betsiamites Can.
121 □D2 Betsiboka r. Madag.
137 E2 Bettendorf U.S.A.
75 C2 Bettiah India
74 B2 Betul India
74 B2 Betwa r. India
99 B3 Betws-y-coed U.K.
100 C2 Betzdorf Ger.
136 C1 Beulah U.S.A.
98 C3 Beverley U.K.
101 D2 Beverungen Ger.
100 B1 Beverwijk Neth.
99 D4 Bexhill U.K.
111 C2 Beykoz Turkey
114 B4 Beyla Guinea
76 B2 Beyneu Kazakh.
80 B1 Beypazarı Turkey
Beyrouth Lebanon see Beirut
80 B2 Beyşehir Turkey
80 B2 Beyşehir Gölü l. Turkey
91 D2 Beysug r. Rus. Fed.
91 D2 Beysugskiy Liman lag. Rus. Fed.
88 C2 Bezhanitsy Rus. Fed.
89 E2 Bezhetsk Rus. Fed.
105 C3 Béziers France
Bhadgaon Nepal see Bhaktapur
75 C2 Bhadrak India
73 B3 Bhadravati India
75 C2 Bhagalpur India
74 A2 Bhairi Hol mt. Pak.
74 B1 Bhakkar Pak.
75 C2 Bhaktapur Nepal
62 A1 Bhamo Myanmar
75 C3 Bhanjanagar India
74 B2 Bharatpur India
74 B2 Bharuch India
74 B2 Bhavnagar India
75 C3 Bhawanipatna India
123 D2 Bhekuzulu S. Africa
74 B1 Bhera Pak.
74 B2 Bhilwara India
73 B3 Bhima r. India
74 B2 Bhind India
123 C3 Bhisho S. Africa
74 B2 Bhiwani India
123 C3 Bhongweni S. Africa
74 B2 Bhopal India
75 C2 Bhubaneshwar India
Bhubaneswar India see Bhubaneshwar
74 A2 Bhuj India
74 B2 Bhusawal India
75 D2 Bhutan country Asia
62 B2 Bia, Phou mt. Laos
59 D3 Biak Indon.
59 D3 Biak i. Indon.
103 E1 Biała Podlaska Pol.
103 D1 Białogard Pol.
103 E1 Białystok Pol.
109 C3 Bianco Italy
74 B2 Biaora India
104 B3 Biarritz France
105 D2 Biasca Switz.
66 D2 Bibai Japan
120 A2 Bibala Angola
53 C3 Bibbenluke Austr.
102 B2 Biberach an der Riß Ger.
155 D2 Bicas Brazil
73 B3 Bid India
115 C4 Bida Nigeria
73 B3 Bidar India
139 E2 Biddeford U.S.A.
96 B2 Bidean nam Bian mt. U.K.
99 A4 Bideford U.K.
Bideford Bay b. U.K. see Barnstaple Bay
Bié Angola see Kuito
120 A2 Bié, Planalto do Angola
101 D2 Biedenkopf Ger.
105 D2 Biel Switz.
101 D1 Bielefeld Ger.
108 A1 Biella Italy
103 D1 Bielsko-Biała Pol.
63 B2 Biên Hoa Vietnam
130 C2 Bienville, Lac l. Can.
100 B3 Bièvre Belgium
118 B3 Bifoun Gabon
111 C2 Biga Turkey
134 D1 Big Belt Mountains U.S.A.
123 D2 Big Bend Swaziland
129 D2 Biggar Can.
96 C3 Biggar U.K.
99 C3 Biggleswade U.K.
134 D1 Big Hole r. U.S.A.
134 E1 Bighorn r. U.S.A.
136 B1 Bighorn r. U.S.A.
136 B2 Bighorn Mountains U.S.A.
143 C2 Big Lake U.S.A.
138 B2 Big Rapids U.S.A.
129 D2 Big River Can.
129 E2 Big Sand Lake Can.
137 D2 Big Sioux r. U.S.A.
143 C2 Big Spring U.S.A.
134 E1 Big Timber U.S.A.
130 B1 Big Trout Lake Can.
130 A2 Big Trout Lake l. Can.
109 C2 Bihać Bos.-Herz.
75 C2 Bihar state India

75 C2 Bihar Sharif India
110 B1 Bihor, Vârful mt. Romania
114 A3 Bijagós, Arquipélago dos is Guinea-Bissau
73 B3 Bijapur India
81 C2 Bijār Iran
109 C2 Bijeljina Bos.-Herz.
109 C2 Bijelo Polje Montenegro
71 A3 Bijie China
74 B2 Bikaner India
66 B1 Bikin Rus. Fed.
66 B1 Bikin r. Rus. Fed.
118 B3 Bikoro Dem. Rep. Congo
79 C2 Bilād Banī 'Alī Oman
75 C2 Bilaspur India
81 C2 Biläsuvar Azer.
90 C2 Bila Tserkva Ukr.
63 A2 Bilauktaung Range mts Myanmar/Thai.
106 C1 Bilbao Spain
109 C2 Bileća Bos.-Herz.
111 C2 Bilecik Turkey
103 E1 Biłgoraj Pol.
119 D3 Bilharamulo Tanz.
90 C2 Bilhorod-Dnistrovs'kyy Ukr.
119 C2 Bili Dem. Rep. Congo
83 M2 Bilibino Rus. Fed.
109 C2 Bilisht Albania
134 E1 Billings U.S.A.
99 B4 Bill of Portland hd U.K.
142 A1 Bill Williams Mountain U.S.A.
115 D3 Bilma Niger
115 D3 Bilma, Grand Erg de des. Niger
51 E2 Biloela Austr.
91 C2 Bilohirs'k Ukr.
90 B1 Bilohir''ya Ukr.
91 C1 Bilopillya Ukr.
91 D2 Bilovods'k Ukr.
140 C2 Biloxi U.S.A.
51 C2 Bilpa Morea Claypan salt flat Austr.
101 E2 Bilshausen Ger.
115 E3 Biltine Chad
90 C2 Bilyayivka Ukr.
114 C4 Bimbila Ghana
118 B2 Bimbo C.A.R.
141 E3 Bimini Islands Bahamas
74 B2 Bina-Etawa India
59 C3 Binaija, Gunung mt. Indon.
53 C1 Bindle Austr.
118 B3 Bindu Dem. Rep. Congo
121 C2 Bindura Zimbabwe
107 D1 Binéfar Spain
120 B2 Binga Zimbabwe
53 D1 Bingara Austr.
100 C3 Bingen am Rhein Ger.
114 B4 Bingerville Côte d'Ivoire
139 F1 Bingham U.S.A.
139 D2 Binghamton U.S.A.
115 D2 Bin Ghanīmah, Jabal hills Libya
81 C2 Bingöl Turkey
62 A1 Bingzhongluo China
60 A1 Binjai Indon.
53 C2 Binnaway Austr.
60 B1 Bintan i. Indon.
60 B2 Bintuhan Indon.
61 C1 Bintulu Malaysia
115 C3 Bin-Yauri Nigeria
70 B2 Binzhou China
109 C2 Biograd na Moru Croatia
118 A2 Bioko i. Equat. Guinea
155 C1 Biquinhas Brazil
115 D2 Birāk Libya
118 C1 Birao C.A.R.
75 C2 Biratnagar Nepal
52 B3 Birchip Austr.
128 C2 Birch Mountains Can.
51 C2 Birdsville Austr.
80 B2 Birecik Turkey
Birendranagar Nepal see Surkhet
60 A1 Bireun Indon.
75 C2 Birganj Nepal
154 B2 Birigüi Brazil
118 C2 Birini C.A.R.
76 B3 Birjand Iran
98 B3 Birkenhead U.K.
99 C3 Birmingham U.K.
140 C2 Birmingham U.S.A.
114 A2 Bîr Mogreïn Maur.
115 C3 Birnin-Kebbi Nigeria
115 C3 Birnin Konni Niger
69 E1 Birobidzhan Rus. Fed.
97 C2 Birr Ireland
96 C1 Birsay U.K.
78 A2 Bi'r Shalatayn Egypt
91 D1 Biryuch Rus. Fed.
88 B2 Biržai Lith.
75 B2 Bisalpur India
142 B2 Bisbee U.S.A.
104 A2 Biscay, Bay of sea France/Spain
141 D3 Biscayne Bay U.S.A.
102 C2 Bischofshofen Austria
77 D2 Bishkek Kyrg.
135 C3 Bishop U.S.A.
98 C2 Bishop Auckland U.K.
69 E1 Bishui China
150 C1 Bisinaca Col.
115 C1 Biskra Alg.
64 B3 Bislig Phil.
136 C1 Bismarck U.S.A.
59 D3 Bismarck Archipelago is P.N.G.
59 D3 Bismarck Sea P.N.G.
107 D2 Bissa, Djebel mt. Alg.
114 A3 Bissau Guinea-Bissau

129 E2 Bissett Can.
128 C2 Bistcho Lake Can.
110 B1 Bistrița Romania
110 C1 Bistrița r. Romania
105 D2 Bitburg Ger.
105 D2 Bitche France
115 D3 Bitkine Chad
81 C2 Bitlis Turkey
111 B2 Bitola Macedonia
Bitolj Macedonia see Bitola
109 C2 Bitonto Italy
101 F2 Bitterfeld Ger.
122 A3 Bitterfontein S. Africa
134 D1 Bitterroot r. U.S.A.
134 C1 Bitterroot Range mts U.S.A.
89 E3 Bityug r. Rus. Fed.
115 D3 Biu Nigeria
67 C3 Biwa-ko l. Japan
77 E1 Biysk Rus. Fed.
Bizerta Tunisia see Bizerte
115 C1 Bizerte Tunisia
92 □A2 Bjargtangar hd Iceland
92 G3 Bjästa Sweden
109 C1 Bjelovar Croatia
92 G2 Bjerkvik Norway
Björneborg Fin. see Pori
82 C2 Bjørnøya Arctic Ocean
114 B3 Bla Mali
137 E3 Black r. U.S.A.
51 D2 Blackall Austr.
98 B3 Blackburn U.K.
134 D2 Blackfoot U.S.A.
102 B2 Black Forest mts Ger.
136 C2 Black Hills U.S.A.
96 B2 Black Isle pen. U.K.
129 C2 Black Lake Can.
129 C2 Black Lake l. Can.
99 B4 Black Mountains hills U.K.
142 A1 Black Mountains U.S.A.
98 B3 Blackpool U.K.
142 B2 Black Range mts U.S.A.
62 B1 Black River r. Vietnam
138 A2 Black River Falls U.S.A.
134 C2 Black Rock Desert U.S.A.
138 C3 Blacksburg U.S.A.
80 B1 Black Sea Asia/Europe
131 D3 Blacks Harbour Can.
97 A1 Blacksod Bay Ireland
97 C2 Blackstairs Mountains hills Ireland
114 B4 Black Volta r. Africa
51 D2 Blackwater Austr.
97 C2 Blackwater r. Ireland
128 B1 Blackwater Lake Can.
50 A3 Blackwood r. Austr.
87 D4 Blagodarnyy Rus. Fed.
111 B2 Blagoevgrad Bulg.
69 E1 Blagoveshchensk Rus. Fed.
129 C2 Blaine Lake Can.
137 D2 Blair U.S.A.
96 C2 Blair Atholl U.K.
96 C2 Blairgowrie U.K.
141 D2 Blakely U.S.A.
105 D2 Blanc, Mont mt. France/Italy
153 B3 Blanca, Bahía b. Arg.
52 A1 Blanche, Lake imp. l. Austr.
152 B1 Blanco r. Bol.
134 B2 Blanco, Cape U.S.A.
131 E2 Blanc-Sablon Can.
92 □A2 Blanda r. Iceland
99 B4 Blandford Forum U.K.
135 E3 Blanding U.S.A.
107 D1 Blanes Spain
60 A1 Blangkejeren Indon.
100 A2 Blankenberge Belgium
100 C2 Blankenheim Ger.
100 C2 Blankenrath Ger.
147 D3 Blanquilla, Isla i. Venez.
103 D2 Blansko Czech Rep.
121 C2 Blantyre Malawi
97 B3 Blarney Ireland
98 C2 Blaydon U.K.
53 C2 Blayney Austr.
54 B2 Blenheim N.Z.
115 C1 Blida Alg.
130 B3 Blind River Can.
123 C2 Bloemfontein S. Africa
123 C2 Bloemhof S. Africa
123 C2 Bloemhof Dam S. Africa
104 C2 Blois France
92 □A2 Blönduós Iceland
97 B1 Bloody Foreland pt Ireland
142 B1 Bloomfield U.S.A.
138 B3 Bloomington IL U.S.A.
138 B3 Bloomington IN U.S.A.
102 B2 Bludenz Austria
137 E2 Blue Earth U.S.A.
138 C3 Bluefield U.S.A.
146 B3 Bluefields Nic.
53 C2 Blue Mountains Austr.
134 C1 Blue Mountains U.S.A.
116 B3 Blue Nile r. Eth./Sudan
126 E2 Bluenose Lake Can.
138 C3 Blue Ridge mts U.S.A.
128 C2 Blue River Can.
97 B1 Blue Stack Mountains hills Ireland
54 A3 Bluff N.Z.
135 E3 Bluff U.S.A.
154 C3 Blumenau Brazil
52 A2 Blyth Austr.
98 C2 Blyth U.K.
135 D4 Blythe U.S.A.
140 C1 Blytheville U.S.A.

114 A4 Bo Sierra Leone
64 B2 Boac Phil.
146 B3 Boaco Nic.
151 E3 Boa Esperança, Açude *resr* Brazil
134 C1 Boardman U.S.A.
151 F3 Boa Viagem Brazil
123 C1 Boatlaname Botswana
150 C2 Boa Vista Brazil
71 B3 Bobadah Austr.
121 □D2 Bobaomby, Tanjona *c.* Madag.
114 A4 Bobo-Dioulasso Burkina Faso
121 B3 Bobonong Botswana
Bobriki Rus. Fed. *see* Novomoskovsk
89 F3 Bobrov Rus. Fed.
91 C2 Bobrovytsya Ukr.
91 C2 Bobrynets' Ukr.
121 □D3 Boby *mt.* Madag.
150 C3 Boca do Acre Brazil
155 C1 Bocaiúva Brazil
154 A2 Bocajá Brazil
137 C3 Bocaranga C.A.R.
141 D3 Boca Raton U.S.A.
146 B4 Bocas del Toro Panama
103 C2 Bochnia Pol.
100 B2 Bocholt Belgium
100 C2 Bocholt Ger.
100 C2 Bochum Ger.
101 E1 Bockenem Ger.
110 B1 Bocşa Romania
118 B2 Boda C.A.R.
83 I3 Bodaybo Rus. Fed.
96 D2 Boddam U.K.
115 D3 Bodélé *reg.* Chad
92 H2 Boden Sweden
Bodensee *l.* Ger./Switz. *see* Constance, Lake
99 A4 Bodmin U.K.
99 A4 Bodmin Moor *moorland* U.K.
92 F2 Bodø Norway
111 C3 Bodrum Turkey
118 C3 Boende Dem. Rep. Congo
63 A2 Bogale Myanmar
140 C2 Bogalusa U.S.A.
114 B3 Bogandé Burkina Faso
118 B3 Bogangolo C.A.R.
80 B2 Boğazlıyan Turkey
68 B2 Bogda Shan *mts* China
53 D1 Boggabilla Austr.
53 D2 Boggabri Austr.
97 B2 Boggeragh Mountains *hills* Ireland
Boghari Alg. *see* Ksar el Boukhari
59 D3 Bogia P.N.G.
100 B3 Bogny-sur-Meuse France
97 C2 Bog of Allen *reg.* Ireland
53 C3 Bogong, Mount Austr.
60 B2 Bogor Indon.
89 E3 Bogoroditsk Rus. Fed.
114 B2 Bogotá Col.
83 G3 Bogotol Rus. Fed.
Bogoyavlenskoye Rus. Fed. *see* Pervomayskiy
83 H3 Boguchany Rus. Fed.
91 E2 Boguchar Rus. Fed.
114 A3 Bogué Maur.
70 B2 Bo Hai *g.* China
100 A3 Bohain-en-Vermandois France
70 B2 Bohai Wan *b.* China
Bohemian Forest *mts* Ger. *see* Böhmer Wald
123 C2 Bohlokong S. Africa
101 F3 Böhmer Wald *mts* Ger.
91 D1 Bohodukhiv Ukr.
64 B3 Bohol *i.* Phil.
64 B3 Bohol Sea Phil.
77 E2 Bohu China
155 C2 Boi, Ponta do *pt* Brazil
123 C2 Boikhutso S. Africa
154 B3 Boi Preto, Serra de *hills* Brazil
154 B1 Bois *r.* Brazil
126 D2 Bois, Lac des *l.* Can.
134 C2 Boise U.S.A.
143 C1 Boise City U.S.A.
129 D3 Boissevain Can.
123 C2 Boitumelong S. Africa
154 C2 Boituva Brazil
101 E1 Boizenburg Ger.
76 B3 Bojnürd Iran
75 C2 Bokaro India
118 B3 Bokatola Dem. Rep. Congo
114 A3 Boké Guinea
118 C3 Bokele Dem. Rep. Congo
93 E4 Boknafjorden *sea chan.* Norway
115 D3 Bokoro Chad
63 A2 Bokpyin Myanmar
89 D2 Boksitogorsk Rus. Fed.
122 B2 Bokspits Botswana
118 C3 Bokungu Dem. Rep. Congo
115 D3 Bol Chad
114 A3 Bolama Guinea-Bissau
63 B2 Bolavén, Phouphiang *plat.* Laos
104 C2 Bolbec France
77 E2 Bole China
118 B3 Boleko Dem. Rep. Congo
114 B3 Bolgatanga Ghana
90 B2 Bolhrad Ukr.
66 B1 Boli China
118 B3 Bolia Dem. Rep. Congo
92 H3 Boliden Sweden
62 B2 Bolikhamxai Laos
110 C2 Bolintin-Vale Romania
137 E3 Bolivar MO U.S.A.
140 C1 Bolivar TN U.S.A.

150 B2 Bolívar, Pico *mt.* Venez.
152 B1 Bolivia *country* S. America
89 E3 Bolkhov Rus. Fed.
105 C3 Bollène France
93 G3 Bollnäs Sweden
53 C1 Bollon Austr.
101 E2 Bollstedt Ger.
93 F4 Bolmen *l.* Sweden
118 B3 Bolobo Dem. Rep. Congo
108 B2 Bologna Italy
89 D2 Bologoye Rus. Fed.
89 D2 Bologoye Rus. Fed.
123 C2 Bolokanang S. Africa
118 B2 Bolomba Dem. Rep. Congo
108 B2 Bolsena, Lago di *l.* Italy
83 H1 Bol'shevik, Ostrov *i.* Rus. Fed.
86 E2 Bol'shezemel'skaya Tundra *lowland* Rus. Fed.
66 B2 Bol'shoy Kamen' Rus. Fed.
Bol'shoy Kavkaz *mts* Asia/Europe *see* Caucasus
83 K2 Bol'shoy Lyakhovskiy, Ostrov *i.* Rus. Fed.
Bol'shoy Tokmak Kyrg. *see* Tokmok
Bol'shoy Tokmak Ukr. *see* Tokmak
144 B2 Bolsón de Mapimí *des.* Mex.
100 B1 Bolsward Neth.
98 B3 Bolton U.K.
80 B1 Bolu Turkey
59 E3 Bolubolu P.N.G.
92 □A2 Bolungarvík Iceland
108 B1 Bolzano Italy
118 B3 Boma Dem. Rep. Congo
53 D2 Bomaderry Austr.
53 C3 Bombala Austr.
Bombay India *see* Mumbai
155 D1 Bom Despacho Brazil
75 D2 Bomdila India
154 B1 Bom Jardim de Goiás Brazil
151 E4 Bom Jesus da Lapa Brazil
155 D2 Bom Jesus do Itabapoana Brazil
115 D1 Bon, Cap *c.* Tunisia
147 D3 Bonaire *mun.* West Indies
134 C1 Bonaparte, Mount U.S.A.
50 B1 Bonaparte Archipelago *is* Austr.
131 E3 Bonavista Can.
131 E3 Bonavista Bay Can.
118 C3 Bondo Dem. Rep. Congo
114 B4 Bondoukou Côte d'Ivoire
Bône Alg. *see* Annaba
61 D2 Bonerate, Kepulauan *is* Indon.
155 C1 Bonfinópolis de Minas Brazil
117 B4 Bonga Eth.
75 D2 Bongaigaon India
118 C2 Bongandanga Dem. Rep. Congo
122 B2 Bongani S. Africa
118 C2 Bongo, Massif des *mts* C.A.R.
121 □D2 Bongolava *mts* Madag.
115 D3 Bongor Chad
114 B4 Bongouanou Côte d'Ivoire
63 B2 Bông Sơn Vietnam
143 D2 Bonham U.S.A.
105 D3 Bonifacio France
108 A2 Bonifacio, Strait of France/Italy
69 F3 Bonin Islands *is* Japan
100 C2 Bonn Ger.
134 C1 Bonners Ferry U.S.A.
105 D2 Bonneville France
50 A3 Bonnie Rock Austr.
129 C2 Bonnyville Can.
108 A2 Bonorva Italy
53 D1 Bonshaw Austr.
61 C1 Bontang Indon.
114 A4 Bonthe Sierra Leone
64 B2 Bontoc Phil.
61 C2 Bontosunggu Indon.
123 C3 Bontrug S. Africa
53 C1 Boolba Austr.
52 B2 Booligal Austr.
53 C1 Boomi Austr.
53 D1 Boonah Austr.
137 E2 Boone U.S.A.
140 C2 Booneville U.S.A.
137 E3 Boonville U.S.A.
52 B2 Booroorban Austr.
53 C2 Boorowa Austr.
117 C3 Boosaaso Somalia
126 G2 Boothia, Gulf of Can.
126 F2 Boothia Peninsula Can.
118 B3 Booué Gabon
100 C2 Boppard Ger.
144 B2 Boquilla, Presa de la *resr* Mex.
109 D2 Bor Serbia
117 B4 Bor S. Sudan
80 B2 Bor Turkey
119 E2 Bor, Lagh *watercourse* Kenya/Somalia
121 □E2 Boraha, Nosy *i.* Madag.
76 B2 Borankul Kazakh.
93 F4 Borås Sweden
81 D3 Borāzjān Iran
150 D3 Borba Brazil
104 B3 Bordeaux France
126 E1 Borden Island Can.
127 G2 Borden Peninsula Can.
52 B3 Bordertown Austr.
107 D2 Bordj Bou Arréridj Alg.
107 D2 Bordj Bounaama Alg.
114 B2 Bordj Flye Ste-Marie Alg.
115 C1 Bordj Messaouda Alg.
114 C2 Bordj Mokhtar Alg.
Bordj Omar Driss Alg. *see* Bordj Omer Driss
115 C2 Bordj Omer Driss Alg.

94 B1 Borðoy *i.* Faroe Is
Borgå Fin. *see* Porvoo
92 □A3 Borgarnes Iceland
143 C1 Borger U.S.A.
93 G4 Borgholm Sweden
100 B2 Borgloon Belgium
108 A1 Borgosesia Italy
87 D3 Borisoglebsk Rus. Fed.
89 E2 Borisoglebskiy Rus. Fed.
91 D1 Borisovka Rus. Fed.
119 C2 Bo River Post S. Sudan
100 C2 Borken Ger.
92 G2 Borkenes Norway
100 C1 Borkum Ger.
100 C1 Borkum *i.* Ger.
93 G3 Borlänge Sweden
101 F2 Borna Ger.
100 C1 Borne Neth.
61 C1 Borneo *i.* Asia
93 F4 Bornholm *i.* Denmark
111 C3 Bornova Turkey
90 B1 Borodyanka Ukr.
77 E2 Borohoro Shan *mts* China
114 B3 Boron Mali
89 D2 Borovichi Rus. Fed.
89 E2 Borovsk Rus. Fed.
76 C1 Borovskoy Kazakh.
51 C1 Borroloola Austr.
110 B1 Borşa Romania
76 B2 Borsakelmas sho'rxogi *salt marsh* Uzbek.
90 B2 Borshchiv Ukr.
69 D1 Borshchovochnyy Khrebet *mts* Rus. Fed.
101 E1 Börßum Ger.
Bortala China *see* Bole
81 C2 Borūjerd Iran
90 A2 Boryslav Ukr.
90 C1 Boryspil' Ukr.
91 C1 Borzna Ukr.
69 D1 Borzya Rus. Fed.
109 C1 Bosanska Dubica Bos.-Herz.
109 C1 Bosanska Gradiška Bos.-Herz.
109 C2 Bosanska Krupa Bos.-Herz.
109 C1 Bosanski Novi Bos.-Herz.
109 C2 Bosansko Grahovo Bos.-Herz.
123 C2 Boshof S. Africa
109 C2 Bosnia-Herzegovina *country* Europe
118 B2 Bosobolo Dem. Rep. Congo
111 C2 Bosporus *str.* Turkey
142 B2 Bosque U.S.A.
118 B2 Bossangoa C.A.R.
118 B2 Bossembélé C.A.R.
140 B2 Bossier City U.S.A.
122 A2 Bossiesvlei Namibia
68 B2 Bosten Hu *l.* China
99 C3 Boston U.K.
139 E2 Boston U.S.A.
140 B1 Boston Mountains U.S.A.
53 D2 Botany Bay Austr.
120 B3 Boteti *r.* Botswana
110 B2 Botev *mt.* Bulg.
80 A1 Botevgrad Bulg.
92 G3 Bothnia, Gulf of Fin./Sweden
110 C1 Botoşani Romania
70 B2 Botou China
123 C2 Botshabelo S. Africa
120 B3 Botswana *country* Africa
109 C3 Botte Donato, Monte *mt.* Italy
136 C1 Bottineau U.S.A.
100 C2 Bottrop Ger.
154 C2 Botucatu Brazil
114 B4 Bouaké Côte d'Ivoire
118 B2 Bouar C.A.R.
114 B1 Bou Arfa Morocco
131 D3 Bouctouche Can.
107 E2 Bougaa Alg.
48 G4 Bougainville Island P.N.G.
Bougie Alg. *see* Bejaïa
114 B3 Bougouni Mali
100 B3 Bouillon Belgium
107 D2 Bouira Alg.
114 A2 Boujdour Western Sahara
50 B3 Boulder Austr.
136 B2 Boulder CO U.S.A.
134 D1 Boulder MT U.S.A.
135 D3 Boulder City U.S.A.
Boulhaut Morocco *see* Ben Slimane
51 C2 Boulia Austr.
104 C2 Boulogne-Billancourt France
104 C1 Boulogne-sur-Mer France
118 C2 Boulouba C.A.R.
118 B3 Boumango Gabon
118 B2 Boumba *r.* Cameroon
107 D2 Boumerdes Alg.
118 B2 Bouna Côte d'Ivoire
114 B4 Boundiali Côte d'Ivoire
134 D2 Bountiful U.S.A.
49 I8 Bounty Islands N.Z.
114 B3 Bourem Mali
105 D2 Bourganeuf France
105 D2 Bourg-en-Bresse France
104 C2 Bourges France
Bourgogne *reg.* France *see* Burgundy
105 D2 Bourgoin-Jallieu France
53 C2 Bourke Austr.
99 C3 Bourne U.K.
99 C4 Bournemouth U.K.
118 C1 Bourtoutou Chad
115 C1 Bou Saâda Alg.
115 D3 Bousso Chad
100 A2 Boussu Belgium
114 A3 Boutilimit Maur.
128 C3 Bow *r.* Can.

Bowa China *see* Muli
51 D2 Bowen Austr.
53 C3 Bowen, Mount Austr.
129 C3 Bow Island Can.
138 B3 Bowling Green KY U.S.A.
137 E3 Bowling Green MO U.S.A.
138 C2 Bowling Green OH U.S.A.
136 C1 Bowman U.S.A.
53 C2 Bowral Austr.
101 D3 Boxberg Ger.
100 B2 Boxtel Neth.
80 B1 Boyabat Turkey
Boyang China *see* Poyang
97 B2 Boyle Ireland
97 C2 Boyne *r.* Ireland
136 B2 Boysen Reservoir U.S.A.
152 B2 Boyuibe Bol.
111 C3 Bozburun Turkey
111 C3 Bozcaada *i.* Turkey
111 C3 Bozdağ *mt.* Turkey
111 C3 Boz Dağları *mts* Turkey
111 C3 Bozdoğan Turkey
134 D1 Bozeman U.S.A.
118 B2 Bozoum C.A.R.
111 C3 Bozüyük Turkey
109 C2 Brač *i.* Croatia
130 C3 Bracebridge Can.
93 G3 Bräcke Sweden
99 C4 Bracknell U.K.
109 C2 Bradano *r.* Italy
141 D3 Bradenton U.S.A.
147 B3 Brades Montserrat
98 C3 Bradford U.K.
139 D2 Bradford U.S.A.
143 D2 Brady U.S.A.
96 C2 Braemar U.K.
106 B1 Braga Port.
151 E3 Bragança Brazil
106 B1 Bragança Port.
155 C2 Bragança Paulista Brazil
89 D3 Brahin Belarus
75 D2 Brahmanbaria Bangl.
75 C3 Brahmapur India
62 A1 Brahmaputra *r.* China/India
53 C3 Braidwood Austr.
110 C1 Brăila Romania
137 E1 Brainerd U.S.A.
99 D4 Braintree U.K.
100 B2 Braives Belgium
101 D1 Brake (Unterweser) Ger.
122 A1 Brakwater Namibia
98 B2 Brampton U.K.
100 D1 Bramsche Ger.
150 C3 Branco *r.* Brazil
101 F1 Brandenburg Ger.
129 E3 Brandon Can.
140 C2 Brandon U.S.A.
97 A2 Brandon Mountain *h.* Ireland
122 B3 Brandvlei S. Africa
103 D1 Braniewo Pol.
130 B3 Brantford Can.
53 D2 Branxton Austr.
131 D3 Bras d'Or Lake Can.
155 D1 Brasil, Planalto do *plat.* Brazil
154 C1 Brasilândia Brazil
154 C1 Brasília Brazil
155 D1 Brasília de Minas Brazil
88 C3 Braslaw Belarus
110 C1 Braşov Romania
103 D2 Bratislava Slovakia
83 H3 Bratsk Rus. Fed.
102 C2 Braunau am Inn Austria
101 E1 Braunschweig Ger.
92 □A2 Brautarholt Iceland
Bravo del Norte, Río *r.* Mex./U.S.A. *see* Rio Grande
135 C4 Brawley U.S.A.
97 C2 Bray Ireland
150 D2 Brazil *country* S. America
158 E6 Brazil Basin S. Atlantic Ocean
143 D3 Brazos *r.* U.S.A.
118 B3 Brazzaville Congo
109 C2 Brčko Bos.-Herz.
96 C2 Brechin U.K.
100 B2 Brecht Belgium
143 D2 Breckenridge U.S.A.
103 D2 Břeclav Czech Rep.
99 B4 Brecon U.K.
99 B4 Brecon Beacons *reg.* U.K.
100 B2 Breda Neth.
122 B3 Bredasdorp S. Africa
102 B2 Bregenz Austria
92 H1 Breivikbotn Norway
92 F3 Brekstad Norway
101 D1 Bremen Ger.
101 D1 Bremerhaven Ger.
Bremersdorp Swaziland *see* Manzini
134 B1 Bremerton U.S.A.
101 D1 Bremervörde Ger.
143 D2 Brenham U.S.A.
105 E2 Brennero Italy
102 C2 Brenner Pass Austria/Italy
99 D4 Brentwood U.K.
108 B1 Brescia Italy
100 A2 Breskens Neth.
105 E2 Bressanone Italy
96 □ Bressay *i.* U.K.
104 B2 Bressuire France
88 B3 Brest Belarus
104 B2 Brest France
Brest-Litovsk Belarus *see* Brest
Bretagne *reg.* France *see* Brittany
140 C3 Breton Sound *b.* U.S.A.

Castiglione della Pescaia

54 C2 Cafelândia Brazil
64 B3 Cagayan de Oro Phil.
64 A3 Cagayan de Tawi-Tawi i. Phil.
108 B2 Cagli Italy
108 A3 Cagliari Italy
108 A3 Cagliari, Golfo di b. Italy
76 B2 Çagyl Turkm.
120 A2 Cahama Angola
97 B3 Caha Mountains hills Ireland
97 A3 Cahermore Ireland
97 C2 Cahir Ireland
97 A3 Cahirsiveen Ireland
Cahora Bassa, Lago de resr Moz. see Cabora Bassa, Lake
97 C2 Cahore Point Ireland
104 C3 Cahors France
90 B2 Cahul Moldova
121 C2 Caia Moz.
151 D4 Caiabis, Serra dos hills Brazil
120 B2 Caianda Angola
154 B1 Caiapó, Serra do mts Brazil
154 B1 Caiapônia Brazil
147 C2 Caicos Islands Turks and Caicos Is
96 C2 Cairngorm Mountains U.K.
96 B3 Cairnryan U.K.
51 D1 Cairns Austr.
116 B1 Cairo Egypt
Caisleán an Bharraigh Ireland see Castlebar
98 C3 Caistor U.K.
120 A2 Caiundo Angola
150 B3 Cajamarca Peru
109 C1 Čakovec Croatia
123 C3 Cala S. Africa
115 C4 Calabar Nigeria
150 C2 Calabozo Venez.
110 B2 Calafat Romania
153 A5 Calafate Arg.
107 C1 Calahorra Spain
120 A2 Calai Angola
104 C1 Calais France
139 F1 Calais U.S.A.
152 B2 Calama Chile
64 A2 Calamian Group is Phil.
107 C1 Calamocha Spain
120 A1 Calandula Angola
60 A1 Calang Indon.
64 B2 Calapan Phil.
110 C2 Călărași Romania
107 C1 Calatayud Spain
64 B2 Calayan i. Phil.
64 B2 Calbayog Phil.
151 F3 Calcanhar, Ponta do pt Brazil
151 D2 Calçoene Brazil
Calcutta India see Kolkata
106 B2 Caldas da Rainha Port.
154 C1 Caldas Novas Brazil
152 A2 Caldera Chile
51 D2 Caldervale Austr.
134 C2 Caldwell U.S.A.
123 C3 Caledon r. Lesotho/S. Africa
122 A3 Caledon S. Africa
153 B4 Caleta Olivia Arg.
98 A2 Calf of Man i. Isle of Man
128 C2 Calgary Can.
150 B2 Cali Col.
Calicut India see Kozhikode
135 D3 Caliente U.S.A.
135 B2 California state U.S.A.
144 A1 California, Gulf of g. Mex.
135 B3 California Aqueduct canal U.S.A.
81 C2 Cälilabad Azer.
122 B3 Calitzdorp S. Africa
145 C2 Calkiní Mex.
52 B1 Callabonna, Lake imp. l. Austr.
135 C3 Callaghan, Mount U.S.A.
97 C2 Callan Ireland
96 B2 Callander U.K.
150 B4 Callao Peru
99 A4 Callington U.K.
108 B3 Caltagirone Italy
108 B3 Caltanissetta Italy
120 A1 Calulo Angola
120 B2 Calunda Angola
120 A2 Caluquembe Angola
117 D3 Caluula Somalia
105 D3 Calvi France
107 D2 Calvià Spain
144 B2 Calvillo Mex.
122 A3 Calvinia S. Africa
109 C2 Calvo, Monte mt. Italy
120 A1 Camabatela Angola
151 F4 Camaçari Brazil
144 B2 Camacho Mex.
120 A2 Camacupa Angola
146 C2 Camagüey Cuba
146 C2 Camagüey, Archipiélago de is Cuba
150 B4 Camana Peru
120 B2 Camanongue Angola
154 B1 Camapuã Brazil
145 C2 Camargo Mex.
63 B3 Ca Mau Vietnam
63 B3 Ca Mau, Mui c. Vietnam
Cambay India see Khambhat
63 B2 Cambodia country Asia
99 A4 Camborne U.K.
105 C1 Cambrai France
99 B3 Cambrian Mountains hills U.K.
138 C2 Cambridge Can.
54 C1 Cambridge N.Z.
99 D3 Cambridge U.K.
139 E2 Cambridge MA U.S.A.
139 D3 Cambridge MD U.S.A.
137 E1 Cambridge MN U.S.A.
138 C2 Cambridge OH U.S.A.
126 E2 Cambridge Bay Can.
131 D2 Cambrien, Lac l. Can.
120 B1 Cambulo Angola
53 D2 Camden Austr.
140 B2 Camden AR U.S.A.
139 F2 Camden ME U.S.A.
139 D3 Camden NJ U.S.A.
137 E3 Camdenton U.S.A.
137 E3 Cameron U.S.A.
118 B2 Cameroon country Africa
118 B2 Cameroon Highlands slope Cameroon/Nigeria
118 A2 Cameroun, Mont vol. Cameroon
151 E3 Cametá Brazil
64 B2 Camiguin i. Phil.
64 B3 Camiguin i. Phil.
152 B2 Camiri Bol.
151 E3 Camocim Brazil
51 C1 Camooweal Austr.
63 A3 Camorta i. India
153 A4 Campana, Isla i. Chile
155 D1 Campanário Brazil
155 C2 Campanha Brazil
122 B2 Campbell S. Africa
54 B2 Campbell, Cape N.Z.
48 H9 Campbell Island N.Z.
156 D9 Campbell Plateau S. Pacific Ocean
128 B2 Campbell River Can.
138 B3 Campbellsville U.S.A.
131 D3 Campbellton Can.
53 D2 Campbelltown Austr.
96 B3 Campbeltown U.K.
145 C3 Campeche Mex.
145 C3 Campeche, Bahía de g. Mex.
52 B3 Camperdown Austr.
110 C1 Câmpina Romania
151 F3 Campina Grande Brazil
154 C2 Campinas Brazil
154 C1 Campina Verde Brazil
108 B2 Campobasso Italy
155 C2 Campo Belo Brazil
154 C1 Campo Florido Brazil
152 B2 Campo Gallo Arg.
154 B2 Campo Grande Brazil
154 C3 Campo Largo Brazil
151 E3 Campo Maior Brazil
106 B2 Campo Maior Port.
150 B1 Campo Mara Venez.
109 C2 Campomarino Italy
154 B2 Campo Mourão Brazil
155 D2 Campos Brazil
155 C1 Campos Altos Brazil
155 C2 Campos do Jordão Brazil
110 C1 Câmpulung Romania
142 A2 Camp Verde U.S.A.
Cam Ranh Vietnam see Ba Ngoi
63 B2 Cam Ranh, Vinh b. Vietnam
Cam Ranh Bay b. Vietnam see Cam Ranh, Vinh
128 C2 Camrose Can.
129 D2 Camsell Portage Can.
111 C2 Çan Turkey
126 F2 Canada country N. America
160 A2 Canada Basin Arctic Ocean
143 C1 Canadian U.S.A.
143 D1 Canadian r. U.S.A.
111 C2 Çanakkale Turkey
144 A1 Cananea Mex.
154 C2 Cananéia Brazil
114 A2 Canary Islands is N. Atlantic Ocean
154 C1 Canastra, Serra da mts Goiás Brazil
155 C1 Canastra, Serra da mts Minas Gerais Brazil
144 B2 Canatlán Mex.
141 D3 Canaveral, Cape U.S.A.
155 E1 Canavieiras Brazil
53 C2 Canbelego Austr.
53 C3 Canberra Austr.
145 D2 Cancún Mex.
111 C3 Çandarlı Turkey
155 C2 Candeias Brazil
145 C3 Candelaria Mex.
154 B2 Cândido de Abreu Brazil
129 D2 Candle Lake Can.
137 D1 Cando U.S.A.
120 A2 Cangamba Angola
106 B1 Cangas Spain
106 B1 Cangas del Narcea Spain
120 B2 Cangombe Angola
152 C3 Canguçu Brazil
70 B2 Cangzhou China
131 D2 Caniapiscau Can.
131 D2 Caniapiscau r. Can.
131 C2 Caniapiscau, Réservoir de resr Can.
Caniçado Moz. see Guija
108 B3 Canicattì Italy
151 F3 Canindé Brazil
144 B2 Cañitas de Felipe Pescador Mex.
80 B1 Çankırı Turkey
128 C2 Canmore Can.
96 A2 Canna i. U.K.
Cannanore India see Kannur
105 D3 Cannes France
99 B3 Cannock U.K.
53 C3 Cann River Austr.
152 C2 Canoas Brazil
129 D2 Canoe Lake Can.
154 B3 Canoinhas Brazil
136 B3 Canon City U.S.A.
52 B2 Canopus Austr.
129 D2 Canora Can.
53 C2 Canowindra Austr.
131 D3 Canso Can.
Cantabrian Mountains mts Spain see Cantábrica, Cordillera
Cantabrian Sea sea Spain see Cantábrico, Mar
106 C1 Cantábrica, Cordillera mts Spain
106 B1 Cantábrico, Mar sea Spain
99 D4 Canterbury U.K.
54 B2 Canterbury Bight b. N.Z.
54 B2 Canterbury Plains N.Z.
63 B2 Cân Thơ Vietnam
151 E3 Canto do Buriti Brazil
Canton China see Guangzhou
137 E2 Canton MO U.S.A.
140 C2 Canton MS U.S.A.
139 D2 Canton NY U.S.A.
138 C2 Canton OH U.S.A.
143 C1 Canyon U.S.A.
134 D1 Canyon Ferry Lake U.S.A.
134 B2 Canyonville U.S.A.
62 B1 Cao Bằng Vietnam
109 C2 Capaccio Italy
154 C2 Capão Bonito Brazil
155 D2 Caparaó, Serra do mts Brazil
139 E1 Cap-de-la-Madeleine Can.
51 D4 Cape Barren Island Austr.
158 F7 Cape Basin S. Atlantic Ocean
52 A3 Cape Borda Austr.
131 D3 Cape Breton Island Can.
141 D3 Cape Canaveral U.S.A.
139 D3 Cape Charles U.S.A.
114 B4 Cape Coast Ghana
139 E2 Cape Cod Bay U.S.A.
141 D3 Cape Coral U.S.A.
127 G2 Cape Dorset Can.
141 E2 Cape Fear r. U.S.A.
137 F3 Cape Girardeau U.S.A.
155 D1 Capelinha Brazil
100 B2 Capelle aan de IJssel Neth.
Capelongo Angola see Kuvango
139 E3 Cape May Point U.S.A.
120 A1 Capenda-Camulemba Angola
122 A3 Cape Town S. Africa
158 E3 Cape Verde country N. Atlantic Ocean
158 D4 Cape Verde Basin N. Atlantic Ocean
51 D1 Cape York Peninsula Austr.
147 C3 Cap-Haïtien Haiti
151 E3 Capim r. Brazil
154 A2 Capitán Bado Para.
58 D1 Capitol Hill N. Mariana Is
154 B2 Capivara, Represa resr Brazil
109 C2 Čapljina Bos.-Herz.
109 B3 Capo d'Orlando Italy
108 A2 Capraia, Isola di i. Italy
108 A2 Caprara, Punta pt Italy
108 B2 Capri, Isola di i. Italy
51 E2 Capricorn Channel Austr.
120 B2 Caprivi Strip reg. Namibia
143 C2 Cap Rock Escarpment U.S.A.
143 C1 Capulin U.S.A.
150 C3 Caquetá r. Col.
110 B2 Caracal Romania
150 C2 Caracaraí Brazil
150 C1 Caracas Venez.
151 E3 Caracol Brazil
155 C2 Caraguatatuba Brazil
153 A3 Carahue Chile
155 D1 Caraí Brazil
151 D3 Carajás, Serra dos hills Brazil
155 D2 Carandaí Brazil
155 D2 Carangola Brazil
110 B1 Caransebeş Romania
131 D3 Caraquet Can.
146 B3 Caratasca, Laguna de lag. Hond.
155 D1 Caratinga Brazil
150 C3 Carauari Brazil
107 C2 Caravaca de la Cruz Spain
155 E1 Caravelas Brazil
129 E3 Carberry Can.
144 A2 Carbó Mex.
107 C2 Carbon, Cap c. Alg.
153 B5 Carbón, Laguna del l. Arg.
108 A3 Carbonara, Capo c. Italy
136 B3 Carbondale CO U.S.A.
138 B3 Carbondale IL U.S.A.
139 D2 Carbondale PA U.S.A.
131 E3 Carbonear Can.
155 D1 Carbonita Brazil
107 C2 Carcaixent Spain
104 C3 Carcassonne France
128 A1 Carcross Can.
146 B2 Cárdenas Cuba
145 C3 Cárdenas Mex.
99 B4 Cardiff U.K.
99 A3 Cardigan U.K.
99 A3 Cardigan Bay U.K.
154 C2 Cardoso Brazil
128 C3 Cardston Can.
110 B1 Carei Romania
104 B2 Carentan France
50 B2 Carey, Lake imp. l. Austr.
155 D2 Cariacica Brazil
146 B3 Caribbean Sea N. Atlantic Ocean
128 B2 Cariboo Mountains Can.
139 F1 Caribou U.S.A.
130 B2 Caribou Lake Can.
128 C2 Caribou Mountains Can.
144 B2 Carichic Mex.
100 B3 Carignan France
53 C2 Carinda Austr.
107 C1 Cariñena Spain
130 C3 Carleton Place Can.
123 C2 Carletonville S. Africa
135 C2 Carlin U.S.A.
97 C1 Carlingford Lough inlet Ireland/U.K.
138 B3 Carlinville U.S.A.
98 B2 Carlisle U.K.
139 D2 Carlisle U.S.A.
155 D1 Carlos Chagas Brazil
97 C2 Carlow Ireland
96 A1 Carloway U.K.
135 C4 Carlsbad CA U.S.A.
142 C2 Carlsbad NM U.S.A.
129 D3 Carlyle Can.
128 A1 Carmacks Can.
129 E3 Carman Can.
99 A4 Carmarthen U.K.
99 A4 Carmarthen Bay U.K.
104 C3 Carmaux France
145 C3 Carmelita Guat.
144 A2 Carmen, Isla i. Mex.
155 C1 Carmo do Paranaíba Brazil
Carmona Angola see Uíge
106 B2 Carmona Spain
104 B2 Carnac France
50 A2 Carnarvon Austr.
122 B3 Carnarvon S. Africa
97 C1 Carndonagh Ireland
129 D3 Carnduff Can.
50 B2 Carnegie, Lake imp. l. Austr.
96 B2 Carn Eige mt. U.K.
55 P2 Carney Island Antarctica
73 D4 Car Nicobar i. India
118 B2 Carnot C.A.R.
52 A2 Carnot, Cape Austr.
96 C2 Carnoustie U.K.
97 C2 Carnsore Point Ireland
151 E3 Carolina Brazil
49 L4 Caroline Island Kiribati
59 D2 Caroline Islands N. Pacific Ocean
122 A2 Carolusberg S. Africa
103 D2 Carpathian Mountains Europe
Carpaţii Meridionali mts Romania see Transylvanian Alps
51 C1 Carpentaria, Gulf of Austr.
105 D3 Carpentras France
108 B2 Carpi Italy
141 D3 Carrabelle U.S.A.
97 B3 Carrantuohill mt. Ireland
108 B2 Carrara Italy
97 D1 Carrickfergus U.K.
97 C2 Carrickmacross Ireland
97 B2 Carrick-on-Shannon Ireland
97 C2 Carrick-on-Suir Ireland
137 D1 Carrington U.S.A.
143 D3 Carrizo Springs U.S.A.
142 B2 Carrizozo U.S.A.
137 E2 Carroll U.S.A.
141 C2 Carrollton U.S.A.
129 D2 Carrot River Can.
135 C3 Carson City U.S.A.
135 C3 Carson Sink l. U.S.A.
Carstensz-top mt. Indon. see Jaya, Puncak
150 B1 Cartagena Col.
107 C2 Cartagena Spain
146 B4 Cartago Costa Rica
54 C2 Carterton N.Z.
137 E3 Carthage MO U.S.A.
143 E2 Carthage TX U.S.A.
131 E2 Cartwright Can.
151 F3 Caruaru Brazil
150 C1 Carúpano Venez.
52 B1 Caryapundy Swamp Austr.
114 B1 Casablanca Morocco
154 C2 Casa Branca Brazil
144 B1 Casa de Janos Mex.
142 A2 Casa Grande U.S.A.
108 A1 Casale Monferrato Italy
109 C2 Casarano Italy
144 B1 Casas Grandes Mex.
134 C2 Cascade U.S.A.
134 B2 Cascade Range mts Can./U.S.A.
106 B2 Cascais Port.
151 F3 Cascavel Brazil
154 B2 Cascavel Brazil
139 F2 Casco Bay U.S.A.
108 B2 Caserta Italy
97 C2 Cashel Ireland
153 B3 Casilda Arg.
53 D1 Casino Austr.
Casnewydd U.K. see Newport
107 C1 Caspe Spain
136 B2 Casper U.S.A.
76 A2 Caspian Lowland Kazakh./Rus. Fed.
81 C1 Caspian Sea Asia/Europe
Cassaigne Alg. see Sidi Ali
154 C2 Cássia Brazil
128 B2 Cassiar Can.
128 A2 Cassiar Mountains Can.
154 B1 Cassilândia Brazil
120 A2 Cassinga Angola
108 B2 Cassino Italy
96 B2 Cassley r. U.K.
151 E3 Castanhal Brazil
152 B3 Castaño r. Arg.
144 B2 Castaños Mex.
104 C3 Casteljaloux France
105 D3 Castellane France
107 C2 Castellón de la Plana Spain
155 D2 Castelo Brazil
106 B2 Castelo Branco Port.
104 C3 Castelsarrasin France
108 B3 Castelvetrano Italy
52 B3 Casterton Austr.
108 B2 Castiglione della Pescaia Italy

Castilla-La Mancha

106 C2 Castilla-La Mancha *aut. comm.* Spain
106 C1 Castilla y León *aut. comm.* Spain
97 B2 Castlebar Ireland
96 A2 Castlebay U.K.
97 C1 Castleblayney Ireland
97 C1 Castlederg U.K.
96 C3 Castle Douglas U.K.
128 C3 Castlegar Can.
97 B2 Castleisland Ireland
52 B3 Castlemaine Austr.
97 C2 Castlepollard Ireland
97 B2 Castlerea Ireland
53 C2 Castlereagh *r.* Austr.
136 C3 Castle Rock U.S.A.
128 C2 Castor Can.
104 C3 Castres France
100 B1 Castricum Neth.
147 D3 Castries St Lucia
154 C2 Castro Brazil
153 A4 Castro Chile
106 B2 Castro Verde Port.
109 C3 Castrovillari Italy
150 A3 Catacaos Peru
155 D2 Cataguases Brazil
154 C1 Catalão Brazil
Catalonia *aut. comm.* Spain *see* Cataluña
107 D1 Cataluña *aut. comm.* Spain
152 B2 Catamarca Arg.
64 B2 Catanduanes *i.* Phil.
154 C2 Catanduva Brazil
154 B3 Catanduvas Brazil
109 C3 Catania Italy
109 C3 Catanzaro Italy
64 B2 Catarman Phil.
107 C2 Catarroja Spain
64 B2 Catbalogan Phil.
145 C3 Catemaco Mex.
120 A1 Catete Angola
Catherine, Mount *mt.* Egypt *see* Kātrīnā, Jabal
147 C2 Cat Island Bahamas
130 A2 Cat Lake Can.
145 D2 Catoche, Cabo *c.* Mex.
139 E2 Catskill Mountains U.S.A.
123 D2 Catuane Moz.
64 B3 Cauayan Phil.
131 D2 Caubvick, Mount Can.
150 B2 Cauca *r.* Col.
151 F3 Caucaia Brazil
81 C1 Caucasus *mts* Asia/Europe
100 A2 Caudry France
109 C3 Caulonia Italy
120 A1 Caungula Angola
150 C2 Caura *r.* Venez.
131 D3 Causapscal Can.
90 B2 Căuşeni Moldova
105 D3 Cavaillon France
151 E4 Cavalcante Brazil
114 B4 Cavally *r.* Côte d'Ivoire/Liberia
97 C2 Cavan Ireland
154 B3 Cavernoso, Serra do *mts* Brazil
151 D2 Caviana, Ilha *i.* Brazil
Cawnpore India *see* Kanpur
151 E3 Caxias Brazil
152 C2 Caxias do Sul Brazil
120 A1 Caxito Angola
151 D2 Cayenne Fr. Guiana
146 B3 Cayman Islands *terr.* West Indies
158 C3 Cayman Trench Caribbean Sea
117 C4 Caynabo Somalia
120 B2 Cazombo Angola
Ceará Brazil *see* Fortaleza
Ceatharlach Ireland *see* Carlow
144 B2 Ceballos Mex.
64 B2 Cebu Phil.
64 B2 Cebu *i.* Phil.
108 B2 Cecina Italy
137 F2 Cedar *r.* U.S.A.
135 D3 Cedar City U.S.A.
137 E2 Cedar Falls U.S.A.
129 D2 Cedar Lake Can.
137 E2 Cedar Rapids U.S.A.
144 A2 Cedros, Isla *i.* Mex.
51 C3 Ceduna Austr.
117 C4 Ceeldheere Somalia
117 C3 Ceerigaabo Somalia
108 B3 Cefalù Italy
145 B2 Celaya Mex.
61 D2 Celebes *i.* Indon.
156 C5 Celebes Sea Indon./Phil.
145 C2 Celestún Mex.
101 E1 Celle Ger.
95 B3 Celtic Sea Ireland/U.K.
59 D3 Cenderawasih, Teluk *b.* Indon.
140 C2 Center Point U.S.A.
150 B2 Central, Cordillera *mts* Col.
150 B4 Central, Cordillera *mts* Peru
64 B2 Central, Cordillera *mts* Phil.
Central African Empire *country* Africa *see* Central African Republic
118 C2 Central African Republic *country* Africa
74 A2 Central Brahui Range *mts* Pak.
137 D2 Central City U.S.A.
138 B3 Centralia *IL* U.S.A.
134 B1 Centralia *WA* U.S.A.
74 A2 Central Makran Range *mts* Pak.
156 D5 Central Pacific Basin Pacific Ocean
134 B2 Central Point U.S.A.
Central Provinces *state* India *see* Madhya Pradesh
59 D3 Central Range *mts* P.N.G.
89 E3 Central Russian Upland *hills* Rus. Fed.
83 I2 Central Siberian Plateau *plat.* Rus. Fed.
140 C2 Century U.S.A.
Ceos *i.* Greece *see* Kea
111 B3 Cephalonia *i.* Greece
Ceram *i.* Indon. *see* Seram
Ceram Sea *sea* Indon. *see* Laut Seram
101 F3 Čerchov *mt.* Czech Rep.
152 B2 Ceres Arg.
154 C1 Ceres Brazil
122 A3 Ceres S. Africa
105 C3 Céret France
106 C1 Cerezo de Abajo Spain
109 C2 Cerignola Italy
Cerigo *i.* Greece *see* Kythira
110 C2 Cernavodă Romania
145 C2 Cerralvo Mex.
144 B2 Cerralvo, Isla *i.* Mex.
145 B2 Cerritos Mex.
154 C2 Cerro Azul Brazil
145 C2 Cerro Azul Mex.
150 B4 Cerro de Pasco Peru
105 D3 Cervione France
106 B1 Cervo Spain
108 B2 Cesena Italy
108 B2 Cesenatico Italy
88 C2 Cēsis Latvia
102 C2 České Budějovice Czech Rep.
101 F3 Český les *mts* Czech Rep.
111 C3 Çeşme Turkey
53 D2 Cessnock Austr.
104 B2 Cesson-Sévigné France
104 B3 Cestas France
109 C2 Cetinje Montenegro
109 C3 Cetraro Italy
106 B2 Ceuta N. Africa
105 C3 Cévennes *mts* France
Ceylon *country* Asia *see* Sri Lanka
79 D2 Chābahār Iran
150 B3 Chachapoyas Peru
89 D3 Chachersk Belarus
63 B2 Chachoengsao Thai.
152 C2 Chaco Boreal *reg.* Para.
142 B1 Chaco Mesa *plat.* U.S.A.
115 D3 Chad *country* Africa
115 D3 Chad, Lake Africa
68 C1 Chadaasan Mongolia
68 C1 Chadan Rus. Fed.
123 C1 Chadibe Botswana
136 C2 Chadron U.S.A.
Chadyr-Lunga Moldova *see* Ciadîr-Lunga
77 D2 Chaek Kyrg.
65 B2 Chaeryŏng N. Korea
74 A2 Chagai Pak.
77 C3 Chaghcharān Afgh.
89 E2 Chagoda Rus. Fed.
56 I10 Chagos Archipelago *is* B.I.O.T.
159 E4 Chagos-Laccadive Ridge Indian Ocean
159 E4 Chagos Trench Indian Ocean
75 C2 Chaibasa India
63 B2 Chainat Thai.
63 A3 Chaiya Thai.
63 B2 Chaiyaphum Thai.
152 C3 Chajarí Arg.
119 D3 Chake Chake Tanz.
131 D2 Chakonipau, Lac Can.
150 B4 Chala Peru
121 C2 Chaláua Moz.
131 D3 Chaleur Bay *inlet* Can.
74 B2 Chalisgaon India
111 C3 Chalki *i.* Greece
111 B3 Chalkida Greece
143 C3 Chalk Mountains U.S.A.
104 B2 Challans France
134 D2 Challis U.S.A.
105 C2 Châlons-en-Champagne France
Châlons-sur-Marne France *see* Châlons-en-Champagne
105 C2 Chalon-sur-Saône France
101 F3 Cham Ger.
142 B1 Chama U.S.A.
121 C2 Chama Zambia
74 A1 Chaman Pak.
74 B1 Chamba India
74 B2 Chambal *r.* India
137 D2 Chamberlain U.S.A.
142 B1 Chambers U.S.A.
139 D3 Chambersburg U.S.A.
105 D2 Chambéry France
121 C2 Chambeshi Zambia
121 B2 Chambeshi *r.* Zambia
Chamdo China *see* Qamdo
119 D2 Ch'amo Hāyk' *l.* Eth.
105 D2 Chamonix-Mont-Blanc France
105 C2 Champagne *reg.* France
138 B2 Champaign U.S.A.
139 E2 Champlain, Lake Can./U.S.A.
145 C3 Champotón Mex.
Chanak Turkey *see* Çanakkale
152 A2 Chañaral Chile
Chanda India *see* Chandrapur
126 C2 Chandalar *r.* U.S.A.
140 C3 Chandeleur Islands U.S.A.
74 B1 Chandigarh India
131 D3 Chandler Can.
142 A2 Chandler U.S.A.
75 D2 Chandpur Bangl.
75 B3 Chandrapur India
63 B2 Chang, Ko *i.* Thai.
Chang'an China *see* Rong'an
121 C3 Changane *r.* Moz.
121 C2 Changara Moz.
65 B1 Changbai China
65 B1 Changbai Shan *mts* China/N. Korea
Changchow China *see* Zhangzhou
Changchow China *see* Changzhou
69 E2 Changchun China
71 B3 Changde China
65 B2 Ch'angdo N. Korea
70 B2 Changge China
65 B3 Changhŭng S. Korea
Chang Jiang *r.* China *see* Yangtze
Changjiang Kou *r. mouth* China *see* Yangtze, Mouth of the
65 B1 Changjin N. Korea
65 B1 Changjin-gang *r.* N. Korea
Changkiang China *see* Zhanjiang
Changning China *see* Xunwu
Ch'ang-pai Shan *mts* China/N. Korea *see* Changbai Shan
71 B3 Changsha China
70 C2 Changshu China
65 B2 Changsŏng S. Korea
Changteh China *see* Changde
71 B3 Changting *Fujian* China
66 A2 Changting *Heilong.* China
65 A1 Changtu China
146 B4 Changuinola Panama
65 B2 Ch'angwŏn S. Korea
65 B2 Changyŏn N. Korea
70 B2 Changyuan China
70 B2 Changzhi China
70 B2 Changzhou China
111 B3 Chania Greece
95 C4 Channel Islands English Chan.
135 C4 Channel Islands U.S.A.
131 E3 Channel-Port-aux-Basques Can.
106 B1 Chantada Spain
63 B2 Chanthaburi Thai.
104 C2 Chantilly France
137 D3 Chanute U.S.A.
82 G3 Chany, Ozero *salt l.* Rus. Fed.
70 B2 Chaohu China
71 B3 Chaoyang *Guangdong* China
Chaoyang China *see* Huinan
70 C1 Chaoyang *Liaoning* China
71 B3 Chaozhou China
144 B2 Chapala, Laguna de *l.* Mex.
76 B1 Chapayevo Kazakh.
87 D3 Chapayevsk Rus. Fed.
152 C2 Chapecó Brazil
141 E1 Chapel Hill U.S.A.
130 B3 Chapleau Can.
89 E3 Chaplygin Rus. Fed.
91 C2 Chaplynka Ukr.
Chapra India *see* Chhapra
145 B2 Charcas Mex.
99 B4 Chard U.K.
Chardzhev Turkm. *see* Türkmenabat
Chardzhou Turkm. *see* Türkmenabat
104 B2 Charente *r.* France
118 B1 Chari *r.* Cameroon/Chad
77 C3 Chārīkār Afgh.
86 E2 Charkayuvom Rus. Fed.
Charkhlik China *see* Ruoqiang
100 B2 Charleroi Belgium
139 D3 Charles, Cape U.S.A.
139 E1 Charlesbourg Can.
137 E2 Charles City U.S.A.
138 B3 Charleston *IL* U.S.A.
137 F3 Charleston *MO* U.S.A.
141 E2 Charleston *SC* U.S.A.
138 C3 Charleston *WV* U.S.A.
135 C3 Charleston Peak U.S.A.
51 D2 Charleville Austr.
97 B2 Charleville Ireland
105 C2 Charleville-Mézières France
138 B1 Charlevoix U.S.A.
141 D1 Charlotte U.S.A.
141 D3 Charlotte Harbor *b.* U.S.A.
139 D3 Charlottesville U.S.A.
131 D3 Charlottetown Can.
52 B3 Charlton Austr.
130 C2 Charlton Island Can.
51 D2 Charters Towers Austr.
104 C2 Chartres France
128 C2 Chase Can.
88 C3 Chashniki Belarus
54 A3 Chaslands Mistake *c.* N.Z.
65 B1 Chasŏng N. Korea
104 B2 Chassiron, Pointe de *pt* France
104 B2 Châteaubriant France
104 C2 Château-du-Loir France
104 C2 Châteaudun France
104 B2 Château-Gontier France
104 B2 Châteaulin France
105 D3 Châteauneuf-les-Martigues France
104 C2 Châteauneuf-sur-Loire France
104 C2 Châteauroux France
105 C2 Château-Thierry France
128 C2 Chateh Can.
100 B2 Châtelet Belgium
104 C2 Châtellerault France
138 C2 Chatham Can.
99 D4 Chatham U.K.
49 J8 Chatham Islands N.Z.
105 C2 Châtillon-sur-Seine France
141 D2 Chattahoochee *r.* U.S.A.
141 C1 Chattanooga U.S.A.
63 B2 Châu Đốc Vietnam
62 A1 Chauk Myanmar
105 D2 Chaumont France
105 C2 Chauny France
Chau Phu Vietnam *see* Châu Đốc
151 E3 Chaves Brazil
106 B1 Chaves Port.
130 C2 Chavigny, Lac *l.* Can.
89 D3 Chavusy Belarus
89 E2 Chayevo Rus. Fed.
86 E3 Chaykovskiy Rus. Fed.
140 C2 Cheaha Mountain *h.* U.S.A.
102 C1 Cheb Czech Rep.
87 D3 Cheboksary Rus. Fed.
138 C1 Cheboygan U.S.A.
65 B2 Chech'ŏn S. Korea
140 A1 Checotah U.S.A.
Chefoo China *see* Yantai
126 B2 Chefornak U.S.A.
114 B2 Chegga Maur.
121 C2 Chegutu Zimbabwe
134 B1 Chehalis U.S.A.
65 B3 Cheju S. Korea
65 B3 Cheju-do *i.* S. Korea
65 B3 Cheju-haehyŏp *sea chan.* S. Korea
89 E2 Chekhov Rus. Fed.
Chekiang *prov.* China *see* Zhejiang
134 B1 Chelan, Lake U.S.A.
103 E1 Chełm Pol.
99 D4 Chelmer *r.* U.K.
103 D1 Chełmno Pol.
99 D4 Chelmsford U.K.
99 B4 Cheltenham U.K.
87 F3 Chelyabinsk Rus. Fed.
101 F2 Chemnitz Ger.
Chemulpo S. Korea *see* Inch'ŏn
134 B2 Chemult U.S.A.
74 B2 Chenab *r.* India/Pak.
114 B2 Chenachane Alg.
134 C1 Cheney U.S.A.
Chengchow China *see* Zhengzhou
70 B1 Chengde China
70 A2 Chengdu China
71 A3 Chengguan China
Chengjiang China *see* Taihe
71 B4 Chengmai China
Chengshou China *see* Yingshan
Chengtu China *see* Chengdu
70 A2 Chengxian China
Chengxiang China *see* Wuxi
Chengxiang China *see* Mianning
Chengyang China *see* Juxian
73 C3 Chennai India
Chenstokhov Pol. *see* Częstochowa
71 B3 Chenzhou China
99 B4 Chepstow U.K.
141 E2 Cheraw U.S.A.
104 B2 Cherbourg-Octeville France
Cherchen China *see* Qiemo
89 E3 Cheremisinovo Rus. Fed.
68 C1 Cheremkhovo Rus. Fed.
89 E2 Cherepovets Rus. Fed.
91 C2 Cherkasy Ukr.
87 D4 Cherkessk Rus. Fed.
89 E3 Chern' Rus. Fed.
91 C1 Chernihiv Ukr.
91 D2 Cherninivka Ukr.
90 B2 Chernivtsi Ukr.
68 C1 Chernogorsk Rus. Fed.
90 B1 Chernyakhiv Ukr.
88 B3 Chernyakhovsk Rus. Fed.
89 E3 Chernyanka Rus. Fed.
69 D1 Chernyshevsk Rus. Fed.
83 I2 Chernyshevskiy Rus. Fed.
Chernyy Rynok Rus. Fed. *see* Kochubey
137 D2 Cherokee U.S.A.
83 L2 Cherskiy Rus. Fed.
83 K2 Cherskogo, Khrebet *mts* Rus. Fed.
91 E2 Chertkovo Rus. Fed.
Chervonoarmeyskoye Ukr. *see* Vil'nyans'k
Chervonoarmiys'k Ukr. *see* Krasnoarmiys'k
Chervonoarmiys'k Ukr. *see* Radyvyliv
90 A1 Chervonohrad Ukr.
88 C3 Chervyen' Belarus
89 D3 Cherykaw Belarus
139 D3 Chesapeake Bay U.S.A.
86 D2 Cheshskaya Guba *b.* Rus. Fed.
98 B3 Chester U.K.
138 B3 Chester *IL* U.S.A.
141 D2 Chester *SC* U.S.A.
139 D3 Chester *VA* U.S.A.
98 C3 Chesterfield U.K.
137 E3 Chesterfield U.S.A.
129 E1 Chesterfield Inlet Can.
129 E1 Chesterfield Inlet *inlet* Can.
139 F1 Chesuncook Lake U.S.A.
108 A3 Chetaïbi Alg.
131 D3 Chéticamp Can.
145 D3 Chetumal Mex.
128 B2 Chetwynd Can.
98 B2 Cheviot Hills U.K.
119 D2 Che'w Bahir *salt l.* Eth.
136 C2 Cheyenne U.S.A.
136 C2 Cheyenne *r.* U.S.A.
136 C3 Cheyenne Wells U.S.A.
75 C2 Chhapra India
75 B2 Chhatarpur India
75 C2 Chhattisgarh *state* India
74 B2 Chhindwara India
75 C2 Chhukha Bhutan
62 A2 Chiang Dao Thai.
120 A2 Chiange Angola
62 A2 Chiang Mai Thai.
62 A2 Chiang Rai Thai.

Cocos Islands

45 C3 Chiapa Mex.
08 A1 Chiavenna Italy
69 F2 Chiba Japan
70 B3 Chibi China
Chibizovka Rus. Fed. see Zherdevka
21 C3 Chiboma Moz.
30 C3 Chibougamau Can.
23 D1 Chibuto Moz.
75 D1 Chibuzhang Co l. China
38 B2 Chicago U.S.A.
28 A2 Chichagof Island U.S.A.
99 C4 Chichester U.K.
50 A2 Chichester Range mts Austr.
43 D1 Chickasha U.S.A.
06 B2 Chiclana de la Frontera Spain
50 B3 Chiclayo Peru
53 B4 Chico Chubut r. Arg.
53 B4 Chico Santa Cruz r. Arg.
35 B3 Chico U.S.A.
39 E2 Chicopee U.S.A.
64 B2 Chico Sapocoy, Mount Phil.
31 C3 Chicoutimi Can.
31 D1 Chidley, Cape Can.
63 A3 Chieo Lan, Ang Kep Nam Thai.
08 B2 Chieti Italy
45 C3 Chietla Mex.
70 B1 Chifeng China
55 D1 Chifre, Serra do mts Brazil
21 C2 Chifunde Moz.
45 C3 Chignahuapán Mex.
21 C3 Chigubo Moz.
62 A1 Chigu Co l. China
74 A1 Chihil Abdālān, Kōh-e mts Afgh.
44 B2 Chihuahua Mex.
88 C2 Chikhachevo Rus. Fed.
67 C3 Chikuma-gawa r. Japan
28 B2 Chilanko r. Can.
74 B1 Chilas Pak.
43 C2 Childress U.S.A.
53 A3 Chile country S. America
58 C6 Chile Basin S. Pacific Ocean
52 B2 Chilecito Arg.
157 G8 Chile Rise S. Pacific Ocean
75 C3 Chilika Lake India
121 B2 Chililabombwe Zambia
128 B2 Chilko r. Can.
128 B2 Chilko Lake Can.
153 A3 Chillán Chile
138 B2 Chillicothe IL U.S.A.
137 E3 Chillicothe MO U.S.A.
138 C3 Chillicothe OH U.S.A.
128 B3 Chilliwack Can.
153 A4 Chiloé, Isla de i. Chile
145 C3 Chilpancingo Mex.
53 C3 Chiltern Austr.
99 C4 Chiltern Hills U.K.
120 B1 Chiluage Angola
71 C3 Chilung Taiwan
119 D3 Chimala Tanz.
121 C2 Chimanimani Zimbabwe
152 B3 Chimbas Arg.
150 B3 Chimborazo mt. Ecuador
150 B3 Chimbote Peru
76 B2 Chimboy Uzbek.
Chimishliya Moldova see Cimişlia
Chimkent Kazakh. see Shymkent
121 C2 Chimoio Moz.
77 C3 Chimtargha, Qullai mt. Tajik.
68 C2 China country Asia
145 C2 China Mex.
150 B4 Chincha Alta Peru
128 C2 Chinchaga r. Can.
145 D3 Chinchorro, Banco Mex.
121 C2 Chinde Moz.
65 B3 Chindo S. Korea
65 B3 Chin-do i. S. Korea
68 C2 Chindu China
62 A1 Chindwin r. Myanmar
65 B2 Chinghwa N. Korea
121 B2 Chingola Zambia
120 A2 Chinguar Angola
65 B2 Chinhae S. Korea
121 C2 Chinhoyi Zimbabwe
Chini India see Kalpa
Chining China see Jining
74 B1 Chiniot Pak.
144 B2 Chinipas Mex.
65 B2 Chinju S. Korea
118 C2 Chinko r. C.A.R.
142 B1 Chinle U.S.A.
Chinnamp'o N. Korea see Namp'o
67 C3 Chino Japan
135 C4 Chino U.S.A.
104 C2 Chinon France
134 E1 Chinook U.S.A.
142 A2 Chino Valley U.S.A.
77 C2 Chinoz Uzbek.
121 C2 Chinsali Zambia
108 B1 Chioggia Italy
111 C3 Chios Greece
111 C3 Chios i. Greece
121 C2 Chipata Zambia
120 A2 Chipindo Angola
Chipinga Zimbabwe see Chipinge
121 C3 Chipinge Zimbabwe
73 B3 Chiplun India
99 B4 Chippenham U.K.
138 A2 Chippewa Falls U.S.A.
99 C4 Chipping Norton U.K.
Chipuriro Zimbabwe see Guruve
145 D3 Chiquimula Guat.
77 C2 Chirchiq Uzbek.
121 C3 Chiredzi Zimbabwe
142 B2 Chiricahua Peak U.S.A.
146 B4 Chiriquí, Golfo de b. Panama
65 B2 Chiri-san mt. S. Korea
146 B4 Chirripó mt. Costa Rica
121 B2 Chirundu Zimbabwe
130 C2 Chisasibi Can.
137 E1 Chisholm U.S.A.
Chisimaio Somalia see Kismaayo
90 B2 Chişinău Moldova
87 E3 Chistopol' Rus. Fed.
69 D1 Chita Rus. Fed.
120 A2 Chitado Angola
Chitaldrug India see Chitradurga
121 C2 Chitambo Zambia
120 B1 Chitato Angola
121 C1 Chitipa Malawi
121 C3 Chitobe Moz.
Chitor India see Chittaurgarh
66 D2 Chitose Japan
73 B3 Chitradurga India
74 B1 Chitral Pak.
146 B4 Chitré Panama
75 D2 Chittagong Bangl.
74 B2 Chittaurgarh India
73 B3 Chittoor India
Chittorgarh India see Chittaurgarh
121 C2 Chitungwiza Zimbabwe
120 B2 Chiume Angola
121 C2 Chivhu Zimbabwe
70 B2 Chizhou China
Chkalov Rus. Fed. see Orenburg
114 C1 Chlef Alg.
107 D2 Chlef, Oued r. Alg.
101 F2 Chodov Czech Rep.
153 B3 Choele Choel Arg.
Chogori Feng mt. China/Pakistan see K2
48 G4 Choiseul i. Solomon Is
144 B2 Choix Mex.
102 C1 Chojna Pol.
103 D1 Chojnice Pol.
117 B3 Ch'ok'ē Mountains Eth.
117 B3 Ch'ok'ē Terara mt. Eth.
Chokue Moz. see Chókwé
83 K2 Chokurdakh Rus. Fed.
121 C3 Chókwé Moz.
104 B2 Cholet France
145 C3 Cholula Mex.
120 B2 Choma Zambia
Chomo China see Yadong
102 C1 Chomutov Czech Rep.
83 I2 Chona r. Rus. Fed.
65 B2 Ch'ŏnan S. Korea
58 A2 Chon Buri Thai.
150 A3 Chone Ecuador
Chong'an China see Wuyishan
65 B1 Ch'ŏngjin N. Korea
65 B2 Chŏngju N. Korea
65 B2 Ch'ŏngju S. Korea
65 B2 Chŏngp'yŏng N. Korea
70 A3 Chongqing China
70 A2 Chongqing mun. China
65 B2 Chŏngŭp S. Korea
121 B2 Chongwe Zambia
71 A3 Chongzuo China
65 B2 Chŏnju S. Korea
153 A4 Chonos, Archipiélago de los is Chile
154 B3 Chopimzinho Brazil
111 B3 Chora Sfakion Greece
98 B3 Chorley U.K.
91 C2 Chornobay Ukr.
90 C1 Chornobyl' Ukr.
91 C2 Chornomors'ke Ukr.
90 B2 Chortkiv Ukr.
65 B2 Ch'ŏrwŏn S. Korea
65 B1 Ch'osan N. Korea
67 D3 Chōshi Japan
153 A3 Chos Malal Arg.
103 D1 Choszczno Pol.
134 D1 Choteau U.S.A.
114 A2 Choûm Maur.
69 D1 Choybalsan Mongolia
69 D1 Choyr Mongolia
54 B2 Christchurch N.Z.
99 C4 Christchurch U.K.
127 H2 Christian, Cape Can.
123 C2 Christiana S. Africa
Christianshåb Greenland see Qasigiannguit
54 A2 Christina, Mount N.Z.
58 B3 Christmas Island terr. Indian Ocean
111 B2 Chrysoupoli Greece
Chu Kazakh. see Shu
Chubarovka Ukr. see Polohy
153 B4 Chubut r. Arg.
89 F3 Chuchkovo Rus. Fed.
90 B1 Chudniv Ukr.
89 D2 Chudovo Rus. Fed.
126 C2 Chugach Mountains U.S.A.
67 B4 Chūgoku-sanchi mts Japan
Chuguchak China see Tacheng
66 B2 Chuguyevka Rus. Fed.
91 D2 Chuhuyiv Ukr.
Chukchi Peninsula pen. Rus. Fed. see Chukotskiy Poluostrov
160 J3 Chukchi Sea sea Rus. Fed./U.S.A.
89 F2 Chukhloma Rus. Fed.
83 N2 Chukotskiy Poluostrov pen. Rus. Fed.
Chulaktau Kazakh. see Karatau
135 C4 Chula Vista U.S.A.
82 G3 Chulym Rus. Fed.
152 B2 Chumbicha Arg.
83 K3 Chumikan Rus. Fed.
63 A2 Chumphon Thai.
65 B2 Ch'unch'ŏn S. Korea
Chungking China see Chongqing
Ch'ungmu S. Korea see T'ongyŏng
83 H2 Chunya r. Rus. Fed.
119 D3 Chunya Tanz.
150 B4 Chuquibamba Peru
152 B2 Chuquicamata Chile
105 D2 Chur Switz.
62 A1 Churachandpur India
83 J2 Churapcha Rus. Fed.
129 E2 Churchill Can.
129 E2 Churchill r. Man. Can.
131 D2 Churchill r. Nfld. and Lab. Can.
129 E2 Churchill, Cape Can.
131 D2 Churchill Falls Can.
129 D2 Churchill Lake Can.
74 B2 Churu India
63 B2 Chư Sê Vietnam
142 B1 Chuska Mountains U.S.A.
86 E3 Chusovoy Rus. Fed.
131 C3 Chute-des-Passes Can.
48 G3 Chuuk is Micronesia
62 B1 Chuxiong China
91 C2 Chyhyryn Ukr.
Chymyshliya Moldova see Cimişlia
Ciadâr-Lunga Moldova see Ciadîr-Lunga
90 B2 Ciadîr-Lunga Moldova
60 B2 Ciamis Indon.
60 B2 Cianjur Indon.
154 B2 Cianorte Brazil
142 A2 Cibuta, Sierra mt. Mex.
80 B1 Cide Turkey
103 E1 Ciechanów Pol.
146 C2 Ciego de Ávila Cuba
147 C3 Ciénaga Col.
146 B2 Cienfuegos Cuba
107 C2 Cieza Spain
106 C2 Cigüela r. Spain
80 B2 Cihanbeyli Turkey
144 B3 Cihuatlán Mex.
106 C2 Cíjara, Embalse de resr Spain
109 C2 Çikës, Maja e mt. Albania
60 B2 Cilacap Indon.
Cill Airne Ireland see Killarney
Cill Chainnigh Ireland see Kilkenny
143 C1 Cimarron r. U.S.A.
90 B2 Cimişlia Moldova
108 B2 Cimone, Monte mt. Italy
Cîmpina Romania see Câmpina
Cîmpulung Romania see Câmpulung
60 B2 Cina, Tanjung c. Indon.
138 C3 Cincinnati U.S.A.
Cinco de Outubro Angola see Xá-Muteba
111 C3 Çine Turkey
100 B2 Ciney Belgium
134 C2 Cinnabar Mountain U.S.A.
145 C3 Cintalapa Mex.
71 B3 Ciping China
153 B3 Cipolletti Arg.
126 C2 Circle AK U.S.A.
136 B1 Circle MT U.S.A.
60 B2 Cirebon Indon.
99 C4 Cirencester U.K.
108 A1 Ciriè Italy
109 C3 Cirò Marina Italy
110 B1 Cisnădie Romania
109 C2 Čitluk Bos.-Herz.
122 A3 Citrusdal S. Africa
135 B3 Citrus Heights U.S.A.
110 C1 Ciucaş, Vârful mt. Romania
145 B2 Ciudad Acuña Mex.
145 B3 Ciudad Altamirano Mex.
150 C2 Ciudad Bolívar Venez.
147 C4 Ciudad Bolivia Venez.
144 B2 Ciudad Camargo Mex.
144 A2 Ciudad Constitución Mex.
145 C3 Ciudad Cuauhtémoc Mex.
145 C3 Ciudad del Carmen Mex.
154 B3 Ciudad del Este Para.
144 B2 Ciudad Delicias Mex.
145 C2 Ciudad de Valles Mex.
150 C2 Ciudad Guayana Venez.
142 B3 Ciudad Guerrero Mex.
144 B3 Ciudad Guzmán Mex.
145 C3 Ciudad Hidalgo Mex.
145 C3 Ciudad Ixtepec Mex.
144 B1 Ciudad Juárez Mex.
145 C2 Ciudad Madero Mex.
145 C2 Ciudad Mante Mex.
145 C2 Ciudad Mier Mex.
144 B2 Ciudad Obregón Mex.
106 C2 Ciudad Real Spain
145 C2 Ciudad Río Bravo Mex.
106 B1 Ciudad Rodrigo Spain
Ciudad Trujillo Dom. Rep. see Santo Domingo
145 C2 Ciudad Victoria Mex.
107 D1 Ciutadella Spain
108 B1 Cividale del Friuli Italy
108 B2 Civitanova Marche Italy
108 B2 Civitavecchia Italy
104 C2 Civray France
111 C3 Çivril Turkey
70 C2 Cixi China
99 D4 Clacton-on-Sea U.K.
128 C2 Claire, Lake Can.
105 C2 Clamecy France
140 C2 Clanton U.S.A.
122 A3 Clanwilliam S. Africa
97 C2 Clara Ireland
52 A2 Clare Austr.
138 C2 Clare U.S.A.
97 A2 Clare Island Ireland
139 E2 Claremont U.S.A.
97 B2 Claremorris Ireland
54 B2 Clarence N.Z.
55 B3 Clarence Island Antarctica
131 E3 Clarenville Can.
128 C2 Claresholm Can.
137 D2 Clarinda U.S.A.
144 A3 Clarión, Isla i. Mex.
123 C3 Clarkebury S. Africa
141 D2 Clark Hill Reservoir U.S.A.
138 C3 Clarksburg U.S.A.
140 B2 Clarksdale U.S.A.
134 C1 Clarks Fork r. U.S.A.
134 C1 Clarkston U.S.A.
140 B1 Clarksville AR U.S.A.
140 C1 Clarksville TN U.S.A.
154 B1 Claro r. Brazil
143 C1 Claude U.S.A.
143 C1 Clayton U.S.A.
97 B3 Clear, Cape Ireland
126 C3 Cleare, Cape U.S.A.
137 E2 Clear Lake U.S.A.
135 B3 Clear Lake l. U.S.A.
128 C2 Clearwater Can.
129 C2 Clearwater r. Can.
141 D3 Clearwater U.S.A.
134 C1 Clearwater r. U.S.A.
143 D2 Cleburne U.S.A.
101 E1 Clenze Ger.
51 D2 Clermont Austr.
105 C2 Clermont-Ferrand France
100 C2 Clervaux Lux.
52 A2 Cleve Austr.
140 B2 Cleveland MS U.S.A.
138 C2 Cleveland OH U.S.A.
141 D1 Cleveland TN U.S.A.
134 D1 Cleveland, Mount U.S.A.
154 B3 Clevelândia Brazil
97 B2 Clew Bay Ireland
141 D3 Clewiston U.S.A.
97 A2 Clifden Ireland
53 D1 Clifton Austr.
142 B2 Clifton U.S.A.
142 B1 Clines Corners U.S.A.
128 B2 Clinton Can.
137 E2 Clinton IA U.S.A.
137 E3 Clinton MO U.S.A.
143 D1 Clinton OK U.S.A.
125 H8 Clipperton, Île terr. N. Pacific Ocean
96 A2 Clisham h. U.K.
98 B3 Clitheroe U.K.
97 B3 Clonakilty Ireland
51 D2 Cloncurry Austr.
97 C1 Clones Ireland
97 C2 Clonmel Ireland
101 D1 Cloppenburg Ger.
137 E1 Cloquet U.S.A.
50 A2 Cloud Break Austr.
136 B2 Cloud Peak U.S.A.
135 C3 Clovis CA U.S.A.
143 C2 Clovis NM U.S.A.
Cluain Meala Ireland see Clonmel
129 D2 Cluff Lake Mine Can.
110 B1 Cluj-Napoca Romania
51 C2 Cluny Austr.
105 D2 Cluses France
54 A3 Clutha r. N.Z.
96 B3 Clyde r. U.K.
96 B3 Clyde, Firth of est. U.K.
96 B3 Clydebank U.K.
127 H2 Clyde River Can.
144 B3 Coalcomán Mex.
128 C3 Coaldale Can.
135 C3 Coaldale U.S.A.
128 B2 Coal River Can.
150 C3 Coari Brazil
150 C3 Coari r. Brazil
141 C2 Coastal Plain U.S.A.
128 B2 Coast Mountains Can.
134 B2 Coast Ranges mts U.S.A.
96 B3 Coatbridge U.K.
129 F1 Coats Island Can.
55 C2 Coats Land reg. Antarctica
145 C3 Coatzacoalcos Mex.
146 A3 Cobán Guat.
53 C2 Cobar Austr.
97 B3 Cobh Ireland
152 B1 Cobija Bol.
Coblenz Ger. see Koblenz
130 C3 Cobourg Can.
50 C1 Cobourg Peninsula Austr.
53 C3 Cobram Austr.
101 E2 Coburg Ger.
152 B1 Cochabamba Bol.
100 C2 Cochem Ger.
Cochin India see Kochi
128 C2 Cochrane Alta Can.
130 B3 Cochrane Ont. Can.
153 A4 Cochrane Chile
52 A2 Cockaleechie Austr.
52 B2 Cockburn Austr.
Cockburn Town Turks and Caicos Is see Grand Turk
98 B2 Cockermouth U.K.
50 B3 Cocklebiddy Austr.
122 B3 Cockscomb mt. S. Africa
146 B3 Coco r. Hond./Nic.
125 J9 Coco, Isla de i. N. Pacific Ocean
159 F4 Cocos Basin Indian Ocean
58 A3 Cocos Islands terr. Indian Ocean

146 C3 Cruz, Cabo *c.* Cuba
152 C2 Cruz Alta Brazil
152 B3 Cruz del Eje Arg.
155 D2 Cruzeiro Brazil
150 B3 Cruzeiro do Sul Brazil
52 A2 Crystal Brook Austr.
135 C1 Crystal City U.S.A.
138 B1 Crystal Falls U.S.A.
140 B2 Crystal Springs U.S.A.
103 E2 Csongrád Hungary
143 D3 Csorna Hungary
121 C2 Cuamba Moz.
120 B2 Cuando *r.* Angola/Zambia
120 A2 Cuangar Angola
118 B3 Cuango *r.* Angola/Dem. Rep. Congo
120 A1 Cuanza *r.* Angola
144 B3 Cuatro Ciénegas Mex.
145 C3 Cuauhtémoc Mex.
145 C3 Cuautla Mex.
146 B2 Cuba *country* West Indies
120 A1 Cubal Angola
120 B2 Cubango *r.* Angola/Namibia
150 B3 Cúcuta Col.
73 B3 Cuddalore India
73 B3 Cuddapah India
50 A2 Cue Austr.
106 C1 Cuéllar Spain
120 A2 Cuemba Angola
150 B3 Cuenca Ecuador
107 C1 Cuenca Spain
107 C1 Cuenca, Serranía de *mts* Spain
145 C3 Cuernavaca Mex.
143 D3 Cuero U.S.A.
104 C3 Cugnaux France
151 D4 Cuiabá Brazil
151 D4 Cuiabá *r.* Brazil
96 A2 Cuillin Sound *sea chan.* U.K.
120 A1 Cuilo Angola
120 B2 Cuito *r.* Angola
120 A2 Cuito Cuanavale Angola
60 B1 Cukai Malaysia
64 B2 Culasi Phil.
53 C3 Culcairn Austr.
100 B2 Culemborg Neth.
53 C1 Culgoa *r.* Austr.
144 B2 Culiacán Mex.
64 A2 Culion *i.* Phil.
107 C2 Cullera Spain
140 C2 Cullman U.S.A.
97 C1 Cullybackey U.K.
139 D3 Culpeper U.S.A.
151 D4 Culuene *r.* Brazil
54 B2 Culverden N.Z.
150 C1 Cumaná Venez.
139 D3 Cumberland U.S.A.
138 B3 Cumberland *r.* U.S.A.
141 D2 Cumberland Island U.S.A.
129 D2 Cumberland Lake Can.
127 H2 Cumberland Peninsula Can.
140 C1 Cumberland Plateau U.S.A.
127 H2 Cumberland Sound *sea chan.* Can.
96 C3 Cumbernauld U.K.
135 B3 Cummings U.S.A.
96 B3 Cumnock U.K.
144 B1 Cumpas Mex.
145 C3 Cunduacán Mex.
108 A2 Cuneo Italy
53 C1 Cunnamulla Austr.
108 A1 Cuorgnè Italy
96 C2 Cupar U.K.
110 B2 Ćuprija Serbia
147 D3 Curaçao *terr.* West Indies
150 B3 Curaray *r.* Ecuador
153 A3 Curicó Chile
154 C3 Curitiba Brazil
52 A2 Curnamona Austr.
135 C3 Currant U.S.A.
51 D3 Currie Austr.
135 D2 Currie U.S.A.
51 E2 Curtis Island Austr.
151 C2 Curuá *r.* Brazil
60 B2 Curup Indon.
151 E3 Cururupu Brazil
155 D1 Curvelo Brazil
150 B4 Cusco Peru
97 C1 Cushendun U.K.
143 D1 Cushing U.S.A.
136 C2 Custer U.S.A.
134 D1 Cut Bank U.S.A.
140 B3 Cut Off U.S.A.
75 C2 Cuttack India
120 A2 Cuvelai Angola
101 D1 Cuxhaven Ger.
64 B2 Cuyo Islands Phil.
Cuzco Peru *see* Cusco
99 B4 Cwmbrân U.K.
119 C3 Cyangugu Rwanda
111 B3 Cyclades *is* Greece
129 C3 Cypress Hills Can.
80 B2 Cyprus *country* Asia
80 B2 Cyprus *i.* Asia
102 C2 Czech Republic *country* Europe
103 D1 Czersk Pol.
103 D1 Częstochowa Pol.

D

Đa, Sông *r.* Vietnam *see* Black River
69 D2 Daban China
103 D2 Dabas Hungary
114 A3 Dabola Guinea
103 D1 Dąbrowa Górnicza Pol.

110 B2 Dăbuleni Romania
Dacca Bangl. *see* Dhaka
102 C2 Dachau Ger.
Dachuan China *see* Dazhou
141 D3 Dade City U.S.A.
Dadong China *see* Donggang
Dadra India *see* Achalpur
74 B2 Dadra and Nagar Haveli *union terr.* India
74 A2 Dadu Pak.
Daegu S. Korea *see* Taegu
64 B2 Daet Phil.
114 A3 Dagana Senegal
119 D2 Daga Post S. Sudan
88 C2 Dagda Latvia
64 B2 Dagupan Phil.
74 B3 Dahanu India
69 D2 Da Hinggan Ling *mts* China
116 C3 Dahlak Archipelago *is* Eritrea
100 C2 Dahlem Ger.
78 B3 Dahm, Ramlat *des.* Saudi Arabia/Yemen
74 B2 Dahod India
Dahomey *country* Africa *see* Benin
Dahra Senegal *see* Dara
81 C2 Dahūk Iraq
60 B2 Daik Indon.
106 C2 Daimiel Spain
Dairen China *see* Dalian
51 C2 Dajarra Austr.
70 A2 Dajing China
114 A3 Dakar Senegal
117 C4 Daketa Shet' *watercourse* Eth.
Dakhla Oasis *oasis* Egypt *see* Wāḥāt ad Dākhilah
63 A3 Dakoank India
88 C3 Dakol'ka *r.* Belarus
Đakovica Kosovo *see* Gjakovë
109 C1 Đakovo Croatia
120 B2 Dala Angola
70 A1 Dalain Hob China
93 G3 Dalälven *r.* Sweden
111 C3 Dalaman Turkey
111 C3 Dalaman *r.* Turkey
68 C2 Dalandzadgad Mongolia
64 B2 Dalanganem Islands Phil.
63 B2 Đa Lat Vietnam
74 A2 Dalbandin Pak.
96 C3 Dalbeattie U.K.
53 D1 Dalby Austr.
93 E3 Dale Norway
141 C1 Dale Hollow Lake U.S.A.
53 C3 Dalgety Austr.
143 C1 Dalhart U.S.A.
131 D3 Dalhousie Can.
62 B1 Dali China
70 C2 Dalian China
96 C3 Dalkeith U.K.
143 D2 Dallas U.S.A.
128 A2 Dall Island U.S.A.
Dalmacija *reg.* Bos.-Herz./Croatia *see* Dalmatia
96 B2 Dalmally U.K.
109 C2 Dalmatia *reg.* Bos.-Herz./Croatia
96 B3 Dalmellington U.K.
66 C2 Dal'negorsk Rus. Fed.
66 B1 Dal'nerechensk Rus. Fed.
Dalny China *see* Dalian
114 B4 Daloa Côte d'Ivoire
71 A3 Dalou Shan *mts* China
51 D2 Dalrymple, Mount Austr.
92 □A3 Dalsmynni Iceland
75 C2 Daltenganj India
141 D2 Dalton U.S.A.
Daltenganj India *see* Daltenganj
60 B1 Daludalu Indon.
71 B3 Daluo Shan *mt.* China
92 □B2 Dalvík Iceland
96 B2 Dalwhinnie U.K.
50 C1 Daly *r.* Austr.
51 C1 Daly Waters Austr.
74 B2 Daman India
74 B2 Daman and Diu *union terr.* India
116 B1 Damanhūr Egypt
59 C3 Damar *i.* Indon.
118 B2 Damara C.A.R.
80 B2 Damascus Syria
115 D3 Damaturu Nigeria
76 B3 Damāvand, Qolleh-ye *mt.* Iran
120 A1 Damba Angola
118 B1 Damboa Nigeria
81 D2 Dāmghān Iran
Damietta Egypt *see* Dumyāṭ
79 C2 Dammam Saudi Arabia
101 D1 Damme Ger.
75 B2 Damoh India
114 B4 Damongo Ghana
50 A2 Dampier Austr.
59 C3 Dampir, Selat *sea chan.* Indon.
75 C2 Damqoq Zangbo *r.* China
Damxung China *see* Gongtang
117 C3 Danakil *reg.* Africa
114 B4 Danané Côte d'Ivoire
63 B2 Đa Năng Vietnam
139 E2 Danbury U.S.A.
70 C1 Dandong China
117 B3 Dangila Eth.
146 B3 Dangriga Belize
70 B2 Dangshan China
89 F2 Danilov Rus. Fed.

89 E2 Danilovskaya Vozvyshennost' *hills* Rus. Fed.
70 B2 Danjiangkou China
79 C2 Ḏank Oman
89 E3 Dankov Rus. Fed.
146 B3 Danlí Hond.
101 E1 Dannenberg (Elbe) Ger.
54 C2 Dannevirke N.Z.
62 B2 Dan Sai Thai.
Dantu China *see* Zhenjiang
110 A1 Danube *r.* Europe
110 C2 Danube Delta Romania/Ukr.
138 B2 Danville IL U.S.A.
138 C3 Danville KY U.S.A.
139 D3 Danville VA U.S.A.
Danxian China *see* Danzhou
71 A4 Danzhou China
Danzig, Gulf of *g.* Pol./Rus. Fed. *see* Gdańsk, Gulf of
Daojiang China *see* Daoxian
115 D2 Dao Timmi Niger
Daoud Alg. *see* Aïn Beïda
114 B4 Daoukro Côte d'Ivoire
71 B3 Daoxian China
64 B3 Dapa Phil.
114 C3 Dapaong Togo
64 B3 Dapitan Phil.
68 C2 Da Qaidam China
69 E1 Daqing China
114 A3 Dara Senegal
80 B2 Dar'ā Syria
81 D3 Dārāb Iran
81 D2 Dārān Iran
Đaravica *mt.* Kosovo *see* Gjeravicë
75 C2 Darbhanga India
Dardo China *see* Kangding
119 D3 Dar es Salaam Tanz.
117 A3 Darfur *reg.* Sudan
74 B1 Dargai Pak.
54 B1 Dargaville N.Z.
53 C3 Dargo Austr.
68 D1 Darhan Mongolia
150 B1 Darién, Golfo del *g.* Col.
Darjeeling India *see* Darjiling
75 C2 Darjiling India
52 B2 Darling *r.* Austr.
53 C1 Darling Downs *hills* Austr.
50 A3 Darling Range *hills* Austr.
98 C2 Darlington U.K.
53 C2 Darlington Point Austr.
103 D1 Darłowo Pol.
101 D3 Darmstadt Ger.
115 E1 Darnah Libya
52 B2 Darnick Austr.
55 H3 Darnley, Cape Antarctica
107 C1 Daroca Spain
99 D4 Dartford U.K.
99 A4 Dartmoor *hills* U.K.
131 D3 Dartmouth Can.
99 B4 Dartmouth U.K.
59 D3 Daru P.N.G.
59 C2 Daruba Indon.
50 C1 Darwin Austr.
153 C5 Darwin Falkland Is
79 C2 Dārzīn Iran
65 A1 Dashiqiao China
Dashkhovuz Turkm. *see* Daşoguz
74 A2 Dasht *r.* Pak.
76 B2 Daşoguz Turkm.
61 C1 Datadian Indon.
111 C3 Datça Turkey
66 D2 Date Japan
71 B3 Datian China
70 B1 Datong China
64 B3 Datu Piang Phil.
74 B1 Daud Khel Pak.
88 B2 Daugava *r.* Latvia
88 C2 Daugavpils Latvia
100 C2 Daun Ger.
129 D2 Dauphin Can.
129 E2 Dauphin Lake Can.
73 B3 Davangere India
64 B3 Davao Phil.
64 B3 Davao Gulf Phil.
137 E2 Davenport U.S.A.
99 C3 Daventry U.K.
123 C2 Daveyton S. Africa
146 B4 David Panama
129 D2 Davidson Can.
126 F3 Davidson Lake Can.
135 B3 Davis U.S.A.
131 D2 Davis Inlet (abandoned) Can.
55 I3 Davis Sea *sea* Antarctica
160 P3 Davis Strait *str.* Can./Greenland
105 D2 Davos Switz.
88 C3 Davyd-Haradok Belarus
78 A2 Dawmat al Jandal Saudi Arabia
79 C3 Dawqah Oman
78 B3 Dawqah Saudi Arabia
126 C2 Dawson Can.
141 D2 Dawson U.S.A.
128 B2 Dawson Creek Can.
128 B2 Dawsons Landing Can.
68 C2 Dawu China
71 C3 Dawu Taiwan
Dawukou China *see* Shizuishan
79 C2 Dawwah Oman
104 B3 Dax France
Daxian China *see* Dazhou
68 C2 Da Xueshan *mts* China
52 B3 Daylesford Austr.
Dayong China *see* Zhangjiajie
81 C2 Dayr az Zawr Syria
138 C3 Dayton U.S.A.

141 D3 Daytona Beach U.S.A.
71 B3 Dayu China
Da Yunhe *canal* China *see* Jinghang Yunhe
79 C2 Dayyer Iran
70 A2 Dazhou China
122 B3 De Aar S. Africa
141 D3 Deadman Bay U.S.A.
80 B2 Dead Sea *salt l.* Asia
99 D4 Deal U.K.
71 B3 De'an China
152 B3 Deán Funes Arg.
128 B2 Dease Lake Can.
126 E2 Dease Strait Can.
135 C3 Death Valley *depr.* U.S.A.
104 C2 Deauville France
61 C1 Debak Malaysia
111 B2 Debar Macedonia
101 E1 Dębica Pol.
103 E1 Dęblin Pol.
114 B3 Débo, Lac *l.* Mali
103 E2 Debrecen Hungary
117 B3 Debre Markos Eth.
119 D2 Debre Sīna Eth.
117 B3 Debre Tabor Eth.
117 B4 Debre Zeyit Eth.
140 C2 Decatur AL U.S.A.
138 B3 Decatur IL U.S.A.
73 B3 Deccan *plat.* India
53 D1 Deception Bay Austr.
71 A3 Dechang China
102 C1 Děčín Czech Rep.
137 E2 Decorah U.S.A.
154 C2 Dedo de Deus *mt.* Brazil
88 C2 Dedovichi Rus. Fed.
121 C2 Dedza Malawi
99 B3 Dee *r.* England/Wales U.K.
96 C2 Dee *r.* Scotland U.K.
130 C3 Deep River Can.
53 D1 Deepwater Austr.
131 E3 Deer Lake Can.
134 D1 Deer Lodge U.S.A.
138 C2 Defiance U.S.A.
140 C2 De Funiak Springs U.S.A.
68 C2 Dêgê China
117 C4 Degeh Bur Eth.
139 F1 Dégelis Can.
102 C2 Deggendorf Ger.
91 E2 Degtevo Rus. Fed.
81 C2 Dehlorān Iran
74 B1 Dehra Dun India
75 C2 Dehri India
69 E2 Dehui China
100 A2 Deinze Belgium
110 B1 Dej Romania
138 B2 De Kalb U.S.A.
116 B3 Dekemhare Eritrea
118 C3 Dekese Dem. Rep. Congo
118 B2 Dékoa C.A.R.
141 D3 De Land U.S.A.
135 C3 Delano U.S.A.
135 D3 Delano Peak U.S.A.
48 I3 Delap-Uliga-Djarrit Marshall Is
123 C2 Delareyville S. Africa
129 D2 Delaronde Lake Can.
139 D3 Delaware U.S.A.
139 D3 Delaware *r.* U.S.A.
139 D3 Delaware *state* U.S.A.
139 D3 Delaware Bay U.S.A.
53 C3 Delegate Austr.
118 C2 Délembé C.A.R.
105 D2 Delémont Switz.
100 B1 Delft Neth.
100 C1 Delfzijl Neth.
121 D2 Delgado, Cabo *c.* Moz.
68 C1 Delgerhaan Mongolia
68 C2 Delhi China
74 B2 Delhi India
60 B2 Deli *i.* Indon.
128 B1 Dĕljine Can.
Delingha China *see* Delhi
101 F2 Delitzsch Ger.
107 D2 Dellys Alg.
135 C4 Del Mar U.S.A.
101 D1 Delmenhorst Ger.
109 B1 Delnice Croatia
136 B3 Del Norte U.S.A.
83 L1 De-Longa, Ostrova *is* Rus. Fed.
De Long Islands *is* Rus. Fed. *see* De-Longa, Ostrova
De Long Strait *sea chan.* Rus. Fed. *see* Longa, Proliv
129 D3 Deloraine Can.
111 B3 Delphi *tourist site* Greece
141 D3 Delray Beach U.S.A.
143 C3 Del Rio U.S.A.
136 B3 Delta CO U.S.A.
135 D3 Delta UT U.S.A.
135 D3 Delta Junction U.S.A.
109 D3 Delvinë Albania
106 C1 Demanda, Sierra de la *mts* Spain
Demavend *mt.* Iran *see* Damāvand, Qolleh-ye
118 C3 Demba Dem. Rep. Congo
119 D1 Dembech'a Eth.
117 B4 Dembī Dolo Eth.
Demerara Guyana *see* Georgetown
91 C3 Demerdzhi *mt.* Ukr.
89 D2 Demidov Rus. Fed.
142 B2 Deming U.S.A.
111 C3 Demirci Turkey
111 C2 Demirköy Turkey
102 C1 Demmin Ger.
140 C2 Demopolis U.S.A.

E

F

Franca

154 C2 **Franca** Brazil
109 C2 **Francavilla Fontana** Italy
104 C2 **France** *country* Europe
118 B3 **Franceville** Gabon
137 D2 **Francis Case, Lake** U.S.A.
155 D1 **Francisco Sá** Brazil
120 B3 **Francistown** Botswana
128 B2 **François Lake** Can.
100 B1 **Franeker** Neth.
101 D2 **Frankenberg (Eder)** Ger.
101 D3 **Frankenthal (Pfalz)** Ger.
101 E2 **Frankenwald** *mts* Ger.
138 C3 **Frankfort** *KY* U.S.A.
138 B2 **Frankfort** *MI* U.S.A.
Frankfurt Ger. *see* **Frankfurt am Main**
101 D2 **Frankfurt am Main** Ger.
102 C1 **Frankfurt an der Oder** Ger.
102 C2 **Fränkische Alb** *hills* Ger.
101 E3 **Fränkische Schweiz** *reg.* Ger.
139 E2 **Franklin** *NH* U.S.A.
139 D2 **Franklin** *PA* U.S.A.
140 C1 **Franklin** *TN* U.S.A.
126 D2 **Franklin Bay** Can.
134 C1 **Franklin D. Roosevelt Lake** U.S.A.
128 B1 **Franklin Mountains** Can.
126 F2 **Franklin Strait** Can.
53 C3 **Frankston** Austr.
82 E1 **Frantsa-Iosifa, Zemlya** *is* Rus. Fed.
54 B2 **Franz Josef Glacier** N.Z.
Franz Josef Land *is* Rus. Fed. *see* **Frantsa-Iosifa, Zemlya**
108 A3 **Frasca, Capo della** *c.* Italy
128 B3 **Fraser** *r.* B.C. Can.
131 D2 **Fraser** *r. Nfld. and Lab.* Can.
122 B3 **Fraserburg** S. Africa
96 C2 **Fraserburgh** U.K.
130 B3 **Fraserdale** Can.
51 E2 **Fraser Island** Austr.
128 B2 **Fraser Lake** Can.
128 B2 **Fraser Plateau** Can.
153 C3 **Fray Bentos** Uru.
93 E4 **Fredericia** Denmark
143 D2 **Frederick** U.S.A.
143 D2 **Fredericksburg** *TX* U.S.A.
139 D3 **Fredericksburg** *VA* U.S.A.
128 A2 **Frederick Sound** *sea chan.* U.S.A.
131 D3 **Fredericton** Can.
Frederikshåb Greenland *see* **Paamiut**
93 F4 **Frederikshavn** Denmark
Fredrikshamn Fin. *see* **Hamina**
93 F4 **Fredrikstad** Norway
138 B2 **Freeport** *IL* U.S.A.
143 D3 **Freeport** *TX* U.S.A.
146 C2 **Freeport City** Bahamas
143 D3 **Freer** U.S.A.
123 C2 **Free State** *prov.* S. Africa
114 A4 **Freetown** Sierra Leone
106 B2 **Fregenal de la Sierra** Spain
104 B2 **Fréhel, Cap** *c.* France
102 B2 **Freiburg im Breisgau** Ger.
102 C2 **Freising** Ger.
102 C2 **Freistadt** Austria
105 D3 **Fréjus** France
50 A3 **Fremantle** Austr.
135 B3 **Fremont** *CA* U.S.A.
137 D2 **Fremont** *NE* U.S.A.
138 C2 **Fremont** *OH* U.S.A.
French Congo *country* Africa *see* **Congo**
151 D2 **French Guiana** *terr.* S. America
French Guinea *country* Africa *see* **Guinea**
134 E1 **Frenchman** *r.* U.S.A.
49 M5 **French Polynesia** *terr.* S. Pacific Ocean
French Somaliland *country* Africa *see* **Djibouti**
French Sudan *country* Africa *see* **Mali**
French Territory of the Afars and Issas *country* Africa *see* **Djibouti**
151 D3 **Fresco** *r.* Brazil
144 B2 **Fresnillo** Mex.
135 C3 **Fresno** U.S.A.
107 D2 **Freu, Cap des** *c.* Spain
105 D2 **Freyming-Merlebach** France
114 A3 **Fria** Guinea
152 B2 **Frias** Arg.
101 D2 **Friedberg (Hessen)** Ger.
102 B2 **Friedrichshafen** Ger.
101 F1 **Friesack** Ger.
100 C1 **Friesoythe** Ger.
143 C2 **Friona** U.S.A.
136 B3 **Frisco** U.S.A.
Frobisher Bay Can. *see* **Iqaluit**
127 H2 **Frobisher Bay** *b.* Can.
101 F2 **Frohburg** Ger.
87 D4 **Frolovo** Rus. Fed.
103 D1 **Frombork** Pol.
99 B4 **Frome** U.K.
52 A2 **Frome, Lake** *imp. l.* Austr.
52 A2 **Frome Downs** Austr.
100 C2 **Fröndenberg** Ger.
143 C3 **Frontera** Mex.
145 C3 **Frontera** Mex.
144 B1 **Fronteras** Mex.
139 D3 **Front Royal** U.S.A.
108 B2 **Frosinone** Italy
92 E3 **Frøya** *i.* Norway
Frunze Kyrg. *see* **Bishkek**
154 C2 **Frutal** Brazil
105 D2 **Frutigen** Switz.
103 D2 **Frýdek-Místek** Czech Rep.
71 B3 **Fu'an** China
71 C3 **Fuding** China
106 C1 **Fuenlabrada** Spain
152 C2 **Fuerte Olimpo** Para.
114 A2 **Fuerteventura** *i.* Islas Canarias
64 B2 **Fuga** *i.* Phil.
79 C2 **Fujairah** U.A.E.
67 C3 **Fuji** Japan
71 B3 **Fujian** *prov.* China
67 C3 **Fujinomiya** Japan
67 C3 **Fuji-san** *vol.* Japan
Fukien *prov.* China *see* **Fujian**
67 C3 **Fukui** Japan
67 B4 **Fukuoka** Japan
67 D3 **Fukushima** Japan
101 D2 **Fulda** Ger.
101 D2 **Fulda** *r.* Ger.
70 A3 **Fuling** China
137 E3 **Fulton** U.S.A.
105 C2 **Fumay** France
49 I4 **Funafuti** *atoll* Tuvalu
114 A1 **Funchal** Arquipélago da Madeira
155 D1 **Fundão** Brazil
106 B1 **Fundão** Port.
131 D3 **Fundy, Bay of** *g.* Can.
121 C3 **Funhalouro** Moz.
70 B2 **Funing** *Jiangsu* China
71 A3 **Funing** *Yunnan* China
115 C3 **Funtua** Nigeria
79 C2 **Fürgun, Küh-e** *mt.* Iran
89 F2 **Furmanov** Rus. Fed.
Furmanovka Kazakh. *see* **Moyynkum**
Furmanovo Kazakh. *see* **Zhalpaktal**
155 C2 **Furnas, Represa** *resr* Brazil
51 D4 **Furneaux Group** *is* Austr.
Furong China *see* **Wan'an**
100 C1 **Fürstenau** Ger.
101 E3 **Fürth** Ger.
66 D3 **Furukawa** Japan
127 G2 **Fury and Hecla Strait** Can.
70 C1 **Fushun** China
65 B1 **Fusong** China
79 C2 **Fuwayriţ** Qatar
Fuxian China *see* **Wafangdian**
70 A2 **Fuxian** China
70 C1 **Fuxin** China
70 B2 **Fuyang** China
69 E1 **Fuyu** China
Fuyu China *see* **Songyuan**
68 B1 **Fuyun** China
71 B3 **Fuzhou** *Fujian* China
71 B3 **Fuzhou** *Jiangxi* China
93 F4 **Fyn** *i.* Denmark
96 B3 **Fyne, Loch** *inlet* U.K.
F.Y.R.O.M. *country* Europe *see* **Macedonia**

G

117 C4 **Gaalkacyo** Somalia
120 A2 **Gabela** Angola
Gaberones Botswana *see* **Gaborone**
115 D1 **Gabès** Tunisia
115 D1 **Gabès, Golfe de** *g.* Tunisia
118 B3 **Gabon** *country* Africa
123 C1 **Gaborone** Botswana
79 C2 **Gābrīk** Iran
110 C2 **Gabrovo** Bulg.
114 A3 **Gabú** Guinea-Bissau
73 B3 **Gadag** India
75 C2 **Gadchiroli** India
101 E1 **Gadebusch** Ger.
140 C2 **Gadsden** U.S.A.
118 B2 **Gadzi** C.A.R.
110 C2 **Găeşti** Romania
108 B2 **Gaeta** Italy
108 B2 **Gaeta, Golfo di** *g.* Italy
141 D1 **Gaffney** U.S.A.
115 C1 **Gafsa** Tunisia
89 E2 **Gagarin** Rus. Fed.
109 C3 **Gagliano del Capo** Italy
114 B4 **Gagnoa** Côte d'Ivoire
131 D2 **Gagnon** Can.
Gago Coutinho Angola *see* **Lumbala N'guimbo**
81 C1 **Gagra** Georgia
122 A2 **Gaiab** *watercourse* Namibia
111 C3 **Gaïdouronisi** *i.* Greece
104 C3 **Gaillac** France
Gaillimh Ireland *see* **Galway**
141 D3 **Gainesville** *FL* U.S.A.
141 D2 **Gainesville** *GA* U.S.A.
143 D2 **Gainesville** *TX* U.S.A.
98 C3 **Gainsborough** U.K.
52 A2 **Gairdner, Lake** *imp. l.* Austr.
96 B2 **Gairloch** U.K.
122 B2 **Gakarosa** *mt.* S. Africa
119 E3 **Galana** *r.* Kenya
103 D2 **Galanta** Slovakia
Galápagos, Islas *is* Ecuador *see* **Galapagos Islands**
125 I10 **Galapagos Islands** *is* Ecuador
157 G6 **Galapagos Rise** Pacific Ocean
96 C3 **Galashiels** U.K.
110 C1 **Galaţi** Romania
93 E3 **Galdhøpiggen** *mt.* Norway
145 B2 **Galeana** Mex.
128 C2 **Galena Bay** Can.
138 A2 **Galesburg** U.S.A.
122 B2 **Galeshewe** S. Africa
89 F2 **Galich** Rus. Fed.
106 B1 **Galicia** *aut. comm.* Spain
80 B2 **Galilee, Sea of** *l.* Israel
78 A3 **Gallabat** Sudan
140 C1 **Gallatin** U.S.A.
73 C4 **Galle** Sri Lanka
157 G6 **Gallego Rise** Pacific Ocean
150 B1 **Gallinas, Punta** *pt* Col.
109 C2 **Gallipoli** Italy
111 C2 **Gallipoli** Turkey
92 H2 **Gällivare** Sweden
142 B1 **Gallup** U.S.A.
117 C4 **Galmudug** *reg.* Somalia
114 A2 **Galtat Zemmour** Western Sahara
97 B2 **Galtymore** *h.* Ireland
143 E3 **Galveston** U.S.A.
143 E3 **Galveston Bay** U.S.A.
143 E3 **Galveston Island** U.S.A.
97 B2 **Galway** Ireland
97 B2 **Galway Bay** Ireland
154 C1 **Gamá** Brazil
123 D3 **Gamalakhe** S. Africa
117 B4 **Gambēla** Eth.
114 A3 **Gambia** *r.* Gambia
114 A3 **Gambia, The** *country* Africa
49 N6 **Gambier, Îles** *is* Fr. Polynesia
52 A3 **Gambier Islands** Austr.
131 E3 **Gambo** Can.
118 B3 **Gamboma** Congo
128 C1 **Gamêtî** Can.
92 H2 **Gammelstaden** Sweden
142 B1 **Ganado** U.S.A.
123 C2 **Ga-Nala** S. Africa
81 C1 **Gäncä** Azer.
61 C2 **Gandadiwata, Bukit** *mt.* Indon.
118 C3 **Gandajika** Dem. Rep. Congo
106 B1 **Gándara** Spain
131 E3 **Gander** Can.
131 E3 **Gander** *r.* Can.
101 D1 **Ganderkesee** Ger.
107 D1 **Gandesa** Spain
74 B2 **Gandhidham** India
74 B2 **Gandhinagar** India
74 B2 **Gandhi Sagar** *resr* India
107 C2 **Gandia** Spain
Ganga *r.* Bangl./India *see* **Ganges**
153 B4 **Gangán** Arg.
74 B2 **Ganganagar** India
62 A1 **Gangaw** Myanmar
68 C2 **Gangca** China
75 C1 **Gangdisê Shan** *mts* China
75 D2 **Ganges** *r.* Bangl./India
105 C3 **Ganges** France
75 C2 **Ganges, Mouths of the** Bangl./India
159 E2 **Ganges Cone** Indian Ocean
75 C2 **Gangtok** India
75 C3 **Ganjam** India
71 B3 **Gan Jiang** *r.* China
71 A3 **Ganluo** China
105 C2 **Gannat** France
136 B2 **Gannett Peak** U.S.A.
122 A3 **Gansbaai** S. Africa
70 A1 **Gansu** *prov.* China
115 D4 **Ganye** Nigeria
71 B3 **Ganzhou** China
114 B3 **Gao** Mali
Gaoleshan China *see* **Xianfeng**
97 B1 **Gaoth Dobhair** Ireland
114 B3 **Gaoua** Burkina Faso
114 A3 **Gaoual** Guinea
71 C3 **Gaoxiong** Taiwan
70 B2 **Gaoyou** China
70 B2 **Gaoyou Hu** *l.* China
105 D3 **Gap** France
64 B2 **Gapan** Phil.
75 C1 **Gar** China
97 B2 **Gara, Lough** *l.* Ireland
76 C3 **Garabil Belentligi** *hills* Turkm.
76 B2 **Garabogaz** Turkm.
76 B2 **Garabogazköl** Turkm.
76 B2 **Garabogazköl Aýlagy** *b.* Turkm.
117 C4 **Garacad** Somalia
53 C1 **Garah** Austr.
151 F3 **Garanhuns** Brazil
123 C2 **Ga-Rankuwa** S. Africa
118 C1 **Garar, Plaine de** *plain* Chad
117 C4 **Garbahaarrey** Somalia
135 B2 **Garberville** U.S.A.
101 D1 **Garbsen** Ger.
154 C2 **Garça** Brazil
154 B2 **Garcias** Brazil
108 B1 **Garda, Lake** *l.* Italy
108 A3 **Garde, Cap de** *c.* Alg.
101 E1 **Gardelegen** Ger.
136 C3 **Garden City** U.S.A.
129 E2 **Garden Hill** Can.
77 C3 **Gardēz** Afgh.
139 F2 **Gardiner** U.S.A.
Gardner *atoll* Micronesia *see* **Faraulep**
135 C3 **Gardnerville** U.S.A.
136 B3 **Garfield** U.S.A.
88 B2 **Gargždai** Lith.
123 C3 **Gariep Dam** *dam* S. Africa
122 A3 **Garies** S. Africa
119 D3 **Garissa** Kenya
88 B2 **Garkalne** Latvia
143 D2 **Garland** U.S.A.
102 C2 **Garmisch-Partenkirchen** Ger.
52 B3 **Garnpung Lake** *imp. l.* Austr.
104 B3 **Garonne** *r.* France
117 C4 **Garoowe** Somalia
74 B2 **Garoth** India
118 B2 **Garoua** Cameroon
118 B2 **Garoua Boulai** Cameroon
Garqêntang China *see* **Sog**
96 B2 **Garry** *r.* U.K.
126 F2 **Garry Lake** Can.
119 E3 **Garsen** Kenya
76 B2 **Garşy** Turkm.
122 A2 **Garub** Namibia
60 B2 **Garut** Indon.
138 B2 **Gary** U.S.A.
145 B2 **Garza García** Mex.
68 C2 **Garzê** China
Gascogne *reg.* France *see* **Gascony**
Gascogne, Golfe de *g.* France *see* **Gascony, Gulf of**
104 B3 **Gascony** *reg.* France
104 B3 **Gascony, Gulf of** France
50 A2 **Gascoyne** *r.* Austr.
118 B2 **Gashaka** Nigeria
115 D3 **Gashua** Nigeria
59 E3 **Gasmata** P.N.G.
131 D3 **Gaspé** Can.
131 D3 **Gaspésie, Péninsule de la** *pen.* Ca
141 E1 **Gaston, Lake** U.S.A.
141 D1 **Gastonia** U.S.A.
107 C2 **Gata, Cabo de** *c.* Spain
88 D2 **Gatchina** Rus. Fed.
98 C2 **Gateshead** U.K.
143 D2 **Gatesville** U.S.A.
139 D1 **Gatineau** Can.
130 C3 **Gatineau** *r.* Can.
Gatooma Zimbabwe *see* **Kadoma**
53 D1 **Gatton** Austr.
129 E2 **Gauer Lake** Can.
93 E4 **Gausta** *mt.* Norway
123 C2 **Gauteng** *prov.* S. Africa
79 C2 **Gāvbandī** Iran
111 B3 **Gavdos** *i.* Greece
93 G3 **Gävle** Sweden
93 G3 **Gävlebukten** *b.* Sweden
89 F2 **Gavrilov Posad** Rus. Fed.
89 E2 **Gavrilov-Yam** Rus. Fed.
122 A2 **Gawachab** Namibia
62 A1 **Gawai** Myanmar
52 A2 **Gawler** Austr.
52 A2 **Gawler Ranges** *hills* Austr.
75 C2 **Gaya** India
114 C3 **Gaya** Niger
114 C3 **Gayéri** Burkina Faso
138 C1 **Gaylord** U.S.A.
86 E2 **Gayny** Rus. Fed.
116 B1 **Gaza** *terr.* Asia
80 B2 **Gaza** Gaza
80 B2 **Gaziantep** Turkey
76 C2 **Gazojak** Turkm.
114 B4 **Gbarnga** Liberia
118 A2 **Gboko** Nigeria
103 D1 **Gdańsk** Pol.
88 A3 **Gdańsk, Gulf of** Pol./Rus. Fed.
88 C2 **Gdov** Rus. Fed.
103 D1 **Gdynia** Pol.
116 B3 **Gedaref** Sudan
101 D2 **Gedern** Ger.
111 C3 **Gediz** Turkey
111 C3 **Gediz** *r.* Turkey
102 C1 **Gedser** Denmark
100 B2 **Geel** Belgium
52 B3 **Geelong** Austr.
101 E1 **Geesthacht** Ger.
75 C1 **Gê'gyai** China
129 D2 **Geikie** *r.* Can.
93 E3 **Geilo** Norway
119 D3 **Geita** Tanz.
71 A3 **Gejiu** China
108 B3 **Gela** Italy
108 B3 **Gela, Golfo di** *g.* Italy
91 D3 **Gelendzhik** Rus. Fed.
Gelibolu Turkey *see* **Gallipoli**
100 C2 **Gelsenkirchen** Ger.
118 B2 **Gemena** Dem. Rep. Congo
111 C2 **Gemlik** Turkey
108 B1 **Gemona del Friuli** Italy
117 C4 **Genalē Wenz** *r.* Eth.
81 C3 **Genāveh** Iran
153 B3 **General Acha** Arg.
153 B3 **General Alvear** Arg.
153 C3 **General Belgrano** Arg.
144 B2 **General Cepeda** Mex.
General Freire Angola *see* **Muxaluando**
General Machado Angola *see* **Camacupa**
153 B3 **General Pico** Arg.
153 B3 **General Roca** Arg.
154 B2 **General Salgado** Brazil
64 B3 **General Santos** Phil.
139 D2 **Genesee** *r.* U.S.A.
138 A2 **Geneseo** *IL* U.S.A.
139 D2 **Geneseo** *NY* U.S.A.
105 D2 **Geneva** Switz.
139 D2 **Geneva** U.S.A.
105 D2 **Geneva, Lake** *l.* France/Switz.
Genève Switz. *see* **Geneva**
106 B2 **Genil** *r.* Spain
100 B2 **Genk** Belgium
53 C3 **Genoa** Austr.
108 A2 **Genoa** Italy
108 A2 **Genoa, Gulf of** *g.* Italy
Genova Italy *see* **Genoa**
Gent Belgium *see* **Ghent**
61 C2 **Genteng** *i.* Indon.
101 F1 **Genthin** Ger.
50 A3 **Geographe Bay** Austr.
131 D2 **George** *r.* Can.
122 B3 **George** S. Africa
52 A3 **George, Lake** Austr.
141 D3 **George, Lake** *FL* U.S.A.
139 E2 **George, Lake** *NY* U.S.A.

Grandview

146 C2 George Town Bahamas
114 A3 Georgetown Gambia
151 D2 Georgetown Guyana
60 B1 George Town Malaysia
138 C3 Georgetown *KY* U.S.A.
141 E2 Georgetown *SC* U.S.A.
143 D2 Georgetown *TX* U.S.A.
55 L2 George V Land *reg.* Antarctica
81 C1 Georgia *country* Asia
141 D2 Georgia *state* U.S.A.
130 B3 Georgian Bay Can.
51 C2 Georgina *watercourse* Austr.
Georgiu-Dezh Rus. Fed. *see* Liski
77 E2 Georgiyevka Kazakh.
87 D4 Georgiyevsk Rus. Fed.
101 F2 Gera Ger.
151 E4 Geral de Goiás, Serra *hills* Brazil
54 B2 Geraldine N.Z.
50 A2 Geraldton Austr.
80 B1 Gerede Turkey
102 C2 Geretsried Ger.
135 C2 Gerlach U.S.A.
103 E2 Gerlachovský štit *mt.* Slovakia
139 D3 Germantown U.S.A.
102 C1 Germany *country* Europe
100 C2 Gerolstein Ger.
101 E3 Gerolzhofen Ger.
53 D2 Gerringong Austr.
101 D2 Gersfeld (Rhön) Ger.
Géryville Alg. *see* El Bayadh
75 C1 Gêrzê China
106 C1 Getafe Spain
139 D3 Gettysburg *PA* U.S.A.
136 D1 Gettysburg *SD* U.S.A.
55 P2 Getz Ice Shelf Antarctica
111 B2 Gevgelija Macedonia
111 C3 Geyikli Turkey
122 B2 Ghaap Plateau S. Africa
Ghadamés Libya *see* Ghadāmis
115 C1 Ghadāmis Libya
75 C2 Ghaghara *r.* India
114 B4 Ghana *country* Africa
120 B3 Ghanzi Botswana
115 C1 Ghardaïa Alg.
78 A2 Ghārib, Jabal *mt.* Egypt
115 D1 Gharyān Libya
115 D2 Ghāt Libya
75 C2 Ghatal India
75 B2 Ghaziabad India
75 C2 Ghazipur India
77 C3 Ghaznī Afgh.
78 B2 Ghazzālah Saudi Arabia
100 A2 Ghent Belgium
Gheorghe Gheorghiu-Dej Romania *see* Onești
110 C1 Gheorgheni Romania
110 B1 Gherla Romania
105 D3 Ghisonaccia France
74 B2 Ghotaru India
74 A2 Ghotki Pak.
75 C2 Ghugri *r.* India
76 C3 Ghūrīān Afgh.
91 E3 Giaginskaya Rus. Fed.
97 C1 Giant's Causeway *lava field* U.K.
61 C2 Gianyar Indon.
109 C3 Giarre Italy
108 A1 Giaveno Italy
122 A2 Gibeon Namibia
106 B2 Gibraltar Gibraltar
106 B2 Gibraltar, Strait of Morocco/Spain
140 B2 Gibsland U.S.A.
50 B2 Gibson Desert Austr.
68 C1 Gichgeniyn Nuruu *mts* Mongolia
117 B4 Gīdolē Eth.
105 C2 Gien France
101 D2 Gießen Ger.
101 E1 Gifhorn Ger.
128 C2 Gift Lake Can.
67 C3 Gifu Japan
96 B3 Gigha *i.* U.K.
76 C2 G'ijduvon Uzbek.
106 B1 Gijón Spain
142 A2 Gila *r.* U.S.A.
142 A2 Gila Bend U.S.A.
51 D1 Gilbert *r.* Austr.
48 I4 Gilbert Islands *is* Kiribati
156 D5 Gilbert Ridge Pacific Ocean
151 E3 Gilbués Brazil
134 D1 Gildford U.S.A.
Gilf Kebir Plateau *plat.* Egypt *see* Haḍabat al Jilf al Kabīr
53 C2 Gilgandra Austr.
74 B1 Gilgit Pak.
74 B1 Gilgit *r.* Pak.
53 C2 Gilgunnia Austr.
129 E2 Gillam Can.
136 B2 Gillette U.S.A.
99 D4 Gillingham U.K.
130 C2 Gilmour Island Can.
135 B3 Gilroy U.S.A.
129 E2 Gimli Can.
64 B3 Gingoog Phil.
117 C4 Gīnīr Eth.
109 C2 Ginosa Italy
109 C2 Gioia del Colle Italy
53 C3 Gippsland *reg.* Austr.
74 A2 Girdar Dhor *r.* Pak.
79 D1 Girdī Iran
80 B1 Giresun Turkey
Girgenti Italy *see* Agrigento
53 C2 Girilambone Austr.
76 C3 Girishk Afgh.
Giron Sweden *see* Kiruna
107 D1 Girona Spain
104 B2 Gironde *est.* France
53 C2 Girral Austr.
96 B3 Girvan U.K.
54 C1 Gisborne N.Z.
93 F4 Gislaved Sweden
119 C3 Gitarama Rwanda
119 C3 Gitega Burundi
Giuba *r.* Somalia *see* Jubba
108 B2 Giulianova Italy
110 C2 Giurgiu Romania
110 C1 Giuvala, Pasul *pass* Romania
105 C2 Givors France
123 D1 Giyani S. Africa
119 D2 Giyon Eth.
116 B2 Giza Egypt
103 E1 Giżycko Pol.
109 D2 Gjakovë Kosovo
109 D2 Gjeravicë *mt.* Kosovo
110 D2 Gjilan Kosovo
109 D2 Gjirokastër Albania
126 F2 Gjoa Haven Can.
93 F3 Gjøvik Norway
131 E3 Glace Bay Can.
134 B1 Glacier Peak *vol.* U.S.A.
143 E2 Gladewater U.S.A.
51 E2 Gladstone *Qld* Austr.
52 A2 Gladstone *S.A.* Austr.
92 □A2 Gláma *mts* Iceland
109 C2 Glamoč Bos.-Herz.
100 C3 Glan *r.* Ger.
97 B2 Glanaruddery Mountains *hills* Ireland
96 B3 Glasgow U.K.
138 B3 Glasgow *KY* U.S.A.
136 B1 Glasgow *MT* U.S.A.
99 B4 Glastonbury U.K.
101 F2 Glauchau Ger.
86 E3 Glazov Rus. Fed.
89 E3 Glazunovka Rus. Fed.
123 D2 Glencoe S. Africa
96 B2 Glen Coe *val.* U.K.
142 A2 Glendale *AZ* U.S.A.
138 B2 Glendale *WI* U.S.A.
53 D2 Glen Davis Austr.
51 D2 Glenden Austr.
136 C1 Glendive U.S.A.
52 B3 Glenelg *r.* Austr.
96 B2 Glenfinnan U.K.
53 D1 Glen Innes Austr.
96 B2 Glen More *val.* U.K.
53 C1 Glenmorgan Austr.
126 C2 Glennallen U.S.A.
134 C2 Glenns Ferry U.S.A.
136 B2 Glenrock U.S.A.
96 C2 Glenrothes U.K.
139 E2 Glens Falls U.S.A.
96 C2 Glen Shee *val.* U.K.
97 B1 Glenties Ireland
142 B2 Glenwood U.S.A.
136 B3 Glenwood Springs U.S.A.
101 E1 Glinde Ger.
103 D1 Gliwice Pol.
142 A2 Globe U.S.A.
103 D1 Głogów Pol.
92 F2 Glomfjord Norway
93 F4 Glomma *r.* Norway
53 D2 Gloucester Austr.
99 B4 Gloucester U.K.
131 E3 Glovertown Can.
101 F1 Glöwen Ger.
77 E1 Glubokoye Kazakh.
101 D1 Glückstadt Ger.
103 C2 Gmünd Austria
102 C2 Gmunden Austria
101 D1 Gnarrenburg Ger.
103 D1 Gniezno Pol.
Gnjilane Kosovo *see* Gjilan
75 D2 Goalpara India
96 B3 Goat Fell *h.* U.K.
117 C4 Goba Eth.
122 A1 Gobabis Namibia
153 A4 Gobernador Gregores Arg.
152 C2 Gobernador Virasoro Arg.
68 D2 Gobi *des.* China/Mongolia
67 C4 Gobō Japan
100 C2 Goch Ger.
122 A1 Gochas Namibia
74 B3 Godavari *r.* India
73 C3 Godavari, Mouths of the India
75 C2 Godda India
117 C4 Godē Eth.
130 B3 Goderich Can.
Godhavn Greenland *see* Qeqertarsuaq
74 B2 Godhra India
129 E2 Gods *r.* Can.
129 E2 Gods Lake Can.
Godthåb Greenland *see* Nuuk
Godwin-Austen, Mount *mt.* China/Pakistan *see* K2
Goedgegun Swaziland *see* Nhlangano
130 C3 Goéland, Lac au *l.* Can.
131 D2 Goélands, Lac aux *l.* Can.
100 A2 Goes Neth.
138 B1 Gogebic Range *hills* U.S.A.
88 C1 Gogland, Ostrov *i.* Rus. Fed.
Gogra *r.* India *see* Ghaghara
119 C2 Gogrial S. Sudan
154 C1 Goiandira Brazil
154 C1 Goianésia Brazil
154 C1 Goiânia Brazil
154 B1 Goiás Brazil
154 B1 Goiás *state* Brazil
154 C1 Goiatuba Brazil
154 B2 Goio-Erê Brazil
111 C2 Gökçeada *i.* Turkey
111 C3 Gökçedağ Turkey
121 B2 Gokwe Zimbabwe
93 E3 Gol Norway
62 A1 Golaghat India
111 C2 Gölcük Turkey
103 E1 Gołdap Pol.
101 F1 Goldberg Ger.
Gold Coast *country* Africa *see* Ghana
53 D1 Gold Coast Austr.
114 B4 Gold Coast *coastal area* Ghana
128 C2 Golden Can.
54 B2 Golden Bay N.Z.
134 B1 Goldendale U.S.A.
128 B3 Golden Hinde *mt.* Can.
97 B2 Golden Vale *lowland* Ireland
135 C3 Goldfield U.S.A.
128 B3 Gold River Can.
141 E1 Goldsboro U.S.A.
103 C1 Goleniów Pol.
135 C4 Goleta U.S.A.
Golfe du St-Laurent *g.* Can. *see* St Lawrence, Gulf of
111 C3 Gölhisar Turkey
Gollel Swaziland *see* Lavumisa
75 D1 Golmud China
81 D2 Golpāyegān Iran
96 C2 Golspie U.K.
Golyshi Rus. Fed. *see* Vetluzhskiy
119 C3 Goma Dem. Rep. Congo
75 C2 Gomati *r.* India
115 D3 Gombe Nigeria
115 D3 Gombi Nigeria
Gomel' Belarus *see* Homyel'
144 B2 Gómez Palacio Mex.
81 D2 Gomīshān Iran
75 C1 Gomo China
147 C3 Gonaïves Haiti
147 C3 Gonâve, Île de la *i.* Haiti
81 D2 Gonbad-e Kāvūs Iran
74 B2 Gondal India
Gondar Eth. *see* Gonder
116 B3 Gonder Eth.
75 C2 Gondia India
111 C2 Gönen Turkey
62 A1 Gonggar China
70 A3 Gongga Shan *mt.* China
68 C2 Gonghe China
115 D4 Gongola *r.* Nigeria
53 C2 Gongolgon Austr.
75 D1 Gongtang China
123 C3 Gonubie S. Africa
145 C2 Gonzáles Mex.
143 D3 Gonzales U.S.A.
122 A3 Good Hope, Cape of S. Africa
134 D2 Gooding U.S.A.
136 C3 Goodland U.S.A.
53 C1 Goodooga Austr.
98 C3 Goole U.K.
53 C2 Goolgowi Austr.
52 A3 Goolwa Austr.
53 D1 Goondiwindi Austr.
134 B2 Goose Lake U.S.A.
102 B2 Göppingen Ger.
75 C2 Gorakhpur India
109 C2 Goražde Bos.-Herz.
111 C3 Gördes Turkey
89 D3 Gordeyevka Rus. Fed.
136 C2 Gordon U.S.A.
51 D4 Gordon, Lake Austr.
115 D4 Goré Chad
117 B4 Gorē Eth.
54 A3 Gore N.Z.
97 C2 Gorey Ireland
81 D2 Gorgān Iran
81 C1 Gori Georgia
100 B2 Gorinchem Neth.
108 B1 Gorizia Italy
Gor'kiy Rus. Fed. *see* Nizhniy Novgorod
89 F2 Gor'kovskoye Vodokhranilishche *resr* Rus. Fed.
103 E2 Gorlice Pol.
103 C1 Görlitz Ger.
Gorna Dzhumaya Bulg. *see* Blagoevgrad
109 D2 Gornji Milanovac Serbia
109 C2 Gornji Vakuf Bos.-Herz.
77 E1 Gorno-Altaysk Rus. Fed.
86 F2 Gornopravdinsk Rus. Fed.
110 C2 Gornotrakiyska Nizina *lowland* Bulg.
66 D1 Gornozavodsk Rus. Fed.
77 E1 Gornyak Rus. Fed.
59 D3 Goroka P.N.G.
52 B3 Goroke Austr.
114 B3 Gorom Gorom Burkina Faso
121 C2 Gorongosa Moz.
61 D1 Gorontalo Indon.
89 E3 Gorshechnoye Rus. Fed.
97 B2 Gorumna Island Ireland
91 D3 Goryachiy Klyuch Rus. Fed.
103 D1 Gorzów Wielkopolski Pol.
59 E3 Goschen Strait P.N.G.
53 D2 Gosford Austr.
74 A2 Goshanak Pak.
66 D2 Goshogawara Japan
101 E2 Goslar Ger.
109 C2 Gospić Croatia
99 C4 Gosport U.K.
111 B2 Gostivar Macedonia
Göteborg Sweden *see* Gothenburg
101 E2 Gotha Ger.
93 F4 Gothenburg Sweden
136 C2 Gothenburg U.S.A.
93 G4 Gotland *i.* Sweden
111 B2 Gotse Delchev Bulg.
93 G4 Gotska Sandön *i.* Sweden
67 B4 Gōtsu Japan
101 D2 Göttingen Ger.
128 B2 Gott Peak Can.
Gottwaldow Czech Rep. *see* Zlín
Gotval'd Ukr. *see* Zmiyiv
100 B1 Gouda Neth.
114 A3 Goudiri Senegal
115 D3 Goudoumaria Niger
158 E7 Gough Island S. Atlantic Ocean
130 C3 Gouin, Réservoir *resr* Can.
53 C2 Goulburn Austr.
53 D2 Goulburn *r. N.S.W.* Austr.
53 C3 Goulburn *r. Vic.* Austr.
114 B3 Goundam Mali
107 D2 Gouraya Alg.
114 B3 Gourcy Burkina Faso
104 C3 Gourdon France
115 D3 Gouré Niger
122 B3 Gourits *r.* S. Africa
114 B3 Gourma-Rharous Mali
53 C3 Gourock Range *mts* Austr.
155 D1 Governador Valadares Brazil
141 E3 Governor's Harbour Bahamas
68 C2 Govĭ Altayn Nuruu *mts* Mongolia
75 C2 Govind Ballash Pant Sagar *resr* India
99 A3 Gower *pen.* U.K.
152 C2 Goya Arg.
81 C1 Göyçay Azer.
80 B1 Göynük Turkey
115 E3 Goz-Beïda Chad
75 C1 Gozha Co *salt l.* China
122 B3 Graaff-Reinet S. Africa
122 A3 Graafwater S. Africa
101 E1 Grabow Ger.
109 C2 Gračac Croatia
87 E3 Grachevka Rus. Fed.
109 C2 Gradačac Bos.-Herz.
104 B3 Gradignan France
101 F2 Gräfenhainichen Ger.
53 D1 Grafton Austr.
137 D1 Grafton U.S.A.
143 D2 Graham U.S.A.
142 B2 Graham, Mount U.S.A.
Graham Bell Island *i.* Rus. Fed. *see* Greem-Bell, Ostrov
128 A2 Graham Island Can.
55 A3 Graham Land *pen.* Antarctica
123 C3 Grahamstown S. Africa
97 C2 Graiguenamanagh Ireland
151 E3 Grajaú Brazil
103 E1 Grajewo Pol.
111 B2 Grammos *mt.* Greece
96 B2 Grampian Mountains U.K.
146 B3 Granada Nic.
106 C2 Granada Spain
97 C2 Granard Ireland
139 E1 Granby Can.
114 A2 Gran Canaria *i.* Islas Canarias
152 B3 Gran Chaco *reg.* Arg./Para.
136 F2 Grand *r. MO* U.S.A.
136 C1 Grand *r. SD* U.S.A.
146 C2 Grand Bahama *i.* Bahamas
131 E3 Grand Bank Can.
158 D2 Grand Banks of Newfoundland N. Atlantic Ocean
Grand Canal *canal* China *see* Jinghang Yunhe
Grand Canary *i.* Islas Canarias *see* Gran Canaria
142 A1 Grand Canyon U.S.A.
142 A1 Grand Canyon *gorge* U.S.A.
146 B3 Grand Cayman *i.* Cayman Is
129 C2 Grand Centre Can.
134 C1 Grand Coulee U.S.A.
152 B1 Grande *r.* Bol.
154 B2 Grande *r.* Brazil
153 B5 Grande, Bahía *b.* Arg.
155 D2 Grande, Ilha *i.* Brazil
150 C2 Grande, Serra *mt.* Brazil
128 C2 Grande Cache Can.
Grande Comore *i.* Comoros *see* Ngazidja
128 C2 Grande Prairie Can.
114 B1 Grand Erg Occidental *des.* Alg.
115 C2 Grand Erg Oriental *des.* Alg.
131 D3 Grande-Rivière Can.
152 B3 Grandes, Salinas *salt flat* Arg.
131 D3 Grand Falls Can.
131 E3 Grand Falls-Windsor Can.
128 C3 Grand Forks Can.
137 D1 Grand Forks U.S.A.
138 B2 Grand Haven U.S.A.
128 C1 Grandin, Lac *l.* Can.
137 D2 Grand Island U.S.A.
140 B3 Grand Isle U.S.A.
136 B3 Grand Junction U.S.A.
114 B4 Grand-Lahou Côte d'Ivoire
131 D3 Grand Lake *N.B.* Can.
131 E3 Grand Lake *Nfld. and Lab.* Can.
137 E1 Grand Marais U.S.A.
130 C3 Grand-Mère Can.
106 B2 Grândola Port.
129 E2 Grand Rapids Can.
138 B2 Grand Rapids *MI* U.S.A.
137 E1 Grand Rapids *MN* U.S.A.
136 A2 Grand Teton *mt.* U.S.A.
147 C2 Grand Turk Turks and Caicos Is
129 D2 Grandview Can.
134 C1 Grandview U.S.A.

Herāt

116 A2 Ḥadabat al Jilf al Kabīr Egypt
79 C2 Ḥadd, Ra's al *pt* Oman
96 C3 Haddington U.K.
115 D3 Hadejia Nigeria
93 E4 Haderslev Denmark
78 B2 Ḥādhah Saudi Arabia
79 B3 Ḥaḑramawt *reg.* Yemen
79 B3 Ḥaḑramawt, Wādī *watercourse* Yemen
91 C1 Hadyach Ukr.
65 B2 Haeju N. Korea
65 B2 Haeju-man *b.* N. Korea
65 B3 Haenam S. Korea
78 B2 Ḥafar al Bāṭin Saudi Arabia
74 B1 Hafizabad Pak.
75 D2 Haflong India
92 □A3 Hafnarfjörður Iceland
78 A3 Hagar Nish Plateau Eritrea/Sudan
59 D2 Hagåtña Guam
101 F1 Hagelberg *h.* Ger.
100 C2 Hagen Ger.
101 E1 Hagenow Ger.
128 B2 Hagensborg Can.
139 D3 Hagerstown U.S.A.
93 F3 Hagfors Sweden
134 D1 Haggin, Mount U.S.A.
67 B4 Hagi Japan
62 B1 Ha Giang Vietnam
97 B2 Hag's Head *hd* Ireland
104 B2 Hague, Cap de la *c.* France
69 F3 Hahajima-rettō *is* Japan
119 D3 Hai Tanz.
Haicheng China *see* Haifeng
70 C1 Haicheng China
128 A2 Haida Gwaii Can.
62 B1 Hai Dương Vietnam
80 B2 Haifa Israel
71 B3 Haifeng China
Haikang China *see* Leizhou
71 B3 Haikou China
78 B2 Ḥā'il Saudi Arabia
Hailar China *see* Hulun Buir
Hailong China *see* Meihekou
92 H2 Hailuoto *i.* Fin.
71 A4 Hainan *prov.* China
69 D3 Hainan Dao *i.* China
128 A2 Haines U.S.A.
128 A1 Haines Junction Can.
101 E2 Hainich *ridge* Ger.
101 E2 Hainleite *ridge* Ger.
Haiphong Vietnam *see* Hai Phong
62 B1 Hai Phong Vietnam
147 C3 Haiti *country* West Indies
116 B3 Haiya Sudan
103 E2 Hajdúböszörmény Hungary
103 E2 Hajdúszoboszló Hungary
67 C3 Hajiki-zaki *pt* Japan
78 B3 Ḥajjah Yemen
81 D3 Ḥājjīābād Iran
103 E1 Hajnówka Pol.
62 A1 Haka Myanmar
81 C2 Hakkâri Turkey
66 D2 Hakodate Japan
122 B2 Hakseen Pan *salt pan* S. Africa
Ḥalab Syria *see* Aleppo
78 B2 Halabān Saudi Arabia
81 C2 Ḥalabja Iraq
116 B2 Halaib Sudan
78 A2 Halaib Triangle *terr.* Egypt/Sudan
79 C3 Ḥalāniyāt, Juzur al *is* Oman
78 A2 Ḥālat 'Ammār Saudi Arabia
Halban Mongolia *see* Tsetserleg
101 E2 Halberstadt Ger.
64 B2 Halcon, Mount Phil.
93 F4 Halden Norway
101 E1 Haldensleben Ger.
75 B2 Haldwani India
79 C2 Hāleh Iran
54 A3 Halfmoon Bay N.Z.
139 D1 Haliburton Highlands *hills* Can.
131 D3 Halifax Can.
98 C3 Halifax U.K.
139 D3 Halifax U.S.A.
65 B3 Halla-san *mt.* S. Korea
127 G2 Hall Beach Can.
100 B2 Halle Belgium
101 E2 Halle (Saale) Ger.
102 C2 Hallein Austria
101 E2 Halle-Neustadt Ger.
48 G3 Hall Islands Micronesia
137 D1 Hallock U.S.A.
127 H2 Hall Peninsula Can.
50 B1 Halls Creek Austr.
59 C2 Halmahera *i.* Indon.
93 F4 Halmstad Sweden
62 B1 Ha Long Vietnam
Hälsingborg Sweden *see* Helsingborg
100 B2 Halsteren Neth.
98 B2 Haltwhistle U.K.
67 B4 Hamada Japan
81 C2 Hamadān Iran
80 B2 Ḥamāh Syria
67 C4 Hamamatsu Japan
93 F3 Hamar Norway
116 B2 Ḥamāṭah, Jabal *mt.* Egypt
73 C4 Hambantota Sri Lanka
101 D1 Hamburg Ger.
123 C3 Hamburg S. Africa
140 B2 Hamburg U.S.A.
78 A2 Ḥamḍ, Wādī al *watercourse* Saudi Arabia
78 B3 Ḥamḍah Saudi Arabia
139 E2 Hamden U.S.A.
93 H3 Hämeenlinna Fin.
101 D1 Hameln Ger.
50 A2 Hamersley Range *mts* Austr.
65 B1 Hamgyŏng-sanmaek *mts* N. Korea
65 B2 Hamhŭng N. Korea
68 C2 Hami China
116 B2 Hamid Sudan
52 B3 Hamilton Austr.
130 C3 Hamilton Can.
Hamilton *r.* Can. *see* Churchill
54 C1 Hamilton N.Z.
96 B3 Hamilton U.K.
140 C2 Hamilton *AL* U.S.A.
134 D1 Hamilton *MT* U.S.A.
138 C3 Hamilton *OH* U.S.A.
115 E1 Hamīm, Wādī al *watercourse* Libya
93 I3 Hamina Fin.
100 C2 Hamm Ger.
115 D1 Hammamet, Golfe de *g.* Tunisia
81 C2 Ḥammār, Hawr al *imp. l.* Iraq
101 D2 Hammelburg Ger.
92 G3 Hammerdal Sweden
92 H1 Hammerfest Norway
140 B2 Hammond U.S.A.
139 E3 Hammonton U.S.A.
139 D3 Hampton U.S.A.
139 E2 Hampton Bays U.S.A.
115 D2 Ḥamrā', Al Ḥamādah al *plat.* Libya
78 A2 Ḥanak Saudi Arabia
66 D3 Hanamaki Japan
101 D2 Hanau Ger.
69 D2 Hanbogd Mongolia
70 B2 Hancheng China
138 B1 Hancock U.S.A.
70 B2 Handan China
119 D3 Handeni Tanz.
135 C3 Hanford U.S.A.
68 C1 Hangayn Nuruu *mts* Mongolia
Hangchow China *see* Hangzhou
Hanggin Houqi China *see* Xamba
Hangö Fin. *see* Hanko
70 B2 Hangu China
70 C2 Hangzhou China
70 C2 Hangzhou Wan *b.* China
79 B2 Ḥanīdh Saudi Arabia
Hanjia China *see* Pengshui
Hanjiang China *see* Yangzhou
93 H4 Hanko Fin.
135 D3 Hanksville U.S.A.
54 B2 Hanmer Springs N.Z.
128 C2 Hanna Can.
136 B2 Hanna U.S.A.
137 E3 Hannibal U.S.A.
101 D1 Hannover Ger.
101 D2 Hannoversch Münden Ger.
93 F4 Hanöbukten *b.* Sweden
Hanoi Vietnam *see* Ha Nôi
62 B1 Ha Nôi Vietnam
130 B3 Hanover Can.
Hanover Ger. *see* Hannover
122 B3 Hanover S. Africa
139 E2 Hanover *NH* U.S.A.
139 D3 Hanover *PA* U.S.A.
92 G2 Hansnes Norway
93 E4 Hanstholm Denmark
88 C3 Hantsavichy Belarus
75 C2 Hanumana India
74 B2 Hanumangarh India
70 A2 Hanzhong China
49 M5 Hao *atoll* Fr. Polynesia
75 C2 Haora India
92 H2 Haparanda Sweden
100 B2 Hapert Neth.
131 D2 Happy Valley-Goose Bay Can.
78 A2 Ḥaql Saudi Arabia
79 B2 Ḥaraḍh Saudi Arabia
88 C2 Haradok Belarus
78 B3 Ḥarajā Saudi Arabia
121 C2 Harare Zimbabwe
79 C3 Ḥarāsīs, Jiddat al *des.* Oman
69 D1 Har-Ayrag Mongolia
115 E3 Haraze-Mangueigne Chad
114 A4 Harbel Liberia
69 E1 Harbin China
138 C2 Harbor Beach U.S.A.
131 E3 Harbour Breton Can.
74 B2 Harda India
92 E4 Hardangerfjorden *sea chan.* Norway
61 C1 Harden, Bukit *mt.* Indon.
100 C1 Hardenberg Neth.
100 B1 Harderwijk Neth.
122 A3 Hardeveld *mts* S. Africa
134 E1 Hardin U.S.A.
128 C1 Hardisty Lake Can.
93 E3 Hareid Norway
100 C1 Haren (Ems) Ger.
117 C4 Härer Eth.
117 C4 Hargeysa Somalia
110 C1 Harghita-Mădăraș, Vârful *mt.* Romania
68 C2 Har Hu *l.* China
88 B2 Hari kurk *sea chan.* Estonia
74 B1 Haripur Pak.
74 A1 Harī Rōd *r.* Afgh./Iran
110 C1 Hârlău Romania
100 B1 Harlingen Neth.
143 D3 Harlingen U.S.A.
99 D4 Harlow U.K.
134 E1 Harlowton U.S.A.
134 C2 Harney Basin U.S.A.
134 C2 Harney Lake U.S.A.
93 G3 Härnösand Sweden
69 E1 Har Nur China
68 C1 Har Nuur *l.* Mongolia
96 □ Haroldswick U.K.
114 B4 Harper Liberia
101 D1 Harpstedt Ger.
130 C2 Harricana, Rivière d' *r.* Can.
53 D2 Harrington Austr.
131 E2 Harrington Harbour Can.
96 A2 Harris *reg.* U.K.
96 A2 Harris, Sound of *sea chan.* U.K.
138 B3 Harrisburg *IL* U.S.A.
134 B2 Harrisburg *OR* U.S.A.
139 D2 Harrisburg *PA* U.S.A.
123 C2 Harrismith S. Africa
140 B1 Harrison U.S.A.
131 E2 Harrison, Cape Can.
126 B2 Harrison Bay U.S.A.
139 D3 Harrisonburg U.S.A.
128 B3 Harrison Lake Can.
137 E3 Harrisonville U.S.A.
98 C3 Harrogate U.K.
110 C2 Hârșova Romania
92 G2 Harstad Norway
122 B2 Hartbees *watercourse* S. Africa
103 D2 Hartberg Austria
139 E2 Hartford *CT* U.S.A.
137 D2 Hartford *SD* U.S.A.
99 A4 Hartland Point U.K.
98 C2 Hartlepool U.K.
Hartley Zimbabwe *see* Chegutu
128 B2 Hartley Bay Can.
123 B2 Harts *r.* S. Africa
141 D2 Hartwell Reservoir U.S.A.
68 C1 Har Us Nuur *l.* Mongolia
136 C1 Harvey U.S.A.
99 D4 Harwich U.K.
74 B2 Haryana *state* India
101 E2 Harz *hills* Ger.
101 E2 Harzgerode Ger.
78 B2 Ḥasan, Jabal *h.* Saudi Arabia
80 B2 Hasan Dağı *mts* Turkey
99 C4 Haslemere U.K.
73 B3 Hassan India
100 B2 Hasselt Belgium
101 E2 Haßfurt Ger.
115 C2 Hassi Bel Guebbour Alg.
115 C1 Hassi Messaoud Alg.
93 F4 Hässleholm Sweden
100 B2 Hastière-Lavaux Belgium
53 C3 Hastings *Vic.* Austr.
54 C1 Hastings N.Z.
99 D4 Hastings U.K.
137 E2 Hastings *MN* U.S.A.
137 D2 Hastings *NE* U.S.A.
Hatay Turkey *see* Antakya
142 B2 Hatch U.S.A.
129 D2 Hatchet Lake Can.
110 B1 Hațeg Romania
52 B2 Hatfield Austr.
68 C1 Hatgal Mongolia
62 B2 Ha Tinh Vietnam
52 B2 Hattah Austr.
141 E1 Hatteras, Cape U.S.A.
157 H3 Hatteras Abyssal Plain S. Atlantic Ocean
140 C2 Hattiesburg U.S.A.
100 C2 Hattingen Ger.
63 B3 Hat Yai Thai.
117 C4 Haud *reg.* Eth.
93 E4 Haugesund Norway
93 E4 Haukeligrend Norway
92 I2 Haukipudas Fin.
54 C1 Hauraki Gulf N.Z.
54 A3 Hauroko, Lake N.Z.
114 B1 Haut Atlas *mts* Morocco
131 D3 Hauterive Can.
Haute-Volta *country* Africa *see* Burkina Faso
114 B1 Hauts Plateaux Alg.
146 B2 Havana Cuba
99 C4 Havant U.K.
101 E1 Havel *r.* Ger.
101 F1 Havelberg Ger.
54 B2 Havelock N.Z.
Havelock Swaziland *see* Bulembu
54 C1 Havelock North N.Z.
99 A4 Haverfordwest U.K.
100 C2 Havixbeck Ger.
103 D2 Havlíčkův Brod Czech Rep.
92 H1 Havøysund Norway
111 C3 Havran Turkey
134 E1 Havre U.S.A.
131 D3 Havre-Aubert Can.
131 D2 Havre-St-Pierre Can.
49 L2 Hawai'i *i.* U.S.A.
156 E4 Hawai'ian Islands *is* N. Pacific Ocean
78 B2 Ḥawallī Kuwait
98 B3 Hawarden U.K.
54 A2 Hawea, Lake N.Z.
54 B1 Hawera N.Z.
98 B2 Hawes U.K.
96 C3 Hawick U.K.
54 C1 Hawke Bay N.Z.
52 A2 Hawker Austr.
52 B1 Hawkers Gate Austr.
122 A3 Hawston S. Africa
135 C3 Hawthorne U.S.A.
52 B2 Hay Austr.
128 C1 Hay *r.* Can.
100 C3 Hayange France
134 C1 Hayden U.S.A.
129 E2 Hayes *r. Man.* Can.
126 F2 Hayes *r. Nunavut* Can.
79 C3 Haymā' Oman
77 C2 Hayotboshi tog'i *mt.* Uzbek.
111 C2 Hayrabolu Turkey
128 C1 Hay River Can.
137 D3 Hays U.S.A.
78 B3 Ḥays Yemen
90 B2 Haysyn Ukr.
135 B3 Hayward U.S.A.
99 C4 Haywards Heath U.K.
81 D2 Hazar Turkm.
74 A1 Hazārah Jāt *reg.* Afgh.
138 C3 Hazard U.S.A.
75 C2 Hazaribagh India
75 C2 Hazaribagh Range *mts* India
104 C1 Hazebrouck France
128 B2 Hazelton Can.
139 D2 Hazleton U.S.A.
135 B3 Healdsburg U.S.A.
53 C3 Healesville Austr.
159 E7 Heard Island Indian Ocean
143 D2 Hearne U.S.A.
130 B3 Hearst Can.
55 A3 Hearst Island Antarctica
70 B2 Hebei *prov.* China
53 C1 Hebel Austr.
140 B1 Heber Springs U.S.A.
131 D2 Hebron Can.
128 A2 Hecate Strait Can.
71 A3 Hechi China
100 B2 Hechtel Belgium
54 C2 Hector, Mount N.Z.
93 F3 Hede Sweden
100 C1 Heerde Neth.
100 B1 Heerenveen Neth.
100 B1 Heerhugowaard Neth.
100 B2 Heerlen Neth.
Ḥefa Israel *see* Haifa
70 B2 Hefei China
70 B3 Hefeng China
69 E1 Hegang China
119 D1 Heiban Sudan
102 B1 Heide Ger.
122 A1 Heide Namibia
101 D3 Heidelberg Ger.
122 B3 Heidelberg S. Africa
69 E1 Heihe China
102 B2 Heilbronn Ger.
69 E1 Heilong Jiang *r.* China
93 I3 Heinola Fin.
Hejaz *reg.* Saudi Arabia *see* Hijaz
92 A3 Hekla *vol.* Iceland
92 F3 Helagsfjället *mt.* Sweden
70 A2 Helan Shan *mts* China
140 B2 Helena *AR* U.S.A.
134 D1 Helena *MT* U.S.A.
96 B2 Helensburgh U.K.
102 B1 Helgoland *i.* Ger.
102 B1 Helgoländer Bucht *g.* Ger.
Heligoland *i.* Ger. *see* Helgoland
Heligoland Bight *g.* Ger. *see* Helgoländer Bucht
Helixi China *see* Ningguo
92 □A3 Hella Iceland
100 B2 Hellevoetsluis Neth.
107 C2 Hellín Spain
Hell-Ville Madag. *see* Andoany
76 C3 Helmand *r.* Afgh.
101 E2 Helmbrechts Ger.
122 A2 Helmeringhausen Namibia
100 B2 Helmond Neth.
96 C1 Helmsdale U.K.
96 C1 Helmsdale *r.* U.K.
98 C2 Helmsley U.K.
101 E1 Helmstedt Ger.
65 B1 Helong China
143 D3 Helotes U.S.A.
93 F4 Helsingborg Sweden
Helsingfors Fin. *see* Helsinki
93 F4 Helsingør Denmark
93 H3 Helsinki Fin.
99 A4 Helston U.K.
97 C2 Helvick Head *hd* Ireland
99 C4 Hemel Hempstead U.K.
101 D1 Hemmoor Ger.
92 F2 Hemnesberget Norway
70 B2 Henan *prov.* China
111 D2 Hendek Turkey
138 B3 Henderson *KY* U.S.A.
141 E1 Henderson *NC* U.S.A.
135 D3 Henderson *NV* U.S.A.
143 E2 Henderson *TX* U.S.A.
49 O6 Henderson Island Pitcairn Is
141 D1 Hendersonville U.S.A.
99 C4 Hendon U.K.
62 A1 Hengduan Shan *mts* China
100 C1 Hengelo Neth.
Hengnan China *see* Hengyang
71 B3 Hengshan China
70 B2 Hengshui China
71 A3 Hengxian China
71 B3 Hengyang China
Hengzhou China *see* Hengxian
91 C2 Heniches'k Ukr.
139 D3 Henlopen, Cape U.S.A.
100 C2 Hennef (Sieg) Ger.
130 B2 Henrietta Maria, Cape Can.
Henrique de Carvalho Angola *see* Saurimo
139 D3 Henry, Cape U.S.A.
143 D1 Henryetta U.S.A.
127 H2 Henry Kater, Cape Can.
101 D1 Henstedt-Ulzburg Ger.
120 A3 Hentiesbaai Namibia
101 D3 Heppenheim (Bergstraße) Ger.
71 A3 Hepu China
76 C3 Herāt Afgh.

Itajubá

Huoxian China see Huozhou
70 B2 Huozhou China
Hupeh prov. China see Hubei
Hurghada Egypt see Al Ghurdaqah
137 D2 Huron U.S.A.
138 C2 Huron, Lake Can./U.S.A.
135 D3 Hurricane U.S.A.
100 C2 Hürth Ger.
92 □B2 Húsavík Iceland
110 C1 Huşi Romania
126 B2 Huslia U.S.A.
78 B3 Ḩuşn Āl 'Abr Yemen
102 B1 Husum Ger.
68 C1 Hutag-Öndör Mongolia
60 A1 Hutanopan Indon.
137 D3 Hutchinson U.S.A.
141 D3 Hutchinson Island U.S.A.
70 B2 Hutuo He r. China
100 B2 Huy Belgium
70 C2 Huzhou China
92 □C3 Hvalnes Iceland
92 □B3 Hvannadalshnúkur vol. Iceland
109 C2 Hvar Croatia
109 C2 Hvar i. Croatia
91 C2 Hvardiys'ke Ukr.
120 B2 Hwange Zimbabwe
Hwang Ho r. China see Yellow River
136 C2 Hyannis U.S.A.
68 C1 Hyargas Nuur salt l. Mongolia
50 A3 Hyden Austr.
73 B3 Hyderabad India
74 A2 Hyderabad Pak.
Hydra i. Greece see Ydra
105 D3 Hyères France
105 D3 Hyères, Îles d' is France
65 B1 Hyesan N. Korea
128 B2 Hyland Post Can.
67 B3 Hyōno-sen mt. Japan
99 D4 Hythe U.K.
67 B4 Hyūga Japan
93 H3 Hyvinkää Fin.

I

114 B2 Iabès, Erg des. Alg.
150 C3 Iaco r. Brazil
110 C2 Ialomiţa r. Romania
110 C1 Ianca Romania
110 C1 Iaşi Romania
64 A2 Iba Phil.
115 C4 Ibadan Nigeria
150 B2 Ibagué Col.
154 B2 Ibaiti Brazil
150 B2 Ibarra Ecuador
78 B3 Ibb Yemen
100 C1 Ibbenbüren Ger.
115 C4 Ibi Nigeria
107 C2 Ibi Spain
155 C1 Ibiá Brazil
155 D1 Ibiaí Brazil
155 D1 Ibiraçu Brazil
107 D2 Ibiza Spain
107 D2 Ibiza i. Spain
151 E4 Ibotirama Brazil
79 C2 Ibrā' Oman
79 C2 Ibrī Oman
150 B4 Ica Peru
Icaria i. Greece see Ikaria
İçel Turkey see Mersin
92 □B2 Iceland country Europe
160 M4 Iceland Basin N. Atlantic Ocean
160 L3 Icelandic Plateau N. Atlantic Ocean
66 D3 Ichinoseki Japan
91 C1 Ichnya Ukr.
65 B2 Ich'ŏn N. Korea
151 F3 Icó Brazil
155 D2 Iconha Brazil
143 E2 Idabel U.S.A.
115 C4 Idah Nigeria
134 D2 Idaho state U.S.A.
134 D2 Idaho Falls U.S.A.
100 C3 Idar-Oberstein Ger.
68 C1 Ideriyn Gol r. Mongolia
116 B2 Idfū Egypt
115 D2 Idhān Murzuq des. Libya
Idi Amin Dada, Lake l. Dem. Rep. Congo/Uganda see Edward, Lake
118 B3 Idiofa Dem. Rep. Congo
80 B2 Idlib Syria
88 B2 Iecava Latvia
154 B2 Iepê Brazil
100 A2 Ieper Belgium
111 C3 Ierapetra Greece
119 D3 Ifakara Tanz.
121 □D3 Ifanadiana Madag.
115 C4 Ife Nigeria
114 C3 Ifôghas, Adrar des hills Mali
118 C3 Ifumo Dem. Rep. Congo
61 C1 Igan Malaysia
119 D2 Iganga Uganda
154 C2 Igarapava Brazil
82 G2 Igarka Rus. Fed.
74 B3 Igatpuri India
81 C2 Iğdır Turkey
108 A3 Iglesias Italy
127 G2 Igloolik Can.
Igluligaarjuk Can. see Chesterfield Inlet
130 A3 Ignace Can.
88 C2 Ignalina Lith.
111 C2 İğneada Turkey
110 C2 İğneada Burnu pt Turkey
111 B3 Igoumenitsa Greece
86 E3 Igra Rus. Fed.
86 F2 Igrim Rus. Fed.
154 B3 Iguaçu r. Brazil
154 B3 Iguaçu Falls Arg./Brazil
145 C3 Iguala Mex.
107 D1 Igualada Spain
154 C2 Iguape Brazil
154 B2 Iguatemi Brazil
154 B2 Iguatemi r. Brazil
151 F3 Iguatu Brazil
118 A3 Iguéla Gabon
114 B2 Iguidi, Erg des. Alg./Maur.
119 D3 Igunga Tanz.
121 □D2 Iharaña Madag.
121 □D3 Ihosy Madag.
92 I2 Iijoki r. Fin.
92 I3 Iisalmi Fin.
67 B4 Iizuka Japan
115 C4 Ijebu-Ode Nigeria
100 B1 IJmuiden Neth.
100 B1 IJssel r. Neth.
100 B1 IJsselmeer l. Neth.
152 C2 Ijuí Brazil
Ikaahuk Can. see Sachs Harbour
123 C2 Ikageleng S. Africa
123 C2 Ikageng S. Africa
111 C3 Ikaria i. Greece
118 C3 Ikela Dem. Rep. Congo
110 B2 Ikhtiman Bulg.
67 A4 Iki-shima i. Japan
118 A2 Ikom Nigeria
121 □D3 Ikongo Madag.
65 B2 Iksan S. Korea
119 D3 Ikungu Tanz.
114 C2 Ilaferh, Oued watercourse Alg.
64 B2 Ilagan Phil.
81 C2 Īlām Iran
75 C2 Ilam Nepal
103 D1 Iława Pol.
79 C2 Ilazārān, Kūh-e mt. Iran
129 D2 Île-à-la-Crosse Can.
129 D2 Île-à-la-Crosse, Lac l. Can.
118 C3 Ilebo Dem. Rep. Congo
119 D2 Ilemi Triangle terr. Kenya
119 D2 Ileret Kenya
99 D4 Ilford U.K.
99 A4 Ilfracombe U.K.
155 C2 Ilhabela Brazil
155 D2 Ilha Grande, Baía da b. Brazil
154 B2 Ilha Grande, Represa resr Brazil
154 B2 Ilha Solteíra, Represa resr Brazil
106 B1 Ílhavo Port.
151 F4 Ilhéus Brazil
Ili Kazakh. see Kapshagay
126 B3 Iliamna Lake U.S.A.
64 B3 Iligan Phil.
Iliysk Kazakh. see Kapshagay
98 C3 Ilkley U.K.
152 A3 Illapel Chile
90 C2 Illichivs'k Ukr.
138 A3 Illinois r. U.S.A.
138 B3 Illinois state U.S.A.
90 B2 Illintsi Ukr.
115 C2 Illizi Alg.
89 D2 Il'men', Ozero l. Rus. Fed.
101 E2 Ilmenau Ger.
150 B4 Ilo Peru
64 B2 Iloilo Phil.
92 J3 Ilomantsi Fin.
115 C4 Ilorin Nigeria
87 D4 Ilovlya Rus. Fed.
53 D1 Iluka Austr.
127 I2 Ilulissat Greenland
Iman Rus. Fed. see Dal'nerechensk
66 B1 Iman r. Rus. Fed.
67 A4 Imari Japan
93 I3 Imatra Fin.
imeni Petra Stuchki Latvia see Aizkraukle
117 C4 Īmī Eth.
65 B2 Imjin-gang r. N. Korea/S. Korea
141 D3 Immokalee U.S.A.
108 B2 Imola Italy
151 E3 Imperatriz Brazil
108 A2 Imperia Italy
136 C2 Imperial U.S.A.
118 B2 Impfondo Congo
72 D2 Imphal India
111 C2 İmroz Turkey
67 C3 Ina Japan
150 C4 Inambari r. Peru
115 C2 In Aménas Alg.
115 C2 In Amguel Alg.
54 B2 Inangahua Junction N.Z.
59 C3 Inanwatan Indon.
92 I2 Inari Fin.
92 I2 Inarijärvi l. Fin.
67 D3 Inawashiro-ko l. Japan
80 B1 İnce Burun pt Turkey
65 B2 Inch'ŏn S. Korea
121 C2 Inchope Moz.
123 D2 Incomati r. Moz.
116 B3 Inda Silasē Eth.
144 B2 Indé Mex.
135 C3 Independence CA U.S.A.
137 E2 Independence IA U.S.A.
137 D3 Independence KS U.S.A.
137 E3 Independence MO U.S.A.
134 C2 Independence Mountains U.S.A.
76 B2 Inderbor Kazakh.
72 B2 India country Asia
139 D2 Indiana U.S.A.
138 B2 Indiana state U.S.A.
138 B3 Indianapolis U.S.A.
129 D2 Indian Head Can.
159 Indian Ocean
137 E2 Indianola IA U.S.A.
140 B2 Indianola MS U.S.A.
135 D3 Indian Peak U.S.A.
135 C3 Indian Springs U.S.A.
86 D2 Indiga Rus. Fed.
83 K2 Indigirka r. Rus. Fed.
109 D1 Inđija Serbia
135 C4 Indio U.S.A.
58 B3 Indonesia country Asia
74 B2 Indore India
60 B2 Indramayu, Tanjung pt Indon.
Indrapura, Gunung vol. Indon. see Kerinci, Gunung
75 C3 Indravati r. India
104 C2 Indre r. France
74 A2 Indus r. China/Pak.
74 A2 Indus, Mouths of the Pak.
159 E2 Indus Cone Indian Ocean
80 B1 İnebolu Turkey
111 C2 İnegöl Turkey
Infantes Spain see Villanueva de los Infantes
144 B3 Infiernillo, Presa resr Mex.
51 D1 Ingham Austr.
53 D1 Inglewood Austr.
102 C2 Ingolstadt Ger.
75 C2 Ingraj Bazar India
123 D2 Ingwavuma S. Africa
120 B2 Ingwe Zambia
123 D2 Inhaca Moz.
121 C3 Inhambane Moz.
121 C2 Inhaminga Moz.
151 D2 Inini Fr. Guiana
Inis Ireland see Ennis
97 A2 Inishbofin i. Ireland
97 B2 Inishmore i. Ireland
97 C1 Inishowen pen. Ireland
54 B2 Inland Kaikoura Range mts N.Z.
Inland Sea sea Japan see Seto-naikai
102 C2 Inn r. Europe
127 H1 Innaanganeq c. Greenland
52 B1 Innamincka Austr.
70 A1 Inner Mongolia aut. reg. China
96 B2 Inner Sound sea chan. U.K.
51 D1 Innisfail Austr.
102 C2 Innsbruck Austria
97 C2 Inny r. Ireland
154 B1 Inocência Brazil
118 B3 Inongo Dem. Rep. Congo
111 D3 İnönü Turkey
Inoucdjouac Can. see Inukjuak
103 D1 Inowrocław Pol.
114 C2 In Salah Alg.
62 A2 Insein Myanmar
110 C2 Însurăţei Romania
86 F2 Inta Rus. Fed.
105 D2 Interlaken Switz.
137 E1 International Falls U.S.A.
63 A2 Interview Island India
130 C2 Inukjuak Can.
126 D2 Inuvik Can.
96 B2 Inveraray U.K.
96 C2 Inverbervie U.K.
54 A3 Invercargill N.Z.
53 D1 Inverell Austr.
96 B2 Invergordon U.K.
128 C2 Invermere Can.
131 D3 Inverness Can.
96 B2 Inverness U.K.
96 C2 Inverurie U.K.
159 F4 Investigator Ridge Indian Ocean
52 A3 Investigator Strait Austr.
77 E1 Inya Rus. Fed.
Inyanga Zimbabwe see Nyanga
119 D3 Inyonga Tanz.
87 D3 Inza Rus. Fed.
111 B3 Ioannina Greece
137 D3 Iola U.S.A.
96 A2 Iona i. U.K.
111 B3 Ionian Islands Greece
109 C3 Ionian Sea Greece/Italy
Ionioi Nisoi is Greece see Ionian Islands
111 C3 Ios i. Greece
137 E2 Iowa state U.S.A.
137 E2 Iowa City U.S.A.
154 C1 Ipameri Brazil
155 D1 Ipatinga Brazil
81 C1 Ipatovo Rus. Fed.
123 C2 Ipelegeng S. Africa
150 B2 Ipiales Col.
151 F4 Ipiaú Brazil
154 B3 Ipiranga Brazil
150 B3 Ipixuna Brazil
60 B1 Ipoh Malaysia
154 B1 Iporá Brazil
118 C2 Ippy C.A.R.
111 C2 İpsala Turkey
53 D1 Ipswich Austr.
99 D3 Ipswich U.K.
127 H2 Iqaluit Can.
152 A2 Iquique Chile
150 B3 Iquitos Peru
Irakleio Greece see Iraklion
111 C3 Iraklion Greece
81 D2 Iran country Asia
61 C1 Iran, Pegunungan mts Indon.
79 D2 Īrānshahr Iran
144 B2 Irapuato Mex.
81 C2 Iraq country Asia
154 B3 Irati Brazil
88 B2 Irbe Strait Estonia/Latvia
80 B2 Irbid Jordan
86 F3 Irbit Rus. Fed.
151 E4 Irecê Brazil
97 C2 Ireland country Europe
118 C3 Irema Dem. Rep. Congo
Iri S. Korea see Iksan
Irian Jaya reg. Indon. see Papua
115 E3 Iriba Chad
114 B3 Irîgui reg. Mali/Maur.
119 D3 Iringa Tanz.
151 D3 Iriri r. Brazil
Irish Free State country Europe see Ireland
95 B3 Irish Sea Ireland/U.K.
68 C1 Irkutsk Rus. Fed.
160 M4 Irminger Basin N. Atlantic Ocean
139 D2 Irondequoit U.S.A.
110 B2 Iron Gates gorge Romania/Serbia
52 A2 Iron Knob Austr.
138 B1 Iron Mountain U.S.A.
138 C3 Ironton U.S.A.
138 A1 Ironwood U.S.A.
130 B3 Iroquois Falls Can.
64 B2 Irosin Phil.
67 C4 Irō-zaki pt Japan
90 C1 Irpin' Ukr.
62 A2 Irrawaddy r. Myanmar
63 A2 Irrawaddy, Mouths of the Myanmar
86 F2 Irtysh r. Kazakh./Rus. Fed.
107 C1 Irun Spain
96 B3 Irvine U.K.
143 D2 Irving U.S.A.
64 B3 Isabela Phil.
146 B3 Isabelia, Cordillera mts Nic.
92 □A2 Ísafjarðardjúp est. Iceland
92 □A2 Ísafjörður Iceland
67 B4 Isahaya Japan
102 C2 Isar r. Ger.
96 □ Isbister U.K.
108 B2 Ischia, Isola d' i. Italy
67 C4 Ise Japan
118 C2 Isengi Dem. Rep. Congo
105 C3 Isère r. France
100 C2 Iserlohn Ger.
101 D1 Isernhagen Ger.
67 C4 Ise-wan b. Japan
114 C4 Iseyin Nigeria
Isfahan Iran see Eşfahān
66 D2 Ishikari-wan b. Japan
82 F3 Ishim Rus. Fed.
67 D3 Ishinomaki Japan
67 D3 Ishioka Japan
67 B4 Ishizuchi-san mt. Japan
74 B1 Ishkoshim Tajik.
138 B1 Ishpeming U.S.A.
111 C2 Işıklar Dağı mts Turkey
111 C3 Işıklı Turkey
123 D2 Isipingo S. Africa
119 C2 Isiro Dem. Rep. Congo
80 B2 İskenderun Turkey
82 G3 Iskitim Rus. Fed.
110 B2 Iskŭr r. Bulg.
117 D3 Iskushuban Somalia
128 A2 Iskut r. Can.
74 B1 Islamabad Pak.
141 D4 Islamorada U.S.A.
52 A2 Island Lagoon imp. l. Austr.
129 E2 Island Lake Can.
54 B1 Islands, Bay of N.Z.
Islas Canarias is N. Atlantic Ocean see Canary Islands
96 A3 Islay i. U.K.
98 A2 Isle of Man i. Irish Sea
Ismail Ukr. see Izmayil
77 D3 Ismoili Somoní, Qullai mt. Tajik.
116 B2 Isnā Egypt
121 □D3 Isoanala Madag.
121 C2 Isoka Zambia
93 H3 Isokyrö Fin.
109 C3 Isola di Capo Rizzuto Italy
Ispahan Iran see Eşfahān
80 B2 Isparta Turkey
110 C2 Isperikh Bulg.
Ispisar Tajik. see Khŭjand
80 B2 Israel country Asia
50 B3 Israelite Bay Austr.
105 C2 Issoire France
Issyk-Kul' Kyrg. see Balykchy
111 C2 İstanbul Turkey
İstanbul Boğazı str. Turkey see Bosporus
103 D2 Isten dombja h. Hungary
111 B3 Istiaia Greece
141 D3 Istokpoga, Lake U.S.A.
Istra pen. Croatia see Istria
105 C3 Istres France
108 B1 Istria pen. Croatia
155 D2 Itabapoana Brazil
151 E4 Itaberaba Brazil
154 C1 Itaberaí Brazil
155 D1 Itabira Brazil
155 D2 Itabirito Brazil
151 F4 Itabuna Brazil
150 D3 Itacoatiara Brazil
155 D2 Itaguaí Brazil
154 B2 Itaguajé Brazil
154 C2 Itaí Brazil
154 C3 Itaiópolis Brazil
154 B3 Itaipu, Represa de resr Brazil
151 D3 Itaituba Brazil
154 C3 Itajaí Brazil
155 C2 Itajubá Brazil

Karakum Desert

93 E3 Jotunheimen *mts* Norway
122 B3 Joubertina S. Africa
123 C2 Jouberton S. Africa
104 C2 Joué-lès-Tours France
93 I3 Joutseno Fin.
134 B1 Juan de Fuca Strait Can./U.S.A.
Juanshui China *see* Tongcheng
145 B2 Juárez Mex.
144 A1 Juárez, Sierra de *mts* Mex.
151 E3 Juazeiro Brazil
151 F3 Juazeiro do Norte Brazil
117 B4 Juba S. Sudan
117 C5 Jubba *r.* Somalia
78 B2 Jubbah Saudi Arabia
Jubbulpore India *see* Jabalpur
145 C3 Juchitán Mex.
155 E1 Jucuruçu Brazil
102 C2 Judenburg Austria
155 E1 Juerana Brazil
101 D2 Jühnde Ger.
146 B3 Juigalpa Nic.
150 D4 Juína Brazil
100 C1 Juist *i.* Ger.
155 D2 Juiz de Fora Brazil
136 C2 Julesburg U.S.A.
150 B4 Juliaca Peru
Julianatop *mt.* Indon. *see* Mandala, Puncak
151 D2 Juliana Top *mt.* Suriname
Jullundur India *see* Jalandhar
107 C2 Jumilla Spain
75 C2 Jumla Nepal
Jumna *r.* India *see* Yamuna
74 B2 Junagadh India
143 D2 Junction U.S.A.
137 D3 Junction City U.S.A.
154 C2 Jundiaí Brazil
128 A2 Juneau U.S.A.
53 C2 Junee Austr.
105 D2 Jungfrau *mt.* Switz.
139 D2 Juniata *r.* U.S.A.
153 B3 Junín Arg.
92 G3 Junsele Sweden
134 C2 Juntura U.S.A.
Junxi China *see* Datian
Junxian China *see* Danjiangkou
154 B2 Jupía, Represa *resr* Brazil
141 D3 Jupiter U.S.A.
154 C2 Juquiá Brazil
117 A4 Jur *r.* S. Sudan
105 D2 Jura *mts* France/Switz.
96 B2 Jura *i.* U.K.
96 B3 Jura, Sound of *sea chan.* U.K.
88 B2 Jurbarkas Lith.
88 B2 Jūrmala Latvia
150 C3 Juruá *r.* Brazil
150 D3 Juruena *r.* Brazil
154 C2 Jurumirim, Represa de *resr* Brazil
151 D3 Juruti Brazil
154 B1 Jussara Brazil
150 C3 Jutaí *r.* Brazil
101 F2 Jüterbog Ger.
154 B2 Juti Brazil
145 D3 Jutiapa Guat.
93 E4 Jutland *pen.* Denmark
146 B2 Juventud, Isla de la *i.* Cuba
70 B2 Juxian China
81 D3 Jūyom Iran
122 B1 Jwaneng Botswana
Jylland *pen.* Denmark *see* Jutland
93 I3 Jyväskylä Fin.

K

74 B1 K2 *mt.* China/Pakistan
Kaakhka Turkm. *see* Kaka
92 I2 Kaamanen Fin.
61 D2 Kabaena *i.* Indon.
119 C3 Kabalo Dem. Rep. Congo
119 C3 Kabambare Dem. Rep. Congo
119 C3 Kabare Dem. Rep. Congo
119 C3 Kabemba Dem. Rep. Congo
130 B3 Kabinakagami Lake Can.
118 C3 Kabinda Dem. Rep. Congo
118 B2 Kabo C.A.R.
120 B2 Kabompo Zambia
119 C3 Kabongo Dem. Rep. Congo
77 C3 Kābul Afgh.
64 B3 Kaburuang *i.* Indon.
121 B2 Kabwe Zambia
109 D2 Kaçanik Kosovo
74 A2 Kachchh, Gulf of India
74 B2 Kachchh, Rann of *marsh* India
83 I3 Kachug Rus. Fed.
81 C1 Kaçkar Dağı *mt.* Turkey
Kadapa India *see* Cuddapah
111 C2 Kadıköy Turkey
52 A2 Kadina Austr.
114 B3 Kadiolo Mali
Kadiyevka Ukr. *see* Stakhanov
73 B3 Kadmat *atoll* India
89 F2 Kadnikov Rus. Fed.
121 B2 Kadoma Zimbabwe
63 A2 Kadonkani Myanmar
117 A3 Kadugli Sudan
115 C3 Kaduna Nigeria
89 E2 Kaduy Rus. Fed.
86 E2 Kadzherom Rus. Fed.
114 A3 Kaédi Maur.
118 B1 Kaélé Cameroon
65 B2 Kaesŏng N. Korea
118 C3 Kafakumba Dem. Rep. Congo
114 A3 Kaffrine Senegal
80 B2 Kafr ash Shaykh Egypt
121 B2 Kafue Zambia
120 B2 Kafue *r.* Zambia
67 C3 Kaga Japan
118 B2 Kaga Bandoro C.A.R.
91 E2 Kagal'nitskaya Rus. Fed.
Kaganovichi Pervyye Ukr. *see* Polis'ke
60 A2 Kagologolo Indon.
67 B4 Kagoshima Japan
Kagul Moldova *see* Cahul
119 D3 Kahama Tanz.
90 C2 Kaharlyk Ukr.
61 C2 Kahayan *r.* Indon.
118 B3 Kahemba Dem. Rep. Congo
101 E2 Kahla Ger.
79 C2 Kahnūj Iran
92 H2 Kahperusvaarat *mts* Fin.
80 B2 Kahramanmaraş Turkey
79 C2 Kahūrak Iran
59 C3 Kai, Kepulauan *is* Indon.
115 C4 Kaiama Nigeria
54 B2 Kaiapoi N.Z.
59 C3 Kai Besar *i.* Indon.
70 B2 Kaifeng China
Kaihua China *see* Wenshan
122 B2 Kaiingveld *reg.* S. Africa
59 C3 Kai Kecil *i.* Indon.
54 B2 Kaikoura N.Z.
114 A4 Kailahun Sierra Leone
Kailas Range *mts* China *see* Gangdisê Shan
71 A3 Kaili China
59 C3 Kaimana Indon.
54 C1 Kaimanawa Mountains N.Z.
72 C2 Kaimur Range *hills* India
88 B2 Käina Estonia
67 C4 Kainan Japan
115 C3 Kainji Reservoir Nigeria
54 B1 Kaipara Harbour N.Z.
74 B2 Kairana India
115 D1 Kairouan Tunisia
100 C3 Kaiserslautern Ger.
55 I2 Kaiser Wilhelm II Land *reg.* Antarctica
54 B1 Kaitaia N.Z.
54 C1 Kaitawa N.Z.
Kaitong China *see* Tongyu
59 C3 Kaiwatu Indon.
65 A1 Kaiyuan *Liaoning* China
71 A3 Kaiyuan *Yunnan* China
92 I3 Kajaani Fin.
51 D2 Kajabbi Austr.
53 C1 Kajarabie, Lake Austr.
76 B3 Kaka Turkm.
122 B2 Kakamas S. Africa
119 D2 Kakamega Kenya
114 A4 Kakata Liberia
91 C2 Kakhovka Ukr.
91 C2 Kakhovs'ke Vodoskhovyshche *resr* Ukr.
Kakhul Moldova *see* Cahul
73 C3 Kakinada India
128 C1 Kakisa Can.
67 B4 Kakogawa Japan
119 C3 Kakoswa Dem. Rep. Congo
126 C2 Kaktovik U.S.A.
Kalaallit Nunaat *terr.* N. America *see* Greenland
59 C3 Kalabahi Indon.
120 B2 Kalabo Zambia
91 E1 Kalach Rus. Fed.
119 D2 Kalacha Dida Kenya
87 D4 Kalach-na-Donu Rus. Fed.
62 A1 Kaladan *r.* India/Myanmar
120 B3 Kalahari Desert Africa
92 H3 Kalajoki Fin.
123 C1 Kalamare Botswana
111 B2 Kalamaria Greece
111 B3 Kalamata Greece
138 B2 Kalamazoo U.S.A.
111 B3 Kalampaka Greece
88 B2 Kalana Estonia
91 C2 Kalanchak Ukr.
115 E2 Kalanshiyū ar Ramlī al Kabīr, Sarīr *des.* Libya
61 D2 Kalao *i.* Indon.
61 D2 Kalaotoa *i.* Indon.
63 B2 Kalasin Thai.
79 C2 Kalāt Iran
74 A2 Kalat Pak.
50 A2 Kalbarri Austr.
Kalburgi India *see* Gulbarga
111 C3 Kale Turkey
80 B1 Kalecik Turkey
118 C3 Kalema Dem. Rep. Congo
119 C3 Kalemie Dem. Rep. Congo
62 A1 Kalemyo Myanmar
86 C2 Kalevala Rus. Fed.
Kalgan China *see* Zhangjiakou
50 B3 Kalgoorlie Austr.
109 C2 Kali Croatia
110 C2 Kaliakra, Nos *pt* Bulg.
60 A2 Kaliet Indon.
119 C3 Kalima Dem. Rep. Congo
61 C2 Kalimantan *reg.* Indon.
Kalinin Rus. Fed. *see* Tver'
88 B3 Kaliningrad Rus. Fed.
91 D2 Kalininskaya Rus. Fed.
88 C3 Kalinkavichy Belarus
134 D1 Kalispell U.S.A.
103 D1 Kalisz Pol.
91 E2 Kalitva *r.* Rus. Fed.
92 H2 Kalix Sweden
92 H2 Kalixälven *r.* Sweden
111 C3 Kalkan Turkey
120 A3 Kalkfeld Namibia
100 C2 Kall Ger.
92 I3 Kallavesi *l.* Fin.
92 F3 Kallsjön *l.* Sweden
93 G4 Kalmar Sweden
93 G4 Kalmarsund *sea chan.* Sweden
73 C4 Kalmunai Sri Lanka
119 C3 Kalole Dem. Rep. Congo
120 B2 Kalomo Zambia
128 B2 Kalone Peak Can.
74 B1 Kalpa India
73 B3 Kalpeni *atoll* India
75 B2 Kalpi India
126 B2 Kaltag U.S.A.
101 D1 Kaltenkirchen Ger.
118 B2 Kaltungo Nigeria
89 E3 Kaluga Rus. Fed.
93 F4 Kalundborg Denmark
74 B1 Kalur Kot Pak.
90 A2 Kalush Ukr.
74 B3 Kalyan India
89 E2 Kalyazin Rus. Fed.
111 C3 Kalymnos Greece
111 C3 Kalymnos *i.* Greece
119 C3 Kama Dem. Rep. Congo
62 A2 Kama Myanmar
86 E3 Kama *r.* Rus. Fed.
66 D3 Kamaishi Japan
80 B2 Kaman Turkey
120 A2 Kamanjab Namibia
78 B3 Kamarān *i.* Yemen
Kamaran Island *i.* Yemen *see* Kamarān
74 A2 Kamarod Pak.
50 B3 Kambalda Austr.
119 C4 Kambove Dem. Rep. Congo
160 C4 Kamchatka Basin Bering Sea
83 L3 Kamchatka Peninsula Rus. Fed.
110 C2 Kamchiya *r.* Bulg.
108 B2 Kamenjak, Rt *pt* Croatia
86 D2 Kamenka Rus. Fed.
87 D3 Kamenka Rus. Fed.
66 C2 Kamenka Rus. Fed.
91 D1 Kamenka Rus. Fed.
Kamenka-Strumilovskaya Ukr. *see* Kam"yanka-Buz'ka
91 E3 Kamennomostskiy Rus. Fed.
91 E2 Kamenolomni Rus. Fed.
Kamenongue Angola *see* Camanongue
83 M2 Kamenskoye Rus. Fed.
Kamenskoye Ukr. *see* Dniprodzerzhyns'k
91 E2 Kamensk-Shakhtinskiy Rus. Fed.
86 F3 Kamensk-Ural'skiy Rus. Fed.
89 F2 Kameshkovo Rus. Fed.
72 C1 Kamet *mt.* China/India
75 B1 Kamet *mt.* China/India
122 A3 Kamiesberge *mts* S. Africa
122 A3 Kamieskroon S. Africa
129 D1 Kamilukuak Lake Can.
119 C3 Kamina Dem. Rep. Congo
129 E1 Kaminak Lake Can.
90 A1 Kamin'-Kashyrs'kyy Ukr.
119 C3 Kamituga Dem. Rep. Congo
128 B2 Kamloops Can.
54 B1 Kamo N.Z.
116 B3 Kamob Sanha Sudan
118 C3 Kamonia Dem. Rep. Congo
119 D2 Kampala Uganda
60 B1 Kampar *r.* Indon.
60 B1 Kampar Malaysia
100 B1 Kampen Neth.
119 C3 Kampene Dem. Rep. Congo
63 A2 Kamphaeng Phet Thai.
63 B2 Kâmpóng Cham Cambodia
63 B2 Kâmpóng Chhnăng Cambodia
Kâmpóng Saôm Cambodia *see* Sihanoukville
63 B2 Kâmpóng Spœ Cambodia
63 B2 Kâmpôt Cambodia
Kampuchea *country* Asia *see* Cambodia
129 D2 Kamsack Can.
86 E3 Kamskoye Vodokhranilishche *resr* Rus. Fed.
117 C4 Kamsuuma Somalia
90 B2 Kam"yanets'-Podil's'kyy Ukr.
90 A1 Kam"yanka-Buz'ka Ukr.
88 B3 Kamyanyets Belarus
91 D2 Kamyshevatskaya Rus. Fed.
87 D3 Kamyshin Rus. Fed.
135 D3 Kanab U.S.A.
118 C3 Kananga Dem. Rep. Congo
87 D3 Kanash Rus. Fed.
138 C3 Kanawha *r.* U.S.A.
67 C3 Kanazawa Japan
62 A1 Kanbalu Myanmar
63 A2 Kanchanaburi Thai.
73 B3 Kanchipuram India
77 C3 Kandahār Afgh.
86 C2 Kandalaksha Rus. Fed.
61 C2 Kandangan Indon.
74 A2 Kandh Kot Pak.
114 C3 Kandi Benin
74 A2 Kandiaro Pak.
74 B2 Kandla India
53 C2 Kandos Austr.
121 □D2 Kandreho Madag.
73 C4 Kandy Sri Lanka
76 B2 Kandyagash Kazakh.
127 H1 Kane Bassin *b.* Greenland
91 D2 Kanevskaya Rus. Fed.
122 B1 Kang Botswana
127 I2 Kangaatsiaq Greenland
114 B3 Kangaba Mali
80 B2 Kangal Turkey
79 C2 Kangān Iran
60 B1 Kangar Malaysia
52 A3 Kangaroo Island Austr.
93 H3 Kangasala Fin.
81 C2 Kangāvar Iran
75 C2 Kangchenjunga *mt.* India/Nepal
70 A2 Kangding China
65 B2 Kangdong N. Korea
61 C2 Kangean, Kepulauan *is* Indon.
119 D2 Kangen *r.* S. Sudan
127 J2 Kangeq *c.* Greenland
127 I2 Kangerlussuaq *inlet* Greenland
127 J2 Kangerlussuaq *inlet* Greenland
127 I2 Kangersuatsiaq Greenland
65 B1 Kanggye N. Korea
131 D2 Kangiqsualujjuaq Can.
127 H2 Kangiqsujuaq Can.
131 C1 Kangirsuk Can.
75 C2 Kangmar China
65 B2 Kangnŭng S. Korea
65 A1 Kangping China
72 D2 Kangto *mt.* China/India
62 A1 Kani Myanmar
118 C3 Kaniama Dem. Rep. Congo
61 C1 Kanibongan Malaysia
86 D2 Kanin, Poluostrov *pen.* Rus. Fed.
86 D2 Kanin Nos Rus. Fed.
86 D2 Kanin Nos, Mys *c.* Rus. Fed.
91 C2 Kaniv Ukr.
52 B3 Kaniva Austr.
93 H3 Kankaanpää Fin.
138 B2 Kankakee U.S.A.
114 B3 Kankan Guinea
75 C2 Kanker India
73 B3 Kannur India
115 C3 Kano Nigeria
122 B3 Kanonpunt *pt* S. Africa
67 B4 Kanoya Japan
75 C2 Kanpur India
136 C3 Kansas *r.* U.S.A.
137 D3 Kansas *state* U.S.A.
137 E3 Kansas City *KS* U.S.A.
137 E3 Kansas City *MO* U.S.A.
83 H3 Kansk Rus. Fed.
Kansu *prov.* China *see* Gansu
63 B2 Kantaralak Thai.
114 C3 Kantchari Burkina Faso
91 D2 Kantemirovka Rus. Fed.
49 J4 Kanton *atoll* Kiribati
97 B2 Kanturk Ireland
123 D2 Kanyamazane S. Africa
123 C1 Kanye Botswana
120 A2 Kaokoveld *plat.* Namibia
114 A3 Kaolack Senegal
120 B2 Kaoma Zambia
118 C3 Kapanga Dem. Rep. Congo
88 C3 Kapatkyevichy Belarus
100 B2 Kapellen Belgium
121 B2 Kapiri Mposhi Zambia
127 I2 Kapisillit Greenland
130 B2 Kapiskau *r.* Can.
61 C1 Kapit Malaysia
63 A3 Kapoe Thai.
117 B4 Kapoeta S. Sudan
103 D2 Kaposvár Hungary
102 B1 Kappeln Ger.
65 B1 Kapsan N. Korea
77 D2 Kapshagay Kazakh.
77 D2 Kapshagay, Vodokhranilishche *resr* Kazakh.
Kapsukas Lith. *see* Marijampolė
61 B2 Kapuas *r.* Indon.
52 A2 Kapunda Austr.
130 B3 Kapuskasing Can.
53 D2 Kaputar *mt.* Austr.
103 D2 Kapuvár Hungary
88 C3 Kapyl' Belarus
77 D3 Kaqung China
114 C4 Kara Togo
111 C3 Kara Ada *i.* Turkey
77 D2 Kara-Balta Kyrg.
76 C1 Karabalyk Kazakh.
81 D1 Karabaur, Uval *hills* Kazakh./Uzbek.
Kara-Bogaz-Gol Turkm. *see* Garabogazköl
80 B1 Karabük Turkey
76 C2 Karabutak Kazakh.
111 C2 Karacabey Turkey
111 C2 Karacaköy Turkey
81 C1 Karachayevsk Rus. Fed.
89 D3 Karachev Rus. Fed.
74 A2 Karachi Pak.
77 D2 Karagandy Kazakh.
77 D2 Karagayly Kazakh.
83 L3 Karaginskiy Zaliv *b.* Rus. Fed.
81 D2 Karaj Iran
Kara-Kala Turkm. *see* Magtymguly
64 B3 Karakelong *i.* Indon.
Karaklis Armenia *see* Vanadzor
77 D2 Kara-Köl Kyrg.
77 D2 Karakol Kyrg.
74 B1 Karakoram Range *mts* Asia
117 B3 Kara K'orē Eth.
Karakum, Peski *des.* Kazakh. *see* Karakum Desert
76 B2 Karakum Desert *des.* Kazakh.
76 C3 Karakum Desert Turkm.

Karakumy, Peski

Karakumy, Peski des. Turkm. see Karakum Desert
80 B2 Karaman Turkey
77 E2 Karamay China
54 B2 Karamea N.Z.
54 B2 Karamea Bight b. N.Z.
80 B2 Karapınar Turkey
122 A2 Karasburg Namibia
86 F1 Kara Sea Rus. Fed.
92 I2 Karasjok Norway
Kara Strait str. Rus. Fed. see Karskiye Vorota, Proliv
111 D2 Karasu Turkey
Karasubazar Ukr. see Bilohirs'k
77 D1 Karasuk Rus. Fed.
77 D2 Karatau Kazakh.
77 C2 Karatau, Khrebet mts Kazakh.
86 F2 Karatayka Rus. Fed.
67 A4 Karatsu Japan
111 B3 Karavas Greece
60 B2 Karawang Indon.
81 C2 Karbalā' Iraq
81 D2 Karbūsh, Kūh-e mt. Iran
103 E2 Karcag Hungary
Kardeljevo Croatia see Ploče
111 B3 Karditsa Greece
88 B2 Kärdla Estonia
122 B3 Kareeberge mts S. Africa
75 B2 Kareli India
88 C3 Karelichy Belarus
92 H2 Karesuando Sweden
Karghalik China see Yecheng
74 B1 Kargil India
Kargilik China see Yecheng
86 C2 Kargopol' Rus. Fed.
118 B1 Kari Nigeria
121 B2 Kariba Zimbabwe
121 B2 Kariba, Lake resr Zambia/Zimbabwe
60 B2 Karimata, Pulau-pulau is Indon.
60 B2 Karimata, Selat str. Indon.
73 B3 Karimnagar India
61 C2 Karimunjawa, Pulau-pulau is Indon.
91 C2 Karkinits'ka Zatoka g. Ukr.
91 D2 Karlivka Ukr.
Karl-Marx-Stadt Ger. see Chemnitz
109 C1 Karlovac Croatia
102 C1 Karlovy Vary Czech Rep.
Karlsburg Romania see Alba Iulia
93 F4 Karlshamn Sweden
93 F4 Karlskoga Sweden
93 G4 Karlskrona Sweden
102 B2 Karlsruhe Ger.
93 F4 Karlstad Sweden
101 D3 Karlstadt Ger.
89 D3 Karma Belarus
93 E4 Karmøy i. Norway
75 D2 Karnafuli Reservoir Bangl.
74 B2 Karnal India
110 C2 Karnobat Bulg.
74 A2 Karodi Pak.
121 B2 Karoi Zimbabwe
121 C1 Karonga Malawi
116 B3 Karora Eritrea
111 C3 Karpathos Greece
111 C3 Karpathos i. Greece
111 B3 Karpenisi Greece
Karpilovka Belarus see Aktsyabrski
86 D2 Karpogory Rus. Fed.
50 A2 Karratha Austr.
81 C1 Kars Turkey
88 C2 Kārsava Latvia
Karshi Uzbek. see Qarshi
111 C3 Karşıyaka Turkey
86 E2 Karskiye Vorota, Proliv str. Rus. Fed.
Karskoye More sea Rus. Fed. see Kara Sea
101 E1 Karstädt Ger.
111 C2 Kartal Turkey
87 F3 Kartaly Rus. Fed.
81 C2 Kārūn, Rūd-e r. Iran
73 B3 Karwar India
83 I3 Karymskoye Rus. Fed.
111 B3 Karystos Greece
111 C3 Kaş Turkey
130 B2 Kasabonika Lake Can.
118 C3 Kasaï, Plateau du Dem. Rep. Congo
118 C4 Kasaji Dem. Rep. Congo
121 C2 Kasama Zambia
120 B2 Kasane Botswana
118 B3 Kasangulu Dem. Rep. Congo
73 B3 Kasaragod India
129 D1 Kasba Lake Can.
120 B2 Kasempa Zambia
119 C4 Kasenga Dem. Rep. Congo
119 C3 Kasese Dem. Rep. Congo
119 D2 Kasese Uganda
Kasevo Rus. Fed. see Neftekamsk
81 D2 Kāshān Iran
Kashgar China see Kashi
77 D3 Kashi China
67 D3 Kashima-nada b. Japan
89 E2 Kashin Rus. Fed.
89 E3 Kashira Rus. Fed.
89 E3 Kashirskoye Rus. Fed.
67 C3 Kashiwazaki Japan
76 B3 Kāshmar Iran
Kashmir terr. Asia see Jammu and Kashmir
74 A2 Kashmore Pak.
119 C3 Kashyukulu Dem. Rep. Congo
89 F3 Kasimov Rus. Fed.
138 B3 Kaskaskia r. U.S.A.
93 H3 Kaskinen Fin.
119 C3 Kasongo Dem. Rep. Congo
118 B3 Kasongo-Lunda Dem. Rep. Congo
111 C3 Kasos i. Greece
Kaspiyskiy Rus. Fed. see Lagan'
116 B3 Kassala Sudan
101 D2 Kassel Ger.
115 C1 Kasserine Tunisia
80 B1 Kastamonu Turkey
Kastellorizon i. Greece see Megisti
111 B2 Kastoria Greece
89 D3 Kastsyukovichy Belarus
119 D3 Kasulu Tanz.
121 C2 Kasungu Malawi
139 F1 Katahdin, Mount U.S.A.
118 C3 Katako-Kombe Dem. Rep. Congo
119 D2 Katakwi Uganda
50 A3 Katanning Austr.
63 A3 Katchall i. India
111 B2 Katerini Greece
119 D3 Katesh Tanz.
128 A2 Kate's Needle mt. Can./U.S.A.
121 C2 Katete Zambia
62 A1 Katha Myanmar
50 C1 Katherine Austr.
50 C1 Katherine r. Austr.
74 B2 Kathiawar pen. India
75 C2 Kathmandu Nepal
122 B2 Kathu S. Africa
74 B1 Kathua India
114 B3 Kati Mali
75 C2 Katihar India
54 C1 Katikati N.Z.
123 C3 Katikati S. Africa
120 B2 Katima Mulilo Namibia
114 B4 Katiola Côte d'Ivoire
123 C2 Katlehong S. Africa
Katmandu Nepal see Kathmandu
111 B3 Kato Achaïa Greece
119 C3 Katompi Dem. Rep. Congo
53 D2 Katoomba Austr.
103 D1 Katowice Pol.
80 B3 Kātrīnā, Jabal mt. Egypt
93 G4 Katrineholm Sweden
115 C3 Katsina Nigeria
115 C4 Katsina-Ala Nigeria
67 D3 Katsuura Japan
77 C3 Kattaqo'rg'on Uzbek.
93 F4 Kattegat str. Denmark/Sweden
100 B1 Katwijk aan Zee Neth.
101 D3 Katzenbuckel h. Ger.
49 L1 Kaua'i i. U.S.A.
93 H3 Kauhajoki Fin.
88 B3 Kaunas Lith.
115 C3 Kaura-Namoda Nigeria
Kaushany Moldova see Căușeni
92 H2 Kautokeino Norway
109 D2 Kavadarci Macedonia
109 C2 Kavajë Albania
111 B2 Kavala Greece
66 C2 Kavalerovo Rus. Fed.
73 C3 Kavali India
73 B3 Kavaratti atoll India
110 C2 Kavarna Bulg.
59 E3 Kavieng P.N.G.
81 D2 Kavīr, Dasht-e des. Iran
67 C3 Kawagoe Japan
54 B1 Kawakawa N.Z.
121 B1 Kawambwa Zambia
67 C3 Kawanishi Japan
130 C3 Kawartha Lakes Can.
67 C3 Kawasaki Japan
54 C1 Kawerau N.Z.
63 A2 Kawkareik Myanmar
62 A1 Kawlin Myanmar
63 A2 Kawmapyin Myanmar
116 B2 Kawm Umbū Egypt
63 A2 Kawthaung Myanmar
Kaxgar China see Kashi
77 D3 Kaxgar He r. China
114 B3 Kaya Burkina Faso
111 C3 Kayacı Dağı h. Turkey
121 C1 Kayambi Zambia
61 C1 Kayan r. Indon.
136 B2 Kaycee U.S.A.
Kaydanovo Belarus see Dzyarzhynsk
142 A1 Kayenta U.S.A.
114 A3 Kayes Mali
77 D2 Kaynar Kazakh.
80 B2 Kayseri Turkey
134 D2 Kaysville U.S.A.
60 B2 Kayuagung Indon.
Kazakhskaya S.S.R. country Asia see Kazakhstan
76 B2 Kazakhskiy Zaliv b. Kazakh.
76 C2 Kazakhstan country Asia
Kazakhstan Kazakh. see Aksay
87 D3 Kazan' Rus. Fed.
Kazandzhik Turkm. see Bereket
110 C2 Kazanlŭk Bulg.
Kazan-rettō is Japan see Volcano Islands
76 A2 Kazbek mt. Georgia/Rus. Fed.
81 D3 Kāzerūn Iran
103 E2 Kazincbarcika Hungary
118 C3 Kazumba Dem. Rep. Congo
66 D2 Kazuno Japan
86 F2 Kazym-Mys Rus. Fed.
111 B3 Kea i. Greece
97 C1 Keady U.K.
137 D2 Kearney U.S.A.
142 A2 Kearny U.S.A.
115 C1 Kebili Tunisia
116 A3 Kebkabiya Sudan
92 G2 Kebnekaise mt. Sweden
117 C4 K'ebrī Dehar Eth.
60 B2 Kebumen Indon.
128 B2 Kechika r. Can.
111 D3 Keçiborlu Turkey
103 D2 Kecskemét Hungary
88 B2 Kėdainiai Lith.
114 A3 Kédougou Senegal
103 D1 Kędzierzyn-Koźle Pol.
128 B1 Keele r. Can.
128 A1 Keele Peak Can.
Keelung Taiwan see Chilung
139 E2 Keene U.S.A.
122 A2 Keetmanshoop Namibia
129 E3 Keewatin Can.
Kefallonia i. Greece see Cephalonia
59 C3 Kefamenanu Indon.
92 □A3 Keflavík Iceland
77 D2 Kegen Kazakh.
128 C2 Keg River Can.
88 C2 Kehra Estonia
62 A1 Kehsi Mansam Myanmar
98 C3 Keighley U.K.
88 B2 Keila Estonia
122 B2 Keimoes S. Africa
92 I3 Keitele l. Fin.
52 B3 Keith Austr.
96 C2 Keith U.K.
128 B1 Keith Arm b. Can.
134 B2 Keizer U.S.A.
103 E2 Kékes mt. Hungary
117 C4 K'elafo Eth.
Kelang Malaysia see Klang
92 J2 Kelesuayv, Gora h. Rus. Fed.
102 C2 Kelheim Ger.
76 C3 Kelif Uzboýy marsh Turkm.
80 B1 Kelkit r. Turkey
128 B1 Keller Lake Can.
134 C1 Kellogg U.S.A.
92 I2 Kelloselkä Fin.
97 C2 Kells Ireland
88 B2 Kelmė Lith.
115 D4 Kélo Chad
128 C3 Kelowna Can.
96 C3 Kelso U.K.
134 B1 Kelso U.S.A.
60 B1 Keluang Malaysia
129 D2 Kelvington Can.
86 C2 Kem' Rus. Fed.
Ke Macina Mali see Macina
128 B2 Kemano (abandoned) Can.
118 C2 Kembé C.A.R.
111 C3 Kemer Turkey
82 G3 Kemerovo Rus. Fed.
92 H2 Kemi Fin.
92 I2 Kemijärvi Fin.
92 I2 Kemijärvi l. Fin.
92 I2 Kemijoki r. Fin.
136 A2 Kemmerer U.S.A.
92 I3 Kempele Fin.
55 G2 Kemp Land reg. Antarctica
55 A2 Kemp Peninsula Antarctica
53 D2 Kempsey Austr.
130 C3 Kempt, Lac l. Can.
102 C2 Kempten (Allgäu) Ger.
123 C2 Kempton Park S. Africa
61 C2 Kemujan i. Indon.
126 B2 Kenai U.S.A.
129 D2 Kenaston Can.
98 B2 Kendal U.K.
141 D3 Kendall U.S.A.
61 D2 Kendari Indon.
60 C2 Kendawangan Indon.
115 D3 Kendégué Chad
114 A4 Kenema Sierra Leone
118 B3 Kenge Dem. Rep. Congo
62 A1 Kengtung Myanmar
122 B2 Kenhardt S. Africa
114 B1 Kenitra Morocco
97 B3 Kenmare Ireland
136 C1 Kenmare U.S.A.
97 A3 Kenmare River inlet Ireland
100 C3 Kenn Ger.
143 C2 Kenna U.S.A.
139 F2 Kennebec r. U.S.A.
Kennedy, Cape c. U.S.A. see Canaveral, Cape
140 B3 Kenner U.S.A.
99 C4 Kennet r. U.K.
137 E3 Kennett U.S.A.
134 C1 Kennewick U.S.A.
130 A3 Kenora Can.
138 B2 Kenosha U.S.A.
142 C2 Kent U.S.A.
77 C2 Kentau Kazakh.
138 B3 Kentucky r. U.S.A.
138 C3 Kentucky state U.S.A.
138 B3 Kentucky Lake U.S.A.
140 B2 Kentwood U.S.A.
119 D2 Kenya country Africa
119 D3 Kenya, Mount mt. Kenya
60 B1 Kenyir, Tasik resr Malaysia
137 E2 Keokuk U.S.A.
75 C2 Keonjhar India
111 C3 Kepsut Turkey
52 B3 Kerang Austr.
91 D2 Kerch Ukr.
59 D3 Kerema P.N.G.
128 C3 Keremeos Can.
116 B3 Keren Eritrea
81 C2 Kerend Iran
Kerepakupai Merú waterfall Venez. see Angel Falls
159 E7 Kerguélen, Îles is Indian Ocean
159 E7 Kerguelen Plateau Indian Ocean
119 D3 Kericho Kenya
54 B1 Kerikeri N.Z.
60 B2 Kerinci, Gunung vol. Indon.
Kerintji vol. Indon. see Kerinci, Gunung
100 C2 Kerkrade Neth.
111 A3 Kerkyra Greece
Kerkyra i. Greece see Corfu
116 B3 Kerma Sudan
49 J7 Kermadec Islands S. Pacific Ocea
79 C1 Kermān Iran
81 C2 Kermānshāh Iran
Kermine Uzbek. see Navoiy
143 C2 Kermit U.S.A.
135 C3 Kern r. U.S.A.
114 B4 Kérouané Guinea
100 C2 Kerpen Ger.
129 D2 Kerrobert Can.
143 D2 Kerrville U.S.A.
97 B2 Kerry Head hd Ireland
Keryneia Cyprus see Kyrenia
130 B2 Kesagami Lake Can.
111 C2 Keşan Turkey
66 D3 Kesennuma Japan
74 B2 Keshod India
100 C2 Kessel Neth.
98 B2 Keswick U.K.
103 D2 Keszthely Hungary
82 G3 Ket' r. Rus. Fed.
60 C2 Ketapang Indon.
128 A2 Ketchikan U.S.A.
134 D2 Ketchum U.S.A.
114 B4 Kete Krachi Ghana
118 B2 Kétté Cameroon
99 C3 Kettering U.K.
138 C3 Kettering U.S.A.
134 C1 Kettle River Range mts U.S.A.
93 H3 Keuruu Fin.
100 C2 Kevelaer Ger.
138 B2 Kewanee U.S.A.
138 B1 Keweenaw Bay U.S.A.
138 B1 Keweenaw Peninsula U.S.A.
141 D3 Key Largo U.S.A.
99 B4 Keynsham U.K.
139 D3 Keyser U.S.A.
141 D4 Key West U.S.A.
123 C2 Kgotsong S. Africa
69 F1 Khabarovsk Rus. Fed.
91 D3 Khadyzhensk Rus. Fed.
75 D2 Khagrachari Bangl.
74 A2 Khairpur Pak.
122 B1 Khakhea Botswana
76 B3 Khalīlābād Iran
86 F2 Khal'mer"yu Rus. Fed.
68 C1 Khamar-Daban, Khrebet mts Rus. Fed.
74 B2 Khambhat India
74 B3 Khambhat, Gulf of India
74 B2 Khamgaon India
79 C2 Khamīr Iran
78 B3 Khamir Yemen
78 B3 Khamīs Mushayṭ Saudi Arabia
77 C3 Khānābād Afgh.
74 B2 Khandwa India
83 K2 Khandyga Rus. Fed.
74 B1 Khanewal Pak.
Khan Hung Vietnam see Soc Trăn
83 J3 Khani Rus. Fed.
66 B2 Khanka, Lake China/Rus. Fed.
115 C2 Khannfoussa h. Alg.
74 B2 Khanpur Pak.
77 D2 Khantau Kazakh.
83 H2 Khantayskoye, Ozero l. Rus. Fed.
86 F2 Khanty-Mansiysk Rus. Fed.
63 A3 Khao Chum Thong Thai.
63 A2 Khao Laem, Ang Kep Nam Thai.
74 B1 Khaplu Pak.
87 D4 Kharabali Rus. Fed.
75 C2 Kharagpur India
79 C2 Khārān r. Iran
Kharga Oasis oasis Egypt see Wāḥāt al Khārijah
74 B2 Khargon India
91 D2 Kharkiv Ukr.
Khar'kov Ukr. see Kharkiv
111 C2 Kharmanli Bulg.
89 F2 Kharovsk Rus. Fed.
116 B3 Khartoum Sudan
87 D4 Khasavyurt Rus. Fed.
79 D2 Khāsh Iran
78 A3 Khashm el Girba Sudan
78 A3 Khashm el Girba Dam Sudan
81 C1 Khashuri Georgia
75 D2 Khasi Hills India
111 C2 Khaskovo Bulg.
83 H2 Khatanga Rus. Fed.
123 C3 Khayamnandi S. Africa
78 A2 Khaybar Saudi Arabia
122 A3 Khayelitsha S. Africa
107 D2 Khemis Miliana Alg.
63 B2 Khemmarat Thai.
115 C1 Khenchela Alg.
81 D3 Kherāmeh Iran
91 C2 Kherson Ukr.
83 H2 Kheta r. Rus. Fed.
69 D1 Khilok Rus. Fed.
89 E2 Khimki Rus. Fed.
74 A2 Khipro Pak.
89 E3 Khlevnoye Rus. Fed.
63 B2 Khlung Thai.
90 B2 Khmel'nyts'kyy Ukr.
Khmer Republic country Asia see Cambodia
Khodzheyli Uzbek. see Xo'jayli
89 E3 Khokhol'skiy Rus. Fed.

Komotini

74 B2 Khokhropar Pak.
89 D2 Kholm Rus. Fed.
89 D2 Kholm-Zhirkovskiy Rus. Fed.
122 A1 Khomas Highland *hills* Namibia
89 E3 Khomutovo Rus. Fed.
79 C2 Khonj Iran
63 B2 Khon Kaen Thai.
62 A1 Khonsa India
83 K2 Khonuu Rus. Fed.
86 E2 Khorey-Ver Rus. Fed.
69 D1 Khorinsk Rus. Fed.
120 A3 Khorixas Namibia
66 B2 Khorol Rus. Fed.
91 C2 Khorol Ukr.
81 C2 Khorramābād Iran
81 C2 Khorramshahr Iran
77 D3 Khorugh Tajik.
86 F2 Khoshgort Rus. Fed.
77 C3 Khōst Afgh.
Khotan China *see* Hotan
90 B2 Khotyn Ukr.
114 B1 Khouribga Morocco
88 C3 Khoyniki Belarus
62 A1 Khreum Myanmar
76 B1 Khromtau Kazakh.
Khrushchev Ukr. *see* Svitlovods'k
90 B2 Khrystynivka Ukr.
123 B1 Khudumelapye Botswana
77 C2 Khŭjand Tajik.
63 B2 Khu Khan Thai.
78 A2 Khulays Saudi Arabia
75 C2 Khulna Bangl.
Khūnīnshahr Iran *see* Khorramshahr
79 B2 Khurayş Saudi Arabia
74 B1 Khushab Pak.
90 A2 Khust Ukr.
123 C2 Khutsong S. Africa
74 A2 Khuzdar Pak.
81 D2 Khvānsār Iran
81 D3 Khvormūj Iran
81 C2 Khvoy Iran
89 D2 Khvoynaya Rus. Fed.
77 D3 Khyber Pass Afgh./Pak.
53 D2 Kiama Austr.
64 B3 Kiamba Phil.
119 C3 Kiambi Dem. Rep. Congo
Kiangsi *prov.* China *see* Jiangxi
Kiangsu *prov.* China *see* Jiangsu
119 D3 Kibaha Tanz.
119 D3 Kibaya Tanz.
119 D3 Kibiti Tanz.
119 C3 Kibombo Dem. Rep. Congo
119 D3 Kibondo Tanz.
119 D2 Kibre Mengist Eth.
119 D3 Kibungo Rwanda
111 B2 Kičevo Macedonia
114 C3 Kidal Mali
99 B3 Kidderminster U.K.
114 A3 Kidira Senegal
74 B1 Kidmang India
54 C1 Kidnappers, Cape N.Z.
102 C1 Kiel Ger.
103 E1 Kielce Pol.
98 B2 Kielder Water *resr* U.K.
119 C4 Kienge Dem. Rep. Congo
90 C1 Kiev Ukr.
114 A3 Kiffa Maur.
119 D3 Kigali Rwanda
119 C3 Kigoma Tanz.
88 B2 Kihnu *i.* Estonia
92 I2 Kiiminki Fin.
67 B4 Kii-suidō *sea chan.* Japan
109 D1 Kikinda Serbia
119 C3 Kikondja Dem. Rep. Congo
59 D3 Kikori P.N.G.
59 D3 Kikori *r.* P.N.G.
118 B3 Kikwit Dem. Rep. Congo
65 B1 Kilchu N. Korea
97 C2 Kilcock Ireland
97 C2 Kildare Ireland
118 B3 Kilembe Dem. Rep. Congo
143 E2 Kilgore U.S.A.
119 D3 Kilifi Kenya
119 D3 Kilimanjaro *vol.* Tanz.
119 D3 Kilindoni Tanz.
73 C4 Kilinochchi Sri Lanka
80 B2 Kilis Turkey
90 B2 Kiliya Ukr.
97 B2 Kilkee Ireland
97 D1 Kilkeel U.K.
97 C2 Kilkenny Ireland
111 B2 Kilkis Greece
97 B1 Killala Ireland
97 B1 Killala Bay Ireland
97 B2 Killaloe Ireland
128 C2 Killam Can.
97 B2 Killarney Ireland
143 D2 Killeen U.S.A.
96 B2 Killin U.K.
131 D1 Killiniq Can.
97 B2 Killorglin Ireland
97 B1 Killybegs Ireland
96 B3 Kilmarnock U.K.
53 B3 Kilmore Austr.
119 D3 Kilosa Tanz.
97 B2 Kilrush Ireland
119 C3 Kilwa Dem. Rep. Congo
119 D3 Kilwa Masoko Tanz.
119 D3 Kimambi Tanz.
52 A2 Kimba Austr.
136 C2 Kimball U.S.A.
59 E3 Kimbe P.N.G.
128 C3 Kimberley Can.
122 B2 Kimberley S. Africa
50 B1 Kimberley Plateau Austr.
65 B1 Kimch'aek N. Korea
65 B2 Kimch'ŏn S. Korea
65 B2 Kimhae S. Korea
127 H2 Kimmirut Can.
89 E3 Kimovsk Rus. Fed.
118 C3 Kimpanga Dem. Rep. Congo
118 B3 Kimpese Dem. Rep. Congo
89 E2 Kimry Rus. Fed.
61 C1 Kinabalu, Gunung *mt.* Malaysia
128 C2 Kinbasket Lake Can.
96 C1 Kinbrace U.K.
130 B3 Kincardine Can.
62 A1 Kinchang Myanmar
119 C3 Kinda Dem. Rep. Congo
98 C3 Kinder Scout *h.* U.K.
129 D2 Kindersley Can.
114 A3 Kindia Guinea
119 C3 Kindu Dem. Rep. Congo
89 F2 Kineshma Rus. Fed.
118 B3 Kingandu Dem. Rep. Congo
51 E2 Kingaroy Austr.
135 B3 King City U.S.A.
130 C2 King George Islands Can.
88 C2 Kingisepp Rus. Fed.
51 D3 King Island Austr.
Kingisseppa Estonia *see* Kuressaare
50 B1 King Leopold Ranges *hills* Austr.
142 A1 Kingman U.S.A.
135 B3 Kings *r.* U.S.A.
52 A3 Kingscote Austr.
97 C2 Kingscourt Ireland
99 D3 King's Lynn U.K.
50 B1 King Sound *b.* Austr.
134 D2 Kings Peak U.S.A.
141 D1 Kingsport U.S.A.
51 D4 Kingston Austr.
130 C3 Kingston Can.
146 C3 Kingston Jamaica
139 E2 Kingston U.S.A.
52 A3 Kingston South East Austr.
98 C3 Kingston upon Hull U.K.
147 D3 Kingstown St Vincent
143 D3 Kingsville U.S.A.
99 B4 Kingswood U.K.
96 B2 Kingussie U.K.
126 F2 King William Island Can.
123 C3 King William's Town S. Africa
67 D3 Kinka-san *i.* Japan
96 B2 Kinlochleven U.K.
93 F4 Kinna Sweden
97 B3 Kinsale Ireland
118 B3 Kinshasa Dem. Rep. Congo
141 E1 Kinston U.S.A.
88 B2 Kintai Lith.
114 B4 Kintampo Ghana
96 C2 Kintore U.K.
96 B3 Kintyre *pen.* U.K.
62 A1 Kin-U Myanmar
119 D3 Kiomboi Tanz.
130 C3 Kipawa, Lac *l.* Can.
119 D3 Kipembawe Tanz.
119 D3 Kipengere Range *mts* Tanz.
129 D2 Kipling Can.
Kipling Station Can. *see* Kipling
119 C4 Kipushi Dem. Rep. Congo
119 C4 Kipushia Dem. Rep. Congo
101 D2 Kirchhain Ger.
101 D3 Kirchheim-Bolanden Ger.
83 I3 Kirenga *r.* Rus. Fed.
83 I3 Kirensk Rus. Fed.
89 E3 Kireyevsk Rus. Fed.
Kirghizia *country* Asia *see* Kyrgyzstan
77 D2 Kirghiz Range *mts* Kazakh./Kyrg.
Kirgizskaya S.S.R. *country* Asia *see* Kyrgyzstan
49 J4 Kiribati *country* Pacific Ocean
80 B2 Kırıkkale Turkey
89 E2 Kirillov Rus. Fed.
Kirin China *see* Jilin
Kirin *prov.* China *see* Jilin
Kirinyaga *mt.* Kenya *see* Kenya, Mount
89 D2 Kirishi Rus. Fed.
48 L3 Kiritimati *atoll* Kiribati
111 C3 Kırkağaç Turkey
98 B3 Kirkby U.K.
98 B2 Kirkby Stephen U.K.
96 C2 Kirkcaldy U.K.
96 B3 Kirkcudbright U.K.
92 J2 Kirkenes Norway
93 H3 Kirkkonummi Fin.
88 B1 Kirkkonummi Fin.
130 B3 Kirkland Lake Can.
111 C2 Kırklareli Turkey
137 E2 Kirksville U.S.A.
81 C2 Kirkūk Iraq
96 C1 Kirkwall U.K.
Kirov Kazakh. *see* Balpyk Bi
89 D3 Kirov *Kaluzhskaya Oblast'* Rus. Fed.
86 D3 Kirov *Kirovskaya Oblast'* Rus. Fed.
Kirovabad Azer. *see* Gäncä
Kirovakan Armenia *see* Vanadzor
Kirovo Ukr. *see* Kirovohrad
86 E3 Kirovo-Chepetsk Rus. Fed.
Kirovo-Chepetskiy Rus. Fed. *see* Kirovo-Chepetsk
91 C2 Kirovohrad Ukr.
86 C2 Kirovsk Rus. Fed.
91 D2 Kirovs'ke Ukr.
Kirovskiy Kazakh. *see* Balpyk Bi
66 B1 Kirovskiy Rus. Fed.
96 C2 Kirriemuir U.K.
86 E3 Kirs Rus. Fed.
87 D3 Kirsanov Rus. Fed.
80 B2 Kırşehir Turkey
74 A2 Kirthar Range *mts* Pak.
92 H2 Kiruna Sweden
67 C3 Kiryū Japan
89 E2 Kirzhach Rus. Fed.
119 D3 Kisaki Tanz.
119 C2 Kisangani Dem. Rep. Congo
118 B3 Kisantu Dem. Rep. Congo
60 A1 Kisaran Indon.
82 G3 Kiselevsk Rus. Fed.
75 C2 Kishanganj India
115 C4 Kishi Nigeria
Kishinev Moldova *see* Chișinău
67 C4 Kishiwada Japan
77 D1 Kishkenekol' Kazakh.
75 D2 Kishoreganj Bangl.
74 B1 Kishtwar India
119 D3 Kisii Kenya
103 D2 Kiskunfélegyháza Hungary
103 D2 Kiskunhalas Hungary
87 D4 Kislovodsk Rus. Fed.
117 C5 Kismaayo Somalia
Kismayu Somalia *see* Kismaayo
119 C3 Kisoro Uganda
111 B3 Kissamos Greece
114 A4 Kissidougou Guinea
141 D3 Kissimmee U.S.A.
141 D3 Kissimmee, Lake U.S.A.
129 D2 Kississing Lake Can.
Kistna *r.* India *see* Krishna
119 D3 Kisumu Kenya
103 E2 Kisvárda Hungary
Kisykkamys Kazakh. *see* Zhanakala
114 B3 Kita Mali
67 D3 Kitaibaraki Japan
66 D3 Kitakami Japan
66 D3 Kitakami-gawa *r.* Japan
67 B4 Kita-Kyūshū Japan
119 D2 Kitale Kenya
66 D2 Kitami Japan
130 B3 Kitchener Can.
93 J3 Kitee Fin.
119 D2 Kitgum Uganda
128 B2 Kitimat Can.
118 B3 Kitona Dem. Rep. Congo
92 H2 Kittilä Fin.
141 E1 Kitty Hawk U.S.A.
119 D3 Kitunda Tanz.
128 B2 Kitwanga Can.
121 B2 Kitwe Zambia
102 C2 Kitzbühel Austria
101 E3 Kitzingen Ger.
59 D3 Kiunga P.N.G.
92 I3 Kiuruvesi Fin.
92 I2 Kivalo *ridge* Fin.
90 B1 Kivertsi Ukr.
88 C2 Kiviõli Estonia
91 D2 Kivsharivka Ukr.
119 C3 Kivu, Lac Dem. Rep. Congo/Rwanda
111 C2 Kıyıköy Turkey
86 E3 Kizel Rus. Fed.
111 C3 Kızılca Dağ *mt.* Turkey
80 B1 Kızılırmak *r.* Turkey
87 D4 Kizlyar Rus. Fed.
Kizyl-Arbat Turkm. *see* Serdar
92 I1 Kjøllefjord Norway
92 G2 Kjøpsvik Norway
102 C1 Kladno Czech Rep.
102 C2 Klagenfurt Austria
88 B2 Klaipėda Lith.
94 B1 Klaksvík Faroe Is
134 B2 Klamath *r.* U.S.A.
134 B2 Klamath Falls U.S.A.
134 B2 Klamath Mountains U.S.A.
60 B1 Klang Malaysia
102 C2 Klatovy Czech Rep.
122 A3 Klawer S. Africa
128 A2 Klawock U.S.A.
128 B2 Kleena Kleene Can.
122 B2 Kleinbegin S. Africa
122 A2 Klein Karas Namibia
122 A2 Kleinsee S. Africa
123 C2 Klerksdorp S. Africa
90 B1 Klesiv Ukr.
89 D3 Kletnya Rus. Fed.
100 C2 Kleve Ger.
88 C3 Klichaw Belarus
89 D3 Klimavichy Belarus
89 D3 Klimovo Rus. Fed.
89 E2 Klimovsk Rus. Fed.
89 E2 Klin Rus. Fed.
101 F2 Klingenthal Ger.
101 F2 Klínovec *mt.* Czech Rep.
93 G4 Klintehamn Sweden
89 D3 Klintsy Rus. Fed.
109 C2 Ključ Bos.-Herz.
103 D1 Kłodzko Pol.
100 C1 Kloosterhaar Neth.
103 D2 Klosterneuburg Austria
101 E1 Klötze (Altmark) Ger.
128 A1 Kluane Lake Can.
Kluang Malaysia *see* Keluang
103 D1 Kluczbork Pol.
Klukhori Rus. Fed. *see* Karachayevsk
128 A2 Klukwan U.S.A.
89 F2 Klyaz'ma *r.* Rus. Fed.
88 C3 Klyetsk Belarus
83 L3 Klyuchi Rus. Fed.
98 C2 Knaresborough U.K.
93 F3 Knästen *h.* Sweden
129 E2 Knee Lake Can.
101 E1 Knesebeck Ger.
101 E3 Knetzgau Ger.
109 C2 Knin Croatia
103 C2 Knittelfeld Austria
109 D2 Knjaževac Serbia
Knob Lake Can. *see* Schefferville
97 B3 Knockboy *h.* Ireland
100 A2 Knokke-Heist Belgium
141 D1 Knoxville U.S.A.
127 H1 Knud Rasmussen Land *reg.* Greenland
122 B3 Knysna S. Africa
60 B2 Koba Indon.
76 B1 Kobda Kazakh.
67 C4 Kōbe Japan
København Denmark *see* Copenhagen
100 C2 Koblenz Ger.
59 C3 Kobroör *i.* Indon.
88 B3 Kobryn Belarus
Kocaeli Turkey *see* İzmit
111 B2 Kočani Macedonia
111 C2 Kocasu *r.* Turkey
109 B1 Kočevje Slovenia
75 C2 Koch Bihar India
89 F3 Kochetovka Rus. Fed.
73 B4 Kochi India
67 B4 Kōchi Japan
87 D4 Kochubey Rus. Fed.
75 C2 Kodarma India
126 B3 Kodiak U.S.A.
126 B3 Kodiak Island U.S.A.
123 C1 Kodibeleng Botswana
117 B4 Kodok S. Sudan
90 B2 Kodyma Ukr.
111 C2 Kodzhaele *mt.* Bulg./Greece
122 A2 Koës Namibia
122 C2 Koffiefontein S. Africa
114 B4 Koforidua Ghana
67 C3 Kōfu Japan
131 D2 Kogaluk *r.* Can.
117 B5 Kogelo Kenya
114 B3 Kogoni Mali
74 B1 Kohat Pak.
72 D2 Kohima India
88 C2 Kohtla-Järve Estonia
128 A1 Koidern Can.
Kokand Uzbek. *see* Qo'qon
88 B2 Kökar Fin.
Kokchetav Kazakh. *see* Kokshetau
122 A2 Kokerboom Namibia
88 C3 Kokhanava Belarus
89 F2 Kokhma Rus. Fed.
92 H3 Kokkola Fin.
88 C2 Koknese Latvia
138 B2 Kokomo U.S.A.
122 B1 Kokong Botswana
123 C2 Kokosi S. Africa
77 E2 Kokpekty Kazakh.
77 C1 Kokshetau Kazakh.
131 D2 Koksoak *r.* Can.
123 C3 Kokstad S. Africa
Koktokay China *see* Fuyun
61 D2 Kolaka Indon.
86 C2 Kola Peninsula Rus. Fed.
92 H2 Kolari Fin.
Kolarovgrad Bulg. *see* Shumen
114 A3 Kolda Senegal
93 E4 Kolding Denmark
119 C2 Kole Dem. Rep. Congo
107 D2 Koléa Alg.
86 D2 Kolguyev, Ostrov *i.* Rus. Fed.
73 B3 Kolhapur India
88 B2 Kolkasrags *pt* Latvia
75 C2 Kolkata India
73 B4 Kollam India
100 C1 Kollum Neth.
Köln Ger. *see* Cologne
103 D1 Koło Pol.
103 D1 Kołobrzeg Pol.
114 B3 Kolokani Mali
89 E2 Kolomna Rus. Fed.
90 B2 Kolomyya Ukr.
114 B3 Kolondiéba Mali
61 D2 Kolonedale Indon.
122 B2 Kolonkwaneng Botswana
82 G3 Kolpashevo Rus. Fed.
89 E3 Kolpny Rus. Fed.
Kol'skiy Poluostrov *pen.* Rus. Fed. *see* Kola Peninsula
78 B3 Koluli Eritrea
92 F3 Kolvereid Norway
119 C4 Kolwezi Dem. Rep. Congo
83 L2 Kolyma *r.* Rus. Fed.
Kolyma Lowland *lowland* Rus. Fed. *see* Kolymskaya Nizmennost'
Kolyma Range *mts* Rus. Fed. *see* Kolymskiy, Khrebet
83 L2 Kolymskaya Nizmennost' *lowland* Rus. Fed.
83 M2 Kolymskiy, Khrebet *mts* Rus. Fed.
122 A2 Komaggas S. Africa
67 C3 Komaki Japan
83 M3 Komandorskiye Ostrova *is* Rus. Fed.
103 D2 Komárno Slovakia
123 D2 Komati *r.* S. Africa/Swaziland
123 D2 Komatipoort S. Africa
67 C3 Komatsu Japan
120 A2 Kombat Namibia
119 C3 Kombe Dem. Rep. Congo
Komintern Ukr. *see* Marhanets'
90 C2 Kominternivs'ke Ukr.
109 C2 Komiža Croatia
103 D2 Komló Hungary
Kommunarsk Ukr. *see* Alchevs'k
118 B3 Komono Congo
111 C2 Komotini Greece

Kompong Som Cambodia see Sihanoukville
Komrat Moldova see Comrat
122 B3 Komsberg mts S. Africa
83 H1 Komsomolets, Ostrov i. Rus. Fed.
89 F2 Komsomol'sk Rus. Fed.
91 C2 Komsomol's'k Ukr.
83 M2 Komsomol'skiy Rus. Fed.
Komsomol'skiy Rus. Fed. see Yugorsk
87 D4 Komsomol'skiy Rus. Fed.
83 K3 Komsomol'sk-na-Amure Rus. Fed.
89 E2 Konakovo Rus. Fed.
75 C3 Kondagaon India
Kondinskoye Rus. Fed. see Oktyabr'skoye
86 F2 Kondinskoye Rus. Fed.
119 D3 Kondoa Tanz.
86 C2 Kondopoga Rus. Fed.
89 E3 Kondrovo Rus. Fed.
127 J2 Kong Christian IX Land reg. Greenland
127 K2 Kong Christian X Land reg. Greenland
127 J2 Kong Frederik VI Kyst coastal area Greenland
65 B2 Kongju S. Korea
119 C3 Kongolo Dem. Rep. Congo
93 E4 Kongsberg Norway
93 F3 Kongsvinger Norway
77 D3 Kongur Shan mt. China
100 C2 Königswinter Ger.
103 D1 Konin Pol.
109 C2 Konjic Bos.-Herz.
122 A2 Konkiep watercourse Namibia
86 D2 Konosha Rus. Fed.
91 C1 Konotop Ukr.
103 E1 Końskie Pol.
Konstantinograd Ukr. see Krasnohrad
102 B2 Konstanz Ger.
115 C3 Kontagora Nigeria
63 B2 Kon Tum Vietnam
63 B2 Kon Tum, Cao Nguyên Vietnam
80 B2 Konya Turkey
77 D2 Konyrat Kazakh.
100 C3 Konz Ger.
86 E3 Konzhakovskiy Kamen', Gora mt. Rus. Fed.
134 C1 Kooskia U.S.A.
128 C3 Kootenay Lake Can.
53 D2 Kootingal Austr.
122 B3 Kootjieskolk S. Africa
92 □B2 Kópasker Iceland
108 B1 Koper Slovenia
93 G4 Köping Sweden
123 C1 Kopong Botswana
93 G4 Kopparberg Sweden
109 C1 Koprivnica Croatia
89 F3 Korablino Rus. Fed.
73 C3 Koraput India
75 C2 Korba India
101 D2 Korbach Ger.
109 D2 Korçë Albania
109 C2 Korčula Croatia
109 C2 Korčula i. Croatia
65 B1 Korea, North country Asia
65 B2 Korea, South country Asia
70 C2 Korea Bay g. China/N. Korea
65 B3 Korea Strait Japan/S. Korea
89 D3 Korenevo Rus. Fed.
91 D2 Korenovsk Rus. Fed.
Korenovskaya Rus. Fed. see Korenovsk
90 B1 Korets' Ukr.
111 C2 Körfez Turkey
114 B4 Korhogo Côte d'Ivoire
Korinthos Greece see Corinth
103 D2 Kőris-hegy h. Hungary
109 D2 Koritnik mt. Albania/Kosovo
Koritsa Albania see Korçë
67 D3 Kōriyama Japan
87 F3 Korkino Rus. Fed.
111 D3 Korkuteli Turkey
77 E2 Korla China
103 D2 Körmend Hungary
49 I5 Koro i. Fiji
114 B3 Koro Mali
131 D2 Koroc r. Can.
91 D1 Korocha Rus. Fed.
119 D3 Korogwe Tanz.
59 C2 Koror Palau
103 E2 Körös r. Hungary
90 B1 Korosten' Ukr.
90 B1 Korostyshiv Ukr.
115 D3 Koro Toro Chad
93 H3 Korpo Fin.
66 D1 Korsakov Rus. Fed.
91 C2 Korsun'-Shevchenkivs'kyy Ukr.
103 E1 Korsze Pol.
116 B3 Korti Sudan
100 A2 Kortrijk Belgium
83 L3 Koryakskaya, Sopka vol. Rus. Fed.
83 M2 Koryakskoye Nagor'ye mts Rus. Fed.
86 D2 Koryazhma Rus. Fed.
65 B2 Koryŏng S. Korea
91 C1 Koryukivka Ukr.
111 C3 Kos Greece
111 C3 Kos i. Greece
91 D2 Kosa Biryuchyy Ostriv i. Ukr.
65 B2 Kosan N. Korea
103 D1 Kościan Pol.
Kosciusko, Mount mt. Austr. see Kosciuszko, Mount

53 C3 Kosciuszko, Mount Austr.
77 E2 Kosh-Agach Rus. Fed.
67 A4 Koshikijima-rettō is Japan
103 E2 Košice Slovakia
92 H2 Koskullskulle Sweden
65 B2 Kosŏng N. Korea
109 D2 Kosovo country Europe
Kosovska Mitrovica Kosovo see Mitrovicë
48 H3 Kosrae atoll Micronesia
114 B4 Kossou, Lac de l. Côte d'Ivoire
76 C1 Kostanay Kazakh.
110 B2 Kostenets Bulg.
123 C2 Koster S. Africa
116 B3 Kosti Sudan
92 J3 Kostomuksha Rus. Fed.
90 B1 Kostopil' Ukr.
89 F2 Kostroma Rus. Fed.
89 F2 Kostroma r. Rus. Fed.
102 C1 Kostrzyn Pol.
91 D2 Kostyantynivka Ukr.
103 D1 Koszalin Pol.
103 D2 Kőszeg Hungary
74 B2 Kota India
90 B1 Kotaagung Indon.
61 C2 Kotabaru Indon.
61 C1 Kota Belud Malaysia
60 B1 Kota Bharu Malaysia
60 B2 Kotabumi Indon.
61 C1 Kota Kinabalu Malaysia
75 C3 Kotaparh India
61 C1 Kota Samarahan Malaysia
86 D3 Kotel'nich Rus. Fed.
87 D4 Kotel'nikovo Rus. Fed.
83 K1 Kotel'nyy, Ostrov i. Rus. Fed.
91 C1 Kotel'va Ukr.
101 E2 Köthen (Anhalt) Ger.
119 D2 Kotido Uganda
93 I3 Kotka Fin.
86 D2 Kotlas Rus. Fed.
126 B2 Kotlik U.S.A.
109 C2 Kotor Varoš Bos.-Herz.
87 D3 Kotovo Rus. Fed.
91 E1 Kotovsk Rus. Fed.
90 B2 Kotovs'k Ukr.
73 C3 Kottagudem India
118 C2 Kotto r. C.A.R.
83 H2 Kotuy r. Rus. Fed.
126 B2 Kotzebue U.S.A.
126 B2 Kotzebue Sound sea chan. U.S.A.
114 A3 Koubia Guinea
100 A2 Koudekerke Neth.
114 B3 Koudougou Burkina Faso
122 B3 Kougaberge mts S. Africa
118 B3 Koulamoutou Gabon
114 B3 Koulikoro Mali
118 B2 Koum Cameroon
118 B2 Koumra Chad
114 A3 Koundâra Guinea
Kounradskiy Kazakh. see Konyrat
151 D2 Kourou Fr. Guiana
114 B3 Kouroussa Guinea
115 D3 Kousséri Cameroon
114 B3 Koutiala Mali
93 I3 Kouvola Fin.
109 D1 Kovačica Serbia
92 J2 Kovdor Rus. Fed.
90 A1 Kovel' Ukr.
Kovno Lith. see Kaunas
89 F2 Kovrov Rus. Fed.
51 D1 Kowanyama Austr.
54 B2 Kowhitirangi N.Z.
Koyamutthoor India see Coimbatore
111 C3 Köyceğiz Turkey
86 D2 Koyda Rus. Fed.
126 B2 Koyukuk r. U.S.A.
111 B2 Kozani Greece
90 C1 Kozelets' Ukr.
89 E3 Kozel'sk Rus. Fed.
73 B3 Kozhikode India
90 B2 Kozyatyn Ukr.
114 C4 Kpalimé Togo
63 A2 Kra, Isthmus of Myanmar/Thai.
63 A3 Krabi Thai.
63 A3 Kra Buri Thai.
63 B2 Krâchéh Cambodia
93 E4 Kragerø Norway
100 B1 Kraggenburg Neth.
109 D2 Kragujevac Serbia
60 B2 Krakatau i. Indon.
103 D1 Kraków Pol.
109 D2 Kraljevo Serbia
91 D2 Kramators'k Ukr.
93 G3 Kramfors Sweden
111 B3 Kranidi Greece
102 C2 Kranj Slovenia
123 D2 Kranskop S. Africa
86 E1 Krasino Rus. Fed.
88 C2 Krāslava Latvia
101 F2 Kraslice Czech Rep.
89 D3 Krasnapollye Belarus
89 D3 Krasnaya Gora Rus. Fed.
89 F2 Krasnaya Gorbatka Rus. Fed.
Krasnoarmeysk Kazakh. see Taiynsha
87 D3 Krasnoarmeysk Rus. Fed.
Krasnoarmeyskaya Rus. Fed. see Poltavskaya
91 D2 Krasnoarmiys'k Ukr.
86 D2 Krasnoborsk Rus. Fed.
91 D2 Krasnodar Rus. Fed.
91 D2 Krasnodarskoye Vodokhranilishche resr Rus. Fed.
91 D2 Krasnodon Ukr.
88 C2 Krasnogorodsk Rus. Fed.

91 D2 Krasnohrad Ukr.
91 C2 Krasnohvardiys'ke Ukr.
86 E3 Krasnokamsk Rus. Fed.
89 D2 Krasnomayskiy Rus. Fed.
87 D3 Krasnoperekops'k Ukr.
87 D3 Krasnoslobodsk Rus. Fed.
86 E3 Krasnotur'insk Rus. Fed.
86 E3 Krasnoufimsk Rus. Fed.
86 E2 Krasnovishersk Rus. Fed.
Krasnovodsk Turkm. see Türkmenbaşy
83 H3 Krasnoyarsk Rus. Fed.
89 E3 Krasnoye Rus. Fed.
83 M2 Krasnoye, Ozero l. Rus. Fed.
89 F2 Krasnoye-na-Volge Rus. Fed.
103 E1 Krasnystaw Pol.
89 D3 Krasnyy Rus. Fed.
Krasnyy Kamyshanik Rus. Fed. see Komsomol'skiy
91 D2 Krasnyy Kholm Rus. Fed.
91 E2 Krasnyy Luch Ukr.
91 E2 Krasnyy Sulin Rus. Fed.
90 B2 Krasyliv Ukr.
Kraulshavn Greenland see Nuussuaq
100 C2 Krefeld Ger.
91 C2 Kremenchuk Ukr.
91 C2 Kremenchuts'ke Vodoskhovyshche resr Ukr.
90 B1 Kremenets' Ukr.
103 D2 Křemešník h. Czech Rep.
Kremges Ukr. see Svitlovods'k
91 D2 Kreminna Ukr.
136 B2 Kremmling U.S.A.
103 D2 Krems an der Donau Austria
89 D2 Kresttsy Rus. Fed.
88 B2 Kretinga Lith.
100 C2 Kreuzau Ger.
101 C2 Kreuztal Ger.
118 A2 Kribi Cameroon
111 B3 Krikellos Greece
66 D1 Kril'on, Mys c. Rus. Fed.
111 B3 Krios, Akrotirio pt Greece
73 C3 Krishna r. India
73 C3 Krishna, Mouths of the India
75 C2 Krishnanagar India
93 E4 Kristiansand Norway
93 F4 Kristianstad Sweden
92 E3 Kristiansund Norway
93 F4 Kristinehamn Sweden
Kristinopol' Ukr. see Chervonohrad
Kriti i. Greece see Crete
111 C3 Kritiko Pelagos sea Greece
110 B2 Kriva Palanka Macedonia
Krivoy Rog Ukr. see Kryvyy Rih
109 C1 Križevci Croatia
108 B1 Krk i. Croatia
92 F3 Krokom Sweden
91 C1 Krolevets' Ukr.
89 E3 Kromy Rus. Fed.
101 E2 Kronach Ger.
63 B2 Krŏng Kaôh Kŏng Cambodia
127 J2 Kronprins Frederik Bjerge nunataks Greenland
123 C2 Kroonstad S. Africa
91 E2 Kropotkin Rus. Fed.
103 E2 Krosno Pol.
103 D1 Krotoszyn Pol.
60 B2 Krui Indon.
122 B3 Kruisfontein S. Africa
109 C2 Krujë Albania
111 C2 Krumovgrad Bulg.
Krung Thep Thai. see Bangkok
88 C3 Krupki Belarus
109 D2 Kruševac Serbia
101 F2 Krušné hory mts Czech Rep.
128 A2 Kruzof Island U.S.A.
89 D3 Krychaw Belarus
91 D2 Krylovskaya Rus. Fed.
91 D3 Krymsk Rus. Fed.
Krymskaya Rus. Fed. see Krymsk
Kryms'kyy Pivostriv pen. Ukr. see Crimea
91 C2 Krystynopol Ukr. see Chervonohrad
90 B2 Kryvyy Rih Ukr.
91 C2 Kryzhopil' Ukr.
114 B2 Ksabi Alg.
107 D2 Ksar el Boukhari Alg.
114 B1 Ksar el Kebir Morocco
Ksar-es-Souk Morocco see Er Rachidia
89 E3 Kshenskiy Rus. Fed.
78 B2 Kū', Jabal al i. Saudi Arabia
61 C1 Kuala Belait Brunei
Kuala Dungun Malaysia see Dungun
60 B1 Kuala Kangsar Malaysia
60 B1 Kuala Kerai Malaysia
60 B1 Kuala Lipis Malaysia
60 B1 Kuala Lumpur Malaysia
60 B1 Kualapembuang Indon.
60 B1 Kuala Terengganu Malaysia
61 C1 Kualatungal Indon.
65 A1 Kuandian China
61 C1 Kuantan Malaysia
91 D2 Kuban' r. Rus. Fed.
89 E2 Kubenskoye, Ozero l. Rus. Fed.
110 C2 Kubrat Bulg.
60 B2 Kubu Indon.
61 C1 Kubuang Indon.
90 B2 Kuching Malaysia
109 C2 Kuçovë Albania
61 C2 Kudat Malaysia
61 C2 Kudus Indon.
102 C2 Kufstein Austria

127 G2 Kugaaruk Can.
91 D2 Kugey Rus. Fed.
126 E2 Kugluktuk Can.
126 D2 Kugmallit Bay Can.
92 I3 Kuhmo Fin.
79 C2 Kūhrān, Kūh-e mt. Iran
122 A1 Kuis Namibia
120 A2 Kuito Angola
92 I3 Kuivaniemi Fin.
65 B2 Kujang N. Korea
66 D2 Kuji Japan
67 B4 Kujū-san vol. Japan
109 D2 Kukës Albania
76 B3 Kükürtli Turkm.
111 C3 Kula Turkey
75 D2 Kula Kangri mt. Bhutan/China
76 B2 Kulandy Kazakh.
88 B2 Kuldīga Latvia
Kuldja China see Yining
122 B1 Kule Botswana
101 E2 Kulmbach Ger.
77 C3 Külob Tajik.
76 B2 Kul'sary Kazakh.
111 C3 Kulübe Tepe mt. Turkey
77 D1 Kulunda Rus. Fed.
77 D1 Kulundinskoye, Ozero salt l. Rus. Fed.
127 J2 Kulusuk Greenland
67 C3 Kumagaya Japan
67 B4 Kumamoto Japan
67 C4 Kumano Japan
110 B2 Kumanovo Macedonia
114 B4 Kumasi Ghana
118 A2 Kumba Cameroon
Kum-Dag Turkm. see Gumdag
78 B2 Kumdah Saudi Arabia
87 E3 Kumertau Rus. Fed.
65 B2 Kumi S. Korea
119 D2 Kumi Uganda
111 C3 Kumkale Turkey
93 G4 Kumla Sweden
115 D3 Kumo Nigeria
62 A1 Kumon Range mts Myanmar
62 B2 Kumphawapi Thai.
Kumul China see Hami
120 A2 Kunene r. Angola/Namibia
77 D2 Kungei Alatau mts Kazakh./Kyrg.
93 F4 Kungsbacka Sweden
118 B3 Kungu Dem. Rep. Congo
86 E3 Kungur Rus. Fed.
62 A1 Kunhing Myanmar
62 A1 Kunlong Myanmar
75 B1 Kunlun Shan mts China
71 A3 Kunming China
65 B2 Kunsan S. Korea
50 B1 Kununurra Austr.
101 D3 Künzelsau Ger.
92 I3 Kuopio Fin.
109 C1 Kupa r. Croatia/Slovenia
59 C3 Kupang Indon.
88 B2 Kupiškis Lith.
111 C2 Küplü Turkey
111 C3 Kupreanof Island U.S.A.
91 D2 Kup"yans'k Ukr.
77 E2 Kuqa China
81 C2 Kür r. Azer.
67 B4 Kurashiki Japan
75 C2 Kurasia India
67 B3 Kurayoshi Japan
89 E3 Kurchatov Rus. Fed.
111 C2 Kürdzhali Bulg.
67 B4 Kure Japan
57 T7 Kure Atoll U.S.A.
88 B2 Kuressaare Estonia
87 F3 Kurgan Rus. Fed.
Kuria Muria Islands is Oman see Ḩalāniyāt, Juzur al
93 H3 Kurikka Fin.
156 C2 Kuril Basin Sea of Okhotsk
69 F1 Kuril Islands is Rus. Fed.
69 F1 Kuril'sk Rus. Fed.
Kuril'skiye Ostrova is Rus. Fed. see Kuril Islands
156 C3 Kuril Trench N. Pacific Ocean
89 E3 Kurkino Rus. Fed.
Kurmashkino Kazakh. see Kurshim
117 B3 Kurmuk Sudan
73 B3 Kurnool India
67 D3 Kuroiso Japan
53 D2 Kurri Kurri Austr.
88 B2 Kuršėnai Lith.
78 B2 Kursh, Jabal mt. Saudi Arabia
77 E2 Kurshim Kazakh.
89 E3 Kursk Rus. Fed.
109 D2 Kuršumlija Serbia
122 B2 Kuruman S. Africa
122 B2 Kuruman watercourse S. Africa
67 B4 Kurume Japan
83 I3 Kurumkan Rus. Fed.
73 C4 Kurunegala Sri Lanka
81 C1 Kuryk Kazakh.
111 C3 Kuşadası Turkey
111 C3 Kuşadası Körfezi b. Turkey
111 C2 Kuş Gölü l. Turkey
91 D2 Kushchevskaya Rus. Fed.
66 D2 Kushiro Japan
Kushka Turkm. see Serhetabat
75 C2 Kushtia Bangl.
126 B2 Kuskokwim r. U.S.A.
126 B2 Kuskokwim Mountains U.S.A.
76 C1 Kusmuryn Kazakh.
66 D2 Kussharo-ko l. Japan
Kustanay Kazakh. see Kostanay

Łuków

108 B3 **Lipari, Isole** *is* Italy
89 E3 **Lipetsk** Rus. Fed.
110 B1 **Lipova** Romania
101 D2 **Lippstadt** Ger.
53 C3 **Liptrap, Cape** Austr.
71 B3 **Lipu** China
119 D2 **Lira** Uganda
108 B2 **Liri** *r.* Italy
76 C1 **Lisakovsk** Kazakh.
118 C2 **Lisala** Dem. Rep. Congo
Lisboa Port. *see* **Lisbon**
106 B2 **Lisbon** Port.
97 C1 **Lisburn** U.K.
97 B2 **Liscannor Bay** Ireland
97 B2 **Lisdoonvarna** Ireland
Lishi China *see* **Dingnan**
71 B3 **Lishui** China
104 C2 **Lisieux** France
99 A4 **Liskeard** U.K.
89 E3 **Liski** Rus. Fed.
53 D1 **Lismore** Austr.
97 C2 **Lismore** Ireland
97 C1 **Lisnaskea** U.K.
97 B2 **Listowel** Ireland
71 A3 **Litang** *Guangxi* China
68 C2 **Litang** *Sichuan* China
138 B3 **Litchfield** *IL* U.S.A.
137 E1 **Litchfield** *MN* U.S.A.
53 D2 **Lithgow** Austr.
111 B3 **Lithino, Akrotirio** *pt* Greece
88 B2 **Lithuania** *country* Europe
111 B2 **Litochoro** Greece
102 C1 **Litoměřice** Czech Rep.
Litovskaya S.S.R. *country* Europe *see* **Lithuania**
146 C2 **Little Abaco** *i.* Bahamas
73 D3 **Little Andaman** *i.* India
141 E3 **Little Bahama Bank** *sea feature* Bahamas
93 E4 **Little Belt** *sea chan.* Denmark
146 B3 **Little Cayman** *i.* Cayman Is
142 A1 **Little Colorado** *r.* U.S.A.
138 C1 **Little Current** Can.
137 E1 **Little Falls** U.S.A.
143 C2 **Littlefield** U.S.A.
99 C4 **Littlehampton** U.K.
122 A2 **Little Karas Berg** *plat.* Namibia
122 B3 **Little Karoo** *plat.* S. Africa
96 A2 **Little Minch** *sea chan.* U.K.
136 C1 **Little Missouri** *r.* U.S.A.
73 D4 **Little Nicobar** *i.* India
140 B2 **Little Rock** U.S.A.
139 E2 **Littleton** U.S.A.
121 C2 **Litunde** Moz.
90 B2 **Lityn** Ukr.
Liuchow China *see* **Liuzhou**
70 B2 **Liujiachang** China
71 A3 **Liupanshui** China
121 C2 **Liupo** Moz.
71 A3 **Liuzhi** China
71 A3 **Liuzhou** China
111 B3 **Livadeia** Greece
88 C2 **Līvāni** Latvia
141 D2 **Live Oak** U.S.A.
50 B1 **Liveringa** Austr.
142 C2 **Livermore, Mount** U.S.A.
53 D2 **Liverpool** Austr.
131 D3 **Liverpool** Can.
98 B3 **Liverpool** U.K.
127 G2 **Liverpool, Cape** Can.
53 C2 **Liverpool Range** *mts* Austr.
96 C3 **Livingston** U.K.
134 D1 **Livingston** *MT* U.S.A.
143 E2 **Livingston** *TX* U.S.A.
143 D2 **Livingston, Lake** U.S.A.
120 B2 **Livingstone** Zambia
55 A3 **Livingston Island** Antarctica
109 C2 **Livno** Bos.-Herz.
89 E3 **Livny** Rus. Fed.
138 C2 **Livonia** U.S.A.
108 B2 **Livorno** Italy
119 D3 **Liwale** Tanz.
99 A5 **Lizard Point** U.K.
108 B1 **Ljubljana** Slovenia
93 G3 **Ljungan** *r.* Sweden
93 F4 **Ljungby** Sweden
93 G3 **Ljusdal** Sweden
93 G3 **Ljusnan** *r.* Sweden
99 B4 **Llandeilo** U.K.
99 B4 **Llandovery** U.K.
99 B3 **Llandrindod Wells** U.K.
98 B3 **Llandudno** U.K.
99 A4 **Llanelli** U.K.
106 C1 **Llanes** Spain
98 A3 **Llangefni** U.K.
99 B3 **Llangollen** U.K.
106 B1 **Llangréu** Spain
99 B3 **Llangurig** U.K.
143 C2 **Llano Estacado** *plain* U.S.A.
150 C2 **Llanos** *plain* Col./Venez.
107 D1 **Lleida** Spain
99 A3 **Lleyn Peninsula** U.K.
107 C2 **Llíria** Spain
128 B2 **Lloyd George, Mount** Can.
129 D2 **Lloyd Lake** Can.
129 C2 **Lloydminster** Can.
152 B2 **Llullaillaco, Volcán** *vol.* Chile
154 B2 **Loanda** Brazil
123 C2 **Lobatse** Botswana
103 D1 **Łobez** Pol.
120 A2 **Lobito** Angola
101 F1 **Loburg** Ger.
96 B2 **Lochaber** *reg.* U.K.
96 B2 **Lochaline** U.K.
Loch Baghasdail U.K. *see* **Lochboisdale**
96 A2 **Lochboisdale** U.K.
104 C2 **Loches** France
96 B2 **Lochgilphead** U.K.
96 B1 **Lochinver** U.K.
96 A2 **Lochmaddy** U.K.
96 C2 **Lochnagar** *mt.* U.K.
Loch nam Madadh U.K. *see* **Lochmaddy**
96 B3 **Lochranza** U.K.
52 A2 **Lock** Austr.
96 C3 **Lockerbie** U.K.
53 C3 **Lockhart** Austr.
143 D3 **Lockhart** U.S.A.
51 D1 **Lockhart River** Austr.
139 D2 **Lock Haven** U.S.A.
139 D2 **Lockport** U.S.A.
63 B2 **Lôc Ninh** Vietnam
105 C3 **Lodève** France
86 C2 **Lodeynoye Pole** Rus. Fed.
74 B2 **Lodhran** Pak.
108 A1 **Lodi** Italy
135 B3 **Lodi** U.S.A.
92 F2 **Løding** Norway
92 G2 **Lødingen** Norway
118 C3 **Lodja** Dem. Rep. Congo
119 D2 **Lodwar** Kenya
103 D1 **Łódź** Pol.
62 B2 **Loei** Thai.
122 A3 **Loeriesfontein** S. Africa
92 F2 **Lofoten** *is* Norway
134 D2 **Logan** U.S.A.
128 A1 **Logan, Mount** Can.
138 B2 **Logansport** U.S.A.
108 B1 **Logatec** Slovenia
115 D3 **Logone** *r.* Africa
106 C1 **Logroño** Spain
93 H3 **Lohja** Fin.
101 D1 **Löhne** Ger.
101 D1 **Lohne (Oldenburg)** Ger.
62 A2 **Loikaw** Myanmar
62 A2 **Loi Lan** *mt.* Myanmar/Thai.
93 H3 **Loimaa** Fin.
104 B2 **Loire** *r.* France
150 B3 **Loja** Ecuador
106 C2 **Loja** Spain
92 I2 **Lokan tekojärvi** *resr* Fin.
74 B1 **Lōkār** Afgh.
100 B2 **Lokeren** Belgium
122 B1 **Lokgwabe** Botswana
91 C1 **Lokhvytsya** Ukr.
119 D2 **Lokichar** Kenya
119 D2 **Lokichokio** Kenya
93 E4 **Løkken** Denmark
89 D2 **Loknya** Rus. Fed.
115 C4 **Lokoja** Nigeria
89 D3 **Lokot'** Rus. Fed.
88 C2 **Loksa** Estonia
127 H2 **Loks Land** *i.* Can.
114 B4 **Lola** Guinea
93 F5 **Lolland** *i.* Denmark
119 D3 **Lollondo** Tanz.
118 C2 **Lolo** Dem. Rep. Congo
122 B2 **Lolwane** S. Africa
110 B2 **Lom** Bulg.
93 E3 **Lom** Norway
119 C2 **Lomami** *r.* Dem. Rep. Congo
153 C3 **Lomas de Zamora** Arg.
50 B1 **Lombardina** Austr.
61 C2 **Lombok** *i.* Indon.
61 C2 **Lombok, Selat** *sea chan.* Indon.
114 C4 **Lomé** Togo
118 C3 **Lomela** *r.* Dem. Rep. Congo
100 B2 **Lommel** Belgium
96 B2 **Lomond, Loch** *l.* U.K.
88 C2 **Lomonosov** Rus. Fed.
160 A1 **Lomonosov Ridge** Arctic Ocean
61 C2 **Lompobattang, Gunung** *mt.* Indon.
135 B4 **Lompoc** U.S.A.
63 B2 **Lom Sak** Thai.
103 E1 **Łomża** Pol.
130 B3 **London** Can.
99 C4 **London** U.K.
138 C3 **London** U.S.A.
97 C1 **Londonderry** U.K.
50 B1 **Londonderry, Cape** Austr.
154 B2 **Londrina** Brazil
135 C3 **Lone Pine** U.S.A.
83 M2 **Longa, Proliv** *sea chan.* Rus. Fed.
61 C1 **Long Akah** Malaysia
141 E2 **Long Bay** U.S.A.
135 C4 **Long Beach** U.S.A.
71 A3 **Longchang** China
99 C3 **Long Eaton** U.K.
97 C2 **Longford** Ireland
96 C1 **Longhope** U.K.
119 D3 **Longido** Tanz.
61 C2 **Longiram** Indon.
147 C2 **Long Island** Bahamas
130 C2 **Long Island** Can.
59 D3 **Long Island** P.N.G.
139 E2 **Long Island** U.S.A.
130 B3 **Longlac** Can.
130 B3 **Long Lake** Can.
71 A3 **Longli** China
71 A3 **Longming** China
136 B2 **Longmont** U.S.A.
70 A2 **Longnan** China
Longping China *see* **Luodian**
138 C2 **Long Point** Can.
71 B3 **Longquan** China
131 E3 **Long Range Mountains** Can.
51 D2 **Longreach** Austr.
Longshan China *see* **Longli**
99 D3 **Long Stratton** U.K.
98 B2 **Longtown** U.K.
105 D2 **Longuyon** France
143 E2 **Longview** *TX* U.S.A.
134 B1 **Longview** *WA* U.S.A.
61 C1 **Longwai** Indon.
70 A2 **Longxi** China
Longxian China *see* **Wengyuan**
71 B3 **Longxi Shan** *mt.* China
63 B2 **Long Xuyên** Vietnam
71 B3 **Longyan** China
82 C1 **Longyearbyen** Svalbard
108 B1 **Lonigo** Italy
100 C1 **Löningen** Ger.
105 D2 **Lons-le-Saunier** France
141 E2 **Lookout, Cape** U.S.A.
119 D3 **Loolmalasin** *vol. crater* Tanz.
50 B3 **Loongana** Austr.
97 B2 **Loop Head** *hd* Ireland
Lopasnya Rus. Fed. *see* **Chekhov**
63 B2 **Lop Buri** Thai.
64 B2 **Lopez** Phil.
118 A3 **Lopez, Cap** *c.* Gabon
68 C2 **Lop Nur** *salt flat* China
118 B2 **Lopori** *r.* Dem. Rep. Congo
92 H1 **Lopphavet** *b.* Norway
74 A2 **Lora, Hāmūn-i-** *dry lake* Afgh./Pak.
106 B2 **Lora del Río** Spain
138 C2 **Lorain** U.S.A.
74 A1 **Loralai** Pak.
107 C2 **Lorca** Spain
51 E3 **Lord Howe Island** Austr.
142 B2 **Lordsburg** U.S.A.
155 C2 **Lorena** Brazil
59 D3 **Lorengau** P.N.G.
59 D3 **Lorentz** *r.* Indon.
152 B1 **Loreto** Bol.
144 A2 **Loreto** Mex.
104 B2 **Lorient** France
96 B2 **Lorn, Firth of** *est.* U.K.
52 B3 **Lorne** Austr.
105 D2 **Lorraine** *reg.* France
142 B1 **Los Alamos** U.S.A.
143 D3 **Los Aldamas** Mex.
153 A3 **Los Ángeles** Chile
135 C4 **Los Angeles** U.S.A.
135 B3 **Los Banos** U.S.A.
152 B2 **Los Blancos** Arg.
89 F3 **Losevo** Rus. Fed.
108 B2 **Lošinj** *i.* Croatia
144 B2 **Los Mochis** Mex.
118 B2 **Losombo** Dem. Rep. Congo
106 B2 **Los Pedroches** *plat.* Spain
147 D3 **Los Roques, Islas** *is* Venez.
96 C2 **Lossiemouth** U.K.
150 C1 **Los Teques** Venez.
59 E3 **Losuia** P.N.G.
152 A3 **Los Vilos** Chile
104 C3 **Lot** *r.* France
96 C1 **Loth** U.K.
134 D1 **Lothair** U.S.A.
Lothringen *reg.* France *see* **Lorraine**
119 D2 **Lotikipi Plain** Kenya/Sudan
118 C3 **Loto** Dem. Rep. Congo
89 E2 **Lotoshino** Rus. Fed.
62 B1 **Louangnamtha** Laos
62 B2 **Louangphabang** Laos
118 B3 **Loubomo** Congo
104 B2 **Loudéac** France
71 B3 **Loudi** China
118 B3 **Loudima** Congo
114 A3 **Louga** Senegal
99 C3 **Loughborough** U.K.
97 B2 **Loughrea** Ireland
105 D2 **Louhans** France
97 B2 **Louisburgh** Ireland
51 E1 **Louisiade Archipelago** *is* P.N.G.
140 B2 **Louisiana** *state* U.S.A.
123 C1 **Louis Trichardt** S. Africa
138 B3 **Louisville** *KY* U.S.A.
140 C2 **Louisville** *MS* U.S.A.
86 C2 **Loukhi** Rus. Fed.
118 B3 **Loukoléla** Congo
106 B2 **Loulé** Port.
118 A2 **Loum** Cameroon
130 C2 **Loups Marins, Lacs des** *lakes* Can.
104 B3 **Lourdes** France
151 D2 **Lourenço** Brazil
Lourenço Marques Moz. *see* **Maputo**
106 B1 **Lousã** Port.
53 C2 **Louth** Austr.
98 C3 **Louth** U.K.
Louvain Belgium *see* **Leuven**
122 A1 **Louwater-Suid** Namibia
89 D2 **Lovat'** *r.* Rus. Fed.
110 B2 **Lovech** Bulg.
136 B2 **Loveland** U.S.A.
136 B2 **Lovell** U.S.A.
135 C2 **Lovelock** U.S.A.
88 C1 **Loviisa** Fin.
143 C2 **Lovington** U.S.A.
86 C2 **Lovozero** Rus. Fed.
119 C3 **Lowa** Dem. Rep. Congo
139 E2 **Lowell** U.S.A.
119 D2 **Lowelli** S. Sudan
128 C3 **Lower Arrow Lake** Can.
Lower California *pen.* Mex. *see* **Baja California**
54 B2 **Lower Hutt** N.Z.
97 C1 **Lower Lough Erne** *l.* U.K.
128 B2 **Lower Post** Can.
137 E1 **Lower Red Lake** U.S.A.
Lower Tunguska *r.* Rus. Fed. *see* **Nizhnyaya Tunguska**
99 D3 **Lowestoft** U.K.
103 D1 **Łowicz** Pol.
139 D2 **Lowville** U.S.A.
52 B2 **Loxton** Austr.
Loyang China *see* **Luoyang**
48 H6 **Loyauté, Îles** New Caledonia
89 D3 **Loyew** Belarus
92 F2 **Løypskardtinden** *mt.* Norway
109 C2 **Loznica** Serbia
91 D2 **Lozova** Ukr.
120 B2 **Luacano** Angola
70 B2 **Lu'an** China
120 A1 **Luanda** Angola
63 B3 **Luang, Thale** *lag.* Thai.
121 C2 **Luangwa** *r.* Zambia
121 B2 **Luanshya** Zambia
Luao Angola *see* **Luau**
106 B1 **Luarca** Spain
120 B2 **Luau** Angola
103 E1 **Lubaczów** Pol.
103 D1 **Lubań** Pol.
64 A2 **Lubang Islands** Phil.
120 A2 **Lubango** Angola
119 C3 **Lubao** Dem. Rep. Congo
103 E1 **Lubartów** Pol.
101 D1 **Lübbecke** Ger.
102 C1 **Lübben** Ger.
143 C2 **Lubbock** U.S.A.
101 E1 **Lübeck** Ger.
69 E2 **Lubei** China
76 B1 **Lubenka** Kazakh.
119 C3 **Lubero** Dem. Rep. Congo
103 D1 **Lubin** Pol.
103 E1 **Lublin** Pol.
91 C1 **Lubny** Ukr.
61 C1 **Lubok Antu** Malaysia
101 E1 **Lübow** Ger.
101 E1 **Lübtheen** Ger.
119 C3 **Lubudi** Dem. Rep. Congo
60 B2 **Lubuklinggau** Indon.
119 C4 **Lubumbashi** Dem. Rep. Congo
120 B2 **Lubungu** Zambia
119 C3 **Lubutu** Dem. Rep. Congo
120 A1 **Lucala** Angola
97 C2 **Lucan** Ireland
120 B1 **Lucapa** Angola
108 B2 **Lucca** Italy
96 B3 **Luce Bay** U.K.
154 B2 **Lucélia** Brazil
64 B2 **Lucena** Phil.
106 C2 **Lucena** Spain
103 D2 **Lučenec** Slovakia
109 C2 **Lucera** Italy
105 D2 **Lucerne** Switz.
66 B1 **Luchegorsk** Rus. Fed.
101 E1 **Lüchow** Ger.
120 A2 **Lucira** Angola
Łuck Ukr. *see* **Luts'k**
101 F1 **Luckenwalde** Ger.
122 B2 **Luckhoff** S. Africa
75 C2 **Lucknow** India
120 A1 **Lucunga** Angola
120 B2 **Lucusse** Angola
Lüda China *see* **Dalian**
100 C2 **Lüdenscheid** Ger.
101 E1 **Lüder** Ger.
120 A3 **Lüderitz** Namibia
119 D4 **Ludewa** Tanz.
74 B1 **Ludhiana** India
138 B2 **Ludington** U.S.A.
99 B3 **Ludlow** U.K.
135 C4 **Ludlow** U.S.A.
110 C2 **Ludogorie** *reg.* Bulg.
93 G3 **Ludvika** Sweden
102 B2 **Ludwigsburg** Ger.
101 F1 **Ludwigsfelde** Ger.
101 D3 **Ludwigshafen am Rhein** Ger.
101 E1 **Ludwigslust** Ger.
88 C2 **Ludza** Latvia
118 C3 **Luebo** Dem. Rep. Congo
120 A2 **Luena** Angola
70 A2 **Lüeyang** China
71 B3 **Lufeng** China
119 C3 **Lufira** *r.* Dem. Rep. Congo
143 E2 **Lufkin** U.S.A.
88 C2 **Luga** Rus. Fed.
88 C2 **Luga** *r.* Rus. Fed.
105 D2 **Lugano** Switz.
121 C2 **Lugenda** *r.* Moz.
97 C2 **Lugnaquilla** *h.* Ireland
106 B1 **Lugo** Spain
110 B1 **Lugoj** Romania
91 D2 **Luhans'k** Ukr.
119 D3 **Luhombero** Tanz.
90 B1 **Luhyny** Ukr.
120 B2 **Luiana** Angola
Luichow Peninsula *pen.* China *see* **Leizhou Bandao**
118 C3 **Luilaka** *r.* Dem. Rep. Congo
Luimneach Ireland *see* **Limerick**
105 D2 **Luino** Italy
92 I2 **Luiro** *r.* Fin.
118 C3 **Luiza** Dem. Rep. Congo
70 B2 **Lujiang** China
Lukapa Angola *see* **Lucapa**
109 C2 **Lukavac** Bos.-Herz.
118 B3 **Lukenie** *r.* Dem. Rep. Congo
142 A2 **Lukeville** U.S.A.
89 E3 **Lukhovitsy** Rus. Fed.
Lukou China *see* **Zhuzhou**
103 E1 **Łuków** Pol.

Molopo

106 B2 Mértola Port.
76 B2 Mertvyy Kultuk, Sor *dry lake* Kazakh.
119 D3 Meru *vol.* Tanz.
122 B2 Merweville S. Africa
80 B1 Merzifon Turkey
100 C3 Merzig Ger.
142 A2 Mesa *AZ* U.S.A.
142 C2 Mesa *NM* U.S.A.
137 E1 Mesabi Range *hills* U.S.A.
109 C2 Mesagne Italy
142 B2 Mescalero U.S.A.
143 C2 Mescalero Ridge U.S.A.
101 D2 Meschede Ger.
89 E3 Meshchovsk Rus. Fed.
Meshed Iran *see* Mashhad
91 E2 Meshkovskaya Rus. Fed.
142 A2 Mesilla U.S.A.
111 B3 Mesimeri Greece
111 B3 Mesolongi Greece
115 C1 Messaad Alg.
121 D2 Messalo *r.* Moz.
109 C3 Messina Italy
109 C3 Messina, Strait of *str.* Italy
Messina, Stretta di *str.* Italy *see* Messina, Strait of
111 B3 Messini Greece
111 B3 Messiniakos Kolpos *g.* Greece
111 B2 Mesta *r.* Bulg.
Mesta *r.* Greece *see* Nestos
150 C2 Meta *r.* Col./Venez.
130 C3 Métabetchouan Can.
127 H2 Meta Incognita Peninsula Can.
140 B3 Metairie U.S.A.
152 B2 Metán Arg.
111 B3 Methoni Greece
109 C2 Metković Croatia
121 C2 Metoro Moz.
60 B2 Metro Indon.
100 C3 Mettlach Ger.
135 C3 Mettler U.S.A.
117 B4 Metu Eth.
105 D2 Metz France
100 B2 Meuse *r.* Belgium/France
143 D2 Mexia U.S.A.
144 A1 Mexicali Mex.
144 B2 Mexico *country* Central America
México Mex. *see* Mexico City
137 E3 Mexico U.S.A.
125 I7 Mexico, Gulf of Mex./U.S.A.
145 C3 Mexico City Mex.
81 D2 Meybod Iran
101 F1 Meyenburg Ger.
83 M2 Meynypil'gyno Rus. Fed.
86 D2 Mezen' Rus. Fed.
86 D2 Mezen' *r.* Rus. Fed.
86 E1 Mezhdusharskiy, Ostrov *i.* Rus. Fed.
103 E2 Mezőtúr Hungary
132 C4 Mezquital *r.* Mex.
144 B2 Mezquitic Mex.
88 C2 Mežvidi Latvia
121 C2 Mfuwe Zambia
89 D3 Mglin Rus. Fed.
123 D2 Mhlume Swaziland
74 B2 Mhow India
145 C3 Miahuatlán Mex.
106 B2 Miajadas Spain
141 D3 Miami *FL* U.S.A.
143 E1 Miami *OK* U.S.A.
141 D3 Miami Beach U.S.A.
81 C2 Miāndowāb Iran
121 □D2 Miandrivazo Madag.
81 C2 Miāneh Iran
71 A3 Mianning China
74 B1 Mianwali Pak.
Mianyang China *see* Xiantao
70 A2 Mianyang China
121 □D2 Miarinarivo Madag.
87 F3 Miass Rus. Fed.
103 D1 Miastko Pol.
128 C2 Mica Creek Can.
103 D2 Michalovce Slovakia
138 B1 Michigan *state* U.S.A.
138 B2 Michigan, Lake U.S.A.
138 B2 Michigan City U.S.A.
138 B1 Michipicoten Bay Can.
130 B3 Michipicoten Island Can.
130 B3 Michipicoten River Can.
Michurin Bulg. *see* Tsarevo
89 F3 Michurinsk Rus. Fed.
156 D5 Micronesia *is* Pacific Ocean
48 G3 Micronesia, Federated States of *country* N. Pacific Ocean
158 E6 Mid-Atlantic Ridge Atlantic Ocean
100 A2 Middelburg Neth.
123 C3 Middelburg *E. Cape* S. Africa
123 C2 Middelburg *Mpumalanga* S. Africa
100 B2 Middelharnis Neth.
134 B2 Middle Alkali Lake U.S.A.
73 D3 Middle Andaman *i.* India
Middle Congo *country* Africa *see* Congo
136 D2 Middle Loup *r.* U.S.A.
138 C3 Middlesboro U.S.A.
98 C2 Middlesbrough U.K.
139 E2 Middletown *NY* U.S.A.
138 C3 Middletown *OH* U.S.A.
78 B3 Mīdī Yemen
138 C2 Midland Can.
138 C2 Midland *MI* U.S.A.
143 C2 Midland *TX* U.S.A.
97 B3 Midleton Ireland
Midnapore India *see* Medinipur
94 B1 Miðvágur Faroe Is
Midway Oman *see* Thamarīt

57 T7 Midway Islands *terr.* N. Pacific Ocean
109 D2 Midzhur *mt.* Bulg./Serbia
103 E1 Mielec Pol.
110 C1 Miercurea-Ciuc Romania
106 B1 Mieres del Camín Spain
101 E1 Mieste Ger.
145 C3 Miguel Alemán, Presa *resr* Mex.
144 B2 Miguel Auza Mex.
144 B2 Miguel Hidalgo, Presa *resr* Mex.
63 A2 Migyaunglaung Myanmar
89 E3 Mihara Japan
Mikhaylovgrad Bulg. *see* Montana
66 B2 Mikhaylov Rus. Fed.
Mikhaylovka Rus. Fed.
87 D3 Mikhaylovka Rus. Fed. *see* Kimovsk
77 D1 Mikhaylovka Rus. Fed.
93 I3 Mikhaylovskoye Rus. Fed.
86 E2 Mikkeli Fin.
67 C3 Mikun' Rus. Fed.
67 C4 Mikuni-sanmyaku *mts* Japan
73 B4 Mikura-jima *i.* Japan
108 A1 Miladhunmadulu Maldives
121 C2 Milan Italy
Milange Moz.
Milano Italy *see* Milan
111 C3 Milas Turkey
137 D1 Milbank U.S.A.
99 D3 Mildenhall U.K.
52 B2 Mildura Austr.
71 A3 Mile China
136 B1 Miles City U.S.A.
139 D3 Milford *DE* U.S.A.
135 D3 Milford *UT* U.S.A.
99 A4 Milford Haven U.K.
54 C1 Milford Sound N.Z.
Milḥ, Baḥr al *l.* Iraq *see* Razāzah, Buḥayrat ar
107 D2 Miliana Alg.
50 C1 Milikapiti Austr.
51 C1 Milingimbi Austr.
134 E1 Milk *r.* U.S.A.
116 B3 Milk, Wadi el *watercourse* Sudan
83 L3 Mil'kovo Rus. Fed.
128 C3 Milk River Can.
105 C3 Millau France
141 D2 Milledgeville U.S.A.
137 E1 Mille Lacs *lakes* U.S.A.
130 A3 Mille Lacs, Lac des *l.* Can.
Millennium Island *atoll* Kiribati *see* Caroline Island
137 D2 Miller U.S.A.
91 E2 Millerovo Rus. Fed.
52 A2 Millers Creek Austr.
96 B3 Milleur Point U.K.
52 B3 Millicent Austr.
140 C1 Millington U.S.A.
139 F1 Millinocket U.S.A.
55 J3 Mill Island Antarctica
53 D1 Millmerran Austr.
98 B2 Millom U.K.
136 B2 Mills U.S.A.
128 C1 Mills Lake Can.
111 B3 Milos *i.* Greece
89 E3 Miloslavskoye Rus. Fed.
91 E2 Milove Ukr.
52 B1 Milparinka Austr.
54 A3 Milton N.Z.
99 C3 Milton Keynes U.K.
138 B2 Milwaukee U.S.A.
158 C3 Milwaukee Deep *sea feature* Caribbean Sea
104 B3 Mimizan France
118 B3 Mimongo Gabon
155 D2 Mimoso do Sul Brazil
79 C2 Mīnāb Iran
61 D1 Minahasa, Semenanjung *pen.* Indon.
Minahassa Peninsula *pen.* Indon. *see* Minahasa, Semenanjung
79 C2 Mina Jebel Ali U.A.E.
Minaker Can. *see* Prophet River
60 B1 Minas Indon.
153 C3 Minas Uru.
79 B2 Mīnā' Sa'ūd Kuwait
155 D1 Minas Gerais *state* Brazil
155 D1 Minas Novas Brazil
145 C3 Minatitlán Mex.
62 A1 Minbu Myanmar
64 B3 Mindanao *i.* Phil.
52 B2 Mindarie Austr.
101 D1 Minden Ger.
140 B2 Minden *LA* U.S.A.
137 D2 Minden *NE* U.S.A.
64 B2 Mindoro *i.* Phil.
64 A2 Mindoro Strait Phil.
118 B3 Mindouli Congo
99 B4 Minehead U.K.
154 B1 Mineiros Brazil
143 D2 Mineral Wells U.S.A.
75 C1 Minfeng China
119 C4 Minga Dem. Rep. Congo
81 C1 Mingäçevir Azer.
131 D2 Mingan Can.
52 B2 Mingary Austr.
70 B2 Mingguang China
62 A1 Mingin Myanmar
107 C2 Minglanilla Spain
119 D4 Mingoyo Tanz.
69 E1 Mingshui China
96 A2 Mingulay *i.* U.K.
71 B3 Mingxi China
Mingzhou China *see* Suide
70 A2 Minhe China

73 B4 Minicoy *atoll* India
114 B3 Minignan Côte d'Ivoire
50 A2 Minilya r. Austr.
131 D2 Minipi Lake Can.
130 A2 Miniss Lake Can.
52 A2 Minlaton Austr.
115 C4 Minna Nigeria
137 E2 Minneapolis U.S.A.
129 E2 Minnedosa Can.
137 E2 Minnesota r. U.S.A.
137 E1 Minnesota *state* U.S.A.
106 B1 Miño r. Port./Spain
107 D1 Minorca *i.* Spain
136 C1 Minot U.S.A.
88 C3 Minsk Belarus
103 E1 Mińsk Mazowiecki Pol.
96 D2 Mintlaw U.K.
131 D3 Minto, Lac l. Can.
130 C2 Minto, Lac l. Can.
68 C1 Minusinsk Rus. Fed.
62 A1 Minutang India
70 A2 Minxian China
155 D1 Mirabela Brazil
155 D1 Miralta Brazil
131 D2 Miramichi Can.
111 C3 Mirampellou, Kolpos b. Greece
152 C2 Miranda Brazil
152 C1 Miranda r. Brazil
Miranda Moz. *see* Macaloge
106 C1 Miranda de Ebro Spain
106 B1 Mirandela Port.
154 B2 Mirandópolis Brazil
154 B2 Mirante, Serra de *hills* Brazil
79 C3 Mirbāṭ Oman
61 C1 Miri Malaysia
153 C3 Mirim, Lagoa l. Brazil/Uru.
79 D2 Mīrjāveh Iran
89 D3 Mirnyy *Bryanskaya Oblast'* Rus. Fed.
83 I2 Mirnyy *Respublika Sakha* Rus. Fed.
101 F1 Mirow Ger.
74 A2 Mirpur Khas Pak.
Mirtoan Sea *sea* Greece *see* Mirtoö Pelagos
111 B3 Mirtoö Pelagos *sea* Greece
65 B2 Miryang S. Korea
Mirzachirla Turkm. *see* Murzechirla
Mirzachul Uzbek. *see* Guliston
75 C2 Mirzapur India
77 E3 Misalay China
66 B1 Mishan China
51 E1 Misima Island P.N.G.
146 B3 Miskitos, Cayos *is* Nic.
103 E2 Miskolc Hungary
59 C3 Misoöl *i.* Indon.
115 D1 Miṣrātah Libya
130 B2 Missinaibi r. Can.
130 B3 Missinaibi Lake Can.
128 B3 Mission Can.
130 B2 Missisa Lake Can.
140 C3 Mississippi r. U.S.A.
140 C2 Mississippi *state* U.S.A.
140 C3 Mississippi Delta U.S.A.
140 C2 Mississippi Sound *sea chan.* U.S.A.
Missolonghi Greece *see* Mesolongi
134 D1 Missoula U.S.A.
137 E3 Missouri r. U.S.A.
137 E3 Missouri *state* U.S.A.
130 C3 Mistassibi r. Can.
130 C2 Mistassini, Lac l. Can.
131 D2 Mistastin Lake Can.
103 D2 Mistelbach Austria
131 D2 Mistinibi, Lac l. Can.
130 C2 Mistissini Can.
51 D2 Mitchell Austr.
51 D1 Mitchell r. Austr.
136 C2 Mitchell *NE* U.S.A.
137 D2 Mitchell *SD* U.S.A.
97 B2 Mitchelstown Ireland
74 A2 Mithi Pak.
67 D3 Mito Japan
119 D3 Mitole Tanz.
109 D2 Mitrovicë Kosovo
53 D2 Mittagong Austr.
101 E2 Mittelhausen Ger.
101 D1 Mittellandkanal *canal* Ger.
101 F3 Mitterteich Ger.
Mittimatalik Can. *see* Pond Inlet
150 B2 Mitú Col.
119 C4 Mitumba, Chaîne des *mts* Dem. Rep. Congo
119 C3 Mitumba, Monts *mts* Dem. Rep. Congo
119 C3 Mitwaba Dem. Rep. Congo
118 B2 Mitzic Gabon
78 B2 Miyah, Wādī al *watercourse* Saudi Arabia
67 C4 Miyake-jima *i.* Japan
66 D3 Miyako Japan
67 B4 Miyakonojō Japan
76 B2 Miyaly Kazakh.
67 B4 Miyazaki Japan
67 C3 Miyazu Japan
115 D1 Mizdah Libya
97 B3 Mizen Head *hd* Ireland
90 A2 Mizhhirr"ya Ukr.
Mizo Hills *state* India *see* Mizoram
75 D2 Mizoram *state* India
93 G4 Mjölby Sweden
93 F3 Mjøsa l. Norway
119 D3 Mkomazi Tanz.
103 C1 Mladá Boleslav Czech Rep.
109 D2 Mladenovac Serbia
103 E1 Mława Pol.

109 C2 Mljet *i.* Croatia
123 C3 Mlungisi S. Africa
90 B1 Mlyniv Ukr.
123 C2 Mmabatho S. Africa
123 C2 Mmathethe Botswana
93 E3 Mo Norway
135 E3 Moab U.S.A.
123 D2 Moamba Moz.
54 B2 Moana N.Z.
118 B3 Moanda Gabon
97 C2 Moate Ireland
119 C3 Moba Dem. Rep. Congo
118 C2 Mobayi-Mbongo Dem. Rep. Congo
137 E3 Moberly U.S.A.
140 C2 Mobile U.S.A.
140 C2 Mobile Bay U.S.A.
140 C2 Mobile Point U.S.A.
136 C1 Mobridge U.S.A.
Mobutu, Lake l. Dem. Rep. Congo/Uganda *see* Albert, Lake
Mobutu Sese Seko, Lake l. Dem. Rep. Congo/Uganda *see* Albert, Lake
121 C2 Moçambicano, Planalto *plat.* Moz.
121 D2 Moçambique Moz.
Moçâmedes Angola *see* Namibe
62 B1 Môc Châu Vietnam
78 B3 Mocha Yemen
123 C1 Mochudi Botswana
121 D2 Mocimboa da Praia Moz.
101 D3 Möckmühl Ger.
150 B2 Mocoa Col.
154 C2 Mococa Brazil
144 B1 Mocorito Mex.
144 B1 Moctezuma Mex.
145 B2 Moctezuma Mex.
144 B2 Moctezuma Mex.
121 C2 Mocuba Moz.
105 D2 Modane France
122 B2 Modder r. S. Africa
108 B2 Modena Italy
135 B3 Modesto U.S.A.
109 B3 Modica Italy
123 C1 Modimolle S. Africa
123 D1 Modjadjiskloof S. Africa
53 C3 Moe Austr.
Moero, Lake l. Dem. Rep. Congo/Zambia *see* Mweru, Lake
100 C2 Moers Ger.
96 C3 Moffat U.K.
117 C4 Mogadishu Somalia
Mogador Morocco *see* Essaouira
106 B1 Mogadouro, Serra de *mts* Port.
123 C1 Mogalakwena r. S. Africa
62 A1 Mogaung Myanmar
Mogilev Belarus *see* Mahilyow
154 C2 Mogi-Mirim Brazil
83 I3 Mogocha Rus. Fed.
123 C1 Mogoditshane Botswana
62 A1 Mogok Myanmar
142 A2 Mogollon Plateau U.S.A.
103 D2 Mohács Hungary
123 C3 Mohale's Hoek Lesotho
74 B1 Mohali India
107 D2 Mohammadia Alg.
142 A2 Mohave Mountains U.S.A.
139 E2 Mohawk r. U.S.A.
62 A1 Mohnyin Myanmar
119 D3 Mohoro Tanz.
90 B2 Mohyliv-Podil's'kyy Ukr.
123 C1 Moijabana Botswana
110 C1 Moineşti Romania
Mointy Kazakh. *see* Moyynty
92 F2 Mo i Rana Norway
88 C2 Möisaküla Estonia
104 C3 Moissac France
135 C3 Mojave U.S.A.
135 C3 Mojave Desert U.S.A.
62 B1 Mojiang China
155 C2 Moji das Cruzes Brazil
154 C2 Moji-Guaçu r. Brazil
109 C2 Mojkovac Montenegro
54 B1 Mokau N.Z.
123 C2 Mokhotlong Lesotho
83 J2 Mokhsogollokh Rus. Fed.
118 B1 Mokolo Cameroon
123 C1 Mokopane S. Africa
65 B3 Mokp'o S. Korea
109 C2 Mola di Bari Italy
145 C2 Molango Mex.
Moldavia *country* Europe *see* Moldova
Moldavskaya S.S.R. *country* Europe *see* Moldova
93 E3 Molde Norway
90 B2 Moldova *country* Europe
110 B2 Moldova Nouă Romania
110 B1 Moldoveanu, Vârful *mt.* Romania
110 B1 Moldovei, Podişul *plat.* Romania
90 B2 Moldovei Centrale, Podişul *plat.* Moldova
123 C1 Molepolole Botswana
88 C2 Molėtai Lith.
109 C2 Molfetta Italy
Molière Alg. *see* Bordj Bounaama
107 C1 Molina de Aragón Spain
107 C2 Molina de Segura Spain
119 D3 Moliro Dem. Rep. Congo
150 B4 Mollendo Peru
93 F4 Mölnlycke Sweden
91 D2 Molochna r. Ukr.
89 E2 Molokovo Rus. Fed.
51 C2 Molong Austr.
122 B2 Molopo *watercourse* Botswana/S. Africa

213

N

P

Saltillo

145 B2 Saltillo Mex.
134 D2 Salt Lake City U.S.A.
154 C2 Salto Brazil
152 C3 Salto Uru.
155 E1 Salto da Divisa Brazil
154 B2 Salto del Guairá Para.
135 C4 Salton Sea salt l. U.S.A.
154 B3 Salto Osório, Represa resr Brazil
154 B3 Salto Santiago, Represa de resr Brazil
141 D2 Saluda U.S.A.
76 B3 Sālūk, Kūh-e mt. Iran
108 A2 Saluzzo Italy
151 F4 Salvador Brazil
79 C2 Salwah Saudi Arabia
62 A2 Salween r. China/Myanmar
81 C2 Salyan Azer.
138 C3 Salyersville U.S.A.
122 A1 Salzbrunn Namibia
102 C2 Salzburg Austria
101 E1 Salzgitter Ger.
101 D2 Salzkotten Ger.
101 E1 Salzwedel Ger.
144 B1 Samalayuca Mex.
66 D2 Samani Japan
64 B2 Samar i. Phil.
87 E3 Samara Rus. Fed.
Samarahan Malaysia see Sri Aman
59 E3 Samarai P.N.G.
61 C2 Samarinda Indon.
77 C3 Samarqand Uzbek.
81 C2 Sāmarrā' Iraq
81 C1 Şamaxı Azer.
119 C3 Samba Dem. Rep. Congo
61 C1 Sambaliung mts Indon.
75 C2 Sambalpur India
60 C2 Sambar, Tanjung pt Indon.
60 B1 Sambas Indon.
121 □E2 Sambava Madag.
74 B2 Sambhar India
90 A2 Sambir Ukr.
61 C2 Samboja Indon.
153 C3 Samborombón, Bahía b. Arg.
65 B2 Samch'ŏk S. Korea
Samch'ŏnp'o S. Korea see Sach'on
81 C2 Samdi Dag mt. Turkey
119 D3 Same Tanz.
121 B2 Samfya Zambia
78 B2 Samīrah Saudi Arabia
65 B1 Samjiyŏn N. Korea
Sam Neua Laos see Xam Nua
48 J5 Samoa country S. Pacific Ocean
156 E6 Samoa Basin S. Pacific Ocean
Samoa i Sisifo country S. Pacific Ocean see Samoa
109 C1 Samobor Croatia
110 B2 Samokov Bulg.
111 C3 Samos i. Greece
Samothrace i. Greece see Samothraki
111 C2 Samothraki Greece
111 C2 Samothraki i. Greece
61 C2 Sampit Indon.
119 C3 Sampwe Dem. Rep. Congo
143 E2 Sam Rayburn Reservoir U.S.A.
62 B2 Sâm Sơn Vietnam
80 B1 Samsun Turkey
81 C1 Samt'redia Georgia
63 B3 Samui, Ko i. Thai.
63 B2 Samut Songkhram Thai.
114 B3 San Mali
78 B3 Şan'ā' Yemen
118 A2 Sanaga r. Cameroon
81 C2 Sanandaj Iran
146 B3 San Andrés, Isla de i. Caribbean Sea
106 B1 San Andrés del Rabanedo Spain
142 B2 San Andres Mountains U.S.A.
145 C3 San Andrés Tuxtla Mex.
143 C2 San Angelo U.S.A.
143 D3 San Antonio U.S.A.
135 C4 San Antonio, Mount U.S.A.
152 B2 San Antonio de los Cobres Arg.
153 B4 San Antonio Oeste Arg.
108 B2 San Benedetto del Tronto Italy
144 A3 San Benedicto, Isla i. Mex.
135 C4 San Bernardino U.S.A.
135 C4 San Bernardino Mountains U.S.A.
142 B3 San Blas Mex.
141 C3 San Blas, Cape U.S.A.
146 C4 San Blas, Punta pt Panama
152 B1 San Borja Bol.
144 B2 San Buenaventura Mex.
64 B2 San Carlos Phil.
147 D4 San Carlos Venez.
153 A4 San Carlos de Bariloche Arg.
147 C4 San Carlos del Zulia Venez.
104 C2 Sancerrois, Collines du hills France
135 C4 San Clemente U.S.A.
135 C4 San Clemente Island U.S.A.
105 C2 Sancoins France
48 H5 San Cristobal i. Solomon Is
150 B2 San Cristóbal Venez.
145 C3 San Cristóbal de las Casas Mex.
146 C2 Sancti Spíritus Cuba
61 C1 Sandakan Malaysia
93 E3 Sandane Norway
111 B2 Sandanski Bulg.
114 A3 Sandaré Mali
96 C1 Sanday i. U.K.
143 C2 Sanderson U.S.A.
150 C4 Sandia Peru
135 C4 San Diego U.S.A.
111 D3 Sandıklı Turkey
93 E4 Sandnes Norway
92 F2 Sandnessjøen Norway
118 C3 Sandoa Dem. Rep. Congo
103 E1 Sandomierz Pol.
89 E2 Sandovo Rus. Fed.
94 B1 Sandoy i. Faroe Is
134 C1 Sandpoint U.S.A.
71 B3 Sandu China
94 B1 Sandur Faroe Is
138 C2 Sandusky U.S.A.
122 A3 Sandveld mts S. Africa
122 A2 Sandverhaar Namibia
93 F4 Sandvika Norway
93 G3 Sandviken Sweden
131 E2 Sandwich Bay Can.
135 D2 Sandy U.S.A.
129 D2 Sandy Bay Can.
51 E2 Sandy Cape Austr.
130 A2 Sandy Lake Can.
130 A2 Sandy Lake l. Can.
141 D2 Sandy Springs U.S.A.
144 A1 San Felipe Mex.
145 B2 San Felipe Mex.
150 C1 San Felipe Venez.
144 A2 San Fernando Mex.
145 C2 San Fernando Mex.
64 B2 San Fernando Phil.
64 B2 San Fernando Phil.
106 B2 San Fernando Spain
147 D3 San Fernando Trin. and Tob.
150 C2 San Fernando de Apure Venez.
141 D3 Sanford FL U.S.A.
139 E2 Sanford ME U.S.A.
141 E1 Sanford NC U.S.A.
152 B3 San Francisco Arg.
135 B3 San Francisco U.S.A.
74 B3 Sangamner India
83 J2 Sangar Rus. Fed.
108 A3 San Gavino Monreale Italy
101 E2 Sangerhausen Ger.
61 C1 Sanggau Indon.
118 B3 Sangha r. Congo
109 C3 San Giovanni in Fiore Italy
59 C2 Sangir i. Indon.
59 C2 Sangir, Kepulauan is Indon.
65 B2 Sangju S. Korea
63 A2 Sangkhla Buri Thai.
61 C1 Sangkulirang Indon.
73 B3 Sangli India
118 B2 Sangmélima Cameroon
121 C3 Sango Zimbabwe
San Gottardo, Passo del pass Switz. see St Gotthard Pass
136 B3 Sangre de Cristo Range mts U.S.A.
75 C2 Sangsang China
144 A2 San Hipólito, Punta pt Mex.
145 D3 San Ignacio Belize
152 B1 San Ignacio Bol.
144 A2 San Ignacio Mex.
130 C2 Sanikiluaq Can.
71 A3 Sanjiang China
Sanjiang China see Jinping
67 C3 Sanjō Japan
135 B3 San Joaquin r. U.S.A.
153 B4 San Jorge, Golfo de g. Arg.
146 B4 San José Costa Rica
64 B2 San Jose Phil.
64 B2 San Jose Phil.
135 B3 San Jose U.S.A.
144 A2 San José, Isla i. Mex.
144 B2 San José de Bavicora Mex.
64 B2 San Jose de Buenavista Phil.
144 A2 San José de Comondú Mex.
144 B2 San José del Cabo Mex.
150 B2 San José del Guaviare Col.
152 B3 San Juan Arg.
146 B3 San Juan r. Costa Rica/Nic.
147 C3 San Juan Dom. Rep.
147 D3 San Juan Puerto Rico
135 D3 San Juan r. U.S.A.
152 C2 San Juan Bautista Para.
145 C3 San Juan Bautista Tuxtepec Mex.
147 D4 San Juan de los Morros Venez.
145 C2 San Juan del Río Mex.
134 B1 San Juan Islands U.S.A.
144 B2 San Juanito Mex.
136 B3 San Juan Mountains U.S.A.
153 B4 San Julián Arg.
75 C2 Sankh r. India
63 B2 San Khao Phang Hoei mts Thai.
100 C2 Sankt Augustin Ger.
105 D2 Sankt Gallen Switz.
105 D2 Sankt Moritz Switz.
Sankt-Peterburg Rus. Fed. see St Petersburg
102 C2 Sankt Veit an der Glan Austria
100 C3 Sankt Wendel Ger.
80 B2 Şanlıurfa Turkey
142 B3 San Lorenzo Mex.
106 B2 Sanlúcar de Barrameda Spain
153 B3 San Luis Arg.
145 B2 San Luis de la Paz Mex.
142 A2 San Luisito Mex.
135 B3 San Luis Obispo U.S.A.
135 B3 San Luis Obispo Bay U.S.A.
145 B2 San Luis Potosí Mex.
144 A1 San Luis Río Colorado Mex.
143 D3 San Marcos U.S.A.
108 B2 San Marino country Europe
108 B2 San Marino San Marino
144 B2 San Martín de Bolaños Mex.
153 A4 San Martín de los Andes Arg.
135 B3 San Mateo U.S.A.
153 B4 San Matías, Golfo g. Arg.
70 B2 Sanmenxia China
146 B3 San Miguel El Salvador
152 B2 San Miguel de Tucumán Arg.
135 B4 San Miguel Island U.S.A.
145 C3 San Miguel Sola de Vega Mex.
71 B3 Sanming China
153 B3 San Nicolás de los Arroyos Arg.
135 C4 San Nicolas Island U.S.A.
110 B1 Sânnicolau Mare Romania
123 C2 Sannieshof S. Africa
114 B4 Sanniquellie Liberia
103 E2 Sanok Pol.
64 B2 San Pablo Phil.
144 B2 San Pablo Balleza Mex.
152 B2 San Pedro Arg.
152 B1 San Pedro Bol.
114 B4 San-Pédro Côte d'Ivoire
144 A2 San Pedro Mex.
142 A2 San Pedro watercourse U.S.A.
106 B2 San Pedro, Sierra de mts Spain
144 B2 San Pedro de las Colonias Mex.
152 C2 San Pedro de Ycuamandyyú Para.
142 A3 San Pedro el Saucito Mex.
146 B3 San Pedro Sula Hond.
108 A3 San Pietro, Isola di i. Italy
96 C3 Sanquhar U.K.
144 A1 San Quintín, Cabo c. Mex.
153 B3 San Rafael Arg.
108 A2 San Remo Italy
143 D2 San Saba U.S.A.
147 C2 San Salvador i. Bahamas
146 B3 San Salvador El Salvador
152 B2 San Salvador de Jujuy Arg.
107 C1 San Sebastián Spain
108 B2 Sansepolcro Italy
109 C2 San Severo Italy
109 C2 Sanski Most Bos.-Herz.
152 B1 Santa Ana Bol.
146 B3 Santa Ana El Salvador
144 A1 Santa Ana Mex.
135 C4 Santa Ana U.S.A.
152 B1 Santa Ana de Yacuma Bol.
144 B2 Santa Bárbara Mex.
135 C4 Santa Barbara U.S.A.
154 B2 Santa Bárbara, Serra de hills Brazil
152 B2 Santa Catalina Chile
135 C4 Santa Catalina Island U.S.A.
154 B3 Santa Catarina state Brazil
150 C3 Santa Clara Col.
146 C2 Santa Clara Cuba
135 B3 Santa Clara U.S.A.
135 C4 Santa Clarita U.S.A.
107 D1 Santa Coloma de Gramenet Spain
Santa Comba Angola see Waku-Kungo
109 C3 Santa Croce, Capo c. Italy
153 B5 Santa Cruz r. Arg.
152 B1 Santa Cruz Bol.
64 B2 Santa Cruz Phil.
135 B3 Santa Cruz U.S.A.
145 C3 Santa Cruz Barillas Guat.
155 E1 Santa Cruz Cabrália Brazil
107 C2 Santa Cruz de Moya Spain
114 A2 Santa Cruz de Tenerife Islas Canarias
152 C2 Santa Cruz do Sul Brazil
135 C4 Santa Cruz Island U.S.A.
48 H5 Santa Cruz Islands Solomon Is
107 D2 Santa Eulalia del Río Spain
152 B3 Santa Fe Arg.
142 B1 Santa Fe U.S.A.
154 B2 Santa Fé do Sul Brazil
154 B1 Santa Helena de Goiás Brazil
153 B3 Santa Isabel Arg.
Santa Isabel Equat. Guinea see Malabo
48 G4 Santa Isabel i. Solomon Is
154 B1 Santa Luisa, Serra de hills Brazil
151 E3 Santa Luzia Brazil
144 A2 Santa Margarita, Isla i. Mex.
152 C2 Santa Maria Brazil
144 B1 Santa María r. Mex.
135 B4 Santa Maria U.S.A.
123 D2 Santa Maria, Cabo de c. Moz.
106 B2 Santa Maria, Cabo de c. Port.
155 C1 Santa Maria, Chapadão de hills Brazil
151 E3 Santa Maria das Barreiras Brazil
109 C3 Santa Maria di Leuca, Capo c. Italy
155 D1 Santa Maria do Suaçuí Brazil
150 B1 Santa Marta Col.
135 C4 Santa Monica U.S.A.
151 E4 Santana Brazil
110 B1 Sântana Romania
106 C1 Santander Spain
108 A3 Sant'Antioco Italy
108 A3 Sant'Antioco, Isola di i. Italy
107 D2 Sant Antoni de Portmany Spain
151 D3 Santarém Brazil
106 B2 Santarém Port.
154 B1 Santa Rita do Araguaia Brazil
153 B3 Santa Rosa Arg.
152 C2 Santa Rosa Brazil
135 B3 Santa Rosa CA U.S.A.
142 C2 Santa Rosa NM U.S.A.
146 B3 Santa Rosa de Copán Hond.
135 B4 Santa Rosa Island CA U.S.A.
140 C2 Santa Rosa Island FL U.S.A.
144 A2 Santa Rosalía Mex.
134 C2 Santa Rosa Range mts U.S.A.
106 B1 Santa Uxía de Ribeira Spain
154 B1 Santa Vitória Brazil
107 D1 Sant Carles de la Ràpita Spain
135 C4 Santee U.S.A.
107 D2 Sant Francesc de Formentera Spa
152 C2 Santiago Brazil
153 A3 Santiago Chile
147 C3 Santiago Dom. Rep.
144 B2 Santiago Mex.
146 B4 Santiago Panama
64 B2 Santiago Phil.
106 B1 Santiago de Compostela Spain
146 C2 Santiago de Cuba Cuba
144 B2 Santiago Ixcuintla Mex.
144 B2 Santiago Papasquiaro Mex.
106 C1 Santillana Spain
107 D2 Sant Joan de Labritja Spain
107 D1 Sant Jordi, Golf de g. Spain
155 D2 Santo Amaro de Campos Brazil
154 B2 Santo Anastácio Brazil
155 C2 Santo André Brazil
152 C2 Santo Angelo Brazil
154 B2 Santo Antônio da Platina Brazil
151 F4 Santo Antônio de Jesus Brazil
150 C3 Santo Antônio do Içá Brazil
155 C2 Santo Antônio do Monte Brazil
147 D3 Santo Domingo Dom. Rep.
144 A2 Santo Domingo Mex.
142 B1 Santo Domingo Pueblo U.S.A.
111 C3 Santorini i. Greece
155 C2 Santos Brazil
155 D2 Santos Dumont Brazil
157 I7 Santos Plateau S. Atlantic Ocean
152 C2 Santo Tomé Arg.
153 A4 San Valentín, Cerro mt. Chile
146 B3 San Vicente El Salvador
144 A1 San Vicente Mex.
64 B2 San Vicente Phil.
150 B4 San Vicente de Cañete Peru
108 B2 San Vincenzo Italy
108 B3 San Vito, Capo c. Italy
71 A4 Sanya China
155 C2 São Bernardo do Campo Brazil
152 C2 São Borja Brazil
154 C2 São Carlos Brazil
155 D1 São Felipe, Serra de hills Brazil
151 D4 São Félix Brazil
151 D3 São Félix Brazil
155 D2 São Fidélis Brazil
155 D1 São Francisco Brazil
151 F4 São Francisco r. Brazil
154 C3 São Francisco, Ilha de i. Brazil
154 C3 São Francisco do Sul Brazil
152 C3 São Gabriel Brazil
155 D2 São Gonçalo Brazil
155 C1 São Gonçalo do Abaeté Brazil
155 C1 São Gotardo Brazil
154 B1 São Jerônimo, Serra de hills Brazil
155 D2 São João da Barra Brazil
155 C2 São João da Boa Vista Brazil
106 B1 São João da Madeira Port.
155 D1 São João da Ponte Brazil
155 D2 São João del Rei Brazil
155 D1 São João do Paraíso Brazil
155 D1 São João Evangelista Brazil
155 D2 São João Nepomuceno Brazil
154 C2 São Joaquim da Barra Brazil
152 D2 São José Brazil
154 C2 São José do Rio Preto Brazil
155 C2 São José dos Campos Brazil
154 C3 São José dos Pinhais Brazil
154 A1 São Lourenço Brazil
155 C2 São Lourenço Brazil
151 E3 São Luís Brazil
154 C2 São Manuel Brazil
154 C1 São Marcos r. Brazil
151 E3 São Marcos, Baía de b. Brazil
155 E1 São Mateus Brazil
154 B3 São Mateus do Sul Brazil
105 C2 Saône r. France
155 C2 São Paulo Brazil
154 C1 São Paulo state Brazil
155 D2 São Pedro da Aldeia Brazil
151 E3 São Raimundo Nonato Brazil
155 C1 São Romão Brazil
São Salvador Angola see M'banza Congo
São Salvador do Congo Angola see M'banza Congo
155 C2 São Sebastião, Ilha do i. Brazil
154 C2 São Sebastião do Paraíso Brazil
154 B1 São Simão Brazil
154 B1 São Simão, Barragem de resr Braz
59 C2 Sao-Siu Indon.
113 D5 São Tomé São Tomé and Príncipe
113 D5 São Tomé i. São Tomé and Princip
155 D2 São Tomé, Cabo de c. Brazil
113 D5 São Tomé and Príncipe country Africa
155 C2 São Vicente Brazil
106 B2 São Vicente, Cabo de c. Port.
59 C3 Saparua Indon.
107 D2 Sa Pobla Spain
89 F3 Sapozhok Rus. Fed.
66 D2 Sapporo Japan
109 C2 Sapri Italy
143 D1 Sapulpa U.S.A.
81 C2 Saqqez Iran
81 C2 Sarāb Iran
63 B2 Sara Buri Thai.
Saragossa Spain see Zaragoza
89 F3 Sarai Rus. Fed.
109 C2 Sarajevo Bos.-Herz.
87 E3 Saraktash Rus. Fed.
62 A1 Saramati mt. India/Myanmar
139 E2 Saranac Lake U.S.A.
109 D3 Sarandë Albania
64 B3 Sarangani Islands Phil.

87 D3 Saransk Rus. Fed.
87 E3 Sarapul Rus. Fed.
141 D3 Sarasota U.S.A.
136 B2 Saratoga U.S.A.
139 E2 Saratoga Springs U.S.A.
61 C1 Saratok Malaysia
87 D3 Saratov Rus. Fed.
79 D2 Sarāvān Iran
61 C1 Sarawak state Malaysia
111 C2 Saray Turkey
111 C3 Sarayköy Turkey
79 D2 Sarbāz Iran
76 B3 Sarbīsheh Iran
74 B2 Sardarshahr India
Sardegna i. Italy see Sardinia
108 A2 Sardinia i. Italy
92 G2 Sarektjåkkå mt. Sweden
77 C3 Sar-e Pul Afgh.
158 C3 Sargasso Sea sea N. Atlantic Ocean
74 B1 Sargodha Pak.
115 D4 Sarh Chad
79 D2 Sarhad reg. Iran
81 D2 Sārī Iran
111 C3 Sarıgöl Turkey
81 C1 Sarıkamış Turkey
61 C1 Sarikei Malaysia
51 D2 Sarina Austr.
65 B2 Sariwŏn N. Korea
111 C2 Sarıyer Turkey
77 D2 Sarkand Kazakh.
111 C2 Şarköy Turkey
104 C3 Sarlat-la-Canéda France
59 D3 Sarmi Indon.
153 B4 Sarmiento Arg.
138 C2 Sarnia Can.
90 B1 Sarny Ukr.
60 B2 Sarolangun Indon.
111 B3 Saronikos Kolpos g. Greece
111 C2 Saros Körfezi b. Turkey
103 E2 Sárospatak Hungary
87 D3 Sarov Rus. Fed.
Sarpan i. N. Mariana Is see Rota
105 D2 Sarrebourg France
106 B1 Sarria Spain
107 C1 Sarrión Spain
105 D3 Sartène France
Sartu China see Daqing
111 C1 Saruhanlı Turkey
103 D2 Sárvár Hungary
81 D3 Sarvestān Iran
77 D1 Saryarka plain Kazakh.
76 B2 Sarykamyshskoye Ozero salt l. Turkm./Uzbek.
77 D2 Saryozek Kazakh.
77 D2 Saryshagan Kazakh.
77 C2 Sarysu watercourse Kazakh.
77 D3 Sary-Tash Kyrg.
75 C2 Sasaram India
67 A4 Sasebo Japan
129 D2 Saskatchewan prov. Can.
129 D2 Saskatchewan r. Can.
129 D2 Saskatoon Can.
83 I2 Saskylakh Rus. Fed.
123 C2 Sasolburg S. Africa
87 D3 Sasovo Rus. Fed.
114 B4 Sassandra Côte d'Ivoire
108 A2 Sassari Italy
102 C1 Sassnitz Ger.
114 A3 Satadougou Mali
136 C3 Satanta U.S.A.
73 B3 Satara India
123 D1 Satara S. Africa
87 E3 Satka Rus. Fed.
75 C2 Satna India
77 C2 Satpayev Kazakh.
74 B2 Satpura Range mts India
63 B2 Sattahip Thai.
110 B1 Satu Mare Romania
63 B3 Satun Thai.
144 B2 Saucillo Mex.
93 E4 Sauda Norway
92 □B2 Sauðárkrókur Iceland
78 B2 Saudi Arabia country Asia
105 C3 Saugues France
137 E1 Sauk Center U.S.A.
105 C2 Saulieu France
88 B2 Saulkrasti Latvia
130 B3 Sault Sainte Marie Can.
138 C1 Sault Sainte Marie U.S.A.
77 C1 Saumalkol' Kazakh.
59 C3 Saumlakki Indon.
104 B2 Saumur France
120 B1 Saurimo Angola
109 D2 Sava r. Europe
49 J5 Savai'i i. Samoa
91 E1 Savala r. Rus. Fed.
114 C4 Savalou Benin
141 D2 Savannah GA U.S.A.
140 C1 Savannah TN U.S.A.
141 D2 Savannah r. U.S.A.
63 B2 Savannakhét Laos
130 A2 Savant Lake Can.
111 C3 Savaştepe Turkey
114 C4 Savè Benin
105 D2 Saverne France
89 F2 Savino Rus. Fed.
86 D2 Savinskiy Rus. Fed.
Savoie reg. France see Savoy
108 A2 Savona Italy
93 I3 Savonlinna Fin.
105 D2 Savoy reg. France
93 F4 Sävsjö Sweden
59 C3 Savu i. Indon.

92 I2 Savukoski Fin.
Savu Sea sea Indon. see Laut Sawu
74 B2 Sawai Madhopur India
62 A1 Sawan Myanmar
62 A2 Sawankhalok Thai.
136 B3 Sawatch Range mts U.S.A.
Sawhāj Egypt see Sūhāj
121 B2 Sawmills Zimbabwe
79 C3 Şawqirah, Dawḩat b. Oman
80 B1 Şawqirah Bay b. Oman
see Şawqirah, Dawḩat
53 D2 Sawtell Austr.
134 C2 Sawtooth Range mts U.S.A.
68 C1 Sayano-Shushenskoye Vodokhranilishche resr Rus. Fed.
76 C3 Saýat Turkm.
79 C3 Saybūt Yemen
93 I3 Säynätsalo Fin.
69 D2 Saynshand Mongolia
144 B3 Sayre U.S.A.
144 B3 Sayula Mex.
145 C3 Sayula Mex.
128 B2 Sayward Can.
Sayyod Turkm. see Saýat
89 E2 Sazonovo Rus. Fed.
114 B2 Sbaa Alg.
98 B2 Scafell Pike h. U.K.
109 C3 Scalea Italy
96 □ Scalloway U.K.
108 B2 Scandicci Italy
96 C1 Scapa Flow inlet U.K.
96 B2 Scarba i. U.K.
130 C3 Scarborough Can.
147 D3 Scarborough Trin. and Tob.
98 C2 Scarborough U.K.
64 A2 Scarborough Shoal sea feature S. China Sea
96 A2 Scarinish U.K.
Scarpanto i. Greece see Karpathos
100 B2 Schaerbeek Belgium
105 D2 Schaffhausen Switz.
100 B1 Schagen Neth.
102 C2 Schärding Austria
100 A2 Scharendijke Neth.
101 D1 Scharhörn i. Ger.
101 D1 Scheeßel Ger.
131 D2 Schefferville Can.
135 D3 Schell Creek Range mts U.S.A.
139 E2 Schenectady U.S.A.
143 D3 Schertz U.S.A.
101 E3 Scheßlitz Ger.
100 C1 Schiermonnikoog i. Neth.
100 B2 Schilde Belgium
108 B1 Schio Italy
101 F2 Schkeuditz Ger.
101 E1 Schladen Ger.
102 C2 Schladming Austria
101 E2 Schleiz Ger.
102 B1 Schleswig Ger.
101 D2 Schloss Holte-Stukenbrock Ger.
101 D2 Schlüchtern Ger.
101 E2 Schlüsselfeld Ger.
101 E2 Schmalkalden, Kurort Ger.
101 E1 Schmallenberg Ger.
Schmidt Island i. Rus. Fed. see Shmidta, Ostrov
101 F2 Schmölln Ger.
101 E1 Schneverdingen Ger.
101 E1 Schönebeck (Elbe) Ger.
101 E1 Schöningen Ger.
100 B2 Schoonhoven Neth.
59 D3 Schouten Islands P.N.G.
97 B3 Schull Ireland
101 E1 Schwabach Ger.
102 B2 Schwäbische Alb mts Ger.
101 F3 Schwandorf Ger.
61 C2 Schwaner, Pegunungan mts Indon.
101 E1 Schwarzenbek Ger.
101 F2 Schwarzenberg Ger.
122 A2 Schwarzrand mts Namibia
Schwarzwald mts Ger. see Black Forest
102 C2 Schwaz Austria
102 C1 Schwedt an der Oder Ger.
101 E2 Schweinfurt Ger.
101 E1 Schwerin Ger.
101 E1 Schweriner See l. Ger.
105 D2 Schwyz Switz.
108 B3 Sciacca Italy
95 B4 Scilly, Isles of U.K.
138 C3 Scioto r. U.S.A.
136 B1 Scobey U.S.A.
53 D2 Scone Austr.
110 B2 Scornicești Romania
55 C3 Scotia Ridge S. Atlantic Ocean
149 F8 Scotia Sea S. Atlantic Ocean
96 C2 Scotland admin. div. U.K.
128 B2 Scott, Cape Can.
123 D3 Scottburgh S. Africa
136 C2 Scott City U.S.A.
136 C2 Scottsbluff U.S.A.
140 C2 Scottsboro U.S.A.
96 B1 Scourie U.K.
139 D2 Scranton U.S.A.
98 C3 Scunthorpe U.K.
105 D2 Scuol Switz.
Scutari Albania see Shkodër
99 D4 Seaford U.K.
98 C2 Seaham U.K.
129 E2 Seal r. Can.
122 B3 Seal, Cape S. Africa
52 B3 Sea Lake Austr.
143 D3 Sealy U.S.A.
140 B1 Searcy U.S.A.

98 B2 Seascale U.K.
134 B1 Seattle U.S.A.
139 E2 Sebago Lake U.S.A.
144 A2 Sebastián Vizcaíno, Bahía b. Mex.
Sebastopol Ukr. see Sevastopol'
Sebenico Croatia see Šibenik
110 B1 Sebeş Romania
60 B2 Sebesi i. Indon.
88 C2 Sebezh Rus. Fed.
80 B1 Şebinkarahisar Turkey
141 D3 Sebring U.S.A.
61 C2 Sebuku i. Indon.
128 B3 Sechelt Can.
150 A3 Sechura Peru
73 B3 Secunderabad India
137 E3 Sedalia U.S.A.
105 C2 Sedan France
54 B2 Seddon N.Z.
114 A3 Sédhiou Senegal
142 A2 Sedona U.S.A.
101 E2 Seeburg Ger.
101 E1 Seehausen (Altmark) Ger.
122 A2 Seeheim Namibia
104 C2 Sées France
101 E2 Seesen Ger.
101 E1 Seevetal Ger.
114 A4 Sefadu Sierra Leone
123 C1 Sefare Botswana
76 C3 Sefid Küh, Selseleh-ye mts Afgh.
93 F3 Segalstad Norway
60 B1 Segamat Malaysia
86 C2 Segezha Rus. Fed.
114 B3 Ségou Mali
106 C1 Segovia Spain
86 C2 Segozerskoye Vodokhranilishche resr Rus. Fed.
115 D2 Séguédine Niger
114 B4 Séguéla Côte d'Ivoire
143 D3 Seguin U.S.A.
107 C2 Segura r. Spain
106 C2 Segura, Sierra de mts Spain
120 B3 Sehithwa Botswana
93 H3 Seinäjoki Fin.
104 C2 Seine r. France
104 B2 Seine, Baie de b. France
105 C2 Seine, Val de val. France
103 E1 Sejny Pol.
60 B2 Sekayu Indon.
114 B4 Sekondi Ghana
134 B1 Selah U.S.A.
59 C3 Selaru i. Indon.
61 C2 Selatan, Tanjung pt Indon.
126 B2 Selawik U.S.A.
61 C2 Selayar, Pulau i. Indon.
98 C3 Selby U.K.
136 C1 Selby U.S.A.
111 C3 Selçuk Turkey
123 C1 Selebi-Phikwe Botswana
120 B3 Selebi-Pikwe Botswana
see Selebi-Phikwe
105 D2 Sélestat France
92 □A3 Selfoss Iceland
114 A3 Sélibabi Maur.
142 A1 Seligman U.S.A.
116 A2 Selima Oasis Sudan
111 C3 Selimiye Turkey
114 B3 Sélingué, Lac de l. Mali
89 D2 Selizharovo Rus. Fed.
93 E4 Seljord Norway
129 E2 Selkirk Can.
96 C3 Selkirk U.K.
128 C2 Selkirk Mountains Can.
142 A2 Sells U.S.A.
140 C2 Selma AL U.S.A.
135 C3 Selma CA U.S.A.
105 D2 Selongey France
99 C4 Selsey Bill h. U.K.
89 D3 Sel'tso Rus. Fed.
Selukwe Zimbabwe see Shurugwi
150 B3 Selvas reg. Brazil
134 C1 Selway r. U.S.A.
129 D1 Selwyn Lake Can.
128 A1 Selwyn Mountains Can.
51 C2 Selwyn Range hills Austr.
60 B2 Semangka, Teluk b. Indon.
61 C2 Semarang Indon.
60 B1 Sematan Malaysia
118 B2 Sembé Congo
81 C2 Şemdinli Turkey
91 C1 Semenivka Ukr.
87 D3 Semenov Rus. Fed.
61 C2 Semeru, Gunung vol. Indon.
77 E1 Semey Kazakh.
91 E2 Semikarakorsk Rus. Fed.
89 E3 Semiluki Rus. Fed.
136 B2 Seminoe Reservoir U.S.A.
143 C2 Seminole U.S.A.
141 D2 Seminole, Lake U.S.A.
61 C1 Semitau Indon.
Sem Kolodezy Ukr. see Lenine
81 D2 Semnān Iran
61 C1 Semporna Malaysia
105 C2 Semur-en-Auxois France
Semyonovskoye Rus. Fed. see Bereznik
Semyonovskoye Rus. Fed. see Ostrovskoye
150 D3 Sena Madureira Brazil
120 B2 Senanga Zambia
67 D3 Sendai Japan
67 D3 Sendai Japan
141 D2 Seneca U.S.A.

114 A3 Senegal country Africa
114 A3 Sénégal r. Maur./Senegal
102 C1 Senftenberg Ger.
119 D3 Sengerema Tanz.
60 B2 Sengkang Indon.
151 E4 Senhor do Bonfim Brazil
103 D2 Senica Slovakia
108 B2 Senigallia Italy
109 B2 Senj Croatia
92 G2 Senja i. Norway
122 B2 Senlac S. Africa
105 C2 Senlis France
63 B2 Senmonorom Cambodia
116 B3 Sennar Sudan
130 C3 Senneterre Can.
123 C3 Senqu r. Lesotho
105 C2 Sens France
109 D1 Senta Serbia
128 B2 Sentinel Peak Can.
123 C1 Senwabarwana S. Africa
75 B2 Seoni India
65 B2 Seoul S. Korea
155 D2 Sepetiba, Baía de b. Brazil
59 D3 Sepik r. P.N.G.
61 C1 Sepinang Indon.
131 D2 Sept-Îles Can.
87 D4 Serafimovich Rus. Fed.
100 B2 Seraing Belgium
59 C3 Seram i. Indon.
60 B2 Serang Indon.
60 B1 Serasan, Selat sea chan. Indon.
109 D2 Serbia country Europe
76 B3 Serdar Turkm.
117 C3 Serdo Eth.
89 E3 Serebryanyye Prudy Rus. Fed.
60 B1 Seremban Malaysia
119 D3 Serengeti Plain Tanz.
121 C2 Serenje Zambia
90 B2 Seret r. Ukr.
87 D3 Sergach Rus. Fed.
86 F2 Sergino Rus. Fed.
89 E2 Sergiyev Posad Rus. Fed.
Sergo Ukr. see Stakhanov
74 A1 Serhetabat Turkm.
61 C1 Seria Brunei
61 C1 Serian Malaysia
111 B3 Serifos i. Greece
80 B2 Serik Turkey
59 C3 Sermata, Kepulauan is Indon.
Sernyy Zavod Turkm. see Kükürtli
86 F3 Serov Rus. Fed.
120 B3 Serowe Botswana
106 B2 Serpa Port.
Serpa Pinto Angola see Menongue
89 E3 Serpukhov Rus. Fed.
155 D2 Serra Brazil
155 C1 Serra das Araras Brazil
108 A3 Serramanna Italy
154 B1 Serranópolis Brazil
100 A3 Serre r. France
111 B2 Serres Greece
151 E4 Serrinha Brazil
155 D1 Sêrro Brazil
154 C2 Sertãozinho Brazil
59 D3 Serui Indon.
120 B3 Serule Botswana
61 C2 Seruyan r. Indon.
68 C2 Sêrxü China
120 A2 Sesfontein Namibia
108 B2 Sessa Aurunca Italy
108 A2 Sestri Levante Italy
105 C3 Sète France
155 D1 Sete Lagoas Brazil
92 G2 Setermoen Norway
93 E4 Setesdal val. Norway
115 C1 Sétif Alg.
67 B4 Seto-naikai sea Japan
114 B1 Settat Morocco
98 B2 Settle U.K.
106 B2 Setúbal Port.
106 B2 Setúbal, Baía de b. Port.
130 A2 Seul, Lac l. Can.
81 C1 Sevan Armenia
76 A2 Sevan, Lake Armenia
Sevana Lich l. Armenia see Sevan, Lake
91 C3 Sevastopol' Ukr.
Seven Islands Can. see Sept-Îles
131 D2 Seven Islands Bay Can.
99 D4 Sevenoaks U.K.
105 C3 Séverac-le-Château France
130 B2 Severn r. Can.
122 B2 Severn S. Africa
99 B4 Severn r. U.K.
86 D2 Severnaya Dvina r. Rus. Fed.
83 H1 Severnaya Zemlya is Rus. Fed.
86 D2 Severnyy Rus. Fed.
86 F2 Severnyy Rus. Fed.
83 I3 Severobaykal'sk Rus. Fed.
86 C2 Severodvinsk Rus. Fed.
83 I3 Severo-Kuril'sk Rus. Fed.
92 J2 Severomorsk Rus. Fed.
86 C2 Severoonezhsk Rus. Fed.
83 H2 Severo-Yeniseyskiy Rus. Fed.
91 D3 Severskaya Rus. Fed.
135 D3 Sevier r. U.S.A.
135 D3 Sevier Lake U.S.A.
Sevilla Spain see Seville
106 B2 Seville Spain
Sevlyush Ukr. see Vynohradiv
89 D3 Sevsk Rus. Fed.
126 C2 Seward U.S.A.
126 B2 Seward Peninsula U.S.A.
128 A2 Sewell Inlet Can.

109 C2 Sinj Croatia
61 D2 Sinjai Indon.
116 B3 Sinkat Sudan
151 D2 Sinnamary Fr. Guiana
Sînnicolau Mare Romania
see Sânnicolau Mare
Sinoia Zimbabwe see Chinhoyi
80 B1 Sinop Turkey
65 B1 Sinp'o N. Korea
61 C1 Sintang Indon.
100 B2 Sint Anthonis Neth.
100 A2 Sint-Laureins Belgium
147 D3 Sint Maarten terr. West Indies
100 B2 Sint-Niklaas Belgium
143 D3 Sinton U.S.A.
65 A1 Sinüiju N. Korea
64 B3 Siocon Phil.
103 D2 Siófok Hungary
105 D2 Sion Switz.
137 D2 Sioux Center U.S.A.
137 D2 Sioux City U.S.A.
137 D2 Sioux Falls U.S.A.
130 A2 Sioux Lookout Can.
65 A1 Siping China
129 E2 Sipiwesk Lake Can.
55 P2 Siple, Mount Antarctica
55 P2 Siple Island Antarctica
Sipolilo Zimbabwe see Guruve
60 A2 Sipura i. Indon.
64 B3 Siquijor Phil.
93 E4 Sira r. Norway
Siracusa Italy see Syracuse
51 C1 Sir Edward Pellew Group is Austr.
110 C1 Siret Romania
110 C1 Siret r. Romania
78 A1 Sirhān, Wādī an watercourse
Saudi Arabia
79 C2 Sīrīk Iran
61 C1 Sirik, Tanjung pt Malaysia
62 B2 Siri Kit, Khuan Thai.
128 B1 Sir James MacBrien, Mount Can.
79 C2 Sīrjān Iran
81 C2 Şırnak Turkey
74 B2 Sirohi India
60 A1 Sirombu Indon.
74 B2 Sirsa India
115 D1 Sirte Libya
115 D1 Sirte, Gulf of Libya
81 C2 Şirvan Azer.
88 B2 Širvintos Lith.
109 C1 Sisak Croatia
63 B2 Sisaket Thai.
145 C2 Sisal Mex.
122 B2 Sishen S. Africa
81 C2 Sisian Armenia
127 I2 Sisimiut Greenland
129 D2 Sisipuk Lake Can.
63 B2 Sisŏphŏn Cambodia
105 D3 Sisteron France
75 C2 Sitapur India
111 C3 Siteia Greece
123 D2 Siteki Swaziland
128 A2 Sitka U.S.A.
100 B2 Sittard Neth.
62 A1 Sittaung Myanmar
62 A2 Sittaung r. Myanmar
62 A1 Sittwe Myanmar
61 C2 Situbondo Indon.
80 B2 Sivas Turkey
62 A1 Sivasagar India
111 C3 Sivaslı Turkey
80 B2 Siverek Turkey
88 D2 Siverskiy Rus. Fed.
80 B2 Sivrihisar Turkey
116 A2 Sīwah Egypt
75 B1 Siwalik Range mts India/Nepal
Siwa Oasis oasis Egypt
see Wāḥāt Sīwah
105 D3 Six-Fours-les-Plages France
70 B2 Sixian China
123 C2 Siyabuswa S. Africa
Sjælland i. Denmark see Zealand
109 D2 Sjenica Serbia
92 G2 Sjøvegan Norway
91 C2 Skadovs'k Ukr.
93 F4 Skagen Denmark
93 E4 Skagerrak str. Denmark/Norway
134 B1 Skagit r. U.S.A.
128 A2 Skagway U.S.A.
92 G2 Skaland Norway
93 F4 Skara Sweden
74 B1 Skardu Pak.
103 E1 Skarżysko-Kamienna Pol.
103 D2 Skawina Pol.
114 A2 Skaymat Western Sahara
128 B2 Skeena r. Can.
128 B2 Skeena Mountains Can.
98 D3 Skegness U.K.
92 H3 Skellefteå Sweden
92 H3 Skellefteälven r. Sweden
97 C2 Skerries Ireland
93 F4 Ski Norway
111 B3 Skiathos i. Greece
97 B3 Skibbereen Ireland
92 □B2 Skíðadals-jökull glacier Iceland
98 B2 Skiddaw h. U.K.
93 E4 Skien Norway
103 E1 Skierniewice Pol.
115 C1 Skikda Alg.
52 B3 Skipton Austr.
98 B3 Skipton U.K.
93 E4 Skive Denmark
92 H1 Skjervøy Norway

Skobelev Uzbek. see Farg'ona
111 B3 Skopelos i. Greece
89 E3 Skopin Rus. Fed.
111 B2 Skopje Macedonia
111 C3 Skoutaros Greece
93 F4 Skövde Sweden
83 J3 Skovorodino Rus. Fed.
139 F2 Skowhegan U.S.A.
92 H2 Skröven Sweden
88 B2 Skrunda Latvia
128 A1 Skukum, Mount Can.
123 D1 Skukuza S. Africa
88 B2 Skuodas Lith.
90 B2 Skvyra Ukr.
96 A2 Skye i. U.K.
111 B3 Skyros Greece
111 B3 Skyros i. Greece
93 F4 Slagelse Denmark
60 B2 Slamet, Gunung vol. Indon.
97 C2 Slaney r. Ireland
88 C2 Slantsy Rus. Fed.
109 C1 Slatina Croatia
110 B2 Slatina Romania
143 C2 Slaton U.S.A.
129 C1 Slave r. Can.
114 C4 Slave Coast Africa
128 C2 Slave Lake Can.
77 D1 Slavgorod Rus. Fed.
88 C2 Slavkovichi Rus. Fed.
Slavonska Požega Croatia
see Požega
109 C1 Slavonski Brod Croatia
90 B1 Slavuta Ukr.
90 C1 Slavutych Ukr.
66 B2 Slavyanka Rus. Fed.
Slavyanskaya Rus. Fed.
see Slavyansk-na-Kubani
91 D2 Slavyansk-na-Kubani Rus. Fed.
89 D3 Slawharad Belarus
103 D1 Sławno Pol.
99 C3 Sleaford U.K.
97 A2 Slea Head hd Ireland
130 C2 Sleeper Islands Can.
97 D1 Slieve Donard h. U.K.
97 B1 Slieve Gamph hills Ireland
96 A2 Sligachan U.K.
Sligeach Ireland see Sligo
97 B1 Sligo Ireland
97 B1 Sligo Bay Ireland
93 G4 Slite Sweden
110 C2 Sliven Bulg.
110 C2 Slobozia Romania
128 C3 Slocan Can.
88 C3 Slonim Belarus
100 B1 Sloten Neth.
99 C4 Slough U.K.
103 D2 Slovakia country Europe
108 B1 Slovenia country Europe
91 D2 Slov"yans'k Ukr.
102 C1 Słubice Pol.
90 B1 Sluch r. Ukr.
100 A2 Sluis Neth.
103 D1 Słupsk Pol.
88 C3 Slutsk Belarus
97 A2 Slyne Head hd Ireland
68 C1 Slyudyanka Rus. Fed.
131 D2 Smallwood Reservoir Can.
88 C3 Smalyavichy Belarus
88 C3 Smarhon' Belarus
129 D2 Smeaton Can.
109 D2 Smederevo Serbia
109 D2 Smederevska Palanka Serbia
91 C2 Smila Ukr.
88 C3 Smilavichy Belarus
88 C2 Smiltene Latvia
137 D3 Smith Center U.S.A.
128 B2 Smithers Can.
141 E1 Smithfield NC U.S.A.
134 D2 Smithfield UT U.S.A.
139 D3 Smith Mountain Lake U.S.A.
130 C3 Smiths Falls Can.
53 D2 Smithton Austr.
53 D2 Smoky Cape Austr.
137 D3 Smoky Hills U.S.A.
92 E3 Smøla i. Norway
89 D3 Smolensk Rus. Fed.
89 D3 Smolensko-Moskovskaya
Vozvyshennost' hills
Belarus/Rus. Fed.
111 B2 Smolyan Bulg.
66 B2 Smolyaninovo Rus. Fed.
130 B3 Smooth Rock Falls Can.
Smyrna Turkey see İzmir
91 D2 Smyrnove Ukr.
92 □B3 Snæfell h. Iceland
98 A2 Snaefell h. Isle of Man
128 A1 Snag (abandoned) Can.
134 C1 Snake r. U.S.A.
134 D2 Snake River Plain U.S.A.
Snare Lakes Can. see Wekweètì
92 F3 Snåsvatn l. Norway
100 B1 Sneek Neth.
97 B3 Sneem Ireland
122 B3 Sneeuberge mts S. Africa
Snegurovka Ukr. see Tetiyiv
103 D1 Snežka mt. Czech Rep.
108 B1 Snežnik mt. Slovenia
103 E1 Śniardwy, Jezioro l. Pol.
Sniečkus Lith. see Visaginas
91 C2 Snihurivka Ukr.
93 E3 Snøhetta mt. Norway
Snovsk Ukr. see Shchors
129 D1 Snowbird Lake Can.

99 A3 Snowdon mt. U.K.
Snowdrift Can. see Łutselk'e
129 C1 Snowdrift r. Can.
142 A2 Snowflake U.S.A.
129 D2 Snow Lake Can.
134 C1 Snowshoe Peak U.S.A.
52 A2 Snowtown Austr.
53 C3 Snowy r. Austr.
53 C3 Snowy Mountains Austr.
143 C2 Snyder U.S.A.
121 □D2 Soalala Madag.
121 □D2 Soanierana-Ivongo Madag.
90 B2 Sob r. Ukr.
65 B2 Sobaek-sanmaek mts S. Korea
117 B4 Sobat r. S. Sudan
89 F2 Sobinka Rus. Fed.
151 E4 Sobradinho, Barragem de resr Brazil
151 E3 Sobral Brazil
91 D3 Sochi Rus. Fed.
65 B2 Sŏch'ŏn S. Korea
49 L5 Society Islands Fr. Polynesia
150 B2 Socorro Col.
142 B2 Socorro NM U.S.A.
142 B2 Socorro TX U.S.A.
144 A3 Socorro, Isla i. Mex.
56 B4 Socotra i. Yemen
63 B3 Soc Trăng Vietnam
106 C2 Socuéllamos Spain
92 I2 Sodankylä Fin.
134 D2 Soda Springs U.S.A.
93 G3 Söderhamn Sweden
93 G4 Södertälje Sweden
116 A3 Sodiri Sudan
117 B4 Sodo Eth.
93 G3 Södra Kvarken str. Fin./Sweden
Soerabaia Indon. see Surabaya
101 D2 Soest Ger.
53 C2 Sofala Austr.
110 B2 Sofia Bulg.
121 □D2 Sofia r. Madag.
Sofiya Bulg. see Sofia
Sofiyevka Ukr. see Vil'nyans'k
75 D1 Sog China
93 E3 Sognefjorden inlet Norway
111 D2 Söğüt Turkey
Sohâg Egypt see Sūhāj
Sohar Oman see Şuḩār
100 B3 Soignies Belgium
105 C2 Soissons France
90 A1 Sokal' Ukr.
65 B2 Sokch'o S. Korea
111 C3 Söke Turkey
81 C1 Sokhumi Georgia
114 C4 Sokodé Togo
89 F2 Sokol Rus. Fed.
101 F2 Sokolov Czech Rep.
115 C3 Sokoto Nigeria
115 C3 Sokoto r. Nigeria
90 B2 Sokyryany Ukr.
73 B3 Solapur India
135 B3 Soledad U.S.A.
89 E2 Soligalich Rus. Fed.
99 C3 Solihull U.K.
86 E3 Solikamsk Rus. Fed.
87 E3 Sol'-Iletsk Rus. Fed.
100 C2 Solingen Ger.
122 A1 Solitaire Namibia
92 G3 Sollefteå Sweden
93 G4 Sollentuna Sweden
107 D2 Sóller Spain
101 D2 Solling hills Ger.
89 E2 Solnechnogorsk Rus. Fed.
60 B2 Solok Indon.
48 H4 Solomon Islands country
S. Pacific Ocean
48 G4 Solomon Sea S. Pacific Ocean
61 D2 Solor, Kepulauan is Indon.
105 D2 Solothurn Switz.
81 D2 Solţānābād Iran
101 D1 Soltau Ger.
89 D2 Sol'tsy Rus. Fed.
96 C3 Solway Firth est. U.K.
120 B2 Solwezi Zambia
111 C3 Soma Turkey
117 C4 Somalia country Africa
Somaliland terr. Somalia
61 C2 Somba Indon.
120 B1 Sombo Angola
109 C1 Sombor Serbia
144 B2 Sombrerete Mex.
138 C3 Somerset U.S.A.
123 C3 Somerset East S. Africa
126 F2 Somerset Island Can.
122 A3 Somerset West S. Africa
110 B1 Someş r. Romania
101 E2 Sömmerda Ger.
75 C2 Son r. India
65 C1 Sŏnbong N. Korea
93 E5 Sønderborg Denmark
101 E2 Sondershausen Ger.
Søndre Strømfjord inlet Greenland
see Kangerlussuaq
108 A1 Sondrio Italy
63 B2 Sông Câu Vietnam
62 B1 Sông Đa, Hồ resr Vietnam
119 D2 Songea Tanz.
65 B1 Sŏnggan N. Korea
65 B1 Songhua Hu resr China
Songjianghe China
Sŏngjin N. Korea see Kimch'aek
63 B3 Songkhla Thai.
65 B2 Sŏngnam S. Korea
65 B2 Songnim N. Korea

120 A1 Songo Angola
121 C2 Songo Moz.
Songololo Dem. Rep. Congo
see Mbanza-Ngungu
69 E1 Songyuan China
Sonid Youqi China see Saihan Tal
74 B2 Sonipat India
89 E2 Sonkovo Rus. Fed.
62 B1 Sơn La Vietnam
74 A2 Sonmiani Pak.
74 A2 Sonmiani Bay Pak.
101 E2 Sonneberg Ger.
142 A2 Sonoita Mex.
144 A2 Sonora r. Mex.
135 B3 Sonora CA U.S.A.
143 C2 Sonora TX U.S.A.
146 B3 Sonsonate El Salvador
117 A4 Sopo watercourse S. Sudan
103 D2 Sopron Hungary
74 B1 Sopur India
108 B2 Sora Italy
130 C2 Sorel Can.
51 D4 Sorell Austr.
106 C1 Soria Spain
90 B2 Soroca Moldova
154 C2 Sorocaba Brazil
87 E3 Sorochinsk Rus. Fed.
Soroki Moldova see Soroca
59 D2 Sorol atoll Micronesia
59 C3 Sorong Indon.
119 D2 Soroti Uganda
92 H1 Sørøya i. Norway
108 B2 Sorrento Italy
92 G2 Sorsele Sweden
64 B2 Sorsogon Phil.
86 C2 Sortavala Rus. Fed.
92 G2 Sortland Norway
65 B2 Sŏsan S. Korea
123 C2 Soshanguve S. Africa
89 E3 Sosna r. Rus. Fed.
153 B3 Sosneado mt. Arg.
86 E2 Sosnogorsk Rus. Fed.
86 D2 Sosnovka Rus. Fed.
88 C2 Sosnovyy Bor Rus. Fed.
103 D1 Sosnowiec Pol.
91 C1 Sosnytsya Ukr.
86 F3 Sos'va Rus. Fed.
91 D2 Sosyka r. Rus. Fed.
145 C2 Soto la Marina Mex.
118 B2 Souanké Congo
111 B3 Souda Greece
104 C3 Souillac France
Sŏul S. Korea see Seoul
104 B2 Soulac-sur-Mer France
104 B3 Soulom France
Soûr Lebanon see Tyre
107 D2 Sour el Ghozlane Alg.
129 D3 Souris Man. Can.
131 D3 Souris P.E.I. Can.
129 E3 Souris r. Can.
151 F3 Sousa Brazil
115 D1 Sousse Tunisia
104 B3 Soustons France
122 B3 South Africa, Republic of
country Africa
99 C4 Southampton U.K.
129 F1 Southampton, Cape Can.
129 F1 Southampton Island Can.
73 D3 South Andaman i. India
52 A1 South Australia state Austr.
140 B2 Southaven U.S.A.
142 B2 South Baldy mt. U.S.A.
130 B3 South Baymouth Can.
138 B2 South Bend U.S.A.
141 D2 South Carolina state U.S.A.
58 B2 South China Sea N. Pacific Ocean
South Coast Town Austr.
see Gold Coast
136 C2 South Dakota state U.S.A.
99 C4 South Downs hills U.K.
159 E6 Southeast Indian Ridge
Indian Ocean
55 O2 Southeast Pacific Basin
S. Pacific Ocean
129 D2 Southend Can.
99 D4 Southend-on-Sea U.K.
54 B2 Southern Alps mts N.Z.
50 A3 Southern Cross Austr.
129 E2 Southern Indian Lake Can.
159 D7 Southern Ocean
141 E1 Southern Pines U.S.A.
Southern Rhodesia country Africa
see Zimbabwe
96 B3 Southern Uplands hills U.K.
55 J2 South Geomagnetic Pole (2008)
Antarctica
149 G8 South Georgia terr. S. Atlantic Ocean
149 G8 South Georgia and the South
Sandwich Islands terr.
S. Atlantic Ocean
138 B3 South Haven U.S.A.
129 E1 South Henik Lake Can.
119 D2 South Horr Kenya
54 B2 South Island N.Z.
65 B2 South Korea country Asia
135 B3 South Lake Tahoe U.S.A.
55 L3 South Magnetic Pole (2008)
Antarctica
149 F9 South Orkney Islands
S. Atlantic Ocean
136 C2 South Platte r. U.S.A.
98 B3 Southport U.K.
141 E2 Southport U.S.A.

67 D4 Sumisu-jima *i.* Japan
131 D3 Summerside Can.
138 C3 Summersville U.S.A.
141 D2 Summerville U.S.A.
137 D1 Summit U.S.A.
128 B2 Summit Lake Can.
103 D2 Šumperk Czech Rep.
81 C1 Sumqayıt Azer.
141 D2 Sumter U.S.A.
91 C1 Sumy Ukr.
75 D2 Sunamganj Bangl.
65 B2 Sunan N. Korea
79 C2 Şunaynah Oman
52 B3 Sunbury Austr.
139 D2 Sunbury U.S.A.
65 B2 Sunch'ŏn N. Korea
65 B3 Sunch'ŏn S. Korea
123 C2 Sun City S. Africa
93 H3 Sund Fin.
60 B2 Sunda, Selat *str.* Indon.
136 C2 Sundance U.S.A.
75 C2 Sundarbans *coastal area* Bangl./India
74 B1 Sundarnagar India
Sunda Strait *str.* Indon.
see Sunda, Selat
Sunda Trench Indian Ocean
see Java Trench
98 C2 Sunderland U.K.
128 C2 Sundre Can.
93 G3 Sundsvall Sweden
123 D2 Sundumbili S. Africa
60 B2 Sungailiat Indon.
60 B2 Sungaipenuh Indon.
60 B1 Sungai Petani Malaysia
80 B1 Sungurlu Turkey
75 C2 Sun Kosi *r.* Nepal
93 E3 Sunndalsøra Norway
134 C1 Sunnyside U.S.A.
135 B3 Sunnyvale U.S.A.
141 D3 Sunrise U.S.A.
83 I2 Suntar Rus. Fed.
74 A2 Suntsar Rus. Fed.
114 B4 Sunyani Ghana
92 I3 Suomussalmi Fin.
67 B4 Suō-nada *b.* Japan
86 C2 Suoyarvi Rus. Fed.
142 A2 Superior AZ U.S.A.
137 D2 Superior NE U.S.A.
138 A1 Superior WI U.S.A.
138 B1 Superior, Lake Can./U.S.A.
63 B2 Suphan Buri Thai.
81 C2 Süphan Dağı *mt.* Turkey
89 D3 Suponevo Rus. Fed.
81 C2 Sūq ash Shuyūkh Iraq
70 B2 Suqian China
78 A2 Sūq Suwayq Saudi Arabia
Suquţrā *i.* Yemen *see* Socotra
79 C2 Şūr Oman
74 A2 Surab Pak.
61 C2 Surabaya Indon.
61 C2 Surakarta Indon.
74 B2 Surat India
74 B2 Suratgarh India
63 A3 Surat Thani Thai.
89 D3 Surazh Rus. Fed.
109 D2 Surdulica Serbia
100 C3 Sûre *r.* Lux.
74 B2 Surendranagar India
82 F2 Surgut Rus. Fed.
64 B3 Surigao Phil.
63 B2 Surin Thai.
151 D2 Suriname *country* S. America
75 C2 Surkhet Nepal
Surt Libya *see* Sirte
Surt, Khalīj *g.* Libya *see* Sirte, Gulf of
60 B2 Surulangun Indon.
81 C2 Süsangerd Iran
89 F2 Susanino Rus. Fed.
135 B2 Susanville U.S.A.
80 B1 Suşehri Turkey
139 D3 Susquehanna *r.* U.S.A.
131 D3 Sussex Can.
101 D1 Süstedt Ger.
100 C1 Sustrum Ger.
83 K2 Susuman Rus. Fed.
111 C3 Susurluk Turkey
74 B1 Sutak India
53 D2 Sutherland Austr.
122 B3 Sutherland S. Africa
136 C2 Sutherland U.S.A.
134 B2 Sutherlin U.S.A.
74 B2 Sutlej *r.* India/Pak.
138 C3 Sutton U.S.A.
99 C3 Sutton Coldfield U.K.
98 C3 Sutton in Ashfield U.K.
66 D2 Suttsu Japan
49 I5 Suva Fiji
Suvalki Pol. *see* Suwałki
89 E3 Suvorov Rus. Fed.
90 B2 Suvorove Ukr.
103 E1 Suwałki Pol.
141 D3 Suwanee Sound *b.* U.S.A.
63 B2 Suwannaphum Thai.
141 D3 Suwannee *r.* U.S.A.
Suways, Qanāt as *canal* Egypt
see Suez Canal
Suweis, Qanâ el *canal* Egypt
see Suez Canal
65 B2 Suwŏn S. Korea
79 C2 Sūzā Iran
89 F2 Suzdal' Rus. Fed.
70 B2 Suzemka Rus. Fed.
70 B2 Suzhou *Anhui* China
70 C2 Suzhou *Jiangsu* China

67 C3 Suzu Japan
67 C3 Suzu-misaki *pt* Japan
82 B1 Svalbard *terr.* Arctic Ocean
90 A2 Svalyava Ukr.
92 H2 Svappavaara Sweden
91 D2 Svatove Ukr.
63 B2 Svay Riĕng Cambodia
93 F3 Sveg Sweden
88 C2 Švenčionys Lith.
93 F4 Svendborg Denmark
Sverdlovsk Rus. Fed.
see Yekaterinburg
111 B2 Sveti Nikole Macedonia
66 C1 Svetlaya Rus. Fed.
88 B3 Svetlogorsk Rus. Fed.
87 D4 Svetlograd Rus. Fed.
88 B3 Svetlyy Rus. Fed.
93 I3 Svetogorsk Rus. Fed.
103 E2 Svidník Slovakia
111 C2 Svilengrad Bulg.
110 B2 Svinecea Mare, Vârful *mt.* Romania
110 C2 Svishtov Bulg.
88 B3 Svislach Belarus
103 D2 Svitavy Czech Rep.
91 C2 Svitlovods'k Ukr.
69 E1 Svobodnyy Rus. Fed.
110 B2 Svoge Bulg.
92 F2 Svolvær Norway
88 C3 Svyetlahorsk Belarus
141 D2 Swainsboro U.S.A.
120 A3 Swakopmund Namibia
52 B3 Swan Hill Austr.
128 C2 Swan Hills Can.
129 D2 Swan Lake Can.
97 C1 Swanlinbar Ireland
129 D2 Swan River Can.
53 D2 Swansea Austr.
99 B4 Swansea U.K.
122 B3 Swartkolkvloer *salt pan* S. Africa
123 C2 Swartruggens S. Africa
Swatow China *see* Shantou
123 D2 Swaziland *country* Africa
93 G3 Sweden *country* Europe
143 C2 Sweetwater U.S.A.
136 B2 Sweetwater *r.* U.S.A.
122 B3 Swellendam S. Africa
103 D1 Świdnica Pol.
103 D1 Świdwin Pol.
103 D1 Świebodzin Pol.
103 D1 Świecie Pol.
129 D2 Swift Current Can.
97 C1 Swilly, Lough *inlet* Ireland
99 C4 Swindon U.K.
102 C1 Świnoujście Pol.
105 D2 Switzerland *country* Europe
97 C2 Swords Ireland
88 C3 Syanno Belarus
89 D1 Syas'stroy Rus. Fed.
89 D2 Sychevka Rus. Fed.
53 D2 Sydney Austr.
131 D3 Sydney Can.
131 D3 Sydney Mines Can.
91 D2 Syeverodonets'k Ukr.
111 B2 Sykia Greece
86 E2 Syktyvkar Rus. Fed.
140 C2 Sylacauga U.S.A.
75 D2 Sylhet Bangl.
102 B1 Sylt *i.* Ger.
138 C2 Sylvania U.S.A.
51 C1 Sylvester, Lake *imp. l.* Austr.
111 C3 Symi *i.* Greece
91 D2 Synel'nykove Ukr.
91 C2 Synyukha *r.* Ukr.
87 D3 Syzran' Rus. Fed.
102 C1 Szczecin Pol.
103 D1 Szczecinek Pol.
103 E1 Szczytno Pol.
Szechwan *prov.* China
see Sichuan
103 E2 Szeged Hungary
103 D2 Székesfehérvár Hungary
103 D2 Szekszárd Hungary
103 E2 Szentes Hungary
103 D2 Szentgotthárd Hungary
103 E2 Szerencs Hungary
103 D2 Szigetvár Hungary
103 E2 Szolnok Hungary
103 D2 Szombathely Hungary
Sztálinváros Hungary
see Dunaújváros

T

117 C4 Taagga Duudka *reg.* Somalia
64 B2 Tabaco Phil.
78 B2 Tābah Saudi Arabia
108 A3 Tabarka Tunisia
76 B3 Ţabas Iran
79 C1 Tabāsīn Iran
81 D3 Tābask, Kūh-e *mt.* Iran
150 D3 Tabatinga Brazil
154 C3 Tabatinga Brazil
114 B2 Tabelbala Alg.

128 C3 Taber Can.
64 B2 Tablas *i.* Phil.
102 C2 Tábor Czech Rep.
119 D3 Tabora Tanz.
114 B4 Tabou Côte d'Ivoire
81 C2 Tabrīz Iran
48 L3 Tabuaeran *atoll* Kiribati
78 A2 Tabūk Saudi Arabia
93 G4 Täby Sweden
77 E2 Tacheng China
102 C2 Tachov Czech Rep.
64 B2 Tacloban Phil.
150 B4 Tacna Peru
134 B1 Tacoma U.S.A.
152 C3 Tacuarembó Uru.
142 B3 Tacupeto Mex.
114 C2 Tademaït, Plateau du Alg.
Tadjikistan *country* Asia
see Tajikistan
117 C3 Tadjourah Djibouti
80 B2 Tadmur Syria
129 E2 Tadoule Lake Can.
Tadzhikskaya S.S.R. *country* Asia
see Tajikistan
65 B2 T'aebaek-sanmaek *mts*
N. Korea/S. Korea
Taech'ŏn S. Korea *see* Poryŏng
65 B2 Taegu S. Korea
65 B2 Taejŏn S. Korea
65 B3 Taejŏng S. Korea
65 B2 T'aepaek S. Korea
107 C1 Tafalla Spain
152 B2 Tafí Viejo Arg.
79 D2 Taftān, Kūh-e *mt.* Iran
91 D2 Taganrog Rus. Fed.
91 D2 Taganrog, Gulf of Rus. Fed./Ukr.
62 A1 Tagaung Myanmar
64 B2 Tagaytay City Phil.
64 B3 Tagbilaran Phil.
64 B2 Tagudin Phil.
51 E1 Tagula Island P.N.G.
64 B3 Tagum Phil.
106 B2 Tagus *r.* Port./Spain
60 B1 Tahan, Gunung *mt.* Malaysia
115 C2 Tahat, Mont *mt.* Alg.
69 E1 Tahe China
49 M5 Tahiti *i.* Fr. Polynesia
143 E1 Tahlequah U.S.A.
135 B3 Tahoe, Lake U.S.A.
135 B3 Tahoe City U.S.A.
126 E2 Tahoe Lake Can.
115 C3 Tahoua Niger
79 C2 Tahrūd Iran
128 B3 Tahsis Can.
116 B2 Ţahţā Egypt
64 B3 Tahuna Indon.
70 B2 Tai'an China
70 A2 Taibai Shan *mt.* China
71 C3 Taibei Taiwan
Taibus Qi China *see* Baochang
70 B2 Taihang Shan *mts* China
54 C1 Taihape N.Z.
71 B3 Taihe China
70 C2 Tai Hu *l.* China
52 A3 Tailem Bend Austr.
71 C3 Tainan Taiwan
111 B3 Tainaro, Akra *c.* Greece
155 D1 Taiobeiras Brazil
Taiping China *see* Chongzuo
60 B1 Taiping Malaysia
Tairbeart U.K. *see* Tarbert
71 B3 Taishan China
70 B2 Tai Shan *hills* China
119 D3 Taita Hills Kenya
153 A4 Taitao, Península de *pen.* Chile
71 C3 T'aitung Taiwan
92 I2 Taivalkoski Fin.
92 H2 Taivaskero *h.* Fin.
71 C3 Taiwan *country* Asia
Taiwan Shan *mts* Taiwan
see Zhongyang Shanmo
71 B3 Taiwan Strait China/Taiwan
77 C1 Taiynsha Kazakh.
70 B2 Taiyuan China
71 C3 Taizhong Taiwan
70 B2 Taizhou *Jiangsu* China
71 C3 Taizhou *Zhejiang* China
78 B3 Ta'izz Yemen
145 C3 Tajamulco, Volcán de *vol.* Guat.
77 D3 Tajikistan *country* Asia
74 B2 Taj Mahal *tourist site* India
Tajo *r.* Spain *see* Tagus
63 A2 Tak Thai.
54 B2 Takaka N.Z.
115 C2 Takalous, Oued *watercourse* Alg.
67 B4 Takamatsu Japan
67 C3 Takaoka Japan
54 B1 Takapuna N.Z.
67 C3 Takasaki Japan
122 B1 Takatokwane Botswana
122 B1 Takatshwaane Botswana
67 C3 Takayama Japan
67 C3 Takefu Japan
60 A1 Takengon Indon.
63 B2 Takêv Cambodia
Takhiatash Uzbek. *see* Taxiatosh
63 B2 Ta Khmau Cambodia
74 B1 Takht-i-Sulaiman *mt.* Pak.
66 D2 Takikawa Japan
128 B2 Takla Lake Can.
128 B2 Takla Landing Can.
Takla Makan *des.* China
see Taklimakan Desert
77 E3 Taklimakan Desert *des.* China

Taklimakan Shamo *des.* China
see Taklimakan Desert
128 A2 Taku *r.* Can./U.S.A.
63 A3 Takua Pa Thai.
115 C4 Takum Nigeria
88 C3 Talachyn Belarus
74 B1 Talagang Pak.
146 B4 Talamanca, Cordillera de
mts Costa Rica
150 A3 Talara Peru
59 C2 Talaud, Kepulauan *is* Indon.
106 C2 Talavera de la Reina Spain
153 A3 Talca Chile
153 A3 Talcahuano Chile
89 E2 Taldom Rus. Fed.
77 D2 Taldykorgan Kazakh.
Taldy-Kurgan Kazakh.
see Taldykorgan
59 C3 Taliabu *i.* Indon.
64 B2 Talisay Phil.
61 C2 Taliwang Indon.
81 C2 Tall 'Afar Iraq
141 D2 Tallahassee U.S.A.
53 C3 Tallangatta Austr.
88 B2 Tallinn Estonia
140 B2 Tallulah U.S.A.
104 B2 Talmont-St-Hilaire France
90 C2 Tal'ne Ukr.
117 B3 Talodi Sudan
74 A1 Tāloqān Afgh.
91 E1 Talovaya Rus. Fed.
126 F2 Taloyoak Can.
88 B2 Talsi Latvia
152 A2 Taltal Chile
129 C1 Taltson *r.* Can.
60 A1 Talu Indon.
53 C1 Talwood Austr.
114 B4 Tamale Ghana
115 C2 Tamanrasset Alg.
99 A4 Tamar *r.* U.K.
Tamatave Madag. *see* Toamasina
144 B2 Tamazula Mex.
145 C2 Tamazunchale Mex.
114 A3 Tambacounda Senegal
60 B1 Tambelan, Kepulauan *is* Indon.
86 G1 Tambey Rus. Fed.
61 C1 Tambisan Malaysia
61 C2 Tambora, Gunung *vol.* Indon.
91 E1 Tambov Rus. Fed.
119 C2 Tambura S. Sudan
62 A1 Tamenglong India
145 C2 Tamiahua, Laguna de *lag.* Mex.
Tammerfors Fin. *see* Tampere
141 D3 Tampa U.S.A.
141 D3 Tampa Bay U.S.A.
93 H3 Tampere Fin.
145 C2 Tampico Mex.
69 D1 Tamsagbulag Mongolia
102 C2 Tamsweg Austria
53 D2 Tamworth Austr.
99 C3 Tamworth U.K.
119 E3 Tana *r.* Kenya
67 C4 Tanabe Japan
92 I1 Tana Bru Norway
60 A2 Tanahbala *i.* Indon.
61 C2 Tanahgrogot Indon.
61 D2 Tanahjampea *i.* Indon.
60 A2 Tanahmasa *i.* Indon.
50 C1 Tanami Desert Austr.
63 B2 Tân An Vietnam
126 B2 Tanana U.S.A.
Tananarive Madag. *see* Antananarivo
108 A1 Tanaro *r.* Italy
65 B1 Tanch'ŏn N. Korea
64 B3 Tandag Phil.
110 C2 Ţăndărei Romania
153 C3 Tandil Arg.
74 A2 Tando Adam Pak.
74 A2 Tando Muhammad Khan Pak.
52 B2 Tandou Lake *imp. l.* Austr.
67 B4 Tanega-shima *i.* Japan
114 B2 Tanezrouft *reg.* Alg./Mali
119 D3 Tanga Tanz.
75 C2 Tangail Bangl.
Tanganyika *country* Africa
see Tanzania
119 C3 Tanganyika, Lake Africa
55 F3 Tange Promontory *hd* Antarctica
114 B1 Tanger Morocco
101 E1 Tangermünde Ger.
75 D1 Tanggulashan China
75 C1 Tanggula Shan *mts* China
Tangier Morocco *see* Tanger
75 C1 Tangra Yumco *salt l.* China
70 B2 Tangshan China
68 C2 Taniantaweng Shan *mts* China
59 C3 Tanimbar, Kepulauan *is* Indon.
64 B3 Tanjay Phil.
61 C2 Tanjung Indon.
60 A1 Tanjungbalai Indon.
Tanjungkarang-Telukbetung Indon.
see Bandar Lampung
60 B2 Tanjungpandan Indon.
60 B1 Tanjungpinang Indon.
61 C1 Tanjungredeb Indon.
61 C1 Tanjungselor Indon.
74 B1 Tank Pak.
48 H5 Tanna *i.* Vanuatu
115 C3 Tanout Niger
75 C2 Tansen Nepal
116 B1 Ţanţā Egypt
114 A2 Tan-Tan Morocco
145 C2 Tantoyuca Mex.

Varanasi

155 D1 Ubaí Brazil
151 F4 Ubaitaba Brazil
118 B3 Ubangi r. C.A.R./Dem. Rep. Congo
Ubangi-Shari country Africa see Central African Republic
67 B4 Ube Japan
106 C2 Úbeda Spain
154 C1 Uberaba Brazil
154 C1 Uberlândia Brazil
106 B1 Ubiña, Peña mt. Spain
123 D2 Ubombo S. Africa
63 B2 Ubon Ratchathani Thai.
119 C3 Ubundu Dem. Rep. Congo
150 B3 Ucayali r. Peru
100 B2 Uccle Belgium
74 B2 Uch Pak.
66 D2 Uchiura-wan b. Japan
76 C2 Uchquduq Uzbek.
83 J3 Uchur r. Rus. Fed.
99 D4 Uckfield U.K.
128 B3 Ucluelet Can.
83 I2 Udachnyy Rus. Fed.
74 B2 Udaipur India
91 C1 Uday r. Ukr.
93 F4 Uddevalla Sweden
92 G2 Uddjaure l. Sweden
100 B2 Uden Neth.
74 B1 Udhampur India
108 B1 Udine Italy
89 E2 Udomlya Rus. Fed.
62 B2 Udon Thani Thai.
73 B3 Udupi India
83 K3 Udyl', Ozero l. Rus. Fed.
67 C3 Ueda Japan
61 D2 Uekuli Indon.
118 C2 Uele r. Dem. Rep. Congo
83 N2 Uelen Rus. Fed.
101 E1 Uelzen Ger.
119 C2 Uere r. Dem. Rep. Congo
87 E3 Ufa Rus. Fed.
119 D3 Ugalla r. Tanz.
119 D2 Uganda country Africa
69 F1 Uglegorsk Rus. Fed.
89 E2 Uglich Rus. Fed.
89 D2 Uglovka Rus. Fed.
66 B2 Uglovoye Rus. Fed.
89 D3 Ugra Rus. Fed.
103 D2 Uherské Hradiště Czech Rep.
Uibhist a' Deas i. U.K. see South Uist
Uibhist a' Tuath i. U.K. see North Uist
101 E2 Uichteritz Ger.
96 A2 Uig U.K.
120 A1 Uíge Angola
65 B2 Ŭijŏngbu S. Korea
65 A1 Ŭiju N. Korea
135 D2 Uinta Mountains U.S.A.
120 A3 Uis Mine Namibia
65 B2 Ŭisŏng S. Korea
123 C3 Uitenhage S. Africa
100 C1 Uithuizen Neth.
131 D2 Uivak, Cape Can.
Ujiyamada Japan see Ise
74 B2 Ujjain India
Ujung Pandang Indon. see Makassar
89 F3 Ukholovo Rus. Fed.
Ukhta Rus. Fed. see Kalevala
86 E2 Ukhta Rus. Fed.
135 B3 Ukiah U.S.A.
127 I2 Ukkusissat Greenland
88 B2 Ukmergė Lith.
90 C2 Ukraine country Europe
Ukrainskaya S.S.R. country Europe see Ukraine
Ulaanbaatar Mongolia see Ulan Bator
68 C1 Ulaangom Mongolia
59 E3 Ulamona P.N.G.
70 A2 Ulan China
69 D1 Ulan Bator Mongolia
Ulanhad China see Chifeng
69 E1 Ulanhot China
87 D4 Ulan-Khol Rus. Fed.
70 B1 Ulan Qab China
69 D1 Ulan-Ude Rus. Fed.
75 D1 Ulan Ul Hu l. China
65 B2 Ulchin S. Korea
Uleåborg Fin. see Oulu
88 C2 Ülenurme Estonia
73 B3 Ulhasnagar India
69 D1 Uliastai China
68 C1 Uliastay Mongolia
59 D2 Ulithi atoll Micronesia
53 D3 Ulladulla Austr.
96 B2 Ullapool U.K.
98 B2 Ullswater l. U.K.
65 C2 Ullŭng-do i. S. Korea
102 B2 Ulm Ger.
65 B2 Ulsan S. Korea
96 □ Ulsta U.K.
97 C1 Ulster reg. Ireland/U.K.
52 B3 Ultima Austr.
145 D3 Ulúa r. Hond.
111 C3 Ulubey Turkey
111 D3 Uluborlu Turkey
111 C2 Uludağ mt. Turkey
126 E2 Ulukhaktok Can.
123 D2 Ulundi S. Africa
77 E2 Ulungur Hu l. China
50 C2 Uluṟu h. Austr.
98 B2 Ulverston U.K.
90 C2 Ul'yanovka Ukr.
87 D3 Ul'yanovsk Rus. Fed.
136 C3 Ulysses U.S.A.
90 C2 Uman' Ukr.
86 C2 Umba Rus. Fed.
59 D3 Umboi i. P.N.G.
59 D3 Umbukul P.N.G.
92 H3 Umeå Sweden
92 H3 Umeälven r. Sweden
123 D2 uMhlanga S. Africa
127 J2 Umiiviip Kangertiva inlet Greenland
126 E2 Umingmaktok (abandoned) Can.
123 D2 Umlazi S. Africa
78 A2 Umm al Birak Saudi Arabia
79 C2 Umm as Samīm salt flat Oman
116 A3 Umm Keddada Sudan
78 A2 Umm Lajj Saudi Arabia
78 A2 Umm Mukhbār, Jabal mt. Saudi Arabia
116 B3 Umm Ruwaba Sudan
115 E1 Umm Sa'ad Libya
134 B2 Umpqua r. U.S.A.
120 A2 Umpulo Angola
Umtali Zimbabwe see Mutare
123 D3 Umtentweni S. Africa
154 B2 Umuarama Brazil
123 C3 Umzimkulu S. Africa
109 C1 Una r. Bos.-Herz./Croatia
155 E1 Una Brazil
154 C1 Unaí Brazil
126 B2 Unalakleet U.S.A.
78 B2 'Unayzah Saudi Arabia
136 B3 Uncompahgre Peak U.S.A.
52 B3 Underbool Austr.
136 C1 Underwood U.S.A.
89 D3 Unecha Rus. Fed.
53 C2 Ungarie Austr.
52 A2 Ungarra Austr.
127 H2 Ungava, Péninsule d' pen. Can.
131 D2 Ungava Bay Can.
Ungeny Moldova see Ungheni
90 B2 Ungheni Moldova
Unguja i. Tanz. see Zanzibar Island
119 E3 Ungwana Bay Kenya
154 B3 União da Vitória Brazil
150 C3 Unini r. Brazil
134 C1 Union U.S.A.
140 C1 Union City U.S.A.
122 B3 Uniondale S. Africa
139 D3 Uniontown U.S.A.
79 C2 United Arab Emirates country Asia
United Arab Republic country Africa see Egypt
95 C3 United Kingdom country Europe
United Provinces state India see Uttar Pradesh
133 B3 United States of America country N. America
129 D2 Unity Can.
100 C2 Unna Ger.
96 □ Unst i. U.K.
101 E2 Unstrut r. Ger.
89 E3 Upa r. Rus. Fed.
119 C3 Upemba, Lac l. Dem. Rep. Congo
122 B2 Upington S. Africa
74 B2 Upleta India
49 J5 'Upolu i. Samoa
134 B2 Upper Alkali Lake U.S.A.
128 C2 Upper Arrow Lake Can.
54 C2 Upper Hutt N.Z.
134 B2 Upper Klamath Lake U.S.A.
128 B1 Upper Liard Can.
97 C1 Upper Lough Erne l. U.K.
137 E1 Upper Red Lake U.S.A.
Upper Tunguska r. Rus. Fed. see Angara
Upper Volta country Africa see Burkina Faso
93 G4 Uppsala Sweden
78 B2 'Uqlat aş Şuqūr Saudi Arabia
Urad Qianqi China see Xishanzui
76 B2 Ural r. Kazakh./Rus. Fed.
53 D2 Uralla Austr.
87 E3 Ural Mountains Rus. Fed.
76 B1 Ural'sk Kazakh.
Ural'skiy Khrebet mts Rus. Fed. see Ural Mountains
119 D3 Urambo Tanz.
53 C3 Urana Austr.
129 D2 Uranium City Can.
86 F2 Uray Rus. Fed.
98 C2 Ure r. U.K.
86 D3 Uren' Rus. Fed.
82 G2 Urengoy Rus. Fed.
144 A2 Ures Mex.
Urfa Turkey see Şanlıurfa
76 C2 Urganch Uzbek.
74 A1 Urgūn-e Kalān Afgh.
100 B1 Urk Neth.
111 C3 Urla Turkey
110 C2 Urlaţi Romania
81 C2 Urmia Iran
81 C2 Urmia, Lake salt l. Iran
Uroševac Kosovo see Ferizaj
144 B2 Uruáchic Mex.
151 E4 Uruaçu Brazil
144 B3 Uruapan Mex.
150 B4 Urubamba r. Peru
151 D3 Urucara Brazil
151 E3 Uruçuí Brazil
151 E3 Uruçuí, Serra do hills Brazil
151 D3 Urucurituba Brazil
152 C2 Uruguaiana Brazil
153 C3 Uruguay country S. America
Urumchi China see Ürümqi
68 B2 Ürümqi China
Urundi country Africa see Burundi
53 D2 Urunga Austr.
119 D3 Uruwira Tanz.
110 C2 Urziceni Romania
67 B4 Usa Japan
86 E2 Usa r. Rus. Fed.
111 C3 Uşak Turkey
120 A3 Usakos Namibia
88 C2 Ushachy Belarus
82 G1 Ushakova, Ostrov i. Rus. Fed.
77 E2 Usharal Kazakh.
77 D2 Ushtobe Kazakh.
Ush-Tyube Kazakh. see Ushtobe
153 B5 Ushuaia Arg.
86 E2 Usinsk Rus. Fed.
99 B4 Usk r. U.K.
88 C3 Uskhodni Belarus
89 E3 Usman' Rus. Fed.
86 D2 Usogorsk Rus. Fed.
104 C2 Ussel France
66 C1 Ussuri r. China/Rus. Fed.
66 B2 Ussuriysk Rus. Fed.
Ust'-Abakanskoye Rus. Fed. see Abakan
Ust'-Balyk Rus. Fed. see Nefteyugansk
91 E2 Ust'-Donetskiy Rus. Fed.
108 B3 Ustica, Isola di i. Italy
83 H3 Ust'-Ilimsk Rus. Fed.
86 E2 Ust'-Ilych Rus. Fed.
102 C1 Ústí nad Labem Czech Rep.
Ustinov Rus. Fed. see Izhevsk
103 D1 Ustka Pol.
83 L3 Ust'-Kamchatsk Rus. Fed.
77 E2 Ust'-Kamenogorsk Kazakh.
86 F2 Ust'-Kara Rus. Fed.
86 E2 Ust'-Kulom Rus. Fed.
83 I3 Ust'-Kut Rus. Fed.
91 D2 Ust'-Labinsk Rus. Fed.
Ust'-Labinskaya Rus. Fed. see Ust'-Labinsk
88 C2 Ust'-Luga Rus. Fed.
86 E2 Ust'-Nem Rus. Fed.
83 K2 Ust'-Nera Rus. Fed.
83 I2 Ust'-Olenek Rus. Fed.
83 K2 Ust'-Omchug Rus. Fed.
83 H3 Ust'-Ordynskiy Rus. Fed.
103 E2 Ustrzyki Dolne Pol.
86 E2 Ust'-Tsil'ma Rus. Fed.
86 D2 Ust'-Ura Rus. Fed.
76 B2 Ustyurt Plateau Kazakh./Uzbek.
89 E2 Ustyuzhna Rus. Fed.
146 B3 Usulután El Salvador
Usumbura Burundi see Bujumbura
89 D2 Usvyaty Rus. Fed.
135 D3 Utah state U.S.A.
135 D2 Utah Lake U.S.A.
88 C2 Utena Lith.
119 D3 Utete Tanz.
63 B2 Uthai Thani Thai.
74 A2 Uthal Pak.
123 D2 uThukela r. S. Africa
139 D2 Utica U.S.A.
107 C2 Utiel Spain
128 C2 Utikuma Lake Can.
93 G4 Utlängan i. Sweden
100 B1 Utrecht Neth.
123 D2 Utrecht S. Africa
106 B2 Utrera Spain
92 I2 Utsjoki Fin.
67 C3 Utsunomiya Japan
87 D4 Utta Rus. Fed.
62 B2 Uttaradit Thai.
75 B1 Uttarakhand state India
75 B2 Uttar Pradesh state India
Uummannaq Greenland see Dundas
127 I2 Uummannaq Greenland
127 I2 Uummannaq Fjord inlet Greenland
93 H3 Uusikaupunki Fin.
120 A2 Uutapi Namibia
143 D3 Uvalde U.S.A.
119 D3 Uvinza Tanz.
123 D3 Uvongo S. Africa
68 C1 Uvs Nuur salt l. Mongolia
67 B4 Uwajima Japan
78 A2 'Uwayriḍ, Ḩarrat al lava field Saudi Arabia
116 A2 Uweinat, Jebel mt. Sudan
83 H3 Uyar Rus. Fed.
115 C4 Uyo Nigeria
79 B2 Uyun Saudi Arabia
152 B2 Uyuni Bol.
152 B2 Uyuni, Salar de salt flat Bol.
76 C2 Uzbekistan country Asia
Uzbekskaya S.S.R. country Asia see Uzbekistan
Uzbek S.S.R. country Asia see Uzbekistan
104 C2 Uzerche France
105 C3 Uzès France
90 C1 Uzh r. Ukr.
90 A2 Uzhhorod Ukr.
Užhorod Ukr. see Uzhhorod
109 C2 Užice Serbia
89 E3 Uzlovaya Rus. Fed.
111 C3 Üzümlü Turkey
111 C2 Uzunköprü Turkey

V

123 B2 Vaal r. S. Africa
92 I3 Vaala Fin.
123 C2 Vaal Dam S. Africa
123 C1 Vaalwater S. Africa
92 H3 Vaasa Fin.
103 D2 Vác Hungary
152 C2 Vacaria Brazil
154 B2 Vacaria, Serra hills Brazil
135 B3 Vacaville U.S.A.
74 B2 Vadodara India
92 I1 Vadsø Norway
105 D2 Vaduz Liechtenstein
94 B1 Vágar i. Faroe Is
94 B1 Vágur Faroe Is
103 D2 Váh r. Slovakia
49 I4 Vaiaku Tuvalu
88 B2 Vaida Estonia
136 B3 Vail U.S.A.
77 C3 Vakhsh Tajik.
Vakhstroy Tajik. see Vakhsh
79 C2 Vakīlābād Iran
108 B1 Valdagno Italy
Valdai Hills hills Rus. Fed. see Valdayskaya Vozvyshennost'
89 D2 Valday Rus. Fed.
89 D2 Valdayskaya Vozvyshennost' hills Rus. Fed.
106 B2 Valdecañas, Embalse de resr Spain
93 G4 Valdemarsvik Sweden
106 C2 Valdepeñas Spain
153 B4 Valdés, Península pen. Arg.
126 C2 Valdez U.S.A.
153 A3 Valdivia Chile
130 C3 Val-d'Or Can.
141 D2 Valdosta U.S.A.
128 C2 Valemount Can.
152 E1 Valença Brazil
105 C3 Valence France
107 C2 Valencia Spain
107 C2 Valencia reg. Spain
150 C1 Valencia Venez.
107 D2 Valencia, Golfo de g. Spain
106 B1 Valencia de Don Juan Spain
97 A3 Valencia Island Ireland
105 C1 Valenciennes France
136 C2 Valentine U.S.A.
64 B2 Valenzuela Phil.
150 B2 Valera Venez.
88 C2 Valga Estonia
109 C2 Valjevo Serbia
88 C2 Valka Latvia
93 H3 Valkeakoski Fin.
100 B2 Valkenswaard Neth.
91 D2 Valky Ukr.
55 G2 Valkyrie Dome Antarctica
145 D2 Valladolid Mex.
106 C1 Valladolid Spain
93 E4 Valle Norway
145 C2 Vallecillos Mex.
150 C2 Valle de la Pascua Venez.
150 B1 Valledupar Col.
145 C2 Valle Hermoso Mex.
135 B3 Vallejo U.S.A.
152 A2 Vallenar Chile
84 F5 Valletta Malta
137 D1 Valley City U.S.A.
134 B2 Valley Falls U.S.A.
128 C2 Valleyview Can.
107 D1 Valls Spain
129 D3 Val Marie Can.
88 C2 Valmiera Latvia
104 B2 Valognes France
88 C3 Valozhyn Belarus
154 B2 Valparaíso Brazil
153 A3 Valparaíso Chile
105 C3 Valréas France
59 D3 Vals, Tanjung c. Indon.
74 B2 Valsad India
122 B2 Valspan S. Africa
91 D1 Valuyki Rus. Fed.
106 B2 Valverde del Camino Spain
81 C2 Van Turkey
81 C2 Van, Lake salt l. Turkey
81 C1 Vanadzor Armenia
83 H2 Vanavara Rus. Fed.
140 B1 Van Buren AR U.S.A.
139 F1 Van Buren ME U.S.A.
Van Buren U.S.A. see Kettering
128 B3 Vancouver Can.
134 B1 Vancouver U.S.A.
128 B3 Vancouver Island Can.
138 B3 Vandalia IL U.S.A.
138 C3 Vandalia OH U.S.A.
123 C2 Vanderbijlpark S. Africa
128 B2 Vanderhoof Can.
122 B3 Vanderkloof Dam dam S. Africa
50 C1 Van Diemen Gulf Austr.
88 C2 Vändra Estonia
Väner, Lake l. Sweden see Vänern
93 F4 Vänern l. Sweden
93 F4 Vänersborg Sweden
121 □D3 Vangaindrano Madag.
Van Gölü salt l. Turkey see Van, Lake
142 C2 Van Horn U.S.A.
59 D3 Vanimo P.N.G.
83 K3 Vanino Rus. Fed.
104 B2 Vannes France
Vannovka Kazakh. see Turar Ryskulov
59 D3 Van Rees, Pegunungan mts Indon.
122 A3 Vanrhynsdorp S. Africa
93 H3 Vantaa Fin.
49 I5 Vanua Levu i. Fiji
48 H5 Vanuatu country S. Pacific Ocean
138 C2 Van Wert U.S.A.
122 B3 Van Wyksvlei S. Africa
122 B2 Van Zylsrus S. Africa
75 C2 Varanasi India

W

Acknowledgements

pages 34-35
Climatic map data:
Kottek, M., Grieser, J., Beck, C., Rudolf, B., and Rubel, F., 2006: World Map of the
Köppen-Geiger climate classification updated.
Meteorol. Z., 15, 259–263.
http://koeppen-geiger.vu-wien.ac.at

pages 36-37
World land cover map data:
© ESA 2010 and UCLouvain
Arino, O., Ramos, J., Kalogirou, V., Defourny, P., Achard, F., 2010.
GlobCover 2009. ESA Living Planet Symposium 2010, 28th June - 2nd July, Bergen,
Norway, SP-686, ESA.
www.esa.int/due/globcover
http://due.esrin.esa.int/prjs/Results/20110202183257.pdf

pages 38-39
Population map data:
Center for International Earth Science Information Network (CIESIN), Columbia
University; and Centro Internacional de Agricultura Tropical (CIAT). 2005. Gridded
Population of the World Version 3 (GPWv3). Palisades, NY: Socioeconomic Data and
Applications Center (SEDAC), Columbia University.
Available at: http://sedac.ciesin.columbia.edu/gpw
http://www.ciesin.columbia.edu

Cover
Coastline © zahradales/Shutterstock